*The Resurrection of
Mary Magdalene*

The Resurrection of Mary Magdalene

Legends, Apocrypha, and
the Christian Testament

JANE SCHABERG

CONTINUUM
New York · London

2002

The Continuum International Publishing Group Inc
370 Lexington Avenue, New York, NY 10017

The Continuum International Publishing Group Ltd
The Tower Building, 11 York Road, London SE1 7NX

Printed in the United States of America

Library of Congress Cataloging-in-Publication Data

Schaberg, Jane.
   The resurrection of Mary Magdalene : legends, apocrypha, and the
Christian testament / Jane Schaberg.
     p. cm.
   Includes bibliographical references and index.
   ISBN 0-8264-1383-8
   1. Mary Magdalene, Saint. I. Title.
BS2485 .S34 2002
226'.092 – dc21

                          2002001875

Contents

Introduction

THIS BOOK HAD ITS ORIGIN in a café on Broadway, on a summer evening. I had wanted to follow up on Elisabeth Schüssler Fiorenza's article, "Mary Magdalene, Apostle to the Apostles,"[1] in which she urged that in order to move from the distortions signaled by images of the Magdalene, we would have to go back to the origin of the trouble, re-write, re-discover. I had spent a frustrating day looking for material in the Union Theological Seminary library, and finding little but a few smarmy, pious treatises on prostitution. I sat in the café over wine with my friend Harvey Klein, discussing Beverly Harrison's appropriate article, "The Power of Anger in the Work of Love."[2] Now, a decade and a half later, books and articles on the Magdalene proliferate,[3] and I have learned that there were some important ones back then too. This book is indebted to those ground-breaking studies.[4] Now even the Magdalene poems are different, hard-edged: Jane Kenyon's "Woman, Why Are You Weeping?"[5] Eilean Ni Chuilleanain's "St. Mary Magdalene Preaching at Marseilles,"[6] Catherine Sasanov's "Las Horas de Belén — A Book of Hours,"[7] Susan Ludvigson's "Trinity."[8]

---

1. "Mary Magdalene, Apostle to the Apostles," *Union Theological Seminary Journal* (April 1975) 5–6.

2. *Making the Connections* (ed. B. W. Harrison and C. S. Robb; Boston: Beacon, 1986); reprinted in *Weaving the Visions* (ed. P. Plaskow and C. P. Christ; San Francisco: Harper & Row, 1989) 214–25.

3. There is even some commercialization and commodification of Mary Magdalene (Elisabeth Schüssler Fiorenza, *Jesus and the Politics of Interpretation* [New York: Continuum, 2000] n. 2, p. 2).

4. See P. Thimmes, "Memory and Revision: Mary Magdalene Research since 1975," *Currents in Research: Biblical Studies* 6 (1990) 198–226.

5. *The Atlantic Monthly* (March 1999) 75–76.

6. *The Magdalene Sermon* (Loughcrew Oldcastle County Meath, Ireland: Gallery Press, 1989).

7. "Las Horas de Belén" (presented by the Mabou Mines in New York City, May 15, 1999) explores the lives of women locked away in the Recogimiento de Belén, "a sanctuary created by the Catholic Church in Mexico City in 1683 to give refuge to single women without means of support."

8. "The Gospel According to Mary Magdalene," *Trinity* (Baton Rouge: Louisiana State University Press, 1996).

The volatile figure of Mary Magdalene is so far too big for Hollywood, which sees her as a mix of lust, loyalty, belief, prostitution, repentance, beauty, madness, sainthood. She is the liminal and strange woman, silent, dominated by the great image of Jesus crucified, resurrected. She symbolizes the belief that women are made only deficiently in the image of God, and are ultimately a symbol of evil and of dependent, sinful humanity. But women can be forgiven;[9] eros can be controlled. Male fantasies about the Magdalene have fired the imagination of artists, made her an instrument of ecclesiastical propaganda, and misshaped lives. We will trace here how through the centuries she is variously ignored, labeled harlot/demoniac/patroness, replaced, appropriated and left behind, conflated, diminished, openly opposed; how she is utilized, unsilenced, rediscovered, resurrected.[10] If you don't care about women's history, or think all history is meaningless, or think Christianity and religion itself are something unevolved, best ignored, I can't tell you why you should care about this figure.

An explanation about the structure of this book is necessary. The chapters proceed in a way (backward) that is unusual in my field of biblical studies, and I trespass into fields other than mine. First, a description of my companion in this project, Virginia Woolf. Second, what little exploration is possible of the site of Migdal (Magdala) in modern Israel/Palestine. Third, analysis of the component parts and mechanism of the Magdalene legends, and of their major shapes, ancient and modern. Fourth, examination of recently available gnostic/apocryphal writings in which Mary (Magdalene) appears as a central character, startlingly different from her legends, praised and opposed as the woman who knew (too) much.[11] Fifth, a survey of major historical and literary difficulties regarding the Christian Testament sources that deal with her, and of the investigations of five contemporary scholars. Sixth, efforts to deal with these difficulties by constructing a set of possibilities, within the framework of feminist thought. Seventh, on the basis of the set of possibilities, my reading of the crucifixion/empty tomb/appearance narratives in the light of Jewish mystical tradition. I end with a reading of John 20 as incorporating a source in which Mary Magdalene was seen as prophetic successor to Jesus.

The book moves this way because I look at the texts of the canonical Gospels through the lenses of their *Nachleben* or afterlife as well as their prelife. I used to think of the whore legends mostly as rubble that had to be cleared. Now I see as the archaeologist does that some stuff is rubble, some precious; a sifting is necessary. Sifting in this case involves self-defining: yes a whore, a prostitute, and yes a madwoman as all of us women are or are in danger of being labeled,

9. E. A. Johnson, *She Who Is* (New York: Crossroad, 1992) 35.
10. See I. Maisch, *Between Contempt and Veneration: Mary Magdalene, The Image of a Woman through the Centuries* (Collegeville, Minn.: Liturgical Press, 1998).
11. See T. Modleski, *The Women Who Knew Too Much: Hitchcock and Feminist Theory* (London: Methuen, 1988).

and yes as we are redefining and claiming our sexuality and our sanity.[12] The harlotization of Mary Magdalene means that the Christian Testament texts that were actually about her[13] have been and still are read differently through the lens of legend. Her witness seen as romantic, emotional, crazed; her influence regarded as inessential, insignificant, minor. Even some modern historical research seems to me tainted with the subliminal thought: O so it all depends on the word of a whore? Anything to avoid it all depending on her word, the word of a looney, a whore, or, in general, on the insight of any woman. Mary Magdalene is the madwoman — angry mad — in Christianity's attic. She was hidden there because of an open and not fully appreciated secret, and its implications, at Christianity's core: that the male disciples fled and the women did not.

I used to think of the apocryphal texts as a branching out of the canonical tree; I see now that both canonical and apocryphal go down to the roots; that their biology is interactive, radically symbiotic. The profile of the gnostic/apocryphal Mary Magdalene seems at first to bear little relation to that of the Christian Testament character. But we are learning that the sources of conflict between different forms of early Christianity, especially those under the names of Mary Magdalene and Peter, are deeper and older than was thought. She represents women's prophetic power in the gnostic/apocrypal literature, as well as in the source I reconstruct behind John 20. Some scholars like Bovon think that the reason gnostic literature was declared heterodox, and therefore fell into disuse, may have less to do with its doctrinal content than with Mary Magdalene's priority among the disciples, especially in relation to Peter. In the Gospel of Mary she encourages and instructs the others (Peter's role in Luke 22:31–32) and he is in open conflict with her. The connections and disruptions between different understandings of body, resurrection, death, life, gender in various texts and families of texts are also receiving careful scholarly analysis. Käsemann's claim that "apocalyptic was the mother of all Christian theology"[14] sounds in a new way when we understand the *basileia* (Kingdom) movement of Jesus and his companions as an apocalyptic/wisdom movement that was inclusive. And when apocalyptic and gnostic motifs, especially the motif of ascent, are seen in the context of Jewish mystical traditions.

One of the tasks I set myself here is to bridge historical criticism and literary criticism, the scholarly and the personal. I came to graduate biblical studies from a literary perspective, and I am a working poet. I studied at Union Theological Seminary with Raymond E. Brown, J. Louis Martyn and J. A. Sanders. My training

---

12. See K. Peterson-Iyer, "Prostitution: A Feminist Ethical Analysis," *JFSR* 14 (1998) 19–44, for analysis of two feminist views on prostitution which she labels the liberal/contractarian approach and the domination/subjection approach, and for the importance of listening to prostitutes themselves.

13. In distinction from the texts that were not about her, but were conflated (see below, pp. 73–77).

14. E. Käsemann, "the Beginnings of Christian Theology," *JTC* 6 (1969) 40.

was in a short-lived Ph.D. program under Sanders in Biblical Studies, that is, in both testaments. Sanders' interest in midrash criticism became an interest of mine, and merged into the study of intertextuality. Historical-critical questions about origins (authors, intentions, settings, ancient meanings, events) and stages of composition are as fascinating to me as questions about literary qualities, the play of language, the coherence of final forms, the relation between text and readers.[15] I choose not to choose between these sets of questions. Straddling alters the questions on both sides, and changes the notion of a successful reading. So do postmodernity's insistence that reason is limited and humility called for, and feminism's instance on the political/personal. I allow myself here a range of voices and moods: there is the irritable, almost pedantic voice of striving after "fact" and precision, of fascination with detail, of exhaustion; and there is the simple voice of puzzlement and reflection and bemusement and horror. Imagination and historical analysis are both in the service of producing a book that is not a novel, but rather a work of sober and sobering scholarship.

I know myself fortunate to work during this phase of the women's movement, when feminist biblical scholarship is breaking new ground and flowering. I owe a tremendous debt to my feminist colleagues and contemporaries, as this book will make clear. I can count on them and those who come after us to make critical use — or not — of the evidence I have assembled and the theories I propose, and to do a better job than I can of reading anew.

Why Virginia Woolf (1882–1941)? Her name and influence appear rarely in biblical scholarship.[16] She has much to offer to Religious Studies, and I think we in Religious Studies have something to offer to Woolf Studies. "Throughout her corpus, Woolf is concerned [as we are] with what can(not) be said, what can(not) be assumed, what can(not) be questioned, and what can(not) be concluded."[17] She regarded Christianity as "the chief enemy" of intellectual freedom,[18] producing preachers and parrots and killers. She also thought that its energies had been and could be used justly. Suspicion and critique of organized religion such as she engaged in are deep and widespread today in Religious Studies, and within religious — as well as Outsider — organizations; they have a long, long history, on part of which Woolf herself drew.[19] The suspicion and

---

15. See Danna Nolan Fewell and David M. Gunn, editors' statement for the series Literary Currents in Biblical Interpretation, in Elizabeth A. Castelli, *Imitating Paul* (Louisville: Westminster/John Knox, 1991) 9.

16. But see E. Schüssler Fiorenza, *Rhetoric and Ethic: the Politics of Biblical Studies* (Minneapolis: Fortress, 1999) 19; Ingrid Rosa Kitzberger, "Introduction" to *The Personal Voice in Biblical Interpretation* (London: Routledge, 1999) 4, 6, 8.

17. K. Ratcliffe, *Anglo-American Feminist Challenges to the Rhetorical Traditions: Virginia Woolf, Mary Daly, Adrienne Rich* (Carbondale: Southern Illinois University Press, 1996) 62.

18. V. Woolf, *Diary*, 1.165.

19. See the work of Jane Marcus, cited in chapter 1, and C. Froula, "St. Virginia's Epistle to an English Gentleman; or, Sex, Violence and the Public Sphere in Virginia Woolf's *Three Guineas*," *Tulsa Studies in Women's Literature* 13 (1994) 27–56; V. Neverow, " 'Tak[ing] our stand openly under

critique grow stronger with the spread of feminist consciousness and response to patriarchal backlash.

In using Woolf to comment from time to time, I do not hold that she is saying what the texts are saying, or vice versa, nor do I intend to appropriate her for my own purposes. But there is a counterpoint here which can be helpful. Her questions about gender, about the boundaries and lack of boundaries between persons, about death and survival ("perhaps — perhaps"[20]) can redirect our attention from the ways issues are treated traditionally. A flawed and experimental spirit, she dealt with anger, the desire for dominance, women's "ancestral memory,"[21] the outsider's split consciousness.[22] What she was after was a radical transformation of culture and society, for men as well as women, and she began an analysis of classism as well as sexism. Leonard Woolf criticized that dimension of her being I deem most valuable: "She does not really know the feeling — which alone saves the brain & the body — that after all nothing matters. She asks too much from the earth & from the people who crawl about it."[23] For a book like this one on death and resurrection, Woolf's great love — exuberant and precise — of the beauty of the world is centering.

She described the ludicrous patriarchal procession and patriarchy's almost demented thinking, and showed in what ways it is everywhere the same: in home, fascist state, church, university. "How difficult it is to write to you! It's all Cambridge — that detestable place and the ap-s-les [Apostles] are so unreal, and their loves are so unreal, and yet I suppose it's all going on still — swarming in the sun — and perhaps not as bad as I imagine. But when I think of it, I vomit — that's all — a green vomit, which gets into the ink and blisters the paper."[24] Sometimes, thinking of other Apostles, earlier and later, I too find my ink turning green.

For all her anger and ridicule and hatred, she showed from time to time a kind of pity, as toward the inhabitants of the "leaning tower," whose education

---

the lamps of Picadilly Circus' Footnoting of the Influence of Josephine Butler on Three Guineas," *Virginia Woolf and the Arts: Selected Papers from the Sixth Annual Conference on Virginia Woolf* (ed. D. F. Gillespie and L. K. Hankins; New York: Pace University Press, 1997) 13–24; C. J. Marshik, "Virginia Woolf and Feminist Intellectual History: The Case of Josephine Butler and *Three Guineas*," *Virginia Woolf and Her Influences; Selected Papers from the Seventh Annual Conference on Virginia Woolf* (ed. L. Davis and J. McVicker; New York: Pace University Press, 1998) 91–97. In the nineteenth century Butler worked to open educational opportunities and the professions to women, and led a successful campaign against the Contagious Diseases Act which oppressed prostitutes. I do not think (against Marshik, 95–96) that in reframing Butler, Woolf really "occluded" the role of religion, or secularized a figure identified with the patriarchal church. Woolf's Society of Outsiders will be discussed below, in chapter 1.

20. Clarissa in V. Woolf, *Mrs. Dalloway* (London: Hogarth Press, 1925) 153.

21. V. Woolf, *Three Guineas* (New York: Harcourt, Brace & World, 1938) 85.

22. V. Woolf, *A Room of One's Own* (New York: Harcourt, Brace & World, 1929) 101.

23. L. Woolf's 1911 description of Virginia Stephen, quoted by G. Spater and I. Parsos, *A Marriage of True Minds: An Intimate Portrait of Leonard and Virginia Woolf* (London: Jonathan Cape, 1977) 61.

24. V. Woolf to L. Strachey, *Letters* (ed. L. Woolf and J. Strachey; London: Hogarth Press, 1956) 38.

and upbringing trap them. "Let us imagine... that we are actually upon a leaning tower and note our sensation." Note that the view is slanting, sidelong, feel the discomfort, the self-pity for that discomfort, the pity turning "to anger against the builder, against society, for making us uncomfortable." Note that you cannot abuse all of society while you continue to profit from it, so you have to find scapegoats. "Anger; pity; scapegoat bleating; excuse finding — these are all very natural tendencies; if we were in their position we should tend to do the same. But we are not in their position.... We have only been climbing an imaginary tower. We can cease to imagine. We can come down. But they cannot." Even when they realize the tower was founded on injustice and tyranny, even when they violently and half-heartedly preach against injustice, even when they long to be human and whole, they are "trapped by their education, pinned down by their capital" and remain on top of their leaning tower.[25] The tower she was describing is the middle-class birth and expensive education of nineteenth-century writers and their inheritors; that tower was steady down to August 1914. Her perceptions apply also to towers more sturdy and more tilting. Some good men and women are trapped inside.

It is my hope also that this book will be a crossover, from feminist Religious Studies/Biblical Studies to Feminist Studies in general. The suspicion on the part of many intellectuals that anyone interested in religion must be a fundamentalist, a reactionary, and/or weak in the head is pervasive, ignorant, and unfortunate. I hope that this book will be useful for feminists who are suspicious of or hostile to religion, as well as to feminists engaged in the study of religion. It is my hope also that the following chapters illustrate each prong of Plaskow's assertions that "(1) religion plays a key role in the dynamics of women's oppression (as well as liberation), and understanding these dynamics is a central task of women's studies; (2) women's studies in religion is a well-established, vital, and exciting field; and (3) to a greater extent than is the case with many other areas of women's studies, feminists in religion maintain strong links to women outside the academy."[26] Feminists need " 'large historical narratives' that detail the particularity of sexism across diverse times and societies" and narratives that can "sketch a vision of the future."[27] And citizens need education in feminist Religious Studies.[28] Concern with spirituality, religious history and ideology, and the immense power of religion

---

25. V. Woolf, "The Leaning Tower," *A Woman's Essays: Selected Essays*, Vol. 1 (ed. R. Bowlby; London: Penguin, 1992) 168–69, 172–73. A paper read to the Workers' Educational Association, Brighton, May, 1940.

26. J. Plaskow, "We Are Also Your Sisters: The Development of Women's Studies in Religion," *Women's Studies Quarterly* 21 (1993) 9–21.

27. E. A. Clark, "Ideology, History and the Construction of 'Woman' in Late Ancient Christianity," *Journal of Early Christian Studies* 2 (1994) 163, citing N. Fraser and L. J. Nicholson, "Social Criticism without Philosophy," *Feminism/Postmodernism* (ed. Nicholson; New York: Routledge, 1990) 34.

28. See the discussion by E. Schüssler Fiorenza, *Jesus and the Politics of Interpretation*, 74–75.

need not be out of bounds, or if it is, "trespass at once."[29] The trespassing has begun, in the work of Alicia Ostriker,[30] Martha Nussbaum[31] and others.

This present book builds on my experiences with a previous one, *The Illegitimacy of Jesus: A Feminist Theological Interpretation of the Infancy Narratives of Matthew and Luke.*[32] I argued that these canonical narratives independently transmit a tradition that Jesus was conceived (normally not miraculously) while his mother was a betrothed virgin, possibly by a rape since the texts allude to the rape law in Deut 22:23–27. I proposed that a nugget of theology is still visible in these Christian Testament texts: that God stands by the endangered woman and child. To follow a book about the Virgin Mary with one on Mary Magdalene might seem a natural move: dealing with the two ends of the spectrum of male misrepresentations of woman, as virgin and whore. Mary of Nazareth and Mary Magdalene are the two most prominent women in the Christian Testament, and their images have had great impact on thought, imagination, art and social arrangements. But other issues are at play here than such a simple progression of ideas.

In *Illegitimacy* I had tried to place "the familiar dimensions of careful textual exegesis ... in the service of a nuanced, feminist reading," recognizing "both the ironies and the potential pitfalls of attempting to reproduce authorial intentions," and acknowledging that intentions and meanings are not fixed and can never be known with certainty. Castelli was among those who found my reading persuasive: "Her exegesis retrieves a repressed story ... it provides the outline for the theological transformation of the figure of Mary."[33] But the book was also regarded by others in the mainstream, such as Raymond E. Brown, John Meier, J. H. Charlesworth, as outrageous and theologically unsound.[34] I became a target

---

29. V. Woolf, "The Leaning Tower," 178. She is quoting her father Leslie Stephen's advice to walkers: "Whenever you see a board up with 'Trespassers will be prosecuted,' trespass at once."
30. A. S. Ostriker, *Feminist Revision and the Bible* (Cambridge, Mass.: Blackwell, 1993); *The Nakedness of the Fathers: Biblical Visions and Revisions* (New Brunswick: Rutgers University Press, 1994).
31. M. Nussbaum, *Women and Human Development: The Capabilities Approach* (Cambridge: Cambridge University Press, 2000) chapter 3. See also P. Chesler, "Introduction Twenty-Fifth Anniversary Edition," *Women and Madness* (New York: Four Walls Eight Windows, 1997) 5, 23; M. F. Katzenstein, *Faithful and Fearless: Moving Feminist Protest Inside the Church and Military* (Princeton: Princeton University Press, 1998), and many articles in the *Journal of Feminist Studies in Religion*.
32. San Francisco: Harper & Row, 1987; paperback editions New York: Crossroad, 1992; Sheffield: Sheffield Academic Press, 1994.
33. Elizabeth A. Castelli, "Heteroglossia, Hermeneutics, and History: a Review Essay of Recent Feminist Studies of Early Christianity," *JFSR* 10 (1994) 88. See also Vernon K. Robbins, "Socio-Rhetorical Criticism: Mary, Elizabeth and the Magnificat as a Test Case," *The New Literary Criticism and the New Testament* (ed. E. S. Malbon and E. V. McKnight; Sheffield: Sheffield Academic Press, 1994) 183–4; G. Lüdemann, *Jungfrauen Geburt: Die wirkliche Geschichte von Maria und ihrem Sohn Jesus* (Stuttgart: Radius, 1997); D. Landry, "Narrative Logic in the Lucan Annunciation Story," *JBL* 114 (1995); L. Schottroff, *Lydia's Impatient Sisters: A Feminist Social History of Early Christianity* (Louisville: Westminster/John Knox, 1995) 200–203.
34. References in J. Schaberg, "Feminist Interpretations of the Infancy Narrative of Matthew," *JFSR* 13 (1997).

of popular and academic anti-feminist backlash, some of it violent, for daring to meddle with the powerful icon of the Virgin, belief in the virginal conception, Roman Catholic emphasis on that belief as central to an understanding of woman as well as of Jesus, and for discussing sexuality in this context.[35] Sensibilities were offended. As Harold Bloom remarks somewhere, there is a huge difference between suggesting Mother Theresa was raped and suggesting the singer Madonna was raped. Or something to that effect.

I had been persuaded before of the importance and inevitability of perspective and interpretive framework, and of institutional/political power at work in scholarship.[36] But now I experienced more personally the truth of Schüssler Fiorenza's statement: "The disagreements between different readings ... can be adjudicated only in a rhetorical-political paradigm of inquiry and not in a 'literalist' scientific one."[37] In this book I am more careful to make it clear I am discussing my reconstructions of historical situations and of the possible mindset of authors, and more careful to lay out my theoretical assumptions and feminist perspectives. I am still unconvinced that the master's tools cannot dismantle the master's house, or at least do it some serious damage in feminist hands. Some of the tenets of historical criticism are clearly unacceptable to feminist and to postmodern thought and unusable: the idea that the scholar can be objective, that his or her social location or standpoint does not influence exegesis; the idea that it is possible to be absolutely certain about past events, meanings, intentions; the idea that such certainty is desirable and a basis for human unity and conformity. And some of the tenets are acceptable: the idea that in some way history matters and is worth doing; that close reading requires and benefits by traditional historical, philological, literary analysis and methodologies. These can provide a common viewpoint from which to criticize readings and enter into dialogue. There is such a thing as striving for a better reading, a better grasp of history. That striving does not have to be a mortal battle, a slaying.

Yes, I was "victimized" a bit, and yes it set me back. But backlash also had the unintended effect of making me more personally and intensely interested in the process of censorship and silencing. It gave me reserves of anger and energy to draw on. I know in my bones how serious the opposition is to women's insight, women's revisioning. I know a little more about strategies of suppression. All this I think can serve me well in dealing with traditions about Mary Magdalene, called whore, possessed, delusional, power hungry, not a real woman, made into a man. I also know more about resilience. Two other aspects of my perspective should be mentioned: I live in Detroit, and I am a Roman Catholic.

35. See J. Schaberg, "Backlash Against Feminism, *BiblIcon* 1 (1999).
36. See E. A. Castelli, "Interpretations of Power in 1 Corinthians," *Semeia* 54 (1992) 199–200.
37. E. Schüssler Fiorenza, *The Book of Revelation. Justice and Judgment* (2d ed.; Minneapolis: Fortress, 1998) 205.; n. 5, p. 229.

Reading from Detroit in this time is reading embedded in experiences of the deep and tangled structures of racism, sexism, poverty, classism, colonialism, and of the despair and courage displayed by those whom these structures have enmeshed. Despite my early efforts to get a "better" job, I am lucky to teach in a non-elite, richly diverse classroom Virginia Woolf would approve of, where some — many — of our students are the poor (or the nearly poor, the recently poor)[38] with whom I try to be a co-learner in the effort to demystify strategies of oppression like "whiteness," and to recognize powers of resistance. Helmut Koester rightly insists: "Interpretation of the Bible is justified only if it is a source for political and religious renewal, or it is not worth the effort.... If the Bible has anything to do with justice and freedom, biblical scholarship must be able to question those very structures of power and expose their injustice and destructive potential."[39] To do this kind of work one must try to be what Osayande Obery Hendricks calls "the guerilla exegete," not waiting for, not expecting "the hegemonic pat on the head."[40]

Standing again at Golgotha[41] in Detroit is a challenge not to turn away from suffering or from the body. It demands a resurrection faith that does not make the suffering all right, does not dull to injustice, does not de-sensitize compassion or fear of death; rather it leads to action in spite of. Mary Magdalene of the Christian Testament is the one who stands by the dying, wrongfully accused, executed; she fails to anoint at an empty tomb of the disappeared. Simply there, she becomes the place, the location, not just the symbol of, the God who is thought to abandon, but does not abandon. Valerie Saiving remarks on "the transformation of the quality of pain by the full presence of other human beings" in our dying.[42] Each of us wishes for one like the Magdalene to go down with us into death, to stay with us to the end. I say this with cancer on my mind, and remembering those I did not stay with until the end, those I love who died alone. More than that: she

---

38. By "poor" I mean here those who have been denied access to economic resources necessary to sustain life in a democratic society. According to M. Orfield (*Detroit Metropolitics: A Regional Agenda for Community and Stability,* report to the Archdiocese of Detroit [January 1999] 5), Detroit is 85% African American, experienced a 93% increase in poverty from 1980–90, and 40% of its citizens live in poverty.

39. H. Koester, "Epilogue," *The Future of Early Christianity* (ed. B. A. Pearson; Minneapolis: Fortress, 1991) 475. Speaking of Brooten's work, *Women Leaders in the Ancient Synagogue* (Chico, Calif.: Scholars Press, 1982) he writes, "To be sure, the political agenda is evident, but it is exactly this political agenda that has led to new scholarly discoveries" (476).

40. O. O. Hendricks, "Guerilla Exegesis: 'Struggle' as a Scholarly Vocation: A Postmodern Approach to African-American Interpretation," *Semeia* 72 (1995) 82. He coins the term "ghetto-centricity," which means using "the naked narrow prism of the ghetto. Where the effects of white supremacy are most acute, both qualitatively and quantitatively" (87). See G. O. West, *The Academy of the Poor* (Sheffield: Sheffield Academic Press, 1999), "What (Socially Engaged) Biblical Scholars Do," 63–78.

41. See J. Plaskow, *Standing Again at Sinai: Judaism from a Feminist Perspective* (San Francisco: Harper & Row, 1990).

42. V. Saiving, "Our Bodies/Our Selves," *JFSR* 5 (1989) 125.

is the one who did not cease to love the dead, who remembered.[43] Reconstruction of her story may help us to stay, not turn away.

I approach the topic of resurrection with trepidation and reluctance. These texts deal with a (perhaps the) foundational belief of Christianity, rooted in the belief of some first-century Jews. What is meant by such belief? And (worse question) is it true? True for me? I do not consider it more sophisticated or intelligent or courageous to dismiss these questions. It is difficult to know what to include in a biblical studies book, of one's own belief or lack of it. This is something scholars like other people rarely talk about, unless they are up-front explicitly orthodox Christians. I belong to a group of survivors "privileged" to experience my mortality: first as a young child with a heart valve problem, then in my forties with Stage 3 breast cancer. But all I remember about the latter experience is the terror of death, the striving to beat death, the will to live, the love of life. Having had to face the fear brought me no closer to an articulated faith, but only sometimes to the grasping of mantra-like phrases ("now and at the hour of our death" and "Shema' Yisrael") and to the presence and support of good friends. Nothing more, nothing less.

My mother, a life-long Catholic who could be more cynical and disinterested in religion than my atheist father, was dying of emphysema. One evening we got into a conversation on a subject we had never discussed before. She asked me if, in light of all my work, I believed that resurrection and life beyond death was true. "Do you believe that any of it is true?" Surprised and somewhat embarrassed by such a question, I stuttered something about not knowing, but hoping it was true. I stuttered something about apocalyptic. I am ashamed — or something like that — of my stuttering answer. This book is in some ways an attempt to continue that conversation. But too late.

I am interested here in trying to think about something Derrida (writing of the work of Louis Marin) describes as "outside the evangelical, doctrinal, or dogmatic space of the resurrection, before it, more originary than it. . . ."[44] I will argue for the resurrection faith as concerned with justice for the whole person, for the body, and for the corporate Human One, Justice, and perhaps mercy. My reconstruction is simple. In making the claim that God raised Jesus, Mary Magdalene was probably in earnest and not insane, not a liar. She was speaking/thinking/creating out of her own experience in the apocalyptically-oriented *basileia* movement, and her experience of the execution of Jesus, and out of what for lack of a better word is called insight or inspiration. Whether one accepts this claim as true or not depends on how it is understood and if it can be experienced in one's own life in any way. Luck and decision seem to be part of acceptance/nonacceptance.

---

43. Cf. the Testamonium Flavianum: Josephus, *Ant.* 18. 63: "those who had in the first place come to love him did not give up their affection for him" (Feldman translation, Loeb).

44. J. Derrida, "By Force of Mourning," *Critical Inquiry* 22 (1996) 180.

Do I believe in the resurrection of the dead? Yes, actually, I do. I also know that I will die. Resurrection is for me a "broken and living myth," as Neil Gillman calls it, an outrageous hope grounded in belief in the God who gives life to the dead.[45] It is grounded also in the invigorating, stubborn moments of struggling against multiple aspects of oppression and against self-righteousness. Scientific knowledge, in my opinion, makes this faith no more outrageous than it was in past ages when people were intimately acquainted with the stink and rot of death, and with injustice. Across centuries and across a lifetime, changing attitudes toward the body, sexuality, selfhood, death, and love influence understandings of resurrection. However absurd the notion of resurrection seems, writes Caroline Walker Bynum, "it is a concept of sublime courage and optimism. It locates redemption there where ultimate horror also resides — in pain, mutilation, death, and decay."[46]

On being a Catholic: First, a disclaimer. I regard religious affiliation, like nationalism, in terms of the "unreal loyalties" Woolf discussed; and in that sense, I want none, and am an Outsider. But I also do not deny being a Catholic, or an American citizen, as long as I continue to benefit from the wealth of either institution, and as long as I responsibly, even loyally oppose their institutional injustices. Drawn to the time before the parting of the ways between Judaism and Christianity, to the integrity of some atheist thought, and to feminist visions, I assert my right to a religion of our own.

For the past forty years, official Catholicism has increasingly identified itself with conservative, right-wing forces, fencing off Catholic social teaching from concern with women and "women's concerns." Meeting the worldwide women's movement with misogyny and fear, the hierarchy and clerical culture of the Church has walled itself up in a tower leaning to the right. Official Roman Catholicism aligned itself at Cairo and Beijing U.N. conferences with Islamic fundamentalists to restrict access of the poor to reproductive health care and family planning, and in the U.S. aligns itself with policy priorities of the GOP and of evangelical Christians and other anti-choice groups. Wealthy conservative Catholics exercise immense influence in private and public ways. During the summer of 1998, when Southern Baptists declared women should be subservient to the "servant leadership" of their husbands, Pope John Paul II made it a part of canon law that there will be no ordination of women in the Roman Catholic church, reaffirming the 1976 ban and later insisting there be no more discussion of this issue. An effort to control U.S. theologians shifted into high gear in 1992,

---

45. N. Gillman, *The Death of Death: Resurrection and Immortality in Jewish Thought* (Woodstock, Vt.: Jewish Lights, 1997) 30–31. "Myths 'are' not true or false, but rather 'become' true or false, if and when we conduct our collective or communal lives in accord with their message" (28). Gillman's stress on the value of the individual person is important in the post-Holocaust context.

46. See C. W. Bynum, *The Resurrection of the Body in Western Christianity, 200–1336* (New York: Columbia University Press, 1995), 343.

eventuating in the present requirement for all Catholics teaching "theology"[47] in Roman Catholic colleges and universities in the U.S. to seek the "Mandatum," official authorization that their teaching conforms to the teaching of the Magisterium[48] of the Church: a loyalty oath. Despite publicity-related efforts to soft peddle the impact of this decree, in the opinion of many it would make serious theological work impossible in Catholic institutions.[49] My ink is turning green.

I do not underestimate this power to enervate, intimidate, destroy work, to harm spirits, consciences, bodies, peoples. When Woolf referred in *Three Guineas* to photographs of the devastation of war, she gave the reader photographs of men in uniforms of the royalty, the law courts, the academy, the military, and the church. At the beginning of the first war of the third millennium (9/11/01), her explorative answers to the question — How do we prevent war? — are still unheard.

At the same time, looking beyond ecclesiastical hierarchy, it seems to some that Christianity is in the throes of a second Reformation, more extensive, more profound than the first. Catholics in high percentages disagree with official church teachings on contraception, abortion, ordination of women, homosexuality. Hierarchical clout proves unable to silence dissenting voices. It becomes clearer than ever that the main obstacle to reform or renewal or recreation is "a problem of structure or church polity that cuts off the avenues of participation, deliberation, and decision making for all but a few men in the monarchical hierarchy. This structural system must be changed."[50] It is a question of dominant and domineering ideologies and high ideals as well.[51] The "official" Roman Catholic Church, increasingly seen as patriarchy writ large, hideously boring, pits itself against egalitarian, communal realities and needs, and against the progressive dimensions of its own history.

The collapse of the idea of a unified and universal world culture based on Euro-American values parallels the collapse of the belief in a unified and catholic religious culture and center of power. The lack of a center is felt: "Most pervasive fact of the world order today is that the plight of the most hungry and most poor is so much worse than once anyone would have imagined and that there is no world center of power willing or able to do anything about it."[52] The Bible and the histories behind it are a source of certain metanarratives that create the belief that

---

47. Including ethics, systematic theology, biblical studies, etc.

48. Narrowly understood to refer to Vatican officials and bishops.

49. See further, M. Dillon, *Catholic Identity* (Cambridge: Cambridge University Press, 1999), especially her chapter 3, on official church teaching on homosexuality, women's ordination, abortion, and the role of the theologian, and chapter 4, on pro-change groups.

50. *A Democratic Catholic Church: The Reconstruction of Roman Catholicism* (ed. E. C. Bianchi and R. R. Ruether; New York: Crossroad, 1992). See 253–60 for their five principles of reform (participation, conciliarity, pluralism, accountability, dialogue).

51. See E. D. Genovese, *The Southern Front* (Columbia: University of Missouri, 1995) chapter 23: "we of the Left" asked to explain ourselves.

52. C. Lemert, *Postmodernism Is Not What You Think* (Oxford: Blackwell, 1997) 33–34.

the world and humanity could become whole, belief in a power that can repair the world. The Qur'an creates that belief as well. Can there be a center — or centers — of democratic power, with commitment to the full humanity of women and men, to multiple perspectives, collective conversation and debate? Can art and theologies and mysticism and action for social justice be produced which free up resources through egalitarian collaboration? Can there be (is there) a religion of Outsiders? "perhaps — perhaps"[53]

Magdalene Christianity offers an alternative and a challenge to Petrine Christianity, which has never been able to silence it. It might move us toward a religion of Outsiders.

Some sections of this book are revised from articles which appeared previously: "Thinking Back Through the Magdalene," *Continuum* 1 (1991) 71–91; "How the Magdalene Became a Whore," *BR* (October 1992); "New Testament Criticism: the Case of Mary Magdalene," *Feminist Approaches to the Bible* (transcription of a panel at the Smithsonian Institution, October 1994; ed. H. Shanks; Washington: Biblical Archaeology Society, 1995); "Fast Forwarding to the Magdalene," *Semeia* 74 (1997); "The F-Word: Feminist Scholarship and the Media," *Journal of Feminist Studies in Religion* (forthcoming).

Due to constraints of space, the index includes only biblical, apocryphal, and gnostic passages. My thanks to those who have read through portions of this book and helped me with their support, critique, suggestions and invitations to speak: among whom are Elisabeth Schüssler Fiorenza (without whose groundbreaking work this book would not be possible); my colleagues Gloria Albrecht and Stephanie Mitchem (for Friday morning editing sessions); the Detroit Writers Guild (especially Anca Vlasopolos, Kathe Koja, Patrick O'Leary); to Christopher Rowland, Alicia Ostriker, Tom Schindler, Harvey Klein, Holly Hearon, Frank Moloney, Carroll Saussy, Gail Godwin, George Aichele, Claire Brown. I am grateful to the Weekapaug Group, and to the Steering Committee of the Women in the Biblical World Section of the Society of Biblical Literature for the sense of connectedness to the wider scholarly world, alleviating the aloneness of this work. Thanks to the Society of Biblical Literature for a research grant in 1999. For generous research assistance: Kat Al-Guweiri (Interlibrary Loans, University of Detroit Mercy); Pat Hall-Thomas and her staff (UDM); Bill Lockwood, Mary Oliver, Stuart Tucker, Kevin Sullivan, Seth Knox; Karla Scanlan. For understanding and encouraging this project: my editor and friend Justus George Lawler. And thanks to Jerry Banninger, for evenings at Baker's Keyboard Lounge and out at the barn with Rappahannock, after a long day's work.

---

53. V. Woolf, *Mrs. Dalloway,* 153.

CHAPTER
ONE
Virginia Woolf and Mary Magdalene
Thinking Back through the Magdalene

> Yet I am now & then haunted by some semi mystic very profound life of a woman, which shall be all told on one occasion; & time shall be utterly obliterated; future shall somehow blossom out of the past.
>
> Virginia Woolf, *Diary*, Tuesday November 23, 1926[1]

M Y INTELLECTUAL COMPANION for this study of the Magdalene, over the years, has been Virginia Woolf. She plays for me a role something like the role played for other biblical scholars by thinkers like Heidegger, Marx, Lonergan, Freud, Kafka, Bakhtin, Foucault, Benjamin, Lacan, Derrida, Lyotard, the ancient Cynics. Compiling an immense Magdalene bibliography of titles ranging from the sickening to the intriguing, many of them novels or biographies or even autobiographies,[2] reading my way through the abstracts, the xeroxes, the volumes, trying to line up the issues and how to deal with them, I found myself distracted — this is how I put it for some time — by Woolf's presence. Her nine novels, her essays and short stories, her five volumes of diaries, her six volumes of letters kept getting into my hands, articles about her and biographies kept getting into my inter-library loan requests, tapes of radio shows produced about her kept getting onto my stereo,[3] her name kept coming up in conversations, her thoughts — unsystematic on purpose, and wide-ranging — kept after me.

Like this one: the Society of Outsiders, she said, by criticizing religion "would attempt to free the religious spirit from its present servitude and would help, if need be, to create a new religion based, it might well be, upon the New Testament, but, it might well be, very different from the religion now erected upon that

---

1. *The Diary of Virginia Woolf* (ed. A. O. Bell, assisted by A. McNeillie (New York: Harcourt Brace Jovanovich, 1980) 3.118.

2. Some examples: E. F. Murphy, *The Scarlet Lily* (Milwaukee: Bruce, 1944); A. Prevos, "The Legend of Mary Magdalene in Afro-Cajun Spirituals," *Pacific Quarterly* (Moana), Hamilton, New Zealand 8 (1984) 25–30; C. Milosz, "Mary Magdalene and I," *The New Yorker* 63 (1987) 40; B. Ingher-Irvin, *The Autobiography of Mary Magdalene* (Nevada City, Calif.: Blue Dolphin, 1989).

3. C. Dalferes, "Va. Woolf & Co.," WTIF, Hershey, Pa., 1980.

21

basis."[4] What exactly are all those tentative qualifiers doing in this sentence, that "if need be," those "might well be"s? She uses them here and elsewhere to convey the optative mood unique to ancient Greek grammar, the mood of wishing, wanting, speculating, longing, expressing something potential or hypothetical.[5] The very uncertainty, the tentativeness delightfully undermine and question. The optative is a mode of doubtful assertion, an expression of possibility rather than probability.[6] What did she have in mind, what was she glimpsing?

The legacy of 2,500 pounds[7] left her by her aunt Caroline Emelia Stephen, Quaker theologian and reformer, gave her the freedom to work, "to think of things in themselves. . . . Indeed my aunt's legacy unveiled the sky to me, and substituted for the large and imposing figure of a gentleman, which Milton recommended for my perpetual adoration, a view of the open sky."[8] "Milton's bogey," the forbidding, patriarchal Christian God,[9] is replaced. For those of us who may not be able to "base" a new religion on the New Testament, what use, what help, if any, will or might the New Testament be? Can it provide, or can it open to a view of the open sky?

There is this statement of hers, too, which makes the feminist critic in me cringe, pause, then read again because it is hers: "[W]hat, we may ask, is 'religion.' What the Christian religion is has been laid down once and for all by the founder of that religion in words that can be read by all in a translation of singular beauty; whether or not we accept the interpretation that has been put on them, we cannot deny them to be words of the most profound meaning. It can thus safely be said that whereas few people know what medicine is, or what law is, everyone who owns a copy of the New Testament knows what religion meant in the mind of its founder."[10] She had a copy, then? Singular beauty? profound meaning? I

---

4. Woolf, *Three Guineas*, 112. Cf. Woolf, "A Society," *Monday or Tuesday* (New York: Harcourt, Brace, 1921) 9–40.

5. See I. B. Anderson, "The Greek Optative in the Narrative Style of *To the Lighthouse*," *Virginia Woolf and Her Influences: Selected Papers from the Seventh Annual Conference on Virginia Woolf* (ed. L. Davis and J. McVicker; New York: Pace University Press, 1977) 195–202.

6. A. T. Robertson and W. H. Davis, *A New Short Grammar of the Greek New Testament* (19th edition; Grand Rapids: Baker Book House, 1979) 309. "It is much more than the wishing mode"; it deals with the future from the standpoint of the past (311). Contrast L. E. Keck, *Who is Jesus? History in the Perfect Tense* (Columbia: University of South Carolina, 2000). "The ancient Greeks used the perfect tense of a verb to distinguish the ongoing import of completed action from its sheer occurrence in the past. . . . [T]o speak of history in the perfect tense is to consider the ongoingness of something from the past, namely Jesus." "The ongoing meaning — the perfect tense . . ." (1–2).

7. M. Leaska (*Granite and Rainbow: The Hidden Life of Virginia Woolf* [New York: Cooper Square, 2000] 137) calculates the 1998 equivalent at 115,000 pounds, roughly $185,000.

8. Woolf, *Room*, 39.

9. J. Marcus, "Quentin's Bogey," *Art & Anger* (Columbus: Ohio State University Press, 1988) 201–3. She suggests Woolf got the idea to use the word "bogey" to mean god from classicist Jane Ellen Harrison.

10. *Three Guineas*, 121. The "founder" is Jesus. Paul is the mind who interprets the mind of the Church, and who changed his own mind (122); she saw him as one of "the virile or dominant type, so familiar at present in Germany, for whose gratification a subject race or sex is essential" (n 38, p. 167, a long note worthy of Antoinette Wire, arguing with Paul's "shifty" reasons for the veiling of women

keep rooting through her work to know more, to find out what she thought "religion meant in the mind of its founder," and what it meant in her mind. A full-length study is needed of her "spiritual vision, the ascetic, moral, practical and political 'religion' which informs her thinking"[11] and of her "subversive, sceptical mysticism."[12]

She was brought up — as my own father was — with an aggressive, humanistic atheism. Her early notions of Christianity were vague. All through her twenties she argued with its hypocrisy, censorship, justification of colonialism, its ethics.[13] Her father Leslie Stephen, one of the most famous rationalists and agnostics of his generation, communicated a strong disdain for and disinterest in religion, from which he had recovered early in life. "I now believe in nothing, to put it shortly; but I do not the less believe in morality, &c. &c." he wrote in 1865.[14] When her mother Julia's first husband died, "she flung aside her religion, and became, as I have heard, the most positive of disbelievers. She reversed those natural instincts which were so strong in her of happiness and joy in a generous and abundant life, and pressed the bitterest fruit only to her lips. She visited the poor, nursed the dying, and felt herself possessed of the true secret of life at last, which is still obscured from a few, though they too must come to know it, that sorrow is our lot, and at best we can but face it bravely. . . . She saw many clever people, and read with a desire to establish her own sad faith, the works of disbelievers who spelt

in 1 Corinthians 11). Contemporary feminist critics share the common methodological confusions about how to get at the mind of the historical Jesus, wondering if this is possible or desirable. Not only is much interpretation patriarchal and sexist, for some, so are the Gospels themselves.

11. J. Marcus, "Niece of a Nun: Virginia Woolf, Caroline Stephen, and the Cloistered Imagination," *Virginia Woolf: a Feminist Slant* (ed. J. Marcus; Lincoln: University of Nebraska, 1983) 7–36. The study of the religious dimension of Woolf's work has begun in the work of Marcus and others. Some examples: M. Moore, *The Short Season Between Two Silences: The Mystical and the Political in the Novels of Virginia Woolf* (Boston: George Allen & Unwin, 1984); R. Blau Du Plessis, *Writing Beyond the Ending* (Bloomington: Indiana University Press, 1985) chapter 10 (n 24, p. 241: "a massive yet tentative revisionary look at Christianity" in *Between the Acts*); S. P. Rosenbaum, "Virginia Woolf and the Intellectual Origins of Bloomsbury," *Virginia Woolf: Centennial Essays* (ed. E. K. Ginsberg and L. M. Gottlieb; Troy, N.Y.: Whitson, 1983) 11–26; M. Hussey, *The Singing of the Real World: the Philosophy of Virginia Woolf's Fiction* (Columbus: Ohio State University Press, 1986) xv–xx; T. C. Caramango, *The Flight of the Mind* (Berkeley: University of California, 1992); C. J. Marshik, "Virginia Woolf and Feminist Intellectual History"; K. Koenigsberger, "Excavating the Elephant and Castle: Joanna Southcott and the Voice of Prophecy in *A Room of One's Own*," *Virginia Woolf and Her Influences*, 99–104; papers on Philosophy and Religion in *Mrs Dalloway* and *To the Lighthouse*, in *Virginia Woolf and Her Influences*; the section "Virginia Woolf and Mysticism," *Virginia Woolf and the Arts; Selected Papers from the Sixth Annual Conference on Virginia Woolf* (ed. D. F. Gillespie and L. K. Hankins; New York: Pace University Press, 1997). Cf. Q. Bell's disappointing discussion in *Virginia Woolf: A Biography* (New York: Harcourt, Brace, Jovanovich, 1972) 2.135.

12. V. Gough, "With Some Irony in Her Interrogation: Woolf's Ironic Mysticism," *Virginia Woolf and the Arts*, 85–97 (88). See also M. Minow-Pinkney, " 'How then does light return to the world after the eclipse of the sun? Miraculously, frailly': A Psychoanalytic Interpretation of Woolf's Mysticism," *Virginia Woolf and the Arts*, 92–98.

13. H. Lee, *Virginia Woolf* (New York: Knopf, 1997) 222–23.

14. F. Maitland, *The Life and Letters of Leslie Stephen* (London: Duckworth, 1906) 144.

God without a capital G."[15] Woolf remembered brutal attempts of her cousins to convert her in her youth: their god she saw as a rapist: "He's got a finger in my mind."[16] Her husband Leonard was a Jew (the only Jew ever to be an Apostle at Cambridge), a lifelong skeptic, socialist, and political activist.

It has been suggested that the "overt use of Christian symbolism in her novels may have constituted a tacit rebellion against an atheistic scepticism she associated with patriarchal intolerance."[17] I think the matter more complicated than this. The symbolism is not "overt," perhaps not symbolism at all. "I meant *nothing* by The Lighthouse. One has to have a central line down the middle of the book to hold the design together. I saw that all sorts of feelings would accrue to this, but I refused to think them out, and trusted that people would make it the deposit for their own emotions — which they have done, one thinking it means one thing another another. I can't manage Symbolism except in this vague, generalized way. Where its right or wrong I don't know; but directly I'm told what a thing means, it becomes hateful to me"[18]

She agrees with the criticisms of religion, she accepts the agnosticism. She places it in tension with something else. Marcus calls Woolf's "communion of saints" "a conspiracy against the aggressive godlessness of Leslie Stephen and Leonard Woolf — it was a political and anti-patriarchal piety in which the materialist worship of solid objects and solid flesh could be combined with the visionary rhapsodies of a Greek chorus demanding justice from the gods."[19] If this is a "conspiracy," it is overt and two-sided. Woolf remembered long hours of talk in her Aunt Caroline Emelia Stephen's room "with the windows opening onto the garden" at her Cambridge cottage called "The Porch." Woolf allowed herself a fascination with the faith of Caroline Emelia Stephen, author of works like *The Light Arising: Thoughts on the Central Radiance*.[20] Woolf wrote that her aunt's life "had about it the harmony of a large design," and yet had something "tender and almost pathetic" about it.[21] Woolf had ambivalence and love for both sides of

15. V. Woolf, *Moments of Being* (2d ed.; New York: Harcourt Brace Jovanovich, 1985) 32–33; see 90 on her mother's sceptical, serious spirit.
16. Quoted by J. Marcus, "Liberty, Sorority, Misogyny," *The Representation of Women in Fiction* (ed. C. G. Heilbrun and M. R. Higonnet; Baltimore: Johns Hopkins, 1983) 70.
17. S. A. Henke, "Mrs Dalloway: the Communion of Saints," *New Feminist Essays on Virginia Woolf* (ed. J. Marcus: Lincoln: University of Nebraska, 1981) n. 8, p. 145. Henke is thinking of such symbols as the dinner party, the scapegoat's death and transfiguration.
18. V. Woolf, *Letters* 3:385; to Roger Fry.
19. J. Marcus, "Thinking Back Through Our Mothers," *New Feminist Essays on Virginia Woolf* (ed. J. Marcus; Lincoln: University of Nebraska, 1981) n. 7, p. 28.
20. Cambridge: Heffner, 1908; see also *The Vision of Faith* (Cambridge: Heffner and Sons, 1911) and *Quaker Strongholds* (Headley Brothers, 1890).
21. V. Woolf's obituary for her aunt, *Guardian* (church weekly) 21 April 1909, quoted by Marcus, "Thinking Back," n. 7, p. 29–30; also in *The Essays of Virginia Woolf* (ed. A. McNeillie; New York: Harcourt Brace Jovanovich, 1986) 1.267–9; see *Letters of Virginia Woolf* (ed. N. Nicolson and J. Trautmann; New York: Harcourt Brace Jovanovich, 1975) 1.229. "Caroline Stephen had one enemy she struggled against all her life as the daughter of an educated man with the power of religious words —

the tension. Some critics, it seems to me, lessen the tension. James Wood places Woolf in the company of Melville, Flaubert, and Joyce, all writers "great enough to move between the religious impulse and the novelistic impulse, to distinguish between them and yet, miraculously, to draw on both." For Woolf, he says, "there was no formal agony of religious belief. The hard work had been done. For her, a kind of religious or mystical belief and a literary belief softly consorted — and yet, for her, the novel still retained its skeptical, inquisitorial function. In her writing the novel acts mystically, only to show that we cannot reach the godhead, for the godhead has disappeared. For her the novel acts religiously but performs skeptically."[22] Rather for her, I think, religion and skepticism are painfully, beautifully intertwined. The hard work is far from finished. Terry DeHay writes that Woolf was ahead of the current debate about community, "already working to create a synthesis between the individualism of liberalism and the collectivism of the communitarian vision, at the same time challenging the fundamental assumptions of nationalism."[23] Her attempted synthesis challenges the fundamental assumptions of religion as well. For her, egalitarianism implies a continuous upheaval of ideas, a rich confusion, and the lack of central, omniscient leadership.[24] Her discussion of religion is in the context of her broader discussion, in *Three Guineas* and elsewhere, How do we prevent war?

Her recent biographer Hermione Lee describes Woolf in the 1930s reading the New Testament, the book of Job and other religious works "with fascination and anger."[25] In her diary Woolf only remarked, "I want, rather vainly, to read the Book of Job."[26] And two weeks later, "Shall I now read the New Testament?"[27] — but we have no reading notes. There are, however, passages like this footnote in *Three Guineas*: she is thankful that "Shakespeare lived too late to be canonized by the Church. Had the plays been ranked among the sacred books they must have received the same treatment as the Old and the New Testaments; we should have had them doled out on Sundays from the mouths of priests in snatches . . . sliced up and interspersed with hymns . . . and Shakespeare would have been as unreadable as the Bible. Yet those who have not been forced from childhood to hear it thus

the Bible and the Book of Common Prayer — to oppress and suppress individual religious feeling. Sermons, the set pieces of preachers, and the traditional forms of protestant worship seemed to imprison her. Silence set her free." Instead of explicating biblical texts or logically explaining doctrine, Qurkers dealt in images and metaphors (Marcus, "Niece of a Nun," 28–29). Leaska (*Granite and Rainbow*, 99) dismisses the "kind but exceedingly dull aunt" and her "sleepy benignity."

22. J. Wood, *The Broken Estate* (New York: Random House, 1999) xvi.

23. T. DeHay, "Gathering Around the Punch Bowl: Woolf's Alternative Narrative Communities," *Virginia Woolf and Communities: Selected Papers from the Eighth Annual Conference on Virginia Woolf* (ed. J. McVicker and L. Davis; New York: Pace University Press, 1999) 179. She is questioning the "hierarchical assumptions that underlie most Western theories of governance" (L. P. Ruotolo, *The Interrupted Moment* (Stanford: Stanford University Press, 1986) 231.

24. Ruotolo, *The Interrupted Moment*, 232, on the experimental college of *Three Guineas*.

25. Lee, *Virginia Woolf*, 631.

26. *Diary*, 4.185.

27. *Diary*, 4.187.

dismembered weekly assert that the Bible is a work of the greatest interest, much beauty, and deep meaning."[28] I read this last remark not as sarcasm, nor some ploy used in order not to appear too radical; she was too honest for that. Certainly she knew the Bible as foremost among the "urtexts of oppression" (Rosenfeld's phrase), providing the West with sanction for violence and oppression, in need of total deconstruction.[29] Lee compares Woolf's criticism of Christianity as agent of repression in *Three Guineas* (1938) with her more mixed feelings about religion (baffled skepticism, enchantment/disbelief) in *The Years* (1937) and *To the Lighthouse* (1927). In the earlier works, "The social injustices carried out in the name of Christianity battle against the allure of its consolatory language."[30] There is change and development in Woolf's views, certainly, and her last novel *Between the Acts* and her last essays (1941) are essential to this discussion. But even the early feelings as mixed. In *Three Guineas* especially we find insight which is still contemporary, still unheeded, although the issue she focused on, of opening the priesthood to women, is decided in favor of opening it in all but the most sexist forms of Christianity.

Woolf identified "the spirit of religion" with the spirit of nationalism, the patriotism and fascism that lead to war, the seductive call of the voice of authority: "the spirit of religion was abroad with her eyes bandaged tight and her lips gaping wide."[31] She could skewer prelates as well as Fellini: "Your clothes in the first place make us gape with astonishment.... Even stranger, however, than the symbolic splendour of your clothes are the ceremonies that take place when you wear them. Here you kneel; there you bow; here you advance in procession behind a man carrying a silver poker; here you mount a carved chair; here you appear to do homage to a piece of painted wood; here you abase yourselves before tables covered with richly worked tapestry. And whatever these ceremonies may mean you perform them always together, always in step, always in the uniform proper to the man and the occasion."[32] It is very important to know who follows whom. Woolf argues that the Church and its literature should be scrutinized, that the Society of Outsiders should "make it their business to have some knowledge of the Christian religion and its history. Further that they would inform themselves of the practice of that religion by attending Church services, by analyzing the intellectual and spiritual value of sermons; by criticizing the opinions of men whose profession is religion as freely as they would criticize the opinions of any other body of men. Thus they would be creative in their activities, not merely critical." She is fascinated by "an experiment in passivity": young women absenting them-

28. *Three Guineas*, n. 29, p. 180.
29. N. Rosenfeld, *Outsiders Together: Virginia and Leonard Woolf* (Princeton: Princeton University Press, 2000) 157.
30. Lee, *Virginia Woolf*, 632.
31. Woolf, *Mrs. Dalloway* (New York: Harcourt Brace Jovanovich, 1953) 20.
32. *Three Guineas*, 20. Not just prelates, but soldiers, kings and queens, prime ministers, judges.

selves from the churches, "obviously the kind of experiment that great numbers of outsiders can practice with very little difficulty or danger ... and this experiment in passivity, whatever our belief in the value of the Church of England as a spiritual agency, is highly encouraging to us as outsiders."[33]

Woolf critically and creatively reads the report of the Archbishops' Commission on the Ministry of Women, "which costs only one shilling and should be in the hands of all educated men's daughters."[34] It puts forth the view that "the Gospels show us that our Lord regarded men and women alike as members of the same spiritual kingdom, as children of God's family, and as possessors of the same spiritual capacities." The prime qualification for the profession of religion was apparently a divine gift of prophecy, given to women as to men, and empowering both to preach. Still, the Commission argued — from 1 Timothy 2:12, from "the mind of the Church" and from the "fact" of its organization in the early centuries when prophet and prophetess became extinct — woman should be excluded from the priesthood on the grounds of her sex. Its conclusion was: "While the Commission as a whole would not give their positive assent to the view that a woman is inherently incapable of receiving the grace of Order, and consequently to admission to any of the three Orders, we believe that the general mind of the Church is still in accord with the continuous tradition of a male priesthood."[35]

Without a footnote to indicate she is doing anything but attacking on her own the pamphlet's logic, Woolf counters that "the profession of religion seems to have been much what the profession of literature is now. It was originally open to anyone who had received the gift of prophecy. No training was needed; the professional requirements were simple in the extreme — a voice and a marketplace, a pen and paper. . . . [P]rophecy was a voluntary and unpaid for occupation. But when the Church became a profession, required special knowledge of its prophets and paid them for imparting it, one sex remained outside; the other was excluded."[36] She compares the salary of an archbishop in England in 1938 (15,000 pounds) with that of a deaconess (150 pounds).

She was especially interested in Appendix I to this pamphlet: "Certain Psychological and Physiological Considerations" by Professor Grensted DD of Oxford. He saw it of "the very greatest practical importance" that strong hostile feeling is aroused by any suggestion that women should be admitted to the threefold Order of the Ministry. "This strength of feeling, conjoined with a wide variety of rational explanations, is clear evidence of the presence of powerful and widespread subconscious motive," based in "infantile fixation. . . . So far as psychology is concerned there is no theoretical reason why this Christian priesthood should

33. *Three Guineas*, 113, 118–19.
34. *Three Guineas*, 118.
35. *Three Guineas*, 124.
36. *Three Guineas*, 123–24.

not be exercised by women as well as men and in exactly the same sense. The difficulties which the psychologist foresees are emotional and practical only."[37] Woolf is pleased with this gift of an explanation — "infantile fixation" — at the root of men's anger, which causes women's fear of speaking. She supplies two motives for denying women the priesthood: first, money ("To pay women more would be to pay men less"), and secondly, women's care of family and household freeing men to withdraw and study (men would lose that total support).

Both this anger and this fear prevent real freedom. Analysis of the profession of religion, which "since it is the highest of all, may be taken as the type of all," throws light on the other professions as it bases itself "on mind and tradition."[38] "Society it seems was a father, and afflicted with the infantile fixation too." But the strong force of the fixation is met with the force of the daughters' opposition — Woolf says we have no word for this force — of tremendous power and inspired by real emotions: "Tears were behind it, of course — bitter tears: the tears of those whose desire for knowledge was frustrated.... Also the desire for an open and rational love was behind it.... But again the desire not to love, to lead a rational existence without love, was behind it ... to travel, to explore Africa; to dig in Greece and Palestine ... to learn music, to paint ... they wanted, like Antigone, not to break the laws, but to find the law."[39]

In other works, Woolf depicts religion's consolatory language as lying about the world. Suddenly Mrs Ramsey in *To the Lighthouse* says to herself, "We are in the hands of the Lord.... What brought her to say that: 'We are in the hands of the Lord'? she wondered. The insincerity slipping in among the truths roused her, annoyed her. She returned to her knitting again. How could any Lord have made this world? she asked."[40] The consolatory language is enchanting, unbelievable. Woolf comments on a marriage ceremony at the Church of St. Bartholomew the Great, Smithfield: "Oh but the inadequacy of the service — the sense of its being the entirely obsolete & primitive voice of a defunct tribal magnate, laying down laws for the government of the tribe: & then these civilized sceptical people letting themselves pretend that they obey. That clogged & diluted all the real feeling ... & the respectability & the wavering watery music: the perpetual compromise."[41] Woolf records feeling at the funeral of the great classicist Jane Ellen Harrison "as usual the obstacle of not believing [which] dulled and bothered me. Who is 'God' & what the Grace of Christ? & what did they mean to Jane?"[42] Woolf described her teacher Harrison as "the flash of some terrible reality leaping,

37. *Three Guineas*, 126.
38. *Three Guineas*, 121, 127.
39. *Three Guineas*, 135, 137–38.
40. Woolf, *To the Lighthouse*, 180.
41. *Diary*, 4.127.
42. *Diary*, 3.181.

as its way is, out of the heart of the spring."[43] In contrast, at the cremation of her Greek teacher Janet Case there were "No words; an adagio from Beethoven, & a text about gentleness & faith, wh. I would have included had I known. But what does my writing matter? There is something fitting & complete about the memory of her, thus consummated . . . Janet was the steadfast contemplative one, anchored in some private faith wh. didn't correspond with the worlds."[44]

In exploring the tension between rationalism and the religious impulse, between real feeling and pretense, Woolf went her own way, beyond family, following "'Imagination' — the quality I most admired & missed most in my father & his agnostic friends."[45] Christianity, she wrote to Ethel Smyth, was "so insistent and so sad . . . such a canting creed."[46] But, defending Leonard's hostility to religion against Ethel's criticism, she could say, "my Jew has more religion in one toe nail — more human love, in one hair." Marder's comment may be correct: "Her tone had lost its satirical edge and become simply indignant. 'My Jew has more religion. . . .' Here she meant exactly what she said."[47] Here is that faith so high that it "believes that it is right to develop your powers to the full," a richer way of looking at the world than the faith whose metaphors of wind and light "solve all personal energy, all irregularity, into one suave stream . . . is wise and harmonious, beautifully simple and innocent."[48]

The tension is dramatized by Woolf for the last time in the tension between adversarial viewpoints, those of Lucy Swithin and her brother Bartholomew Oliver in *Between the Acts:* "He would carry the torch of reason till it went out in the darkness of the cave. For herself, every morning, kneeling, she protected her vision."[49] Whether or not in Virginia Woolf's skull, as in Lucy's, there existed what Bart calls "a prayable being . . . a force or radiance,"[50] Woolf was deeply interested

43. *Room*, 17.
44. *Diary*, 5.102–3.
45. *Diary*, 3.246.
46. *Letters*, 5.319.
47. H. Marder, *The Measure of Life: Virginia Woolf's Last Years* (Ithaca: Cornell University Press, 2000) 160.
48. V. Woolf, "The Inward Light," review in *TLS*, February 27, 1908, of *The Inward Light* by H. F. Hall (Macmillan & Co, 1908) about a European who had become "a Burman in religion"; in *The Essays of Virginia Woolf* (ed. A. McNeillie; New York: Harcourt Brace Jovanovich, 1986) 1.173.
49. V. Woolf, *Between the Acts* (New York: Harcourt Brace Jovanovich, 1941) 205–6. It is a mistake to reduce this to conflict between Virginia and Leonard Woolf, to reduce Virginia to one side of the tension; but R. Poole does see her trying to protect her vision here "firstly against the terrifying approach of total war, and secondly in spite of a lifetime's belittlement, disappointment, fear and effort" (*The Unknown Virginia Woolf* [London: Cambridge University Press, 1978] 243, 235). I. Coates, *Who's Afraid of Leonard Woolf: A Case for the Sanity of Virginia Woolf* (New York: Soho, 1998) reads in a rage, and sees Leonard as getting away with "a slow and subtle form of murder" (349). Although Woolf's "black, sardonic story," "The Legacy," her earlier story "Lappin and Lapinova," and the battle of Isa and Giles in *Between the Acts* are "harsh, ironic version[s] of the dark side of her own marriage" (Lee, *Virginia Woolf*, 736), I think Rosenfeld is right to emphasize "both the irritation, and the inspiration provided by Leonard Woolf" to Virginia; she argues that their marriage "played a vital role in the engagement with injustice" that informs her works (*Outsiders Together*, 3, 5).
50. *Between the Acts*, 25.

in it, and in the tension. Lucy Swithin is indeed "a potentially redemptive figure who falls short," whose "visions of unity are too easily achieved,"[51] but to me she, like Miss LaTrobe who re-writes Genesis, and Reverend Streatfield who claims we are members of one another, is more than "a reminder of the effortless epiphanies — and certitudes — of the past."[52] The past and the failure of its visions are part of the future toward which Woolf aims.

She "made up for her lack of an integrated, meaningful, and above all comforting vision by literally making it up, creating it not out of conviction or even theory, but out of sheer will and imagination, and she gave it to all her characters.... [I]n doing so she was both exerting power over the imagined life, and giving the vision to herself as she existed in her characters."[53] This I take as part of our feminist religious heritage and future. For Woolf, the individual imagination is not alone; it expresses the collective consciousness. "Masterpieces are not single and solitary births, they are the outcome of thinking in common, of thinking by the body of the people, so that the experience of the mass is behind the single voice"[54] She regarded all of us human beings as part of the work of art that is the whole world. "Hamlet or a Beethoven quartet is the truth about this vast mass that we call the world. But there is no Shakespeare, there is no Beethoven; certainly and emphatically there is no God; we are the words; we are the music; we are the thing itself And I see this when I have a shock."[55] The "absentmindedness" of a character such as Mrs. Ramsey in *To the Lighthouse*, "forgetfulness" of her own being at the center, and the readers' experience of this, "brings us closer to what Woolf called 'life.' In her novels, thought radiates outward, as a medieval town radiates outward — from a beautifully neglected center."[56]

Perhaps unsolvable is the question of how her suicide in 1941 relates to her powerful vision of life, to her mental/emotional condition, and to the monstrous war. Heilbrun thinks Kenney's description of the vision quoted above is perfect except for *Between the Acts*: "Woolf believed that life would begin again, but not that she would ever be a part of it, even in her imagination. She did not wish to be a part of it, and her characters could not act for her. Thus *Between the Acts* ends

---

51. Rosenfeld, *Outsiders Together*, 164; cf. Ruotolo, *The Interrupted Moment*, 211–12.

52. M. DiBattista, *"Between the Acts*: The Play of Will," in *Virginia Woolf: Modern Critical Views* (ed. H. Bloom; New York: Chelsea House, 1986) 143,quoted by Rosenfeld, *Outsiders Together*, 164; see A. Zwerdling, *Virginia Woolf and the Real World* (Berkeley: University of California, 1986) 313, for the view that Streatfield and Lucy Swithin do not speak for Woolf; they do not take note of the airplanes above. Though the possibility of a return to community is never denied in the pageant, "the forces of dispersal" are shown to be ascending "with the power of historical inevitability.... In reality, the pageant fails to unite the spectators" (320).

53. S. M. Kenney, "Two Endings: Virginia Woolf's Suicide and *Between the Acts*," *University of Toronto Quarterly* (summer 1975) 275.

54. Woolf, *Room*, 98.

55. V. Woolf, *Moments of Being* (2d ed.; ed. J. Schulkind; New York: Harcourt Brace Jovanovich, 1985) 72.

56. Wood, *Broken Estate*, 99.

with the possibility of a childbirth she had not risked, an act unconnected with herself at that time.... She did not find within herself great powers of renewal" after she exhausted herself embodying woman's anger in her fifties. "She chose to end her life before the chance to make that decision for herself could be taken from her." Madness, Heilbrun thinks, was the easiest way Woolf had to describe her despair, given the conditions of her world.[57] Lee argues that the act of suicide was "rational, deliberate, and courageous."[58] Poole sees it as a beautiful, creative, responsible, idealistic choice.[59] Without claiming she was a war casualty, or one who gave up the fight against fascism, Marder stresses Woolf's perceptions of Britain under siege, squarely facing the rising violence and her own suffering.[60] With our own world at war again, and the ethics of suicide again a subject of open debate, her action at the River Ouse takes on new meanings. Whether or not she could imagine or wish to be a part of the future, she *is* a part of it.

Zwerdling analyzes the end of Woolf's life as despairing: "her old faith in human betterment," her hope of a radically transformed world, could not be sustained in the face of present realities of human solitude and alienation and chaos. She could not see what anyone could have done or do to make a difference. "What eluded her was any understanding of how the present could conceivably lead to the future she imagined." He sees her giving up hope in the short run, but thinks that her longer historical sense "convinced her that even the radical transformations she had in mind — of feminine and masculine identity, of the aggressive 'instinct' — might well come about." Despair seen in the larger pattern of her life and thought brings new generations of readers to "a searching, non-utopian account of the relation between the individual life and the life of the community, and a belief in the possibility — even the inevitability — of society's eventual responsiveness to the criticism of the human beings who constitute it."[61] Why non-utopian? I see her dying poised, in the optative mood, rather than with a belief in inevitability. She does not reach beyond the world, beyond the human, toward an answer, and does not write of any answer coming to her. This is an apocalyptic context, even an apocalyptic moment, if/though not an apocalypse.

It is not unusual, I know, for Woolf to exercise a deep fascination over writers in other fields, and to lead them in new directions in those fields. The philosopher Sara Ruddick details how Woolf was the personal, direct agent of change in Ruddick's own life. Conferring a mysterious gift of authenticity, Woolf freed her from dependence on men's judgment and from professionalism, made women real for her, and helped her find her own mind, eyes, and voice. She taught her

---

57. C. G. Heilbrun, "Virginia Woolf in Her Fifties," *Virginia Woolf: A Feminist Slant* (ed. J. Marcus; Lincoln: University of Nebraska, 1983) 248–49.
58. Lee, *Virginia Woolf*, 744.
59. See Poole, *The Unknown Virginia Woolf*, 245; cf. Marcus, *Art & Anger*, 150–51.
60. Marder, *Measure*. Coates sees her as virtually if not actually murdered by Leonard.
61. Zwerdling, *Virginia Woolf and the Real World*, 326–29.

to allow feeling to inform her most abstract thinking. "She showed me a place outside of charmed circles where I could stand."[62] Woolf's influence has been felt in many disciplines; but to my knowledge not yet much in Religious Studies. In my own case, she functions something like the mentor I never had. "Consulting" her, reading her avidly in the course of writing this book, is part of the feminist methodology I use here, infusing and refreshing the conventional methodologies of my discipline, oxygenating the masculinist atmosphere. Woolf puts me in the mood to think and write; she somehow keeps me going. She teaches the writer's life of concentration and commitment, and makes it happier, by repudiating the sacrifice of friendship, love, and simple social pleasures, and of the needs of others. Scorning "adultery of the brain" or "intellectual harlotry" (writing what one does not want to write, for the sake of money rather than in the interests of culture and intellectual liberation[63]), she urges connected thinking, and political savvy. "[S]he did not escape to fantasy. In her life she fought despair and comforted others."[64] Woolf's blend of artistry, feminism, socialism, and pacifism,[65] and "her insistence on the sexual inflection of all questions of historical understanding and literary representation,"[66] her practice of working in the context of collaborative friendships, set an integrated critical ideal for me. She knew how to plot the twists and turns of patriarchal logic; how to condemn yet understand the "father."[67] Her tolerance of ambiguity, of multiple, provisional points of view, is freeing. In her insistence that our knowledge of anyone and anything is tentative and incomplete, she was epistemologically modest.[68] I am aware of the dangers of overreading, of presuming, of speaking "proprietarily about her life."[69] I make no claim, of course, that Woolf's writings accurately interpret biblical material or vice versa. But my claim is that they can be good, useful, and beautiful together: an oblong standing on a square.[70]

---

62. S. Ruddick, "New Combinations: Learning from Virginia Woolf," *Between Women* (ed. C. Ascher, L. deSalvo, S. Ruddick; Boston: Beacon, 1980) 138.

63. *Three Guineas*, 81, 94.

64. S. Ruddick, "Private Brother, Public World," *New Feminist Essays on Virginia Woolf* (ed. J. Marcus; Lincoln: University of Nebraska, 1981) 209.

65. See N. Black, "Virginia Woolf and the Women's Movement," *Virginia Woolf: A Feminist Slant* (ed. J. Marcus; Lincoln: University of Nebraska, 1983) 180–97; *The Cambridge Companion to Virginia Woolf* (ed. S. Roe and S. Sellers; Cambridge: Cambridge University Press, 2000).

66. R. Bowlby, *Virginia Woolf: Feminist Destinations* (London: Blackwell, 1988) 15.

67. On her reconciliation with the memory of her father, see Caramango, *The Flight of the Mind*, 244.

68. Ruddick, "Private Brother," 192.

69. Lee, *Virginia Woolf*, 4; D. Royer, "Remaking Virginia: A Caution for Readers," *Virginia Woolf & Communities: Selected Papers from the Eighth Annual Conference on Virginia Woolf* (ed. J. McVicker and L. Davis; New York: Pace University Press, 1999) 187.

70. Rhoda in V. Woolf, *The Waves* (New York: Harcourt Brace Jovanovich, 1931) 288: "The structure is now visible, what is inchoate is here stated; we are not so various or so mean, we have made oblongs and stood them upon squares. This is our triumph; this our consolation." It is the structure of art.

Woolf liked romantically to see herself a redeemer of lost lives, the deliverer of the stranded ghosts of history — women and the working class: "I ... have a plan already to get historical manuscripts & write Lives of the Obscure." "It was, I think, the only romantic indulgence she allowed herself," says Marcus.[71] Woolf insists on herself also in my imagination as in some way a counterpart or companion of the ghost I am hunting, the all-but-erased woman from the first Christian century, whose traditions need untangling. Virginia Woolf and Mary Magdalene. Why not? Both "mad" or "ill" women: one "neurotic" or "manic-depressive," one "possessed." Both exorcised or self-exorcised.[72] Both talking about "moments of vision." Both Outsiders to "the patriarchal circus," and neither of them Apostles. Woolf's Outsiders have four great teachers from whom they should refuse to be separated: poverty, (intellectual) chastity, derision, and lack of rights and privileges, which can lead to freedom from unreal loyalties (from pride of nationality, religion, school, family, sex). They should be combined with some wealth, some knowledge, and some service to real loyalties.[73] These four, it seems to me, can be thought to have taught with Jesus of Nazareth. Many of the males of Woolf's family and circle were members of the Cambridge University semi-secret Conversazione Society called the Apostles who, though they voted in 1894 to admit women, did not do so until 1970.[74] Woolf mocked this society by creating a "parallel sisterhood of intellectual inquiry and social conscience" in her London conversazione society of fictional females, which had no restriction on the number of members.[75] Woolf's model as a parallel concept 'had to confront male concepts of female chastity and brutality and violence against women, as well as its own lack of an institutional power base."[76] Mary Magdalene was not an apostle in the Lucan sense (Acts 1:21–22), and never even called a disciple in the canonical texts, though as we will see later there is ample evidence she fulfilled the roles and was denied the titles. But then, maybe the lack of titles is important; maybe she was something else, which was given no name. As Woolf's aunt Carolyn Stephen put it, mystics are "indisposed to discipleship. ... They sit at no man's feet and do not ... greatly care to have anyone sit at theirs."[77] Luke 8:1–3 mentions those who travelled with Jesus in the Galilee: first the Twelve men, and then (as though they

71. *Diary*, 3.129. J. Marcus, "Invisible Mending," *Between Women*, 39.

72. "[In her novels] I found that Virginia had herself documented the reasons for her own mental distress, and very intelligently 'exorcised' certain key persons and passages from her conscious or unconscious life by writing them fully out" (Poole, *The Unknown Virginia Woolf*, 3.

73. *Three Guineas*, 78.

74. A. Banfield, *The Phantom Table: Woolf, Fry, Russell and the Epistemology of Modernism* (New York: Cambridge University Press, 2000) 20–21; P. Levy, *Moore: G. E. Moore and the Cambridge Apostles* (London: Weidenfeld and Nicolson, 1979.

75. See J. Marcus, "Liberty, Sorority, Misogyny," *The Representation of Women in Fiction* (ed. C. G. Heilbrun and M. R. Higonnet; Baltimore: Johns Hopkins, 1983) 67.

76. Marcus, "Liberty, Sorority," 67. "[I]t was Woolf's revolutionary goal to storm the gates of Cambridge to steal the secret of what sociologists call 'same-sex bonding'" (68).

77. C. Stephen *The Light Arising*, 47 quoted by Marcus, "Niece of a Nun," 27.

were some sort of parallel society like Philo's Therapeutrids to the Therapeutae) many women, three of whom are named, Mary Magdalene, Joanna, and Susanna.

Mary Magdalene is one of the three Marys, at least in the Johannine crucifixion scene and in harmonizations of Synoptic texts. So too is Woolf one of three, when in *A Room of One's Own* she revives for herself three Marys from the Elizabethan "Ballad of Mary Hamilton." Mary Hamilton, a lady in waiting to the Queen of Scotland, is singing from the gallows; she is about to die for killing the baby born of her rape by the King. "Last night there were four Marys / Tonight there'll be but three / There's Mary Beton and Mary Seton / and Mary Carmichael and me." Woolf says, "Call me Mary Beton, Mary Seton, Mary Carmichael, or by any name you please — it is not a matter of any importance."[78] The first two of these Marys, in Woolf's reading, supply money and space for the third Mary to become an author, and in a hundred years, a poet. Mary Hamilton, unmentioned by Woolf, is "an uncannily powerful presence," lost to most readers who are unfamiliar with the ballad. Her story parallels that of Woolf's tragic Judith Shakespeare who lives on "in you and in me, and in many other women who are not here tonight, for they are washing up the dishes and putting the children to bed."[79] All these Marys "embody Woolf's collective self; together they enact 'the common life which is the real life.' "[80] The posthumous lives of Mary Magdalene and Virginia Woolf are parallel too, the stuff of myth and legend. Both "went on living and changing after death,"[81] becoming icons put to many different uses, "symptomatic of embedded layers of cultural anxiety."[82]

These are two of the mothers through and toward and beyond whom I want to think back and forward and beyond. "[W]e think back through our mothers if we are women. It is useless to go to the great men writers for help, however much one may go to them for pleasure." The mind "can think back through its fathers or through its mothers, as I have said that a woman writing thinks back through her mothers."[83] Woolf tells us mental matricide is not necessary for the woman artist, the woman thinker.[84] She can think also through the absence of mothers[85] and through fathers. And sideways, back through sisters and brothers.

---

78. Woolf, *Room*, 5.

79. Woolf, *Room*, 113; see M. DeKoven, "The Community of Audience: Woolf's Drama of Public Woman," *Virginia Woolf & Communities*, 240; Du Plessis, *Writing Beyond the Ending*, 31; P. M. Spacks, *The Female Imagination* (New York: Knopf, 1975) 155. The ballad (Child 385) is on Joan Baez's first Vanguard album, *Joan Baez*.

80. L. Rusk, "The Collective Self: Maxine Hong Kingston and Virginia Woolf," *Virginia Woolf and Her Influences*, 182, quoting Woolf, *Room*, 113.

81. Lee, *Virginia Woolf*, 755.

82. B. R. Silver, *Virginia Woolf Icon* (Chicago: University of Chicago, 1999) 5; cf. S. Haskins, *Mary Magdalen: Myth and Metaphor* (London: Harper Collins, 1993).

83. Woolf, *Room*, 72–73, 79, 101. See Marcus, "Thinking Back," 1–30.

84. Marcus, "Thinking Back," 21.

85. Bowlby, *Feminist Destinations*, 27. G. E. Lyon ("Virginia Woolf and the Problem of the Body," *Virginia Woolf: Centennial Essays* [ed. E. K. Ginsberg and L. M. Gottlieb; Troy, N.Y.: Whitson, 1983] 112) remarks that motherlessness permeates Woolf's characters.

"As a socialist she urged women writers to think back through their mothers. As a feminist she urged them to think sideways through their sisters."[86] The family metaphors, of course, are soiled and inadequate; we think through friends and colleagues and lovers and enemies, and sometimes we think we think alone. B. London warns against perpetuating genealogical thinking that "reinscribes, from the distaff side, the structures of patriarchal authority," and against the family model that reinforces a binary, heterosexist framework.[87] "Thinking back through" the Magdalene means thinking through iconic images and misrepresentations, legends and half-truths, discoveries of ancient documents, the palimpsests of familiar texts, the reconstructions of history; thinking through what to save, what to toss, thinking and rethinking.

But this kind of thinking back can be dangerous. It might involve the creation of a mother who needs to be destroyed,[88] or a mother who disappoints,[89] who is a limitation of creativity. But if we are to learn to "'to think back through our mothers,' we must matter-of-factly endure their weaknesses so that we may concentrate our energies on their strengths,"[90] redeem them "from their compromises with the patriarchy."[91] There is the danger too that "thinking back" might lead to mistakenly imagining the past as a long-lost home. Studying history then would become an indulgence in nostalgia, in the dream of return and reunion, identification with faraway times, places and people, the creation of heroines and heroes.[92] This kind of thinking might seduce us into genealogical reasoning, reasoning like that about "apostolic succession." Buell argues that second and third century Christians made claims to legitimacy and authenticity by appealing to lineages, and that scholars have inadequately theorized and historically contextualized such claims by not paying attention to this appeal as a rhetorical strategy to define and control what would count as authentic Christian discourse.[93]

Treating the Magdalene as mother or sister is particularly susceptible to this, and difficult to avoid as we will see in chapter 7. In some modern treatments,

---

86. Marcus, "Liberty, Sorority, Misogyny," 87.

87. B. London, "Guerrilla in Petticoats or Sans-Culotte? Virginia Woolf and the Future of Feminist Criticism," *diacritics* 21 (1991) 18.

88. E. Showalter argues in *A Literature of Their Own* (Princeton: Princeton University Press, 1977) that Woolf was an unfit mother for women writers. Her idea of androgynous and anonymous art Showalter regards as a flight, not a liberation, from the dilemma of a polarized sexual existence. "Androgyny was the myth that helped her evade confrontation with her own painful femaleness and enabled her to choke and repress her anger and ambition."

89. Sapphire, "Breaking Karma: A Conversation with Sapphire," *Poets & Writers* (January/February 2000) 31.

90. Ruddick, "Private Brother," 213.

91. Marcus, "Thinking Back," 21.

92. See the discussion in M. Peskowitz, *Spinning Fantasies: Rabbis, Gender and History* (Berkeley: University of California, 1997) 154–55. To nostalgia she contrasts nostomania, an intense homesick desire that can never be met. On the Magdalene as heroine, see J. A. Grassi, *The Hidden Heroes of the Gospels: Female Counterparts of Jesus* (Collegeville, Minn.: Liturgical Press, 1998).

93. D. Buell, *Generative Polemics* (Princeton: Princeton University Press, forthcoming).

there is a an effort to make her the source of authority for twentieth- and twenty-
first-century ecclesiastical changes. Haskins ends her survey of the figure of the
Magdalene in art history and legend with reflections on her "rightful role" and
her existence as a "touchstone" in relation to such issues as the ministry and
ordination of women in Christian churches. She is "a symbol of women's right
to resume their place and role in the Church."[94] This, to my mind, can seduce
us into simplistic genealogical thinking. It also limits and confines the uses of
historical reconstruction, in this case to ecclesiastical reform, when this can be
put to much broader uses. The creation of a myth of origins produces too linear,
too confident reconstructions of the way things were, especially of too pristine
beginnings, and the privileging of those beginnings. We might forget that "these
are metaphorical mothers, or mothers of metaphorical invention,"[95] forget the
rhetorical struggles that produce and reproduce them; or forget Woolf's own idea
of collective character, and her refusal to create characters with whom the reader
can egotistically identify.[96] We might forget her tentativeness: archival records
tell many stories and the past can be rewritten in many ways. Thinking back —
through Woolf herself and through the Magdalene — can be the creation of
a mother or sister who is only oneself, nothing but oneself. "[T]hat the Woolf
'discovered' in the material of history turns out to be one precisely suited to
the critic's own 'radical feminist need' for what Gilbert and Gubar have called
'the most empowering, the most authoritative' ancestor is a coincidence worthy of
further iniquity."[97] Feminism's desire for a committed feminist and deeply political
Woolf corresponds to its desire (or the desire of some feminists) for a feminist
Mary Magdalene, an ancestor with whose help we might construct a religion
or a spirituality of one's own, or — better — something not yet named, along
those lines, restructured, reconceived, something outside these lines. Something
creating a new system "that does not shut out."[98]

   Aware of these risks and vulnerabilities, I nevertheless see the Magdalene as
someone through whom to think back, with whose nearly lost histories and whose
legends we need to connect, in our struggle for the past and future. If we see our
own image reflected in the past, and make the Magdalene in our image, we can
at least be aware of what we are doing, hunt for what disturbs that image, and
see it as a communal not individualistic image. See her as a figure about whom
we need to disagree.[99] Albert Schweitzer pointed to the mirror in our work, the
mirror as part of our equipment; but he showed it could be tipped toward the

94. Haskins, *Mary Magdalen*, 393–400, 397.
95. Bowlby, *Feminist Destinations*, 47.
96. Marcus, "Thinking Back," 9.
97. London, "Guerrilla," 14, citing S. M. Gilbert and S. Gubar, *No Man's Land* (New Haven: Yale
University Press, 1988) 1.200.
98. *Diary*, 4.127.
99. London, "Guerrilla," 27: If we must continually 'rescue' Woolf, if we continue to need her
name to stake our identity, it may be that we need her as a figure about whom to disagree."

future, in his case toward Lambarene. To lessen anxiety about our own attacks on the patriarchy, our efforts to destructure and restructure — for which there is always retaliation — I imagine some connection between Woolf's spirit and the Magdalene of history, so that the past might offer some protection as well as some precedent. This imagined link exemplifies Woolf's stress on the connected "thing itself," beyond separate egos. This book, in fact, is a kind of act of faith or an experiment in Woolf's vision of connectedness.[100] The vision serves to energize the research and writing — which, in the long run, is for the sake of imagining "a religion very different from that now erected on [the] basis [of the New Testament]."

Imagining the Magdalene as "this poet who never wrote a word and was buried at the crossroads [and who] still lives," who is a "continuing presence,"[101] may help exploration of the crossroads itself, and of roads not taken in the first Christian centuries, and now.[102] Studying her exclusion from the patriarchal procession leads to reflection on the types of power best shunned; the desire to join that procession is destroyed.[103] Woolf's feminism challenges patriarchy as a form of lunacy, ranting, losing its grip, on the verge of collapse.[104] She created in the character of Louis in *The Waves* one "who embodied those personal and political characteristics she most feared: envious hatred, frantic egocentricity, and a dangerous, compulsive will to dominate."[105] And yet she could still think even of patriarchs as brothers. Bernard imagines taking the arm of Rhoda who has committed suicide: "'Wait till these omnibuses have gone by. Do not cross so dangerously. These men are your brothers.' In persuading her I was also persuading my own soul."[106]

That all this need not be "necrophilic investment" is the subject of this book.[107] Historical work need not cripple the imagination by the creation of an idealized past or a flattering, distorting, magnifying mirror of limited, limiting possibilities. Rather, solidarity with the dead can energize solidarity with the living, and the

---

100. I owe this insight to Alicia Ostriker.

101. Woolf, *Room*, 171. Marcus ("Liberty, Sorority," 78) calls this a prediction of Judith Shakespeare's resurrection.

102. Before 1823 suicides were buried at crossroads so that the sign of the cross and traffic over it would keep their ghosts down. Judith Shakespeare is the figure of the criminalized female suicide, epitomizing the marginalization of women; see V. Gough, "'A Responsible Person Like her'" Woolf's Suicide Culture," *Virginia Woolf: Turning the Centuries: Selected Papers from the Ninth Annual Conference on Virginia Woolf* (ed. A. Ardis and B. K. Scott; New York: Pace University Press, 2000) 187.

103. *Three Guineas*, 60–62.

104. J. Rose, "Smashing the Teapots," review of Lee, *Virginia Woolf*, London Review of Books January 23, 1997, 6.

105. Ruddick, "Private Brother," 206.

106. Woolf, *The Waves*, 372.

107. London ("Guerilla," 17) argues that in feminist literary criticism "Woolf has become the dead body in whose name feminism erects its monuments and dates its history. Breathing life into her spirit, responding to her words, resurrecting her image, do we become *Woolf'* s other sister? More important, do we want or need this kinship . . . these prescribed possibilities? In this respect we would do well to ask whose interests are served by this necrophilic investment and whether there are roles available to us other than sister or daughter to our great predecessor."

political action that expresses that solidarity. The artist, the thinker, needs pre-decessors; and she needs to be one of a group of free discussion and practice.[108] Feminist historical reconstruction aims to rob history of its power to oppress.

I have tried to orientate this book toward a future for religion which Woolf may have glimpsed. In an effort to understand the traditions of Mary Magdalene and the other women at the empty tomb, and scholarly explorations of those traditions, I draw in the following pages on several of Woolf's major, interlocking motifs or ideas. The "anonymous and secret" Society of Outsiders[109] is crucial. Outsiders are marked by the denial of access to education, professions, and socio-cultural power. Woolf calls for a vow to remain Outsiders, to give up loyalties to militarism, hierarchy, authoritarianism and whatever benefits and rewards accrue from the male-centered world. And she tells us why we should take that vow, describing the immense peace she gained by the writing of *Three Guineas:* "I am an outsider. I can take my way: experiment with my own imagination in my own way. The pack may howl, but it shall never catch me. And even if the pack — reviewers, friends, enemies — pays me no attention or sneers, still I'm free. This is the actual result of that spiritual conversion (I cant bother to get the right words) in the autumn of 1933 — or 4 — when I rushed through London, buying, I remember, a great magnifying glass, from sheer ecstasy, near Blackfriars: when I gave the man who played the harp half a crown for talking to me about his life in the Tube station."[110] We should take that vow also as a vow to avoid becoming the Dictator, a figure from which we cannot disassociate ourselves, since women as well as men are responsible for tyranny.[111] The call to be an Outsider comes from the Society of Outsiders itself, not from the establishment. It is not a call to be excluded, be sacrificed, be crucified, but to live, and to connect. Fleishman sees that Woolf's portrait of the Outsider is related to the archetype of the scape-goat "which has traditionally accompanied the communal ideal. By the exclusion, sacrifice, or crucifixion of one of its members the group establishes or reaffirms its own organic ties."[112] From the standpoint of the establishment, the Outsider is a necessary victim; but from the standpoint of Outsiders, she or he is forming a new community; marginality is exploited "for collective political purposes."[113] Outsiders — " 'We' . . . all waifs and strays"[114] — are not responsible for the actions

---

108. V. Woolf, *New Statesman* 16 Oct 1920, responding to criticism of "A Society"; cited by Marcus, "Thinking Back," 2.

109. Woolf, *Three Guineas*, 109.

110. *Diary*, 5.141.

111. See N. Knowles, "A Community of Women Looking at Men: the Photographs in Virginia Woolf's *Three Guineas*," *Virginia Woolf & Communities*, 95–96.

112. A. Fleishman, *Virginia Woolf: A Critical Reading* (Baltimore: Johns Hopkins University Press, 1975) 77.

113. Marcus, "Niece of a Nun," 8.

114. *Diary*, 5.135.

of the patriarchs, but they are complicit if they remain silent. They must fight for freedom "with the mind."[115]

The Outsider's perspective and determination to remain outside causing trouble[116] are important to conversation over false boundaries, creating good confusion about what is central, centrality itself, and what is inside. The Outsiders' Society, if it existed, would reject the culture of violence; it would be without regimentation and formality, without leaders, dues, offices. "[I]ts name would be shorthand for many spontaneous private acts, or a way of reinventing society itself by introducing the values of domestic life into the public domain," setting women free for careers they choose and to receive equal pay for their work, including their domestic work.[117] And it does exist. The Society of Outsiders is no mere utopian invention; it is "in being and at work." It is elusive, but can be documented in newspapers, sometimes openly, sometimes between the lines.[118] It is a community of women — and perhaps of some men — with whom women can work and think and love as "outsiders together."[119] Negative markers can be turned into positive markers of difference, and marginal status turned to political advantage and political power. Outsiders "are critical inheritors."[120]

The question of inclusiveness is important. A. Zwerdling comments, "As in the first feminists, there is a residual conservative element in her identity that makes her reluctant, even in her most radical phases, to abandon altogether the ideal of women and men working in harmony for the same goals.... [S]he consistently idealizes a future world in which the sexes are no longer at cross-purposes.... The cooperative ideal is based on the belief that men's aggression is as much a product of false training as is women's submission." Zwerdling says this is Woolf at her most optimistic, and argues that in her later career, in the context of the rise of Fascism and war, her view that men are not willing or able to change is at least as powerful and dominates her works. "Despite Woolf's frequently expressed hope for a revolution in the relation between the sexes, she was more

---

115. V. Woolf, "Thoughts on Peace in an Air Raid" (August 1940) *The Death of the Moth and Other Essays* (New York: Harcourt Brace & Co., 1942) 244; see discussion by Rosenfeld, *Outsiders Together*, 156.

116. C. Exum points out that when women are viewed as inside the border of the phallocentric symbolic order — between men and chaos — they are seen to have protective qualities; when viewed as outside, they are dangerous ("Second Thoughts about Secondary Characters," *A Feminist Companion to Exodus and Deuteronomy* [ed. A. Brenner; Sheffield: Sheffield Academic Press, 1994] 86); T. Moi, *Sexual/Textual Politics* (London: Methuen, 1985) 167. Cf. E. Schüssler Fiorenza's resident alien troublemaker, Trin T. Min-ha's inappropriate(d) other.

117. Marder, *Measure*, 249–50.

118. *Three Guineas*, 119. Against Marder, *Measure*, 249.

119. Rosenfeld, *Outsiders Together*, 4: "In opposed yet complementary ways, the Woolfs were outsiders together — she privileged by her background but excluded from centers by her gender, he privileged by gender and marginalized through background." See below on Schüssler Fiorenza's definition of wo/men (pp. 103, 258).

120. DuPlessis, *Writing Beyond the Ending*, 170, 40.

deeply convinced of the unlikeliness of such a transformation."[121] Woolf's hope, however, must be put in the context of her mysticism which was an experience of oneness, as Zwerdling sees.[122] I do not see her death as a denial of this experience, though her "sense of the pervasiveness of human isolation" was acute in the final years.[123] The mysticism and hope are linked too with whatever in Woolf might be considered "resurrection." Clarissa Dalloway thinks unsystematically on death and survival and streets and trees and people and mist. "Did it matter, then, she asked herself, walking towards Bond Street, did it matter that she must inevitably cease completely; all this must go on without her; did she resent it; or did it not become consoling to believe that death ended absolutely? but that somehow in the streets of London, on the ebb and flow of things, here, there, she survived, Peter survived, lived in each other, she being part, she was positive, of the trees at home; or the house there, ugly, rambling all to bits and pieces as it was; part of people she had never met; being laid out like a mist between the people she knew best, who lifted her on their branches as she has seen the trees lift the mist, but it spread ever so far, her life, herself."[124]

The freedom Woolf urged from unreal loyalties led her to write "[A]s a woman I have no country. As a woman I want no country. As a woman my country is the whole world."[125] She can teach us to say, As a woman I have no religion. I am not Jew or Christian or Muslim or pagan — or — As a woman I am Jew, and Christian, and Muslim and pagan — a move which may bring us closer to appreciating aspects of first century c.e. pluralisms and identity constructions, as well as possibilities for the future. (I am thinking here of John Chrysostom's tirade against Christian women in fourth-century Antioch who were celebrating Jewish festivals of Rosh Hashanah, Yom Kippur, Sukkoth, probably with Jewish and pagan women.[126])

Woolf's mysticism is a topic some have avoided, as a trap: as a mystic she can be dismissed as a crank, irrational, eccentric,[127] apolitical. But the mysticism is there. I can't see that it matters what we call it: "agnosticism with mystery

121. Zwerdling, *Virginia Woolf and the Real World*, 260–61.
122. Zwerdling, *Virginia Woolf and the Real World*, 280–81. "Hope" in his chapter heading, "Pacifism without Hope" refers to hope that the war can be prevented. In 1939 she "had come to the end of her idealism and was forced to recognize the barrenness of the faith she could not bring herself to give up" (289) as "in perhaps the darkest moment of her country's history," she faces the madness of international conflict and the waste of another generation. He calls this a crisis of her secular faith in community and in the possibility of emancipating men (323, 290, 297–301).
123. Zwerdling, *Virginia Woolf and the Real World*, 321.
124. Woolf, *Mrs. Dalloway*, 11–12.
125. *Three Guineas*, 109.
126. *Against Judaizing Christians*, 2.3.3–2.3.6; 4.7.3; in R. S. Kraemer, *Maenads, Martyrs, Matrons, Monastics* (Philadelphia: Fortress, 1988) 31; discussed on pp. 59–60 and in R. S. Kraemer, *Her Share of the Blessings* (New York: Oxford, 1992) 108.
127. Marcus, "Niece of a Nun," 27.

at the heart of it"[128] or a philosophy or a secular vision,[129] or the experience of what Freud called "the oceanic feeling."[130] It is revolutionary, materialist, erotic and chaste, nonviolent, "based on ethics and morality, a vision of history and socialist community."[131] Woolf had the courage required for the "mystical side of solitude," for the insights that "it is not oneself but something in the universe that one's left with"[132] and that "The thing is in itself enough." "Often down here I have entered into a sanctuary; a nunnery; had a religious retreat; of great agony once; and always some terror; so afraid one is of loneliness; of seeing to the bottom of the vessel."[133] "[M]y happiness isn't blind. That is the achievement, I was thinking between 3 & 4 this morning, of my 55 years. I lay awake so calm, so content, as if I'd stepped off the whirling world into a deep blue quiet space, & there open eyed existed, beyond harm; armed against all that can happen. I have never had this feeling before in all my life; but I have had it several times since last summer: when I reached it, in my worst depression, as if I stepped out, throwing aside a cloak, lying in bed, looking at the stars, those nights at Monks House."[134]

Her courage to look at the body as squarely as she could, her desire to tell the truth about it, her "reason rooted in the bowels of the earth," saved her mysticism from tapering off into transcendentalism.[135] Catherine Smith insisted a generation ago that studying mysticism and feminism together is a way of learning more "about the links between envisioning power and pursuing it. Idealist analogues of transcendence may shape political notions of sexual equality as much as materialist or rationalists arguments do." But study of the intellectual history of feminism still "lacks a developed consideration of its debts to nonrational, nonmaterialist traditions. As a result, we know too little about the structure of vision in feminist politics."[136] Certainly central to Woolf's mysticism is her sense

---

128. See Marcus, "Niece of a Nun," 23, 29. These are phrases Caroline Stephen used to describe herself (*Vision of Faith*, cxi). Marcus thinks of mysticism as "the purest religious concept. It allows access to the community of saints without the dogmas and disciplines of organized religion" ("Niece," 10; cf. "Liberty, Sorority," 71).

129. M. Cunningham prefers the term "a secular visionary" for Woolf: ("Virginia Woolf: The Quiet Revolutionary," salon.com June 22, 2000).

130. Zwerdling, *Virginia Woolf and the Real World*, 279.

131. Marcus, "Niece," 15.

132. *Diary*, 3.113. See also 62, 114, 235

133. *Diary*, 3.196.

134. *Diary*, 5.78.

135. Talking about illness, melancholia, fever: "To look these things squarely in the face would need the courage of a lion tamer; a robust philosophy; a reason rooted in the bowels of the earth. Short of these, this monster, the body, this miracle, its pain, will soon make us taper into mysticism, or rise, with rapid beats of the wings, into the raptures of transcendentalism." V. Woolf, *The Moment and Other Essays* (New York: Harcourt Brace and Co., 1948) 10. See Marcus, "Mothering, Madness and Music," *Virginia Woolf Centennial Essays*, 40.

136. C. F. Smith, "Jane Lead: The Feminist Mind and Art of a Seventeenth-Century Protestant Mystic," *Women of Spirit: Female Leadership in the Jewish and Christian Traditions* (ed. R. R. Ruether and E. McLaughlin; New York: Simon and Schuster, 1979) 184–85.

of the transpersonal, impersonal, collective "We" — so often gathered together at a dinner party. "Now all the candles were lit, and the faces on both sides of the table were brought nearer by the candlelight, and composed, as they had not been in the twilight, into a party round a table...."[137] The cook and the serving girl participate in the party's success, but Woolf does not think to invite them to sit. Though it is a flawed claim, Woolf makes a "feminist, socialist and pacifist claim to a global self."[138] Her dread of egotism, her conviction that the boundaries around what look like discrete personal egos are arbitrary or even false give entry into the ancient idea of a corporate Human One (Son of Man). Selves overlap, but without loss of distinctive personality; individuality is not contaminated by individualism. There are freedom and darkness at the core, and a "summoning together."[139]

Death is something through the eyes of which Woolf sees.[140] Several of her books "composed themselves about an absence," as Beer puts it.[141] In *To the Lighthouse*, after the death of Mrs. Ramsey Lily Briscoe sees that "Suddenly, the empty drawing room steps, the frill of the chair inside, the puppy tumbling on the terrace, the whole wave and whisper of the garden became like curves and arabesques flourishing around a centre of complete emptiness."[142] Death is de-centered in *Jacob's Room*,[143] where it is death in war, an unavoidable outcome of institutionalized violence in a world governed by divisions.[144]

Woolf's notion of "the private brother" is particularly helpful to me in re-conceptualizing the figure of Jesus, thinking about the participation of women in the early Christian movement, and thinking about the crucifixion/resurrection materials. "Inevitably, we look upon societies as conspiracies that sink the private brother, whom many of us have reason to respect, and inflate in his stead a monstrous male, loud of voice, hard of fist, childishly intent upon scoring the floor of the earth with chalk marks."[145] My study of the Magdalene is not undertaken in order to better understand Jesus,[146] or to use her as one of the women who "have

137. *To the Lighthouse*, 105.
138. J. Marcus, "Wrapped in the Stars and Stripes: Virginia Woolf in the U.S.A.," *The South Carolina Review* (1996) 17.
139. *To the Lighthouse*, 79: "...being oneself, a wedge-shaped core of darkness, something invisible to others...this self having shed its attachments was free for the strangest adventures....This core of darkness could go anywhere, for no one saw it. They could not stop it, she thought, exulting. There was freedom, there was peace, there was, most welcome of all, a summoning together, a resting on a platform of stability. Not as oneself did one find rest ever, in her experience (she accomplished here something dexterous with her needles) but as a wedge of darkness."
140. Rose, "Smashing the Teapots," 5.
141. G. Beer, "Hume, Stephen and Elegy in *To the Lighthouse*," *Essays in Criticism* 34 (1984) 183.
142. *To the Lighthouse*, 169.
143. Caramango, *The Flight of the Mind*, 251.
144. See Ruddick, "Private Brother," 193.
145. *Three Guineas*, 105.
146. Contrast E. de Boer, *Mary Magdalene: Beyond the Myth* (Harrisburg, Pa.: Trinity Press International, 1997) forward. Her book "has been written out of a desire to learn more about the significance of Jesus in a new way, by means of Mary Magdalene."

served all these centuries as looking-glasses possessing the magic and delicious power of reflecting the figure of man at twice its natural size."[147] Jesus reconceived as a brother: a male who is not a father, not a lover; a male who might be a guide to the limited male world, or who might even be guided into women's spheres, thus confusing private and public. Who might use the power and privilege he has to defend and foster, to open doors. Not hero or leader or God, but companion, "comrade-twin," moving toward an early, pointless death.[148] Ruddick quotes Adrienne Rich's poem "Natural Resources": "It was never the rapist: / It was the brother, lost. // the comrade-twin whose palm / would bear a life-line like our own: . . . //merely a fellow-creature / with natural resources equal to our own."[149]

Woolf's brother Thoby Stephen, older than she by seventeen months, dead of typhoid in 1906 at the age of twenty-six before conspiracies could sink him, inspired the absent characters of Jacob in *Jacob's Room* and Percival in *The Waves*.[150] Thoby stands in contrast to her two half-brothers George and Gerald Duckworth who abused her sexually and tried to force her into their superficial social world.[151] Thoby offered his sister his Cambridge friends, the Greeks, Shakespeare. "He was melancholy; original; not able to take ordinary ambitions seriously."[152] "Who was Thoby?" Ruddick asks. "What promises did he make to his sister? What promises would he have kept? Whose side was he on?" She muses that Shakespeare could have helped the sister Woolf created for him run away, but "despite his efforts there would have been no place in his world for a person with a woman's body who wished to practice a man's art."[153] Woolf's husband Leonard, like her sister Vanessa, was never really a direct and sustained subject of her writing; a silence surrounds these two most important connections. But she wrote enough to persuade some, including me, that Leonard was neither angel nor murderer, that they achieved companionship and worked together, provoked and sustained each other. Whatever the sexual realities of their marriage, which may have fluctuated, and however contradictory his character, which was hard, he too may be seen as a private brother.

Some of what the private brother cannot do for a woman, her women friends can do, and Woolf's were many, intimate, and varied (Violet Dickinson, Margaret Llewelyn Davies, Ethel Smyth, Vita Sackville-West, her sister Vanessa Bell, and others). Most interesting is what Woolf can do for the private brother: "Having

---

147. Woolf, *Room*, 35–36.

148. See Zwerdling, *Virginia Woolf and the Real World*, chapter 3, on *Jacob's Room*.

149. A. Rich, *The Dream of a Common Language* (New York: Norton, 1978), quoted by Ruddick, "Private Brother," n. 1, p. 214.

150. *Three Guineas* is an argument with and sort of elegy for Woolf's nephew Julian Bell, killed as an ambulance driver in the Spanish Civil War, at the age of twenty-nine.

151. Louise De Salvo, *Virginia Woolf: The Impact of Childhood Sexual Abuse on Her Life and Work* (Boston: Beacon, 1989).

152. Woolf, *Moments of Being,* 120.

153. Ruddick, "Private Brother," 191.

adopted maternal vision while refusing a motherly identity of life, Woolf freed herself both to give birth to and to appropriate a benign maleness — a protective brotherliness, a realistic camaraderie" without judgment and alluring might.[154]

In line with my interest in the contributions of women to the earliest Christian movement, I am interested also in Woolf's interest in the recovery of female tra-dition and female prophecy; in the thought and the "sentence that could hold its own against the male flood,"[155] in silence and ellipsis and the unfinished sentence, in the "little language," in the disorderly voice of the charwoman, moaning and crooning,[156] — that "bent figure with the knobbed hands and the bleared eyes, who, in spite of the poets, is the true figure of womanhood."[157] Woolf's approval of Coleridge's perception that the great mind must be androgynous[158] — when not hardened into a doctrine[159] — is helpful in discussion of the insistance that the gnostic Magdalene must be made a "man." "For this is not one life"; says Bernard in *The Waves.* "nor do I always know if I am man or woman." He refuses to "reduce to order."[160] As some gnostics were, but in different ways, Woolf was trying (at least trying) here and in other works "to theorize the transcendence of gender."[161]

She was criticized in her time and is still in ours as an intellectual lightweight who avoided moral, sexual, political and social issues, a classbound snob, an irritatingly "difficult" writer[162] who can be stripped of her feminism. But all of Woolf's creative work is a feminist subversion of a patriarchal social order. Her essays and diaries and letters show this subversion at work in her own life. "[I]n

---

154. Ruddick, "Private Brother," 211–12: she sees Woolf having given herself in Bernard "a voice which is that of a male inheritor who is trustworthy and moral."

155. V. Woolf, *The Pargiters: The Novel-Essay Portion of "The Years"* (ed. M. A. Leaska; London: Hogarth Press, 1978) 164.

156. See Jane Marcus, "A Rose for Him to Rifle," *Virginia Woolf and the Languages of Patriarchy* (Bloomington: Indiana University Press, 1987) 10–17. The charwoman is the "unacknowledged bearer of culture in her fiction" (12). See Woolf, *Mrs. Dalloway*, 91: the "rude mouth" of the battered old woman by the tube sings; Miller thinks her song is a version of Strauss's "Aller Seelen," about the day of collective resurrection, a lament in which a bereaved woman imagines meeting her dead lover on All Souls' Day (J. H. Miller, "Virginia Woolf's All Souls' Day," *The Shaken Realist* [ed. M. J. Friedman and J. B. Vickery; Baton Rouge: Louisiana State University Press, 1970] 114–15); J. H. Miller, *Fiction and Repetition* (Cambridge: Harvard University Press, 1982) 189–90.

157. Virginia Woolf, "Men and Women" quoted by Marcus, "Thinking Back," 17.

158. *Room*, 98.

159. See J. Marcus, "Tintinnabulations," *Marxist Perspectives* 2 (1979/80) 159.

160. *The Waves*, 342.

161. Rosenfeld, *Outsiders Together*, 118.

162. Cunningham, "Virginia Woolf." See Marcus, "Wrapped in Stars and Stripes," 19–23 for discussion of works which continue to denigrate, scapegoat or ignore Woolf's social and political contributions, especially in England. Also Silver, *Virginia Woolf Icon*, part 1. The image of Woolf as the "twentieth-century madwoman with a bedroom of her own — witty and malicious, yes, and pro-ductive, but again, all of the above: delicate, ethereal, asexual, apolitical, etc — ...survived well into the 1990s and still surfaces today" (123). In *Virginia Woolf and Her Influences*, H. Lee ("Responses to a Life of Virginia Woolf," 13–15) details the hostility; B. R. Silver ("Retro-Anger and Baby-Boomer Nostalgia," 221) discusses Woolf's absence in "intellectual" journals like the *New Yorker*, the *New Republic, Commentary, The Nation,* the *New York Review of Books.*

her adult life Woolf became increasingly wise,... her capacities for indignation, charity and political acuity steadily grew.... [She] was among the sanest, the strongest, the most joyful of women."[163] She issues her challenge: "...I am asking you to live in the presence of reality...."[164] It was a reality which was singing something indescribable.

Here I am using Woolf for a project I don't think she would have scorned, though she might have hooted with laughter to learn of it. (Elizabeth Bowen remembers, "And her laughter was entrancing, it was outrageous laughter, almost like a child's laughter. Whoops of laughter, if anything amused her. As it happened, the last day I saw her I was staying at Rodmell and I remember her kneeling back on the floor — we were tacking away, mending a torn Spanish curtain in the house — and she sat back on her heels and put her head back in a patch of sun, early spring sun. Then she laughed in this consuming, choking, delightful, hooting way. And *that* is what has remained with me."[165])

I hope my use of Woolf may serve to highlight an aspect of her thought and imagination not yet thoroughly explored, and to show its value for the study of religion. Especially in this field, we need her scorn, her hatred of pomposity and of all preaching. We need her intolerance of social injustice (flawed though that was by her antisemitism[166] and class biases). Her tentativeness and uncertainty can aid our efforts to avoid falling into assertion. Her freedom from and modifications of romance, her powerful anger[167] and "madness," her puzzled ruminations about the body, her interest in the strategies of domination make her a good guide and companion for this particular project, thinking back through the Magdalene. Woolf mocked and criticized but valued Cambridge University. "Though the dons of Cambridge may provoke Woolf's satire, its beauty, friendship and respect for ideas do not.... [Hers is] a bitter loving protest against a destructive world whose beauty is never denied. "[168] We might learn to do the same for church.

Alice Walker inserts Phillis Wheatley's story into Woolf's story of Shakespeare's sister, into which I insert that of Mary Magdalene:

Virginia Woolf wrote further, speaking of course not of our Phillis (insert 'or our Mary Magdalene'), that 'any woman born with a great gift in the sixteenth cen-

---

163. Ruddick, "Private Brother," 213.

164. Woolf, *Room*, 110.

165. E. Bowen, Adapted from an interview in the BBC Television film, *A Night's Darkness. A Day's Sail*, in *Recollections of Virginia Woolf* (ed. J. Russell Noble; New York: William Morrow & Co., 1972) 49–50.

166. See Lee, *Virginia Woolf*, 308, 668–69.

167. Righteous indignation (not the same as bitterness and spite) and also misplaced reaction to insult and attack (see Marcus, *Art & Anger*, 132–35). "We know from *A Writer's Diary* how often anger was the primary impulse of Woolf's art" (138). See also J. Marcus, "Daughters of anger/material girls: con/textualizing feminist criticism," *Women's Studies* 15 (1988) 281–308; P. Lyman, "The Politics of Anger: On Silence, ressentiment, and Political Speech," *Socialist Review* 11 (1981) 55–74; B. R. Silver, "The Authority of Anger: *Three Guineas* as a Case Study," *Signs* 16 (1991) 340–70.

168. Ruddick, "Private Brother," 197.

tury [insert 'eighteenth century,' (insert 'first century'), insert 'black woman' (insert 'Jew'), insert 'born or made a slave' (insert 'of unknown social origin, unknown occupation')] would certainly have gone crazed (insert 'been considered possessed by demons'), shot herself, or ended her days in some lonely cottage (insert 'some cave high in the mountains') outside the village, half witch, half wizard [insert 'Saint' (insert 'reformed prostitute, exorcised demoniac, preacher, saint')], feared and mocked at (insert 'leered at, abused, revered, appropriated'). For it needs little skill and psychology to be sure that a highly gifted girl (insert 'or old woman') who had tried to use her gift for poetry (insert 'theology') would have been so thwarted and hindered by contrary instincts [add 'chains, guns, the lash, the ownership of one's body by someone else, submission to an alien religion' (insert 'the use of one's body by painters, sculptors, photographers, submission to a deforming religion')], that she must have lost her health and sanity to a certainty (insert 'or that she survived for a time among the like-minded,' insert 'and that she can be resurrected').[169]

Woolf was and was not speaking of Phillis, of Mary Magdalene, or of herself or of ourselves. Her thought is open to multiple readings and incarnations.

I have happily trespassed into the wealth of Woolf studies. I hope Woolf scholars who read this book will be curious, generous, indulgent, and that biblical scholars will be curious, drawn to Woolf across our false boundaries.[170] Several photographs of Woolf capture her ironical, humorous expression — like the one by Gisele Freund, where Woolf holds her cigarette in a holder, and the one by an unknown photographer, where she rests her face in her hand.[171] Her expression conveys to me a certain amusement and doubt about this whole Magdalene project, a little curiosity, a tentative approval about the use to which it might be put, the hope that it might be something interesting. She asks, Are you up to this? I hope she looks out quizzically from the contents of this book.

169. A. Walker, *In Search of Our Mothers' Gardens* (San Diego: Harcourt Brace Jovanovich, 1983) 235. As London remarks ("Guerrilla," 26), "Walker's 'insertions' disrupt Woolf's text, asserting simultaneously identify and difference; even as she attests to the usefulness of Woolf's model, Walker thus exposes its raced, classed, and cultured positioning. Walker's new 'voiced over' text records, among other things, its distance from the 'original' — the wrenching required to rehistoricize Woolf's imaginary history. Yet Walker speaks powerfully for the enfranchisement 'Woolf' continues to offer many feminists, and, particularly, for the power of identification to those who have been culturally dispossessed of their 'mothers.'"
170. See *Virginia Woolf Out of Bounds: Selected Papers from the Tenth Annual Conference on Virginia Woolf* (ed. J. Berman and J. Goldman; New York: Pace University Press, 2001).
171. See Silver, *Virginia Woolf Icon*, figures 8 and 17.

CHAPTER

TWO

Meditations at Migdal

May the Lord make us truly thankful.
But who is the Lord.
A transparency appears.
10,000 a year. The Arch. of Cant.
The dappled dawn.
The
Do not raise monuments.
Let us not praise famous women.

Virginia Woolf, notebook 1935
(Monk's House Papers/B 16b)[1]

"[P]ausing there she looked out to meet the stroke of the Lighthouse.... She looked up over her knitting and met the third stroke and it seemed to her like her own eyes meeting her own eyes, searching as she alone could search into her mind and her heart, purifying out of existence that lie, any lie. She praised herself in praising the light, without vanity, for she was stern, she was searching, she was beautiful like that light."

Virginia Woolf, *To the Lighthouse*, 1927[2]

MAGDALA, THE TOWN OF MARY MAGDALENE, is generally identified with the site of Migdal on the western shore of the Sea of Galilee, five kilometers north of Tiberias. This is probably the town called Migdal Nunya or Nunayah (Tower of Fish) in the Babylonian Talmud (*b. Pesah.* 46b), Taricheae (Place of Salted Fish) by Josephus (*Ant.* 14.120; 20. 159; *J.W.* 1. 180; 2. 252), and also Migdal Seb'iya (Tower of Dyers) in the Jerusalem Talmud (*y. Ta'an.* 4.8).[3] The

---

1. Quoted by B. R. Silver, "Three Guineas Before and After," *Virginia Woolf: A Feminist Slant*, 258.
2. V. Woolf, *To the Lighthouse* (ed. S. Kemp; London: Routledge, 1994) 79–80; first British edition Hogarth Press 1927.
3. Magadan (Matt 15:39) and Dalmanutha (Mark 8:10) — mentioned as the area to which Jesus went after the feeding of four thousand — are possibly corrupt forms of Magdal and Magdal Nuna. On the misidentification of Taricheae (by Pliny the Elder and E. Robinson and others) as south of Tiberias (Khirbet Kerak), see A. Brunot, "Magdala," *Bible et Terre Sainte* 192 (1977) 5.

47

place is marked by a road sign running with rust, stating that this was the birth-place of Mary Magdalene, a city that flourished toward the end of the second temple period, and one of the cities fortified by Joseph ben Matityahu (Jose-phus) during the great revolt of the Jews against the Romans. It is not mentioned in major guidebooks such as Jerome Murphy O'Connor's *The Holy Land: An Archaeological Guide from Earliest Times to 1700*.[4] A popular guidebook claims in-accurately — and typically — that "nothing but ruined masonry overgrown with weeds" marks the town, and that "a small white-washed dome near the road is a reminder of the meeting between Jesus and Mary Magdalene (Mark VI, 53)."[5]

The neglect apparent in this sentence is interesting. The dome actually covers an old, unidentified Islamic tomb, inside of which snuffed-out candles and remains of meals and bedding may be evidence of some sort of sporadic occupation and/or veneration. No meeting with Mary Magdalene is recounted in Mark VI, 53. Maybe it means to say Mark XV, 40–41, or XVI, 1. And the weeds are growing over a dig that was directed by Franciscans, the late Virgilio Corbo and Stanislao Loffreda, on behalf of the Custodia di Terra Sancta — a dig which was suspended after five campaigns (1971, 1973, 1976–77) because of a problem with water from underground springs. The difficulty of knowing what was here, and the neglect, signal a feminist task.

I have visited this place often since 1986 with students from the University of Detroit Mercy, and we joke about establishing an institute of feminist studies here, with no budget, no authorization, no permission even to enter. We joke about it as we try to overcome the difficulties of finding out about the dig and even getting a decent look at it. "Why in the world would you be interested in that place?" asked archaeologist Lee Levine. "Oh" (bored with the answer). Presently closed to the public, the site is surrounded by both an inner stone wall with chain link and curled barbed wire on top, and another outer fence of barbed wire. It is "too dangerous, not possible" to enter, said Corbo when we interviewed him at Capernaum in 1988. According to Corbo, the Israeli government forced him to stop the dig: there is water under the surface, and they are the only ones who can drain it. He said he suspected they really wanted to make a beach there. "Entry forbidden," reads the blue and white sign. Snarling watchdogs are on pa-trol; bales of hay are stacked high, covered with plastic sheets. A stone house, once a Franciscan friary, stands empty. The family of Marwan Assadi (parents, son, daughters, sons-in-law) and friends are the caretakers, living in a small cor-rugated shack. According to Rami Arav, director of the Bethsaida excavations, the Franciscans own the small parcel of the excavated Migdal occupied by the Arab family, the Greek Orthodox Church own another small piece, and the Jew-

---

4. 4th edition; New York: Oxford University Press, 1998
5. *The Sea of Galilee and Its Holy Sites: A Pictorial Guide* ([Herzlia, Israel]: Palphot, n.d.).

ish National Fund owns the bulk of it. The JNF leases parts of the land on bids.[6] The head Franciscan at Capernaum is said to have said (1995) they will not open the place to visitors; perhaps they should clean it, but it's a lot of work. It has to be cleaned twice a year as it is, and it's a lot of work. The water is the problem; and the dam at the south end of the lake raised the water table.

Our taped interview with Marwan in the summer of 1989 was punctuated with loud bleating of a dozen or so sheep, and discussion concerning one hugely bloated and dying sheep. We sat around a table in the shade in front of their home, eating the chunks of watermelon and drinking the strong coffee in tin cups offered with gracious hospitality. There is something haunting about the site. Surprised by my own question, I asked if there were any ghosts here. "Yes," said Marwan, pointing, "she sits over there."

On each subsequent visit, the place becomes more desolate and depressing from an archaeological perspective. The sheep are gone, all sold, replaced by many chickens scratching up what is left of mosaics, then by only a few chickens and a rooster, baby chicks in a milk crate, a duck or two. Certain stones I remember are gone. The snarling dogs remain. Even with the connection with Marwan, who studied to be a truck driver and tells me he will call me when he comes to the US, it is more and more difficult to enter because sometimes he is not there. The hospitality is constant, however, when we do. What my photographs show, from year to year, is the scattering and sinking of stones, rearrangements, accumulation of trash — cigarette butts, plastic bottles. The green weeds and wildflowers taking over fallen columns, pedestals and low walls. Palm trees and eucalyptus trees. The breeze rumbles on my videocam tape. Graffiti is sprayed on the steel gate to the sea: "Do not go in, Do not go in" with the skull-and-crossbones flag meaning "You can die here." Another sign with drawings of waves and palm trees: "Magdala Beach, History Place," but we never see anyone on this beach, and the history is mute. Just south of the site along the west side of the road are sarcophagi carved out of the rocks, ancient Migdal's cemetery.

Written materials about the dig are not extensive,[7] and almost every aspect is confusing, including the recent history of the site. The excavations are in the area once occupied by the Arab village of Al Medgel or Mejdel, bulldozed by the Israelis in 1948. (Where are the people who remember that bulldozing, in the year

6. Private communication from John Rousseau, February 1995. There is nothing about the site on the web site of the Franciscan seminary in Jerusalem (http://198.62.75.1/www1/ofm/sites/TScpmain.html).

7. See V. Corbo, "Scavi archeologici a Magdala (1971–1973)," *Studii Biblici Francescani Liber Annuus* 24 (1974) 55–37; "La città romana di Magdala," *Studia Hierosolymitana* I (Jerusalem, 1976) 355–78; "Piazza e Villa Urbana a Magdala," *Studii Biblici Francescani Liber Annuus* 28 (Jerusalem: Franciscan Printing Press, 1978) 232–40, photos and drawings 71–76; "La città romana di Magdala, repporto pre-liminare dopo la IV campagna del 1975," *Studia Hierosolymitana* I (Jerusalem, 1986) 355–78. See also B. Bagatti, *Antichi Villaggi Christiani di Galilea* (Jerusalem: Tipografia dei PP. Francescani, 1971) 80–83.

of Deir Yassin?) This village had been settled in the nineteenth century by several Egyptian fellahin; nothing remains of that village but the Muslim grave (*weli*). At the beginning of the twentieth century, a German architect, R. Lendle, purchased land from the Arabs of Mejdel and began excavating; I know of no reports of this effort. In April of 1935, two Franciscans, Saller and Bagatti, visited Mejdel as guests of Muktar Mutlaq, whose numerous descendants, born of his nine wives, made up almost all the population of the village. A little later, the Custodians of the Holy Land acquired property here, and the Italian Ministry of Foreign Affairs financed the digs.[8] Referring to another portion of this area (possibly part of what locals call Upper Migdal, on the road up to Mount Arbel) *Carta's Guide* reports that in 1909 Migdal was established as a farm on land originally purchased by a German Catholic order which had attempted to settle in Biq'at Ginnesar; the site was abandoned because of the prevalence of malaria. In 1920 private farms were set up, with mainly citrus and banana groves. In 1921 a work camp was located here for workers on the Tiberias — Rosh Pinna Road. Here the Joseph Trumpeldor labor battalion was established. In 1983 Migdal was a moshav with an area of 3700 dunam and a population of 730, approximately 200 families.[9]

The difficulties the archaeologists faced were great, especially three: underground water; the reuse of materials over the centuries; and the radical destruction by bulldozers which aimed to wipe out all traces of the Arab village, and in the process pushed ancient materials toward the sea. The archaeologists found the following. (1) On the northern edge of the excavations, a large structure near the sea, with badly damaged mosaic floors of geometric and cross designs, using white, blue, various red and ash-colored stones. It was possibly a Byzantine monastery.

(2) On the eastern side of the main paved road which crossed through the Roman town, the Cardo Maximus, a complex of public and private buildings[10] believed to be early Roman first century C.E.. These include one (B-1) that was identified as either a first century mini-synagogue of the early Galilean basilican type, or a nymphaeum. It is only 26.8 by 23.8 feet, with less than 60m of enclosed space. It was constructed of finely hewn basalt blocks laid on a foundation of roughly hewn rocks, the interstices filled with mortar and chips of stone. There were seven basalt columns in this structure, three on each of three walls, with the SE and SW corner columns heart shaped, as in the synagogue (?) at Gamla,[11] and

---

8. Brunot, "Magdala," 5. The Franciscans, founded in 1209, were made Custodians of the Holy Land in 1335. Their two main duties were "to ensure the performance of the Latin liturgical services" at Jerusalem's Holy Sepulchre and Bethlehem's Church of the Nativity, and to oversee and guide pilgrimages to the holy places (see J. Murphy-O'Connor, "The Geography of Faith," *BR* 12 [1996] 37).

9. See *Carta's Official Guide to Israel* (Jerusalem: Israel Ministry of Defense and Carta, 1983) 319.

10. Chiat 116: seven "rooms" block D.

11. Michael Avi-Yonah once stated these were peculiar to synagogues, but Chiat notes they appear as early as the second century B.C.E. in the bouleterion of Miletos built by Antiochus Epiphanes IV

the pedestals and two surviving capitals, beautifully austere. On the fourth side facing north, there is a step-like series of five benches; the focal point may have been the opposite southern wall facing Jerusalem. The interior, with its pavement of basalt flagstone, was probably entered from the west. It could be seen to have the form of a small basilica with nave and two aisles the length of the building and an aisle across the back or south side. Interpreted this way, the size of the building implies a small congregation, with room, for perhaps 30 on the risers, and the nave accommodating around 25 comfortably.[12] The building's "iconographic silence" contrasted with Roman emphasis on iconography enables it to speak more clearly for Judaism, as a non-Roman element.[13] In the second phase of construction, the pavement level was raised to the second tier of benches; under the raised pavement was a collection channel for water, and waterways were situated between the three walls and the columns.[14] Adjoining B-1's east wall, was a building (D-2) which had a water channel located below its pavement, carrying water to a small (swimming?) pool to its east. Near the northern part of this building's east wall was an open court paved with large basalt stones, furrowed on three sides to collect water that flowed along a channel into B-1 (i.e., into the mini-synagogue[?] used as a reservoir?).

All this led the Franciscan excavators to suppose the synagogue was changed into a nympheum (a city fountain house or water storage building, a reservoir?) during the first century C.E. because of springs of water, still much in evidence, that flooded the synagogue. And/or to suppose that the synagogue, destroyed in 70 C.E., became a reservoir, in use until the second century, when it was replaced by a water tower. But some scholars now consider the identification as a synagogue erroneous, arguing that the building was always a nympheum, or well house, or the portico of a villa, or some sort of meeting hall.[15] Brunot notes, however, that

---

(M. J. Chiat, "First Century Synagogue Architecture: Methodological Problems," *Ancient Synagogues: The State of Research* (ed. J. Gutmann; Chico, Calif.: Scholars Press, 1981) 52.

12. J. F. Strange, "Magdala," *IDBSup* (1976) 561.

13. J. F. Strange, "Some Implications of Archaeology for New Testament Studies," *What Has Archaeology to Do With Faith?* (ed. J. H. Charlesworth and W. P. Weaver; Philadelphia: Trinity Press International, 1992) 39–40.

14. Corbo argued the first-century synagogue was converted into a water installation in the second century.

15. See Corbo, "Piazza e Villa Urbana" (1976) see also M. J. Chiat, *Handbook of Synagogue Architecture* (Chico, Calif.: Scholars Press, 1982) 116; E. Netzer, "The Synagogues in Massada, Herodium, Gamla and Magdala (?) — from the Architect's Viewpoint," *Synagogues in Antiquity* (ed. A. Kasher et al.; Jerusalem: Yad Izhak Ben Zvi, 1987) xi; L. Levine, *The Ancient Synagogue: the First Thousand Years* (New Haven: Yale University Press, 2000) 67. Netzer argues that the first-century building was a water facility, with water channels on 3 sides. Later the floor was raised to correct the problem of flooding, and the building continued to function as a nymphaeum (Netzer, "Water Installation in Magdala," 165–72). B. J. Brooten, *Women Leaders in the Ancient Synagogue* [Chico, Calif.: Scholars Press, 1982] nn. 6, 14, pp. 250–51) says Chiat makes a good case for questioning the identity of buildings at Gamla, Migdal and elsewhere as synagogues in the narrow sense, "but one must then ask if what seem in any case to be public meeting halls might not have been used for worship services" (see also Chiat, "First Century Synagogue Architecture," 55–56). Brooten accepts without discussion

there are no characteristics of a nympheum — no niches, not even a fountain, only the water.[16] In any case, a "synagogue" building in the first century C.E. would have been used for several types of community assembly, from public prayer to fundraising to local governance.[17]

There is also a tower, an aqueduct, a large paved court enclosed by colonnades to the south of the residential quarter, and to the north, an urban villa. The villa was in use from the first century C.E. until the beginning of the Byzantine period, and was probably built by a wealthy resident of Migdal. Its vestibule had a first-century mosaic floor with the Greek inscription *kai su* ("and you" or "you too") closest to the southern door step, and a square panel within which seven objects are represented in blue, red, white, brown. Some regard these as magical symbols,[18] and indeed the inscription — the only one of its kind found in Israel — may be some sort of invocation against the evil eye; the phrase *kai su* is known from private houses in Antioch.[19] Or, perhaps it is a quotation like that Epiphanius mentions from the *Gospel of Eve*, the words spoken on a high mountain: "*ego su kai su ego*" ("I am you and you are me" [*Panarion* 26, 3, 1]).[20]

The symbols in the mosaic probably represent aspects of the fishing trade. The major item is a sailboat, a five person workboat (four rowers and one helmsman who uses the rear oar as a rudder[21]). This is a merchant sailing vessel, used for crossing the lake carrying cargo, not a fishing boat or a warship, and certainly not a symbol of the cross or of the church, as Bagatti thought.[22] Like the boat depicted on a coin of Tiberias from the reign of Caracalla, this is a distinct Kinneret type of vessel, developed to face the dangers particular to this lake with its sudden storms and change of wind direction. It seems to be a modified type of the Mediterranean vessel called the myoparo, known as a fast and efficient pirate ship and auxiliary war vessel, whose hull has a cutwater at its bow. It is also like the boat discovered behind the breakwater at Migdal[23] in 1986 and preserved

Corbo's 1976 suggestion that the mini-synagogue may have been the portico of the Roman villa, in which case the five risers would be seen as steps.

16. Brunot, "Magdala," 6.

17. See R. A. Horsley, *Galilee* (Valley Forge, Pa.: Trinity Press International, 1995) 222–33.

18. M. Piccirillo, *Studium Biblicum Franciscanum Jerusalem Museum* (Jerusalem: Franciscan Printing Press, 1983) 31. R. Reich, "A Note on the Roman Mosaic from Magdala on the Shore of the Sea of Galilee" [Hebrew], *Qadmoniot* 22 (1989) 43–44; *NTA* 34 (1990) 213.

19. A. Raban, "The boat from Migdal Nunia and the anchorages of the Sea of Galilee from the time of Jesus," *The International Journal of Nautical Archaeology and Underwater Exploration* 17 (1988) 313.

20. "I stood on a high mountain and I saw a tall man and another short one and I heard something like the sound of thunder and I approached to hear and he spoke to me and said, '*ego su kai su ego*' and where you are I am there and in everything I am sown. And if you wish you can collect me and when you collect me you collect yourself." See S. Benko, "The Libertine Gnostic Sect of the Phibionites according to Epiphanius," *VC* 21 (1967) 107.

21. Raban, "The boat," 319, citing a letter to him from Mendel Nun.

22. B. Bagatti, *The Church of the Circumcision* (Jerusalem: Franciscan Printing Press, 1971) 219.

23. M. Nun, *The Sea of Galilee and Its Fishermen in the New Testament* (EinGev: Kibbutz Ein Gev, 1989) 61.

in a tank at Nof Ginnosar 1.5 km north. That boat was worn out, stripped, and pushed out to the Sea to sink beside a boat repair center at Magdala.[24] A sailboat, we will see, turns up again in the legends of the Magdalene from Provence, but there it is rudderless.

The other items in the mosaic are these: a flower or bud lying on its left side between two leaves; a black disc behind which are two containers or baskets attached by a pole, perhaps for carrying loads on a pack animal's back; a large kantharos with two handles and a triangular base; and a fish whose head is preserved, out of whose mouth juts a branch or piece of seaweed. The mosaic as a whole may illustrate the production and trade in salted fish to distant customers. Perhaps the villa owner was advertising the source of his or her wealth, or thanking for it. Or perhaps this is not a villa at all, but a commercial structure.

Josephus says the city was surrounded by a great wall which he built, and mentions there were two grain markets, a large aqueduct system a theatre and a hippodrome, the latter holding 100,000 men (*J.W.* 2. 598–99) — but Josephus' numbers here as elsewhere are wildly inflated ("His concern is not accurate numbers, but is aimed more at self-aggrandizement in presenting himself, his army, and his nation as a worthy foe for Vespasian, his legions, and Rome."[25]). These structures have not been found. He writes also of "the residence of the nobles," from which he made a canal leading to the lake, in one of his action-packed escapes (Life 153). This may be Corbo's urban villa.

The reports also list from the digs at Migdal one needle for repairing nets, lead weights for nets, pottery dated from 63 B.C.E. to the second revolt against Rome in 135 C.E.. Many coins were found from the first revolt (66–70 C.E.), four coins from the third century, and the latest coin, found in the top layer, comes from the time of Constantine. A hoard of coins was also found containing 74 coins from Tyre, 15 from Ptolemais, 17 from Gadara, 14 from Scythopolis, 10 from Tiberias, 9 from Hippos, 8 from Sepphoris, and 2 from Gaba.[26] More artifacts have been

24. *The New Encyclopedia of Archaeological Excavations in the Holy Land* (ed. E. Stern; New York, 1993) 2.520. J. H. Charlesworth notes that the shallow draft of this boat would have made it precarious during the sudden storms on the Sea of Galilee ("Archaeological Research and Biblical Theology," *Geschichte — Tradition — Reflexion* [ed. P. Schafer; Tübingen: Mohr/Siebeck, 1996] 1.12).

25. J. L. Reed, "Population Numbers, Urbanization and Economics: Galilean Archaeology and the Historical Jesus," *SBL Seminar Papers* (Atlanta: Scholars Press, 1994) 206. No census figures survive for the Galilee of this period. On Josephus and myth-making, see J. A. Overman, "Jesus of Galilee and the Historical Peasant," *Archaeology and the Galilee* (ed. D. R. Edwards and C. T. McCollough (Atlanta: Scholars Press, 1997) 67–73.

26. Y. Meshorer, "A Hoard of Coins from Migdal," *Atiqot ES* 11 (1976) 54–71. See Reed, "Places," 78 on the importance of Tyre as the major mint for Galilee; and D. E. Oakman, "The Archaeology of First-Century Galilee and the Social Interpretation of the Historical Jesus," *SBL Seminar Papers* 1994, 229: the Temple tax was paid in Tyrian money and he thinks it likely Herodian rents and taxes were also paid in this currency.

found in the muddy silt of the shoreline, with the waterline now 3–4 feet above the ancient coast.[27]

Earlier Franciscan excavators had not detected the ancient harbor, into which they dumped their rubble, as they did at Capernaum.[28] Examination of the schematic plan of the costal structures, anchorage and quays at Migdal, based on an IUES survey 1971–75, shows that the structures near the lake included a basalt wharf, from which protrudes a mooring stone for ships. A street constructed on the wharf was found at a depth of 3m. Cooking vessels and storage jars from the Herodian period were found there, along the northern end of the breakwaters, which closed off an area of over one acre, making this the largest of the ancient anchorages of the Sea found by 1977, and one of the largest of the sixteen found by 1999.[29] Migdal's location east of the mouth of the Arbel rift meant there was no need to provide protection from rough waves during most of the year, so ships moored along the wharf built south of the anchorage, opposite the open water.[30] The port consisted of a promenade which ran parallel to the shore and a sheltered basin; these outlines were clear and complete in the 1970s, but now the topography has been altered by rapid silting and development.[31]

In 1991 when the waters of the Sea were low after a severe drought (1989–91), a tower appeared about 150 feet from the shore at Migdal. Basalt pillars that apparently supported it were uncovered by the Antiquities Authority's Marine Archaeology Division, headed by Ehud Galili. Archaeologists believe that this was — yes — a lighthouse, for the fishermen working at night on the sea. It is now submerged again,[32] unlike this other one. "The place had gone to rack and ruin. Only the Lighthouse beam entered the rooms for a moment, sent its sudden stare over bed and wall in the darkness of winter, looked with equanimity at the thistle and the swallow, the rat and the straw. Nothing now withstood them; nothing said no to them. Let the wind blow; let the poppy seed itself and the carnation mate with the cabbage. . . . "[33]

Literary sources concerning the spot have been compiled by Frederic Manns.[34] Rabbinic literature mentions a synagogue and a famous beth midrash (study house), famous scribe (Niqai) and rabbis (Isaac, Judan) at Magdala. The priestly

---

27. See M. Nun, "Ports of Galilee," *BAR* 25 (1999) 22, 26. He discusses several of the 16 bustling ports from the first century C.E..

28. Nun, "Ports," 29.

29. See Nun's reconstruction, "Ports," 21.

30. Raban, "The Boat," 323.

31. Nun, "Ports," 29: the promenade starts below the ruins of the Arab village of Migdal and continues north for about 300 feet.

32. "New Highlights on the Sea of Galilee," *Israel: A Letter from the Holy Land* 4 (July 1991) 2.

33. Woolf, *To the Lighthouse*, 138.

34. F. Manns, "Magdala dans les Sources litteraires," *Studia Hierosolymitana* I 22 (Jerusalem: Franciscan Printing Press, 1976) 307–37. Cf. J. Wilkinson, *Jerusalem Pilgrims before the Crusades* (Warminster, England: Ais & Phillips, 1977) and D. Baldi, *Enchiridion Locorum Sanctorum* (2d ed.; Jerusalem: Franciscan Printing Press, 1982) 260–64.

order of Ezekiel is said to have had its seat there.[35] The Talmud mentions that the
city had a small harbor[36] and a boat-building industry. The names Migdal Nunya
and Taricheae reflect the city's importance as the main center of the prosperous
fishing, fish-processing and exporting industries in eastern Galilee,[37] specializing in
pickled sardines.[38] Strabo (*The Geography*, XIV, 2, 45) reported that "In Taricheae
the sea provides the finest fish for pickling, and on its banks grow fruit trees which
resemble appletrees."

The town had a reputation for opulence and immorality. According to *y.
Ta'anit* 4, 69c, "Magdala was destroyed because of prostitution (*znut*)"; according
to *Midrash Ekha* 2,2, 4, because of the profound corruption of its inhabitants.
Neubauer comments illogically that the corruption "trouve une confirmation
partielle et tres-curieuse dans l'episode de la pecheresse des Evangiles, 'Maria
Magdalena.' "[39] So strong is the Magdalene's legend that some have suggested that
"Mary the Magdalene" might be the equivalent of "Mary the Harlot," since "by
the Jews, the word Magdala was used to denote a person with plaited or twisted
hair, a practice then much in use among women of loose character."[40] Since the
Aramaic for hairdresser is *megaddlela'*, some sort of pun may have linked the city
and that profession, but I have found no description of prostitutes wearing their
hair plaited, or working as beauticians, though that occupation may have been
regarded as disreputable. In *b. Sabb.* 104b and *b. Sanh.* 67a, the mother of the "son
of Stada" or "son of Pandira" (a reference to Jesus) is called Mary the hairdresser,
an adulteress; apparently she has been confused with Mary Magdalene. Other
scholars have asked if there is a correlation between Magdala's depravity and
the seven demons cast out of Mary.[41] The Christian legend of Mary Magdalene
appears to have seeped somehow into rabbinic writings.

An ancient, well attested rabbinic tradition says that the daughters of Job died
at Migdal Seb'iyah (*Pesiqa de Rab Kahanah* [*Pisqa* 7]; *Wayyikrah Rabbah* 17:4;
Ruth Rabbah 1:5). This means Migdal is an important site with connections to

35. G. Dalman, *Sacred Sites and Ways* (London, SPCK, 1935) 127.

36. See J. J. Rousseau and R. Arav, *Jesus and His World* (Minneapolis: Fortress, 1995) map on
p. 27; on 247 they say archaeological surveys have revealed sixteen ancient harbors around the sea
of Galilee, but Magdala is not listed there.

37. Rousseau and Arav, *Jesus*, 94–95. This area was connected by roads with Syria and
Mesopotamia, the Mediterranean coast, Samaria, Judea (p. 248). Jn 6:1–24 locates the feeding of
5000 in the area of Magdala-Ginnosar: Tiberias on one side, Capernaum on the other (p. 29).

38. M. Nun, "Cast Your Net Upon the Waters: Fish and Fishermen in Jesus' Time," *BAR* 19
(1993) 49.

39. The corruption "finds a partial and very curious confirmation in the episode of the sinner of
the Gospels, 'Mary Magdalene.' " A. Neubauer, *La Geographie du Talmud* (Hildesheim: Georg Olms,
1967) 217.

40. See *A Dictionary of Christ and the Gospels* (ed. James Hastings; New York: 1917) 2: 139; cited
by H. M. Garth, *Saint Mary Magdalene in Mediaeval Literature* (Baltimore: Johns Hopkins, 1950) 77.
The suggestion about hair is Garth's, who gives no reference to support the connection between plaits
and a reputation for immorality.

41. Rousseau and Arav, *Jesus and His World*, 189.

women's mystical and literary traditions. The biblical book of Job simply says that in the blessing of his latter days Job had seven sons and three daughters. Only the daughters are named: Jemimah (Dove), Keziah (Cinnamon), and Keren-happuch (Horn of Kohl). "In all the land there were no women so beautiful as Job's daughters; and their father gave them an inheritance along with their brothers" (42:14–15). That inheritance is described in the first century B.C.E.–C.E. pseudepigrapha, *The Testament of Job,* as the gift of three multicolor cords or sashes. When the sisters (now named Day, Kasia, and Amaltheia's Horn) put them on, they can speak and sing in the language of the angels. And they can see and celebrate the heavenly chariot come for the soul of their father (T. Job 46–52).[42] File that in the back of your mind.[43]

As a site of military history, Migdal and the area around it ran with blood. In 161 B.C.E., partisans of the Maccabees were slaughtered in the caves at Arbela near Tarichaeae by the Syrian general Baccides (1 Macc 9:2; Josephus, *Ant.* 12. 11.1 [421]), and in 38 B.C.E. soldiers of Herod the Great slaughtered supporters of his rival Antigonus who had taken refuge in those caves (Josephus, *Ant.* 14:423–26). Cassius, who governed Syria from 53–51 B.C.E., attacked Taricheae and took 30,000 men slaves. During the war of 66–70 (74) C.E., when Josephus was commander of the Galilean revolutionaries' army, he made Taricheae-Magdala his headquarters and fortified it (*Life* 18.32). He asserts that the men of the city were on his side, his supporters numbering 40,000 men (*J.W.* 2.608). On the eve of the Sabbath he was able to mobilize 230 vessels and overcome his pro-Roman enemies from the city of Tiberias, imprisoning 600 members of the council of Tiberias at Taricheae (*J.W.* 2. 21, 4 [2.634–38, 641]). It was a Zealot stronghold and refuge for rebels, until it fell to the Romans (*Life* 463–504). In the great naval battle at Tarichaeae, 6,700 Jews were killed by Vespasian's army in 67 C.E.. Titus,

---

42. See R. P. Spitter, "Testament of Job," *Old Testament Pseudepigrapha* (ed. J. H. Charlesworth; Garden City: Doubleday, 1983) 1.829–68; Rebecca Lesses, "The Daughters of Job," *Searching the Scriptures* (ed. E. Schüssler Fiorenza; New York: Crossroad, 1994) 2.139–49. See further, below, pp. 311–13. R. S. Kraemer has reservations about the date and Jewishness of this text ("Jewish Women and Women's Judaism(s) at the Beginning of Christianity," *Women and Christian Origins* [ed. R. S. Kraemer and M. R. D'Angelo; New York: Oxford, 1999] n. 5, p. 74) but she does not discuss them.

43. Legend has it that kabbalists from Safed centuries later claimed that they rediscovered Miriam's Well near the Sea of Galilee. "One drink from its pure waters was said to alert the heart, mind and soul and make the meanings of the Torah become more clear." This was the well of sparkling water, created at twilight on the second day of creation, said to belong throughout history to those who know how to draw its waters: to Abraham, Hagar, Isaac, and to Miriam during the Exodus "because of the power of her voice and her intimate understanding of water." The well accompanied the people on their wanderings, but disappeared when they entered Canaan. Water from that well "was taken in pouches to wherever Jews settled. In each generation, it was believed, there lived wise men and women who would sprinkle these waters on the ground and cause new wells to spring forth. Centuries later, the Hasidim of Eastern Europe attested to its ability to reappear, whenever Jews sang to it. In our own time it is said Miriam's Well is near those who cast their buckets into any well at the end of the Sabbath as all wells are filled with those refreshing waters at that time." See P. V. Aldeman, *Miriam's Well: Rituals for Jewish Women Around the Year* (Fresh Meadows, N.Y.: Biblio, 1986) 63–64.

on horseback, led his troops through the lake side into the town, killing those who were caught there, or boarding boats, or swimming away. He then launched a flotilla to defeat those who had escaped by boat. "One could see the whole lake red with blood and covered with corpses, for not a man escaped." A stench hung over the region, and the beaches were strewn with corpses. The Jews were plunged into mourning, and the conquerors revolted (*J.W.* 3, 10:1–6/462–505). Vespasian, sitting on his tribunal at Tarichaeae, granted the rebels "an amnesty in equivocal terms": he let them leave the city but only by the road to Tiberias. In Tiberias they were led to the stadium where 1200 — "the old and unserviceable" — were executed, 6000 youths sent to Nero, and the rest — 30,400 except for those of whom he made a present to Agrippa — were sold (*J.W.* 3. 532–42). Nero included the city in the territory of Agrippa II (*Ant.* 20, 8.4/159); after he died, the city was attached to the province of Judea.

I know of no full-scale analysis of all this archaeological and written material which would give us a sense of the dimensions of Migdal in the first century c.e., some sense of its class structures, its wealth and poverty, the labor requirements suggested by the extant buildings, how it compared to other places like Sepphoris and Tiberias, founded by Herod Antipas in 4 b.c.e. and 18 c.e. respectively.[44] Meyers and Strange comment only that the architectural remains indicate that Migdal, like Tiberias, seems "to have been more Romanized (and perhaps paganized?)" than Capernaum or Chorazin.[45] Strange notes that "in the archaeology of the villages of Galilee and in the archaeology of Sepphoris, Tiberias, Acco-Ptolemais, Beth Shean and Magdala we have an excellent source for understanding the social context of the Galilean ministry of Jesus and the emergence of the gospels." At Migdal and elsewhere "one can lay eyes on the imprint of the Roman idea of the city" in the respect for a geometric grid in the archaeological remains.[46] The Roman passion for entertainment is represented by the theatre and hippodrome Josephus mentions, where cultural, class and economic differences would have been prominent.[47] Migdal was a place where Jews and non-Jews met, an urban center on the main road than ran from Philoteria at the south end of the Sea of Galilee, along the western side of the Sea to fork: north to Damascus before Capernaum, east through Capernaum to Bethsaida-Julias and points eastward. Its location "implies traffic, commerce, and the flow of ideas and information, in-

---

44. Sepphoris is thought to have had a population of around 18,000, Tiberias around 24, 000 (J. L. Reed, *Places in Early Christianity: Galilee, Archaeology, Urbanization, and Q*, dissertation Claremont Graduate School, 1994, 70). Dalman (*Sacred Sites and Ways*, 127) calls Magdala "the most important city on the western bank of the lake, contributing a wagon-load of taxes (Gen R 79 [1706]), until Herod Antipas raised up a rival on the lake by building Tiberias."

45. E. M. Meyers and J. F. Strange, *Archaeology, the Rabbis and Early Christianity* (Abingdon: Nashville, 1981) 26.

46. J. F. Strange, "Implications," 29, 36.

47. Dalman (*Sacred Sites and Ways*, 126) thought that this showed the inhabitants were probably non-Jews for the most part.

cluding gossip."[48] Overman says that as "the capital of a toparchy," Migdal would have possessed "some administrative apparatus and personnel, though not to the extent of a Sepphoris or Tiberias." Josephus' estimate of 40,000 for the city's population [actually, the estimate of the men who supported him] is unlikely, though it was probably "quite large" and "did have some impressive institutions and apparatus which would have established it as an important regional center."[49]

Christian pilgrim sources, from the ninth to the thirteenth centuries, Crusader period, speak of a church there, in which was found the house of Mary Magdalene, which could be entered. This church (or temple [*naos, templum*]) is said to have been built in the fourth century by Queen Helena, who is said to have found the house of Mary Magdalene. In the thirteenth century, in the period of the Mamelukes, according to these sources the beautiful church was not destroyed but transformed into a stable. (Contrast Saxer:[50] the first church dedicated to Mary Magdalene was in the Jewish quarter of Jerusalem at the beginning of the twelfth century [the century in which her legend was completed]). By the seventeenth century, only ruins are reported at Migdal. In 1871 Captains Wilson and Warren say they found "a heap of ruins" there.[51] Manns remarks that it is important to note the silence of the first pilgrims: the Bordeaux Pilgrim (333 C.E.), Egeria (381–84 C.E.) and Jerome (386 C.E.) do not mention Mary Magdalene's house or church. Neither does Willibald (722 C.E.) who passed by "the village of Magdalum."[52] This silence is explained in part, he argues, by the fact that many places which recalled the memory of Jesus were in the hands of Jewish Christians, who were separated and alienated from Gentile Christians, especially after the council of Nicea took strongly anti-Judaic positions.[53] Galilee at this time was still a strongly Jewish area.[54] But what else does the silence say? Only about a third of Egeria's work is extant;[55] the Bordeaux Pilgrim did not go to the Galilee; Jerome shows no familiarity with the Galilee, and probably depended on Eusebius for most of his knowledge of it.[56]

---

48. Strange, "Implications," 42–43. See also *Archaeology and the Galilee.*
49. "Who Were the First Urban Christians? Urbanization in Galilee in the First Century," *SBL Seminar Papers* (Atlanta: Scholars Press, 1988) 163.
50. V. Saxer, *Le Culte de Marie Madeleine en Occident des origines à la fin du moyen age* (Paris, 1959) 344; followed by S. Haskins, *Mary Magdalen,* 193.
51. Capt. Wilson and Capt. Warren, *The Recovery of Jerusalem* (ed. W. Morrison; New York: Appleton, 1871) 275.
52. Wilson and Warren, *Recovery,* 299.
53. The Bordeaux Pilgrim, however, may have been a Jewish Christian (see H. Donner, *Die ersten Palestinapilger* [Stuttgart: Catholic Bibelwerk, 1983] 41–42. Further, the Jewish Christian house church at Capernaum may have been visited by Egeria (see below).
54. J. Wilkinson, *Egeria's Travels* (London: SPCK, 1971), 19.
55. On Peter the Deacon's twelfth-century treatment of Tiberias, Capernaum, Nazareth, Mount Tabor, Capernaum, Tabgha, the "cave" of the Beatitudes, and perhaps Chorazin, possibly following Egeria, and certainly using as his outline *On the Holy Places* by the venerable Bede (ca. 673–735), see Wilkinson, *Egeria's Travels,* 193–201.
56. Wilkinson, *Egeria's Travels,* n. 7, pp. 192–93.

And why am I, who deal with texts for a living, squeezing through the barbed wire? Why am I, who do feminist biblical studies, reading archaeology when "Almost no one does it. Almost no one attempts to integrate the results of archaeological research into the various projects of biblical study that might be called feminist"[57] Why are we driving, then climbing up the cliff of Mount Arbel which overlooks Migdal? Why are we sitting here on the edge of a sheer drop, in rebel territory, thinking of the ancient city whose name translates "Tower" (for defense? for observation? for warning sailors?), and of present challenges? Surely this "pilgrimage" is like the relief parties Woolf led to ferret out the lives of the obscured, to rescue a stranded ghost. Our trespass is meant as an act of usurpation. We are here to insist on the flesh and blood, the bone and rock of our own women's history. Our desire — impossible though it may be — is to connect over past time in present space with a real and historical forerunner.

But the evidence is lost, or all but lost. It is gone to ground. Carted off, scattered. In the Studium Biblicum Franciscanum Museum at the Church of the Flagellation back in Jerusalem, you can see a few marble fragments decorated with a vine leaf, possibly from what may have been the mini-synagogue or nymphaeum, some Roman pottery and bronze objects from Migdal. In the glassware room, blown vessels from Migdal — goblets, beakers, bottles, flasks, tablewear, jewelry, lamps, perfume bottles, kohl vases. Nothing is carefully marked. To the west of Migdal, up the Arbel mountain range in the modern town of Upper Migdal, archaeological artifacts probably from the Migdal dig decorate homes: a telephone rests on an ancient column in one yard, a wine press sits in another. Who knows what was ground up by bulldozers, pushed into the Sea? We have a Netzer beer in the roadside bar and think about this.

"A transparency appears." Superimpose over the ruins here at Migdal a slide of what goes on eleven km. up the road at Capernaum (Kefar Nahum), one of the most important Christian excavations in Israel/Palestine. There a modern church (magnificent? tasteless? expensive) was under construction for some years. Slabs of concrete with iron rods protruding; wood and metal scaffolding; great puffs and snorts of dust marked the quick movement of the tractor driven energetically by Corbo and his crew: moving, removing, reconstructing, covering. Finally finished, the 22 foot high church supported on eight columns now incorporates the remains of a fifth-century memorial structure of three concentric octagons, considered by some archaeologists to have been built over the actual house of Peter, which in the mid-first century c.e. became a house church that survived

<hr />

57. C. Meyers, "Recovering Objects, Re-Visioning Subjects: Archaeology and Feminist Biblical Study," *A Feminist Companion to Reading the Bible: Approaches, Methods and Strategies* (ed. A. Brenner and C. Fontaine; Sheffield: Sheffield Academic Press, 1997) 270. Meyers shows that it can and should be done. Her aim is to prevent anachronistic readings and judgments, in the light of the assumption that the biblical world-view is radically different from ours, "that the biblical past is dead, extinct, gone forever. So too are its ways of thinking, doing, living (271)." I accept this assumption as only a half-truth.

four hundred years. The single large room of that house was plastered, and graffiti mention Jesus as "Lord" and "Christ." There are also etched crosses, a boat, and over one hundred Greek, Aramaic, Syriac, Latin and Hebrew graffiti from the second and third centuries. Some may mention Peter, but this is unconfirmed. Fish hooks were found between layers of the floor; pieces of broken lamps and storage jars were recovered in the room, but no domestic pottery. The reasonable but cautious conclusion has been that "this may be the earliest evidence for Christian gatherings that has ever come to light."[58] The pilgrim Egeria did visit this site in the fourth century and reported in her diary, "In Capernaum a house church (*domus ecclesia*) was made out of the home of the prince of the apostles, whose walls still stand today as they were."[59] The modern church, like a space ship with eight rocket launchers, perches over the remains, which are visible though windows in the floor and from the outside. *"Tu es Petrus et super hanc petram aedificabo ecclesiam meam et portae inferi non praevalerunt adversus eam,"* proclaims a huge carved panel. Four color charts depict the excavation in stages and from different views; a mosaic floor of banded circles is partially restored, and the walls of the house-church finished off at about two feet.

This oldest Christian sanctuary, contained in a fancy modern church welcoming the tour busses, offers a striking contrast to the barbed wire of Midgal, the sheep and chickens walking down its Roman road and through its paved court. "And I thought how unpleasant it is to be locked out; and I thought how it is worse perhaps to be locked in."[60] To Capernaum, Corbo carted the *kai su* inscription and the mosaic from Migdal of the boat and six other objects, and put them on display, along with some carved marble stones, maybe lintels, with a blue sign: FIRST CENT. AD MAGDALA. The politics of archaeology; the sexual politics of archaeology.[61] Who digs where, and why, and with what money? I naively ask. "Let us not praise famous women." There is no need to travel in imagination to Rome's great basilica of St. Peter's to illustrate the contrast in attention and honor paid currently and earlier to the two biblical figures of Peter and Mary Magdalene. There is no rivalry between the sites along the Sea of Galilee, because it is no contest. But open rivalry is in the ancient Gnostic texts, with roots that twist and turn deep in the Christian Testament, as we will see.

Superimpose another transparency. Monk's House at Rodmell in East Sussex, England, home of Virginia and Leonard Woolf from 1919 until her death in 1941,

58. J. F. Strange and H. Shanks, "Has the House Where Jesus Stayed in Capernaum Been Found?" *BAR* 8 (1982) 26–37; J. H. Charlesworth, *Jesus Within Judaism* (New York: Doubleday, 1988) 109–15: "The possibility [that this is the house of Peter] is so remarkable that it elicits from an audience the charge of slipping from the rigors of scholarship into sensationalism. Yet it is not the claim, but the discovery, which may well be sensational" (109).

59. Wilkinson, *Egeria's Travels*, 194.

60. Woolf, *Room*, 24.

61. See C. Meyers, *Discovering Eve* (New York: Oxford, 1988) 16–18 on the male bias in archaeology.

Leonard's until his death in 1969. The National Trust cares for the house, with its apple green sitting room, its paintings and drawings and books, its 3/4 acre gardens and orchards overlooking the Downs, its two ponds.[62] "It is an unpretending house, long & low, a house of many doors...."[63] You can walk to the River Ouse, where she drowned herself. You can come back and look into her little writing shed, the Lodge, by the churchyard of twelfth-century St. Peter's with its grey flint tower and "cursed Xtian bells...""intermittent, sullen, didactic."[64] Her sheets of blue writing paper sit on her desk; windows give a view across the valley to Mount Caburn. You can sit with your friends outside that cottage under the huge dark horsechestnut tree, and rest. People are sketching, writing, strolling, having tea. Some of the women are wearing big hats and long dresses and an abstracted, focused air, like Woolf. It is tempting, writes Hermione Lee, to think one can enter the past, but " 'Her' Monk's House, 'her' Rodmell, exist and do not exist."[65]

I am puzzled by my return to Migdal year after year, by my fascination or obsession with the details of this dig. Does it matter, what more might have been learned here, with more money and attention, more care? Does it matter that there is no memorial to Mary Magdalene — I mean not a monument, and certainly not a church, but a place of access, of respect? Something by Maya Lin, perhaps, just a partially erased name, a dishonored name, in process of being restored, in basalt. But for now, the memorial is this place of high walls and weeds.

I want to buy it (a middle-class American's crass solution) from the Commissariat of the Holy Land, Casa Generalizia, Frati Minori, Rome, Italy; or from Father Alviero Niccacci, Custodium Biblicum Franciscanum, Convent of the Flagellation, B.P. 19424, Jerusalem 91193; or from the Studium Biblicum Franciscanum, Via Dolorosa POB 19424, 91193 Jerusalem; email sbfnet@netvision.net.il. (Dear Sir, If you have no plans for the site at Migdal, once excavated by Virgilio Corbo, would you consider....) Or at least to lease it (To the Jewish National Defense Fund; Dear Sir: I would like to make a bid....) I want to make a video for the Biblical Archaeology Society: shots of the weeds and chickens, illustrating and voicing the loss of women's history. (Dear Hershel Shanks, Would you be interested....) I want to negotiate with Marwan's family about their living space, to interest some university's archaeology department, interest the Israeli Department of Antiquities, interest some women's cooperative, some philanthropist, interest even some Franciscan archaeologist, and eventually — what? Have the dig resumed, expanded, done more carefully, adequately controlled, have the

---

62. On the gardens, see R. W. Apple, Jr., "Bloomsbury in Bloom," *Garden Design* (May, 1998) 78–87.

63. *Diary* 1.286–87; 3 July 1919.

64. V. Woolf, "In the Orchard," *The Collected Shorter Fiction of Virginia Woolf* (ed. Susan Dick; Hogarth Press, 1985, 1989) 149.

65. Lee, *Virginia Woolf*, 416.

clear, informative blue and white signs and the diagrams, create a small museum of Jewish and Christian women's history.

A dig of one's own. I want it to produce studies of gendered archaeology or ethnoarchaeology,[66] or feminist archaeology,[67] focusing on the Second Temple period and slightly beyond. I want to bring up the submerged lighthouse ("it was a stark tower on a bare rock"[68]), restore the harbor. And the mini-synagogue, or nymphaeum, or portico — into which springs keep bubbling. Make use of all this information; expand it. Imagine the streets and buildings, the promenade and shops filled with women and children and men, the elderly and the young, wealthy and poor, the marginal and the respected, not just with Josephus strutting along with his men and mobs, not just male rabbis with their male students. A town with faces.[69] Imagine with the help of feminist anthropologists the social dynamics of the fish industry and other businesses and technologies, the home, the synagogue. There would be a garden as at Rodmell, and "fruit trees which resemble appletrees," a place to sit and commune with ghosts, to consider the dominance of male interests, and the agency of women and wo/men. There would be a clean beach from which we and those who come after us could swim around the lighthouse, tie up our skiffs at the mooring stone. Listen for the music of the daughters of Job. Coffee and watermelon, and for the non-vegetarians pickled sardines. In this artistic and intellectual community all are at the table, in the discussion.

But no — in all likelihood Migdal will go further back into the earth, its artifacts lie there neglected, or become the trash thrown out if or when a resort hotel is built over it. A water slide; Muzak blaring; a huge plastic lobby; drinks with decorated swizzle sticks. Migdal will be a clear or a blurred statement of what is lost, irretrievably lost to history, buried and overgrown and overbuilt, as the voices and actions and lives of the first century c.e. women are buried and overgrown and overbuilt by the Christian Testament words and centuries of interpretation. Past events and historical persons, what really happened and who dead persons really were — I know these are irretrievable in any absolute sense,

---

66. Sometimes called social archaeology. See Meyers, "Recovering Objects," 278–79. On the many archaeologies of gender, see R. P. Wright, "Introduction: Gendered Ways of Knowing in Archaeology," *Gender and Archaeology* (ed. R. P. Wright; Philadelphia: University of Pennsylvania, 1996) 1–19. Most interesting is the premise that teaching and fieldwork, as knowledge-producing acts, must be investigated. Essays in this volume focus on more subtle matters than where to dig, when to keep digging, and why, the matters that interests me in this chapter.

67. See I. Hodder, *Reading the Past* (Cambridge: Cambridge University Press, 1986) 168–72. See also R. A. Horsley, "The Historical Jesus and Archaeology of the Galilee: Questions from Historical Jesus Research to Archaeologists," *SBL Seminar Papers* 1994, 91–135.

68. Woolf, *To the Lighthouse,* 187.

69. See R. E. Tringham, "Households with Faces: the Challenge of Gender in Prehistoric Architectural Remains," *Engendering Archaeology* (ed. J. M. Gero and M. W. Conkey; Cambridge, Mass.: Blackwell, 1991) 93–131. "The problem has been that 'faces' are not demonstrable in the archaeological record, they cannot be 'operationalized' archaeologically, they are not testable, and thus they cannot be taken seriously by respectable scientists. It moreover takes a great deal of effort and imaginative power to consider them. But they *are* there" (117).

and in some sense irrelevant. Connection in any literal sense is impossible. But I will still ask historical questions and still visit this site as long as it is a site, and even if, especially if, it becomes a hotel. I am looking for something, maybe for what used to be called my spirit or my immortal soul. Something for my imagination. I allow myself that. Even though "The aims of the imagination are not the aims of history," as Cynthia Ozick has said,[70] these aims are congruent. History and imagination interact. I know that "History is the fruit of power, but power itself is never so transparent that its analysis becomes superfluous. The ultimate mark of power may be its invisibility; the ultimate challenge, the exposition of its roots."[71] This is true, I think, for both the power that suppresses and the power that is suppressed. Even though certainty always eludes us, the possibilities and the probabilities of women's historical contributions should be honored by examination, enjoyment, use, imagination; and their lack of historical contributions, where that can be shown, should be mourned and imagined.[72] Both the contributions and the lack of contributions, and the images of contribution and of lack, have shaped how historical actors in the past and present live their lives.[73] They shape us.

"Irresistible Decay: Ruins Reclaimed" was an exhibition of photographs and texts held at the Getty Center in Los Angeles December 16, 1997, through February 22, 1998. In its companion volume, Salvatore Settis writes,

> Ruins signal simultaneously an absence and a presence; they show, they *are*, an intersection of the visible and the invisible. Fragmented, decayed structures, which no longer serve their original purpose, point to an absence — a lost, invisible whole. But their visible presence also points to durability, even if that which is no longer what it once was.... Ruins potently epitomize the perennial tension between what is preserved and what is lost, what seems immediately understandable (or usable) and what needs interpretation (or reconstruction). As we have learned that trauma and discontinuity are fundamental for memory and history, ruins have come to be necessary for linking creativity to the experience of loss at the individual and collective level. Ruins operate as powerful metaphors for absence or rejection and hence, as incentives for reflection or restoration.[74]

70. Quoted at the conference at Boston University, "The Claims of Memory" (S. Boxer, "Giving Memory Its Due in an Age of License," *New York Times*, Wed. Oct. 28, 1998, B1).

71. M-R Trouillot, *Silencing the Past: Power and the Production of History* (Boston: Beacon, 1995) xix.

72. On the work of Torjesen, Corley, Kraemer, Schüssler Fiorenza, Brooten, Wire and others underscoring "the centrality of historical reconstruction as a foundational tool for feminist interpretation of early Christianity," and the work of Joan Kelly, see Castelli, "Heteroglossia," 91–93.

73. On the shaping of all historical evidence in cultural codes embedded in language, and on how image shapes reality, see M. Y. MacDonald, *Early Christian Women and Pagan Opinion: The Power of the Hysterical Woman* (Cambridge: Cambridge University Press, 1996) 120–21.

74. S. Settis, Forward to M. S. Roth with C. Lyons and C. Merewether, *Irresistible Decay: Ruins Reclaimed* (Los Angeles: The Getty Institute for the History of Art and the Humanities, 1997) vii.

The curators discuss a variety of perspectives: the ruin as constructed by the beholder as a decayed trace of the past; how ruins connote loss and mortality but promise connection; how documentation makes scholarly work possible and effects the ways we frame the past. Ruins that seem to be returning to the landscape signal a deep belonging to the natural world, welcome or devouring.

When we contemplate the luxury hotel that might or might not rise at Migdal, it seems true that ruins "persist, whether beneath the ground or above."[75] Ruins beneath the imagined hotel, a ruin in its own way, and a short distance from the church at Capernaum, a ruin in its own way,[76] Migdal's ruins persist in photographs, in memory, in curiosity, in sadness, in desire. Migdal is our irresistible decay, our necessary ruin. Like the oasis in the Negeb at 'Ain El-Qudeirat with its three springs, which is possibly Kadesh or Kadesh-barnea, the burial place of Miriam (Num 20:1),[77] Migdal has no memorial, and is the focus of no reconstruction. The site stands for me as a reminder of loss, of the possibility of knowing nothing or nearly nothing. It is a reminder of distance, of the inexorability of time and death, of massive indifference and resistance. It teaches that even if we are convinced of women's agency and power, even if we desire an ancestor of historical greatness, we may not be able to reconstruct our history convincingly; our reconstructions may be wrong. We have to be open to nothingness and disappointment. We are chickens scratching the remnants of mosaics. But still we scratch. I'll write it again. Migdal is our irresistible decay, our necessary ruin.

---

75. Merewether, *Irresistible Decay*, 25.
76. My colleague Gloria Albrecht comments on the latter: "the decay of kyriarchal posturing."
77. See R. Cohen, *Kadesh-barnea: a Fortress from the Time of the Judaean Kingdom* (Jerusalem: the Israel Museum, 1983). No relics from the Exodus period have been found there.

CHAPTER	Silence, Conflation,
THREE	**Distortion, Legends**

Silence, Conflation, Distortion, Legends

"Do people always get what they deserve, & did KM[1] do something to deserve this cheap posthumous life?"

V. Woolf, *Diary* 2.238

" 'What is chastity, then? I mean is it good, or is it bad, or is it nothing at all?' [Castalia] replied so low that I could not catch what she said. 'You know I was shocked,' said another,' for at least ten minutes.' 'In my opinion,' said Poll . . . 'chastity is nothing but ignorance — a most discreditable state of mind. We should admit only the unchaste to our society. . . . It is as unfair to brand women with chastity as with unchastity. . . . ' "

V. Woolf, "A Society"[2]

"I must not settle into a figure."

V. Woolf, *Diary* 4.85

I F WE CANNOT DIG AT MIGDAL, where there is "no entry," we can scratch away at the overlay of legends, and deconstruct the stories built in Western Christianity on the meagre material in the Christian Testament and other ancient works, about — and not about — Mary Magdalene. Clearing the site is preparation for the work of the following chapters: examining the most ancient literary fragments and offering literary and historical reconstructions, discussing their possible uses for some at the beginning of the twenty-first century.

These fragments about her in the Christian Testament are of course still visible and ready-to-hand, since it is a living document, and the so-called gnostic[3] materials about her have been available since their rediscovery in the twentieth century. According to all four Christian Testament gospels, Mary Magdalene is a — perhaps the — primary witness to the fundamental data of the early Christian

---

1. Katherine Mansfield.
2. V. Woolf, "A Society, *Monday or Tuesday* (New York: Harcourt, Brace and Company, 1921).
3. See below, pp. 122–24, for discussion of this term.

faith. She is said to have participated in the Galilean career of Jesus of Nazareth, followed him to Jerusalem, stood by at his execution and burial, found his tomb empty and received an explanation of that emptiness. Two texts mention that seven demons had come out of her (Luke 8:2; Mark 16:9[4]]). According to three accounts (Mark 16:7; Matthew 28:7; John 20:17) she is sent with a commission to deliver the explanation of the empty tomb to the disciples. Also according to three accounts (Matt 28:9–10; John 20:14–18; Mark 16:9) she was the first to experience a vision or appearance of the resurrected Jesus. Gnostic materials present her as a leading intellectual and spiritual guide of the early, post-Easter community, as a visionary, the Savior's beloved companion, a conduit for and interpreter of his teachings.

In spite of her importance in the Gospel narratives and noncanonical works, there is silence and confusion around this figure. In spite of the paucity of information about her, there is a great deal of tension or anxiety about her role. There exists no narrative of her call by Jesus (or of any other woman's call), nor in the Christian Testament is there any teaching during the ministry that involves her. Luke 8:1–3 reports that Mary Magdalene and other women travelled with Jesus and the Twelve, and "ministered to (or: served) them out of their means." This passage raises many questions we will examine later about the social/economic makeup and lifestyle of this movement and the nature of women's contributions. Where she is mentioned by name, Mary Magdalene is identified only by her city — she is the Mary from Magdala — and not by any relationship with father or husband or son. She is also mentioned first among women (except in John 19:25), indicating her prominence.

But she is one of many Marys in the narratives, all of whom are hard to keep straight. Why so many Marys? For whom are they named? Perhaps for the prophet Miriam, or for Mariamme the Hasmonean, married in 37 B.C.E. to Herod the Great and murdered by him eight years later. The name Mary, associated with the hopes of Hasmonean nationalists or sympathizers for independence, became suddenly common after her murder, in the generation before Jesus and into first century C.E. in Palestine.[5] A study of the recorded names of Jewish women in Palestine from 330 B.C.E. to 200 C.E. shows that 47.7 percent were called either Salome or Mary (Mariamme or Maria). Mary is the name of 23.4 percent,[6] roughly a fourth

---

4. The Markan Appendix is the longer ending of Mark (vv. 9–20); is canonical, but not by the author of Mark.

5. M. Sawicki, "Magdalenes and Tiberiennes: City Women in the Entourage of Jesus," *Transformative Encounters: Jesus and Women Re-Viewed* (ed. I. R. Kitzberger; Leiden: Brill, 1999) 3, 5, 7. Note that two of Jesus' disciples were named Judas, probably after Judas Maccabee.

6. T. Ilan, "Notes on the Distribution of Jewish Women's Names in Palestine in the Second Temple and Mishnaic Periods," *JJS* 40 (1989) 188–200; R. Bauckham, *Jude and the Relatives of Jesus* (Edinburgh: T. & T. Clark, 1990) 43. Ilan notes that discrimination against women is indicated by that fact that the total of all these women known by name in this period is 247, in comparison with 2040 men known by name; in the Christian Testament, it is 16 women named, in comparison to 92 men (187–88). There are 61 women named Salome (or its longer version Salomezion) and 58 named

of all women; in the Christian Testament the number is nearly half, 6 out of 16, 42.5 percent. Jesus' mother was named Mary, as were perhaps as many as five (or as few as three) other women associated with him: Mary of Bethany, Mary the mother of James the Less and of Joses, "the other Mary" (Matthew's phrase), Mary Cleophas (only in John), and Mary Magdalene.[7] The last four names are given in various Gospel accounts of the crucifixion. Only three other women in this circle are named: Joanna, Suzanna and Salome. Matthew's mother of the sons of Zebedee may be another Mary, or one of the others. And in legends, add Mary Jacobus, Mary Salome. This "overdose of scriptural Marys"[8] certainly led to confusion, especially on the part of those harmonizing and attempting to reconcile discrepancies, further exacerbated by readings which attributed to the Virgin Mary all powerful female roles and attributes, in order to heighten her praise.[9]

In the Gospels Mary Magdalene is spoken to only by the figure(s) at the empty tomb and by the risen Jesus. She speaks only to and of them, or of the empty tomb. Dialogue with her as an individual occurs only in the Gospel of John, in the garden tomb scene. Mark 16:8 depicts her and the other women fleeing from the empty tomb and saying nothing to anyone because of their fear, so that that Gospel ends in their silence. In Luke 24:34 (as in 1 Cor 15:5) the first vision of the resurrected one is said to be Peter's; John 20:8 presents the mysterious figure of the beloved disciple as the first to believe.

Outside the Gospels, she is mentioned by name nowhere else in the Christian Testament, not even in 1 Cor 15:5–8 which lists those to whom the risen Jesus appeared. In the gnostic materials, as we will see in chapter 4, her role is larger: she converses with the risen Jesus, relates visionary experiences and teachings she received, and encourages the dejected disciples after the resurrection. But she is also a source of open conflict: her authority is criticized by the disciples, especially by Peter, and she is defended. Erotic intimacy between her and Jesus, read by some in John 20 — in her weeping, the calling of her name and the refusal of her touch — is an even stronger, more open element in the gnostic texts.

Analysis of the differences among the four Gospel accounts of the crucifixion, empty tomb, and post-resurrection visions indicates that as early as the second half of the first century her role and its implications were already disputed or ignored or perhaps unknown. In the memories and rethinking of the Pauline and Lukan communities, she was overshadowed by Peter; in Johannine circles, by

---

Mariamme (or its shorter version Maria [191–92]). The name Salome may have been given after the Hasmonean Queen Salomezion Alexander.

7. On the addition of Mary the mother of Jesus to the crucifixion scene see M. Proctor-Smith, "A Choice of Marys," *Academy* 38 (1982) 30.

8. K. L. Jansen, "Maria Magdalena: *Apostolorum Apostola*," *Women Preachers and Prophets Through Two Millennia of Christianity* (ed. B. M. Kienzle and P. J. Walker; Berkeley: University of California, 1998) 59.

9. Jansen, "Maria Magdalena," 59–60.

someone called the Beloved Disciple. The gnostic materials show other dimensions of gender conflict within communities whose delineations and influence we cannot yet decipher, and whose relation to the Christian Testament communities and their literature is still uncertain.

My primary interest in this book lies with these ancient texts. But for contemporary Western readers and those who inherited or had foisted on them Western interpretations, the Mary Magdalene passages have scrawled over them the word WHORE. Repentant whore. Whore who loved and was forgiven by Jesus. Saved whore (a relatively rare figure in literature).[10] There are other elements of her legends, to be sure, but this is the one most people today free-associate with the name Mary Magdalene. Her sexual "biography" has a long history, featuring in the Middle Ages stress on her penitence and apostleship; the Renaissance and Reformation, and nineteenth and twentieth centuries offered multiple assessments of her as a representative of female sexuality. Cleaning off the texts is an interesting task, and turns the mind to ask about the scrawling and the scrawlers. I am interested in this chapter in how the Magdalene become a whore, and when, and why.

No other biblical figure — including Judas, and perhaps even Jesus[11] — has had such a vivid and bizarre postbiblical life in the human imagination, in legend and in art. If Mary Magdalene the Whore did not exist, we who are interested in the history of man's idea of woman would have to invent her, as complement and contrast to the Virgin Mother. A survey of the postbiblical images of the Magdalene, literary and visual, leads to disturbing insights. Successive epochs, beginning with the times of the Evangelists, have found their own thoughts in her, created her in accord with their own characters and needs. The effect — and perhaps in some sense the intent — was that the memory of the historical woman and the Christian Testament character did not live but die, or nearly die. Fundamental questions concerning sexuality and the spirit, guilt and transcendence, authority and love, and unspoken questions too, have been addressed by her changing image.

Elisabeth Schüssler Fiorenza has remarked that post-Christian Testament distortion of the image of Mary Magdalene signals a deep distortion in the attitudes toward, and in the self-understanding and identity of, the Christian woman and man.[12] That distortion, which amounts at times to a pathology, has begun to

10. See P. L. Horn and M. B. Pringle, *The Image of the Prostitute in Modern Literature* (New York: Ungar, 1984) 3–6.

11. And certainly not Joseph of Arimathea. R. E. Brown characterizes the post-biblical career of Mary Magdalene as "not unlike the legends that grew up around Joseph from Arimathea" (*Death of the Messiah*, 2. n. 81, p. 1276). It is very unlike those legends.

12. E. Schüssler Fiorenza, "Mary Magdalene: Apostle to the Apostles," 5; see also her earlier work *Der Vergessener Partner* (Dusseldorf: Patmos-Verlag, 1964) 57–59. Haskins sees the victimization of Mary Magdalene as a metaphor for the historically subordinate position of women in Christianity (*Mary Magdalen*, 392).

receive precise documentation and analysis. We can be sure that the image func‐ tioned differently for women and for men, and the legend of her whoring was given different emphases in different contexts. Women may have emphasized Mary Magdalene's constant and courageous suffering, men her conversion and repentance.[13] Certainly, given the legend's strength and durability, and its com‐ plexity, it empowered in some ways as well as imprisoned. Elisabeth B. Davis, for example, sees the legendary Magdalene presented in sixteenth‐ and seven‐ teenth Spanish texts as a woman with a rich, human life marked by passion and self‐determination rather than passivity.[14]

Multiple issues raised by women's history, women's studies, historical Jesus research, and gnostic studies, and issues important to the women's movement (sexuality, prostitution, leadership, ordination) can be focused through the lens of this figure. From the perspective of art history, two works have attempted to analyze the complex Magdalene traditions from the Christian Testament period to the present: Marjorie M. Malvern's *Venus in Sackcloth: the Magdalene's Origins and Metamorphoses* (1975)[15] and Susan Haskins' best‐selling monumental study *Mary Magdalen: Myth and Metaphor* (1993).[16] In this regard, see also the works Diane Apostolos‐Cappadona,[17] Jane Dillenberger,[18] and Margaret Miles.[19] Sessions and papers on Mary Magdalene in canonical and non‐canonical literature have been given at the Society of Biblical Literature/American Academy of Religion for

---

13. See C. W. Bynum, "'And Women His Humanity': Female Imagery in the Religious Writing of the Later Middle Ages," *Gender and Religion: On the Complexity of Symbols* (ed. C. W. Bynum, S. Harrell, P. Richman; Boston: Beacon, 1986) 260. Raymond of Capua says that Mary Magdalene was a model for Catherine of Siena because the Magdalene fasted for thirty‐three years; but Catherine herself presents her as a model because she stood under the cross (C. W. Bynum, *Holy Feast and Holy Fast* (Berkeley: University of California, 1987) 166.

14. E. B. Davis, "'Woman, Why Weepest Thou?' Re‐visioning the Golden Age Magdalen," *Hispania* 76 (1993) 40. I'm grateful to my colleague Anton Donoso for this reference.

15. Carbondale, Illinois: Southern Illinois University Press. This study is flawed by its treatment of the gnostic material, but it is valuable as a first step and for its reproduction of twenty works of art.

16. London: Harper Collins. The subject of this book is for the most part "the mythical aspects of her figure and their meaning" (xi). Its strength lies in the author's speciality as an art historian; the treatment of biblical materials is unfortunately marred by anti‐Judaic perspectives on women in Judaism, especially in chapter 1.

17. D. Apostolos‐Cappadona, *Dictionary of Christian Art* (New York: Continuum, 1994) 233–37; "Images, Interpretations, and Traditions: A Study of the Magdalene," *Interpreting Tra‐ dition* (ed. J. Kopas; Chico, Calif.: Scholars Press, 1983); "When the Magdalene Reads: Nudity and Sacramentality in Christian Art," paper delivered at the 1990 AAR/SBL Meeting, New Orleans.

18. J. Dillenberger, *Style & Content in Christian Art* (New York: Crossroad, 1988) 83–84, 92–95; "The Magdalen: Reflections on the Image of Saint and Sinner in Christian Art," *Image & Spirit in Sacred & Secular Art* (ed. D. Apostolos‐Cappadona; New York: Crossroad, 1990) 28–50. "There is no biblical figure other than the Magdalen who has borne a comparable breadth of humanity in all its many facets" (50).

19. M. R. Miles, *Image as Insight* (Boston: Beacon, 1985) 75–81; "Nudity, Gender and Religious Meaning in the Italian Renaissance," *Art as Religious Studies* (ed. D. Adams & D. Apostolos‐ Cappadona; New York: Crossroad, 1987) 101–16.

over a decade,[20] dissertations have been finished and are in progress in Finland, the Netherlands, Germany, the US, and elsewhere, and important treatments of her have begun to appear in the works of several biblical scholars, feminist and otherwise.

While it is now common scholarly knowledge that the image of the Magdalene as a repentant whore is a distortion, that image is still alive and powerful in contemporary novels, plays, films, and TV presentations. Robert Stone's journalist character Lucas, in *Damascus Gate*, muses in the creepy Holy Sepulchre:

> There were icons of the Magdalen on the walls and paintings in the Western manner, all kitsch, trash. Mary M., Lucas thought, half hypnotized by the chanting in the room beside him; Mary Moe, Jane Doe, the girl from Migdal in Galilee turned hooker in the big city. The original whore with the heart of gold. Used to be a nice Jewish girl, and next thing she's fucking the buckos of the Tenth Legion Fratensis, fucking the pilgrims who'd made their sacrifice at the Temple and were ready to party, the odd priest and Levite on the sly.
>
> Maybe she was smart and funny. Certainly always on the lookout for the right guy to take her out of the life. Like a lot of whores, she tended toward religion. So along comes Jesus Christ, Mr. Right with a Vengeance, Mr. All Right Now! Fixes on her his hot, crazy eyes and she's all, Anything, I'll do anything. I'll wash your feet with my hair. You don't even have to fuck me.
>
> You had to wonder what she'd make of her picture on the wall times seven. Amusing to show her around the place. What do you think, kid? Like it? Everybody remembers you and your old gang. We talk about you all the time.[21]

Contrast the mystery, *A Letter of Mary* (Magdalene), by Laurie R. King, who knows the scholarship. Here Mary is depicted as formerly mad but not formerly a whore; it is the only example of such a treatment that I have found. An amateur archaeologist finds an inlaid box with an ancient letter on stained papyrus; it is from "Mariam, an apostle of Jesus the Messiah" written in haste during the destruction of Jerusalem in 70 C.E., in the expectation of her death. Mary Russell, Sherlock Holmes' colleague, decides not to release the letter until ten years after her death. "I suppose that the Christian world at the close of the twentieth century will be better equipped to deal with the revelations contained in Mary's letter than it was in the century's earlier decades."[22] Unfortunately, the only bombshell the letter contains is the word "apostle."

---

20. At the 1989 meeting of the AAR/SBL in Anaheim, the Female and Male in Gnosticism Section presented papers by G. Franklin Shibroun, K. L. King, A. Pasquier and H. J. McEvoy on the theme "Mary Magdalene in Christianity and Gnosticism." At the meeting in 2000 in Nashville, the Christian Apocrypha Section presented papers by J. Knight, S. Shoemaker, K. L. King and F. Bovon on the theme "There's Something about Mary(s)." Papers concerning Mary Magdalene have been read in other sections, such as Women in the Biblical World.

21. R. Stone, *Damascus Gate* (Boston: Houghton Mifflin, 1998) 291. "When they passed Migdal, where Mary Magdalene had been a country girl before she went wrong in the big city, a single faint bell was sounding near the lake" (386).

22. L. R. King, *A Letter of Mary* (New York: St. Martin's, 1996) 276.

The historical novel for children, *Mary Magdalene: A Woman Who Showed Her Gratitude* is part of the series "Outstanding Women of the Bible," "designed to communicate a positive identity as a woman." "Mary Magdalene was not famous for the great things she did or said, but she goes down in history as a woman who truly loved Jesus with all her heart and was not embarrassed to show it despite criticism from others." Tales of her lustful early life and repentance take up half the text.[23] Donna Jo Napoli's novel for young readers, *Song of the Magdalene,* was created by working backward, "starting with every biblical episode I could find that might possibly involve Mary Magdalene . . . and then creating for her a history that would prepare her for and make sense of the actions she takes in the New Testament." Apparently this means using the repentant sinner of Luke 7 and other texts, since the author writes that "Mary Magdalene first appears in the New Testament with Jesus, either anointing his feet or coming forth among the afflicted, asking to be healed. Biblical scholars disagree over this"[24] but that is unimportant to Napoli. Her Mary Magdalene has fits; she initially thinks of herself as a demoniac, filthy and impure, but learns better from her friend Abraham who has palsy (he is regarded by people as "the idiot"), and who fathers her child before he dies. Her reputation as a prostitute is based on this pregnancy and on her rape[25] by a man of her home town, who slanders her as lustful. In a scene that seems modelled on John 8 and on an exorcism, Joshua prevents her from being stoned and she joins him. The whore legend is used here to illustrate that "If the Creator saw fit to ruin a woman's family — unless shelter was offered to her, unless work was extended to her, unless the community protected her — that woman, any woman, could become a prostitute. Any woman at all. Any one of us."[26]

Tim Rice and Andrew Lloyd Webber presented Mary Magdalene in the early 1970s in "Jesus Christ Superstar" as a prostitute in love with Jesus "mentally," having an ambiguous sexual relationship with him. Obsessed and baffled by him, she strokes and anoints him in a soothing massage.[27] In this rock opera later made into a film (1973), she is the foil for Judas; both characters sing "I Don't Know How to Love Him." In Zeffirelli's made-for-TV movie *Jesus of Nazareth,* Anne Bancroft played her in 1977 as a prostitute of angry intelligence. The Scorsese film *The Last Temptation of Christ,* based on Kazantzakis' 1955 novel, depicted the

23. M. Alex, *Mary Magdalene* (Grand Rapids: Eerdmans, 1987).

24. D. J. Napoli, *Song of the Magdalene* (New York: Scholastic, 1996) 243. I thank C. Brown for this reference.

25. Cf. the gang-rape in M. Roberts' novel, *Wild Girl* (1984), summarized by Haskins, *Mary Magdalen*, 385.

26. Napoli, *Song,*196.

27. *Jesus Christ Superstar,* the authorized version compiled by Michael Braun et al. (New York: Ballantine, 1972); transcript of an interview by David Frost; see G. E. Forshey, American Religious and Biblical Spectaculars (London: Praeger, 1992) 107; the way the resurrection is presented is also "at best ambiguous."

Magdalene in 1988 as a tattooed prostitute to whom Jesus is attracted physically, and *as* his last temptation — the temptation to become ordinary, sensual, domestic, fettered. As originally shot, the Scorsese film began with the young Jesus breaking his engagement to the Magdalene, his decision forcing her, dishonored, into prostitution (compare to the legend associated with Ephesus, treated below, where it is John the Evangelist who breaks off his betrothal to her and jilts her).

Denys Arcand's film *Jesus of Montreal* (1989) is the story of a small troupe of five professional actors hired to do a Passion Play on church property. Their conflict with church authorities and forces in the advertising industry lead to the cancellation of the play and the accidental death of the actor playing Jesus. Arcand gives us a sensitive and sweet-faced Magdalene who is not exactly a whore, but "comes from the tarnished background of commercialism that traditionally employs sexuality and sensuality in order to sell products"[28] ("I used to show my ass to sell soap and beer"). Her abusive boyfriend says she has (only) a nice ass. She is saved by Jesus from a having to take off her clothes for a job in a beer commercial, in a rage he overturns cameras, TVs and tables, cleansing the studio. They kiss and she says, "I love you, you crazy nut."

In Hal Hartley's "hip religious fable," "The Book of Life" (1998) P. J. Harvey plays "Jesus' assistant and gal Friday, Magdalena, a witchy-looking vixen wearing knee-high black boots and toting a backpack."[29] She hardly ever speaks, and understands without being given instructions. She met Jesus when he prevented people from stoning her. Is she a whore?, she is asked. "Self-employed." "I thought he had fallen in love with me,"she says wistfully. A "coming attraction" is the Jesus film from writer/director Paul Verhoeven, tentatively titled *Fully Human*. Asked if he planned to include a love interest for Jesus in this film, a Magdalene, Verhoeven is reported to have replied with a grin, "Of course. But I'm aware that the feminist scholars emphasize the fact that Jesus had female disciples, so it will probably be platonic. Besides, Jesus doesn't have time. He's always on the run."[30]

Each film's Magdalene is the conflated figure of legend, the repentant whore. Barbara Hershey, who played her in *The Last Temptation,* speaks in a scary way to the fascination of this conflated figure: "The thing that fascinated me about Mary Magdalene is that she represents all aspects of womanhood: she's a whore and a victim, a complete primal animal, and then she's reborn and becomes virginal and sisterlike. She evolves through all phases of womanhood, so it was a wonderful

---

28. R. C. Stern, C. N. Jefford, G. DeBona, *Savior on the Silver Screen* (New York: Paulist, 1999) 311.

29. S. Holden, "The Millennium in Fable and Reality," *New York Times* Arts and Ideas (Saturday, Oct 10, 1998) A24.

30. C. Allen, "Away with the Manger," *Lingua Franca* (Fev 22–30, 1995) 28. Allen says she was mentally casting Sharon Stone as Mary Magdalene. Verhoeven's other work includes "Robo-Cop," "Basic Instinct," and "Showgirls." See Haskins, *Mary Magdalen,* 376–77 on Kieslowski's 1989 film *A Short Film about Love.*

role in that way.... I felt that I was put on earth to play this part."[31] Scorsese introduces Mary Magdalene at work, watched at her work by the viewer and by a waiting room full of men including Jesus. "My most important scene, as a prostitute in Magdala, was also the most difficult because I was going to show Magdalene with a series of men. Even though Marty's films have a lot of sexuality, there hadn't been any nudity in them — and he asked me if I wanted a double, so at first I said sure. Every atom of me wanted a double. But I didn't feel a double would be Magdalene. I didn't feel she would move like I would move. I knew if I did the scene, I'd really feel like a whore."[32] Really feeling like a whore was essential to her portrayal. This Magdalene does not represent a disdain for female sexuality, but an inability to see women as other than sexual, that is, as female and spiritual.[33]

TV documentaries for Lifetime (1996) and A&E (1999) show, in my opinion, the enduring strength of the legend and how it still overpowers feminist scholarship.[34] Only Zeffirelli's and Arcand's films, to which we will return at the end of this chapter, contain startling images that threaten to break out of the legend, images of the Magdalene as Outsider. Marina Warner remarked in 1976 that with contemporary interest in the historical Jesus, Magdalene mythology analogous to that of the Gnostics is on the increase in our time.[35] I'm not sure what she meant by this, other than growing popularity, since there is little similarity between twentieth-century Magdalenes and gnostic Magdalenes, as we will see. Most recent Magdalenes are created mainly to serve an interest in the sexuality of Jesus, to save him from his asexual or (covertly) homosexual or inhuman image. They are examples of one major effort over the centuries to erase a figure and a memory more threatening, examples of what Alicia Ostriker calls the erasure that has to be obsessively repeated because it is never complete, never finished.[36]

How Mary Magdalene became a whore involved a process of powering and depowering texts, ignoring some and focusing on others. An ancient form of backlash, the assumption that she was a whore is accomplished by the conflation of several gospel stories. Conflation is not the same as harmonization, an attempt to smooth out difficulties and discrepancies, often in the service of a literalistic

---

31. P. Lemos, "Divine Duo," *MS.* (January/February 1989) 126, 124.

32. Hershey in M. Scorsese, *Scorsese on Scorsese* (ed. D. Thompson and I. Christie; London: Faber and Faber, 1989) 225.

33. B. Babington and P. W. Evans, *Biblical Epics* (Manchester: Manchester University Press, 1993) 165.

34. See J. Schaberg, "Mary of Nazareth and Mary Magdalene: Lifetime TV and A&E," paper for the Women in the Biblical World Section, SBL meeting in Nashville, 2000; forthcoming in *JFSR*. The theme of the session was "The 'F' Word: Biblical Female Figures and Feminist Scholars in the Media."

35. M. Warner, *Alone of All Her Sex* (New York: Knopf, 1976) 229.

36. A. Ostriker, "A Triple Hermeneutic: Scripture and Revisionist Women's Poetry," in *A Feminist Companion to Reading the Bible: Approaches, Methods and Strategies* (ed. A. Brenner and C. Fontaine; Sheffield: Sheffield Academic Press, 1997) 164. Ostriker is talking here of the text of the covenant depending on a subtext of female erasure.

or fundamentalistic understanding of Scripture or revelation. Conflation merges and strings together texts to make a kind of novelistic whole, and in this case is in the service of certain gender ideologies. Joseph Brodsky uses the word "contamination" for Rilke's conflation of Mary Magdalene with Mary the mother of Jesus, in "Pieta."[37] Mary Magdalene's name appears in the Christian Testament only in Luke 8:2, in all four crucifixion and empty tomb scenes, in resurrection vision narratives in Matthew and John, and in the list in the Markan Appendix of those who received resurrection appearances. However, she early acquired a biography when seven other pericopae which are *not* about her were combined with those that *do* mention her.

Her unsuccessful attempt to anoint Jesus in the tomb (in Mark, Luke, and the Gospel of Peter) was linked to three other anointing scenes. (1) Jesus' head is anointed by an unnamed woman in Mark 14:3–9 par Matt 26:6–13; this is a prophetic gesture, interpreted by Jesus as anticipating his burial. (2) John tells the story of a woman who anointed Jesus' feet with perfume (12:1–8), again a prophetic gesture interpreted as an anointing for burial. The anointing woman is named Mary, the sister of Lazarus and Martha of Bethany in John 11:1. (3) Most important is Luke's account of an unnamed "woman in the city, who was a sinner" who wets Jesus' feet with her tears, wipes them with her hair, kisses his feet and anoints them with ointment. She is forgiven by Jesus because (or with the result that) she had loved much (7:36–50). The commonly accepted scholarly hypothesis, accepted here, is that Mark is the earliest Gospel (ca. 65–70), used by Matthew and Luke in the composition of their Gospels in the 80s, along with Q (material these two have in common) and other material available only to each of them (M and L respectively). The Gospel of John is widely regarded as independent of the Synoptics, even if this view is not a consensus.[38] I have argued elsewhere[39] that the anointing stories are three versions of an ancient story, already depoliticized by Mark. Luke has radically rewritten Mark's account and turned the anointing prophet into a woman most readers have seen as a prostitute,[40] forgiven for her great love. Even though the Markan and Matthean

---

37. J. Brodsky, "A hidden duet: the intimate connection between the 'Magdalene' poems of Boris Pasternak and Marina Tsvetaeva," *TLS* August 27, 1999, 14.

38. See further, below, pp. 214, 225, 246–47.

39. See J. Schaberg, "Luke," *The Women's Bible Commentary* (ed. S. Ringe and C. Newsom; Philadelphia: Westminster/John Knox, 1992) 285–86.

40. I think it is Luke's intent that she be seen as such. T. Hornsby ("Why Is She Crying? A Feminist Interpretation of Luke 7:36–50," *Escaping Eden* (ed. H. C. Washington, S. L. Graham and P. Thimmes; New York: New York University Press, 1999) 91–103) quite rightly sees that a feminist interpretation of this passage can present the woman's renown, her lavish sensuality, her tears and her sin in a different light. My point here is that Luke's own design, and subsequent androcentric, misogynistic interpretation present her as a repenting whore, and that is how this passage has functioned in the Magdalene legends, as degrading. It is, of course, not how we have to keep reading it. Feminist scholarship both points out sexism and offers alternative readings. In Hornsby's reading, based on a positive evaluation of women's bodies, the woman is "someone who understands that physicality may be the ultimate display of love and that passion may be given as a gift to God" (92). My suggestion

versions carry the remark of Jesus that "wherever the good news is proclaimed in the whole world, what she [the prophet] has done will be told in remembrance of her," Luke's story — without the remark and without the prophetic dimension of anointing — overpowered the other two by means of its dangerous artistry and its ideology. The prophet is morphed into the whore. This moment of forgiveness for sexual sin all but obliterated the political anointing,[41] and later became the central moment of the Magdalene legends. Joined also to the Magdalene complex at times were the stories of (4) Mary of Bethany who sits at Jesus' feet while her sister Martha waits on him (Luke 10:38–42); (5) the woman taken in adultery (John 7:53–8:11); (6) the Samaritan woman (John 4:4–42), these latter two often mistaken for prostitutes; and (7) the anonymous bride of the wedding feast at Cana (John 2:1–11).

The logic of this conflation can be appreciated. It is still operating for many readers and viewers, and even for some scholars.[42] The most important motif that links the stories is, of course, that of anointing. Jesus, the Anointed One (*Christos*) is anointed (that is, literally made the Christ or Messiah, not just recognized as the Christ) only by a woman in the Christian Testament narratives. At least this is so in the Markan and Matthean accounts. In Luke the gesture is one of hospitality, gratitude, lavish sensuality, love. In fact, the anointing itself is not central in this version. Rather, there is a shift of focus: to the emotional extravagance of the woman's actions, to Jesus' prophetic awareness and acceptance of such a person, and to his forgiving her.

Apart from the anointing motif, the seven stories are linked in other ways. The name Simon appears in (1) and (3), and Bethany in (1) and (2). Sexual "sin" is a motif in (3) (5) and (6).[43] The motif of rebuke addressed to a woman, and her defense by Jesus appears in (1) (2) (3) (5) and (6). The motif of intimacy is found in (1) (2) (3) (4) (6)and (7); of a woman at Jesus' feet in (2) (3) (4). A woman's tears are mentioned in (3), perhaps presumed in (1) and (2), the prophetic anointing for burial; these function as a link with Mary Magdalene in the Synoptic accounts of her presence at the cross and tomb, where again one can presume tears were shed; Mary Magdalene weeps at the tomb of Jesus in John 20:11–15; and Mary of Bethany at Lazarus' tomb in 11:31–33. A woman's touch is mentioned in (3) where Simon muses that if Jesus were a prophet, "he would have known who and what kind of woman this is who is touching him — that she

is that the prostitute aspect of the Magdalene's legend needs rethinking and reincorporation in a feminist perspective: this attempt to degrade can be turned around into an opportunity for solidarity (see below, pp. 103–7, 113–14).

41. See the anointing of kings by prophets in 1 Sam 15:1; 16:13; 1 Kings 1:45; 19:15–16; 2 Kings 9:1–13, and the eschatological prediction in Dan 9:24.

42. See below, pp. 101–2.

43. The Samaritan woman's sexual past has been usually read as "sinful," and she is characterized by interpreters as "a five-time loser" or a "tramp," but see G. O'Day, "John," *Women's Bible Commentary*, 295–96 on this as a misreading.

is a sinner," and in John 20:17, where the risen Jesus says to Mary Magdalene, "Do not touch me (or: hold on to me)." A woman's love is praised in (3), and although love is not mentioned in the other texts, it may be the dominant feeling readers imagined to be that of these women characters, as of the Magdalene. The name Mary appears in (2 [John 11:1]) and (4).

A primary or initial reason for this conflation of texts may have been the desire to read or hear the Gospels with intelligence and imagination, and with sensitivity to echoes, to what appear to be allusions within the texts, and to harmonize. Silences in narratives are gaps in which the readers question, link texts, and create. The process of conflating and legend-making yields one actual anointing of Jesus: by Mary Magdalene, "the sinner," whose act is penitential and loving, not prophetic. The scholar, in contrast, may argue that historically speaking only one anointing occurred during the ministry of Jesus, a prophetic action by an unnamed woman. The tradition of this anointing then most likely proliferated into three versions, *none* of which concerned Mary Magdalene. Her connection with anointing, we must remind ourselves, is merely that according to Mark 14:1; Luke 24:1 she *intended* to anoint the corpse of Jesus, but found the tomb empty. Another reason the conflation of texts was and is so popular is that it responds to the desire to know about the life of Mary Magdalene. Conflation produced the beginnings of a biography of this woman who — like the unnamed woman prophet — was clearly more important to the story of Jesus than the Gospel writers explicitly indicated. Conflation shows us a narrative, dramatic necessity: the character who is so essential to the action and resolution at the end of the story as the basic witness to the crucifixion, burial, and empty tomb cannot — should not — come out of nowhere (as she does in Mark, Matthew, and John; and almost in Luke except for 8:1–3). These motives behind the conflation may be regarded as benign, even creative.

However, the fact that this biography gave the Magdalene a past of sexual "sin" that could be exploited and expanded is another matter. Even initially, there is much more to this process than confusion.[44] It was Luke, in my opinion, who downgraded the anointing woman in Mark 14 from prophet to "sinner," implying that her sin was sexual promiscuity, or prostitution. Luke 7, which may have some basis in a separate, independent story about another woman, has overpowered and overwritten the story in Mark 14 about the prophet. The prophetic anointing just before the arrest of Jesus is omitted only by Luke. Luke's juxtaposition of the story of the "sinner" with the first mention of Mary Magdalene in 8:2 suggests *her* denigration as well. It is strange that this is the only Synoptic mention of women followers placed during the ministry of Jesus, in Luke's "loosely written

---

44. Contrast the following with Haskins' analysis of the anointing stories (*Mary Magdalen*, 16–26). Haskins comments on Luke 7 that "the act of anointing opened the way to the confusion about the figures which were conflated to create the image of Mary Magdalen" (18).

and rambling sentence."[45] But I am not sure that this juxtaposition is internal commentary. Not sure, that is, that the slur on the Magdalene should be traced to Luke, that he is such a master of insidious subliminal messages.

There is one more important factor, besides the multiplicity of Marys and the split-off anointing scenes. That is the tradition, found in Luke 8:2 and Markan Appendix 16:9 that Mary Magdalene had been possessed by seven demons.[46] Luke says only that they had come out of her; the Markan Appendix that Jesus had cast them out. Here is the great imaginative opportunity: what kind of demons would a woman have? Sexual, of course. And seven, indicating intensity, totality, voracious lust. Her demon-possession is variously interpreted today as epilepsy or mental illness, an obsession or addiction, a not understood compulsion, a binding by the spirits of unfreedom, a sign of the lack of the Holy Spirit. Her exorcism, linked with her first encounter with Jesus, is thought to have set her free from what oppressed her, made her a new woman, made her holy and pure. Still the sexual dimension clings.[47] And the demonic is often associated in film and video with senseless sound, garbled or improper speech, a roaring that must be silenced.

Robert Price has argued, I think rightly, that the claim that Mary Magdalene had been demon-possessed may not be based on historical memory. It may be, rather, a trace of early polemics against what was regarded as her heresy, and hence her authority. "[I]t is hard to see how being tagged with the reputation of sevenfold demon-possession would not seriously undermine one's credibility as an apostle"[48] — even if it is only what she was healed from, what she used to be. Ruth Padel notes that in early Greek thought, because a female body has more openings than a male's, the female was considered to be more permeable, and so women more susceptible to the entrance of spirits.[49] Even if this conceptuality may be "nowhere explicitly present in early Christianity...nonetheless, the continued emphasis in other texts on the sexual purity or impurity of women prophets may carry this conceptuality subliminally."[50] In a kind of lesbian rape fantasy, Athanasius describes the Arian movement as the daughter of the devil, identifying "Woman Heresy" with the serpent who "forces her way back into the church's paradise." He introduces "the penetrable harlot Eve" as the archetype

45. J. Meier, *A Marginal Jew: Rethinking the Historical Jesus* (New York: Doubleday, 1994) 2.657.

46. B. Chilton, *Rabbi Jesus: An Intimate Biography* (New York: Doubleday, 2000) 145: "The enumeration of her demons suggests that Jesus exorcised her repeatedly."

47. N. Mailer (*The Gospel according to the Son* [New York: Random House, 1997] 180–81) identifies Mary Magdalene with the woman caught in adultery, and has Jesus cast out her seven powers and demons (the powers are Darkness, Desire, Ignorance, Love of Death, Whole Domain, Excess of Wisdom and Wisdom of Wrath; cf. the powers in the *Gospel of Mary*, below, p. 169).

48. R. Price, "Mary Magdalene, Gnostic Apostle?" *Grail* 6 (1990) 73–74. See below, pp. 199, 232.

49. R. Padel, "Woman: Model for Possession by Greek Daemons," *Images of Women in Antiquity* (ed. A. Cameron and A. Kuhut; Detroit: Wayne State University Press, 1983) 3–19. In the early third century, Tertullian characterized woman as "the devil's gateway" (cf. Sir 26:10–12).

50. K. King, "Prophetic Power and Women's Authority: the Case of the Gospel of Mary (Magdalene)," *Women Preachers and Prophets*, 30.

of the deceived fool and counterpart to the "impenetrable virgin Mary."[51] Medieval society made the connection between women's preaching and demonic possession.[52]

So did the Hebrew Bible and the Christian Testament. The pattern is a common one: the powerful woman disempowered, remembered as a whore or whorish. It operates in the memory of Elijah's opponent Jezebel (1 Kings 18, 19, 21; 2 Kings 9) with her painted eyes and adorned head (2 Kings 9:30), of the Samaritan woman and her multiple relationships (John 4), and of the prophet of Thyatira, "that woman Jezebel, who calls herself a prophet... [and] refuses to repent of her fornication" (Rev 2:20–23). Even when the harlot is heroine, as is the case in three Hebrew Bible stories studied and in the legends of the Magdalene, the social status of the harlot is always "that of an outcast, though not an outlaw, a tolerated, but dishonored member of society."[53] Haskins draws out the parallels between Mary Magdalene and Moses' sister Miriam (Numbers 12), both demoted from prominence to repentance.[54] Religious apostasy is represented by imagining Jerusalem, Samaria, Israel as whore or adulteress — uncontrolled, obscene.[55] As Phyllis Bird points out, the metaphorical use of the root *znh* in Hosea, envoking the image of the common prostitute and the promiscuous daughter or wife, is a rhetorical device to expose men's sin: "It is easy for patriarchal society to see the guilt of a 'fallen woman': Hosea says, 'You [male Israel] are that woman!'"[56] The Hebrew word *min* (heretic, sectarian) also means kind, species (Gen 1:11–12, 24–25 and elsewhere). Alan Segal argues it also means sex/gender, and associates it with the Hebrew *nh,* to commit adultery; heresy and sexual unfaithfulness/idolatry are thus linked and gendered in the traditions inherited by the rabbis and the "fathers."[57]

---

51. Athanasius, First Discourse Against the Arians 1.1; see V. Burrus, "Word and Flesh: The Bodies and Sexuality of Ascetic Women in Christian Antiquity," *JFSR* 10 (1994) 37.

52. K. King, "Preface: Authority and Definition," *Women Preachers and Prophets,* xv on Sigewize, a woman inspired by Hildegard of Bingen. Sigewize was considered possessed because of her desire to preach publicly. Tertullian condemns the prophet Philumene as "an enormous prostitute," associating her "erroneous" teachings with penetration by evil spirits and hence sexual pollution (*De Praescriptione hereticorum* 6 and 30). On the belief that false prophets were inspired by the devil and his demons, see Tertullian, *De Anima* 11 (King, "Prophetic Power," 28–29). Possession by having sex with the devil and heresy are part of the profile of the witch (see A. L. Barstow, *Witchcraze* (San Francisco: HarperCollins, 1995).

53. P. A. Bird, "The Harlot as Heroine," *Semeia* 46 (1989) 119–39.

54. Haskins, *Mary Magdalen,* 47. Miriam is not said to repent, but she is punished.

55. On the post-exilic creation of a new dimension to the harlot, now not just impure in her lewdness but a creature of malevolent power and danger to men, see L. J. Archer, "The Virgin and the Harlot in the Writings of Formative Judaism," *History Workshop Journal* 24 (1987) 1–16.

56. P. Bird, "'To Play the Harlot': An Inquiry into an Old Testament Metaphor," *Missing Persons and Mistaken Identities* (Minneapolis: Fortress, 1997) 236. See R. Weems, *Battered Love* (Minneapolis: Fortress, 1995).

57. A. Segal, *Two Powers in Heaven: Early Rabbinic Reports about Christianity and Gnosticism* (Leiden: Brill, 1977) n. 3, p. 5; cited by E. Schüssler Fiorenza, "Transgressing Canonical Boundaries," *Searching the Scriptures,* 2.13, n. 14. Ambrose and Jerome link harlotry and heresy in several works (Burrus, "Word and Flesh," 43).

And so too did Luke make this connection between female prophecy and possession (though not heresy), in Acts. Almost all scholars hold that the same person wrote Luke and Acts, and they should be read together. Acts 16:16–19 is the curious story of the slave girl, said not to be a prophet but to be "possessed with a spirit of divination" (*pneuma puthona*). She had brought her masters much profit by "fortune-telling" (*manteuomenē*). In Philippi she followed Paul and Silas, crying out "'These men are the servants of the Most High God, who proclaim to you[58] the way of salvation.' But Paul, greatly annoyed (*diaponētheis*[59]), turned and said to the spirit, 'I command you in the name of Jesus Christ to come out of her.' And it came out that very hour." Her masters were distressed at having lost their hope of profit, and brought Paul and Silas before the authorities. Luke passes on without comment on the girl's message or Paul's annoyance. Indeed, his own editorial techniques in his Gospel have a similar effect, of silencing women in the traditions he inherited.[60] At least the women whom Ezekiel "exorcised" in 13:17–23 were said to be prophesying even if "out of their own imagination" (v. 17, cf. 13:2). At least their "divination" had to do with a message different from his own.[61] What a woman *thinks* and what she has to *say* can be every bit as alarming as her genital sexuality.[62] The heightening of and focus on her sexuality may be a way of decapitating her, removing her mind, identity, voice.[63]

Whether Luke created her seven demons, or they were traditional, Mary Magdalene is the madwoman in Christianity's attic. Her madness — historical or not — is open to feminist analysis. It could stand for resistance and subversion, for rage and brave protest against patriarchy, that is, for a kind of sanity. In this sense, her madness would be a preferable alternative to healing, unless with the healing came further power and speech, not taming and submission. Unless the protest of her madness was successful, and the former madwoman spoke and was heard, creating possibilities for the transformation of the social order.[64] As it stands, however, in Luke 8:1–3, Mary Magdalene's demon-possession is in the past. She appears with "certain women who had been healed of evil spirits and infirmities (*tetherapeumenai apo pneumatōn povñrōn kai astheneiōn*)." The implica-

---

58. Other ancient authorities read "to us."

59. The same verb is used in 4:2 of "the people, the priests, the captain of the temple, and the Sadducees," vexed because Peter and John were "teaching the people and proclaiming that in Jesus there is resurrection of the dead."

60. See Schaberg, "Luke."

61. See N. R. Bowen, "The Daughters of Your People: Female Prophets in Ezekiel 13: 17–23," *JBL* 118 (1999) 417–33.

62. See R. S. Kraemer, *Her Share of the Blessings* (New York: Oxford, 1995) chapter 11: "Heresy as Women's Religion: Women's Religion as Heresy."

63. H. Eilberg-Schwartz, "Introduction: The Spectacle of the Female Head," *Off with Her Head! The Deial of Women's Identity in Myth, Religion, and Culture* (ed. H. Eilberg-Schwartz and W. Doniger; Berkeley: University of California, 1995) 1–13.

64. See M. Carminero-Santangelo, *The Madwoman Can't Speak: Or Why Insanity Is Not Subversive* (Ithaca: Cornell University Press, 1998).

tion is clear that she and they follow Jesus out of gratitude (no such motivation is suggested for male disciples). The women are silent, serving Jesus and the Twelve (contrast Mark 15:41 where the Galilean women are said to have followed and served *him* in Galilee). They will be accused later of speaking nonsense (*leros*, 24:11) about an empty tomb, but the reader knows better.[65]

Warner considers the Magdalene of legend as "brought into existence by the powerful undertow of misogyny in Christianity, which associates women with the dangers and degradation of the flesh. *For this reason* [emphasis mine] she became a prominent and beloved saint." Her prominence, Warner insists, was "assisted but not caused by" the frequency and significance of her appearances in the Gospels. Rather, the need for a penitent whore-heroine in Christian mythology shaped the understanding of passages that did and (in Christian imagination) might concern her. This need is not to be reduced to the human appetite for "romance" or drama; it contains "Christianity's fear of women, its identification of physical beauty with temptation, and its practice of bodily mortification."[66] However, only if we see the story of the "sinner" as almost obliterating the story of the woman prophet, and then added to the story of Mary Magdalene, do we realize, as Warner and Haskins do not or do not emphasize, that the process was reaction against the female power and authority of a major witness.

Inclusion of the element of prostitution in the later Magdalene legends responds to the desire to downgrade her and deny her authority, as well as the desire to attach to female sexuality the notions of evil, repentance, and male mercy. It also serves to divide and conquer women, alienating those who are prostitutes from those who are not or say they are not. (I am a whore / I am not a whore. And so what if I am? What is a whore anyway? "We are neither of us chaste."[67]) "The division of women into the honorable and the dishonorable is perhaps the most insidious political function of the stigma 'whore.' "[68] The issue of "real loyalties" is raised. Unless one would hold that the anointing prophet historically *was* Mary Magdalene — and I do not see how that possibility can be supported — it appears that the Magdalene inherited the slur Luke directed against the unnamed prophet. Backlash against the Magdalene builds on backlash against the woman prophet.

In this analysis of Magdalene traditions from the first century onward, what we are looking at and for is not "conspiracy"[69] but neither is it a series of inno-

---

65. On possible links between gnostic/apocryphal traditions of Mary as the companion of Jesus and the development of the legend of her as whore, see below, p. 155.

66. Warner, *Alone*, 225–26, 232.

67. Woolf, "A Society," 23.

68. G. Pheterson, *The Prostitution Prism* (Amsterdam: Amsterdam University Press, 1996) 11.

69. See R. R. Ruether, "No church conspiracy against Mary Magdalene," *National Catholic Reporter* (February 9, 2001) 17; in reaction to such articles as Heidi Schlumpf, "Who Framed Mary Magdalene?" *US Catholic* (April 2000) 12–17. For another view of this issue, see a 1998 article from the ultra-conservative Catholic newspaper *The Wanderer*, in which it is argued that the new scholar-

cent mistakes and confusions. Analysis of gender constructions is not primarily concerned with the intent of writers or painters or filmmakers, nor even with the effect of their works on historical or modern audiences. It calls rather for a disobedient reading or viewing which looks for "the ways in which gender constructions are embedded in communications so naturalistically that the author [or artist] can count on them to move an argument, to persuade, or to seduce."[70] The traditions are extremely complex and varied, with positive and negative dimensions. It is important to note the many transformations of her image, and the variety of their political/social/ecclesiastical contexts. Conflation is "exegetically untenable," as Peter Ketter puts it, and the whole process may be in its beginnings one of "wilful misinterpretation, to suit the purposes of an ascetic Church," creating from the Gospel woman "a manageable, controllable figure, and effective weapon and instrument of propaganda against her own sex." Her sin, fornication, bodies forth the feared and abhorred female sexuality,[71] and she stands also for intelligence and authority. She must be creatively honored and punished.

She became a whore for many reasons: sexism, never simple, and misogyny; the struggle to create and maintain a male hierarchy with its male models and precedents; unconscious or semi-conscious androcentrism; asceticism and the increasingly high value put on celibacy; intolerance of difference; the genuine fear of one's opponents within and without; political and social and cultural pressures; the liking for a good story; anger.

"There was always an element of heat. This heat took many forms; it showed itself in satire, in sentiment, in curiosity, in reprobation. But there was another element which was often present and could not immediately be identified. Anger, I called it. But it was anger that had gone underground and mixed itself with all kinds of other emotions To judge from its odd effects, it was anger disguised and complex, not anger simple and open."[72]

What role women had in the creation of the legends, and how they heard them, may be unknowable. The sanctity of a (former) whore and the apostleship of a woman may say some positive things about female sexuality and leadership ability, and may have supported women's self-determination. But one fact remains as a substratum of the legends and the purposes they served: that "every prominent stream of theology and practice within early [and later] Christianity that supported women's leadership was sharply opposed, even described as heretical."[73]

---

ship about "the historical Magdalene" is a distorted "crusade for a laywoman-run church" (quoted by Schlumpf, 16).

70. M. R. Miles, *Carnal Knowing: Female Nakedness and Religious Meaning in the Christian West*, (Boston: Beacon, 1989) xiv.

71. P. Ketter, *The Magdalene Question* (Milwaukee: Bruce, 1935) 36; this pamphlet is still worth reading.

72. Woolf, *Room*, 32.

73. K. King, "Prophetic Power and Women's Authority," 29.

How early conflation produced the legend of Mary Magdalene the repentant whore, we do not know. R. M. Grant thought that already by the end of the second century Mary Magdalene was being identified with the sister of Lazarus (John 11:3) and the woman in Luke 7:36–50 "who expressed her love for Jesus"; he cites Clement, *Excerpta* 50, 1 and Origen, *Joh. comm.*, fr.78, pp. 544–45 (Preuschen) in support of this dating.[74] Mary Rose D'Angelo writes that "This image appears to have arisen in the sixth century, when the example of penitent whores became fashionable in the West, producing legendary lives of Pelagia, Thais and Mary of Egypt."[75] Haskins also regards Mary Magdalene the repentant whore as a late sixth-century creation, serving the purposes of ecclesiastical hierarchy.[76] In that century Pope Gregory the Great (ca. 540–604) gave prestige, authoritative sanction and wide promulgation to the conflation of texts about Mary Magdalene, the "sinner" of Luke 7, and Mary of Bethany who anointed Jesus before his arrest in John 12 (cf. Mark 14): the Pope declared that these three were one person:

> She whom Luke calls the sinful woman, whom John calls Mary, we believe to be the Mary from whom seven devils were ejected according to Mark. And what did these seven devils signify, if not all the vices.... It is clear, brothers, that the woman previously used the unguent to perfume her flesh in forbidden acts. What she therefore displayed more scandalously, she was now offering to God in a more praiseworthy manner. She had coveted with earthly eyes, but now through penitence these are consumed with tears. She displayed her hair to set off her face, but now her hair dries her tears. She had spoken proud things with her mouth, but in kissing the Lord's feet, she now planted her mouth on the Redeemer's feet. For every delight, therefore, she had had in herself, she now immolated herself. She turned the mass of her crimes to virtues, in order to serve God entirely in penance, for as much as she had wrongly held God in contempt.[77]

Note that the demonic and the erotic are the elements emphasized; the demonic and erotic are perhaps even identified. Haskins comments that Gregory was offering her "as an example of conversion to the people of Rome, beset by famine, plague and war, for each individual to reflect on his own sins and seek his salvation."[78] Her locution is important here: "his" sins, "his" salvation, as is Gregory's choice of a female saint rather than a male — say, Peter — to serve as an example for males. This is the Magdalene who came to the tomb at Easter

---

74. R. M. Grant, "The Mystery of Marriage in the Gospel of Philip," *VC* 15 (1961) 138. H Lesetre ("Marie-Madeleine," *Dictionnaire de la Bible* 4 [1908] c.809–18) says the tradition of identifying the three Marys also goes back to Clement of Alexandria (ca. 150–215), *Paidagogos* 2.8.

75. M. R. D'Angelo, "Reconstructing 'real' women from the gospels: the case of Mary Magdalene," *Women and Christian Origins*, 105.

76. Haskins, *Mary Magdalen*, 11, 26.

77. *Homily XXXIII* (PL 76:1239–40) on Luke 7, quoted by Haskins, p. 96; see also Homilies XXV (PL 76: 1180); II.25 (PL 76:1188–96). See V. Saxer, "Les Origines du Culte de Marie-Madeleine en Occident," *Marie Madeleine dans la mystique, les arts et les lettres* (ed. E. Duperray; Paris: Beauchesne, 1989) 33–47.

78. Haskins, *Mary Magdalen*, 96.

in the liturgies of Holy Week and was popular in homilies during the following centuries.

What Haskins and others call "confusion" about the identity of the figures is earlier than conflation, documented, she says, from at least the third century in the West in the writings of Ambrose (ca. 339–97), Jerome (ca. 342–420) and Origen (ca. 185–ca. 254). The fact that the Magdalene was not depicted as a whore in gnostic traditions of the late first to fourth centuries suggests to her that the conflation is later. She attributes the few references to Mary Magdalene by so-called "orthodox" writers in the second and third centuries to reticence in the face of her prominence in gnostic writings, which will be examined in the next chapter.

But much more than confusion and reticence preceded official conflation, and this much more is important to probe. Gregory the Great's Magdalene is not a "new" Magdalene.[79] First of all, we should not imagine "a state of equality" between men and women lasting a few generations after Jesus' death,[80] nor even existing in the movement during his career.[81] The earliest traditions indicate gender conflict and struggle, and the Jesus of the Gospel tradition and probably the historical Jesus did not explicitly champion what we call women's rights.[82] Rooted in questions of authority, asceticism, and reputation, this conflict took different forms, one of which was labelling the women in the movement. Already in Matt 21:31–32 there is a saying attributed to Jesus about whores: "Truly I tell you, the tax-collectors and the prostitutes are going into the Kingdom of God ahead of you. For John came to you in the way of righteousness and you did not believe him; but the tax collectors and the prostitutes believed him; and even after you saw it, you did not change your minds and believe him." Although the saying is not in Luke, it has been argued that some form of this saying may have occurred in Q, the hypothetical document reconstructed from agreements between Matthew and Luke, and dating perhaps to the 40s. If Luke found the saying in Q, he has reworked part of it in 7:29–30 (a contrast between tax collectors baptized by John and Jewish leaders), and then a few verses later illustrated the part about prostitutes in the story of the "sinner" who weeps at Jesus' feet (7:36–50).[83] The saying about prostitutes may represent the memory of actual women in this kind of work among the followers of John and Jesus, and/or the memory of women among them who were slaves, freedwomen or legal

---

79. Against Jansen, "Maria Magdalena," 60.

80. Contrast Haskins, *Mary Magdalen*, 53.

81. Contrast Haskins, *Mary Magdalen*, 16, 38, 90. She hopes that Mary Madalene will be recognized as "a full member of the revolutionary community created by the one who considered men and women equal" (399), the chief female disciple, apostle to the apostles, first witness to the resurrection.

82. J. Plaskow, "Anti-Judaism in Feminist Christian Interpretation," *Searching the Scriptures* (ed. E. Schüssler Fiorenza; New York: Crossroad, 1993) 1.119.

83. Meier, *A Marginal Jew*, 2.169 thinks we are not dealing with Q; but he does not discuss the story of the "sinner" in this regard.

concubines, and/or reflect how all women among them were slandered (cf. Mark 2:15–17 pars). Kathleen Corley has suggested that in this saying Jesus used the insult probably in jest, to deflect the criticism.[84] However, an insult has to be reused by the insulted themselves in order for it to be truly drained of power.

Against Celsus was written by Origen around 248, making use of Celsus' *True Doctrine*, written around 178 and probably making use of older Jewish sources. Here Origen documents the accusation of the pagan Celsus (put in the mouth of a Jew) that "Jesus went about with his disciples collecting their livelihood in a shameful and importunate way." Origen counters the accusation of "beggary" by alluding to Luke 8:1–3: "For in the gospels certain women who had been healed from their ailments, among whom was Suzanna, provided the disciples with meals out of their own substance. But what philosopher who was devoted to the benefit of his pupils did not receive from them money for his needs? Or was it proper and right for them to do this, whereas when Jesus' disciples do it, they are accused by Celsus of collecting their means of livelihood in a disgraceful and importunate way?"[85]

From Origen's reply, we can gather Celsus' original critique probably mentioned women, and insinuated that Jesus took more than money from them: "it is possible that allegations of living off prostitutes were involved."[86] Of the three women mentioned in Luke 8:1–3 — Mary Magdalene, Joanna the wife of Herod's steward Chuza, and Suzanna — Origen mentions only Suzanna, who has the same name as the pure, maligned woman of Daniel 13 LXX Old Greek version and Theodotion, the chaste wife falsely accused.[87] We can only wonder if there is a studious avoidance here of the other names, perhaps especially one. Celsus, and/or Celsus' Jew does not call Mary Magdalene a whore, but he does — without naming her — refer to her as hysterical, and give a raft of unwholesome reasons for her claim that Jesus was raised:

> But we must examine this question whether anyone who really died ever rose again with the same body. Or do you think that . . . the ending of your tragedy is to be regarded as noble and convincing — his cry from the cross when he expired, and the earthquake and the darkness? While he was alive he did not help himself, but after death he rose again and showed the marks of his punishment and how his hands had been pierced. But who saw this? A hysterical female (*gynē paroistros*), as you say, and perhaps some other one of those who were deluded by the same sorcery, who either dreamt in a certain state of mind and through wishful thinking had a hallucination

84. K. Corley, *Private Women, Public Meals* (Peabody, Mass.: Hendrickson, 199) 154–58. "Luke has a tendency to cast the women around Jesus as respectable" (156), so he might have omitted it. See also K. Corley, "Were the Women around Jesus Really Prostitutes? Women in the Context of Greco-Roman Meals," *SBL Seminar Papers* (Atlanta: Scholars Press, 1989) 487–521.
85. *C. Cels.* I.65.
86. MacDonald, *Early Christian Women and Pagan Opinion*, 103.
87. See B. Halpern-Amaru, "The Journey of Susanna Among the Church Fathers," *The Judgment of Susanna* (ed. E. Spolsky; Atlanta: Scholars Press, 1996) 21–34; 26–27 on Origen.

due to some mistaken notion (an experience which has happened to thousands), or, which is more likely, wanted to impress others by telling this fantastic tale, and so by this cock-and-bull story to provide a chance for other beggars (*aguptais*).[88]

The reference to "other beggars" (like her) links the hysterical woman with the disreputable lifestyle of this movement described in I.65. Celsus makes one other comment about this woman in 2.70: Jesus "appeared secretly to just one woman and to those of his own confraternity." In his response, Origen refers to Matt 28:1, naming Mary Magdalene and the other Mary — not one but two. All this suggests that in the second century the Magdalene may have been tarred with the accusation of disreputability directed against all of Jesus' women associates.

In addition, women involved in early Christianity as in other eastern cults, were open to the accusation of whore — whether married or unmarried, unconventional or conventional.[89] The rabbinic traditions about R. Eliezer (fl. 70–100), assenting to some heretical teaching "in the name of Jesus the son of Panteri" about what to do with the wages of prostitutes, are tantalizing in this regard. The original form of the saying may have been "from filth they came, and to filth they shall return," possibly with a reference to Micah 1:7 ("All [Samaria's] images shall be beaten to pieces, all her wages shall be burned with fire, and all her idols I will lay waste; for as the wages of a prostitute she gathered them, and as the wages of a prostitute they shall again be used").[90]

In an unpublished paper, Kathleen Corley has collected references to Mary Magdalene in patristic literature.[91] There are some indications that the conflation of the figures of the Magdalene and the "sinful" woman of Luke 7 is early. Most interesting is the reference of Tertullian (ca. 160–225) to the touch of "the woman which was a sinner" to prove that Jesus was "not an empty phantom but a really solid body."[92] (Cf. the use of John 20:17 by Irenaeus [ca. 130–200] to show that Jesus' risen body had substance.[93]) Elsewhere, referring to the scene in which the Magdalene sees the risen Jesus in the garden (John 20:11–18), Tertullian speaks of the faithful woman who approached Jesus to touch him "out of love" (*ex dilectione*), not out of curiosity nor out of the incredulity of Thomas.[94] There is no mention of love in John 20, but love is the trademark of the "sinner" in Luke 7.[95] A sermon once attributed to Hippolytus (ca. 170–235) depicts Martha and Mary

---

88. *C. Cels.* 2.55; cf. 2.59. For MacDonald's translation of *paroistros* as "hysterical," see *Early Christian Women*, 168.

89. See MacDonald, *Early Christian Women*, 68–69, 250.

90. *T. Hullin* II.24; *b. Zarah* 16b–17a; *Midrash Qohelet Rabba'* I.8.3. See M. Smith, *Jesus the Magician* (New York: Harper & Row, 1978) 46, 178.

91. K. Corley, "'Noli Me Tangere': Mary Magdalene in the Patristic Literature" unpublished paper 1984, Claremont Graduate School.

92. *Against Marcion* 4.18.9:16–17.

93. *Against Heresies* 5.7.1; 5.31.1.

94. *Against Praxeas* 25.2.19–21

95. Origen also comments on John 20:17 in regard to the status of Jesus after the resurrection. *Commentary on John* 6.37; 10.21.

(the sisters from Luke 10 and John 11) seeking Christ in the garden (as Mary Magdalene does in John 20). The conflated women represent the Synagogue and the woman the Canticle of Canticles who searches for her lover and finds him. In them, the sin of the first Eve has been compensated for by their obedience, and "Eve has become apostle." They are "apostles to the apostles" sent not only by angels but by Christ himself, who then appears to the males to confirm the women's message.[96]

Tertullian, Irenaeus, Hippolytus, and Origen are the only major "fathers" of the second and third centuries to deal with Mary Magdalene. Origen's remarks seem to be responses to questions about secrecy, to the perception by pagans, familiar with the role that women play in the resurrection stories,[97] that the initiative of women — and Mary Magdalene in particular — was central to the development of Christianity, and to questions about the morality of these women. Tertullian and Hippolytus inject an erotic element into John 20, and with Hippolytus the link is made with Eve and her sin (not, however, via the "sinner" of Luke 7). Only Irenaeus calls Mary Magdalene the first to see and worship the risen Jesus; and he is silent about the implications of this.

In the fourth century, there is more discussion of Mary Magdalene, with over thirty references to her by Ambrose, Jerome, the Cappadocians, Chrysostom, Augustine, and others, almost all direct references to John 20:17.[98] Obsession — then and earlier — with her attempt to touch or hold Jesus in John 20:17 may be a part of discussions of the nature of the body of Jesus (was he truly a man? did he rise physically from the dead?), but the context or subcontext is also the body of the Magdalene. In the fourth-century texts we begin to see two developments that will be important for the full-blown legends: (1) criticism of the Magdalene's faith and intelligence (e.g., Jerome's statement that since she did not believe Jesus had risen and thought him to be still in the tomb, she was not worthy to touch him[99]) and emphasis on the distance between him and her;[100] and (2) the further merging of her image and role with that of Eve. The second is a way of accepting her status as messenger from the risen Jesus: to consider it an appropriate redemption of the offense of woman in general, as it was a woman who first brought the message of sin (Ambrose[101]). In a saying of Gregory of Nyssa (ca. 330–395), the Magdalene *is* Eve, not her antithesis: "[S]he is the first witness of the resurrection, that she

---

96. Hippolytus, *Commentary on the Canticle of Canticles* 8.2; 24.60. See Jansen, "Maria Magdalena," 58.

97. MacDonald, *Early Christian Women*, 106.

98. Corley, "'Noli'" 8.

99. Jerome, *To Pammachius against John of Jerusalem*, 35; cf. *To Marcella* (letter 59); Ambrose, *Of the Christian Faith* 4.2.25. In *Ep.* 127, 5, however, Jerome considers her "first worthy to see Christ rising, even before the apostles. For we judge moral excellences not by people's sex, but by their quality of spirit." Ephraem Syrus (ca. 306–73) makes Mary the Mother of Jesus the woman in the garden in John 20:17: she is the resurrection witness and the one who is prohibited from touching Jesus.

100. See E. de Boer, *Mary Magdalene*, 64.

101. Ambrose, *Of the Holy Spirit* 3.11.74; cf. similar sayings of Augustine and Chrysostom.

might set straight again by her faith in the resurrection, what was turned over by her transgression."[102] Corley comments, "Gregory pictures Mary Magdalene as a fallen woman, who is instrumental in the redemption of the rest of her fallen sex."[103] While in the tradition Eve was not considered a whore, and her sin and Adam's not considered by most to be the sexual act, still she was the tempted temptress, and the fall was imagined to take sexual form. Her submission was the appropriate punishment.[104]

With the gnostic documents, to which we will turn in the next chapter, we can begin to hear conversations full of static, long silences, and broken connections. Even in the near-silences of the second and third centuries concerning her, there are whispers about the Magdalene and her body, her authority, her mind, her spirit (are they cancelled by her body?) and about Jesus' body, his authority (but on a different wavelength, with different things at stake). When the relevant patristic literature is set beside the gnostic materials discovered in the past century, there is an initial puzzlement. The "fathers" apparently did not directly and explicitly attack or respond to contemporary gnostic views of the Magdalene as a leader of primary importance and insight. Celsus mentions those "who follow Mariamme" as well as other leaders, but Origen dismisses this with a wave of his hand — "he pours on us a heap of names."[105] Perhaps these are most effective indirect methods of response: silence, focus on other issues and other personalities, ignoring of certain texts, highlighting and counterinterpreting others, and the early conflations. Crumbs of acknowledgement; criticism of her intelligence, of the female intelligence in general; provocation of unreal class loyalties; assertions about the place and fate of women. Without these preparations, Gregory's homily and the fullblown legends of the redeemed whore hardly seem possible. With these preparations, Mary Magdalene is already nicely reduced and demeaned.

The full-blown legends are powerful, entertaining stories. The earliest extant text that assembles the harmonizing into a single, concise, coherent narrative appears to be a tenth- or eleventh-century sermon once attributed to Odo of Cluny.[106] Between 875 and 900, legendary materials circulating in Europe about Mary Magdalene took two main forms: the *vita eremitica* (conflating her with the desert hermit Mary of Egypt) and the *vita apostolica* (concerning the evangelization of Gaul). Eventually these were blended into the *vita apostolico-eremitica*

---

102. Gregory of Nyssa, *Against Eunomius* 3.10.16; cf. Tertullian, *De Cultu Feminarum* I, 12: "Do you not know that every one of you is an Eve? The sentence of God on your sex lives on in this age; the guilt, of necessity, lives on too."

103. Corley, " 'Noli," 11.

104. See E. Pagels, *Adam, Eve and the Serpent* (New York: Random House, 1988) 27–28, 68.

105. C. Cels. V.62. H. Chadwick comments (*Origen: Contra Celsum* [Cambridge: Cambridge University Press, 1953] 312): The Ophites held that their doctrines were taught to Mariamme by James the Lord's brother (Hippolytus, *Ref.* V.7.1; X.9.3). Her connection with them appears in the Acts of Philip (M. R. James, *Apocryphal New Testament*, 446) where Philip and Mariamme go to the land of the Ophites. See below.

106. BHL 5439; printed in *Acta Sanctorum*, July V: 218–21; also in PL 133:713–21.

(eleventh century), forming the "crazy quilt of a vita" included in the Legenda aurea, the Golden Legend, and lively material for sermons in the later Middle Ages.[107]

David Mycoff, building on the work of Victor Saxer, has classified popular Magdalene legends from the first through the seventeenth century.[108] Different writers created different emphases within the same basic story, depending on whether their interest was in the roles of women, disputes over ecclesiastical privilege and material assets, the mystery of grace and the nature of the contemplative or active vocations, the individual layperson's spiritual aspirations, or conflict between conservatives and reformers. From the tenth century through the Reformation, the Magdalene literature burgeoned. In addition to her role as penitent and as "apostle to the apostles" (based on her role in the Gospel narratives, especially John 20), she was said to have had a post-Ascension career as evangelist of Gaul, preaching and converting pagans. The stress on her as preacher can be traced to Rabanus Maurus (ca. 844),[109] who said that by her preaching (*praedicando*) she had filled the universe with the scent of the news of Christ; he is nicely conflating her with Mary of Bethany who anointed Jesus in John 12 ("The house was filled with the fragrance of the perfume" v. 3). In the twelfth century Abbot Hugh of Semur (d. 1109), Peter Abelard (d. 1142), Geoffrey of Vendome (d. 1132) and others referred to Mary Magdalene as the sinner who merited the title *apostolorum apostola*.[110] The title became a commonplace in twelfth- and thirteenth-century hagiography, exegesis, hymnody and art. Jansen suggests that veneration of the Magdalene as an apostle emerged in the twelfth century for two reasons. (1) Luke's "sinner" had been successfully conflated with her. She became "the paradigmatic sinner, whose personal history of sin allied her with her sinful sister Eve. Divine symmetry demanded that a female penitent rectify the sin of her sinful predecessor." (2) The twelfth-century "rediscovery of the individual" led to emphasis on history and biography, and on historical rather than figurative analysis. Gregory the Great's composite figure and legendary sources dating back at least to the eighth century were drawn on. "Peter of Celle could say that the Lord had made a saint from a sinner and an *apostola* from a whore, and no one

---

107. See Jansen, "Maria Magdalena," 65–67.

108. D. Mycoff, *The Life of Saint Mary Magdalene and of Her Sister Saint Martha* (Kalamazoo, Mich.: Cistercian Publications, 1989); *A Critical Edition of the Legend of Mary Magdalene from Caxton's Golden Legend of 1483* (Salzburg: Universität Salzburg, Institut für Anglistik und Amerikanistik, 1985); Victor Saxer, *Le culte de Marie Madeleine en Occident des origines à la fin du moyen age* (2 vols.; Auxerre/Paris: Clavreuil, 1959); *Le dossier Vézélien de Marie Madeleine* (Brussels: Soc. de Boll., 1975); and numerous articles by Saxer mainly in *Recherches de Science Religieuse*. See also H. Garth, *Saint Mary Magdalene in Medieval Literature* (Baltimore: Johns Hopkins, 1950).

109. PL 111, col. 84; Jansen, "Maria Magdalena," n. 19, p. 82.

110. See Jansen, "Maria Magdalena," 61, 83. Bernard of Clairvaux (d. 1153) used the title *apostolae apostologum* for the three Marys (Sermo 75, PL 183, col. 1148).

batted an eye."[111] The counterweight of her sinfulness had made it safe to speak of her power and authority.

Mycoff classifies the patristic and medieval legends of Mary Magdalene in three ways. (1) Heretical and orthodox early materials. His definition of these two categories is particularly interesting. "What defines the orthodox as a group is their belief that Mary Magdalene is a mortal creature who only witnesses or perhaps plays a minor role in the salvation of mankind [sic]. What unites the various gnostic traditions is their higher estimate of Mary's significance." In an attempt to pinpoint the heresy, he says they base "her status on a special and unique knowledge she possesses rather than on some gracious gesture Christ makes to her."[112] Within the orthodox range, he identifies one extreme represented by Christianus Druthmarus (who attributes to her the status of evangelist and apostle, by dint of her being the first human being to whom the risen Christ appeared), and the other extreme represented by John Chrysostom (who emphasizes Mary's obtuseness: due to lack of faith and feminine frailty, she did not recognize the risen Lord at first glance).[113]

(2) Theories of unity and theories of multiplicity. By and large, the Western church held that the women in all or most of the Christian Testament stories listed above are one woman, Mary Magdalene. But the Eastern church held that Mary Magdalene, Mary of Bethany, and the "sinner" are different women. All the Magdalene legends involved in the transmission of the story to the English vernacular are based on the unity theory.

(3) Versions of the Magdalene's post-Ascension career. Legends differ according to whether they locate the site of her last days in Palestine, Ephesus, Les Saintes-Maries-de-la-Mer in the Camargue in southeastern France, or Aix or Marseilles in Provence. The most widely accepted in the East was the Ephesian legend, which plays on the tradition that Mary Magdalene was engaged to John the Evangelist, who abandoned her when he was called away from their wedding at Cana — as she was not — to be a disciple of Christ.[114] Honorius of Autun (early twelfth century) summarizes: "She fled to Jerusalem, where, unmindful of her birth, forgetful of the law of God, she became a common prostitute and of her own free will set up a brothel of sin and made it in truth a temple of demons, for seven devils entered into her and plagued her continually with foul desires."[115]

111. Jansen, "Maria Magdalena," 64–65. *"de peccatrice sanctam, de meretrice apostolam constituit"*; *Sermo LXIV (in festo S. Mariae Magdalenae)*, PL 202, col. 839, quoted by Jansen, n. 33, p. 85.

112. Mycoff, *Critical Edition*, 5, 6; n. 6, p. 46.

113. Christianus Druthmarus, *Expositio in Matthaeum Evangelistam* (PL 106:1497–1500); John Chrysostom, *Homilies on St. John* (Washington: Catholic University Press, 1957–60) 2.46–49, Homilies 85 and 86.

114. See Haskins, *Mary Magdalen*, 106–7. In Umberto Eco's *Foucault's Pendulum* (San Diego: Harcourt, 1989) Jesus and Mary Magdalene are married at Cana.

115. Honorius of Autun, *Speculum Ecclesiae: De Sancta Maria Magdalena*, PL 172, col 979. Quoted by B. Ward, *Harlots of the Desert: A Study of Repentance in Early Monastic Studies* (Kalamazoo, Mich.: Cistercian Publications, 1987) 16.

(Marguerite Yourcenar makes use of this story in *Fires*, spicing it up in the Western fashion. John's abandonment causes her prostitution and an unsuccessful attempt at Simon's house to seduce Jesus [God]. She becomes a disciple who rivals John. At the empty tomb: "For the second time in my life, I was standing in front of a deserted bed."[116]) After the ascension and pentecost, she is said in the Greek tradition to have followed her former lover and then fellow disciple John to Ephesus, to have died there and been buried in the cave of the Seven Sleepers. Her relics and those of John were later taken to the church of St. Lazarus in Constantinople by Emperor Leo VI.

As Ward puts it, the post-ascension Western tradition was more lively.[117] The Provençal legend was the most influential in the West, particularly after the twelfth century. Its fully-developed and relatively stable thirteenth-century form is that told by Jacobus de Voragine (d. 1298), the Dominican archbishop of Genoa, in the popular *Golden Legend* (*Legenda aurea*), probably not later than 1267.[118] Its popularity is seen in the fact that over 700 manuscripts and 173 printed editions survive; the last figure includes translations, of which there is one for almost every Western European language.[119] In Western Europe, over 190 shrines were dedicated to Mary Magdalene, and more than 600 of her relics venerated. In pre-Reformation England, there were 170 churches bearing her name.[120] Caxton's *Golden Legende* of 1483, a prose legend in Middle English, was the last full-scale hagiographical compendium published in English before the Reformation. It disappeared "a victim of a conscious policy of the Protestant state, bent on obliterating all material associated with Catholicism, and not a change in popular taste."[121] The most original and interesting drama of Middle English on the Magdalene is the Digby Play, which makes some dramatic changes in the legend; the scene at Simon the Pharisee's house, for example, is the occasion of Mary Magdalene's exorcism.[122]

Since the *Golden Legend* is not readily accessible but indispensable for reading the iconography of the Magdalene, let me summarize it here. The account begins with interpretations of the names "Mary" and "Magdalene," with stress on penance (most accented), contemplation, and enlightenment, and with mention but

---

116. M. Yourcenar, *Fires* (New York: Farrar, Straus and Giroux, 1981) 75.

117. Ward, *Harlots*, 17.

118. Jacobus de Voragine, *Legenda aurea* (ed. T. Graesse; Dresden, 1846); ET *The Golden Legend of Jacobus de Voragine* (trans. G. Ryan and H. Rippergar; New York: Longmans, 1941; reprint New York: Arno, 1969) 355–64.

119. Mycoff, *Critical Edition*, n. 37, p. 55.

120. S. Eberly, "Margery Kempe, St. Mary Magdalene, and Patterns of Contemplation," *The Downside Review* 368 (1989) 210.

121. Mycoff, *Critical Edition*, 2.

122. Haskins, *Mary Magdalen*, 165, 168. See *Late Medieval Religious Plays of Bodleian MSS Digby 133 and E Museo 160* (ed. D. Baker, J. Murphy, L. Hall; Oxford: The Early English Text Society, 1982) 47. See also P. Happe, "The Protestant Adaptation of the Saint Play," *The Saint Play in Medieval Europe* (ed. C. Davidson; Kalamazoo, Mich.: Medieval Institute Publications, 1986).

no real stress on discipleship or witness to the crucifixion and resurrection. Mary Magdalene, her sister Martha and her brother Lazarus were born of royal, wealthy parents. So entirely had Mary "abandoned her body to pleasure that she was no longer called by any other name than 'the sinner.'" But one day by divine inspiration, she entered the house of Simon the leper, the Pharisee of Bethany, where the Lord was at dinner. She bathed his feet with her tears of penance, dried them with her hair, anointed them with precious ointment. (The prophetic anointing before the arrest of Jesus is later omitted.) Although the Pharisee objected, the Lord forgave her.

"And thenceforth there was no grace that He refused her, nor any mark of affection that He withheld from her" (there is no indication as far as I can see that this is meant erotically). He delivered her from seven devils, "admitted her to His friendship, condescended to dwell in her house, and was pleased to defend her whenever the occasion arose" (before the Pharisee, Martha, and Judas). He raised Lazarus from the dead "for love of her" whom he could not see in tears without himself weeping. "Magdalene also had the honour of being present at the death of Jesus, standing at the foot of the Cross; and it was she that anointed His body with sweet spices after His death, and who stayed at the sepulchre when all the disciples went away. And to her first the risen Jesus appeared and made her apostle to the apostles."

Thus the great bulk of the pre-Ascension part of the story concerns the narratives conflated with the Christian Testament references to Mary Magdalene. Only the two sentences quoted above pay attention to the passion and resurrection scenes. The notion of her great wealth is not connected to financial support of Jesus and the Twelve (Luke 8:1–3), but rather serves to emphasize her prior life of luxury. The figures with which the Magdalene was conflated have overwhelmed the Magdalene. Emphasis is on her sin and repentance, and on love.

The story continues fourteen years after the Ascension. When the disciples went out worldwide to preach, St. Peter entrusted Mary Magdalene to St. Maximinus, one of the seventy-two disciples. With Maximinus, Lazarus, Martha, Martilla (Martha's servant), and other Christians, Mary Magdalene was put out to sea by "the infidels" (i.e., the Jews) in a boat without a rudder, in the hope that all would drown. (The rudderless boat appears also in the legend of the three seaborne Marys, associated with the Camargue.) But they landed safely at Marseilles and were sheltered under the portico of a pagan temple. "And when Mary Magdalene saw the pagans going into their temple to offer sacrifice to their gods, she arose with calm mien and prudent tongue," and began to preach Christ to them. "And all wondered at her, not only for her beauty, but for her eloquence, which eloquence was not indeed a matter of surprise on lips that had touched the Lord's feet." She converted the prince and princess of Marseilles and successfully threatened them with punishment for their neglect of the poor "servants of God."

One day when the Magdalene was preaching, the ruler asked if she could give proof of the faith she preached. She answered that it was confirmed by miracles "and through the preaching of Peter, my master, the bishop of Rome!" Even though she interceded with God to obtain the conception of a child for him, the prince wished to consult St. Peter "in order to know whether all that Magdalene said of Christ were true." On the journey to Rome, during a storm at sea, the princess gave birth prematurely and died. Her body and the living newborn infant were abandoned on a hilly coast. Blaming Mary Magdalene, but commending his wife and child to her and to God, the prince continued on to Rome and was received there by St. Peter, who accompanied him on a pilgrimage to Jerusalem. After two years' instruction in the faith by Peter, the prince started back to Marseilles. Along the way, the child ("whom Mary Magdalene had taken into her care, watching over him from afar to keep him alive") was found. As the prince offered a short prayer to Mary Magdalene, the body of the princess came alive. She announced that Mary Magdalene had also escorted her on a trip to Jerusalem: "when Saint Peter led thee about Jerusalem, showing thee scenes of Christ's life and death, I too was there, with Mary Magdalene as my guide."

Finally back in Marseilles, the family found Mary Magdalene "busy at preaching with her disciples." The royal couple were baptized by Maximinus, and the citizens of Marseilles replaced all pagan temples with Christian churches. Lazarus was chosen to be bishop of Marseilles, and when Mary and her followers went to Aix, Maximinus was elected bishop there. This portion of the legend is interesting for its subordination of Mary Magdalene to Peter (without conflict), its attribution to her of fertility powers, and its emphasis on her preaching.

The last phase of this story concerns the retirement of Mary Magdalene, "moved by her wish to live in contemplation of the things of God," to a mountain cave, where she spent her last thirty years in isolation. Without friends, family, animals, without even ravens to feed her like Elijah. Her lack of "earthly satisfaction" there is not explicitly explained as punishment or penance, through shortly before her death she introduced herself to a priest in the wilderness in this way: "Dost thou recall having read in the Gospel the story of Mary, the notorious sinner who washed the Savior's feet, wiped them with the hairs of her head, and obtained pardon for all her sins?. . . . I am that sinner." She sent him to Maximinus to tell him to expect her to appear with angels in his oratory on the day after Easter. When she appeared, raised two cubits above the earth and surrounded by angels, her face was radiant. After she received the viaticum, "her body fell lifeless before the altar and her soul took its flight to the Lord." Maximinus buried her and commanded that he be buried beside her at his death. The legend ends with an alternate, less dramatic death account, an account of the theft of her relics from Aix to Vézelay, the author's insistence that the story of Mary's betrothal to John is "a false and frivolous tale," and five stories of her post-burial miracles.

A remote source of the account of her thirty-year solitude is the legend of the fifth century prostitute-actress from Alexandria, Mary of Egypt, who did penance naked and wrapped in her hair in a desert retreat east of Palestine.[123] This story had been blended into Mary Magdalene's by the ninth century, though the provenance and first appearances of this account of the final phase of her life are uncertain. The long penitential seclusion became one of the best known aspects of her story in the Middle Ages and later. It was exploited by the monastery at Vézelay in Burgundy, which made the loudest claim to possess her bones, becoming for a time the site of the most celebrated and economically productive pilgrimage in France. The cave was localized in the twelfth century as the grotto of Ste. Baume (Holy Balm[124]), high up in the massif of Provence, east of Marseilles, near the town of St. Maximin. A flood of hagiographical materials evolving over two hundred years developed different versions of how she got from Palestine to France and with whom, and how her bones got from Marseilles to Vézelay. In the thirteenth century Vézelay was upstaged by St. Maximin's claim to possess the body, and the pilgrims came to Provence, as they still do today, to see her skull paraded about encased in gold during her feast days in July.

Later in the fifteenth century, the bodies of her companions were said to be discovered at a town at the mouth of the Rhone, Notre Dame de la Mer, renamed Les Stes Maries de-la-Mer.[125] The shrine there is dedicated to Mary Salome, Jary Jacobe, and Mary Magdalene. Even today the Marys (two or three or four of them) are celebrated there in May, with their companion or servant or host black Sara, patron saint of the Gitanes or Roma (gypsies). Sara is mysterious: "Son origine est plutôt obscure. On a parlé d'une ancienne déesse ... (ou) d'une reine des Terres de Camargue ... (ou d') une Egyptienne...."[126] On feast days the dressed-up statues are carried back to the Mediterranean, their escort mounted on the white Camargue horses, thousands of onlookers lining the beach.

The Christian Testament Magdalene has all but disappeared by the dramatic end of this version of her story, which developed in the context of ecclesiastical financial dealings, monastic rivalries, the cult of relics, the politics of pilgrimage, and idea(l)s of feminine asceticism and sin. It refused to conclude neatly, but burgeoned into artistic and social reform expressions.

---

123. See Ward, *Harlots*, 26–56. Ward holds wrongly that the "unfortunate mistake" of confusing Mary Magdalene and Mary of Egypt perhaps was the link that "provided material for the idea of sexual sin as Mary Magdalene's main concern, as distinct from possession by all seven devils" (15). She speculates also that it is possible that the idea of Mary Magdalene as a prostitute "was affected by a tradition found in some fragments, which may come from a gnostic milieu in which Mary Magdalene is referred to as the lover of Christ" (referring to the *Gospel of Philip*).
124. *Baoumo* is Provençal for "cave," but in the high French used by ecclesiastics, *baume* is "balm."
125. See Haskins, *Mary Magdalen*, 111–33; Saxer, *Le Culte*, 2.238–39.
126. P. Cordlier, *Les Gitanes* (Rennes: Editions Ouest-France, 1983) 27. My thanks to Professor W. G. Lockwood of Wayne State University for conversations about Sara and her feast, and for acquainting me with patrin-roma-culture@igc.topica.com.

A bit earlier than the *Legenda aurea* is the relatively little known *De vita Beatae Mariae Magdalenae et sororis ejus Sanctae Marthae*, influenced by the spiritual, mystical doctrine of Bernard of Clairvaux.[127] Like the more popular *Legenda aurea*, this work, which is fifty chapters long, harmonizes Christian Testament texts. But its tone and emphases are quite different and interesting in terms of how those who considered themselves the spiritual elite imagined the Magdalene.

The bulk (chapters 4 through 36) is a retelling of the Gospels and Acts 1–7, with only parts of five chapters given to the post-Ascension career of Mary Magdalene. Dismissed as false are the stories of her naked solitude in the cave and angelic transport, and nothing is said about a rudderless boat or the prince and princess of Marseilles. This author is primarily interested in what was believed to be the Christian Testament profile of the Magdalene. Five chapters, instead of two sentences, are devoted to summarizing separately and harmonizing the empty tomb and appearance stories, with awareness of the different details: this yields four appearance to Mary of six angels, and two appearances to her of the risen Jesus, first alone, and then with other women.

Her unmeasured friendship (*familiaritas*) and intimacy with Christ is celebrated, their "mutual love" (chap. 15), linked with reflection on his humanity. She is his "first servant" (*premiceria*; chaps. 24, 26), "special friend" (*amica specialis*), "the most tenderly loved among all women except for the Virgin Mother of God" (chap. 27). This love is usually presented erotically (chaps. 17–18 [caressing massage of his feet and hair], 33 [her grief like that of a forsaken lover; his "sweet embraces" finally given her "in the rest of eternal contemplation"]) and as bridal (chap. 45), but is said to be chaste (chap. 8). Sexual imagery is used: "Impregnated [by Jesus] with [the seven gifts of the] Spirit, by faith she conceived a good hope within herself, and gave birth to a fervent charity" (chap. 6). But the Magdalene does not become a spiritual mother of souls.

Her early life of sexual sin is explained as the result of youth, physical attractiveness, "the weakness of the [female] sex," and wealth. An extended contrast with Eve is drawn (chap. 27). The first anointing at the house of Simon is described with allusions to the prodigal son, and, illustrating the notion of prevenient grace, as a kind of call ("for in truth, [Jesus] came to her first, through the seven-fold gifts of the spirit . . . drawing her to himself"; (chap. 5). This suggests that the story in the conflated biography takes the place of a call by Jesus such as male disciples receive in the Christian Testament. Her role as a traveller with Jesus in his career is acknowledged, but she is later said to stay behind at home often with her sister Martha, sending supplies to Jesus and his followers (chaps. 9, 11).

Mary Magdalene is depicted as eye-witness to all the events of the passion of Jesus, from the garden, to the hearings and "trial," the way of the cross, death,

---

127. Mycoff, *Life of Saint Mary Magdalene*; cf. Mycoff, "The Legend of Mary Magdalene in a Twelfth-Century Context," *Cistercian Studies* 23 (1988) 310–18.

entombment (chaps. 20–23); she is, however, excluded from the last supper. (The medieval mystery plays often presented the resurrection through her eyes, following her from the shop where she buys the embalming unguents to the garden where she sees the risen Christ.[128]) "Loyalty did not forsake Mary Magdalene. The skin of her flesh adhered to the bones of the Saviour, for when Judas betrayed him, Peter denied him, and the ten apostles fled from him, there was still found in Mary Magdalene the courage of the Redeemer" (chap. 20). Her loyalty illustrates that "love is as strong as death. This was seen in the Lord's passion, when Mary's love did not die" (chap. 21). Almost identified with Christ on the cross ("Christ was pierced with nails on the cross; the soul of Mary was pierced with sharp grief," chap. 21), she is once said to be a "man" ("a man's soul was manifested in a woman") because she fulfills a passage attributed to Solomon ("My hands dripped with myrrh," chap. 23).

It is not Peter, but Mary Magdalene who is the first to see the risen Lord (no allusion is made to 1 Cor 15:5). She, not the Beloved Disciple, is the first to believe. And she is the first to announce the resurrection and predict the ascension (chaps. 25–27, 29). All this makes her an apostle, evangelist, and prophet, and, because of her conversion and intimacy with Christ, more than a prophet (chaps. 29, 32).

In chap. 21 she is present for the commission, but in the post-Ascension section of this work she is not at first a preacher (rather, her penitence is often the subject of male preaching). She becomes instead a maid to the Virgin Mary, and her companion in contemplation, "frequently enjoying angelic visions and visitations" (chaps. 34–35). Peter, who sets up his "patriarchal throne" in Antioch, delegates the Western regions to male preachers, and Maximinus is sent to Gaul. Mary Magdalene joins and entrusts herself to him (chaps. 36–37). While Maximinus preaches and new faith springs up, Mary still devotes herself primarily to contemplation ("for she was in fact the most ardent lover of the Redeemer, the woman who had wisely chosen the best part which — witness God — was never taken from her once she received it from Christ at his feet"). But "also mindful of the well-being of her friends," she "from time to time" leaves the joys of contemplation and preaches to the unbelievers and believers, presenting herself to sinners as an example of conversion, and becoming "an evangelist for believers throughout the world" (chap. 38).

On the whole, it is difficult to say which the author has emphasized more, her sin/conversion/penitence (symbolized by her alabaster jar), or her role as witness/apostle/prophet. But in the post-Ascension section, the former receives the heavier weight. In chapter 30 the author writes, "most happy by far [is] the one who has been so moved by and who has taken such delight in the surpassing fragrance of Mary's deeds that he has followed the example of her conversion,

---

128. Warner, *Alone*, 228.

has imprinted in himself the image of her repentance, and has filled his spirit with her devotion, to the degree that he has made himself a partaker of that best part which she chose." Again, the women from the other stories have overwhelmed the Christian Testament Mary Magdalene. In this case, the power to tame her comes most strongly from the story of Mary of Bethany, listening and silent at the feet of Jesus. It comes from the story which many have thought of as promoting the liberation of women, but which Elisabeth Schüssler Fiorenza has shown promotes with dangerous subtlety the patriarchal separation and restriction of women.[129]

In a final irony which escapes the author, in death the Magdalene is removed from women. When Maximinus was laid beside her, the place became "so holy that no king, prince, or other person, no matter what earthly pomp attended him, would enter the church to pray for help without making some sign of humble devotion, first disposing of his weapons and all other marks of brutal ferocity. No woman was ever so audacious as to enter that temple, no matter what condition, order, or dignity she enjoyed. That monastery is called the Abbey of Saint Maximin.... " (chap. 50). Has the author had in mind all along as reader only the individual contemplative monk, whose soul is a "she" urged to strive to imitate the Magdalene?

By the twelfth century, her legend was complete, and by the thirteenth she had become a character in her own right,[130] almost free of her scriptural origins. Her story illustrated the church's emphasis on sin, repentance and individual responsibility, as she became a model for all, for taking the sacraments of penance and the eucharist. She was also regarded as the great exception to the prohibition against women preaching (1 Timothy 2).[131] Her life of sin and penance allowed her to be honored and extolled in the late thirteenth, fourteenth and fifteenth century by preachers and writers as an apostle and more (*praedicatrix et annunciatrix fidei, praedicatrix privilegiata, doctrix, magistra, prenuncia, testis veritatis, seminatrix and sapientiae schola*[132]) without fear that she would become a model for women in this regard. Like the Virgin Mary, she was "alone of all her sex." "The powerful [but restricted] image of [only one] woman...which emerged in the eleventh century, only to bloom in the twelfth and succeeding centuries, was part of the common conceptual economy at least until the Council of Trent. Thus for a good five hundred years Mary Magdalene was represented as *apostolo-*

129. E. Schüssler Fiorenza, "A Feminist Critical Interpretation for Liberation: Martha and Mary: Lk. 10:38–42," *Religion & Intellectual Life* 3 (1986) 21–36.

130. Haskins, *Mary Magdalen*, 163.

131. From the fourth century into the twelfth, the *noli me tangere* of John 20:17 was taken to mean women were forbidden to teach in church or perform other important functions. Still, the Dominican Moneta of Cremona contended that Waldensian women were justifying their own claims to preach by appealing to Mary Magdalene's role as *nuncia* in John 20. Jansen, "Maria Magdalena," 67, 68.

132. Jansen, "Maria Magdalena," 71.

rum apostola."[133] After the Reformation, in Protestant and many Catholic works the attribution to her of apostleship disappeared. She was no longer typically associated with preaching or evangelism, but became almost exclusively a figure of penitence for Protestants, and of penitence and contemplation for Catholics. "The private aspects of her cult, i.e., the aspects dealing with interior 'acts,' dominate the public aspects, which deal with ministry."[134] Jo Ann McNamara's title for her final chapter on nuns in the high Middle Ages, "The Tears of the Magdalene," details ecclesiastical and secular attacks on women in convents because of their chastity and because of their lack of chastity; it suggests that interesting studies could be done on the correlation between men's perception of these women and the Magdalene legends, as between these women's self understanding and their understanding of the Magdalene.[135]

What can we say that is not utterly obvious about the sexual politics of these two medieval versions of her legend? The conflations and accretions successfully reduce the significance of the Christian Testament Magdalene, with focus even in the *Life of Saint Mary Magdalene* on penitence and contemplation, rather than on prophetic action, courage, perception. Single, she functions as a sexual being only as a whore, a freelance whore. Five reasons are given for her whoredom: she is young, beautiful, female, weathy, and (in the Ephesian version) abandoned by her fiance John. She has no child to feed, no abuse to escape, is not a widow or foreigner or lesbian or person of color or businesswoman — all of which might provide more or other realistic motivations.[136]

Using scriptural citations, four reasons are given in the *Legenda aurea* to explain why the risen Jesus appeared first to her: because she loved ardently (Luke 7:47); because he died for sinners (Matt 9:13); to show harlots precede the wise in the kingdom (Matt 21:31); to show that just as a woman was the messenger of death, so she should be the messenger of life (Genesis 3). Some sort of sudden insight or "grace" is responsible for the Magdalene's conversion and repentance ("from that moment she was the most chaste of women" [chap. VIII]). Forgiven, she chooses the better part, as she formerly chose whoring. When Jesus is killed, her love will not give him up; he returns to her; he leaves again. She lives on as a contemplative, and/or as a naked, isolated penitent, weeping. The guilt never really goes away. Her love becomes spiritual and her beauty — especially her

---

133. Jansen, "Maria Magdalena," 78. She points out that Susan Haskins "misrepresents the historical record when she speaks of the 'brief resurgence' of the title in the Middle Ages" (n. 108, p. 95; Haskins, *Mary Magdalen,* 67)

134. Mycoff, *Critical Edition,* 169.

135. J. A. McNamara, *Sisters in Arms: Catholic Nuns through Two Millennia* (Cambridge: Harvard University Press, 1996). "Dominican control of the Inquisition had always been balanced by a willingness to promote some women as champions of orthodoxy" (361).

136. Cf., for example, the case of Angela, wife of Nofri di Francesco: in 1398 she was reported to have chosen prostitution for economic reasons, and not to have been ashamed of it (E. A. Petroff, *Body and Soul: Essays on Medieval Women and Mysticism* [New York: Oxford University Press, 1994] 29).

hair—one is allowed to admire. In the *Legenda aurea*, she has miraculous power to aid others in conception, and is in this sense a "mother."

As long as the legend emphasizes her Easter role and her apostleship, she is contrasted with the fearful and unbelieving male disciples, and so is a somewhat or potentially subversive character. Garth implies that her popularity in the Middle Ages had something to do with anticlericalism, when she argues that her superiority over the other apostles was a major factor.[137] The Magdalene's preaching in the south of France enlarges her role of apostle to the apostles.[138] But she offers no real challenge to the hierarchy of the church, subordinating herself in the story to Peter and to Maximinus (who are not threatened by her), and living a life more contemplative than active. Authorized by the risen Christ, she strangely has no authority. Even though her characteristic is extravagant love for Christ, from whom she draws all her meaning, and her life is depicted as one of extremes, there is a controlled calmness and prudence about her in these legends. She is a woman of warm emotion and loyalty, but not of ideas or great intelligence. She is presented as understanding herself as a sinner who has been given mercy, and in the end she has nothing much to say to others except to point to herself as a sinner.[139] Weeping replaces speaking; or weeping is her form of speech, as for the woman in Luke 7.[140] This replacement invalidates "what is most hers, the ability to express her truth through language."[141] In short, even though she is acknowledged as the most extraordinary woman, she does not disturb but rather confirms the patriarchal ideology and structures. She is at their service.

For men, there is a reassurance here: you have nothing to fear from such a strong woman. For women, a message concerning salvation (from female sexuality) and protection by the male (Jesus, the church authorities). This is the destiny of even the greatest women, and in fact this is their greatness. For all, the story of this great sinner reconciled to God makes the promise that no one is beyond the reach of God's mercy. But the sins women name as theirs are not the same as the sins of men or the sins men name as women's.[142] For the sins of women, as known by women, the Magdalene legend offers no definition and no remedy.

137. Garth, *Saint Mary Magdalene*, 105.
138. K. L. Jansen, "Mary Magdalen and the Mendicants: The preaching of penance in the late Middle Ages," *Journal of Medieval History* 21 (1995) 22.
139. In the South English Legendary version of the Magdalene legend (written probably in 1276 or 1279) there is a twenty-two-line speech purporting to be her sermon (II.199–238); neither the *Legenda aurea* nor any other legends related to it has a corresponding passage. Its theme is the greatness, eternity, and lordship of God the creator (Mycoff, *Critical Edition*, 91–92).
140. For J. Kristeva milk and tears are both "metaphors of non-language, of a 'semiotic' that does not coincide with linguistic communication" ("Stabat Mater," *The Female Body in Western Culture* [ed. S. R. Suleiman; Cambridge: Harvard, 1986] 109).
141. E. B. Davis, " 'Woman, Why Weepest Thou' " 47.
142. Valerie Saiving, "The Human Situation: a Feminine View," *Journal of Religion* 40 (1960) 100–112.

The tenacity and force with which the imagination has clung to the portrait of the harlot-saint is shown not only in modern media presentations, and in the richness of artistic portraits of the Magdalene of legend. It can be seen in sixteenth-, seventeenth-, and nineteenth-century reactions against attempts to deharmonize the texts. In 1517, the year Luther nailed up his theses in Wittenberg, the leading French Christian humanist Dominican Jacques Lefèvre d'Etaples published a critique of the then-traditional Magdalene, *De Maria Magdalene & triduo Christi Disceptatio.* Within three years, fifteen major treatises had been written on the controversy and Lefèvre had been accused of heresy, censured by the theological faculty of the Sorbonne and his works placed on the Index. His supporter Clichtoue testified before the faculty that both he and Lefèvre rejected their earlier opinions, but they stood condemned.[143]

The issue was raised fiercely again in the seventeenth century, and serious debate continued until after the end of the nineteenth century. It was not simply a scholarly debate. In the mid-nineteenth-century upper- and middle-class Evangelical women working with prostitutes refuted the traditional view of Mary Magdalene, emphasizing her as the woman at the cross.[144] Today, both Roman Catholicism and Protestantism officially agree with Eastern Orthodoxy in distinguishing among Mary Magdalene, Mary of Bethany, and the "sinner"/penitent of Luke. We are reminded how recent this official stance is of rehabilitating Mary Magdalene when we note that not until 1969 were changes in the Roman Calendar promulgated, and not until 1978 were deletions made in the Roman Breviary wiping out her sinful reputation. She was reinstated as one of many followers of Jesus, her role of apostle to the apostles and preacher erased, and her feast-day reduced from a "duplex, one of the most elaborate of all liturgies reserved for the most important saints," to a "memorial, a simple remembrance."[145] We are reminded how softpeddled even this official stance is by John Meier's comments: "it goes without saying — or should — that Mary Magdalene is not to be equated with either the 'sinful woman' of Luke 7:36–50 or the Mary of Bethany from the Johannine tradition (John 11–12). This is a commonplace in exegesis today [referring to the Anchor Bible Commentary article on "Mary (Person)"]....Indeed, even in 20th-century Catholic exegesis this view is nothing new" (referring to Ketter's 1929 monograph).[146] "It goes without saying — or should" but doesn't.

The stranded ghost of Migdal is trapped in two stories by Luke: that of the anointing woman who was a "sinner" (7:36–50) and that of Mary of Bethany who chooses silent contemplation rather than service (10:38–42). Lucan artistry,

---

143. Haskins, *Mary Magdalen,* 250–51.
144. Haskins, *Mary Magdalen,* 328, 364.
145. K. L. Jansen, *The Making of the Magdalen: Preaching and Popular Devotion in the Later Middle Ages* (Princeton: Princeton University Press, 2000) 334–35; Haskins, *Mary Magdalen,* 399.
146. Meier, *Marginal Jew,* n. 57, p. 673.

at the service of misogynistic impulses, provided the distorting lenses. At bottom, as Woolf puts it in another, similar context, romantic "Love was the only possible interpreter"[147] of a woman of power. "And when we are writing the life of a woman, we may, it is agreed, waive our demand for action, and substitute love instead. Love, the poet has said, is woman's whole existence . . . (and as long as she thinks of a man, nobody objects to a woman thinking). . . . But love — as the male novelists define it — and who, after all, speak with greater authority? — has nothing whatever to do with kindness, fidelity, generosity, or poetry. Love is slipping off one's petticoat and — But we all know what love is"[148]

What kind of love is this? First it's self-love, self-indulgence, seen as the cause of her whoring. Then, if Luke 7:47 ("her sins, which were many, have been forgiven, for she has loved much") is read in all its ambiguity, instead of being smoothed out with v. 42 ("I suppose the one for whom he cancelled the debt [will love the creditor more]"), it might be the love of a whore for her johns — or at least her enjoyment of them. Then it becomes love based on guilt about her freely-chosen sexual behavior, and on gratitude for the lifting of that burden of guilt by forgiveness. She switches the object of her love, from the johns to Jesus. Sex with Jesus, or at least an erotic relationship with Jesus, is suggested by the use of poetry from the Song of Songs to express this love.

Sex between Mary Magdalene and Jesus is explicit in theologies and opinions that build on the legends (the Catharists or Albigensians [who held that she was his concubine], Luther [who assumed a sexual relationship existed between them], Brigham Young [who suggested in a sermon that Christ was a polygamist with Mary, Martha, and Mary Magdalene][149] and the Rosicrucians [who are interested in the descendants of Christ and Mary Magdalene]). It appears in some late nineteenth-century and twentieth-century art, novels, poetry (Rodin, Rilke, D. H. Lawrence, erotic paintings of the crucifixion) and film (*The Last Temptation*), fictional autobiographies[150] and in scholarship, pseudo-scholarship and journalistic works. William E. Phipps holds that Jesus may have married Mary Magdalene when he was in his twenties; she may have been unfaithful to him but he forgave her, an experience that influenced his views on divorce and human relationships.[151] Barbara Thiering argues (or rather, asserts) from fantastic con-

147. Woolf, *Room*, 87.

148. V. Woolf, *Orlando* (New York: Harcourt Brace & Co., 1928) 268–69. L. Faschinger's Magdalene is a wacky modern adventurer who chooses to be a murderess of seven lovers over being a madwoman (the only two choices open to her in Catholic Austria). She is constantly swept away by passion, never seeking anything but love (*Magdalena the Sinner* [New York: HarperCollins, 1997). E. Cunningham's *Maeve* (*Daughter of the Shining Isles* [Station Hill, 2000]) is a Celtic Harry Potter, twin of Esus, and focused on the need for "touch."

149. See Haskins, *Mary Magdalen*, n. 42, pp. 485–86.

150. S. Ludvigson, *Trinity* (Baton Rouge: Louisiana State University Press, 1996) "The Gospel according to Mary Magdalene."

151. W. E. Phipps, *Was Jesus Married?* (New York: Harper & Row, 1970) see also E. Moltmann-Wendel, *The Women around Jesus* (New York: Crossroad, 1982). Contrast E. Moltmann-Wendel,

flations and code-breaking of Christian Testament and Dead Sea Scrolls passages that Mary Magdalene was married to Jesus and they had three children, a girl and two boys. She left him and he married again.[152] Michael Baigent, Richard Leigh, and Henry Lincoln's popular book, *Holy Blood, Holy Grail*, based on investigative TV reporting and "common sense," spins a fascinating mystery about Jesus' marriage to Mary Magdalene, her arrival with their child or children in the south of France, and the finding and decoding of secret documents from the Knights Templars, the Cathars, the Rosicrucians, the Masons and others, tracing the bloodline of Jesus and the Magdalene (the Holy Grail dynasty) in the royal houses of Europe. "[O]ur arguments were eagerly seized upon by American feminists, who were quick to discern the implications of what we had said — implications which were indeed considerable regarding a number of controversial contemporary issues, such as clerical celibacy and the role of women in both Church and society."[153] This sensationalistic and influential book reminds us, if we need reminding, of the world of difference between scholarship and journalism.

And then some contemporary scholars and clerics remind us that the difference is not so great. It is surprising to find treatments of Mary Magdalene that still conflate the texts, though modern motivation differs from that of the past. Spong highlights hints in the Gospels that she was linked with Jesus "in a romantic way." He can entertain the idea that they might have been married, but not that they were lovers, since that latter idea "would fly in the face of the moral values espoused by the church through the ages, and it would deeply violate our understanding of Jesus as incarnate Lord and the Holy Sinless One." Cana becomes he marriage of Jesus and Mary Magdalene, whom Spong identifies with Mary of Bethany, the anointing woman in Mark 14, and the "sinner" of Luke 7: "If this Mary can in fact be identified with Mary Magdalene, as many scholars suggest [sic], then the intimate role of anointing Jesus' head with oil, kissing Jesus' feet, and wiping Jesus' feet with her hair would have been things done to Jesus by Mary Magdalene. These actions would be appropriate only in one of two roles: Mary was either his wife or she was a prostitute." Spong asks, "Why is there still a continuing sense, ranging from dis-ease to revulsion, that arises in us when we hear the suggestion that Jesus might have been married? I suggest that far more than any of us realize we are subconsciously victimized by the historic negativity toward women that has been a major gift of the Christian church to the world. So pervasive is this negativity that unconsciously we still regard holy matrimony to be less than the ideal, and we still operate out of an understanding

---

"Motherhood or Friendship," *Concilium* 168 (1983) 17–22. J. K. Coyle ("Mary Magdalene in Manichaeism?" *Muséon* 104 [1991] 39) holds only that the theory that Jesus was married favors Mary Magdalene as "the prime spousal candidate."

152. B. Thiering, *Jesus and the Riddle of the Dead Sea Scrolls* (San Francisco: Harper, 1992).

153. *Holy Blood, Holy Grail* (New York: Dell, 1983) 16, 21. See the use made of this book by M. Starbird, *The Woman with the Alabaster Jar: Mary Magdalene and the Holy Grail* (Santa Fe: Bear & Co., 1993).

of women that defines them as the source of sin, the polluter of otherwise moral men."[154] This is the patriarchal "we," that does not move out of patriarchialism by simply accepting marriage (for Jesus and others) as a good. Bruce Chilton argues that "There is no evidence that Jesus did or did not enjoy sexual contact during his life, but seven-demoned Miriam remains the most likely candidate if he did so, because she is the only woman, apart from his mother, with whom he had persistent contact. Indeed, her status made her the kind of woman Jesus' mother might once have hoped her *mamzer* son would marry." Jesus' itinerant life precluded marriage and children, and the Torah forbade adultery, "[b]ut sexual contact with an unmarried woman who was not a virgin, particularly a sinner or a formerly demon-possessed person, did not fall under the definition of adultery or seduction."[155] It is not clear that Chilton identifies her with the "sinner" of Luke 7, whose elaborate gesture with her hair he thinks makes it likely she pursued "the forbidden profession of a hairdresser, which many rabbis saw as just a step away from prostitution." But he does identify her with the anointing woman of Mark 14 and its Matthean parallel.[156] Kitzberger reads Luke 7:36–50; John 12:1–8 (and 13:1) together, intertextually, making very different points.[157]

The making of Mary Magdalene into Jesus' wife or lover seems to me a patriarchal attempt to complete the process of her "redemption" from a whore into the form of a "normal" woman, reabsorbed into society. It is an assertion or acknowledgement of heterosexual female sexuality, true, and this is why it has some appeal to women. But primarily it is about Jesus. It serves to make him into a "real man," with satisfied sexual urges, the ability to love fully, human like we are. The films especially find it is not easy to humanize him without denying his divinity; not possible to humanize him without reference to his active heterosexuality; and it is important in some ages like ours to humanize him by de-divinizing him. The Magdalene is used in a variety of ways in different periods in order to think about Jesus, and about men in general. She is one of those looking-glasses "possessing the magic and delicious power of reflecting the figure of man at twice its natural

---

154. J. S. Spong, *Born of a Woman* (San Francisco: Harper, 1992) 187–99. His treatment is flawed by a lack of familiarity with feminist and other current scholarship, and overconfident statements about "rules governing women in first century Jewish society" (191); see also his *Resurrection: Myth or Reality* (San Francisco: HarperCollins, 1994). A. Feuillet identifies all three Marys in "Les deux onctions faites sur Jésus et Marie-Madeleine," *Revue Thomiste* 74 (1975) 357–94.

155. Chilton, *Rabbi Jesus*, 145. He thinks Jesus was regarded as a *mamzer* (an Israelite of suspect paternity or of "uncertain ethnic paternity," a "silenced one," without a voice in the social/political/religious life of Israel) because Mary and Joseph had sex during their betrothal while she lived in Nazareth and he lived in (northern) Bethlehem, and "it was virtually impossible for her to prove that he [and not some prohibited man] was the father" (5–8, 12–13).

156. Chilton, *Rabbi Jesus*, 134, 250. He does not identify her with "the widowed sisters Miriam and Martha, no longer young" (235).

157. I. R. Kitzberger, "Love and Footwashing," *BibInt* 2 (1994) 190–206. She holds that John knew and used the Synoptics. My preference is to read the Lukan text by itself, freeing it up for an interpretation of its own.

size," mirrors "essential to all violent and heroic action."[158] This is something like the way Toni Morrison has shown white American literature using the black character as a "metaphorical shortcut." "The fabrication of an Africanist persona is reflexive; an extraordinary meditation on the self; a powerful exploration of the fears and desires that reside in the writerly conscious. It is an astonishing reve-lation of longing, of terror, of perplexity, of shame, of magnanimity. It requires hard work *not* to see this."[159]

But thinking about Jesus and gender is not all that easy, outside a patriarchal framework. As Outsider, Jesus in the Christian Testament is a representation of a wo/man, urging other men to become wo/men — Schüssler Fiorenza's term that includes all women, and oppressed and marginalized men.[160] He is reported to have engaged in gender bending, in what Sarah Ruddick calls maternal think-ing: he nurtures, is concerned for children, he wishes to comfort and stop the violence. He feeds, washes feet, he weeps, he experiences intimacy. More im-portantly, in his career and execution he struggles against oppression "at the bottom of the kyriarchal pyramid."[161] Not a "real man," he represents Sophia as a wo/man. Susannah Heschel writes of Jesus as "Theological Transvestite," who destabilizes the boundaries between male and female. "From the Gospel accounts, modern scholars found that Jesus' teachings laud gentleness, the meek, and [turn-ing] the cheek; he is himself pierced, wounded; he bleeds, suffers and dies. At the same time, however, [according to the canonical texts] he is a man whose closest associates are men, not women; who proclaims himself one with the Fa-ther, whose death is overcome by the erection of resurrection."[162] He "queers" our understanding of boundaries. Heschel uses recent queer theory to turn away from fictive binary views (Jew and Christian, male and female) to categories of overlap and confusion and inseparability. Gender is seen not as identifiable essence or even as social construction, but as performance.[163] Then what to make of Mary Magdalene? I let this question hang over the following chapters.

Outside a feminist framework, all this talk in the legends of love and whoring serves other purposes as well. Illusion or partial illusion is perpetuated by societies

---

158. Woolf, *Room*, 35–36.

159. T. Morrison, *Playing in the Dark: Whiteness and the Literary Imagination* (Cambridge: Harvard, 1992) x, 17. Blackness stimulates "notions of excessive, limitless love, anarchy, or routine dread." "Whiteness, alone, is mute, meaningless, unfathomable, pointless, frozen, veiled, curtained, dreaded, senseless, implacable. Or so our writers seem to say" (59).

160. I use this term also to express my sense that females are not naturally, innately, or essentially superior to males, although as a group women have different histories and have been socialized in different ways than men, which can carry valuable strengths.

161. E. Schüssler Fiorenza, *Jesus: Miriam's Child, Sophia's Prophet* (New York: Continuum, 1994) 14.

162. S. Heschel, "Jesus as Theological Transvestite," *Judaism Since Gender* (ed. M. Peskowitz and L. Levitt; New York: Routledge, 1997) 192. Her primary interest in this article is in how the transvestism of Jesus questions the constructs, and destabilizes the boundaries between Judaism and Christianity.

163. Heschel, "Jesus," 191.

that need and condone prostitution, blame and glamorize the individual victim, ignore the pimps and customers, hide systemic oppression, the spectrum of female sexual slavery, male dominance, abuse, the whole marketplace context.[164] (Slavery and prostitution, for example, were correlated in the Greco-Roman world,[165] as in sectors of our world.) Gail Pheterson argues that prostitution "functions much as a prism in deviating attention, decomposing understanding and deforming reality. An ultimate projection object from the outside, prostitution can be a privileged site of observation and analysis from within."[166] The Magdalene becomes from the twelfth century on associated with charitable activities directed at women. Her legends inspire hospices for old women, at-risk girls, other marginals; and reformatories, convents, and other institutions for her specialty — repentant prostitutes. They are objects of compassion and pity, but generally not accepted back into society. Even when viewed in secular terms, their sexual activity is still "sin" requiring penance. Mary Magdalene continues to represent and be represented by these women believed to menace society with diseases of the body, mind, spirit. They are punished but their clients are not.

The repentant whore who became a lover of Christ and a saint is needed in the church as the prostitute is needed in secular society of dominators and dominated. She was needed in the Reformation and post-Reformation periods as a symbol of sin and salvation to exemplify traditional Roman Catholic teachings on the use of images and the sacraments. The emphasis on Mary Magdalene's past life and her repentance in the cave, i.e., on the non-scriptural elements, was most useful as propaganda against Lutheran tenets and was used to uphold the idea of merit after the Council of Trent, when "the repentant sinner, voluptuous and weeping, came into her own."[167] The broad church context in which all this operates is that of male culture and hypermasculinity: valuing obedience to male authority, sexual control or chastity, hierarchy. It is a culture marked by misogyny, devaluation of sexuality, fear of homosexuality, ambivalent attitudes toward the body, the split between body and soul. A sinful, fallen condition is projected on women, making the prostitute, represented by Mary Magdalene, the archetypal sinner unless she chooses to be saved by divine grace. As Thistlethwaite and Brock remark, "Sin is not a concept adequate to explaining the condition of women and children who

---

164. S. B. Thistlethwaite and R. N. Brock (*Casting Stones: Prostitution and Liberation in Asia and the United States* [Minneapolis: Fortress, 1996]) expose and analyze multiple aspects of the sex industry. See also A. M. Jaggar, "Prostitution," *The Philosophy of Sex* (2nd revised ed.; ed. Alan Soble; Savage, Md.: Rowman and Littlefield, 1991) 259–80; J. Anthony, "Prostitution as 'Choice,'" *MS.* (January/February 1992) 86–87; J. Wells, *A Herstory of Prostitution in Western Europe* (Berkeley: Shameless Hussy, 1982); K. Barry, *Female Sexual Slavery* (Englewood Cliffs, N.J.: Prentice-Hall, 1979); *Sex Work: Writings by Women in the Sex Industry* (ed. F. Delacoste and P. Alexander; Pittsburgh: Cleis, 1987).

165. See J. A. Glancy, "Prostitution as a Barrier to Slaves' Participation in Pauline Churches," *JBL* 117 (1998) 481–501; A. Rouselle, *Porneia: On Desire and the Body in Antiquity* (Oxford: Blackwell, 1988) 94.

166. G. Pheterson, *The Prostitution Prism* (Amsterdam: Amsterdam University Press, 1996) 7.

167. Haskins, *Mary Magdalen*, 251.

are exploited sexually."[168] In this inadequate concept, and its companion, repentance, the Magdalene and those who symbolize her are imprisoned. Repentant, hers is "a restored female sexuality... that is not threatening to masculinity: a femininity that does not assert its own desires."[169]

As real prostitutes were offered the paternalistic help of the church, under the leadership of men who created/promoted/acquiesced in the ideology of lustful male and tempting female, the Magdalene in the imagination of the church was offered the paternalistic help of Jesus. In the early legends, he is immune to her temptations, leaving her alone with her body and her memories. Whether the identification of Mary Magdalene and the "sinner" of Luke 7 was beneficial to real prostitutes over the centuries is an important question that cannot be answered easily. On the one hand, the legend illustrates the belief that prostitution is an undesirable life from which it is possible to turn, and the truth that prostitutes are loveable persons capable of greatness. Who knows to what extent the legend inspired people to try to help women out of "the life," and who knows to what extent these efforts, flawed as they were and are, actually empowered and empower some. On the other hand, this aspect of the legend (which undercut the apostolic authority of Mary Magdalene) underplays the moral agency and survival skill of the Magdalene and those she represents, emphasizing instead the power of Jesus and his forgiveness. Splitting off sexuality from spirituality, it made the prostitute the sinner par excellence. Ignored are all the dynamics of the sex industry in peace and in war, the processes of scapegoating, controlling and abuse, the economic conditions and gender stereotypes that make prostitution a reasonable choice for some women. The complex interaction between victimization and initiative of the prostitute is also ignored. Every woman — transgressive or not — is vulnerable to the whore stigma which the prostitute embodies, but especially women "who show too much, say too much, know too much, and do too much. Too much of anything is unchaste for women."[170] Demonizing whores blurs the social reality that wives and whores can be seen as "the respective legitimized and illegitimized prototypes of a common female condition."[171]

We need to view the developing Magdalene legends in the contexts of the toleration of prostitution in the twelfth century, its institutionalization in the fourteenth and fifteenth, and its condemnation in the sixteenth[172] and beyond,

---

168. Thistlethwaite and Brock, *Casting Stones*, 18, 236.

169. See J. A. Glancy, "Unveiling Masculinity: The Construction of Gender in Mark 6:17–29," *Biblical Interpretation* 2 (1994) 49.

170. Pheterson, *Prism*, 84. Some may be more vulnerable than others on the basis of their group identity, personal appearance or history of abuse: women of color, working class women, divorced women, fat women, battered women (67).

171. Pheterson, *Prism*, 55.

172. See L. L. Otis attempts to explain these changes in *Prostitution in Medieval Society: The History of an Urban Institution in Languedoc* (Chicago: University of Chicago, 1985) 100–113. See also N. Orme, "The Reformation and the Red Light," *History Today* 37 (1987) 36–41; L. Roper, "Discipline and Respectability: Prostitution and the Reformation in Augsburg," *History Workshop* 19 (1985)

and its reexamination/rehabilitation by some in the twentieth and twenty-first who call for the abolition of prostitution or for prostitutes' political rights. For modern feminism the very concept of prostitute has meaning only within the ideology of male sexual domination and is produced by this system of sexual values. "Men have created the group, the type, the concept, the epithet, the insult, the industry, the trade, the commodity, the reality of woman as whore."[173] The "oldest profession" is accepted as an inevitable aspect of patriarchal society: the whore's sexual services to married or unmarried men maintain an illusion of monogamy or even polygamy, the myth of the male's greater sexual needs, and the possibility of fulfilling these needs without violating another male's "rights" to his wife. The professional prostitute may have no husband, no sexual obligation to any other male. She has no protection; she is vulnerable and out of bounds. Reduced to her sexuality, she is experienced as dangerous to those men who want to and do resist her temptation, and who don't. Blamed for provoking their sexual desire, enflaming their lust, she is often the target of male sexual aggression and hostility, moral outrage and condemnation. The prostitute is seen in this context primarily as victimized (listening to former prostitutes' description of their experiences in organizations such as Whisper); but she is also sometimes seen as an entrepreneur, with a right to her form of sexual freedom (listening to women in organizations such as Coyote).[174] The prostitute is viewed today with ambivalence and discomfort, probably in part because of the realization that "male domination of the female body is the basic material reality of [all] women's lives," and all struggle for dignity and self-determination is rooted in the struggle for actual control of one's body. A sexist interpretation of this solidarity distinguishes the prostitute from other women not in kind but by degree.[175]

Only a prostitute's commentary on the legends, seen "from the vantage point of branded women" and from the vantage point of solidarity, would lay bare the mechanisms of injustice in the context of women's struggles for autonomy.[176] Thistlethwaite has heard repeatedly from women who work for or are

---

3–28; M. E. Perry, "Deviant Insiders: Legalized Prostitutes and Consciousness of Women in Early Modern Seville," *Comparative Studies in Society and History* 27 (1985) 138–58.

173. See A. Dworkin, *Pornography* (New York: Perigee, 1979) 200, 9.

174. M. St. James is founder of COYOTE (Call Off Your Tired Old Ethics), and E. Giobbe founder of WHISPER (Women Hurt In Systems of Prostitution Engaged in Revolt). These organizations, with Prostitutes Anonymous, are three different and contradictory prostitute discourses, discussed by S. Bell, *Reading, Writing and Rewriting the Prostitute Body* (Bloomington: Indiana University Press, 1994). All three agree that prostitution is problematic, and all three support the struggle of women to control their own bodies. See also K. Peterson-Iyer, "Prostitution: A Feminist Ethical Analysis," *JFSR* (1998) 19–44.

175. See Dworkin, *Pornography*, 203.

176. Pheterson, *Prism*, 7. Pheterson herself has worked with the prostitute activist Margo St. James and others, to make that vantage point clear, founding and directing the International Committee for Prostitutes Rights, and chairing the First and Second World Whores' Congress.

clients of Chicago's Genesis House that "prostitutes themselves identify with Mary Magdalene and find her supposed closeness to Jesus a source of empowerment."[177]

The life in art of the legendary Magdalene, and the visual language used to describe her is richly varied. She is *vanitas*, a gaunt ascetic maenad, a voluptuous penitent reading in her cave,[178] a Venus, a pitiful woman contemplating death, a weeper, a masochist who has turned against her own body, a figure melded to the crucified Jesus. Sometimes she is hideous, anorexic and haunted, more often beautiful, sensual. Almost always through the thirteenth to the nineteenth century she is nude or partially nude. "The exposed breast alone is a complex symbol."[179] Often it signals the Magdalene's seductiveness, "a 'pathological' sexual interest lurking in the background" of her sanctity, her love of God; her inability to attain a pure, disinterested contemplation.[180] An object of legitimized voyeurism, Mary Magdalene's eroticism could express pious emotionalism, or pious pornography, or secular pornography.

One of the most striking images in Haskins' book, the one I think of most often, belongs in the last category. It is the photograph made in the 1864 of Hannah Cullwick posed as the Magdalene, now in the collection of Trinity College Library, Cambridge. There was a long tradition going back to the eighteenth century of men having their mistresses or wives or illegitimate daughters, royal beauties or unknowns painted in this fashion. Hannah Cullwick (1833–1909), born and raised in Shropshire, "entered service" when she was eight years old, ending her three years of education at a Charity School. In her late teens she was orphaned and moved to London, and became a "maid of all work," mostly dirty work as she could not keep herself clean enough to be on call to serve food. She was the secret mistress (if that is the right word) of Arthur Munby, a London lawyer and writer (who married her in 1873, keeping this cross-class marriage a secret). He arranged sessions in which James Stodart photographed her as different types of working women, e.g., half naked as a chimney sweep with Munby towering over her. Munby saw in Hannah "a noble and gentle woman" to be raised to "spiritual beauty" by "toil and servile labor." Redemption, he thought, was through "voluntary debasement." Watching Stodart push Hannah into position or rub dirt on her roughly to achieve greater realism, Munby observed that "she obeyed him as a thing of course, and [I] saw him blacken and besmear her.... It made my

177. For some of the foregoing analysis, see Thistlethwaite and Brock, *Casting Stones*, 236, 239, and n. 5, p. 357. Los Angeles has a Mary Magdalene House, Phoenix a Dignity House.

178. On the variety of other messages conveyed in different periods by the Magdalene reading, see Apostolos-Cappadona, "When the Magdalene Reads."

179. Haskins, *Mary Magdalen*, 244. Even dressed, the Magdalene is naked: "Her chestnut-brown hair curls in rings / And covers her back, strong, almost virile, / Rests on her shoulder, on a dark-blue dress / Under which her nakedness phosphoresces" (C. Milosz, "Mary Magdalene and I," *New Yorker* February 23, 1987, 40. She is also silent, with "A voice that is low, husky, as if hoarse. / But she will say nothing."

180. See S. Žižek, *The Metastases of Enjoyment* (London: Verso, 1994) 138, on the thought of O. Weininger, that woman is entirely dominated by sexuality.

blood tingle, but it made me bow in spirit more than ever, before *so divine an abnegation of self*" (emphasis mine).[181] Munby asked that she be photographed as the Magdalene wearing nothing but a white shift. Her diary — written at Munby's behest, and compiled and edited by him[182] — describes the session:

> I had to strip off my servant's things — to my shift, what I hardly liked, but still I knew there was no harm in that, & Mr S. was a serious sort o' man & we neither of us laugh'd or smil'd over it. He took me in a kneeling position as if I was praying with my hair down my back & looking up. The side face was good for it, but the *hands* was too big & coarse he said, so it wouldn't do as a picture. And so it's best for me to be done as a drudge what I am, for my hands & arms are tho' chief to *me*, to get my living with, & I don't care about my face if Massa [Munby] likes it. . . . When I was stripp'd for the Magdalene I was a little confused, having my steel chain & padlock around my neck, for Mr S. said, "Oh take that chain off." I said, "I canna sir." He said, "Is it lock'd?" I blush'd a bit as I said, "Yes, & I've not got the key." "Ah, there's some mystery about that," he said. And so it was done wi' the chain on. . . .[183]

In the photo Hannah's hair is stringy, her exposed breast flattened or sagging, her lips slightly parted, though she does not appear about to speak. Her hands and arms are just fine; they do look like they could do a day's work. Hannah also wore a leather strap on her right wrist, like a dog collar,[184] but it is not visible in this photo. Her expression is hard to read — it is not anger or disappointment, nor is it quite a kind of dazed patience, dullness, or disassociation. Reading several entries in her diary convinces me of her intelligence, though it was enslaved, not free. This enslaved intelligence must be what Munby saw as a divine abnegation of self. Hannah Cullwick here is looking at something or someone (is it Munby, with his blood tingling?) off to the side and above her, but not very tall. The chain looks like a necklace. There's no mystery about it.

I place beside this photo several I have taken of the pilgrimage points of the Magdalene legends ("What am I who deal with texts for a living . . . ?"). First, the photos of the cave La Sainte Baume. "Le pèlerin ou le visiteur devra, pour acceder à la grotte de la Madeleine, monter pendant plus d'une demi-heure à travers une forêt bien étrange et quelque peu 'inquiétante. . . . ' [L]a lumière pourtant

181. Thistlethwaite and Brock, *Casting Stones*, 107, quoting from Munby's diary; see A. Heath, *The Sexual Fix* (Basingstoke: Macmillan, 1982) n, p. 12–13; cited in *Body Matters* (ed. S. Scott and D. Morgan; London: Falmer, 1993) 91–92.

182. See *Munby, Man of Two Worlds: Life and Diaries of Arthur J. Munby* (ed. D. Hudson; London, 1972).

183. Hannah Cullwick's Diary, quoted in H. Dawkins, "The Diaries and Photographs of Hannah Cullwick," *Art History* 10 (1987) 180–81, cited by Haskins, *Mary Magdalen*, 346–47. The photo is on p. 347.

184. *Victorian Women: A Documentary Account of Women's Lives in Nineteenth-Century England, France and the United States* (ed. E. O. Hellerstein, et al.; Stanford: Stanford University Press, 1981) 350.

éclantante de la Provence ne pénètre pas."[185] Much more than a half-hour. The sign at the bottom commands: "Tenue décente exigée. Eviter les cris. Pensez à monter un vêtement chaud." The path is steep and rocky but well tended; the forest dense and silent. My companion on this expedition is the poet Madeleine Tiger, who has written a chapbook on Mary Magdalene.[186] Madeleine falls and gashes her leg badly. We climb on, the only climbers. We can see the site way above us, looming, dizzying, perched in the grey sheer rock. The Dominican monastery is more than 1,000 meters up, near the top. It is closed by the time we get there, but the monk on duty lets us in; he tells us there are only six monks living here, and takes us to the cave.

It is chilling. Beneath a rough stone altar lies a stone female statue, covered from the waist down with a clear plastic sheet. Around it kneel statues that are headless, armless, some also swathed. It is like I imagine the morgue, or the scene of a crime. Against the jagged, dripping, rough walls other nineteenth-century statues are arranged or not arranged: a Magdalene kneeling, a Magdalene reclining with one hand to her face, a crucifix with a Magdalene off to the side, a Magdalene lifted up by angels, a Virgin and child, the French king Louis XI; there are electrical wires about, and, strangely, lit tapers. Three garish stained-glass windows from 1978 and the 80s (the converted sinner; Jesus' meal at Martha's house; Noli me tangere) are not illuminated.

I know this place. It is my nightmare, women's fear, of utter isolation. It *is* the morgue, and the scene of a crime.

Higher up, too far, on the edge of the crest of Saint-Pilon — leave it for another trip — is some sort of shack, "où sept fois par jour, Marie Madeleine est elevée par les Anges." These are the lengths to which people went to try to banish her; and to find her. "And Creon said: 'I will take [Antigone] where the path is loneliest, and hide her, living, in a rocky vault.' And he shut her not in Holloway or in a concentration camp, but in a tomb."[187]

More photographs: 60 km from Ste. Baume, in Saint Maximin on the 21st of July the feast of Mary Magdalene is opened with an evening procession of her relics through the streets to the Dominican convent. We stand with tourists and townspeople in front of the grill in the unfinished Gothic basilica and look at the tobacco-colored skull encased in what resembles an astronaut's helmet or the helmet of someone engaged in some dangerous industrial work: gold hair, neck, shoulders, a plastic face shield. Something that looks like a piece of scalp with flat dreadlocks sits on top of the skull. The eye sockets are deep, the chin strong, the mouth slightly opened; all in all, very well preserved for what is said to be the skull of a first-century woman.

---

185. P. De Voncoux du Buysson, *La Sainte Baume haut-lieu de la Provence* (Marseilles: Editions PEC, 1992) 1.

186. *Mary of Migdal* (Galloway, N.J.: Still Waters Press, 1991).

187. Woolf, *Three Guineas*, 141.

This is — I assume — part of the skeleton, complete except for a leg, discovered in 1279 in a marble sarcophagus here in the crypt; the skeleton from which came forth a "fragrant scent," the skull from whose mouth a green plant was growing, fennel or palm. (But now no "green leaf of language comes twisting out of her mouth."[188]) This is the skull whose identity was attested to not only by scent and plant but by "an inscription so ancient that it could scarcely be deciphered 'even with help of a crystal,'" by a forged piece of parchment which dissolved to dust, by divine inspiration to Louis X's nephew Charles of Salerno, and by a barely legible Latin document, a cartellus, wrapped in wax, stating: "Here lies the body of the blessed Mary Magdalene."[189] And so the cult and the pilgrimages moved from Vézelay to St. Maximin, though valuable bits of bone and hair said to be hers were treasured in other locations as well. In a reliquary beneath the skull here in Saint Maximin is something maybe even more disgusting to modern sensibilities, a shred of skin or boney tissue which adhered to the frontal bone of Mary Magdalene "où le Sauveur avait posé ses doigts au matin de la Resurrection."[190] This is the "Noli (me tangere)," removed from the skull in 1789. (Calvin called it a piece of wax, "said to be the mark of a blow which our Savior gave her in anger when she wished to touch him."[191])

The Travel Section of the *New York Times* has described the crypt where the relics are usually kept, the nineteenth-century statue of the Magdalene reclining ("like an effigy of Shirley Temple doing penance for the sins of the flesh"), and the graffiti of names, initials, lovers' hearts, and horseshoe shaped drawings meant to resemble a cave. "[T]here was more than a vague whiff of the pagan, as though perhaps Mary had been as much the converted as the converter."[192]

For the procession, a gold face is snapped or screwed in place onto the helmet by men who clamber up onto the stand. Gladioli and marigolds and daisies in vases and lying on the steps, thrown through the grill, are moved aside. The skull and its helmet, with four gold angels holding it up, and a gold canopy above it, is shakily lifted on poles by seven burly men in T-shirts and sports shirts issuing orders to one another, sweating. We go out into the sunset, streets lit for a tiny carnival, one machine with little cars ready to spin tomorrow, past people who had been sitting in their doorways for hours. The crowd of maybe a hundred sings its way in ancient Provençal ("Madaleno, o bello Santo, / Que l'amour mene tant

188. Eilean Ni Chuilleanain, "Pygmalion's Image," *The Magdalene Sermon* (Loughcrew, Ireland: Gallery Press, 1989) 9.

189. Haskins, *Mary Magdalen*, 130–33. Saxer, *Culte*, 2.230–33, 350; L. Duchesne, *Fastes episcopaux de l'ancienne Gaulle* (Paris: Albert Fontemoing, 1907) 350–53.

190. M. Moncault, *La Basilique Sainte-Marie-Madeleine et le Couvent Royal Dominicain* (Aix-en-Provence: Edisud, 1985) 38.

191. J. Calvin, *Tractates and Treatises on the Reformation of the Church* (Grand Rapids: Eerdmans 1958) 1.330.

192. W. B. Logan, "Provence Pilgrimages, High and Low," *New York Times*, Sunday June 26, 1988, 14.

aut!") to the convent where nuns, young and old, greet the procession with litany
("Sainte Marie-Madeleine, Modèle de pénitence, priez pour nous.... Vous qui,
d'argile ténébreuse, etes devenue pur cristal, priez pour nous.... Marqué au front
par le contact de sa main glorieuse, priez pour nous") and sermon and socializing.
The "marvelous hoax"[193] is alive and well. A Fellini could document its vitality.

My last set of photographs is from Les Saintes Marie de-la-Mer, west of
Marseilles in the wetlands of the Camargue where the Rhone flows into the
Mediterranean. Mixed in with shots of the sparking sea and beach, of the spirited
white Camargue horses, flamingoes in flight, signs welcoming nomads, of "Valerie
acrobate et Salvi clown et musicien," a family of street performers riding a bike
that looks like a giant cocoon, and other Roma plying their trades, are photos of
the plaques and paintings. They are *ex votos,* thanking for favors. From the sixteenth century to the present, they have been hung in the twelfth-century church
in the town square. A man is squashed by a huge barrel, a man and woman kneel
in distress beside a cradle, a man is thrown by his horse, another attacked by a
dog, a woman tumbles from a tower, flails her arms in fire. Someone is in bed in
a room with mourners; someone falls through the floor, is hit by a falling tree.
And above it all, coming down from the sky, beaming in through windows, are
the Maries in their rudderless, oarless, sailless boat, coming to the rescue. Light
streams down modestly. Usually there are two, Marie Jacobe and Marie Salome,
but sometimes more, Marie Magdalene, and the sister of the first two, Mary the
mother of Jesus. They are very cute. Black Sara is not with them. The bones of
Marie Jacobe and Marie Salome are said to be in the little caskets hung high up
in the nave.

And in the basement crypt where three sets of bones were found in 1448,
the statue and casket of Sara, servant and/or companion of the "white" Maries,
or a gypsy herself who welcomed them to Provence: Kali Sara. She may be a
survival of Hinduism among the Roma, a powerful black goddess living in the
grotto underneath. Her face is like a little brown berry, on top of her voluminous
dresses and copes and capes. A small child lifts and peeks under the outermost
one as her mother whispers not to.[194] Beside Sara is a collection box for prayers
and notes to her, and below that some children's crutches and baby shoes. "Her
obscure origin authorizes the most diverse interpretations,"[195] which is as it should
be. The second century *Epistula Apostolorum* 10 lists Mary Magdalene, Martha and

193. Haskins, *Mary Magdalen,* 131.

194. Cf. C. Galland, *Longing for Darkness: Tara and the Black Madonna, a Ten-Year Journey* (New
York: Viking 1990) 178–79. She describes a family of Gypsies visiting the crypt, the man going up to
"St. Sara with a complete lack of self-consciousness, and as he must have done many times before—
the movement is so intimate, so familiar—he parts her elaborate robes and finds a way through her
dress to the statue underneath. She is suddenly flesh, the way he touches her underneath and gently
strokes her. Then he leans over closer, whispers something to her, kisses her on the lips, and steps
away."

195. A. Albaric, *Les Saintes Maries de-la-Mer* (Aigues-Mortes: Editions du Vent Large, 1993) 16.

Sara as those to whom the risen Jesus appeared near the sepulchre, and narrates how the resurrection message of all three was rebuffed. But Black Sara has had her own procession only since 1933, has been "authorized" to be venerated only since 1935. Never canonized by Rome, she is the beloved patron of the Roma who since the sixteenth century have come from all over the world to live here or to make the pilgrimage to their "sainte et amie."[196] Her casket is taken with her statue for the procession to the sea on May 25; the ceremony is repeated a week later for the "white" Marys. The Roma do not participate in this ceremony as they do for Sara.

To me, these photos above all are imaginative resources for the future: women partners working together, celebrated together, perhaps someday in procession together.

The legends of Mary Magdalene are deeply, deeply ambiguous. Her courage and loyalty are stressed at the crucifixion and tomb; but almost always rationalized and explained away as expressing (only) romantic love and gratitude. In some versions she preaches and teaches; but what she says — if anything is given her to say — simply repeats what men say. She becomes represented by and represents prostitutes; but both she and they are degraded and blamed, in a social context that goes virtually unanalyzed. In the Magdalene legends a woman independent of children, marriage and family is celebrated; but she winds up dramatically alone, punished forever for her autonomy. She is contemplative, spiritually talented; but the price for this is removal from human society. Her "morbid (and theologically incoherent) legend did . . . give rise to some splendid art."[197] Through her, female sexuality is sometimes presented as saucy, never quite tamed ("She does not become bland, restrained, or polite after her conversion, nor does she cut or cover her flaming hair"[198]). But the presentation is of male views only, with the sensual and the spiritual and the intellectual split apart. She is a failed attempt to meld these human dimensions, failed because she remains punishable by the memory of that from which she was "reformed." She represents something I can't quite see.

The prostitute Magdalene of legend occupies a place in the imagination difficult to understand, between Mary and Eve: between the virgin mother — asexual, morally pure, sacrificing, devoted to her son — and the temptress — sexual, morally weak, responsible for the fall of humanity. These two are culturally desirable to men, for obviously different purposes.[199] Mary Magdalene is like

---

196. Conversation with Pere Jean Morel, cure of Les Saintes Maries de-la-Mer (July 1994).

197. B. Shullenberger," Mary Magdalene: A Misunderstood 'Apostle,'" *The Living Church* (July, 1994) 8.

198. Miles, *Image as Insight*, 81.

199. V. Sapiro, *Women in American Society* (4th edition; Mountain View, Calif.: Mayfield, 1999) 118–19.

a bridge or a compromise between the two, or a blend of the two. Or is she some-thing totally different? She begins as an Eve, and in some ways remains always an Eve, deserving whatever bad consequences come her way. Then she also becomes saintly, asexual and sacrificing, but with no son. What cultural purposes does she serve to men who are celibate and those who are sexually active?[200] At once sexually available and not available, object of voyeuristic, pious prayer, she seems to embody love. Her legends bring us, however, "face to face with the intractable misogyny of Western culture, the fear and loathing for the unnamable — love."[201] The legendary Magdalene is a life sacrificed to that fear and loathing.

But the central aspect of the legend, the identification of the Magdalene as a whore, has untapped power. It is not only a slur to be scraped off the historical figure, but an "event" of interpretation — "exegetically untenable" though it was, a product of bad faith though it was. It invites pondering and reuse. Especially in the light of feminist analysis of prostitution and of the various voices of prostitutes themselves as they come to political speech today, it can be read as creating good confusion, an opportunity for subversion. When the divide and conquer policy no longer works, when the social control of women is demystified, when women listen to each other over great differences, and form alliances,[202] there are new powers, new questions. Not only What is a whore?[203] but also " 'What is chastity then?"[204] For Taslima Nasreen — condemned to death by Islamic fundamentalists in Bangladesh — the word "whore" is a "virile and fatal weapon. . . . If I evoke [it] here, it is to show [men] that we [women] know what strategies they use. And a strategy becomes ineffective when it loses all its mystery."[205] Unlike the Victorian ideal The Angel in the House, the prostitute in the street is a "woman men wished women to be." But no inkpots need be flung to kill her.[206] A reworked image of the Magdalene as prostitute can function as a mirror for women, and help us tell the truth about our own experiences as bodies.[207] It can also raise

200. Brodsky reasons: Pasternack "was a man, and his love had always been addressed to women. Therefore, he could not experience Christ's death on the cross as a personal loss — that is, not until he assumed Magdalene's role" ("A hidden duet," 16)

201. A. Vlasopolos, "Venus Live! Re-membering Sarah Bartman in Late-19th-Century Fashions and Late-20th-Century Reflections," paper given at the Interdisciplinary Nineteenth-Century Studies Conference, Ohio State University Press, April 1999.

202. See Pheterson, *Prism*, Appendix B, p. 132 on the Alliance between Whores, Wives and Dykes, a proposal for a work group to demystify and eliminate the division of women into bad, good and perverse.

203. Bell (*Reading, Writing*, 136) calls "prostitute" an ambiguous identity containing partially actualized possibilities in a negative reality.

204. V. Woolf, "A Society," *Monday or Tuesday* (New York: Harcourt Brace & Co., 1921) 25.

205. T. Nasreen, *Femmes, Manifestez-Vous* (Paris: Des Femmes, 1994) 65–67, quoted by Pheterson, *Prism*, 13.

206. V. Woolf, "Professions for Women," *The Death of the Moth and Other Essays* (New York: Harcourt Brace & Co, 1942) 236–38.

207. Woolf, "Professions," 241: "These were two of the adventures of my professional life. The first — killing the Angel in the House — I think I solved. She died. But the second, telling the truth

the question why any population of women should be "assigned to take all the ugliness to protect the rest of us."[208]

Shannon Bell argues that performance art is an excellent contemporary medium for the presentation of the individual lives of prostitutes. The overriding theme in the six artists' works she examines — among them, the work of Annie Sprinkle and Scarlet Harlot — is "the reunification of the sacred and the obscene in the same female body."[209] In Detroit, performance artist and poet Janet Young Webster has created the ongoing "Witness Project," to remember eleven black women found strangled in this city and in Highland Park throughout 1991–92. The project involved the writing of poetry and the placing of handprints in the terrifying locations in which the women's bodies were found: crammed upside down in shower stalls in the abandoned Monterey Motel, or flung onto box springs and piles of garbage in empty rooms of vacant buildings along Woodward Avenue. These women were poor, and said to be addicted to crack, with histories of prostitution. "They're still human beings. They deserved to live," said a member of the jury that convicted Benjamin Atkins of the crimes. Atkins, who was "abandoned at age 2, raped from the age of 10 on, and forced to watch his mother turn tricks in the front seat of a car," was sentenced to life. "Society cannot be blamed for these deaths, but he should have gotten help," said another juror.[210] The Witness Project involves also an outdoor art and writing called "Soul," about a fourteen-year-old girl's sexual abuse and about the power of beauty to restore the self to wholeness. Young writes, "The story is recreated in the public domain to create an opening through which the community can begin to take responsibility for what happens within our common human culture."[211] In the context of this art, a surreal and frightening dimension, a serious dimension, of the Magdalene legends is highlighted. By means of attention to realities such as these from Detroit, we might get beneath the pious to what is glossed over, denied, trivialized.[212]

The continuing value of her legends and art is due as well to the depiction of an exuberant and irrepressible female sexuality, of a transcendent and spiritual dimension of the beauty of the body. She is the only official saint — "a very

about my own experiences as a body, I do not think I solved. I doubt that any woman has solved it yet."

208. Question poignantly raised in the National Film Board of Canada's video on the pornography industry, "Not a Love Story."

209. Bell, *Reading, Writing,* 137.

210. J. Wilson, "Atkins convicted of killing 11 Women," *Detroit Free Press,* April 22, 1994, 1A, 6A. The women were Debbie Ann Friday, Bertha Jean Mason, Patricia Cannon George, Vickie Truelove, Valerie Chalk, Juanita Hardy, unknown female, Brenda Mitchell, Vicki Beasley-Brown, Joanne O'Rourke, Ocinena Waymer. A twelfth woman, Darlene Saunders, was raped and survived.

211. Janet Young Webster, performance notes. The Center for Impact Research reports on prostitution of women and girls in metropolitan Chicago: http://www.impactresearch.org

212. See A. Bach, "Reading the Body Politic: Women and Violence in Judges 21," *Biblical Interpretation* 6 (1998) 16–17: on the reader's feeling of an emotional connection between the virgins of Shiloh and the Muslim women of Bosnia.

physical saint" — who represents that, however distorted, costly and punished it is. Her emotional range is enormous. "Bitter tears . . . she often sheds, but she evidently knows love and fury, spiritual transport, thoughtful concentration, great dignity, and deep anxiety." "I believe . . . ," writes Hollander, "that the sinful, colorful, mythical Mary still has good work to do. . . . I wouldn't want to do without the ambivalence she represents. . . . [W]hat we get from her composite image is a more realistic picture of human female experience than was ever intended."[213]

That work may be more than representing ambivalence. Two of the movies mentioned above give us images of a Magdalene moving into the future. They are worth a closer look as a bridge to discussions in the next chapter. The more recent film *Jesus of Montreal* depicts the Magdalene character (named Mireille, played by Catherine Wilkening) encouraging Jesus and the others when they meet opposition ("What's with you guys? You can't let it get to you. You saved me; you can't let me down. What we have here is precious. We have to keep going"). In a subsequent temptation scene parallel to the temptations offered earlier to the actor Daniel Coulombe who plays Jesus, the actors playing disciples are approached with a marketing idea: to found a theatre company in the name of the dead and now famous Coulombe, with the one who plays Peter as the founding president. Two of them insist that they could continue as a troupe only if they remain faithful to Coulombe's ideas, and if this is not to be a commercial mainstream theatre. The show biz lawyer agrees this can be done, "Yes, and turn a profit." Mireille quietly says, "Excuse me." The camera follows her as she calmly walks out of the negotiations and up a stairway. Sandwiched between this scene and the one in which Mireille last appears, a woman who has received the transplanted corneas of Coulombe opens her eyes and the doctor asks, "How many fingers?" She sees.

Mireille walks alone and silent in the dark outside on the church terrace above Montreal, the city lights below her. The camera follows her as she closes her eyes and leans on a railing, turning her back to the camera and the audience. The movie's final scene is a return to the subway platform where Coulombe fell dying. Two women sing Pergolesi's "Stabat Mater" (for money?) to music from a boom box. Looming over them is a poster of another actor, who played a suicide to great applause in the opening segment. These women are not, I think, the two actors of the original troupe, but the women seen in a choir early on in the film, and later at the beer commercial tryouts. An escalator rises and descends against a black wall.

Arcand's layering of past and present, acting and reality, expresses his deep and pessimistic criticism of the corporate business world, the word of buying and selling, talk shows and inane, sentimental superficiality, enthusiasms and fads.

---

213. A. Hollander, "Woman of Extremes," review of Haskins, *Mary Magdalen* in the *New Yorker* (1994) 113, 117.

He offers deep and pessimistic criticism of clerical culture as well, as part of that business world. The main priest in the film, Raymond Leclerc, almost belongs to the troupe. He is having an affair with the other woman actor ("It gives him so much pleasure and me so little pain," she says). Invited to join them, he declines. He is paralyzed with fear of having nothing, of winding up either as chaplain to a nursing home in Winnepeg or like his "pitiful" friends who have left the priesthood. "Even a bad priest is still a priest. If I'm not that, I'm nothing." He's "too old to learn," so he sends his lover away. The official church in this film is afraid of Jesus, afraid of the modernization of his story, afraid of scholars. It demands restrictions, modifications, the old script, comfort. Arcand is saying that the real community, the real church, is elsewhere. Or at least it tries to be elsewhere, was for a time elsewhere, might be somewhere again.

How we read the visually interesting final scene in the subway station determines our view of Arcand's Magdalene. What does the viewer make of the two women with the boom box? Are they a new idealistic troupe, or promoters of the compromised the theatre company? In the end Mireille may be the only one who understands. Or she may not be the only one.[214]

The Magdalene from Zeffirelli's *Jesus of Nazareth* lingers differently in my mind and imagination. For his former prostitute Zeffirelli chose Anne Bancroft, an intelligent actress with a short fuse. It is casting that backfires, I think, if Zeffirelli wanted his regular ending as filmed to be powerful. Or perhaps there is miswriting here, or misdirecting, or (I like to think) subversive acting. Mary Magdalene's final scene begins with a knock and ends with a door banging shut. It contains the Magdalene's only self-defense — as far as I know — in the history of interpretation. When she is disbelieved in Luke 24:11 and Markan Appendix 16:11, there is no defense. In the gnostic literature, Jesus or Levi defends her. Here she comes to the hiding disciples and they sit around her as she narrates how she has "seen the Lord." They are silent, then embarrassed, evasive. She turns to John as the one who will surely believe her, but he does not. Mary Magdalene and John face to face are in a power struggle; the lighting is harsh, suddenly overexposed; she is old, washed out by the light, wrinkled.[215] He tells her she's tired: "Please, please go." As she gives up and moves angrily toward the door, one of them mutters, "women's fantasies." Here the anger of the Bancroft Magdalene comes to a healthy head. Medusa-like, she glares with contempt on the disciples and turns around the movie game of gazing. She growls, "Was his death a fantasy? . . . Why

---

214. The assessment of Stern, Jefford and DeBona is negative, and does not link them with Mireille: "Their presence in these several scenes mimics the journey of faith that many have taken, from participation in organized religion to the surrender to more immediate gratification to an amorphous faith in either some guru or simply faith in faith, faith in anything" (*Savior*, 319).

215. Barbara Hershey commented on the months of delay in making *The Last Temptation*: "My inner fear was that I might someday be too old to play Mary Magdalene" (M. P. Kelly, *Martin Scorsese: A Journey* [New York: Thunder's Mouth, 1991] 205).

should he not appear to me? . . . [then coldly] He told me to tell you, and I have done so." This is also the only instance I know of the Magdalene's anger.

She flings back the bar of the door, and slams out. The door slowly springs back open. The doorway is empty. The movie, however, is not over. It proceeds to its ending in an all-male world where the viewer is supposed to follow. First we have discussion about who among the disciples believes and who doesn't. Eventually it becomes clear that Peter believes ("because he [Jesus] said so"). "I have always believed," he says.[216] Talk turns to forgiveness, and Peter speaks of a "we" that excludes the women: a we who are all cowards, all betrayed, all abandoned. But "we" are all forgiven. The viewer is supposed to be drawn into that "we" by Peter's direct look at the camera.

The Magdalene's message about an empty tomb is disappearing under the weight of Peter's belief. Her meaning is reduced again to forgiveness, and even that appropriated, blotted out, by the character of Peter.

Big deal: he's forgiven, we're all forgiven, and the Magdalene is gone. Her function has been to bring a message to the men who matter. She confronts, she leaves; they appropriate her belief; they go on. It's not like she left an outfit she was a part of. No one has asked her to stay; no one goes after her; her absence isn't mourned; no one in the story gives her a thought when she's gone. Domination of her is easy dismissal, the culmination (just as violent and crude, but smoother) of the rejections of her in earlier scenes. She was a woman who knew too much.[217]

In the final moments of the film, Jesus comes to the disciples; they gather around him and are sent out to make disciples. Visually echoing the scene in which the Bancroft Magdalene attempts to teach (Jesus has become her, become a woman), he teaches. I am with you always, blah, blah, blah. The power of the Magdalene's last scene and the empty door, for me as a viewer, has drained all power from these all-male scenes that follow it. It makes them look hokier than usual, even more false. It de-ends the ending. The film cannot end on the note it seems intended to end on, of firm resolution which would enable the spectator to put it out of her/his mind. In spite of Peter's attempt to pull us in, the resistant viewer has been long gone, out the door with the Magdalene.

Where does she go? into pre-Christian, and/or post-Christian space. At the cross she joined a family with the other women; is she alone again now, or in the potentially subversive world of female bonding? There has been a glimpse in this film of female self-empowerment and female bonding — and most importantly, more than a glimpse of female anger. The female spectator has been allowed to feel anger. The ideal viewer, the viewer the film tries to create, is not meant to follow the Magdalene in imagination out the door. But the powerful absence she

---

216. Contrast the view of G. E. Forshey, *American Religious and Biblical Spectaculars* (Westport, Conn.: Praeger, 1992) 167: Peter believes *her* because Jesus predicted it.

217. See T. Modleski, *The Women Who Knew Too Much: Hitchcock and Feminist Theory* (New York: Methuen, 1988).

leaves in the final scene lingers in the memory of the resistant spectator. Mary Magdalene has made her exodus, her escape. Angry, in Zeffirelli's version; sadly, in Arcand's.

The patriarchal/kyriarchal structure is not "cleanly sealed," to use theatre critic Jill Dolan's phrase.[218] "Patriarchal texts," says Cheryl Exum, "can neither fully nor successfully ignore or suppress women's experience."[219] And, as Regina Schwartz put is, it is empowering to acknowledge that "victimization is inherently unstable, that the foundations of patriarchy are everywhere not only cracked but ruptured."[220] Even in films based on her legend, the Magdalene is a focalizer of the experience of early Christian women. And her absence in the open, empty doorway is a focalizer of the experience of many women and men with patriarchal religions. I read the doorway as leaving open the possibility not that she will come back, but that the men can get out.[221] It is the exit to a tomb that is not (yet) empty. The resistant viewer wonders: what is she doing out there? As the movie moves on, we move out.

To ponder the sadness, yes, but most importantly the anger and its relation to creativity and authority. "Anger had snatched my pencil while I dreamt. But what was anger doing there? Interest, confusion, amusement, boredom — all these emotions I could trace and name as they succeeded each other throughout the morning. Had anger, the black snake, been lurking among them? Yes, said the sketch, anger had. . . . I had been angry because [the professor] was angry. Yet it seemed absurd, I thought, turning over the evening paper, that a man with all this power should be angry. Or is anger, I wondered, somehow, the familiar, the attendant sprite on power? Rich people, for example, are often angry because they suspect that the poor want to seize their wealth. The professors, or patriarchs, as it might be more accurate to call them, might be angry for that reason partly, but partly for one that lies a little less obviously on the surface. Possibly they were not 'angry' at all; often, indeed, they were admiring, devoted, exemplary in the relations of private life. Possibly when the Professor insisted a little too emphatically upon the inferiority of women, he was concerned not with their inferiority, but with his own superiority."[222]

Woolf carefully analyzed the source of her own anger. She knew how often the anger heaped on us women from above is deflected to those below. She learned to direct it at the enemy, and spit it out. She was able to harness its creative energy and make it incandescent, without letting it become preaching, without

218. J. Dolan, *The Feminist Spectator as Critic* (Ann Arbor: University of Michigan, 1988) 201.
219. C. Exum, *Fragmented Women: Feminist (Sub)versions of Biblical Narratives* (Valley Forge, Pa.: Trinity Press International, 1993) 201.
220. R. Schwartz, "Rethinking Voyeurism and Patriarchy: The Case of *Paradise Lost*," *Representations* 34 (1991) 86.
221. Thanks to Norman Gottwald and Alice Bach for their questions about this symbolism.
222. Woolf, *Room*, 31–32, 34–35.

worrying about upsetting or shocking men. She urged women to overcome their fear of anger and let it out, so that every generation need not relearn to express it and relearn the hostility it provokes. "When she urges us to fight tooth and nail for power in our professions she also urges us to keep a sense of humor and offers fantasies to make us laugh. . . . Woolf's idea of healthy anger is 'a separable spite,' separable from the attempt to live a joyful life. . . . [I]t was anger that impelled her art, and intellect that combed out the snarls, dissolved the blood clots and unclogged the drains of that great sewer of the imagination, anger."[223] Anger about injustice and oppression becomes a political act, the Outsider's act of insubordination, "the expression of an ethical or moral stance," and of a collective social consciousness.[224]

Mary Magdalene was not labeled whore or sinner in the gnostic materials we will examine in the next chapter, nor was her story conflated with those of other women. Instead, other traits of the Magdalene legends examined here — focus on her apostleship and speaking — have parallels and perhaps roots in gnostic memories. This other heritage has its own set of ambiguities and compromises, but it lived as an underground spring. The church "fathers" had second-hand knowledge of non-canonical traditions about Mary Magdalene. According to Hippolytus, the Naassenes passed down discourses of the Savior from James the brother of the Lord to her (*Ref.* 5.7.1). Origen, as we have seen, mentioned groups named after Miriamme and other women, Marcellina, Salome, and Martha (*Contra Celsum* 5.62). Epiphanius claimed to know about books attributed to Mary Magdalene, *Questions of Mary*, in which she is said to have received from the risen Savior secret teaching about interrupted intercourse and eating semen (*Panarion* 2.8.1–6).

It may be that we can even see in the "fathers" traces of second-hand knowledge of texts such as the *Gospel of Mary* and the *Gospel of Philip*. The homily once attributed to Odo of Cluny puts her on an equal footing with the male apostles. The author says "she removed doubt and incredulity of [the Lord's] Resurrection from their hearts," and calls her *apostolorum consors*[225] — partner of the apostles, or equal of the apostles. An anonymous Cistercian calls her the *ascensionis eius*

223. Marcus, "Art and Anger," 139.

224. Silver, "The Authority of Anger," 361–63. Silver quotes Heilbrun's reassessment of *Three Guineas*: "For many years I was made uncomfortable by [the angry tone of] *Three Guineas*, preferring the 'nicer' *Room* where Woolf never presses against the bounds of proper female behavior — where, it could seen, her art prevailed. I say this to my shame. What prevailed was not her art alone, but her fear (and mine) of arousing the patriarchy to disgust, or acting wholly apart from the 'script' assigned to women. . . . [Woolf's extraordinary action in *Three Guineas* was] "to search out a new creative vein, to allow one's anger to drive one to the discovery of new forms. This measures the terrible daring of Woolf's, and all the best, feminist writing: by its nature it opposes what we have learned from the great art of the patriarchy, that anger is inimical to creation" ("Virginia Woolf in Her Fifties," 236–53, esp. 241, 245; quoted by Silver, 266–67).

225. *Sermo II (In veneratione Sanctae Mariae Magdalenae)* PL 133, col 721, 714. Jansen, "Maria Magdalena," 61.

prophetessa: "She witnessed the ascension on the mountain."[226] Wipo of St. Gall's *Victimae paschali,* written in the eleventh century, contains a dialogue between Mary Magdalene and the male apostles: they ask her, "Tell us, Mary, what did you see on the way?" She answers "I saw the sepulchre of the living Christ and the glory of the risen one."[227] In a sermon the abbot Geoffrey of Vendome (d. 1132) remarked that Saint Peter denied what Mary Magdalene preached (*praedicavit*) about the Resurrection.[228] Or perhaps these things — her role as encourager and as *consors,* the link between her status as prophet and ascension, a question from the males to her, and opposition from Peter — are simply free-floating imaginative elements that occurred naturally and independently to many as they dramatized the Easter story.

In some of the gnostic materials we will examine, the anger of the male disciples flares up. The reader of the twenty-first century may experience anger too, over a heritage pushed outside.

---

226. Like John the Baptist, she was more than a prophet (PL 112, cols 1495, 1474–75. See Jansen, "Maria Magdalena," n. 41, p. 85 for the list of others who associate her with prophecy.

227. Jansen, "Maria Magdalena," n. 27, p. 84.

228. *Sermo 64 (in festo S. Mariae Magdalenae)* PL, 202, cols 273–74; Jansen, "Maria Magdalena," 61.

The Woman Who Understood (Too) Completely

The Gnostic/Apocryphal Mary Magdalene

"The future ... depends very much upon what extent men can be educated to stand free speech in women."
V. Woolf, notes for the original speech, "Professions for Women"[1]

Texts and Definitions

I N 1945, THIRTEEN CODICES were accidentally found by Muhammad 'Ali, a peasant digging for nitrates for fertilizer, near the town of Nag Hammadi in Upper Egypt. These contained fifty-two religious tractates[2] — Jewish, Christian and pagan — forty of them nowhere else preserved. Most of them expressed ideas formerly known only second-hand, through the harsh criticisms and ridicule of the heresiologists writing against their opponents. The codices had been hidden in a jar around 400 C.E., possibly to preserve them from Roman Christian "heresy" hunters (the "orthodox" monastery of St. Pachomius was nearby at Chenoboskia). The treatises are translations into Coptic[3] from originally Greek works, usually dated to the second century C.E., though the sources of some may be even earlier. In these texts, the ancient voices of some gnostics, on their own terms, are once more audible, partially, in texts that survived through historical accident. But as only two or three generations of scholars so far have worked on these texts in little more than fifty years,[4] and as the texts themselves are damaged, the study is in its infancy, and the voices are garbled. They are, however, revolutionizing the understanding of early Christianity.

---

1. V. Woolf, *Women and Writing* (ed. M. Barrett; New York: Harcourt, Brace, Jovanovich, 1979) 13. The future here means the future of fiction.
2. There are forty-five separate titles, as some are duplicates.
3. Coptic is the Egyptian language as it existed at the end of the second century C.E. (already containing many Greek loan words). It was written in a modified form of the Greek alphabet and with additional Greek loan words by Christian missionaries translating the Bible into Egyptian. T. O. Lambdin, *Introduction to Sahidic Coptic* (Macon: Mercer University Press, 1983) vii.
4. See *The Nag Hammadi Library after Fifty Years: Proceedings of the 1995 Society of Biblical Literature Commemoration* (ed. J. D. Turner and A. McGuire; Leiden: Brill, 1997).

Within the Nag Hammadi library, five texts give Mary Magdalene a startlingly prominent role, startlingly unlike the roles she plays in the legends and in the Christian Testament. These texts are the Gospel of Thomas, the Dialogue of the Savior, the First Apocalypse of James, the Gospel of Philip, and the Sophia of Jesus Christ.[5] They are not grouped together in a single codex. From what kind or kinds of Christianity did they come?

To call them gnostic is not to give much of an answer, because gnosticism is not a unified phenomenon, but extremely varied and complex.[6] Perhaps it is not a phenomenon at all. Clark provides a succinct and unsatisfactory definition, as it applies to Christianity: she calls gnosticism an umbrella term for a variety of sects and movements flourishing in the first four centuries C.E. "that offered to enlightened adherents escape from the evils of the natural world and the celestial tyrants who governed it."[7] (Note that this offer can be found also in Colossians and Ephesians and several other Christian Testament works or passages.) Escape in gnosticism is said to be by means of knowledge (*gnōsis*) rather than by faith or obedience to the law. (However, in some works gnosis seems to be a kind of faith and a kind of obedience.) This is knowledge of one's own divine, inner self, the perfect "man," whose origin and home are transcendent. (Not unlike Christian Testament notions of the corporate Human One [Son of Man], and the body of Christ, body of the church.) Dualism between spirit and the body/matter is sometimes grounded in or expressed by the belief that the cosmos was created not by the supreme God but by an inferior power or God; matter is sometimes considered destined to destruction. (Here there is no Christian Testament parallel, however, this belief does not appear in all the works designated gnostic.) Robinson writes of the sense of estrangement and despair of the world, affinity to a transcendent ideal order, yearning for ultimate liberation, and a radical lifestyle of withdrawal that mark the works in the Nag Hammadi Library — a stance "too radical to establish itself within the organized religions or philosophical schools of the day"[8] although it has much in common with apocalyptic and mystical strains in primitive Christianity and other religions and spiritualities. More than fifty years after the find, it is important to reexamine this description and ask what gnostic radicality and liberation entailed, if and how the ideal was linked with despair.

---

5. This last work had been known earlier as part of Papyrus Berolinensis 8502 (=BG) discovered in Egypt and purchased for the Berlin Museum in 1896, but not published until 1955.

6. For a discussion of gnosticism in general, see C. W. Hedrick, "Introduction: Nag Hammadi, Gnosticism, and Early Christianity — A Beginner's Guide," *Nag Hammadi, Gnosticism and Early Christianity* (ed. C. W. Hedrick and R. Hodson, Jr.; Peabody, Mass.: Hendrickson, 1986) 1–11.

7. E. A. Clark, *Ascetic Piety and Women's Faith* (Lewiston, N.Y.: Edwin Mellen, 1986) 33.

8. James M. Robinson, "Introduction," *The Nag Hammadi Library in English* (ed. J. M. Robinson; 3d ed.; San Francisco: Harper & Row, 1988=*NHL*) 1–2. "It is not an aggressive revolution that is intended, but rather a withdrawal from involvement in the contamination that destroys clarity of vision" (1).

Merkur warns that a definition of gnosticism in terms of its anticosmic, matter-rejecting dualism results in a different history than a definition in terms of its esoteric practice of visionary and unitive mysticism. The dualism was most important to Christian "heresy"-hunters, but can be seen as "an occasional extravagance," since "most gnostics have been content to adhere to Christian, Jewish or Muslim views of matter and the body."[9] What mattered more to the history of monotheistic religions of the West, he argues, was gnosticism's distinctive type of visionary experience, and its attempt to understand this neither as perception of objectively existing external realities (i.e., with mythological objectivity) nor as allegory or metaphoric presentation of abstract ideas (with allegorizing subjectivity), but paradoxically according the same reality to the world as to their visions.[10] The "occasional extravagance" of dualism may be part some of the texts examined in this chapter, and the mysticism may have become in some instances only or mainly a literary tradition used to deliver a teaching. But Merkur's insistence on their mystical content and context — experiential religious knowledge and thought — is crucial, in my opinion, for interpretation of the gnostic Magdalene traditions, and, as we will see in the next chapters, of the Christian Testament resurrection traditions.

The terms "gnosticism," "heresy," "marginal," "heterodoxy" and "orthodoxy," "central," "mainline," "traditional," "ecclesiastical" are all increasingly unsatisfactory to the scholar, implying as they do that the lines between various Christian groups were clear, and that it was clear to the neutral observer which groups were "truly" Christian and which were not, which were original and healthy, and which parasitical or viral. Further, the term "gnosticism" — even as an umbrella term — wrongly implies some sort of monolithic system or movement. It is so linked to the perceptions and polemics of the heresiologists, and so linked to vague cliches (like hatred of the body, and world rejection), that some scholars prefer not to use it.[11] Attridge can refer to "the phenomena once known as Gnosticism,"[12]

---

9. De Boer (*Mary Magdalene*, 92) speaks of the "specific characteristic of ancient gnosis [as] radical dualism, hostility towards matter. Modern gnosis [in contrast] is characterized by the notion of holism: everything is connected." But that interconnectedness, I would argue, is seen in ancient texts like the Gospel of Mary.

10. They were desiring to reconcile visionary and unitive experiences by affirming doctrinally the manifest contents of both. D. Merkur, *Gnosis* (Albany: SUNY Press, 1993) 113–15. "Ascensions could be understood as internal and transformative within human beings [before death], even though the ideas remained external and objectively given, due to their existence in the divine mind (*logos, nous,* and the like)" (126). A. DeConick in a number of works has explored early Christian disagreements over whether pre-mortem ascension and visionary experience were thought of as necessary to salvation (see, for example, "The Dialogue of the Savior and the Mystical Stayings of Jesus," VC 50 [1996] 178–99).

11. M. A. Williams, *Rethinking "Gnosticism": An Argument for Dismantling a Dubious Category* (Princeton: Princeton University Press, 1996); K. King, "Is There Such a Thing as Gnosticism?" paper given at the annual meeting of the Society of Biblical Literature, Washington, D.C., 1993, abstract in AAR/SBL Abstracts 1993, p. 176.

12. H. W. Attridge, "Gnosticism and Apocalypticism," paper delivered at the SBL Annual Meeting, 1998, 2.

like the Artist Formerly Known as Prince, who is now known as something else. However, in lieu of the present lack of better terms to refer to the Nag Hammadi material and material that may be related to it in distinctive ways, I will use gnosticism/gnostic here without quotation marks and without capitalization. I use these terms as problematic and provisional, and with the reservations that (1) all or even most of the elements of the above descriptions do not appear in every gnostic text; (2) gnostics were never a clear-cut group or sect or movement or religion;[13] (3) the relationship among the texts, grouped in this chapter because they mention Mary, is not at all clear. (4) Some of the texts — for example, the Gospel of Mary — are not gnostic according to anything but the widest use of the term: that is, they are gnostic only in that they seem to share an emphasis on the saving significance of experiential religious knowledge, *gnōsis*.[14] (5) Their relationship to the Christian Testament and its traditions is at present uncertain.

I will put the other terms in quotation marks to indicate the groups which came to dominate or be dominated, and to indicate at the same time that people from a variety of viewpoints were claiming authenticity for their teachings and their organizations, their understandings of gender and related practices. Jesus in the Coptic gnostic Apocalypse of Peter (from the end of the second century or beginning of the third) criticizes those who "cleave to the name of a dead man, thinking that (through this name) they will become pure.... Some do not know (the true) mysteries (and) speak about things which they do not understand. But they will pride themselves that the mystery of the truth is in their hands alone.... But there are others of those who are outside of your number, who are called "bishop" and "deacon," as if they had received authority from God. They recline (at table, and thus fall) under the judgment of the first places.[15] They are the canals without water" (74, 76, 79).[16] Fascinating here — in a work which describes Peter's vision of the crucifixion of Jesus (81) without mentioning the presence of women — is reference to a sisterhood that seen as a counterfeit of the brotherhood, and as oppressing the brothers (79). This sisterhood is charged with having a false understanding of the crucifixion and resurrection, recognizing only material reality. As the main opponents in the Apocalypse of Peter appear to

---

13. Contrast the continued use of the term by B. A. Pearson, "From Apocalyptic to Gnosis," unpublished paper delivered at the SBL Annual Meeting, 1998, 1–3, 9–10: he defines Gnosticism as "a religion" in its own right. Also Pearson, *The Emergence of the Christian Religion* (Harrisburg, Pa.: Trinity International, 1997) especially chapter 7. Williams, in contrast, thinks the texts are best understood as sources from a variety of religious movements; the category "gnosticism" (which seems to have originated in the eighteenth century) has to be dismantled and replaced (*Rethinking*, 5, 28).

14. See A. McGuire, "Women, Gender, and Gnosis in Gnostic Texts and Traditions," *Women and Christian Origins*, 258. Williams (*Rethinking*, 41–42) notes that gnostic as a self-designation meant intellectual.

15. Cf. Matt 23:6.

16. Cf. 2 Peter 2:17; Jer 15:18. Translation by A. Werner, "The Apocalypse of Peter," *New Testament Apocrypha* (=NTA) 2.706–8. My references to NTA are to the 1991/1992 edition unless otherwise noted.

be the bishops and deacons of the orthodox church,[17] attacking the "sisterhood" may be like scorning male football players as "girls." Or it may be scorn actually heaped on women and women's traditions. Werner[18] compares this text with the negative assessment of "female prophecy" in the Pseudo Clementines, especially Hom. III 23–25. "Proclaiming what pertains to the present world, female prophecy [Eve] desires to be considered male On this account she steals the seed of the male, envelops them with her own seed of the flesh and lets them — that is, her words — come forth as her own creations. . . . She not only ventures to speak and hear of many gods, but also believes that she herself will be deified; and because she hopes to become something that contradicts her nature, she destroys what she has. . . . Those who desire to get to know the truth from her, are led by many opposing and varied statements and hints to seek it perpetually without finding it, even unto death. for from the beginning a cause of death is certain for blind men; for she prophesies errors, ambiguities and obscurities, and thus deceives those who believe her."[19]

Before the Nag Hammadi find, several other ancient texts had already been discovered in the eighteenth, nineteenth, and early twentieth centuries that mention Mary Magdalene: the Pistis Sophia, Gospel of Peter, Gospel of Mary, Psalms of Heracleides, Epistula Apostolorum, Apostolic Church Order, Acts of Philip.[20] These works and others are listed and described in Appendix A. In the first years of their discoveries, many were treated somewhat casually, and without a full sense of their significance for the study of women in early Christianity. They can now be used to add to our knowledge of Mary Magdalene's non-patristic, non-canonical profiles. Surely there is more to come: more discoveries of what lies buried in libraries or in the ground, more reexamination of earlier discoveries, more discussion about what is classified as gnostic and what is not, about whether the classification is useful or not, what relationship these materials have to the canonical gospels, and how they expand and correct our understanding of early

---

17. F. Wisse, "Peter, Apocalypse of," *ABD* 5.269.

18. Werner, "Apocalypse of Peter," NTA 2. n. 30, p. 711. Cf. D. Hellholm, "The Mighty Minority of Gnostic Christians," *Mighty Minorities* (ed. D. Hellholm, H. Moxnes, T. K. Seim; Oslo: Scandinavian University Press, 1995) 42–66.

19. NTA 2.532–33.

20. The role of Mary in these and other texts discussed in this chapter is treated by F. Bovon ("Mary Magdalene's Paschal Privilege," *New Testament Traditions and Apocryphal Narratives* [Allison Park, Pa.: Pickwick, 1995] 147–57, 228–35; originally published in French in *NTS* 30 [1984] 50–62) and on a larger, more technical scale by A. Marjanen (*The Woman Jesus Loved: Mary Magdalene in the Nag Hammadi Library and Related Documents*, dissertation University of Helsinki, 1995; published with slight revisions as Nag Hammadi and Manichaean Studies 40 [Leiden: Brill, 1996]). Marjanen carefully points out errors made by Malvern and Haskins. See also de Boer, *Mary Magdalene*, a more popular book with some interesting insights. R. Atwood (*Mary Magdalene in the New Testament Gospels and Early Tradition* [Bern: Peter Lang, 1993] 186–204) treats two late texts not mentioned by Marjanen or Bovon, the Coptic Bartholomew text (Lacau IV) whose traditions may go back to the third or fourth centuries (NTA 1.555–56) and the mid-sixth-century Gospel according to Nicodemus 10; 11 (NTA 1.503).

Christianities.[21] The Nag Hammadi find, of course, throws new light on all these materials and makes them of much wider interest[22] and somewhat more coherent.

We have available now late-first (?), second, third and fourth century Mary Magdalene traditions and fragments of traditions very different from the ones discussed in the previous chapter, and very different from those in the Christian Testament. There is heavy drudgery involved in accessing and analyzing these materials, what Woolf called "donkey work," but it is energized by the excitement of dawning insights. We can hear gnostics and near-gnostics and others, and those who disagreed with them (or those critics who were imagined) talking about her, and giving voice to their ideas of her. What we hear changes the future.

The Name Mary

Her name is found in several forms, sometimes even within the same document. — Already in the Christian Testament two forms of the name Mary were found, Maria and Mariam. The first was preferred in milieux in contact with the Romans, then in Christian families; the second was popular in the Jewish milieux of Palestine and the Hellenistic diaspora. Both forms appear in epigraphic sources; the second is generally used in literary documents.

- Josephus uses the form Mariam(m)e especially for Miriam, Moses' sister.[23]
- In the Gospel of Thomas Mary is twice called Mariham, as in Pistis Sophia IV.
- In Pistis Sophia I–III she is usually called Maria, sometimes Mariham, and once Mary of Magdala (chap. 96).
- She is Mary Magdalene in the Gospel of Peter 12:50;
- Mariahamme in the Sophia of Jesus Christ;
- Mariamme in the Greek fragments of the Gospel of Mary.
- In the Dialogue of the Savior she is sometimes Marihamme, sometimes Mariham.[24]
- In the Manichaean Psalm Book she is called Marihama (the last letter is uncertain, according to Bovon) and Marihamme.
- In the Acts of Philip VIII she is Mariamne, Mariamme or Maria the Magdalene.[25]

---

21. For further discussion of introductory questions of dating, provenance, original language, manuscript variations, gnostic and non-gnostic characteristics, and so forth, see *NHL*, NTA, Marjanen, *The Woman*, and recent editions of the individual texts.

22. See Marjanen, *The Woman*, 3–4 on C. Schmidt's studies of Pistis Sophia (1892) and the Gospel of Mary (1896).

23. Bovon, "Paschal Privilege," n. 1, p. 228.

24. Bovon, "Paschal Privilege," 153 thinks this corresponds to the use of different sources. Contrast Marjanen, *The Woman*, n. 7, p. 65.

25. Hippolytus calls her Mariamme (so also Origen) and Mariamne (Bovon, "Paschal Privilege," 232).

Only in the Gospel of Philip, the Pistis Sophia, Gospel of Peter, and the Acts of Philip VIII, then, is Mary identified as Mary Magdalene, the Mary from Magdala. This fact, and the variant forms of the name, are puzzling, but do not mean different characters named Mary are always or often indistinguishable ("a universal Mary"[26]), nor that full conflation of characters has taken place,[27] nor probably even that we are dealing with different sources within individual documents. Most scholars (Marjanen, King, Bovon) hold that it is reasonably clear in most cases when Mary Magdalene is meant.[28] The gradual replacing of Mary Magdalene by Mary of Nazareth is documented by Brock[29] in Syriac literature especially, but it has not been accomplished in the works discussed in this chapter.[30] Silke Peterson argues that in many of these texts Mary Magdalene is identified by her appearance in conflicts over her being a woman, and her special relationship with Jesus and hidden knowledge. She represents resistance to gender subordination. Mary of Nazareth, on the other hand, represents that subordination.[31] I agree that a cluster of traits, or what I call a profile, indicates when Mary Magdalene is in mind.

Aspects of a Profile

It is clearly impossible here in the confines of one chapter to examine fully each of the texts mentioned above and to set about trying to identify trajectories or spirals about the ways that thinking about this figure developed or did not develop. But although the materials in which Mary Magdalene appears have distinctive and

---

26. "Perhaps the safest conclusion is that a 'universal Mary' is in mind, and that specific historical Marys are no longer clearly distinguished." M. W. Meyer, "Making Mary Male," *NTS* 31 (1985) 562, on the Gospel of Thomas. A. Pasquier views Mary in the Gospel of Mary as representing a corporate personality (J. K. Coyle, "Mary Magdalene in Manichaeism?" *Museon* 104 [1991] n. 20, p. 42, says she informed him that this was her reconsidered view).

27. S. J. Shoemaker, "Rethinking the 'Gnostic Mary': Mary of Nazareth and Mary of Magdala in Early Christian Literature," paper delivered at the SBL annual meeting 2000 in Nashville, argues that a conflation of figures or "universal Mary" is in mind in gnostic materials such as the Gospel of Philip and Pistis Sophia. Mary of Nazareth is part of the composite, as is clear in the Syriac Dormition and Assumption apocrypha from the end of the fifth century, which may depend on works as early as the second century. He does not, however, think the forms of the name show a distinction between these figures.

28. On Jesus' mother, her sister, and Mary Magdalene in the Gospel of Philip 59, 6–18, see below, pp. 132–33.

29. Ann Graham Brock, *Authority, Politics, and Gender in Early Christianity: Mary, Peter, and the Portrayal of Leadership*, dissertation Harvard University, 2000.

30. On the omission of "Magdalene": at John 20:1 OS sin, see R. E. Brown, *The Gospel according to John* (New York: Doubleday, 1970)) 2.981: from the time of Tatian's Diatessaron in the second century, there are traces of a tradition that Mary the mother of Jesus came to the tomb.

31. See S. Petersen, *"Zerstört die Werke der Weiblichkeit!" Maria Magdalena, Salome und Andere Jüngerinnen Jesu in Christlich-Gnostischen Schriften* (Leiden: Brill, 1999) 104. She holds that the tension implicit in the Christian Testament between protophany traditions (to Mary Magdalene or to Peter) could be a connecting point for the motif of direct conflict between them in the gnostic texts (98).

sometimes conflicting emphases,[32] it is possible to sketch an overarching profile. Precision is unattainable, even with regard to the individual works. The major texts have lacunae, others are only fragments, there are many serious translation difficulties, and next to nothing is known except by inference of the social situations of various gnostic groups and their interactions, their leadership conflicts, their gender ideologies, stereotypes and schemas.[33] The very attempt to sketch a profile is valuable, however, because the effort exposes the inconsistencies, blind spots, expectations, assumptions, weaknesses of each scholar. Through critique the conversation advances.

Bovon lists aspects that "various marginal circles of early Christianity" insisted upon "in turns": "(1) the virtue and purity of Mary Magdalene; (2) the affection of Jesus for this woman; (3) the first, immediate, and privileged contact she had with the resurrected Lord as a source of revelation; (4) the disciples' jealousy of this paschal privilege; (5) the responsibility given her to regroup the disciples and to send them out on mission; (6) the virile character, in the spiritual sense, of this chosen and cherished woman."[34] Marjanen, on the other hand, declares that "Common to all [the] Gnostic sources is the fact that they scarcely build on canonical Mary Magdalene traditions"[35] — including, I suppose him to mean, the "paschal privilege" (Bovon's 3 and 4). I see Marjanen's point, but think the question of "scarcely build[ing]" requires more analysis, as building may be subtle. He has not paid enough attention to the canonical material. Other points of Bovon's profile are also problematic: I find his (1) to be like a photographic negative: it is something that he sees because he is *not* seeing in the gnostic materials the "impurity" of the Western Magdalene legends. Actually, there seems to me to be here no issue at all about her "purity." And as for (5): it needs more distance from the language world being analyzed: what is "virile character, in the spiritual sense"? Further, Bovon has grouped his discussion of the non-canonical texts under the heading, "The Heretical Impulse," following discussion of the New Testament material under the heading "The First Witnesses and Official Disdain," a neat but anachronistic arrangement and (even if intended ironically)

---

32. Marjanen especially emphasizes this in *The Woman*. He insists that each writing must be studied separately before any general conclusions are drawn (25).

33. On gender schemas, see Virginia Valian, *Why So Slow? The Advancement of Women* (Cambridge, Mass.: MIT Press, 1998). They are implicit, or nonconscious, thus usually unarticulated, hypotheses about sex and gender differences, shared by men and women alike. They affect expectations, evaluations, and performance. "Their most important consequence for professional life is that men are consistently overrated, while women are underrated. Whatever emphasizes a man's gender gives him a small advantage, a plus mark. Whatever accentuates a woman's gender results in a small loss for her, a minus mark" (2). The term schema is a better, more inclusive term than stereotype. The content of gender schema, which she calls "nonconscious beliefs," may even be disavowed by those who explicitly and sincerely profess egalitarian beliefs. Gender schema grow by accumulation of advantage and disadvantage over time.

34. Bovon, "Paschal Privilege," 154.

35. Marjanen, *The Woman*, 20.

one that presupposes boundaries and definitions that can no longer be taken for granted.

My own attempt at a profile of the gnostic/apocryphal Mary Magdalene will be followed by sharper focus on one text, the Gospel of Mary — in which all the profile's aspects are found together. This will lead to discussion of the issues I think most significant and interesting for my particular study, and will entail some speculation about trajectories and spirals, especially those proposed by Bovon and Price.[36] The speculation — like the profile — is offered as tentative, provisional, and very likely inaccurate in some respects.

My profile has nine points: (1) Mary is prominent among the followers of Jesus; (2) she exists as a character, as a memory, in a textual world of androcentric language and patriarchal ideology;[37] (3) she speaks boldly; (4) she plays a leadership role vis-à-vis the male disciples; (5) she is a visionary; (6) she is praised for her superior understanding; (7) she is identified as the intimate companion of Jesus; (8) she is opposed by or in open conflict with one or more of the male disciples; (9) she is defended.[38] Several of my points (prominence, bold speech, leadership role, visionary experience [sometimes involving spiritual journey], and conflict) can be seen as characteristics of a prophet or an apocalyptic seer. But I have separated these components.

I have created the nine out of aspects that appear[39] in at least four texts. Only in one text, the Gospel of Mary, do we find all nine elements. The elements, moreover, have different values and meaning from text to text, when seen in the context of each work as a whole, and then when seen in the context of the codex in which a work may appear.[40] I do not see any evidence of intertextuality among them, nor evidence of any other literary or social connections. It is true that if we look at the Nag Hammadi tractates as somebody's holy texts, we might speak of his or her canonical portrait of Mary, drawn only from the five texts found there that mention her. As Robinson reminds us, we know almost nothing about the persons who translated, copied, used and buried (were buried with?) the Nag Hammadi tractates — except that they seem to have revered these writings.[41]

---

36. Bovon, "Paschal Privilege," and Price, "Mary Magdalene: Gnostic Apostle?" 54–76.

37. See H. W. Attridge, "Gnosticism and Apocalypticism," paper read at SBL annual meeting 1998.

38. Cf. K. King, "The Gospel of Mary Magdalene," *Searching the Scriptures*, 2.620. She writes of several "scenarios" concerning Mary that had become traditional by the second century: "her role as a preeminent disciple of Jesus, her privileged reception of special visions and teaching from the risen Lord, her role as comforter and teacher of the other disciples, and the conflict with the male disciples over the reliability of her testimony."

39. Sometimes, for example with regard to #7 (intimate companion) and the Manichaean Psalm Book II, the appearance depends on a debated interpretation, in this case of Mary as the Spirit of Wisdom.

40. Williams, *Rethinking*, 261 argues that each writing from Nag Hammadi "had its own function and could be interpreted in terms of that function in relation to other works within the codex."

41. Robinson, "Introduction," 13.

The Mary of Nag Hammadi and of my broader profile looks very unlike the Mary Magdalene of Western legend. In all the texts dealt with in this chapter her prominence is apparent. One might wonder at first glance if this is some sort of mid-to-late twentieth-century feminist hoax, based on apocryphae forged in and for our own times, the creation of a figure needed by one side in Christianity's current critical debates about gender and leadership. And in several of the texts, especially the Gospel of Thomas, the Gospel of Philip, the Gospel of Mary, and Pistis Sophia I–III and IV, male protests against Mary's importance and even presence are early, angry foreshadowings of current debates. Only the first two of these were found at Nag Hammadi.

Usually generalizations about the gnostic Magdalene are based on only three sources: the Gospel of Mary, the Pistis Sophia, and the Gospel of Philip. But in the following pages, I will comb and recomb through all the apocryphal Magdalene materials for examples of each point in my profile, taking time to explore important aspects. The profile in the Gospel of Mary will be treated last, as a whole. Extensive quotations from texts rather than summaries will, I hope, put the raw material into the hands of more readers. The diversity of ways in which the Magdalene appears under each point in the different documents will be readily apparent. No firm dating and hence no real chronological order can be established at this stage of research. What we hear is a chorus of voices whose different times (late first century to fourth century) and different places (Syria, Egypt, Palestine?) we cannot pinpoint; a chorus from still hidden speakers.[42]

1. Mary's Prominence

The category, prominence, arches over the other categories in this profile. It usually has to do with Mary being named as among the disciples, and with her being spoken to and/or speaking. It has also to do with the tasks she performs and with challenges to and complaints about her. It is not the same thing as leadership, or formal titles, or success or empowerment or ruling, though it is sometimes linked with these. In some of these works, she is prominently disparaged or diminished.

In the Gospel of Thomas, Mary is one of six disciples who are named, five of whom speak; the other speakers are Simon Peter, Matthew, Thomas and Salome. James the Just is designated by Jesus as the one to be "great over us"[43] after Jesus' departure (12). Thomas is the one to whom Jesus gave special secret teachings (13; cf. 108). He is seen by Perkins as "the model for those who have attained the goal of drinking from the wisdom that flows from Jesus. This person no longer needs teachers."[44] Mary is not depicted as a leader, or receiving special revela-

---

42. Translations of texts from Nag Hammadi are from *NHL* unless otherwise noted; if a work does not appear in the *NHL*, translations are from NTA unless otherwise noted.

43. Beate Blatz translation, NTA 1. NHL: "who is to be our leader?"

44. P. Perkins, "The Gospel of Thomas," *Searching the Scriptures*, 2.538. Thomas calls Jesus "Master," but Jesus replies "I am not your master, for you have drunk, you have become drunk from the

tion; her role is more modest. But as one who questions Jesus (21), she may be considered at least at this point a spokesperson for the entire group.[45] That she is indeed a member of the group — a community or a leadership echelon — is emphasized by Peter's desire that she be excommunicated, "leave us" (114; see below, under point 8).

In the Sophia of Jesus Christ 90, 17–19, Mary is the only woman named, of the seven who followed the Redeemer into Galilee after he rose from the dead. The seven are gathered with the twelve male disciples to hear him before his ascension. (Note that the time frame — after resurrection and before ascension — is the same in the Gospel of Mary and for her appearance in John 20.) She may represent these seven gnostic women.[46] Mary is also the only woman who asks Jesus questions; the four named males who ask are Philip, Matthew, Thomas and Bartholomew.

In the First Apocalypse of James 40, 22–26 (NHL translation and restoration by Schoedel) the Lord tells James, "when you speak these words of this [perception], encourage these [four]: Salome and Mariam [and Martha and Arsinoe . . .]."[47] Marjanen convincingly offers a different reading: instead of being told to encourage the women, James is told "When you speak these words of this [perception/knowledge], be persuaded by this [testimony/word of] Salome and Mary [and Martha and Ars]inoe. . . . " He thinks it is clear the text "is meant to read that James can learn something from Mary Magdalene and the other three women," considered as spiritual authorities who could provide guidance to James in the tasks entrusted to him.[48] These four women probably belong to the seven James asks the Lord about: "who are the [seven] women who have [been] your disciples? And behold all women bless you. I also am amazed how [powerless] vessels have become strong by a perception which is in them" (38, 16–23). In the context of this work's focus on the suffering of James and the Lord,[49] it is possible that the women's strength may have to do with their suffering, being

---

bubbling spring which I have caused to gush forth (?)." In logion 108 Jesus says, "He who will drink from my mouth will become like me. I myself shall become he, and the things that are hidden will be revealed to him" (NHL, Lambdin translation).

45. Marjanen, *The Woman*, 36.

46. Seven gnostic women are spoken of also in First Apocalypse of James 38, 16–18 (NHL Schoedel's reconstruction) and seven in the Manichaean Psalm Book II, 192, 21–24. In First Apocalypse of James 40, 22–26 (see below) four women are singled out and named. We get a full list of seven names in the gnostic literature only in the Manichaean Psalm Book (see below).

47. Cf. the Manichaean Psalm Book II 194, 19–22; 192, 21–24 where the same four are mentioned. In Pistis Sophia I–III, the four are Martha, Salome, Mary Magdalene and Mary the mother of Jesus.

48. Marjanen, *The Woman*, 115–16. His tasks are to answer before the three toll collectors during his ascent, to communicate the Lord's revelation to Addai, and to rebuke the twelve. The Naassenes are said to claim that their teaching came from James through Mary Magdalene (Hippolytus, *Ref.* 5,7,1).

49. The Lord says, however, "I am he who was within me. Never have I suffered in any way, nor have I been distressed" (31, 17–29).

reviled and persecuted (41, 22–23). Note that it is said James "heard of" the sufferings of Jesus and was much distressed; it is not said from whom he heard of the sufferings. With Judas (probably Judas Thomas) and Matthew, Mary questions Jesus in the Dialogue of the Savior. She also dialogues with her "brothers" (131, 19–21) about where they are "going to put [these things] about which you ask the son [. . . [50]]?" Calling her "Sister" (131,22–23), Jesus responds, speaking of putting them in the heart.

In the Gospel of Philip, Mary Magdalene, the "companion" of the Lord, is said to have "always walked with" him (59, 6–11) as did Mary his mother, and her sister, who may be called "his" sister in the next sentence: "His sister and his mother and his companion were each a Mary."[51] This reference to three women, perhaps three Marys, may be a rare allusion to the presence of women at the cross[52] or tomb. Cf. Mark 15:41; 16:1 where the three women are Mary Magdalene, Mary the mother of James and of Joses, and (however) Salome;[53] and John 19:25 where there are three or four women: Jesus' mother (unnamed in this Gospel), his mother's sister, Mary the wife of Clopas, and Mary Magdalene. This passage in the Gospel of Philip may be as well an allusion to the women following Jesus ("always") from Galilee. "Always" certainly implies steadfastness and loyalty, closeness to the Lord, and perhaps a contrast to the male disciples,[54] of whom only Philip and Levi are mentioned by name.

More is going on in this work, of course, than simply remembering historical women. The three Marys may also be seen as three manifestations of one person called Mary. If this is the case, it is a strange conflation, quite unlike the conflations found in the legendary Magdalene materials which basically serve to weaken and lower the figure of the Magdalene.[55] The Gospel of Philip's "elusive Mary," the three blurred and interchangeable personalities, is/are sometimes

50. B. Blatz in NTA 1.305 fills in the lacuna here with "of Man." Koester and Pagels in their introduction to this work in *NHL* (25) hold that "Son of Man" is a a title which the Dialogue of the Savior never uses of Jesus; it is used of a figure (angelic, say Koester and Pagels) who explains the apocalyptic vision in 134,24–137, 2.

51. See Epiphanius, *Pan.* 78.8,1; 78.9,6 for the tradition that one of Jesus' sisters was named Mary. Isenberg (*NHL*) thinks these are three Marys. Cf. the legends of the three Marys from Provence treated in the previous chapter.

52. It is also unique to find "My God, my God, why, O lord, have you forsaken me?" (Mark 15:34 par Matt) quoted in 68, 26–28.

53. Cf. Matt 27:58: Mary Magdalene, Mary the mother of James and Joseph, and the mother of the sons of Zebedee. Salome becomes Mary Salome by means of conflation with this text. See J.-É. Ménard, *L'Evangile selon Philippe* (Strasbourg: Université de Strasbourg, 1967) 150.

54. J. J. Buckley, " 'The Holy Spirit is a Double Name': Holy Spirit, Mary and Sophia in the Gospel of Philip," *Images of the Feminine in Gnosticism* (ed. K. King; Philadelphia: Fortress, 1988) 214.

55. Marjanen (*The Woman*, 138) comments that this Mary who plays three different roles in the Savior's life — his sister, his mother, his companion — is no historical person, but a mythical figure from the transcendent realm, manifesting herself in the women who accompanied Jesus. For him, the text either states that Mary Magdalene was one of the three Marys accompanying Jesus, *or* the text contains an allegorical commentary showing the three women are in fact one Mary. This either/or seems too sharp to me.

identified with the Holy Spirit and the double Sophia, all three the female *syzygos* (partner) of Christ/Jesus,[56] with Mary Magdalene in this role as his bride, the church.[57] Marjanen, who splits off the historical from the mythical, thinks that the human Mary Magdalene is represented in this work as the most spiritually mature of the followers of Jesus during his earthly ministry, but one who has, however, no significant role as transmitter of spiritual mysteries, no special leadership or authority after the appearance of the risen Jesus.[58] But in this work, Jesus kisses Mary Magdalene (63, 34–36), making her capable of conceiving spiritual offspring. Whatever else the kiss may mean,[59] it does indicate her unique position as transmitter to future generations. Further, elevation into a mythical figure, via her characterization as the companion of the Savior means that apostolic witness is borne somehow to her as well as to the Savior. One might be tempted to speak of a kind of divinization of Mary Magdalene, especially if there is a correlation between her and Sophia in 63, 31–34: "As for the Wisdom who is called 'the barren,'she is the mother [of the] angels. And the companion of the [...] Mary Magdalene."[60] But the point I want to make here is that in her prominence in this work, humanness is united with the transcendent, not obliterated by it.

In Pistis Sophia[61] (both in I–III and IV), Mary Magdalene is the most prominent disciple of Jesus and the chief questioner of Jesus, asking more questions than all the other disciples (seven men named [Philip, Peter, John, Andrew, Thomas, Matthew, James] and four women, [besides her, Martha, Salome and Mary the mother of Jesus]).[62] At her request the risen Jesus recounts the adventures and lamentations of Pistis Sophia, whom he met on his heavenly journey. By my count she asks 67 of the 115 questions in I–III, and 4 of the 12 questions asked by named questioners in the extant parts of IV.[63] She also gives in I–III the major interpretations[64] of the post-ascension teachings of the returned Jesus: about his ascent, and about the thirteen repentances, the deliverance, and praises of the Pistis Sophia. She is the first of the disciples to speak (I, 17–18) and is often their

---

56. Buckley, "The Holy Spirit," 211. Kurt Rudolph, in his response to her paper, agrees (p. 323).

57. E. Pagels, "Pursuing the Spiritual Eve: Imagery and Hermeneutics in the Hypostasis of the Archons and the Gospel of Philip," *Images of the Feminine in Gnosticism*, 202.

58. Marjanen, *The Woman*, 139, 145–46. The author, says Marjanen, is emphasizing the collective witness of all the apostles.

59. See King, "The Gospel of Mary Magdalene," 2. n. 42, p. 631, and below p. 154.

60. See Buckley, "'The Holy Spirit,'" 221.

61. Translation is by V. MacDermot, *Pistis Sophia* (ed. C. Schmidt; Leiden: Brill, 1978). Reference is made here to the chapter divisions in this edition. Faith Wisdom is creatively derived from the figure of Wisdom in the Hebrew Bible. See D. Good, *Reconstructing the Tradition of Sophia in Gnostic Literature* (Atlanta: Scholars Press, 1987) for the various gnostic versions of Sophia; E. Schüssler Fiorenza, *Sharing Her Word* (Boston: Beacon, 1998) 161–63 on G*ddess language and traditions integrated into the biblical image of Sophia.

62. In Pistis Sophia IV, a separate work, the women disciples are mentioned as a group (IV, 136).

63. See below, n. 233 on the missing pages in IV.

64. Interpretations are also given by Salome, Mary the mother of Jesus, John, Peter, James, Martha and Philip.

spokesperson. Her questions and interpretations make her "the most capable one among the disciples,"[65] insightful and courageous.

Her prominence in this work, besides involving intellectual and spiritual leadership, has further dimensions. It appears that she does "rule," and does preach and perform ritual acts. As Deirdre Good puts it, the women in Pistis Sophia exemplify discipleship, and Mary takes on the corporate identity of the gnostic community behind the text.[66] Since the number twelve is not connected in Pistis Sophia to twelve male disciples of Jesus as it is in the Synoptics, Mary should probably be understood as included in the twelve who "will save the whole world" (I, 9).[67] In response to Matthew, Jesus speaks of himself sitting in the Treasury of Light, and promises "you yourselves will sit on twelve light-powers." Mary comes forward to explain this as a reference to the saying we find in Luke 22:28–30: those who have endured with him will share in the kingdom and sit on twelve thrones judging the twelve tribes of Israel (I, 50). In II, 96, the Savior says that all who receive mysteries in the Ineffable will become fellow-rulers with him in his kingdom; his throne, however, will be superior to theirs, and the thrones of the "twelve servers" will be joined to his. "But Maria Magdalene and John the Virgin[68] will be superior to all my disciples," that is, will be the two highest of the twelve (or, less likely, if twelve is a symbolic number, above the twelve). There seems to be some sort of ranked egalitarianism here; the passage continues to depict all who receive mysteries in the Ineffable on his right and on his left. "And I am they and they are I."

In III, 108 and elsewhere, Mary asks what "we" shall do in the community, as though she is involved in its leadership. In III, 102, the commission is given to all the disciples to preach to the whole world (cf. III, 111; III, 121; III, 125) there is no reason to think she is not included. Mary asks questions about preaching in III, 105 ("...from now I will begin to question thee concerning everything regarding the manner in which we will preach to mankind"); III, 110 ("...when we go to places of the country and they do not believe us and they do not listen to our words, and we perform a mystery of this kind in those places, then they know truly and verily that we are preaching the words <of the God> of All"). The term "mystery" refers here and in some other passages (e.g., II, 98; III, 109, 111, 112) to ritual activity, like baptism, which the disciples are taught to perform.

It has been noted, however, that some passages in this work seem to show that it is not Mary Magdalene but the male disciples who are supposed to preach and

---

65. Marjanen, *The Woman* 153.
66. Good, "Pistis Sophia," 2.680, 682.
67. Counting the four women, eleven disciples are named in I–III, twelve in I–III, IV (which adds Bartholomew). Marjanen, *The Woman*, n. 28, p. 152 thinks it probable that the twelve is "simply a traditional term which no longer has any clear function in Pistis Sophia I–III."
68. See the praise of John in I, 40 where he kisses (lit. worships) the breast of Jesus (as James does in I, 51); I, 41; II, 90. John also functions as the disciples' spokesperson.

perform the mysteries — whether special revelation or a ritual acts.[69] She says, for example, "I question all things with assurance and certainty, for my brothers preach them to the whole race of mankind..." (II, 88); and in III, 114 she questions "for the sake of the manner in which my brothers will preach to the whole race of mankind." It seems to me, rather, that she may be talking not about something she does not do, but about something her brothers might do better than they are now doing it. Andrew, for example, clearly has trouble understanding what is to be preached (II, 100). With regard to the performance of the mysteries, Mary speaks of her brothers giving the mysteries after someone has repented (III, 123[70]); in III, 122 Peter is put to the test to see if he will be merciful to a woman who came to repent, or whether he will perform the mystery which cuts her off from "the inheritance of the light." Peter is forgiving and wins the Savior's praise. In IV, 139 Mary asks the Lord to "reveal to us in what manner the souls are carried off by theft, so that my brothers also understand." Her statement "implies that she does not need this information for herself but asks here on behalf of her brothers, who do not comprehend the mysteries as easily as she does."[71] These texts do not, to my mind, indicate that Mary and the other women are excluded from the performance of the mysteries, but on the contrary imply they perform them well. Their roles do not appear to be limited or subordinate.

There are two lists of disciples in the Manichaean Psalm Book II 192, 5–193, 3 and 194, 7–22. In both passages the list of the men precedes the list of the women. Peter is first in the list of the men, and Mary Magdalene first in the list of the women. As we have seen, both lists of women include also Martha, Salome, Arsinoe (as in First Apocalypse of James 40, 25–26). Besides these, there are seven others in the first list: Thecla, Maximilla, Iphidama, Aristobula, Eubula, Drusiane, and Mygdonia, names derived from second- and third-century Acts. The separation of men and women in the lists, and the listing of women after men seem to reflect a separation of roles, and a subordination of the women's roles to the men's.[72] Women were part of the Elect, the spiritual group of the Manichaeans, but they had no access to the more powerful roles of apostles, bishops, presbyters. Mary's prominence, however, involves power.

In the first catalogue, Mary is characterized in this way: "A net-caster is Mary (Marihama), hunting for the eleven others that were wandering"[73] (192, 21–

---

69. Marjanen, *The Woman*, 154.
70. Jesus replies here in the same terms, about the brothers.
71. Marjanen, *The Woman*, 160.
72. This conforms to what is known of roles in Manichaeanism (Mirecki, *ABD*, 4.596), an ascetic religious movement founded in the third century c.e. by Mani, combining elements of Jewish Christianity and Zoroastrianism.
73. Translation by C. R. C. Allberry, *A Manichean Psalm-Book. Part II. Manichean Manuscripts in the Chester Beatty Collection*, Vol. II (Stuttgart: W. Kohlhammer, 1938). Marjanen prefers to translate "lost" instead of "wandering" (*The Woman*, n. 10, p. 176, 181); but both seem to be almost technical terms for the soul led astray.

22). She is the fisher of these men. In the second catalogue it is said that the Son "chose Mary (Marihamme), the spirit of wisdom (*r^ma ^ntsophia*)" (194, 19). Marjanen argues that "spirit" is to be understood here as referring to a disciple (cf. the reference to the Son of God as the "Savior of Spirits" in 194,13; 190, 21), and that "wisdom" be understood as a God-given human quality, given to Mary because she was the first "to recognize the real character of the Risen Jesus"[74] as she does in II,187,1–35, a midrash on John 20:11–18 (see below). But Coyle reads this description of Mary quite differently: he argues that it identifies her with the Spirit of Wisdom. Personifying Sophia, she is the essential feminine complement to the Christ-Savior figure. This relationship Coyle thinks may be "meant to enlarge on the Sophia/Savior couple of Gnostic writings." Sophia in Manichaeism is never regarded as having fallen, nor as "a manifestation of feminine instability"; rather she is closely associated and often identified with Jesus himself, perhaps intended to express a feminine aspect in him.[75] If Coyle is right, this text is another instance of element 7 in my profile (intimate companion).

Manichaean Psalm Book II, 187: 2–35[76] carefully and closely adapts John 20:11–18, expanding on the risen Jesus' words to Mary Magdalene at the empty tomb. In John 20, Jesus speaks three times: to ask her why she is weeping and for whom she is looking; to speak her name; and to tell her not to touch him and to commission her. But here she is told to "know me . . . know me"; know, that is, that he is her master, her God who was not stolen away, and did not die but mastered death; know that he is not the gardener. In this knowledge, she is to cast away her sadness. She is commissioned to go to the "wandering orphans," using "all [her] skill (*technē*) and advice" to bring "the sheep to the shepherd," the Risen Jesus. She is not only to deliver a message, but to make sure it is understood. She accepts the commission with dedication and enthusiasm, becoming the model gnostic.

A heroic Mary appears in the Acts of Philip VIII, 2–4. She stands beside Christ when he commissions his apostles, encourages her brother Philip who is moaning and weeping about the city to which he is sent. She holds the register of the regions to be evangelized, and prepares the bread and salt and the breaking of the bread. She is told to accompany him. Dressed as a man, she does so and stands by him when he is martyred.[77] In The Great Questions of Mary, she receives a vision on a mountain, depicted in ways reminiscent of the transfiguration in Luke.

---

74. Marjanen, *The Woman*, 185. Compare the description of James in the same list.

75. Coyle, "Mary Magdalene" 54–55. He sees the Marihamme of Manichaeism "as a continued or revived Gnostic tradition" (48). He reads the terms "sister" and "mother" applied to Mary in the Gospel of Philip (see above) as evidence also of her identification with Wisdom, since those are terms which designate Wisdom. Cf. Petersen, " 'Zerstört die Werke,' " 192–93.

76. This is printed in NTA 1.403 in the section, "The Gospel of Mani" in the chapter by Puech, revised by Beate Blatz, "Other Gnostic Gospels and Related Literature." I am using the translation by Allberry.

77. Bovon, "Paschal Privilege," 156–57; *Acta Philippi, 241–47.*

In the last four texts to be mentioned in this section, Mary's prominence is somewhat blurred and diminished. The Gospel of Peter 12:50–13:57 shows Mary Magdalene, called "a disciple of the Lord" coming with her unnamed and unnumbered women friends to the sepulchre, which they find opened. They flee afraid when a young man in shining robes tells them the crucified one is risen and gone. Her prominence as a disciple is underlined by a triple mention of her fear of "the Jews." Since a crowd from Jerusalem and environs, and soldiers guarding the tomb have already witnessed the resurrection, the women's discovery of the empty tomb and the announcement of the young man in bright clothing that the one who was crucified "is risen and gone" is anticlimactic. They have no commission (as in Luke's account), and flee in fear (as in Mark's account).[78] The Epistula Apostolorum has the Lord buried in "the place of the skull" to which three women come: Sarah, Martha and Mary Magdalene in the Ethiopic version; Mary, the daughter of Martha and Mary Magdalene in the Coptic version. At the empty tomb, the Lord appears to them and sends them to tell their "brothers" that he is risen from the dead. In the Ethiopic version, Mary and Sarah deliver the message in turn and are rebuffed; in the Coptic, Martha and Mary. The third attempt is to be made by Mary and her sisters in the company of Jesus; the women fade out, however ("the Lord said to Mary and to her sisters, 'Let us go to them.' And he came . . . "); it is the Lord alone who finally convinces the men of his resurrection. Also in the Apostolic Order, Martha and Mary appear together; Mary's laughter is possibly related in some garbled way to the exclusion of women from ordination. The woman "whose brother was dead' in the Secret Gospel of Mark is "the sister of the young man Jesus loved." She requests and wins the mercy of Jesus and her brother's revival in his tomb; but she and his other sister(s), Jesus mother and Salome are not received by Jesus in Jericho.

2. A Character in a Textual World of Androcentric Language and Patriarchal Ideology

The prominence of the literary character, the gnostic/apocryphal Mary Magdalene, is achieved in a textual world of androcentric language and patriarchal ideology. From language, we can only infer something of the gender schemas and sexism of the social world of those who produced the texts and those who read them. In some texts, the authors may be simply adopting "the pattern of gender language typical of Mediterranean culture, in which the male represents that which is perfect, powerful, and transcendent and the female what is incomplete, weak and mundane."[79] In others, misogyny is not far beneath the surface, sometimes leaping out in ways that suggest response to the challenge of specific events

---

78. J. D. Crossan (*The Cross That Spoke* [San Francisco: Harper & Row, 1988] 285–86) thinks that the material about Mary may be a second-century addition, influenced by the canonical Gospel tradition.

79. Marjanen, *The Woman*, 61, on the Sophia of Jesus Christ.

unknown to us, or that suggest the atmosphere of closed male groups. In some texts, too, androcentrism is in tension with androgynous or female imagery and language for the divine. In all of the texts, women characters are a minority, and men do most of the talking.[80] In them, as in all patriarchal/kyriocentric societies, women speak for — in favor of — oppression, but they also struggle against it, and speak out against it.

It is extremely important to note that this struggle also has a context in the long-lived notion from Greek and Roman times of "male-female Sameness: that certain women, specifically those from families possessing power and privilege, shared qualities and traits with men, a notion which in turn facilitated and justi-fied elite women's participation in what were ordinarily deemed to be masculine pursuits."[81] Hallett notes that this notion of Sameness appears in pagan depic-tions not only of elite women, but of female worshippers, slaves, former slaves, victims, lovers, married women, lower class women. It is traced to early Greek conceptualizations of divinity, of the Sameness of gods and goddesses. Bravery, physical strength, intelligence, powerful speech, strong affection and initiative are the characteristics of this Sameness, which coexisted with the male supremacist tradition and which should not be confused with notions of gender equality.[82]

Patriarchal language patterns are used to define salvation in the Gospel of Thomas 114: women are said by Simon Peter to be unworthy of life; Jesus responds that they can become "male." Women's experience as such is devalued in this work, and its image of God is "entirely patriarchal."[83] In the Sophia of Jesus Christ, Jesus calls the future gnostic Christians "the masculine [multitude]" (III/4,118,6), and speaks of "the defect of the female" (BG118, 16).

For the Gospel of Philip only "free men and virgins" are "Christians" (74, 13–16), excluding "defiled women," who have participated in "the marriage of defilement" (81, 34–82, 10) which some scholars read as all or any sexual inter-course;[84] others, as we will see, stress the ambiguity of the sexual language in this work. When one drinks "the cup of prayer which contains wine and water and is full of the holy spirit, one receives "the perfect man." When one goes down into the water, one puts on "the living man" (75, 14–25). "If anyone becomes a son of the bridal chamber, he will receive the light" (86, 45).

---

80. This is true even for the Gospel of Mary, since the missing sections in the beginning and middle contained words of the Savior.
81. J. P. Hallett, "Women's Lives in the Ancient Mediterranean," *Women and Christian Origins*, 20–21. She argues that Greek and Roman efforts to stress this Sameness, in imagining the gods and defining appropriate human behavior, is all too often overlooked. More scholarly attention is given to the notion of difference and female "Otherness," which indeed was more pronounced, especially in the area of Roman political and legal rights (18).
82. Hallett, "Women's Lives," 33.
83. P. Perkins, "The Gospel of Thomas," 2.539, 560.
84. Isenberg, *NHL*, 140.

In the Dialogue of the Savior, when Judas asks, "When we pray, how should we pray," the Lord answers, "Pray in the place where there is no woman" (144, 16). The disciple Matthew interprets this to mean "Destroy the works of womanhood," that is, cease giving birth. The next several lines which are full of lacunae seem to be further discussion of "the works of womanhood."[85] In 144, 22 Mary says "They will never be obliterated"; she might be seen here as objecting, standing up for "the works of womanhood," but more likely she is going along with the discussion, voicing her pessimism. (Cf. the Greek Gospel of the Egyptians [not identical with the one found at Nag Hammadi] contained a saying of the Savior: "I am come to undo the works of the female," interpreted by Clement of Alexandria this way: female=lust, works=birth and decay[86]). Marjanen comments:

> Although being a woman and a spiritual authority in the writing, [Mary] is made to accept uncritically, even to wish, that the works of womanhood be destroyed. Thus, the women readers of the text had to consent to the fact that their most prominent female paragon gave her approval to the use of gender imagery which emphasized women's inferiority and subordination typical of the dominant male construction of gender in Mediterranean society. Thereby Mary Magdalene herself was made to undermine the positive impact which her own role as major interlocutor of Jesus might have had on furthering a new ideology of women's position in society and religious life.[87]

Further, ascetic renunciation did and does not mean the same thing for women as for men. For women, destroying the works of womanhood in a cultural order in which women's sexuality is synonymous with their identity "is to make a far more profound demand for alienation and renunciation of self than any demand for continence on the part of men."[88] McGuire makes what seems to me an odd argument against this alienation that ironically proves its truth.

"The symbolic association of the category of the female ('femaleness' or 'womanhood') with the negative pole of sexuality and reproduction does not necessarily devalue women, lead to a negative attitude toward women, or exclude women from leadership, as some have implied. Such an association may, of course, lead in that direction and has frequently been used to justify such devaluation and exclusionary practice. Individual women, however, can become free of such devaluation and exclusion, as the example of Mary Magdalene makes clear. Even groups that question women's authority as a matter of course may nonetheless value and legitimate the authority of a woman who exemplifies religious ideals, as

---

85. Koester and Pagels, *NHL*, 246, think that "emphasis upon the tasks of Christian life in the world implies that the 'dissolution of the works of womanhood' does not suggest a metaphysically motivated sexual asceticism, but the secret birth through the one who 'is coming from the Father.'"

86. Clement of Alexandria, *Stromateis* III 63; NTA 1.209.

87. Marjanen, *The Woman*, 78–79.

88. E. Castelli, "Virginity and its Meaning for Women's Sexuality in Early Christianity," *JFSR* 2 (1986) 86. While asceticism and virginity may have appeared as liberating options to some women, the choice for them involved self-dissolution, self-destruction.

Mary Magdalene clearly did within several varieties of Christianity in the ancient world."[89] It seems to me that these "religious ideals," would "free" some women from most women, thus dividing and conquering.

In the First Apocalypse of James, femaleness is used to describe existence in the perishable material world. It is not to be obliterated or rejected, but assimilated to the imperishable male element (41, 15–19: "The perishable has [gone up] to the imperishable and the female element has attained to this male element"). Female terminology, however, is also used for the transcendent powers: the Lord calls upon "the imperishable knowledge, which is Sophia who is in the Father (and) who is the mother of Achamoth" (35, 5–9). James is amazed that the seven women "[powerless] vessels have become strong by a perception which is in them" (38, 20–23).

In the Pistis Sophia I, 33, 7–8 Mary says "My Lord, there are ears to my man of light, and I hear in my light power" (cf. I, 43, 4–5: "my man of light has ears and I am prepared to hear by means of my power").[90] In III, 113: "my man of light has guided (me), and has rejoiced and has welled up within me, wishing to come forth from me, and to go towards thee." Has she become male? Good notes that "Light-power is the Gnostic element inside a person that enhances perception, insight, and the interpretation of texts."[91] The enlightened soul is identical to Jesus (II, 96: "that person is I and I am that person"). But he — in his connection with Pistis Sophia as a christological figure,[92] and in his wearing of the "body" of the female Barbelo in the height (I,8) — is both male and female. "Jesus' male/female nature makes it possible for everyone who receives mysteries and completes them in the appropriate ways to become part of the world and, at the same time, to be exalted far beyond it.... [T]he gender of Jesus is as incidental to the text as the gender of the disciples who apprehend Jesus' teaching."[93] In this work, however, androcentric language is used to describe not only Mary's achievements, but also the function of the disciples in the kingdom: the "brothers" of Andrew, his fellow-disciples, will become rulers (II, 100; cf. I, 50). This term leads some critics to think — mistakenly — that this means that only the male disciples will rule.[94]

The Epistula Apostolorum can address its readers as "our sons and daughters" (1), and speak of them as "the children of the light (Ethiopic; Coptic: of life [28]). But it purports to be "the letter of the council of the apostles, the disciples of

89. McGuire, "Women, Gender and Gnosis," 277.
90. Thomas speaks about his "man of light" in II, 69.
91. Good, "Pistis Sophia," n. 11, p. 705.
92. Good, "Pistis Sophia," 688, 690, 698–99.
93. Good, "Pistis Sophia," 699–700.
94. Marjanen, *The Woman*, n. 26, p. 151; he thinks the differences between Mary and the males are overemphasized by H. Koivunen, *The Woman Who Understood Completely. A Semiotic Analysis of the Mary Magdalene Myth in the Gnostic Gospel of Mary* (Imatra: International Semiotics Institute, 1994) 177–78. This work has not been available to me.

Jesus Christ, to the Catholics" (1); eleven named male disciples are the authors and only ones in conversation with the risen Jesus.

3. Her Bold Speech

The gnostic Mary has been given a voice that is powerful, insistent and courageous. She enters into dialogue with Jesus, questioning him and giving theological explanations on her own. In some texts she dialogues with the male disciples. Gospel of Thomas 21: "Mary said to Jesus: 'Whom are your disciples like?'" This question, a request for an image,[95] seems to replace or parallel the question about the nature of the kingdom of heaven in the Synoptics, which is asked by the disciples in 20; Jesus asks what he himself is like in 13. Mary's question does not indicate that she has less understanding than the other disciples, even Thomas.[96] She is not asking about a group of men ("disciples") but a group of men and women.[97]

In the Sophia of Jesus Christ, Mary and the members of what Parrott calls "the Philip group" (Matthew, Philip, Thomas and Bartholomew)[98] each ask the Savior two questions apiece. She asks about how the disciples will know the difference between the imperishable and the perishable (III/4, 98, 9–10). She also asks the final, important question, "Holy Lord, where did your disciples come from and where are they going and (what) should they do here?" (III/4 114,8–13).

Matthew, Judas, and Mary are in conversation with the earthly Savior[99] or — less likely — the risen Savior[100] in the Dialogue of the Savior. She speaks to the Lord thirteen times (Judas speaks to him sixteen times and Matthew ten times). For example, in III,5, 126, 18–20: "[Mary] said, 'Lord, behold! Whence [do I] bear the body [while I] weep, and whence while I [...]?" The response of the Lord has to do with "weeping on account of its works" and the mind laughing. She also questions the brothers (131, 25) about where they are going to "put [these things] about which you ask the son...[...]."

In the Pistis Sophia her freedom or boldness (*parrēsia*[101]) of speech is most evident. In I, 17, 5–9, she asks to be commanded[102] to speak openly, and Jesus responds, "Mariam, thou blessed one, whom I will complete in all the mysteries

95. Perkins, "Gospel of Thomas," 546.
96. Contrast Marjanen, *The Woman*, 35–36, with Perkins "Gospel of Thomas," 558. Marjanen sees her as disciple in the ordinary sense, like Salome, one who need to be exhorted to become "a person who understands." Perkins regards the women as having insight similar to that of Thomas.
97. Petersen, "'Zerstört die Werke,'" 107; she uses the translation *JüngerInnen* here.
98. D. M. Parrott, "Gnostic and Orthodox Disciples in the Second and Third Centuries," *Nag Hammadi, Gnosticism, and Early Christianity*, 193–219.
99. H. Koester and E. H. Pagels, "The Dialogue of the Savior," *NHL*, 245–46.
100. Marjanen, *The Woman*, 67.
101. Cf. Mark 8:32; Acts 4:13, 29; Eph 6:20 and elsewhere.
102. Cf. I, 59; I, 61 where the mother of Jesus asks to be commanded to give an explanation; and Matthew in II, 62; John in II, 71. In I, 62 Mary Magdalene adds to an interpretation of Mary the mother of Jesus. In I, 22 Philip asks for authority to speak in Jesus' presence, and is given it. In I, 38, Martha responds to the invitation of Jesus that someone speak, and humbly, cringingly asks to be allowed to give her interpretation, using Ps 69 (70); she is bolder in I, 57.

of the height,[103] speak openly." Cf. I, 19, 11–12, where he tells her, "Speak openly and do not fear. I will reveal all things which thou seekest." She asks to be reassured in I, 24, 4–9: "My Lord, suffer me that I speak in thy presence, an be not angry with me because I trouble thee many times, questioning thee"; and she is reassured. Her first question is theologically profound and basic. It concerns the fall of the Pistis Sophia below the thirteenth aeon. Mary is puzzled by this, as the Pistis Sophia — who is a paradigm of the soul and the human condition, and who is/is not Jesus — belongs above. She is an aeon enmeshed in matter whose plight mirrors that of the disciples, male and female. Mary, as a woman, has a special affinity for the role of this female aeon.[104] Her interpretations are vigorous and technical; her questions direct, insistent, spunky. Usually she "springs up" to speak (e.g., I, 52; I, 60). She and the other disciples catch allusions in Pistis Sophia's *pesherim*[105] to the biblical Psalms, the Psalms and the Odes of Solomon, and they use these works to interpret the repentances and praises of the Pistis Sophia.[106] Mary has a confident voice: "My Lord, this is the interpretation of the mystery of the repentance of the Pistis Sophia" (I, 34). She is called "the beautiful in her speech" (I, 24, 2), "thou [who] dost seek everything with certainty and with accuracy" (I, 25, 2–3), "spiritual one." Most often she recalls Synoptic sayings of Jesus which explain what he is now teaching. She can, that is, follow the radical gnostic reinterpretation and root it in the older traditions. She is irrepressible, speaks for herself and the others, and speaks to others as well, for example, interpreting Salome's words for her (III, 132). Mary carefully organizes her comments (e.g., her four thoughts in III, 113). She speaks also about the mysteries of the Ineffable, and about community life — renouncing, preaching, forgiving, punishments and so forth. When Jesus asks his disciples "Do you understand in what manner I have spoken to you?" Mary answers, "Yes, O Lord, I have understood the discourse which thou hast spoken" (I, 46, 42–45; III, 113; III, 120; III, 121).

In the Manichaean Psalm Book II, 187, the risen Jesus coaches Mary on what she is to say to the Eleven: "'Arise, let us go, it is your brother that calls you.' If they scorn my brotherhood, say to them, 'It is your master.' If they disregard my

103. Cf. I, 54 where Jesus tells Salome he will complete her in all mysteries of the Kingdom of Light.
104. Good, "Pistis Sophia," 684–85, 699–700.
105. Commentary on and application of quoted parts of biblical texts.
106. It is possible that the use of the Psalms of lament and thanksgiving in the Christian Testament Gospels is behind the use of psalms here. There are references in I, 33 to Ps 68 (69 Hebrew) — one of the psalms used in all four of the Christian Testament crucifixion narratives (Mark 15:36, pars.), and to Ps 30 (31) which is used in Luke 23:46, in I, 49. But Psalm 22, the psalm most used by the Christian Testament evangelists to shape the narrative, may have been the hermeneutical model here, but — strangely — it is never used in the story of Pistis Sophia's repentance. See Good, "Pistis Sophia," 698. The psalms of lament have been reinterpreted "to explain the plight of Sophia, her present condition, her innocence as a basis for an appeal, and her pleas for redress and final restoration to the Light above" and to "give corporate voice" to the gnostic mired in matter (694).

mastership, say to them 'It is your Lord.' "[107] She is to " 'use all skill and advice until thou hast brought the sheep to the shepherd.' " There is no account of her efforts with the Eleven, but she does respond to Jesus, "Rabbi, my master, I will serve thy commandment in the joy of my whole heart. I will not give rest to my heart, I will not give sleep to my eyes, I will not give rest to my feet until I have brought the sheep to the fold." Here, as Coyle notes, she gives no teaching of her own, and there is [therefore?] no open conflict between her and the Eleven, though she is charged with leading them back.[108] In the Acts of Philip VIII, 2–3 Mary speaks up on behalf of her cowardly brother Philip. She wins a backhanded complement from the Savior, who says he knows she has a virile and valiant mentality, in contrast to Philip's womanly mentality. In one manuscript, she also speaks (preaches?) to women.[109] Though women are said to have become strong by a "perception" in them in the First Apocalypse of James (39, 22), there are no sayings attributed to them; this is a dialogue between only James and the Lord.[110]

The following sayings of the Magdalene contrast to those above in this section. She speaks, but not boldly. The Gospel of Peter 12:52–54 has Mary Magdalene and her women friends speaking to one another at the sepulchre. In this case, the speech is fearful. "Although we could not weep and lament on that day when he was crucified, yet let us now do so at his sepulchre. But who will roll away for us the stone also that is set on the entrance to the sepulchre, that we may go in and sit beside him and do what is due? — For the stone was great, — and we fear lest any one see us. And if we cannot do so, let us at least put down at the entrance what we bring for a memorial of him and let us weep and lament until we have again gone home" (12:52–54). In the Ethiopic version of the Epistula Apostolorum 10, the only direct speech Mary has is her statement to the Lord, "None of them believed me concerning your resurrection."

In the Apostolic Church Order, the topic under discussion is whether the Eucharistic ministry should be open to women.[111] John argues that it should not because at the Last Supper Jesus did not permit women to stand with the apostles. Martha says that it — the reason women were not permitted to stand with the

---

107. The risen Jesus is "God" and "Rabbi" to her (line 7); it is not clear what he will be to the Eleven — brother? master? lord? (lines 18–20).

108. Coyle, "Mary Magdalene," 54.

109. Bovon, "Paschal Privilege," 156. He says (n 61, p. 234) in Vaticanus graecus 808, f. 185r-185v (=APh #109) she preaches encratism to them. See *Acta Apostolorum Apocrypha* (ed. M. Bonnet; Darmstadt: Wissenschaftliche Buchgesellschaft, 1959) n. 57, p. xv, lin. 12ff.

110. In the Great Questions of Mary she is speechless, falling to the ground "abashed" at the vision of Jesus. He criticizes her when he raises her up: "Why did you doubt, O you of little faith?" (cf. Matt 14:31).

111. Cf. the Didascalia Apostolorum 3.6.2 where the author points out that although there were women disciples of Jesus (Mary Magdalene, Mary the daughter of James, and the "other" Mary), the Master did not command that they "instruct the people" together with the male disciples. Also Epiphanius, *Pan.* 79.7, 1–4.

men at the supper,[112] and/or the reason they should not be Eucharistic ministers — is because of Mary, "because I (or: he) saw her smile." Mary defends herself against the charge, responding that she did not laugh (or no longer laughed; or never again laughed: Gk: *ouketi egelasa;* 1.26:2). An emendation has been proposed for this puzzling statement: instead of *ouketi,* read *oux hoti:* "(it was) not because of this that I laughed."[113] The passage continues in a saying that may be part of her speech and may connect it to the topic under discussion: Jesus himself taught that "the weak will be saved through the strong." It would then be unnecessary for women (the weak) to take part in the Eucharist performed by men (the strong).[114] The Syriac seems to agree with this reading: "Martha said (concerning Mary): 'I saw her laughing between her teeth exultingly.' Mary said: 'I did not really laugh, only I remembered the words of our Lord and I exulted; for ye know that He told us before, when He was teaching: "the weak shall be saved through the strong."'"[115] Here there is no boldness, as she takes back her laughter[116] and speaks for the secondary status of women.[117] Note that in the Dialogue of the Savior, Mary — later called "a woman who had understood completely" (139, 12–13) — seeks from Jesus the meaning of her tears and her laughter (126, 13).[118]

4. Her Leadership Role vis-à-vis the Male Disciples

Her leadership does not necessarily or always mean that Mary has followers, that she is successful, or that she has power to go with her authority or vice versa, but that she is depicted as showing the way. Often this involves comforting and encouraging the others to move on, correcting them, urging them to believe and act.

In Sophia of Jesus Christ, the risen Savior himself comforts and teaches the perplexed disciples. But in her second and final question, Mary voices concern for the mission of the disciples: "Holy Lord, where did your disciples come from and where are they going, and (what) should they do here?" (III,4, 114, 8–13).

---

112. So Schüssler Fiorenza, *In Memory of Her,* 307. In this reading, Martha is saying that the reason Jesus did not allow women to stand at the Last Supper is (simply) because of Mary's laughter. Mary denies she laughed, and then herself supplies the argument against the ministry of women with her quotation of the words of Jesus.

113. See Schermann, *Die allegemeine Kirchen-ordnung,* note p. 32:=the Latin, *non quia risi;* Cf. Bovon, "Paschal Privilege," n. 63, p. 234: "I have not yet laughed."

114. Marjanen, *The Woman,* n. 87, p. 23 reads it this way, though the saying is not explicitly connected to the topic of the Eucharist. Maclean (*Ancient Church Orders,* 27) calls all this "a curious side-remark about Martha and Mary" and a saying of the Lord. Bovon ("Paschal Privilege," n. 63, p. 234), following A. Harnack (*Die Quellen der sogenannten Apostolischen Kirchenordnung* [TU 2, 5; Leipzig, 1886] 28–31), thinks of the conversation of Martha and Mary as a digression.

115. Arendzen, "An Entire Syriac Text," 73.

116. Cf. the laughter of Mary the mother of Jesus in the Ethiopic version of the Epistula Apostolorum 14: "she believed and laughed" (also Sibylline Oracles 8, 466).

117. See K. J. Torjesen, "The Early Christian *Orans,*" *Women Preachers and Prophets Through Two Millennia of Christianity,* 49–51.

118. See Bovon, "Paschal Privilege," 153.

His response to her ends with a commissioning in language surely meant to be inclusive ("I have given you authority over all things as Sons of Light..."), his disappearance, the disciples' joy, and the beginning of their preaching (119). In the Dialogue of the Savior she expresses concern about the conservation of the discussions of the Savior (131, 19–21); here she might be talking about writing down his words, about preserving scrolls, or about understanding and practicing. Mary is one of four women in the First Apocalypse of James who serves "as a model for how James is supposed to go about his own mission."[119] The four are recognized as spiritual authorities, though their influence is less direct than that of James, who in this work receives the basic revelation. In the Epistula Apostolorum, Mary Magdalene and two other women experience an appearance of the Lord at the empty tomb. First Mary is sent to tell the "brothers" that the Lord has risen from the dead, then Sarah (Ethiopic; in the Coptic, first Martha and then Mary); both are rebuffed in turn and met with doubt that is overcome only when the "brothers" touch him (chaps. 10–11).

The Pistis Sophia has no scene in which Mary explicitly encourages the disciples, but the situation at the beginning of I–III is one in which the disciples are in fear and agitation, after Jesus' ascension in a fabulous light display. They gaze after him in silence as he ascends, and then the powers of heaven shake for more than a day; all humans are agitated including the disciples who think, "Perhaps the world will be rolled up" (I, 3). He himself ("the compassionate and tender-hearted" I, 6) comes back to comfort and teach them. But in her constant questioning and explication, Mary functions in this work as a team-teacher with him. In II, 94, the disciples are told by Jesus to listen with perception and assurance, "For from now I will speak to you of the whole place of truth of the Ineffable and of the manner in which it is." Hearing this, they retire and despair "completely."[120] Mary Magdalene comes forward, prostrates herself at his feet, worships, cries out and weeps.[121] She seems to be interceding here for her "brothers," telling Jesus of their despair and explaining their lack of perception, insisting that he had said he would (only) *"begin* to speak ... of the whole knowledge of the *mystery* of the Ineffable" (emphasis mine), and asking him to explain how,

---

119. Marjanen, *The Woman,* 118.
120. Till translation: they became discouraged and they ceased to listen (*Koptisch-gnostische Schriften; Bd. 1: Die Pistis Sophia* [ed. Carl Schmidt; 3d rev. ed. W. Till; Berlin: Akademie-Verlag, 1959).
121. Cf. III, 108, where she worships at the feet of Jesus and kisses them. This passage (mistakenly cited as II, 108) is understood by Good ("Pistis Sophia," 696) to "loosely reflect" the language of several gospel passages: Luke 7:38 (where the "woman of the city" kisses Jesus' feet); John 11:32 (where Mary of Bethany does the same); and Matt 28:9 (where Mary Magdalene and the other women at the tomb grasp the feet of the risen Jesus and worship him). In my opinion, it is more likely that only Matt 28:9 is being alluded to. (Good recognizes that this is "perhaps the closest passage" to Pistis Sophia III, 108.) The other texts become a part of the Magdalene legend later and in different circumstances. If Luke 7 were being alluded to, this would be the only place in the gnostic literature where his "woman of the city" is conflated with Mary Magdalene.

then a human being can understand the mystery. "Now it happened when Jesus heard these words which Maria said and he knew that the disciples had heard and that they had begun to despair, he encouraged them," telling them that the mystery does indeed belong to them and to everyone who will hear them, and urging them to "renounce the world, all the matter in it, every wicked thought, and all the cares of this aeon" (II,95). In this passage, then, Mary does more than comfort her brothers here; she teaches and instructs the risen Jesus.

Mary's "service" (*leitourgia*) in the Manichaean Psalm Book II, 187 is to be a messenger from the risen Jesus to the Eleven. She is told she will find them, "those wandering orphans," gathered on the bank of the Jordan.[122] They have given up fishing for humans and gone back to fishing for fish: "The traitor persuaded them to be fishermen as they were at first and to lay down their nets with which they caught men to life." Her commission is to bring these sheep to the fold. She is told what to do if they scorn Jesus' brotherhood and disregard his mastership. If she sees that their "wits are gone," she is to remind Peter of a saying of Jesus to him on the Mount of Olives: "I have something to say, I have no one to whom to say it." Marjanen argues that Mary Magdalene is not the most prominent and authoritative person in the circle of the disciples. Overshadowed by Peter in this work, "[h]er task is [only] to transmit the master's call" to the males, and she will have no significant leadership position on the basis of that task.[123] The message Mary is to deliver to Peter is interpreted by Marjanen to mean that Jesus anticipated this post-resurrection situation in which the male disciples and Peter their leader are absent; in their absence, Jesus cannot say what he wants to say. He cannot say it, that is, to Mary.[124] But see below for a different interpretation of the message to Peter.[125]

5. A Visionary

I make no distinctions in this section between having a vision and receiving a resurrection appearance.[126] I am using the term "visionary" here to mean not one who receives private revelations and keeps them private, but one whose

---

122. At the southern end of the Sea of Galilee? See Marjanen, *The Woman*, 182–83 on the symbolic and metaphoric meanings of the Jordan.

123. Marjanen, *The Woman*, 183.

124. Marjanen thinks that there is no tension or rivalry in this work between Mary and the eleven, who are on the same side. This indicates the work is not intended to be an instrument of polemics. It may be, however, from a time and/or a place in which Mary and women in general had lost out.

125. P. 165.

126. E. Pagels points out in her important article on the significance of visions within gnosticism ("Visions, Appearances, and Apostolic Authority: Gnostic and Orthodox Traditions," *Gnosis* [ed. U. Bianchi et al.; Göttingen: Vandenhoeck & Ruprecht, 1987] 413) that traditions about the appearances of the risen Christ by the mid-second century had developed in at least two different lines: (1) ecclesiastical writers increasingly used and expounded those elements of the Christian Testament tradition that attested the "reality" of the resurrection, and (2) gnostic writers characteristically used and adapted those that lent themselves to being interpreted as visions.

visionary and auditory experiences of direct communication with the Savior entail messages for others or are themselves messages for others. I see the visionary as encompassing the roles of prophet[127] and apocalyptic seer. Mary's direct contact with the Savior is the source of her gnosis, her authority and her teaching. In Dialogue of the Savior 134, 24–25 she is mentioned with Judas and Matthew at the beginning of an account of an apocalyptic vision, which was originally received by one person,[128] perhaps Mary.[129] Fragments of the vision, which is recognizable from 134, 24 to 137,3,[130] or 142, 80, are reminiscent of the Christian Testament transfiguration scenes, and of the final pericope of Matthew (28:16–20). Besides three special disciples, these fragments involve a high mountain from which all of heaven and earth can be seen, the touch of the Lord, Son of Man imagery, the garment, and "two spirits bringing a single soul" in light. Originally, the vision may have been about "the rescue of a soul and its installation before God in a new garment," but the final author placed the dialogue in the context of baptismal initiation.[131] Bovon thinks that in 137, 4–11 the Savior seems to be speaking to Mary of two kinds of vision.[132] "But when you see the Eternal Existent, that is the great vision." To all the disciples a few lines further on, a transient vision is contrasted with an eternal vision (137, 12–16).

In the Gospel of Philip, Mary is one of the three women who "always walked with the Lord" (59. 6–10). In the Hebrew Bible, only Enoch and Noah are said to "walk with God": "Enoch walked with God, and he was not, because God took him" (Gen 5:24); "Noah was a righteous man, blameless in his generation; Noah walked with God" (Gen 6:9). These two figures are visionaries in later apocalyptic literature such as the Books of Enoch I, II, III, and the Apocalypse of Adam. It is possible that the resonances of this phrase from Jewish mystical tradition should be heard here with regard to Mary.

In several instances, the visionary experience of Mary is linked to mourning. The appearance of Jesus to her in the Manichaean Psalm Book II, 187 based on John 20, is a response to her tears and her grief ("I appeared[?] [not] to thee, until I saw thy tears and thy grief . . . for [?] me").[133] In the Epistula Apostolorum 9–10, Mary and two other women carry ointment to pour on the dead body of Jesus, "weeping and mourning over what had happened." Not finding his body, "as they were mourning and weeping, the Lord appeared to them and said to them, (Coptic: For whom are you weeping? Now) do not weep; I am he whom

---

127. See King, "Prophetic Power and Women's Authority," 22–23.
128. The first person singular is used in 135, 13–15; 136, 17. See Blatz, "The Dialogue of the Saviour," NTA 1.302. In 135, 4–11 Judas has a vision of a high place and of the underworld; he turns to Matthew to speak
129. Against Marjanen, *The Woman*, 65.
130. Koester and Pagels, *NHL*, 245.
131. Koester and Pagels, *NHL*, 245.
132. Bovon, "Paschal Privilege," 153.
133. See below (pp. 150–51), on the preference for the word "grief" here rather than "weakness."

you seek." The weeping and lamenting of Mary and her women friends in the Gospel of Peter 12–13 are also the occasion for an appearance, this time of a young man at the tomb.[134]

In Epiphanius' reference[135] to a work of so-called libertine gnostics,[136] the Great Questions of Mary, it is asserted that Jesus gave Mary a revelation on "the mountain" of what Epiphanius calls "the obscenity" (*aisxrourgia*). Jesus is said to have taken her aside, prayed, and produced a woman from his side. He began to have sex with this woman, but then to eat his semen[137] to show that " 'we must so do, that we may live'. . . . And when Mary was abashed and fell to the ground, he raised her up and said to her, 'Why didst thou doubt, O thou of little faith?' " Some texts relate the eating of semen and menstrual blood to the eucharist — the body of Christ, the blood of Christ (*Pan.* 26.8,5; 26.4, 1–8 on *coitus interruptus;* and perhaps 26.5,7). It is debated whether or not this is a description of actual gnostic behavior, a misreading of a sexual metaphor, or wild accusation and polemics on the part of the enemy vowed to destroy them.[138] This behavior remains a mystery, and not typical of gnostic Christianity.[139] From what Epiphanius says, however, the act seems to be explained as a way of freeing the soul, considered to be in the semen and the menses, and taking it to the heavens (26, 9, 4; 10, 8–9), as well as a way of preventing conception (see 26, 5,2).[140] Mary's reaction, falling down, is a typical reaction to a vision (cf. Ezek 1:28). She is not said to be the woman with whom he has sex in this scene, which reenacts the creation of Eve from Adam (Genesis 2) and then depicts their union, the prototype of a mystery rite. Mary is apparently being shown how the new Eve is taken from Jesus, the new Adam (cf. 1 Corinthians 15), and shown that Eve is his partner — but not for procreation. Mary, however, may also be thought to be seeing herself as Jesus' partner in this vision,[141] represented by the new Eve.

---

134. On mourning and weeping as "preludes" to visions, see D. Merkur, "The Visionary Practices of Jewish Apocalyptists," *The Psychoanalytic Study of Society* 14 (1989) 119–48.

135. *Pan* 26.8.1–3; ANT 1.390–91.

136. Borborites, "filthies, muddies," may be the nickname given by their opponents. See B. Layton, *The Gnostic Scriptures* (New York: Doubleday, 1987) 200. Cf. Williams, *Rethinking 'Gnosticism,'* on the Phibionites.

137. How did he do that? lick his hands or the woman? ejaculate into a container?

138. See J. E. Goehring, "Libertine or Liberated: Women in the So-called Libertine Gnostic Communities," *Images of the Feminine in Gnosticism*, 329–44; McGuire, "Women, Gender and Gnosis," 266.

139. Layton, *Gnostic Scriptures*, 200. See Pistis Sophia IV, 147 in which Jesus angrily condemns the practice Thomas says he has heard of: taking semen and menstrual blood and making a dish of lentils of it, and eating it. As Good says, this passage may be used to question the accuracy of Epiphanius's description; or it could be self-conscious apologetic directed against such practices ("Pistis Sophia," 696).

140. The practice is criticized in Pistis Sophia IV 381, 6–20; 2 Book of Jeu 100, 16–23. See Marjanen, *The Woman*, 172–73.

141. Enoch sees himself in the vision of the Son of Man in 1 Enoch 71 (see Appendix B). See below, element 7 in this profile of Mary.

Her menstrual blood, however, is not mentioned here with his semen.[142] Unlike the Eve who is re-joined with Adam, their unity restored, however, this Eve is brought forth, dis-joined in a kind of de-androgynization process that may be some form of "protest exegesis."[143]

In the Pistis Sophia, Mary both experiences and interprets visions. In a passage with some dramatic affinities to the Gospel of Mary and to the Gospel of John, she and the other disciples see the risen but pre-ascended Jesus engulfed in a great light reaching from earth to the heavens. Jesus rises to heaven in this light. In the ninth hour of the next day the heavens open and he descends in even more light (I, 2–4) which he then turns off at the disciples' request. He begins to tell them what he has seen in his ascent. Mary is not said to have had a special, private vision, but in II, 17 she stares into the air for one hour before she speaks, using Isaiah 19, to interpret the Savior's words about his removal of power from the archons. At the beginning of Book IV (136), the male and female disciples stand with Jesus beside the ocean and hear him speak intelligible prayers and mysterious words. They see the heavens contorted, the sun turn to a great dragon drawn by the likeness of white horses, the moon as a boat steered by dragons and drawn by bulls, the likeness of a child at the back of the moon, a cat face in front of it. The disciples are up in the air in the Midst with Jesus, as they receive his explanations. Mary, weeping, asks for Jesus' compassion and protection in this experience, and receives it (IV, 137). Pistis Sophia II, 96 speaks of a throne for Mary in heaven (see below), perhaps a link with the tradition that can be traced back to the description of the chariot-throne of Ezekiel 1.

6. Praise for Her Superior Understanding

Mary's understanding is insight, gnosis. In Dialogue of the Savior 139, 12–13 she is praised by the narrator or redactor as "a woman who had understood completely."[144] This praise follows her use of traditional Jesus-statements (the "wickedness of each day," "the laborer is worthy of his food," and "the disciple resembles his teacher") as interpretations of his saying in 139, 5 about the path by which one leaves to get to the place of reward. Mary herself says "I want to understand all things, [just as] they are" (141, 12–14). In response to her request, "Tell me, Lord, why I have come to this place to profit or to forfeit," she is praised by the Lord: "You make clear the abundance of the revealer!" (140, 14–18). In the First Apocalypse of James 39, 20–23, Mary is understood as one of the seven women who James says "have become strong by a perception which is in them."

---

142. See Goehring, "Libertine or Liberated," 341–42, on the interest in menses as well as semen as indicating the high regard in which the Phibionites held women.

143. Williams, Rethinking 'Gnosticism,' chapter 3.

144. On this and two other translations of this phrase ("the woman who knew the All," and "the woman who had understood everything") see Marjanen, *The Woman*, 72–73. Cf. 142, 12–13 where all the disciples are said to "have understood all the things I have said to you," and 140, 3–4 where Matthew is praised for his perceptive question.

If the disciples' question to Jesus ("Why do you love [Mary] more than all of us?") and Jesus' question to them in the Gospel of Philip, ("Why do I not love you like her?") are not unanswered, the implied answer to both seems to be that Mary Magdalene is loved by the Savior because in contrast to the other disciples she is not blind, but sees the light (64, 5–9).[145] Marjanen thinks this means that "It is only Mary Magdalene, the favorite of the Savior, who is able to see what the others can see only after the resurrection." She is "a paragon of apostleship whose spiritual maturity is reached by other followers of Jesus only later."[146]

Pistis Sophia II, 96 speaks of the throne of Mary Magdalene. "But Mary Magdalene and John the virgin (*parthenos*) will surpass all my disciples and all men who shall receive mysteries in the Ineffable, they will be on my right hand and on my left, and I am they and they are I, and they will be equal with you in all things, save that your thrones will surpass theirs, and my own throne will surpass yours and those of all men who shall find the word of the Ineffable."[147] The formula "I am they and they are I" is the same as the formula in the prayer of Marcus, a disciple of Valentinus, for the authority of women prophets.[148] (Compare the inscription *kai su* in the mosaic floor at Midgal, and in the Gospel of Eve.[149]) In the Pistis Sophia, Jesus gives a mark of "excellent" to almost every disciple who speaks, but Mary is praised enthusiastically and constantly by Jesus for her spiritual understanding. She is "blessed beyond all women on earth, because [she] shall be the pleroma of all pleromas and the completion of all completions" (I, 19),[150] "blessed among all generations" (I, 34). The Savior marvels at her answers — as he does at those of no others — "because she had completely become pure Spirit" (II, 88). Jesus says to her in I, 17, "You are she whose heart is more directed to the Reign of Heaven than all your brothers." The term "heart" clearly carries here the integration of mind and emotion that the Hebrew word *leb* does. What she knows and understands in Pistis Sophia is the risen, ascended, and (even) returned Jesus, and this is also presented as self-knowledge and knowledge of authentic Christian community life.

In the Manichaean Psalm Book II, 187, 10 the risen Jesus says he did not appear to Mary "until I saw thy tears and thy grief." Marjanen thinks the Coptic word *pesone* should be translated "thy weakness" instead of "thy grief."[151] This may be correct, since *sone* is "illness." It is true that she is said to have had

---

145. That is, if we take the passage about blindness as part of his answer to the question, "Why do I not love you like her?"
146. Marjanen, *The Woman*, 145.
147. ANT 1.366.
148. E. Schüssler Fiorenza, "Word, Spirit and Power;: Women in Early Christian Communities," *Women of Spirit*, 53; Irenaeus, *Adv. Haer.* 13:3.
149. Above, p. 52.
150. Cf. I, 27 where all the disciples say, "We are blessed beyond all men." In I, 46 Thomas is told "all generations of the world will bless you upon the earth...you have become understanding and Pneumatic, since you have understood what I said."
151. Marjanen, *The Woman*, 180.

"thoughts of littleness" — thoughts, that is, that her God (Jesus' soul?) had been stolen away (by hostile powers?), that he had died. She is told that he was not stolen, nor did he die, but mastered death (lines 7–8).[152] Nevertheless, "grief" instead of "weakness" seems a better choice in line 10, since in the next line she is told to cast away "this sadness" (cf. line 4: "stem the tears of thy eyes and know me...."). Moreover, Jesus' perception of her grief moves him to appear, as his perception of Mary of Bethany's grief in John 11:33 moves him to act for Lazarus; it is possible this sort of conflation of Marys is at work here.[153] She is more a mourning woman who ceases to mourn, than a spiritually inadequate woman, as she is often portrayed by the "church fathers." There is implicit praise for her in the command that she use "all skill and advice" to deliver her message to the Eleven. The narrator praises her: "Glory to Mariamme, because she hearkened to her master, [she] served commandment in the joy of her whole heart" (34–35).[154]

Mary speaks to the Savior on behalf of her brother Philip in Acts of Philip VIII, 3 and receives his praise: "I know that you are a good and courageous soul and blessed among women;[155] here is Philip, possessed by the mentality of a woman, while in you resides a virile and courageous mentality (*to phronēma to arrenikon kai andreion*)."[156] Like Humphrey Bogart's praise of his secretary in "The Maltese Falcon," "You're a good man, sister."

The works mentioned in this section stress as well as illustrate the integrated intellectual/spiritual/emotional ability of Mary. These affirmations "are all the more striking in view of the association in late antiquity of women with lower forms of mental activity, such as sense perception."[157]

7. Identified as an (or the) Intimate Companion of Jesus

The most famous example of this aspect of the gnostic Magdalene's profile occurs in the Valentinian[158] Gospel of Philip 63, 32–64, 9, a tantalizingly corrupt passage, which I will treat here at some length. "And the companion (*koinōnos*) of the [...] Mary Magdalene [... loved] her more than [all] the disciples [and used to] kiss her [often] on her [...]. The rest of [the disciples ...]. They said to him, 'Why do you love her more than all of us?' The Savior answered and said to them,

---

152. Marjanen rightly points out that in this work, in contrast to John 20, Mary is not weeping because she thinks *his body* has been stolen (*The Woman*, n. 20, p. 180).

153. See below, p. 200, for a discussion of conflation of this type in the gnostic texts.

154. On the praise of "Maria" in line 36 ([Glory and] victory to the soul of blessed Mary," see Allberry, *A Manichean Psalm-book*, xx (this Mary may have been a Manichaean martyr). Coyle ("Mary Magdalene," 51–53) thinks Mary Magdalene is mirrored in this Mary, contrast Marjanen, *The Woman*, n. 11, p. 178.

155. Cf. Luke 1:42, on Mary the mother of Jesus.

156. Bovon, "Paschal Privilege," 157; *Acta Philippi*, 243.

157. Good, "Pistis Sophia," 681.

158. On the teachings of Valentinus (ca. 115–65 C.E.), see Hultgren and Haggmark, *The Earliest Christian Heretics*, 82–83. On the affinities of the Gospel of Philip with Valentinian teaching, see W. Foerster, *Gnosis* (Oxford: Clarendon, 1974) 2.77.

'Why do I not love you like her?'" The rest of this saying may imply, as we have seen, that the other disciples are blind, but she is one who sees.[159] In Gospel of Philip 59, 6–11, Mary is one of "three who always walked with the Lord: Mary his mother, her sister and the Magdalene, the one who was called his companion (*tef-koinōnos*). For Mary is his sister and she is his mother and she is his companion (*tef-hotre*)."[160] She is not called the "companion" of the Lord anywhere else in the extant gnostic literature,[161] and no one else is called his "companion."

The Greek term *koinōnos* has a wide range of meanings in the Bible and elsewhere: marriage partner, participant, co-worker in evangelization, companion in faith, business partner, comrade, friend.[162] The notion of sharing (interests, enterprises, material possessions, education, meals) is central to it. It is not used in Gen 2:18LXX for Eve. Other terms of the group *koinōn-rkoinōnei, koinōnia* as well as their Coptic equivalent *hōt^er* (to join, to hire, to be joined, to be in harmony[163]) are used in three ways in the Gospel of Philip: (1) in contexts in which they have a pejorative sense referring to illicit or adulterous intercourse; (2) as referring to "the literal pairing of man and woman in marital (and sexual) relationship," but always as "a metaphor for a deeper, spiritual partnership"; (3) to describe the salvific experience of a gnostic Christian, which takes place when unity with the divine realm is reestablished, an experience "depicted as union with an angelic counterpart in the pleroma or as its ritual anticipation with another Gnostic of opposite sex in the sacrament of the bridal chamber."[164]

The contexts in the Gospel of Philip that refer to Mary Magdalene have no negative implications, and so rule out the first meaning. The second meaning, consort or spouse/wife, may be intended in 59, 8–9: Mary Magdalene is the earthly partner of Jesus. Schüssler Fiorenza comments, "Since the Valentinian system knew three Christs and perceived the divine and the world in syzygies (couples), it is possible that Mary Magdalene was thought of as consort of the earthly Jesus, as the Holy Spirit was the consort of the aeon Christ in the Pleroma and Sophia was the consort of the Savior."[165] And the third meaning may also be evoked: the syzygy of Mary Magdalene and Jesus may function as "the prototype

159. See Bovon, "Paschal Privilege, 153.
160. Translation by McGuire, "Women, Gender, and Gnosis," 275.
161. H.-M. Shenke thinks it is Sophia who is his "companion" in 63, 31–33 and not Mary Magdalene ("Die Arbeit am Philippus-Evangelium," *TLZ* 90 [1965] 328). But see Marjanen, *The Woman*, n. 27, p. 131.
162. Marjanen, *The Woman*, 131; Hauck, "*koinonos, koinoneo*," TDNT 3.797–809; Liddell and Scott, *Greek-English Lexicon* (7th edition; Oxford: Clarendon, 1975) 441.
163. Lambdin, *Sahidic Coptic*, 338; cf. W. E. Crum, *A Coptic Dictionary* (Oxford: Clarendon, 1939) 726a. See Gospel of Philip 59:6–11, above, in which both terms are used.
164. Marjanen, *The Woman*, 132. On the mystery of the bridal chamber, see 69, 1–4; 70, 12–22. Irenaeus, *Adv. Haer.* I 21,3 speaks of the mystic rite of the bridal chamber performed by the Valentinian school of the Marcosians: "they claim that what they are effecting is a spiritual marriage, after the image of the syzygies above."
165. Schüssler Fiorenza, "Word, Spirit, and Power," 50.

which the readers of the Gospel of Philip try to imitate in the sacramental act of the bridal chamber."[166]

It is debated whether or not this sort of partnership—between the male and female gnostics envisioned by the Gospel of Philip and therefore also between Jesus and Mary Magdalene as depicted here—involves actual marriage and/or sexual intercourse. Some argue that the viewpoint of this work is exclusively encratic, even promoting celibate marriage. Others argue that in this work sexual intercourse is the prerequisite of spiritual union or an expression of it for the true gnostic. Pagels, reviewing the debate, argues that the Gospel of Philip is intentionally ambiguous and enigmatic on this point. The author, she says, entirely rejects the question being asked by many second-century Christians concerning sexual practice. This refusal is based on an understanding of the ambiguity of language and a consequent rejection of dualistic thought patterns. The alternatives (marriage vs. celibacy), posed as opposites, present a false dichotomy which distracts from the author's ethical interest in how to reconcile the freedom gnosis brings with love.[167] In this, Pagels is following Klaus Koschorke, who saw that "[t]he entire thinking and phraseology of the Gospel of Philip is marked by ambiguity."[168] As it invites readers to maturity, this ambiguity may be the author's way of rejecting the possibility of becoming *a* or *the* voice of authority in sexual matters.

This presentation in the Gospel of Philip of Mary Magdalene's companionship with Jesus as ambiguous and enigmatic strikes me as extremely important and profound. Such ambiguity avoids two alternatives which both buy into patriarchal notions of the female body: (1) that any male-female relationship must involve sexual relations; or (2) that "sacred" or "spiritual" male-female relations must not.[169] It also opens up examination of the broader range of meaning of the term, "companion": Philo in *Moses* 1.155–58 says God rewarded Moses by appointing him a partner (*koinonon*) of God's own possessions, giving the whole world into his hand.

The jealous disciples in the Gospel of Philip are fixated on the literal, sexual sense. The ambiguity is also difficult for modern scholars to hold on to, and the

---

166. Marjanen, *The Woman*, 133. Buckley ("'The Holy Spirit,'" 213) says Jesus' "interactions with her may allude to the goal, the bridal chamber." She sees earthly marriage as a symbol and a prerequisite for the bridal chamber sacrament.

167. E. Pagels, "The 'Mystery of Marriage' in the Gospel of Philip Revisited," *The Future of Early Christianity* (ed. B. A. Pearson; Minneapolis: Fortress, 1991) 442–54. (See Pagels p. 449 on the author's refusal also to engage the question about resurrection: in the flesh or not in the flesh. Cf. Paul's similar refusal, about mystical experience, in 2 Cor 12:2–4 "whether in the body or out of the body, I do not know. God knows"). Irenaeus knew of those Valentinians who celebrated marital intercourse as a symbol of divine pleromic harmony, and also those who tried to live in celibate marriages (*Adv. haer.* 1.6,3–4).

168. K. Koschorke, "Die 'Namen' im Philippusevangelium," *ZNW* 64 (1973) 310, quoted also by K. Rudolph, "A Response to 'The Holy Spirit is a Double Name,'" 230.

169. King, "The Gospel of Mary Magdalene," 2.616.

Magdalene legend hard to shake. Ménard, commenting on Gospel of Thomas 61, where Salome speaks of Jesus as having "come up on my couch and eaten from my table," slips and calls her Mary. "Perhaps Ménard expects Mary Magdalene, and not Salome," says Buckley, who, however, is aware of the ambiguity of the imagery of the couch.[170]

In the Gospel of Philip, Jesus is said to love Mary Magdalene "more than [all] the disciples" and to "kiss her [often] on her [. . .]" (63, 33–35). That last lacuna is particularly tantalizing; how is it to be filled? With mouth? lips? head? hand? genitals? feet? Layton lists four possibilities: mouth, feet, cheek, forehead.[171] The passage exists at present in only this one flawed manuscript, in Codex II from Nag Hammadi. But internal evidence indicates that mouth may be the best choice: 59, 1–6 juxtaposes talk of nourishment from the mouth and the kiss by which "the perfect conceive and give birth . . . from the grace which is in one another" (Cf. John 20:22 where the risen Jesus breathes on the disciples and gives them the Holy Spirit; and cf. Gen 2:7).

It is debated whether or not the kiss is connected to the ritual of the bridal chamber. Buckley, for example,[172] thinks the kiss alludes to some secret activity in the bridal chamber; Rudolph[173] thinks it does not. Irenaeus' quotation of a formula used in the bridal chamber ("Place the seed of light in your bridal chamber"; *Adv. Haer.* 1,13,3) may be evoked in the discussion about light in 64, 4–9, which seems to be an explanation offered by Jesus for his kissing and loving Mary Magdalene (see also 79, 1–3 "If you become light, the light will become your companion [*koinōnei*]).[174] If so, this argues for a connection between the kiss and the bridal chamber. In either case, however, the kiss could be a metaphor of spiritual intercourse, *or* a sign for sexual intercourse. King argues that the Gospel of Philip never denies that kissing may have a literal sense; but 58, 34–59, 6 shows that it clearly has a metaphorical meaning. She distinguishes three possible understandings of kissing in the metaphorical sense, which are not mutually exclusive: "(1) reference to teaching through the word; (2) a metaphor for an intimate and personal reception of the word of teaching; and (3) the Christian practice of the kiss of fellowship."[175] One or all of these may be intended in Jesus kissing Mary in the Gospel of Philip, meaning that Mary is seen as one who accepted and understood his teaching and was therefore loved by him; she is a wise pupil kissed by her teacher.[176]

---

170. J. J. Buckley, "An Interpretation of Logion 114 in the Gospel of Thomas," *NovT* 27 (1985) 269.
171. *Nag Hammadi Codex II,2–7* (ed. B. Layton; Leiden: Brill, 1989) 1.169.
172. Buckley, " 'The Holy Spirit,' " 225.
173. Rudolph, "Response," 232.
174. Translation by Pagels, "The 'Mystery of Marriage,' " 450–51.
175. King, "The Gospel of Mary Magdalene," 2. n. 42, p. 631. Cf. McGuire, "Women, Gender and Gnosis," 275–76.
176. D'Angelo, "Reconstructing 'Real' Women" 120.

So the kiss too is ambiguous, enigmatic. The jealousy of the male disciples (see below) does not settle the issue.[177] Asking whether this is either a spiritual love between a master and disciple, or an erotic love creates a false dichotomy, especially if eroticism is seen in Audre Lorde's sense, as a deep source of power, knowledge, joy, bravery, and the energy to change the world.[178] "Jesus' kissing Mary is a cunning, paradoxical action, which gives rise to opposed interpretations by different audiences."[179]

It is tempting to speculate that the gnostic use of this terminology for Mary Magdalene, and the inability of some of the "orthodox" and their later followers to live with ambiguity, may have had something to do with the characterization of her in Western legend as (repentant) whore. It might have been, say, a catalyst for the conflation of Luke 7 (a conflation I think is not found in extant gnostic materials[180]) with the Christian Testament texts that do speak of her. But as far as I can see, there is no clear evidence that the patristic writers or legend-makers were responding to the gnostic portrait. The links are missing.

Only in the Gospel of Philip and the Gospel of Mary, which will be treated below, is Jesus' love for Mary Magdalene explicitly stated. Marjanen thinks that the beloved disciple motif linked with Mary Magdalene in these two works, which also contrast her to all the other disciples, "speaks for a connection between these writings," but he does not explore this idea in detail. In any case, there are other traces of the love theme. As we have seen above,[181] Mary's (sexual though nonorgasmic, unconsummated?) partnership with Jesus may be implied in the vision of the new Eve in the Greater Questions of Mary. Not enough of this work has been preserved, however, in its hostile context in Epiphanius' *Panarion*, to be sure of this. The Manichaean Psalm Book II 194, 19 refers to "Mary, the spirit of wisdom," as "chosen" by the Son. Coyle reads this as elevation of her to a personification of Sophia and partner of the Savior.[182] The Gospel of Peter 12:50 says that Jesus was beloved of Mary Magdalene: she "had not done at the sepulchre of the Lord what women are wont to do for those beloved of them who die."[183]

---

177. Against Marjanen, *The Woman*, 137.

178. A. Lorde, "Uses of the Erotic: the Erotic as Power" in *Weaving the Visions* (ed. Judith Plaskow and Carol Christ; San Francisco: Harper & Row, 1989) 208–13.

179. Buckley, " 'The Holy Spirit,' " 217. She does not think the saying about light is a response to the disciples' question; it goes unanswered. See further, below, pp. 160–61.

180. As we have seen, Good ("Pistis Sophia," 696, 703) holds that Mary worshipping at the feet of Jesus and kissing them (III 108 [the reference given is incorrect]) is a "composite figure" who reflects the language of several passages: Luke 7:38; John 11:32; Matt 28:9. I think only the last passage is evoked here, and Good regards that as the strongest allusion. See above, n. 121.

181. Pp. 148–49.

182. See above, p. 136.

183. In the second fragment of the Secret Gospel of Mark the unnamed woman who may be Mary is not herself loved by Jesus; she is only "the sister of the youth whom Jesus loved," and she is not received by him.

8. Opposed by and in Open Conflict with One or More of the Male Disciples[184]

In the Gospel of Thomas 114 Simon Peter said to the other disciples, " 'Let Mary leave us, for women are not worthy of life.' Jesus said,' I myself shall lead her in order to make her male, so that she too may become a living spirit [cf. Gen 2:7] resembling you males. For every woman who will make herself male will enter the kingdom of heaven.' " Peter is not just asking that Mary — and all women — be excluded from the community, but from salvation, from the kingdom of heaven. The term "kingdom" in the Gospel of Thomas is "virtually synonymous with belonging to the Thomas group/community."[185] As Beata Blatz points out, however, there are scarcely any signs of the formation of a community in this work. It has no ecclesiology, and it is to individuals that it promises access to the kingdom.[186] The question of who is in and who is out is answered in terms of gender.

It is debated whether this Peter is a literary device, representing an exaggerated view of obtuseness, or whether he is meant to represent an actual contemporary view of women, either "a caricature of a major ecclesiastical view with its clear subordination of women" (the "mainstream" view vs. the gnostic view) or "a mischaracterized [?sic] representative of a developing ascetic perspective in which male celibates view the presence of women as threatening." Marjanen thinks the last suggestion is most probable, in which case the whole saying would pit two different encratic positions against one another: one emphasizing that an ascetic group should be male only, excluding women as spiritually inferior; the other (which is the view of the writer of the logion) insisting that both male and female ascetics have the right to be in the same community as long as the females "become male."[187] In each and any case, the saying represents conflict that had arisen over place of women in the community.[188] Note that the accusation that James is "not worthy of life" occurs in the mouth of those who martyr him in the First Apocalypse of James 43, 13. Peter's objection to Mary, and Jesus' response which seems to indicate "a subtle agreement with Peter's point," form a statement which "at some level operates only on the basis of an unremitting patriarchalism."[189] Women as women are outsiders. At issue here and elsewhere is whether women as women could be seen by men as part of a human ideal, in

---

184. For an attempt to discern stages of conflict, see Marjanen, *The Woman*, 223.

185. K. King, "Kingdom in the Gospel of Thomas," 53. Other sayings which deal with to whom the kingdom belongs are logia 3 and 113; with how one gets into the kingdom, logia 21, 22, 46, 49, 99. S. Davies argues that the Kingdom is also identified with Wisdom (*The Gospel of Thomas and Christian Wisdom* [New York: Seabury, 1983] 36–61). Logion 114, then, implicitly links women with foolishness, lack of understanding.

186. B. Blatz, "The Coptic Gospel of Thomas," NTA 1.114.

187. Marjanen, *The Woman*, 45–46.

188. See Perkins, "Gospel of Thomas" 558.

189. King, "Kingdom in the Gospel of Thomas," 66.

or as the Human One. Obviously some men could not see them this way; but the very conflict indicates that some women could.[190]

The apocryphal Peter is often associated with hostility toward women. He is portrayed in one version of Acts of Philip as a man who "fled from all places where there was a woman."[191] Elsewhere in the fifth-century ascetic work, the Pseudo-Titus Epistle, Peter is shown eliminating the sexual threat of a young girl by his prayer "that the Lord bestow on her what is expedient for her soul." She drops dead.[192] In the Acts of Peter, he also causes his own daughter to become paralyzed in order to preserve her virginity: "For this (daughter) will wound many souls if her body remains healthy."[193]

There are three major lines of interpretation of the phrases in Gospel of Thomas 114 "being made/making oneself male,"[194] and their overlap is apparent. (1) The first involves a female's concrete impersonation of a male, by means of cross-dressing and cutting her hair short. As well as symbolizing a radical ascetic choice, this could be an act of self defense, a minimization of female vulnerability in a patriarchal world. For example, in the case of Thecla (Acts of Thecla 25.40), her disguise keeps her safe as a traveller with Paul, but also "hints that Thecla is taking up a 'manly' way of life and must leave her 'female' self behind."[195] This text, from the second half of the second century, or the oral tradition behind it, may be the first witness we have of an interpretation of Gospel of Thomas 114 in terms of what Marjanen calls "a concrete male interpretation."[196] Burrus points out how Thecla "shatters the spatial boundaries which define women's social roles. In the course of the narrative Thecla moves first to gaze out of the window, then to leave the house alone at night, then to leave her town in the company of a strange man, and finally to travel independently and speak publicly as a man would."[197] In the Acts of Philip VIII, 4 Christ tells Mary, "[C]hange your dress and appearance: take off everything external to yourself which is reminiscent of a woman, the summer dress you are wearing. Do not let the hem of your clothing trail along the ground, or drape it, but cut it off."[198] This is to protect her from the serpents of the village Opheorymos, who might otherwise take her for Eve. According to one recension of the Acts of Philip VIII, 125, Mary says, "I am not a

---

190. See below, Appendix B on 1 Enoch 70–71 and "identification mysticism."

191. 142; Lipsius & Bonnet II, 81; see Marjanen, *The Woman*, 46.

192. See A. de Santos Otero, "Pseudo-Titus Epistle," NTA 2.57. The girl is raised at the insistance of her father, and is later seduced.

193. Acts of Peter, BG 8502,4; NHL pp. 529–31. See Marjanen, *The Woman*, 46.

194. The framework of this section is drawn from Marjanen, *The Woman*, 40–44.

195. S. E. McGinn, "The Acts of Thecla," *Searching the Scriptures*, 2. n. 81, p. 827.

196. Marjanen himself thinks the Acts of Philip may provide this first witness.

197. V. Burrus, "Word and Flesh: the Bodies and Sexuality of Ascetic Women in Christian Antiquity," JFSR 10 (1994) 47.

198. Bovon, "Paschal Privilege," 156–57; *Acta Philippi*, 245.

woman" (*ouk eimi gunē*).[199] As Woolf puts it, "the change of clothes ... change[s] our view of the world and the world's view of us."[200] This meaning involving disguises is clearly not intended in the Gospel of Thomas.

(2) "Making oneself male" in Logion 114 can be interpreted in light of the Platonic myth of the androgyne, as reflected in the creation stories of Genesis. The woman is made male by reentering Adam, restoring the pre-fall state before gender division. (Gen 2:22). To make oneself "neither male nor female" (logion 22) is somehow related to "becoming male" (114). However, the word for male (*hoout*) appears in 114, instead of the word for human (*rōme*), signaling that there is a difference or dissonance between the ideals of the two logia. Buckley suggests therefore that a two-stage process is imagined here for women: "an initiation ritual [is] required for the female so that she may be restored to the lost unity of Adam [the living spirit] in Genesis 2." Mary must return "via the male element" to the unity of the spiritual being of Gen 2:7 (cf. logion 22 where "a totally new creation is demanded, which abolishes the pattern of opposites"). Female salvation is seen as more complicated than that of the male.[201] This logion is often read to hint at primordial androgyny, with pre-Paradisial Adam, the living spirit, enclosing both male and female. But rather than being a movement beyond gender, this looks like becoming a "male androgyne,"[202] the male Adam become autonomous, not in need of a 'helper' because the 'helper' is within. DeConick therefore thinks a two-stage process is not necessary for women: to make oneself "neither male nor female" (logion 22) is the same as "becoming male" (114). Both have to do with return to the pristine state of the first *Man* who was neither gender but was "in the male form with woman concealed inside of him."[203] This might be called androcentric androgyny. The male disciples, apparently, are thought of as already having become "living spirit" which Mary will resemble; but they are still called "males."

(3) In the conceptual framework of contemporary culture, "female" meant earthly, sensual, imperfect, passive;[204] "male" meant transcendent, chaste, perfect, active, autonomous, rational, virtuous, courageous. The movement of salvation

199. Recension DELTA (ed. Bonnet, *Acta apostolorum* 54 line 26; cited by Bovon, "Paschal Privilege," n. 64, p. 235: Bovon reads this as Mary pretending not to be a woman.
200. V. Woolf, *Orlando* (New York: Harcourt Brace & Co, 1928) 187.
201. Buckley, "An Interpretation of Logion 114," 245–72. She reads in terms of transformation, not imitation. Mary must become like Salome, who Buckley says is initiated in logion 61. Cf. W. Meeks, "The Image of the Androgyne: Some Uses of a Symbol in Earliest Christianity," *History of Religions* 13 (1974) 165–208.
202. King ("Kingdom in the Gospel of Thomas," 66) attributes this suggestion to H. Attridge and D. McDonald in conversation; she links it as DeConick does to Philo's ideal of a male androgyne in his interpretation of Genesis 1.
203. A. D. DeConick, *Seek to See Him* (New York: Brill, 1996) 19–20; she refers to Philo, *Op. mundi*. 134: "the heavenly man" of Gen 1:27 was "neither male nor female." She argues that the Gospel of Thomas is not gnostic but mystical.
204. Philo derides femaleness as "weak, easily deceived, cause of sin, lifeless, diseased, enslaved, unmanly, nerveless, mean, slavish, sluggish" (see Meeks, "The Image of the Androgyne," 176).

for women and men, then, is from what is physical and earthly to that which is spiritual and heavenly.[205] While "becoming male" might be imagined by and even perhaps for a woman as the movement of a woman away from traditional femininity but not necessarily femaleness — that is, as becoming androgynous, crossing and balancing gender roles, the breaking of stereotypes — this was not the goal, according to this reading of Logion 114. By making women male, gender distinction, seen as characteristic of the fallen status of humans, is undone; if there is only one gender, there is no gender distinction. Asexuality is the goal, not androgyny.[206] Castelli points to the differentiation in gnostic texts "between a notion of 'oneness,' where sexual or gender identity is erased, and a notion of an 'androgyne,' where genders are blended. In these texts, androgyny is seen as monstrous and problematic, not as a state to be embraced."[207] The only exception I see is the depiction of Mary in the Gospel of Mary, an exception which will be explored below.

However it is interpreted, the goal of a woman "becoming male" reinscribes traditional gender hierarchies of male over female, masculine over feminine. But the possibility that women can "become male" also stretches the boundaries of the hegemonic gendered order, if only for a moment. It paradoxically "also re-veals the tenuousness and malleability of the naturalized categories of male and female."[208] Gender identity and gender difference are seen as not fixed. The "ma-nipulation of the constraints of gender and the social conventions linked to them" are illustrated for Castelli in the account of Perpetua whose visions lead her to actually cast off the female body and its social roles and ties.[209] The third-century Martyrdom of Perpetua and Felicitas incorporates Perpetua's own diary (which may come from 203 C.E.[210]), in which she sees herself made male in a final vision

---

205. So M. Meyer, "Making Mary Male: The Categories 'Male' and 'Female' in the Gospel of Thomas," *NTS* 31 (1985) 554–70.

206. Meyer, "Making Mary Male," 561 on logion 22 and Philo. This might involve the acceptance of a celibate/virginal lifestyle. Homosexuality does not seem to have been envisioned in this regard. See D. Boyarin, " 'Behold Israel According to the Flesh' " On Anthropology and Sexuality in Late Antique Judaisms," *Yale Journal of Criticism* 2 (1992) 34–35 on Philo's idea of incorporeal androgyny.

207. E. Castelli, " 'I Will Make Mary Male' " Pieties of the Body and Gender Transformation of Christian Women in Late Antiquity," *Body Guards: the Cultural Politics of Gender Ambiguity* (ed. J. Ep-stein and K. Straub; New York: Routledge, 1991) 32. Meyer ("Making Mary Male, 560) distinguishes between "the mutual elimination of sexual characteristics" (a goal of asexual unity which he finds in logion 22) and "the hermaphroditic manifestation of complete sexual features."

208. Castelli, " 'I Will Make Mary Male,' " 33.

209. Castelli, " 'I Will Make Mary Male,' " 34. She notes how the narrator reinserts her into the gendered order and resolves the gender ambiguities and tensions in Perpetua's first-person narrative. Early Christian women's refusal to participate in conventional sexual roles Castelli thinks was "not as an attempt to undercut the patriarchal social order, but in order to achieve perfection" (a distinction that I think some women may not have made so clear-cut). The refusal was perceived ambivalently (46). Apocryphal depictions of Mary's spiritual achievement, and the hostility of Peter for her illustrate this ambivalence.

210. See M. A. Tilley, "The Passion of Perpetua and Felicity," *Searching the Scriptures* 2.833, and references there.

of her martyrdom, a vision of a fight to the death with an Egyptian: "My clothes were stripped off, and suddenly I was a man" (10).[211] In her waking life, she stands up to her father; she leaves behind her child; her breast milk dries up; she bravely dies a martyr. The outward appearance as male is not a disguise, but the embracing of a form of piety that resists dominant cultural expectations for women. Her vision of being male can be seen as a recognition of her female strength, not primarily an expression of the alienation of self from the female body or rejection of her worth as a woman.[212] "[T]his asymmetrical process of transformation" only for women which we find in these apocryphal texts was an important early "moment of slippage," says Castelli.[213] We can hope it allowed for some androgynous behavior of women (and maybe even of men), some performance of a broad spectrum of roles, some unexpected conduct. "For it was this mixture in her of man and woman, one being uppermost and then the other, that often gave her conduct an unexpected turn.... Whether, then, Orlando was most man or woman, it is difficult to say and cannot now be decided."[214]

The disciples' jealousy of Mary Magdalene, the Lord's "companion," is apparent in the Gospel of Philip 63, 31–64, 9. Faced with the fact that the Lord "[...loved] her more than [all] the disciples [and used to] kiss her often on her [...]," the rest of the disciples ask him "Why do you love her more than all of us?" The text is usually emended so that the question is mean-spirited, springing from sexual and spiritual jealousy: "Do they wish to be kissed as Mary is?"[215] It challenges his preference for her, and as competition for the attention of a male Savior, it has a homoerotic cast, which may be a signal understanding of high-level spirituality in terms of penetration.[216] An expression of their offense and disapproval, it pits them against her, and indicates their lack of regard for her, and/or their fear of her "theologically threatening position."[217] Jesus' response is either the indirectly responsive question alone, "Why do I not love you like her?" which goes unanswered, or this question plus the little parable that follows: "When a blind man and one who sees are both together in darkness, they are no different from one another. When the light comes, then he who sees will see the light, and he who is blind will remain in darkness."

Without the parable, Jesus' response has been read by Buckley as a deliberate provocation of the disciples' jealousy, "in order to demonstrate that they do

211. On hair cutting and transvestism, see further Castelli, "Virginity, 75–76.
212. See Burrus, "Word and Flesh," 30, following P. C. Miller, "The Devil's Gateway: An Eros of Difference in the Dreams of Perpetua," *Dreams* 2 (1992) 62. Cf. K. Aspergren, *The Male Woman: A Feminine Ideal in the Early Church* (Stockholm: Almqvist & Wiksell International, 1990) 142: in her male and female qualities are woven together; she fights as a man and conquers as a woman.
213. Castelli, "'I Will Make Mary Male,'" 46–47.
214. Woolf, *Orlando*, 189–90.
215. Buckley, "'The Holy Spirit," 215.
216. See King, "Prophetic Power and Women's Authority," 30–31.
217. Buckley, "'The Holy Spirit,'" 215.

not understand the kiss" that makes Mary "spiritually" pregnant (cf. 58–59).[218] Buckley argues that the kiss carries sexual connotations here because Mary is a woman. I understand her correctly, she implies that this obscures its spiritual meaning for the rest of the disciples. As we have seen, ambiguity and a refusal of the questions that obsess others are marks of this author's thought. The disciples, then, can be understood as intolerant of ambiguity. The parable, as part of Jesus' answer, depicts Mary as able to see the light, and the disciples as blind. He loves her and kisses her because she is different; and vice versa. Because the disciples are portrayed elsewhere in the Gospel of Philip in a mostly positive way — as anointed spiritual authorities, bearers of the tradition — Marjanen relegates their hostility to Mary to the time before the resurrection, before they had revelation of Jesus "in glory on the mountain" (reading 58, 5–10 in the light of other gnostic revelation dialogues[219] as a post-resurrection scene, not as a transfiguration). "He became great, but he made the disciples great, that they might be able to see him in his greatness." Before the resurrection, according to this interpretation, only Mary Magdalene could "see." She is granted this superiority to the others by the author of the Gospel of Philip because the role of Jesus' "companion" could not be assigned to a disciple without understanding.[220] While this seems to me a plausible interpretation, so too is one which stresses the post-resurrection superiority of Mary Magdalene and the post-resurrection hostility of the rest of the disciples. Or, even better, an interpretation which sidesteps this question. Resurrection and pre-resurrection states — even, presumably, of Jesus — are not sharply distinguished in an ordinary way in this work: resurrection must be experienced before one dies. "Those who say they will die first and then rise are in error. If they do not first receive the resurrection while they live, when they die they will receive nothing" (73,1–4). Furthermore, there is no indication that the disciples are thought of here as perfect, even after receiving revelation.

In the Pistis Sophia, Peter is mentioned three times as opposing Mary. (1) In I, 36–37, when Jesus has spoken about the second repentance of the Pistis Sophia, he asks the disciples if they understand in what manner he is speaking with them. "Peter leapt forward, he said to Jesus: 'My Lord, we are not able to suffer this woman who takes the opportunity from us, and does not allow anyone of us to speak, but she speaks many times.'" Peter here protests for all the males, accusing Mary of denying them opportunity, and attributing to her the power to silence them. Jesus answers, mollifying and coddling Peter: "'Let him in whom the power of his Spirit has welled up so that he understands what I say, come forward and speak. Nevertheless, thou Peter, I see thy power within thee understands the interpretation.... Now at this time do thou, Peter, speak the thought

---

218. Buckley, "'The Holy Spirit,'" 217. The kiss is seen by Buckley as alluding to the secret activity of the bridal chamber.
219. In the Sophia of Jesus Christ, the Letter of Peter to Philip, and Pistis Sophia I–III.
220. Marjanen, The Woman, 142–46.

of her [Sophia's] repentance in the midst of thy brethren." Peter quotes Psalm 70, and is praised, "'Well done, Peter, this is the interpretation of her repentance. You are blessed beyond all men upon earth, for I have revealed to you these mysteries.... And I will fill you with Spirit so that you are called Pneumatics, fulfilled in every pleroma.'" The response of Jesus evokes Matt 16:19; 18:18.[221] Note that Peter calls Mary "this woman," not his fellow-disciple[222] or sister. He thus verbally pushes her away, creating a distinction or difference, which is in effect a rift, a separation. It is not clear how Mary has taken the opportunity from the males — by the speed and enthusiasm of her responses? She does not speak again until I, 43 when she springs up to explain that Philip, Thomas and Matthew are in their writings the three witnesses of which Moses spoke (Deut 19:15).

(2) In II, 72 she is wary, "My Lord, my mind is understanding at all times that I should come forward and give the interpretation of the words which [Pistis Sophia] spoke, but I am afraid of Peter, for he threatens me and hates our race."[223] She is afraid not only for herself, but for the "race" (*genos*) of women.[224] The First Mystery replies that "Everyone who will be filled with the Spirit of light to come forward and give the interpretation of those things which I say, him will no one be able to prevent." King comments, "Here the issue of gender is sidestepped in favor of nongendered spirituality."[225] Good argues that the text's care not to countenance either Peter's or Mary's grievance "by having Jesus/the First Mystery speak directly to it, perhaps is an attempt by the author of the text to prevent a rift between the two newly defined and not yet separated groups," gnostics and the proto-orthodox.[226] Marjanen, in contrast, thinks we have here two different gnostic views about spiritual hierarchy.[227] Mary is told to give her interpretation, and she does, again in II, 74 and again and again.

In III, 122 Peter is put to the test by Jesus to see if he is compassionate to a repentant woman; there is no indication this is meant to represent Mary. He passes the test. It is interesting to note that Thomas also appears to be afraid of his brothers: he comes forward to speak in I, 46, saying, "rejoice greatly because thou hast revealed to us these words. Nevertheless I have suffered my brothers up till now lest I cause anger in them." Furthermore, Peter's anger seems to have

---

221. Cf. IV, 141 where the keys of the kingdom of heaven are given to all the disciples, undercutting the power of Peter as understood in some circles; IV, 142 where the power of forgiving and binding are given to all of them.

222. Good, "Pistis Sophia," 2. 684.

223. Marjanen (*The Woman*, 151) thinks that other sayings of Mary (e.g. II, 72) suggest that Mary could have spoken even more frequently, but was remaining silent out of consideration for or fear of the others.

224. Marjanen (*The Woman*, 156) understands *genos* here as the female sex, not a self-designation of gnostics.

225. King, "The Gospel of Mary," 2.623.

226. Good, "Pistis Sophia," 685. She thinks that Peter represents a group that the text is eager to include, and that the gnostic group is egalitarian and non-competitive (695–96).

227. Marjanen, *The Woman*, 158.

made Mary more afraid of Jesus. The passage in II, 83 is worth quoting at length for the neurotic-sounding rationalization Mary presents (you told us to ask; and there is no one else to ask but you; and I [we] do ask out of spiritual knowledge) and Jesus' firm reply.

> She says, " 'My Lord, be not angry with me, that I question thee, for we question all things with assurance and certainty. For thou hast once said to us, 'Seek and ye shall find, and knock and it shall be opened to you, for everyone that seeks will find, and to everyone that knocks it will be opened to him.'[228] Now at this time, my Lord, whom will I find, or to whom shall we knock, or rather who is able to say to us the answer to the words on which we question thee, or rather who knows the power of the words which we will question? Because with understanding (mind) thou hast given us understanding (mind) of the light; and thou hast given us perception and greatly elevated thought. For this reason now there is no one who exists in the world of mankind, nor who exists in the height of the aeons who is able to say to us the answer to the words which we question, except thyself alone who knowest the All, and art complete in the All. Because I[229] do not question in the manner in which the men of the world question, but we question with the knowledge of the height which thou hast given to us, and we question with the type of superior questioning with which thou hast taught us, that we should question therewith. Now at this time, my Lord, be not angry with me, but reveal to me the subject on which I will question thee.' " Jesus answers her, "Question that which thou dost wish to question, and I will reveal it with assurance and certainty. Truly, truly, I say to you: rejoice with great joy and be exceedingly glad. If you question everything with assurance, I will be exceedingly glad because you question everything with assurance, and you ask about the manner in which one should inquire. Now at this time question that which thou dost question, and I will reveal it with joy."

In the very next chapter, however, she is springing up to say again, "My Lord, be not angry with me for questioning thee, for we question all things with assurance." He responds that she should ask what she wants, and he will reveal it openly "without parable." (II, 85). Again in II, 88 she says, "My Lord, be not angry with me that I question thee because I have troubled thee many times." Many times her speaking is prefaced with this warding off of Jesus' anger (II, 97; II, 98 [speaking for all: "be not angry with me for questioning thee, but have mercy on us . . . "]; III, 108). The fear of Jesus' anger — ironic in this work which emphasizes his compassion over and over — is catching: John has it in II, 90; III, 107: "Be not angry with me that I question thee on all things with assurance and certainty." and Andrew in II, 100 (but with good reason: the Savior is angry with his lack of understanding about the material world and renunciation of it).

Marjanen comments accurately that "Peter's problem with Mary Magdalene is that she is spiritually more advanced than his male colleagues and that she is

---

228. Matt 7:7–8; Luke 11:9–10.
229. The manuscript reads "I" but Schmidt/MacDermot emend to "we."

a woman."[230] He is envious, contentious, and misogynistic — traits, as we have seen, associated with him elsewhere. The tension between them does not involve doctrinal issues. It is about the position of Mary within the group of disciples, her right to act as a spiritual and intellectual authority, her right to take the lead, to represent. In contrast, the conflict in Gospel of Thomas concerns "the possibility of women to gain salvation."[231] Also in contrast, the conflict in Gospel of Philip concerns love: why Mary is loved more, or loved too much.

(3) The issue of Mary speaking too much is resolved in Pistis Sophia IV, which is independent of, and only secondarily attached to, I–III. Book IV may be older than books I–III,[232] but it makes a certain narrative sense to place it here, bringing to a conclusion the theme of hostility between Peter and Mary, now expanded to all "the women." If IV were placed before I–III, we would have a work rehabilitating the voices of women — which may in fact have been the purpose of I–III. In arranging the traditions as we now have them, the author may have used an older tradition to try to virtually silence women.

In IV, 146, after Mary has spoken briefly three times and Salome once in the extant text,[233] "Peter said, 'My Lord, let the women cease to question, that we also may question.'" (Cf. 1 Tim 2:11–12 [ca. 125 C.E.?]: "Let a woman learn in silence with full submission. I permit no woman to teach or to have authority over a man; she is to keep silent."[234]) Jesus — the Jesus who in I, 36–37 said that the one whom the Spirit empowers to understand should come forward and speak up — "said to Mariam and the women, 'Give way to the men, your brothers,[235] that they may question also.'" Mary does not "cease to question" as Peter desired, but as the advanced star pupil she is slowed down and restrained so that the less bright students can catch up.[236] She does not speak again until 148, after Peter, Andrew, Thomas, Bartholomew and John have asked their questions. This is her last question, and the last question by any woman; it is followed by a question of John's and by the disciples' weeping and pleas for mercy. Mary receives no special praise or promise or blessing in IV. It is important to note that in this

---

230. Marjanen, *The Woman*, 159. Note that here the accusation that Peter is misogynistic comes from Mary.

231. Marjanen, *The Woman*, 157.

232. So Bovon, "Paschal Privilege," 152: "said to be older."

233. There is a lacuna of 6 pages (4 leaves) between chapters 143 and 144, which may have contained questions asked by the women.

234. Some critics claim this passage is about wives and husbands, not all women and men. Cf. 1 Cor 14:33–36 (mid-50s C.E.): "As in all the churches of the saints, women should be silent in the churches. For they are not permitted to speak, but should be subordinate, as the law also says. If there is anything they desire to know, let them ask their husbands (or: men) at home. For it is shameful for a woman to speak in church. Or did the word of God originate with you? Or are you the only ones it has reached?" On these passages, see A. C. Wire, *The Corinthian Women Prophets* (Minneapolis: Fortress, 1990) 149–52; "1 Corinthians," *Searching the Scriptures*, 2.185–89; Linda M. Maloney, "The Pastoral Epistles," *Searching the Scriptures*, 2.369–70.

235. Lit.: leave place to your male brothers.

236. Kevin Sullivan, private communication.

book Jesus blesses the wine and speaks the words of institution of the Eucharist
(IV, 141); the mystery (ritual) of forgiveness is also stressed. In the near-silencing
of Mary, "sacerdotal magic" seems to be on the way to becoming the exclusive
property of males.[237] Mary and the other women have been swallowed up by
"all the disciples," whose questions do not show any insight but merely serve to
highlight the authority of Jesus as the only revealer. All Mary's questions, all her
springing up to speak, all that vitality is over: the author may think of Jesus'
rebuke of her as justified.

Even though there are no individual male "spiritual heroes" in Pistis Sophia IV,
the maleness[238] and male-bondedness of the "reasonable" Jesus in this text boosts
the authority of the male disciples. A text by another hand is written in the
first column of the recto of the last unpaginated leaf, about the preaching of the
Gospel of the Kingdom in the whole world, with Christ working with them (cf.
Markan Appendix 16:20). Two lines following are erased, probably the title. The
title of IV with I–III might have been: Jesus becomes a wimp, a waffle. Or better:
Jesus is busy; he is no longer interested in gender roles or the roles of women.

There is no narration of conflict between Mary and the male disciples in the
Manichaean Psalm Book II, 187, but it is predicted by the risen Jesus that the
Eleven "wandering orphans" will, through scorn and disregard, necessitate that
her message to them be changed in order to reach them and move them to action:
"Say to them, 'Arise, let us go, it is your brother that calls you.' If they scorn my
brotherhood, say to them, 'It is your master.' If they disregard my mastership, say
to them, 'It is your Lord'" (18–22). If she sees that "their wits are gone," she
is to draw Simon Peter to herself and remind him of a saying of Jesus to him,
"'Remember what I uttered between thee and me...in the Mount of Olives: 'I
have something to say, I have none to whom to say it'" (24–29). Peter is singled
out for mention in Mark 16:7, where no special message is given. The apocryphal
saying here is puzzling. It does not, I think, imply that Peter, as the leading disciple,
not Mary Magdalene, is the one who should receive now some important message,
which Jesus cannot deliver to him while he is at the Jordan.[239] It seems, rather,
to remind Peter of some past failure, perhaps his betrayal, in order to bring him
back to his "wits." A similar saying appears in the Acts of John 97–98: John says
"I saw him suffer, and did not wait by his suffering, but fled to the Mount of
Olives and wept at what had come to pass." He receives a vision of Jesus who
shows him a Cross of light with the Lord above it as a voice which says, "John,
there must (be) one man (to) hear these things from me; for I need one who is

---

237. See and contrast Good, "Pistis Sophia," 704; she does not deal with IV as a work distinct
from I–III.

238. Contrast the male/female aspect of Jesus prominent in Pistis Sophia I–III. See above, p. 140.

239. So Marjanen, *The Woman*, 182–83, if I understand him correctly. He says "The conversation
appears to anticipate the very post-resurrection situation where Peter and the other disciples have left
for the Jordan and the Risen Jesus cannot under those circumstances speak the important message
he has to say....Mary Magdalene who is present is not the one to hear it."

ready to hear." What follows is a description of the gnostic understanding of the crucifixion as paradox and mystery ("You hear that I suffered, yet I suffered not; and that I suffered not, yet I did suffer").[240] Mary's delivering of the message and the male disciples' scorn are not narrated in the Manichaean Psalm Book.

They are both narrated, however, in the Epistula Apostolorum, where three women come in turn to tell the men. Mary is disbelieved in the Ethiopic version: "And we said to her, 'What have we to do with you, O woman? He that is dead and buried, can he then live?' And we did not believe her, that our Saviour had risen from the dead." Sarah's report is met with the accusation that she is lying. When the Savior goes with Mary and her sisters on the third try, the men doubt it is he, but he eventually convinces them of his resurrection. The women in the Gospel of Peter flee afraid from the tomb; they have been given no message, and they tell no one (13:55–57).

In the Apostolic Church Order, Peter initiates a discussion about the eucharist: " 'We have gone too fast in making ordinances; let us signify accurately concerning the offering of the body and the blood.' John said: 'Ye have forgotten, brethren, when the Teacher asked for the bread and the cup, and blessed them, saying: This is my body and my blood, that he permitted not these women to be (stand) with us.' Martha said: 'It was because of Mary, because he saw her smiling.' Mary said: 'I laughed not yet (or: I laughed no more): for he said unto us before that: "That which is weak shall be saved by means of that which is strong." ' " In this text, we have the only instance in which John excludes women (here, from the priesthood), and in which a woman appears hostile to Mary.[241]

9. Defended

Jesus comes to Mary's defense in Gospel of Thomas 114: "Look, I will lead her that I may make her male, in order that she too may become a living spirit resembling you males." As King notes, the reply is odd. Women do not seek and find, but are "led" (*sōk*) — a verb elsewhere used in this work to describe persons who lead others astray. "This odd usage seems to indicate a subtle agreement with Peter's point that women are somehow less worthy than men. Jesus, however states that with special help they could make it."[242] Helmut Koester understands "maleness" as "solitary existence" (*monakhos*) leaving behind everything that binds human beings to this world.[243] Williams wonders if this term means reunification of elements within the individual, a reuniting of male and female, restoration of a primordial androgyny, childlike, pre-sexual innocence; or if

---

240. NTA, 2.185–87, translation by K. Schaeferdiek.

241. M. R. James translation, *The Apocryphal New Testament* (Oxford: Clarendon, 1960) 35–36. See above, for different readings of the dynamics of this discussion and of Martha and Mary's roles in the exclusion of women from the Eucharistic ministry, pp. 137, 143–44.

242. King, "Kingdom in the Gospel of Thomas," 65.

243. H. Koester, "Introduction to the Gospel of Thomas," NHL, 126.

it means social solitariness, separation and celibacy.[244] Buckley, as we have seen, thinks that the hierarchical order of female, male and "living spirit" interprets Genesis 2, and that this logion speaks of an initiation ritual required only for the female, a first step to the abolition of sexual divisions altogether.[245] DeConick, on the other hand, interprets Gospel of Thomas 114 in terms of androcentric androgyny.[246] However maleness is understood here,[247] "Mary's spiritual status is defended against Peter's attack, but his categorical sexism is at best moderated, not opposed: women *as women* are apparently not worthy of life."[248] This falls far short of being a rebuke of Peter.[249] However the saying is understood, the basic logic of belonging by means of a transformation from female to male "works only against the mode of patriarchal presuppositions current in antiquity and Jesus' statement does nothing to contravene these."[250] Becoming an insider, with access to social identity, order, power, salvation, has a high price for women.

The Savior's defense of Mary against the question of the disciples ("Why do you love her more than all of us?") in the Gospel of Philip 55 is quite different. It is not a proposal or promise that she will be brought up to their level, but a question ("Why do I not love you like her?") and a little parable that both imply she is beyond them. The parable speaks of all, the blind and the sighted, being "no different from one another" in the darkness. But in the light, the blind remain blind, and the sighted see. If the disciples' question concerns gender issues, by implying perhaps that as a woman she should be loved less, the defense levels the field. "Why do I not love you like her?" is an invitation to self-reflection. The parable suggests that as the sighted see in the light, the loveable (spiritually talented?) are loved. Jesus' question goes unanswered.

In Pistis Sophia I–III, Jesus/First Mystery defends Mary's right to speak — though he does not mention Mary personally — by saying that those who understand should speak. "Let him in whom the power of his Spirit has welled up so that he understands what I say come forward and speak" (I,3). Moreover, he says such speech cannot be silenced: "Everyone who will be filled with the Spirit of light to come forward and give the interpretation of those things which I say, him will no one be able to prevent" (II, 72). In IV, 146, however, when Peter asks that Jesus silence the women so that the men (who have been asking questions) may question, Jesus does so: "Give way (lit: Leave place) to the men, your brothers, that they may question also." Mary is never directly defended when Peter attacks her and never directly spoken to about this, except in the last instance. Nor is her

---

244. Williams, *Rethinking*, 146.
245. Buckley, "An Interpretation of Logion 114," 245–72.
246. See above, p. 158.
247. See further, McGuire, "Women, Gender and Gnosis," 279–81.
248. King, "The Gospel of Mary Magdalene," 2.623.
249. Contrast Pagels, "Visions, Appearances, and Apostolic Authority," 425, who also reads the response of the Lord in the Pistis Sophia this way (but see below pp. 167–68).
250. King, "Kingdom in the Gospel of Thomas," 66.

charge addressed, that Peter hates her and hates women ("our race"). Instead, Jesus shows concern for the attacker.

In the Manichaean Psalm Book II, 187, Jesus coaches Mary on how to change her message when it is scorned. In the Epistula Apostolorum 11, Jesus himself goes with the women in the third attempt to tell of the resurrection; he rebukes Peter for denying him again (presumably by not believing the women, who, however, disappear from the story before the male disciples believe). Mary defends herself — if that is what she is doing — only in the Apostolic Order: accused of smiling at the Last Supper, she says she did not laugh.

The Gospel of Mary

Each of the nine points of my Magdalene profile is illustrated in the Gospel of Mary. She is prominent, exists in a textual world of androcentric language and sexist ideology, speaks boldly, plays a leadership role *visà vis* the male disciples, is a visionary, is praised for her superior understanding, is identified as the intimate companion of Jesus, is opposed by and in open conflict with one or more of the male disciples, and is defended.

Originally written in Greek in the late first or early second century C.E., the Gospel of Mary[251] was not present in the Nag Hammadi find.[252] It is preserved only in three fragmentary copies: a Coptic translation, and two Greek papyri.[253] The Greek fragments are both from Oxyrhynchus, but not from the same manuscript, as the handwriting and format differ. They also differ in important ways from the Coptic; and where they do, the Greek is preferred, not only because these fragments are written earlier and in the original language, but also because they appear to present earlier controversy. Comparison of the Greek and the Coptic indicates that objections raised about Mary originally focused on the content of her teaching, and later on her being a woman. The later version also appears to correct misreadings of the earlier. The following translation by Karen King privileges the Greek.[254]

The first six pages of this work are missing; they may have included a reference to the location of the scene. What we do have begins with what is probably a

---

251. It is generally read as the Gospel of Mary (Magdalene). Some scholars, however, have argued this Mary is Mary the mother of Jesus. So E. Lucchesi, "Evangile selon Marie ou Evangile selon Marie-Madeleine?" *Analecta Bollandiana* 103 (1985) 366; but see Marjanen, *The Woman*, n. 2, p. 80.

252. However, it is translated by G. W. MacRae and R. McL. Wilson, and edited by D. M. Parrott, in *NHL*, 524–27.

253. The Coptic translation was discovered in Cairo by Schmid in 1896, and not published until 1955 by Till (P. Berolinensis gnosticus [BG] 8502,1). Originally having 19 pages, it is missing at least pages 1–6 and 11–14, perhaps half the text. The Greek fragments are P. Rylands III 463 (=BG 17.5–21; 18. 5–19.5) found in 1917 and published in 1938, and P. Oxyrhynchus 3525 (=BG 9.5–10.14), identified and published in 1983.

254. K. King, "Gospel of Mary," *The Complete Gospels* (ed. R. J. Miller; Sonoma, Calif.: Polebridge, 1994) 359. Hereafter cited as CG. Her chapter and verse divisions are used also.

postresurrection dialogue between the Savior and the disciples concerning matter ("Will matter then be utterly destroyed or not?") and sin ("What is the sin of the world?"). The answer to the first question seems to most readers to be negative, but seems to me ambiguous: "every nature, every modeled form, every creature [matter], exists in and with each other. They will dissolve again into their own proper root" (2:2–3).[255] The second question is answered by the denial that there is such a thing as sin in itself. Rather, human beings produce sin when they act according to a passion contrary to nature and its true image; when they uproot, so to speak (3:3–13). Then after commissioning them to "Go then, preach the good news of the domain," the risen Savior "departs."

> The disciples were distressed and wept greatly. "How are we going to go out to the rest of the world to preach the good news about the domain of the seed of true humanity[256] ?" they said. "If they did not spare him, how will they spare us?" Then Mary stood up. She greeted them all, and addressed her brothers: "Do not weep and be distressed nor let your hearts be irresolute. For his grace will be with you all and will shelter you. Rather we should praise his greatness, for he has joined us together and made us true human beings."[257] When Mary said these things, she turned their minds [to]ward the Good, and they began to [as]k about the wor[d]s of the Savi[or]. Peter said to Mary, "Sister, we know that the Savior loved you more than any other woman. Tell us the words of the Savior that you know but which we haven't heard." Mary responded, "I will re[port to you as much as] I remember that you don't know." And she began to speak these words to them. She said, "I saw the Lord in a vision and I said to him, 'Lord, I saw you today in a vision.' He said to me "Congratulations to you for not wavering at seeing me. For where the mind is, there is the treasure." I said to him, 'Lord, how does a person who sees a vision see it — [with] the soul [or] with the spirit?' The Savior answered, 'The <visionary> does not see with the soul or with the spirit, but the mind which exists between these two — that is [what] sees the vision and that is w[hat]' (5:1–7:6)

Four pages are missing at this point. The text resumes in the midst of a description by Mary of the ascent of the soul past the four powers (the four elements of matter), the last of which takes seven forms (representing the seven astrological spheres), "the seven Powers of Wrath." They are Darkness, Desire, Ignorance, Zeal for Death,[258] Domain of the Flesh, Foolish Wisdom of the Flesh, Wisdom of the Wrathful Person. When the goal is achieved, the soul says, "From now on, for the rest of the course of the [due] measure of the time of the age, I will rest

---

255. King, "Prophetic Power and Authority," n. 35, p. 37 says "Whether that root is matter or nothingness cannot be determined with certainty from the text." But 3:5–6, in which the Good sets "what belongs to every nature" within its root, gives me the impression the root may be something else: something (not nothing) positive, a true image of nature (3:13). King thinks that while the body in this work is not considered evil, ultimately it will not be saved or resurrected. "While the soul ascends to its immortal rest, the material body returns to its root" (25). But perhaps this is an interpretation of the body's salvation. In any case, the soul does not return to it.

256. King, CG, 359.

257. Lit: made us into men.

258. NHL: "the excitement of Death."

i[n] silence."[259] There is no description of the goal, no description of the highest heaven as temple or anything else.

> When Mary had said these things, she fell silent, since it was up to this point that the Savior had spoken to her. But Andrew sai[d, "B]rothers, what is your opinion of what was just said? I for one don't believe that the S[a]vior said these things, be[cause] these opinions seem to be so different from h[is th]ought." After reflecting on these ma[tt]ers, [Peter said,] "Has the Sa[vior] spoken secretly to a wo[m]an and [not] openly so that [we] would all hear? [Surely] he did [not wish to indicate] that [she] is more worthy than we are?" Then Mary wept and said to Peter, "Peter, my brother, what are you imagining about this? Do you think that I've made all this up secretly by myself or that I am telling lies about the Savior?" Levi said to Peter, "Peter, you have a constant inclination to anger and you are always ready to give way to it. And even now you are doing exactly that by questioning the woman as if you're her adversary. If the Savior considered her to be worthy, who are you to disregard her? For he knew her completely <and> l oved her devotedly. Instead, we should be ashamed and, once we clothe ourselves with perfect humanity, we should do what we were commanded. We should announce the good news as the Savior ordered, and not be laying down any rules or making laws." After he said these things, Levi left <and> began to announce the good news (9:30–10:14).

The nine points of my profile are apparent in this work. Mary's prominence is indicated by her standing in the assembly to address the quaking, grieving disciples. She need not be imagined as the only woman present. She is not identified as wife or mother, and nothing is said of her sexuality or anyone else's. The fear of the others indicates that they have only partially understood[260] the teaching of the Savior: they are right that they will not be "spared" as he was not, but they are wrong to fear death and to let their fear paralyze them. Mary, not afraid of death and not afraid of the disciples, comforts them in language reminiscent of Jesus' Last Supper discourse (5:5 with John 14:1 "Let not your hearts be troubled"). She insists that they are all united and will be protected, and focuses them on the greatness of the Savior and their own spiritual community and inner strength.

Though the language is androcentric (lit: "son of man" in 4:5; "he has ... made us into men" in 5:8; "put on the perfect man" in 10:11), King has chosen to translate inclusively ("seed of true humanity" in 4:5 [*pšēre mprōme*]; "true human beings" in 5:8 [*rōme*]; and "perfect humanity" in 10:11 [*prōme ntelios*]) because the language here has a different connotation than it has in other contexts.[261] The term "seed" is used by King as a pointer to the androcentric nature of the

---

259. On the sub-genre of apocalypses that takes the form of ascent of the visionary through the heavens (1 Enoch's Book of Watchers; Aramaic Levi 4Q213a; Testament of Levi), see J. J. Collins, "The Afterlife in Apocalyptic Literature," *Judaism in Late Antiquity* (ed. A. J. Avery-Peck and J. Neusner; Leiden: Brill, 2000) 4.131.

260. Contrast Marjanen, *The Woman*, 91 who argues that they have misunderstood the Savior who "tried to teach that deliverance from the body results in the removal of suffering and death."

261. The terms used here can be generic or refer to the male. In contrast, as we have seen, in Gospel of Thomas 114, Jesus speaks of making Mary *hoout*, a term which means male.

original.[262] "True" is added[263] to indicate the reference is not to a male person but to "the archetypal Image of humanity in each person,"[264] "the heavenly model and the spiritual progenitor of all humanity." Joined together,[265] Mary and the males are both to be "made true human beings" (5:8), and at the end of the work Levi urges the males to "clothe themselves with the perfect humanity" (10:11).

The point King makes with her translation is an important one. Here meaning is in conflict with language, is straining against ordinary usage. I see no indication that the viewpoint of the author is sexist, that men are valued more than women, or that in order to become true human beings women must overcome their femaleness more than men must overcome their maleness. In fact, that viewpoint, Peter's, is explicitly rejected.[266] The use of the masculine as a generic, to refer to humanity as a whole, springs from values which this gospel does not hold. In fact, the neuter term "the Good (*pagathon*)," to which Mary turns the disciples' minds in 5:9, may be a parallel to "the seed of true humanity." Marjanen comments that "the Good" is not Christological, since the neuter form is used, which, he says, citing Stern and Till, denotes non-humans.[267] But if the neuter is used here in a way that breaks out of androcentrism (not referring to the Savior but to the "perfect humanity") the inclusive ideal is changing the language. In 4:5–6 King translates with the English neuter to refer to the "seed of true humanity": "Follow it! Those who search for it will find it." Identifying with the archetypal image of the perfect humanity, recognizing oneself in it, conforming to it, is what this gospel presents as "following" the heavenly ideal that exists within each person. I do not see the Savior in this work as fully identical with perfect humanity or the seed of true humanity; rather, he seems to be an aspect of it. The Savior is (part of) and is not (the whole of) perfect humanity. Something similar may be described in 1 Enoch 71, treated in an appendix to this chapter. In her discussion of "identification mysticism," Pagels distinguishes between "identification between the soul and some sort of 'given,' essentially divine self" and identification (as in her reading of the Gospel of Philip) between the initiate and Christ, characterized there as perfect human (55:14).[268]

Mary's initial speech in the Gospel of Mary boldly names the disciples' weaknesses: they grieve, they weep, they are "irresolute" or doubtful.[269] She promises the Savior's grace will "shelter" them, and calls them to know themselves as joined

---

262. King, "The Gospel of Mary," 2.606–7.

263. Cf. *ptelios ˤrrōme* Gospel of Philip 55:14.

264. King, CG, 362.

265. Greek: *sunērtēken* P Oxy 3525. See Marjanen, *The Woman*, n. 37, p. 92. The Coptic reads "he has prepared us" in 5:8.

266. As it is not in the Gospel of Thomas, where the objection to Mary is countered by the mollifying statement that can be read: she will become like you (males).

267. Marjanen, *The Woman*, 92.

268. E. Pagels, "Ritual in the Gospel of Philip," *The Nag Hammadi Library After Fifty Years*, 186–87.

269. Note that their grief does not occasion visionary experience. Cf. Matt 28:17: "but some doubted."

together, made "true human beings." She calls them, that is, to a sense of their present unity and power, rather than to a hope of perfection and strength in some future time. Later, Peter asks Mary to teach that which she knows but which the others have not heard. She does so willingly,[270] describing a conversation with the Lord about her vision of him; she asks him about the experiential dynamics of vision, what aspect of consciousness receives it. When the text resumes after the four missing pages, she is in the midst of describing the ascent of the soul, and its dialogues with each of the Powers. When she has no more to say about the teachings of the Savior, she falls silent. When she is attacked by Andrew and Peter, weeping she counters Peter's objections.

Mary's leadership is clear at the beginning of the gospel, as she takes over the Savior's role when he departs, much like the Paraclete in the Gospel of John. Comforting and encouraging them (and in the Greek: kissing each of them[271]), she "turns their minds toward the Good." Her leadership at first seems to be accepted by the males who begin to ask her about the words of the Savior; Peter acknowledges that the Savior loved her, and that she knows words of the Savior that they do not know, and he asks her to tell them. His request may refer to pre-or post-resurrection teaching. When her teaching is challenged, Levi's intervention on her behalf validates her leadership — for himself at least, in the Greek text, as he leaves alone on the mission; for all, in the Coptic text, as they leave together.

It is not certain whether Mary's vision of the Savior is a pre-resurrection vision, or post-resurrection.[272] It clearly has a different status than the appearance to all of the disciples at the beginning of this work. She seems to be reporting to him in somewhat normal conversation — note her stuttering beginning ("'I,' she said, 'I' saw....")[273] — that she had seen him in vision earlier that day.[274] Or, this might be a vision within a vision, that is, Mary speaking *in* it of an earlier vision.[275] The Gospel itself is about events on the day the Savior "left" them, but no time frame is given for the interval between his death and the leaving, and no time

---

270. Marjanen thinks Mary enters the discussion only after Peter ("one of the apostles — in fact, the most important one") gives her permission by his invitation (*The Woman*, 93–94). But no one is an "apostle" in this text, and Peter — while obnoxious — seems no more important than any other male.

271. See Marjanen, *The Woman*, 86; the Coptic may also denote a kiss or an embrace. The kiss may imply the giving of spiritual nourishment.

272. E. Pagels ("Visions, Appearances and Apostolic Authority: Gnostic and Orthodox Traditions," *Gnosis* [ed. U. Bianchi et al.; Göttingen: Vandenhoeck & Ruprecht, 1978] 425) thinks that here "Instead of recounting events and sayings she recalls from her former companionship with the earthly Jesus, as Peter apparently expects, Mary reveals what she has *just seen* in a vision (*horama*)" (emphasis mine). I agree that the expectation may be there that she will speak about the earthly Jesus; but it may or may not be met.

273. The *NHL* translation retains this (525). Or perhaps the repetition is for emphasis.

274. That is, she saw the Lord in a vision, and later she said to him.... The Greek reads "Once when the Lord appeared to me in a vision," implying, as King says, that he may have appeared to her more than once ("Gospel of Mary," n. 27, p. 2.630).

275. King in *NHL*, 523: a vision and a private dialogue.

frame for her visions. If the time frame is thought of as long, there is opportunity for people, including her, to have had many post-resurrection visions. This text is certainly related to the tradition of a post-resurrection appearance of Jesus to Mary Magdalene (John 20:18: "I have seen the Lord"),[276] as we will see below in chapter 7. It might also have another dimension, represented as memory from the pre-resurrection career of Jesus. Morton Smith suggested visionary activity was a feature of the career of the historical Jesus. A mystic (Smith says magician) himself, Jesus taught mystical (magical) practices to some of his disciples.[277] In vision, the pre- and post-resurrection perspectives blur. The words of the Savior that Mary recounts in Gospel of Mary might, then, be thought of as (in our terms) words of the earthly Jesus.[278] My own attitude toward such "hallucinations" is not as negative Smith's. I also do not see the choice between understanding visionary material as experiential or understanding it as literary as a clear-cut either/or. In any case, the Savior is depicted as "the teacher of ascent wisdom to Mary Magdalene."[279]

Mary is represented as not knowing how one experiences visions, as she asks the Savior if it is with the soul or with the spirit.[280] The Savior tells her the vision is seen with the mind (*nous*), which is between the soul and spirit,[281] and acts as a mediator between sensory perceptions and divine spirit.[282] The visionary experience is not understood as penetration or loss of control; Mary is not "feminized" by it.[283] The Greek word *horama* may indicate the vision came to Mary in a dream. The information about the ascent of the soul is information she is relaying from the Savior, perhaps about his own post-mortem ascent, and/or perhaps about pre-mortem ascents in general.[284] It may also be information from her own mind's experience, of following the seed of true humanity within her,

276. Pasquier (*L'Evangile selon Marie*, n. 96, p. 71) points out that in contrast to John 20, here Mary recognizes the Savior immediately, and takes the initiative to speaks to him.

277. M. Smith, *Jesus the Magician* (New York: Harper & Row, 1978). See for example, p. 124 on ascent to the heavens; 121 on the transfiguration. Smith finds traces of stories that credited Jesus with the feat during his lifetime (Jn 3:13; Phil 2:5ff; 1 Tim 3:16; 2 Cor 12:2–5 [Paul understood by Smith as referring to Jesus; he later considered "favorably the hypothesis that Paul speaks of himself" (See Segal, *Paul the Convert*, n. 7, p. 314]). See Dialogue of the Savior 5, 135, 2–4 for certain prayers, instruction and laying on of hands after which the disciples "hoped that they would see it." Pagels says "This may reflect a liturgical setting in which the initiate expects to see visions" ("Visions, Appearances, and Apostolic Authority," 427).

278. Against Marjanen, *The Woman*, 94.

279. DeConick, *Seek to See Him*, 60.

280. De Boer (*Mary Magdalene*, 109) reads this as the question: revelation or projection? Does the vision come from the divine Spirit or from her own soul?

281. Merkur (*Gnosis*, 136) sees the contrast as pertaining to the different functions that the human mind and the divine spirit had during visionary experiences; a lack of consubstantiality is not implied.

282. King, "Prophetic Power," 26. But if it is a mediator, I do not see how it is "not associated with the senses."

283. King, "Prophetic Power," 31. It is not said to be a "flight out of the body," though it well may be.

284. Cf. Gospel of Philip 75, 22: "[It is proper] that we [by all means] become [perfect human beings] before we leave [the world]" (Marjanen, *The Woman*, 101). In the Gospel of Philip the means

searching for it and finding it. The missing pages prevent a judgment on exactly whose ascent is being described. The seven Powers of Wrath, which are the last to be overcome as the soul ascends, may be compared to — maybe even related to — the seven demons expelled from the Christian Testament Mary (Luke 8:2; Mark 16:9 with Jesus mentioned as the exorcist).[285] Surely the point of Mary telling the disciples about her vision of the Lord, and about the teaching on ascent, is to move them to vision and gnosis, to set them on that ascent. As a seer, she presents a vision of unity, for which she is opposed.

The Savior praises Mary for "not wavering at seeing me" in her vision. "For where the mind is, there is the treasure" (7:6). Her mind is stable, fixed on the eternal and spiritual. Peter's request — that Mary tell of the words of the Savior that she knows but that the males have not heard — acknowledges her as a teacher, the favorite woman. Mary responds that she will report what she remembers but they do not know (the Coptic of 6:3 makes it clearer that Mary has esoteric knowledge: "I will inform you about what is hidden from you"). The teaching that Mary gives in this work is not in conflict with the teaching of the Savior about matter and sin in 2–4, but Andrew accuses her of having "opinions... different from" the Savior's thought (10:2). In Levi's defense of her, he says "If the Savior considered her to be worthy, who are you to disregard her? For he knew her completely <and> loved her devotedly" (10:9–10). The verb *sōk* translated "considered" can be translated "guided" or "led" (cf. Gospel of Thomas 114). The Coptic of 10:10 reads, "Assuredly the Savior's knowledge of her is completely reliable." She is not praised by the men for her understanding, but the Savior's knowledge of her is thought by Levi — and by the author — to validate it.

Peter in 6:1 acknowledges that the Savior loved Mary "more than any other woman," which may imply that she knows something that other women do not know. But in 10:3–4, after hearing her teach he is incensed at the thought that the Savior might have spoken secretly to her, and that this might be an indication that she "is more worthy than we are." She knows too much. The Coptic heightens what he sees as an absurdity: "Did he, then, speak with a woman in private without our knowing about it?... Did he choose her over us?" Levi's response in the Greek ("he knew her completely <and> loved her devotedly") is also heightened in the Coptic: "Assuredly the Savior's knowledge of her is completely reliable. Because of this he loved her more than <he loved> us" (10:10).[286] The linking of love and knowledge in 6:1 is reprised here. As King has noted, Peter

---

are sacramental acts (eucharist, baptism, the bridal chamber, anointment); here in the Gospel of Mary 10:11, the reference to being "clothed" may be an allusion to baptism.

285. Peter in his wrath represents the seven Powers of Wrath (see below); but he is not exorcised.

286. Cf. Gospel of Philip 63:34–35: he loved her "more than [all] the disciples [and used to] kiss her [often] on her [. . .]."

is able to accept Mary as the most loved woman, but not as the chosen or most loved person/disciple.[287] This is a power struggle.

Love in this work is based on intimate knowledge, mind to mind. It is love between a master and his most beloved disciple.[288] That it is not thought of as between equals is signaled by Mary's reference to the "Savior" and "Lord." But Schoedel points out with reference to the First Apocalypse of James, the difference between the redeemer and the redeemed is "significantly less pronounced in Gnosticism" than in "catholic Christianity." The two figures of the Lord and James in that work "complement rather than rival one another in ways that are difficult for catholic Christianity to contemplate."[289] I think that is the case here in the Gospel of Mary, though I would not call it complementarity since she functions as the Savior's replacement, not by being named his replacement but by being able to function as such, like the Paraclete in the Gospel of John. Love is erotic in the broad sense, but has no overtly sexual overtones.[290] It is basically a recognition of spiritual worth. The disciples in the Gospel of Philip ask the natural follow-up question: "Why do you love her more than us?" And the answer there too, as we have seen, has to do with insight, spiritual worth, undercutting the competitiveness. "Why do I not love you like her?" (58, 34–59, 6).

The "logic" of the hostility Mary faces is hard to follow. It is clear that "Mary's account does not correspond to [the disciples'] expectations at all."[291] She is opposed by two of them, first by Andrew who addresses the "brothers," asking for their opinion of what she has just said but not waiting for it. He himself is unconvinced that her teaching comes from the Savior because "these opinions seem to be so different from h[is th]ought" (10:2). In the Coptic Andrew contrasts his evaluation of Mary with that of the others (they might believe her, but he does not), and then perhaps to separate the truth of her words from their origin (her words may be true, but they are not words of the Savior, and anyway they are strange). "Say what you will about the truth of the things she has said, but I do not believe that the Savior said these things. For indeed these teachings are strange ideas!" Her words are unacceptable not only because they are different from the Savior's, but also because they are strange in themselves.[292] They come

---

287. King, "The Gospel of Mary," 2.616.

288. Marjanen, *The Woman*, 99.

289. W. R. Schoedel, Introduction to The (First) Apocalypse of James," *NHL* 261.

290. So King, "Gospel of Mary," 2.616, who notes also that "the text is quite ambiguous and certainly does not directly condemn sexual relations." Ambiguity, it has been argued, is the key to this issue in the Gospel of Philip. Above, pp. 153–54.

291. Marjanen, *The Woman*, 97.

292. On the breakdown of "the apparent binary of wise-strange" in the Hebrew Bible, more complex and more interesting than the virgin-whore dichotomy, see C. Camp, *Wise, Strange and Holy: the Strange Woman and the Making of the Bible* (Sheffield: Sheffield Academic Press, 2000) 15, 17, 27–28. "Strange" is a root metaphor for all that is "not-Us" (n 6, p. 22, 323). The modern ikon of Mary Magdalene pointing to an egg, symbol of the resurrection, is used on the cover of this book.

from somewhere else — where? — not from the Savior. There is no discussion of their origin or their substance.

From what we have of the document, the words of Mary are not strange, nor are they different from the Savior's. The teachings of the Savior at the beginning of this work have to do with the dissolving, interconnected nature of matter, and with freeing oneself from the body and following after "the seed of true humanity" which exists within. Mary's teachings are an application or example of this: the soul follows, searching within and travelling through the realms of the Powers (Darkness, Desire, Ignorance, Wrath), conquering attachment to the world and therefore the fear of death, and ultimately reaching rest. Andrew's objections are illogical, a smoke screen, as the reader of the Gospel of Mary can clearly see. It is an early, bad-faith charge of "false prophecy" and "heresy." Implicitly, he is hostile to her teachings because they are hers. But he does not attack her personally.

The second objection, Peter's, comes from a completely different direction, making the implication explicit. He rejects the thought that the Savior would have spoken secretly[293] to a woman, rather than openly to all. In 6:1, however, he had asked for instruction concerning the words of the Savior that Mary knew but the men did not — apparently meaning words that they happened not to have heard, not words that the Savior directed privately to Mary. The contrast here is not only between secret speech and open speech, but also between secret speech to a woman and speech of any kind to the males. Secret teaching to a woman is unthinkable because it might indicate "that [she] is more worthy than we are."[294] The Coptic version makes it even clearer that this concerns authorization and leadership. "Did he, then, speak to a woman in private without our knowing about it? Are we to turn around and listen to her? Did he choose her over us?"[295] The males supposedly oversee what goes on in private; but they did not know about this. Further, such secret teaching would mean that she should be listened to, that she was chosen over them, and that is unacceptable. The questions are rhetorical. The attack again is not personal; Mary is not attacked as unworthy, unmarried, unveiled, demon-possessed, impure, or whatever — but as a woman.

Mary does not respond to Andrew, but she is hurt by Peter's attack and weeps. She defends herself in a conciliatory manner, without anger, calling Peter him "brother" as he had earlier called her "sister."[296] She asks if he imagines she "made all this up secretly by myself" or that she is "telling lies about the Savior."

---

293. See Marjanen, *The Woman*, n. 71, p. 94.
294. See King, "Gospel of Mary," 2.615 on the other type of private activity that might involve secrecy: some kind of immoral meeting. I don't see here any implied recognition here of this second type.
295. *NHL*: "Did he prefer her to us?"
296. R. Schmid (*Maria Magdalena in Gnostischen Schriften* [Munich: Arbeitsgemeinschaft fur Religions-und Weltanschauungsfragen, 1990] 16) notes that this is the only time in gnostic materials that Peter speaks the word "sister."

Her defense relies on Peter's good assessment of her character and Peter's good will toward her. But he does not know her, and his good will does not exist.

Levi's defense of Mary is a counterattack on Peter's character: "you have a constant inclination to anger and you are always ready to give way to it" (Coptic: "you have always been a wrathful person"). Levi sees Peter's objection as an expression of his anger, "questioning the woman as if you're her adversary." The Coptic compares his behavior to that of heretical Christians or more likely that of the Powers themselves: "Now I see you contending against the woman like [one of] the Adversaries." Levi's defense rests on the Savior's apparent evaluation of Mary. This implies the rhetorical questions of Peter are to be answered: yes. Note that this is the only time in the extant literature that Peter is criticized when Mary is defended, and that Levi does not respond to Andrew. What Levi does not say is important. He does not address the issue of Mary as a woman. Perhaps the reader/hearer is meant to understand without comment or repetition that in the Gospel of Mary the body as the location of self has been rejected, that her leadership has been supported but at the price of her body, her identity as a woman.

Levi calls for the disciples to be ashamed (of opposing Mary? and/or of their lack of understanding, their fears and hesitancy?). Taking over or paralleling Mary's role after the departure of the Savior, he brings them back to the Savior's last words, telling them to clothe themselves with that perfect humanity whose seed he had said exists within them. They were to follow it, search for it, find it. Mary, it is implied, was wrong to think they — or at least two of them — had achieved it (5:8). Levi reminds them they were to go and preach the good news "and not be laying down any rules or making laws" (10:11–13). There are indeed rules or laws just under the surface of what Peter had said, rules that "dominate" him (4:10). Such as: Women's spiritual experience is to be subject to male approval and control. Women will not teach men. Women will not lead men. Women will not claim roles the Savior did not choose them for. Men will be in charge of determining the authenticity of all teaching about the Savior, whether based on memory and interpretation of his career and person, or on subsequent experience.[297] Andrew, Peter and the other males do not reply to Levi, who departs alone (contrast the Coptic where "they began to go forth" but without assenting to Mary's teaching or Levi's defense of it).

A Tightly Woven Work

Some have argued that this work was originally two separate pieces, oral or written. Because of Peter's change of attitude to Mary, Pasquier suggests that the

---

297. See King, "Gospel of Mary," 2.608–9: the best historical reading of polemic against further law-making is inner-Christian conflict, not anti-Judaism or Roman colonialism.

Gospel originally would have contained Jesus' final teaching and departure, the disciples' consternation, Mary's assumption of a leadership role by means of her encouragement, objections against her, and Levi's defense of her. The theme of "androgynous unity as the goal of salvation"[298] (5:8) is what raises Peter's ire, in Pasquier's reconstruction and interpretation of this first version. His request that Mary tell them the words of the Savior that they have not heard is a secondary transition to another early tradition, the revelation to Mary (her seeing the Lord in a vision, talking to him about how a person sees a vision, and then her recounting of the ascent of the soul).[299] Whether this is so[300] or not[301] (as I tend to think), the combination of the narrative and the account of the vision — and the further tightening in the Coptic version[302] — makes for a brilliant commentary on the gender struggles within some early Christian community or communities. Some accepted women's leadership up to a point, but drew the line at women's teaching; others drew no such lines.

Ancient traditions are combined here with great skill. The sections of the Gospel of Mary as we have it are very tightly interwoven, and the theme of human unity pervades the work. The consternation and fear of the male disciples after Jesus' departure, and the hostility Mary faces both illustrate "adultery": the wrongful combining of the material and the spiritual, with the material overcoming or contaminating the spiritual. Fear of death ("If they didn't spare him, how will they spare us?") appears as a kind of zeal for death, as they see no way to begin their job in face of danger. They turn toward death. They love what deceives them (3:8): physical safety, their physical lives. Mary's teaching applies the teaching of Jesus to the difficult ascent of the soul. And then the hostility she faces from Andrew and Peter concretizes and illustrates the difficulties of ascent. The Adversaries or Powers take human form.

Andrew's evaluation of Mary's teaching as "strange" means that he has not understood the Savior's teaching, nor understood himself. Or that he did not know that the Savior experienced and taught the ascent of the soul. Something blinds Andrew so that he cannot recognize the truth of her words; he passes judgment on them. If they are strange or alien, then he is alien to her, to the Savior, to himself.

---

298. Marjanen, *The Woman*, 88.

299. Pasquier, *L'Evangile selon Marie*, 7–10. Mary's vision discourse, she thinks, is an early tradition, to which the transition in 6:1–4 has been added.

300. See the criticism of Pasquier's suggestion by Marjanen, *The Woman*, 87–88: the change in Peter's attitude may be "plot development" (a suggestion he owes to King). Other suggestions of literary disunity are summarized and argued against on pp. 85–87. De Boer (*Mary Magdalene*, 94) thinks the author is deliberately emphasizing Peter's inconsistency. "It may be that his changing attitude is meant to demonstrate something."

301. M. Tardieu (*Ecrits Gnostiques: Codex de Berlin* [Paris: Cerf, 1984]) regards the work in the form in which it was discovered as a unity.

302. Using the plural (Adversaries) in 10:8.

In the Greek, Peter's wrathful objections are based on pride of leadership, "unreal" loyalty to his gender, desire for domination. He cannot believe that the males have not been given all wisdom, that Mary might be "more worthy" than they of knowing more and therefore may have something to tell them. He is objecting not only to the validity of secret versus open teaching by the Savior, but to the very idea that the Savior would give esoteric teaching to a woman. In fact, the teaching to all at the beginning of this work is esoteric, but it is open insofar as the special males are present. Peter did not know that the Savior taught a woman privately. What surfaces here is Peter's low esteem and scorn for woman. He is conforming to the body and further, to sexist evaluations of the body (his which he thinks is powerful, hers which he believes is weak). He is deceived by his body, loving it, thinking of it as something permanent and allied with the spiritual. He is ignorant that these bodies "exist in and with each other" (2:3) and are destined to dissolve into their root. He is ignorant also that the Savior has "joined us together[303] and made us true human beings" (5:8). Like the second Power, Desire, he mistakes the garment" she wears for her true self, and his own for his true self (9:5). He does not know "that other image of nature" in the presence of which he should form himself: "the seed of true humanity" (3:13; 4:3). King comments, "the body is a false image of the human self" and not the true self.[304] Peter all along has seen Mary (only) as a woman. His mind is on penises and vaginas, on power/status and lack. It is not an androgynous mind, being without "that curious sexual quality that comes only when sex is unconscious of itself."[305]

The Coptic account of Peter's objections heightens his ignorance. He seems to be thinking of the Savior as a male whose exchanges with the female Mary should have been monitored or chaperoned by other males: "Did he then speak with a woman in private without our knowing about it?"[306] When he asks if they are to "turn around" and listen to Mary, he shows he has not been facing her, does not know her, though she had tried to "turn their minds toward the Good" (5:9). He voices then what is unthinkable to him: "Did he choose her over us?" That is, could she have been chosen instead of the males as leader? He is still deceived by the voices "Look over here!" or "Look over there!" for a leader (4:3–4); buying into the structures of domination ("you belong to me," says Desire" [9:3]). Peter in fact *is* that voice of deception the Savior warned about. This is a gospel which proposes there be no leadership but that leadership which urges an

---

303. So the Greek; the Coptic has "prepared us."
304. King, CG, 362.
305. Woolf, *Room*, 93.
306. De Boer (*Mary Magdalene*, 78) compares this to the disciples surprise in John 4:27: they "marvelled that he was taking with a woman, but none said, 'What do you wish?' or 'Why are you talking to her?' "

interiority that would put all on the same level, and make something approaching egalitarian community possible.

Mary's response to Peter is not really a defense. She calls him ("my brother") to the bond which he does not at this point recognize, though he called her "sister" before. She points out he is imagining her a lone, delusional hysteric ("I've made all this up secretly by myself"[307]) or a liar ("I am telling lies about the Savior"), in either case unstable, unconnected to the Savior, and, perhaps, power hungry. The seed of true humanity within her is not recognized by Peter who has not searched for nor found it in himself. "You did not see me nor did you know me," says the soul to Desire; "nor did you recognize me" (9:4, 6). Mary is a soul set free, having conquered, resting in silence. She is the visionary whose mind is focused on the Good (5:9). Her weeping before Peter contrasts, however, with the soul's jocular sparring with the Powers, the soul's saucy attitude and cunning. It contrasts also with her bold encouragement of the weeping disciples: "Do not weep and be distressed nor let your hearts be irresolute" (5:5).

Why does Mary weep before Peter? Her weeping can be read in many different ways. It may indicate that at this point she is reduced by him from a human to a woman.[308] That she is, that is, only what he thinks she is. Her suffering from this encounter does not seem to be a sign that she is weak and has lost her inner peace; it is not the "disturbing confusion" of 3:11. It may be a kind of suffering that has some other meaning, such as grief over Peter's lack of understanding.[309] Whatever it means, it does not change Peter's mind. *He* is attached to the body, but *she* is the one suffering. I read her weeping as a positive strength. It has gender implications. I am using the term gender here as *not* totally reduceable to the schemas, roles, and values of patriarchal ideology. Gender, of course, has to do with socially constructed definitions of "masculine" and "feminine," wrongly said to be connected, even confined, to the biological differences of male and female. But it also involves the historical (over)development of specific, assigned strengths (such as compassion, vulnerability for the female; such as courage, reason for the male), and the burdens of historical experience. These have not been transcended in the Gospel of Mary, so much as incorporated and transmuted. Both Mary's apparent "femininity," in contrast to Peter's arrogant "masculinity," and her suffering, in contrast to his cruelty, like her wisdom in contrast to Andrew's stupidity, are aspects for the author of the truly human. Levi's "masculinity" as he stands up for her and berates Peter marks him as a "private brother."

---

307. NHL: "that I thought this up myself in my heart."

308. King ("Gospel of Mary," 2.615) thinks that Mary keeps here to the "traditional role of female modesty and passivity." Actually, she is not passive here, since she does speak up. She may be "modest," in that in her challenges to Peter's way of looking at her, she implies but does not state that she is an authentic disciple and teacher.

309. King, "Gospel of Mary," 2.610 argues that "The Savior came to alleviate suffering, not to chart a path to salvation by bringing it upon his disciples." His own death has no salvific meaning, and neither does martyrdom.

Levi's and Mary's lack of anger (in this work so full of anger, so interested in anger as a defect — that of the Powers, that of Peter) may be meant to illustrate their peace and equilibrium, although *apatheia* is clearly not an ideal.[310] The feminist critic may prefer or wish for a flash of the sharp, righteous anger that energizes Woolf's *Three Guineas:* "But I had been angry because he was angry. Yet it seemed absurd, I thought, turning over the evening paper, that a man with all this power should be angry. Or is anger, I wondered, somehow, the familiar, the attendant sprite on power? . . . Possibly when the professor insisted a little too emphatically upon the inferiority of women, he was concerned not with their inferiority, but with his own superiority."[311] The absence of righteous anger in the Gospel of Mary may be another indication of the precariousness of women's leadership. Mary is not "spared" suffering, as the Savior was not spared (5:3); and like him she may be presented as surviving it. The reader/hearer cannot overlook that Mary is a woman, and is being oppressed. If the Mary of 10:5–6 is seen as a woman *and* a true human being, or even a true human being *as* a woman, then gender does remain a point in this work. It is not, it seems to me, blotted out by a focus on nongendered spirituality.[312] Mary has not been "made male." Gender *bias* — thinking with your penis, your unearned privilege and power — and gender *hierarchy* have been attacked, whether conscious or unconscious,[313] but Mary and Levi as a "woman" and a "man" are both true human beings. Further analysis of the weeping, the courage, and the lack of anger seems to me some of our unfinished business with this text. As King says, "transcendence is not bought at the expense of ignoring or erasing awareness of injustice and suffering. Instead, the ideal of transcendence is tied to a sharp criticism of social injustice and illegitimate domination. . . . Transcendence and justice are linked, so that authority is based on spiritual maturity rather than bodily differentiations."[314] I would say transcendence and gender justice are linked. Gender (as I am using the term, to include women's and men's historical experience) may be both transcended and embraced.

---

310. See de Boer, *Mary Magdalene,* 99. Contrast Gregory of Nyssa's idealization of *apatheia* in his biography of Macrina, and his equation of pathos and femininity (*Vita Macrinae* 10–12; 22 cited in Castelli, "Virginity," 74). Righteous anger is not an ideal in this work either.
311. Woolf, *Three Guineas,* 34–35. See J. Marcus, "Art and Anger," 122–54.
312. Contrast McGuire, "Women, Gender and Gnosis," 275: "gender differentiation is insignificant in the true identify of an anthropos." Gender exists only in material bodies which will cease to exist. Also King, "Gospel of Mary," 2.624: she argues that while this work affirms that women can and did have legitimate authority, "it seems to deny that women could hold that authority *as women.* Women were either expected in some way to become male, or their legitimacy was seen as a matter of nongendered spiritual progression. In the first case, it would seem that male patriarchal authority is not really challenged on the symbolic level: the male alone symbolizes full humanity. In the second case, women's leadership in some sense becomes a nonissue. Gender is not the point; spirituality is." But King's own translations (see above) recognize that the symbol system is strained.
313. See above, p. 128, n. 33, for Valian's understanding of gender schemas.
314. King, "Prophetic Power and Authority," 32.

Levi breaks ranks with the men to stand with Mary against Peter, and against Andrew also, though he does not respond to him. (Why does Levi not respond to Andrew?) In the Greek text, Levi already probably links Peter to the Powers by identifying his anger and his "questioning the woman as if you're her adversary." Peter's questions, however, have not been directed to Mary but to the males, about her. Both the Greek and the Coptic versions stress anger as his constant characteristic. This kind of anger is the opposite of peace, the sign of a lack of inner peace (4:1–2). Without Levi's intervention, Peter's words could be read in as "reasonable" a tone as Andrew's. Levi brushes aside the objections to Mary as worthless spite. He has recognized in them the dynamic of the Powers opposing the ascent of the soul (Coptic: "Now I see you contending against the woman like the Adversaries"). That is, he has seen a sociological/anthropological context in the mystical tradition. It is not about the ascent of the lonely, individual one to the transcendent One, but about that ascent in the context of human interaction, and toward a recognition of corporate identity—beyond the material corpus. Salvation may be "found within oneself";[315] but once within, one finds oneself joined. The isolated, individual self is an illusion. Mary's opponent Peter is "like" the opponents of the soul, and they are like those who did not spare the Savior. Levi speaks up to free Mary from male disparagement and domination, as the soul speaks up to free itself from the Powers, as the disciple is freed from the fear of death: the processes of liberation merge.[316] Recognition of Mary's authority and the authenticity of her vision and teaching are a matter of moving from the realm of death to the realm of life.

What is Peter angry about? The soul's freedom, the freedom of one whom he had thought belonged to him (cf. 9:3). His anger is the anger of desire and death and ignorance, the body's own anger. It is a murderous anger, the "passion" born of matter "which has no <true> image[317] because it derives from what is contrary to nature" (3:10). It is jealous and competitive, worried about being "replaced"[318] or about losing illusory power. It blusters; it has not achieved "silence" (9:29). The very structure of the gospel as we have it indicates why: the dialogue of the Savior with Peter and the other disciples "seems to function as a preparation for the revelation through Mary Magdalene. This plan of the work clearly suggests that the full and definitive revelation of the Saviour is accessible only through Mary

315. Marjanen, *The Woman*, 95.
316. King ("Gospel of Mary," 2.624–25) sees that this work "opposes illegitimate domination — whether by self-made entrapments, enslavement to the Powers of materiality, or the exclusion of women from leadership. Moreover, it offers powerful images of liberation in its portrait of Mary's ministry and the soul's journey to freedom." I think this work shows how dominations overlap and intertwine. That is, Levi sees that the soul's entrapments are not all "self-made." King speaks (627) of a doubling of opponents (those who killed the Savior and may kill the disciples, and those who oppose Mary). I see a tripling here (the killers, Mary's opponents, the Powers). Marjanen, *The Woman*, does not discuss Mary's report of the vision in any detail.
317. NHL: equal.
318. Marjanen, *The Woman*, 99. Or having to work with, learn from, share authority with her.

Magdalene . . . [I]f even the post-Easter revelations given to Peter were incomplete and insufficient, this would the more be true of the teaching of the 'earthly' Jesus."[319]

The author of this work accepts a world view that disparages matter and the body (which is only a "garment" [9:5]); the Seven Powers of Wrath can even regard the soul as a "human killer" (9:26).[320] This acceptance, it seems to me, is not only because of "a deep sensitivity to the connection of suffering and death with the physical body,"[321] but because of the body's insensitivity to other (different) bodies, its insistence on separation and domination, its blindness; because of the body's rejection of human unity. Gender wars belong to matter; the soul is perhaps somehow gendered, perhaps androgynous, perhaps wo/man. Mary herself is androgynous, in that she is courageous, active, intelligent, gentle, sensitive; she acts like a "man" *and* like a "woman." And Levi also: forceful, protective, confrontative, encouraging. Sexist structures are undermined by a deeply democratic spirituality. The legitimacy of woman's leadership and authority is affirmed "on the basis of superior spiritual qualifications"[322] but without making her (only) a man.

Levi asks, "If the Savior considered (or: guided) her to be worthy, who are you to disregard[323] her?" Levi aligns the Savior and Mary, and lets the Savior's evaluation of Mary as "worthy" stand against Peter's. "Who are you?" is a question, the central question, that Peter cannot answer, anymore than he could answer the questions "Where do you come from?" and "Where are you going?" Levi the gnostic knows that the Savior knew Mary "completely <and> loved her devotedly." Levi is a "true human" who recognizes Mary as another. In the Coptic version, Levi can also recognize distinctions and differences and gradations: because of the Savior's "completely reliable" knowledge of Mary, "he loved her more than (he loved) us." Levi is a better "man" than analytical, narrow, illogical Andrew and bullying, aggressive Peter. Levi uses his privileged position to stand up against Peter. Masculinities and femininities are in the process of deconstructing here, as is linguistic androcentrism.[324] How — besides with flat statements or with neologisms — could it be shown that women can hold authority *as women*, if not as here, with Mary and Levi behaving as both "woman" and "man," and as true human beings, though not as actively sexual beings. There is more than

---

319. G. P. Luttikhuizen, "The Evaluation of the Teaching of Jesus in Christian Gnostic Revelation Dialogues," *NovT* 30 (1988) 164.
320. The soul responds, "What binds me has been slain" — that is, matter, the body. But not what is "human"?
321. King, "Gospel of Mary," 2.605.
322. King, "Gospel of Mary," 2.623.
323. *NHL*: "to reject her."
324. See K. King, "Ridicule and Rape, Rule and Rebellion, The Hypostasis of the Archons," *Gnosticism & the Early Christian World* (ed. J. E. Goehring et al.; Sonoma, Calif.: Polebridge, 1990) 4–6, on the cultural construction of gender in antiquity.

a glimmer here of the new notion of "person." Perhaps if Mary behaved like Levi and vice versa (Levi wept, Mary confronted) the reversal of expected roles could have communicated change more clearly.

In an inversion of conventional, material values, Levi urges the disciples to be "ashamed." They are to "clothe" themselves with "perfect humanity" which — in contrast to the "garment" of the body (9:5) — joins them together (5:7) in their true self (9:5). He urges them to go within, that is, as they go out to announce the good news, which has to do with liberation from bondage to the material world, with the recognition of true selves, and most importantly with overcoming the fear of death ("If they didn't spare him, how will they spare us?"). As we have seen, only Levi leaves in the Greek text; "they" go forth to preach and teach in the Coptic version. Presumably they are thought to have been convinced by Levi's defense of Mary, but in the absence of a statement to that effect, the reader of the Coptic is left with a feeling of uneasiness about their message. "The reader must wonder what kind of good news such proud and ignorant men will announce."[325] The reader would know that announcing and preaching and teaching should be authenticated by certain things: by an absence of new rules or laws, and by silence, the silence of the soul who is at rest and of the person who has come to the end of what the Savior said to her or him (9:29–30).

Mary seems to have been almost replaced by Levi. She is championed by him, but never addressed. Whereas the soul defended itself before the Powers, Mary has been defended by another. What does "Levi" mean in this work? Mary had exhorted the fearful disciples to courage in the face of their suffering, as they would be sheltered by the Savior's grace (5:6); here Levi shelters Mary. But as he or as the disciples leave at the end of the gospel, where is Mary? She and Levi are not said to leave together as partners,[326] and it is difficult to imagine her — last seen weeping, and never told not to weep[327] — tagging along with the others. She seems to have been forgotten in the forward focus on ministry. And in the departing, there is no space for an apology by Andrew or by Peter, no space for them to realize and confirm that they have been "joined together" (5:8).[328] Mary might be read here as an apostle sent only to the other apostles, and not to the world. She is, however, apparently regarded as present among the apostles for the commission in 4:8–10. She herself says the Savior "has made us true human

---

325. King, CG, 357. C. H. Roberts (*Catalogue of the Greek and Latin Papyri in the John Rylands Library* [London, 1938] 3.19,22) thought that the Gospel proper only began where our text ends; so he concludes they "began to preach the Gospel according to Mary." But in the Berlin text, the treatise ends with the last five words forming a colophon (see R. McL. Wilson, "The New Testament in the Gnostic Gospel of Mary," NTS 3 [1957] 239).

326. However, Marjanen (*The Woman*, 102) thinks this is a possibility.

327. Contrast her words to them in 5:5: "Do not weep and be distressed. . . . "

328. Pagels ("Visions, Appearances, and Apostolic Authority," 425) mistakenly says that "Finally, the others override Peter's objection, and the disciples consent to receive this revelation from Mary, acknowledging that her direct contact with the Lord though visions surpasses their own. Strengthened by her vision, the disciples go out and preach."

beings" (5:8) and she is among those who are clothed "with perfect humanity" (10:11) and are free of the fear of death, thereby ready to preach. Hers is not a quasi-apostolic role; but, on the other hand, she is not depicted as going forth.

As King comments, the ending of this gospel is ambiguous, and the controversy is far from resolved, but it has let us hear the voices of those who spoke for women's leadership in antiquity.[329] Those men, I used to think, were and are speaking to men.[330] Maybe; now I'm not sure.

The Gospel of Mary, lost for centuries, is one of those rediscovered texts that seriously challenges the canon, not just for scholars. Unencumbered by complex gnostic systems and terminology, it is accessible to contemporary readers. Luckily for some, it has ten or more missing pages (over half the work) and many gaps, which are opportunities for creativity whether or not the missing pages are ever found. Wrapped in feathers, the codex containing it was found in a niche in a wall in a burial place near Akhmim.[331] Who placed it there, and with whose body? Why feathers, and what kind of feathers? I wouldn't mind having it buried with me too, with my ashes. On a disc or whatever is technologically available. I'd like to hear its words ring out in Christian — especially Catholic — assemblies: "If the Savior considered her to be worthy, who are you to disregard her?" (10:9). "Who are you?" is a call for gnosis.

Questions

Many intriguing questions are raised by the texts discussed in this chapter. Two questions (which sometimes overlap) are: (1) What, if anything, do the roles given to Mary Magdalene reflect of the actual social/sexual/religious/spiritual life of women and men in some early Christian communities? (2) What is the relationship between the traditions found in these works and the Christian Testament materials that mention Mary Magdalene, or that are conflated in her subsequent legends?

1. Roles

The first and main thing to be said about the role of Mary and the roles of actual women is that no sweeping generalizations are valid. "After fifty years of Nag Hammadi study we are finally learning...to drop generalizations...and speak instead about specific texts."[332] Only tentative suggestions can be made,

---

329. King, CG, 357; "Gospel of Mary," 2.601.
330. King, "Gospel of Mary," 2.628 thinks it possible to speculate that it was written by a woman, but "the gender of an author cannot be determined solely by stylistic characteristics or content (at least not without reifying patriarchally constructed gender differences or assuming that women's perspectives are never present in scribal writings by men").
331. De Boer, *Mary Magdalene*, 75.
332. Pagels, "Ritual in the Gospel of Philip," 280.

as Marjanen has attempted, based on an analysis of each work in itself, with a recognition of the different ways Mary is depicted. It is too early for more than that.

Anne McGuire remarks that "the task of reconstructing the social roles of women in 'gnosticism' remains one of the most challenging in the study of ancient Mediterranean religions." She helpfully distinguishes three distinct positions on the relation between gender imagery and the social roles of women in "gnostic" communities.[333]

A. The first holds that the preponderance of positive female imagery may correlate directly with prominent, positive social roles for women. Pagels early on argued that the evidence "clearly indicates a correlation between religious theory and social practice,"[334] between images and attitudes, even though "symbolism is not sociology."[335] Considering not only the extensive use in gnostic materials of feminine imagery for the divine,[336] but also the heresiologists' tirades against women who teach, argue, exorcise, cure, baptize,[337] proselytize,[338] and prophesy,[339] the claim has been made that we should see in gnosticism an egalitarian form of Christianity, pitted against patriarchal "orthodoxy," even though the "Gnostics were not unanimous in affirming women — nor were the orthodox unanimous in denigrating them."[340] Michael A. Williams makes his point very cautiously: "Due especially to enhanced sensitivities of the most recent generation of scholarship to the correlation between androcentric religious symbolism and social dominance by males, there has been an interest in the possibility that Gnostic mythology was making a statement rejecting traditional forms of androcentrism and asserting the equality of female and male, women and men."[341] He noted in 1986 that no consensus had emerged on this question. It has still not emerged.

The elevated role given to Mary Magdalene in the Gospel of Mary and elsewhere in gnostic or near-gnostic literature might represent the authoritative roles

---

333. A. McGuire, "Women, Gender, and Gnosis in Gnostic Texts and Traditions," *Women and Christian Origins*, 258–59; she puts the term "gnostic" in quotation marks to refer to "the traditional conception of a unified phenomenon, religion, or movement (n 1, p. 288).
334. Pagels, *The Gnostic Gospels*, 60.
335. E. Pagels, "Pursuing the Spiritual Eve," *Images of the Feminine in Gnosticism*, 188. "The way gnostic and orthodox Christians use, or avoid, feminine images certainly connects with and expresses social and sexual attitudes" (187).
336. See Pagels, *The Gnostic Gospels*, "God the Father/God the Mother," 48–69.
337. Tertullian, *De Praescr. Haer.* 41.
338. Epiphanius speaks of women under the gnostic delusion offering him "this line of talk" and divulging this sort of things to him, and trying to seduce him (*Haer.* 26.17.4–9).
339. Irenaeus, *Adv Haer* 1.13.3–4.
340. Pagels, *The Gnostic Gospels*, 66. See the reviews by R. E. Brown in the *New York Times Book Review* (January 20, 1980) and by J. A. Fitzmyer in *America* (February 16, 1980); R. J. Hoffman, "De Statu Feminarum: The Correlation Between Gnostic Theory and Social Practices," *Église et Théologie* 14 (1983) 293–304, for early, vehement reactions to Pagels.
341. M. A. Williams, "Uses of Gender Imagery in Ancient Gnostic Texts," *Gender and Religion: On the Complexity of Symbols* (ed. C. W. Bynum, S. Harrell, P. Richman; Boston: Beacon, 1986) 197.

of women (such as prophet, teacher, healer, priest, bishop) in some — not all — actual gnostic communities, in which women and men might have been considered equal. That would mean that Mary Magdalene was chosen as a major character and speaker in part or in great part because she was a woman. She was presented as a role model and one on whose memory later women based their successful claims to power in some communities.[342] The tradition of the Magdalene as a sinner can then be seen as developed in other Christian circles primarily to displace the apostolic authority claimed for women through her name, that is, it developed as backlash.[343]

B. A second view also sees a direct correlation, but emphasizes the negative references to "femaleness" in the gnostic sources, arguing that these images indicate that women and the female gender were devalued and subordinated, both in theory and in practice in gnostic communities. Femaleness was reduced to a focus on sexuality and procreation; against which warnings were issued.[344] "Male" and "female" represent cosmic, unequal religious principles or archetypes, not real men and women. It is unlikely, according to this second view, that women functioned as bishops or priests or enjoyed high status in real gnostic groups.[345]

McGuire warns against these first two positions because they "reflect a generalizing conception of 'gnosticism' as a single religious movement with a fairly unified body of imagery, thought and practice."[346] That generalizing is also apparent sometimes in the position that the figure of Mary is purely symbolic and has no correlation with the lives of women. Mary is chosen, according to this view, simply because her non-apostolic role in the canonical texts fitted her to represent those who opposed the "orthodox." Perkins, for example, is skeptical of those like Pagels who use the picture of Mary in gnostic literature to claim that gnostics upheld community leadership by women, in opposition to the male-dominated hierarchy of the "orthodox" church. Mary, Perkins explains, is the hero in gnostic texts "not because of an extraordinary role played by women in Gnostic communities, but because she is a figure closely associated with Jesus to whom esoteric tradition may be attached." She thinks that the polemics in the Gospel of Mary are general and no indication of the sociological makeup of the various groups.[347] Mary's "close association" makes her a more obvious choice than Lazarus or Nicodemus or Joseph of Arimathea or Barabbas — all of whom had post-canonical legendary lives.

---

342. Celsus, as we have seen, knows of some "who follow Mariamme" as well as those who follow Salome or Martha (Origen, *Contra Celsus* 5.62).

343. R. R. Ruether, *Women-Church* (San Francisco: Harper & Row, 1985) n. 1, p. 286.

344. See F. Wisse, "Flee Femininity: Antifemininity in Gnostic Texts and the Question of Social Milieu," *Images of the Feminine in Gnosticism*, 297–307.

345. D. L. Hoffman, *The Status of Women and Gnosticism in Irenaeus and Tertullian* (Lewiston, N.Y.: Mellen, 1995) 3–4.

346. McGuire, "Women, Gender and Gnosis," 259.

347. P. Perkins, *The Gnostic Dialogue* (New York: Paulist, 1980) n. 10, p. 136.

C. A third, more nuanced position is now developing; it sees a varied and complex relation between gendered image and social roles. There may be a direct correlation, an inverse relation, or no apparent relation at all — depending on each text's ideological framework and what can be determined of the social location of the early writers and readers. In radical gnostic dualism, the female is secondary, involved in the created world and history, and must be destroyed. But "in the moderately dualistic systems, salvation means the reunification of the male and female principle to an androgynous or asexual unity"[348] Buckley regards the majority of texts attributing contradictory, ambiguous characteristics to single female figures whether these are mythological beings, or human women, or the female component of humanity. The gamut runs from advocation of the outright abolition of the female to the view that male and female are united in the Lightworld. Further, "surface depreciation of females frequently masks a profound concern with these figures because they are ambiguous, possessing outrightly positive — and therefore surprising — qualities."[349] McGuire herself thinks that it is possible some of the authors and readers chose images of male and female "because they were engaged in a process of contesting, revising categories of gender and the social roles of women and men." More importantly, she thinks, they chose these images as helpful metaphors for reflection on such issues as difference, unity, spirit and matter, creation and redemption.[350]

Although some of the texts may have been written by women, and although they contain a large amount of feminine imagery, the current tendency seems to be toward the view that women did not necessarily have a large and powerful social role. How women were attracted and/or repelled by gnostic practices and ideas, what parts women might have played in ritual practices and rites of initiation, what difference social class made, how gender roles were played and valued, how real sexuality functioned, and whether there are resources here for human liberation — these are some of the issues debated.[351] More significant perhaps than the authoritative, formal roles some women may have played in gnostic communities, is the impact various evaluations of matter and the earth, of the body, of sexuality and procreation and marriage, had on the lives of ordinary gnostic women: in terms of the options open to them, for travel and work, for sexual expression and companionship, for family, for intellectual and spiritual development. In comparison to lives in other groups, were these lives restricted and choices narrowed, or were they expanded and choices widened? How were asceticism and so-called libertinism[352] experienced and evaluated by women in

---

348. Schüssler Fiorenza, *In Memory of Her*, 278–79; "Word, Spirit and Power," 50.

349. J. J. Buckley, *Female Fault and Fulfillment in Gnosticism* (Chapel Hill: University of North Carolina, 1986) xi.

350. McGuire, "Women, Gender and Gnosis," 287.

351. See King, "Editor's Foreword," *Images of the Feminine in Gnosticism*, xiv–xvii.

352. J. J. Buckley ("Libertines or Not: Fruit, Bread, Semen and Other Body Fluids in Gnosticism," *JECS* 2 [1994] 15) says "The ovarian question remains . . . whether the actions and theology of the

terms of their own understandings of body, sexuality, physical suffering, social oppression? How were their experiences and evaluations different from those of men? Burrus notes, for instance, that ascetic women of antiquity were most concerned with the problems of resistance to male control of female sexuality, social relationships and intellectual strivings. They were not concerned with the problems of the preservation of virginity and sexual purity, and resisting their own female sexual desire. Ascetic culture freed women to seek new expressions of their sexuality and erotic power.[353] Goehring argues that women in so-called libertine groups were neither simpletons nor victims, as Epiphanius would have it, but women who might have taken the initiative in free communal sexual interchange, finding release from social constraints, and knowing themselves as representatives of the divine.[354] Regarding avoidance of procreation, alternatives to or modifications of marriage, the search for community, roles in community: each text differently answers or — more commonly — refuses a clear answer to the question of actual women's experience.

Mary, whether representing woman as a stage to be left behind as in the Gospel of Thomas 114, or identified with earthly/otherworldly creative entities as in the Gospel of Philip, or speaking sanely, charismatically and compassionately as in the Gospel of Mary, is a paradigm of the saved. In some texts her appearance leads to reflection about the position of women in general (Peter "hates our race"); in others there is no such reflection. In some the depiction of her energy and intelligence provides a contrast to and alleviation of standard notions of the weakness of the female. Marjanen notes that some of the texts show "hardly any interest in the concrete reality women experienced in Gnostic communities." He argues that Mary is "an ideal heroine from the distant past" in such texts as the Sophia of Jesus Christ, the Dialogue of the Savior, the Gospel of Philip and the Manichaean Psalm Book. He overstates the case, I think, especially when he says that "She is acknowledged as an important transmitter and proclaimer of the Gnostic tradition, but nothing indicates that the women of the contemporary Gnostic groups would or could claim the same or similar status. As a matter of fact, the pejorative feminine gendered language in the Sophia of Jesus Christ and the Dialogue of the Savior suggests that the authors of the writings would not necessarily be even aware of such strivings."[355] I suggest, rather, that awareness of strivings or even engagement in strivings is not always — is rarely — neatly coordinated with awareness of linguistic and ideological sexism. The context is not a thought-world made by women or by men and women together. It is a world in which women learned to double-think and see themselves as included even

---

so-called Libertine Gnostic can be adequately understood." But she does not offer any gender analysis in this article.
353. See Burrus, "Word and Flesh," 31–32, 50–51.
354. Goehring, "Libertine or Liberated," 340–44.
355. Marjanen, *The Woman*, 192.

(and especially) when they were not; where they had to deal with the craziness of symbols such as the androgynous Man or the male androgyne,[356] to learn to tune out. Ideas, concepts, language, practices could not have meant the same thing for women as for men. Language in many cases is straining and failing to express clearly the unconventional, as our language is today.[357]

In her rivalry with male disciples, primarily Peter, Mary probably "functioned in Gnostic circles simultaneously as the representative of the female followers of Jesus and as a symbol of the importance of women among the [sic; some] Gnostics"[358] Depending on the text, the rivalry may reflect the debate between different groups of Christians, or debate internal to one group. Marjanen, for example, thinks that the Gospel of Mary reflects disagreement between "Gnostic and non-Gnostic, orthodox Christians over the position of women with regard to the question of spiritual authority."[359] In Pistis Sophia III, however, the issue is "inter-Gnostic controversy" over "the credibility of Mary Magdalene as a transmitter of authoritative traditions."[360] In the Gospel of Thomas 114 the debate is between two different models of asceticism in conflict among Thomasine Christians.[361]

The "concreteness of the controversy" between Mary and Peter in the Gospel of Mary persuades Marjanen that there is a clear correspondence between the significant position of Mary in the text world and the sociohistorical reality of women. This gospel was at least partly written, he thinks, in defense of "women wanting to take part in spiritual leadership but being prevented by those who regarded it as an illegitimate enterprise.... It is not only the role of Mary as a transmitter of a visionary revelation which is at stake but the spiritual authority of women in general."[362] "The concreteness of the controversy" clicks with some

356. On the "complete male" into which the female has been reintegrated in kabbalistic thought, and the one-sex theory behind it (the feminine is just an extension of the masculine), see E. R. Wolfson, "On Becoming Female: Crossing Gender Boundaries in Kabbalistic Ritual and Myth," *Gender and Judaism: The Transformation of Tradition* (ed. T. M. Rudavsky; New York: New York University Press, 1995) 210–11.

357. We have at present, for examples, no adequate word for the pro-feminist man; no words besides feminism and womanism for striving toward our common humanity.

358. See D. M. Parrot, "Gnostic and Orthodox Disciples in the Second and Third Centuries," *Nag Hammadi, Gnosticism, and Early Christianity*, 197, 218–19. He thinks she is not, however, regarded as *the* spokesperson or founder.

359. Compare King, "Gospel of Mary," 2.621–5. Peter and Mary represent groups that oppose each other on the issues of the validity of postresurrection teaching and visionary revelation, and of the authority of women.

360. Good ("Pistis Sophia," 2.695) argues that Mary may represent the nascent Gnostic community of that text, while Peter may stand for a more orthodox group which the text is eager to include. The community is egalitarian and non-competitive. It seems to me that the eagerness to include is destroying whatever egalitarianism and non-competitiveness it had.

361. Marjanen, *The Woman*, 190–91. He notes that the envy of the males in the Gospel of Philip does not really lead to conflict with Mary; "instead, their dissatisfaction is more directed to Jesus" (191).

362. Marjanen, *The Woman*, 193. So also King, "Gospel of Mary," 2.624: the Gospel of Mary provides evidence that women were exercising leadership and exerting their authority over men; this work "unequivocally advocated women's leadership based on spiritual merit." The only other work

twenty-first century readers. The charge made by Andrew, that Mary's ideas are "strange ideas" — I've heard that charge about my own ideas and those of other feminists. And the rage of Peter — I've heard that too, just this week. Controversy in the other documents feels "concrete" to me too: ridicule and disbelief meeting the women's announcement; the complaint that Mary speaks too much; the Savior siding with her critics.

Perhaps more significant also than whatever official positions women may have held, is the fact that some may have spoken out, in the name of Mary, about visionary traditions, their own experience, their own reasoning, their own reading of the past. That there was clear recognition of injustice, of hostility faced by women, of the dismissive scorn with which some men treated them. That some men, weakly or strongly, might have defended women thinking and speaking, and defended women's presence and leadership. There seems to have been also some perception of what we would call the social construction of gender and its fluidity: women are spoken of as being made male, becoming male, becoming human. This perception is one-sided, since there is no corresponding change imagined for males.

General lines of what constituted the "heresy" or "heresies" some wo/men stood for can be sketched: direct access to the divine through the Spirit; the possibility of — reality of — transcendent human unity now in the risen Savior; bypassing external authorities; ignoring gender hierarchies; communal expression of divine authority.[363] In works like the Gospel of Mary, there is no focus on the death of Jesus, or on guilt, repentance, atonement, lawmaking; order. The risen Jesus is a teacher, not a judge or ruler.[364] We have few other materials from antiquity with which to compare the sharpness of these insights.

The presence in the same texts of a Mary who is enlightened and strong, and of language that absorbs or assimilates the female into the male shows that we are not dealing in any of the texts with egalitarianism in any full sense. But some of the evidence provides glimpses of egalitarianism struggling within a system or systems that cannot accommodate it; glimpses of women in positions of authority within dualistic, patriarchal systems. K. Thrade suggests that gnostic dualism of "male and female" developed in reaction to the actual leadership of women in gnosticism.[365] It might be more accurate to say it hardened rather than developed.

Marjanen thinks has such a correspondence with the social reality of women is the Great Questions of Mary, which, with Epiphanius' remarks, indicates women in a libertine group claimed to derive their authority and the group's existence from an encounter between the risen Jesus and Mary. But the fragmentary nature of that text and Epiphanius' polemic make this argument unpersuasive to me. Cf. Williams, *Rethinking 'Gnosticism,'* 179–88.

363. Cf. King, "Prophetic Power and Authority," 31–33; she refers to "views that are enabling for women's leadership."
364. K. King, "Canonization and Marginalization: Mary of Magdala," *Concilium* 3 (1998) 34.
365. K. Thrade, "Frau," *RAC*, 8.237.

To a certain extent the gnostic Mary Magdalene may be a man in disguise and/or the mouthpiece of men.[366] But I am not persuaded that the status of women in communities in which and for which these texts were produced and valued was more or less the same as their status in "mainline" Christianity, or that the figure of Mary in such texts as the Pistis Sophia, the Gospel of Philip and the Gospel of Mary simply represents male theology- or authority-as-usual. Even when gnostic anti-feminism, sexism, misogyny and androcentrism are recognized, there are still indications in the texts we have examined here of more powerful roles for women in some gnostic circles than in "orthodox." Mary, like other female figures in gnostic texts, is often charged with sexual power, and with female power to act and create. Contact with this figure must have communicated this power.[367] A claim that Mary was uniquely prominent, historically, seems to me embedded in the profile of the apocryphal Mary. What is debated is what authority flows from this, for her and other women.

In sum, the hypothesis that Mary reflects the more extensive roles women played in gnostic communities, as leaders and as sources of revelation and authority, is an hypothesis increasingly seen as difficult to test.[368] But it is one that still demands exploration. Also difficult to test yet demanding exploration, is the hypothesis that these gnostic roles are related in some way to, perhaps developed from, roles for women in the Jesus movement, themselves rooted in roles for women in egalitarian form(s) of Judaism. The struggle for egalitarianism requires some sort of vision, some ideal, however vaguely or inadequately articulated. I find that vision and ideal expressed in Son of Man or Human One language, threaded through Daniel, the Christian Testament, and some of the apocryphal/gnostic works that feature Mary. Woolf's work, I think like the Gospel of Mary, shows how ideals of human unity and androgyny can coalesce. The six characters in *The Waves*, for example, three men and three women, themselves androgynous, are friends who appear to represent different aspects of a single androgynous being. The dead Percival is the mystical seventh, the transfiguring element which unites them.[369] He is not, to Bernard, a god or a hero or a leader, but a companion. He is "too small a mark" to bear the width and breadth of the feelings of communion; is only one petal of a seven sided flower, that "whole flower to which every eye brings its contribution."[370] Together, Bernard says, "I saw for a moment laid out among us the body of the complete human being whom we have failed to be, but

---

366. Brown, *New York Times* review of Pagels, *The Gnostic Gospels*.

367. See Buckley, *Female Fault*, xii on the positive and negative motif of female creativity, which can lead to the elevation of the female to divine levels, embodying a "dynamic monism."

368. See R. S. Kraemer, *Maenads, Martyrs, Matrons, Monastics* (Philadelphia: Fortress, 1988) 415.

369. H. Richter, "Hunting the Moth: Virginia Woolf and the Creative Imagination," *Virginia Woolf, Revaluation and Continuity* (ed. R. Freedman; Berkeley: University of California, 1980) 21.

370. "Let us commit any blasphemy of laughter and criticism rather than exude this lily-sweet glue; and cover him with phrases" (*The Waves*, 365). See Ruddick, "Private Brother," 210.

at the same time, cannot forget."[371] Woolf explained, "I did mean that in some vague way we are the same person, and not separate people. The six characters were supposed to be one."[372]

Woolf explored the notion of common mind, the composite self, how minds are joined together, and how "illuminations" or "moments of being" could be drawn out of the individual memory, allowing the artist to touch the collective memory.[373] She invoked the anonymous self — not limited to the human, while holding to a sense of individual rights and liberties and mutual integrity.[374] " 'I' rejected; 'We' substituted . . . 'we' . . . waifs and strays — a rambling, capricious but somehow unified whole."[375] The images she used to convey this varied: rooms open to each other, actors playing different parts, Orlando through his/her life through the centuries. And most of all, Woolf insisted that "music makes us see the hidden, join the broken," hear "the voice that was no one's voice."[376] Woolf set her vision squarely within the political and personal struggle for women's rights, for radical social change.

2. Relationships

The second question raised by our analysis of the gnostic/apocryphal works concerns the relationship between the traditions found in them, and the Christian Testament materials that mention Mary Magdalene, or that are conflated in her legends. It is too simplistic to regard the gnostic/apocryphal traditions as interpretations of or responses to the finished Christian Testament Gospel stories or sayings, which they quote or to which they allude,[377] and/or to think of the "heretics" as building on some Christian Testament traditions while the "orthodox" played them down. Some of the gnostic/apocryphal traditions may indeed have been formed along these lines; but others may be rooted in parallel or earlier traditions, which the Christian Testament materials may respond to, or develop, or censor.

371. Woolf, *The Waves*, 277.
372. Woolf, *Letters* 4, 397. The quote continues: "I am getting old myself — I shall be fifty next year; and I come to feel more and more how difficult it is to collect oneself into one Virginia; even though the special Virginia in whose body I live for the moment is violently susceptible to all sorts of separate feelings. Therefore I wanted to give the sense of continuity, instead of which most people say, no you've given the sense of flowing and passing away and that nothing matters. Yet I feel things matter quite immensely. What the significance is, heaven knows I cant guess; but there is significance — that I feel overwhelmingly."
373. Marcus, "Thinking Back," 6; Marder, *Measure of Life*, 51–52.
374. See Du Plessis, *Writing Beyond the Ending*, 166, 171, 173, 177.
375. Woolf, *Writer's Diary*, April 26 1938, 279.
376. Woolf, *Between the Acts*, 120, 181.
377. On Christian Testament echoes in the Gospel of Mary, see C. Tuckett, "Synoptic Traditions in Some Nag Hammadi and Related Texts," *VC* 36 (1982) 178–82; he does not discuss any of the passages mentioned below. See L. Painchaud, "The Use of Scripture in Gnostic Literature," *JECS* 4 (1996) 131–32 on the importance of allusions, which are often put aside in favor of study of possible explicit quotations.

With regard to Mary Magdalene's prominence, Coyle argues that to suggest that great attention is given to her in the gnostic writings "merely because of her role in announcing the resurrection in Matthew, Mark [i.e., Markan Appendix], Luke and John is to beg the question, for the early streams of what became orthodox Christianity chose to perceive no special significance in this."[378] I cannot follow his logic here, since some groups may have perceived significance and others not; moreover the choices of perception and non-perception may be interrelated. Other reasons given for attention to her, according to Coyle, "fall into four main categories, each of which may be valid, depending on the Gnostic system in question: (1) *Sociologically*, Mary's presence is highlighted in an attempt to restore the position of women suppressed in society and in what came to be known as the 'orthodox' church, with the latter represented by Simon Peter; (2) *allegorically*, it symbolizes the feminine aspect of salvation — specifically, as the fallen and restored Sophia; (3) *mythologically*, it is an extension (through the couple Jesus/Mary) of the old Gnostic view of humanity as primordially androgynous, a view at one time symbolized by Simon Magus/Helen; or (4) *literarily*, the story of Jesus and 'Mary' displays the hallmarks of the hellenistic romance novel."[379]

  R. E. Brown holds "that it was probably John's portrait of Mary Magdalene [in John 20] which sparked the gnostic Gospels to make her the chief recipient of post-resurrectional revelation and the rival of Peter."[380] He notes that in the Gospel of Mary, Peter becomes jealous of Mary even as he is jealous of the beloved disciple in John 21:20–23.[381] But as far as I can see, concrete allusions to John 20–21 are lacking in regard to both themes (revelation and rivalry) in most of the works discussed in this chapter. There are some possible relationships: touching in John 20 might be related to kissing; Jesus calling Mary's name might be related to her gnosis, being known by him; her ultimate recognition of him might be related to high estimates of her insight and knowledge; the charge that she go tell the disciples might relate to her leadership. In John 20:18, she tells the disciples, "'I have seen the Lord'; and she told them that he had said these things to her." The vague phrase "these things" may have functioned as a kind of catch-all gap. Pasquier notices that in the Gospel of Mary it is Mary, not the Lord, who engages in dialogue: "I saw the Lord in a vision and I said to him . . ." [7:2]). But these interpretive possibilities and opportunities do not show literary connection.[382] King thinks Mary's vision of the Savior in the Gospel of Mary probably reflects

378. Coyle, "Mary Magdalene in Manichaeism?" 44.

379. Coyle, "Mary Magdalene in Manichaeism?" 44, developing Bovon, "Paschal Privilege," 154–55. But see below, on Bovon's suggestions about paleo-Christian traditions.

380. R. E. Brown, *The Community of the Beloved Disciple* (New York: Paulist, 1979) 154.

381. Brown, *Community*, n. 300, p. 155.

382. See K. King, "The Jesus tradition in the *Gospel of Mary*," paper read at the SBL meeting, New Orleans, 1996: the Jesus traditions in this work are independent of any known literature. Contrast R. McL Wilson, "The New Testament in the Gnostic Gospel of Mary," *NTS* 3 (1957) 236–43;

the same tradition known to John 20:16–18 (emphasis mine).[383] But the absence of extensive, explicit Johannine allusions, except in the Manichaean Psalm Book, strikes me as strange and important. In chapter 7 I will come back to this puzzle.

In four works that mention Mary, I find clusters of motifs that may bear some relationship to Matthew 28: mountain,[384] Galilee, vision, reaction, Son of Man-type language and imagery, empowerment, commission, promise of presence, reference to law or commands, Father-Son-Holy Spirit linked. These clusters are found in the Sophia of Jesus Christ, the Dialogue of the Savior, the Gospel of Mary and the Gospel of Philip. For example, in the Sophia of Jesus Christ the risen Savior appears "not in his previous form, but in the invisible spirit" to "his twelve disciples and seven women" on a mountain in Galilee called "Divination and Joy." They marveled and were afraid (90:13–91:24). Part of the revelation discourse has to do with the revelation of "Man . . . Immortal Androgynous Man . . . the interpreter who was sent, who is with you until the end of the poverty of the robbers" (109–15), "First Man" (102:20), "designated in the Gospel 'Man' and 'Son of Man' " (104:1–2). This work ends with the Savior telling them "I have given you authority over all things as Sons of Light" (119:4–5); then he disappears. They go out to preach. Marjanen claims that the depiction of the Savior's appearance and the reference to his perpetual presence "can hardly have been written without knowledge of Matt 28, 16–20, although its use may have been indirect." The "strange combination of the Mount of Olives and the Mount of Galilee . . . seems to suggest that use of Matt 28, 16–20 has been indirect, perhaps based on an oral tradition *resultant from* the finished version of the Gospel of Matthew" (emphasis mine).[385] However, the mountain referred to in 91:20 as "Of Olives" in Galilee is not necessarily the same mountain referred to above; in the second case, the author may be referring to an earlier teaching in another place, about which he or she is confused. Luttikhuizen thinks the author of the Sophia of Jesus Christ was familiar with Matthean traditions indirectly, through earlier Gnostic traditions or revelation texts.[386]

The Gospel of Mary unites the themes of vision, Human One (Son of Man) language, presence (within), commission, and the instruction to lay down no further rules. Mary urges the disciples not to be double-minded (*hēt snau*); some consider that the idea of doubtful, irresolute disciples derives from Matt 28:17.[387]

Tuckett, "Synoptic Tradition" thinks there was access to the Gospels of Matthew and Luke, and no use of pre-synoptic sources.

383. King, *CG*, 358.

384. Only one resurrection appearance in the Christian Testament Gospels takes place on a mountain, Matt 28:16–20. Luke sets the ascension scene in Acts 1:12 on the mount called Olivet.

385. Marjanen, *The Woman*, 51.

386. G. P. Luttikhuizen, "The Evaluation of the Teaching of Jesus in Christian Gnostic Revelation Dialogues," *NovT* 30 (1988) 158–68.

387. D. Lührmann, "Die griechischen Fragmente des Mariaevangeliums: POx 3525 und PRyl 463," *NovT* 30 (1988) 326; Marjanen, *The Woman*, n. 53, p. 91.

"The rest of the world" (King translation) in Gospel of Mary 5:2 may also bear some relation to Matt 28:19's "all nations." Matt 28:16–20 and the traditions behind it do not concern the fleshiness of the resurrected Jesus. His final appearance is abrupt as though from heaven, and without description; and the Gospel ends with his promise of continual presence, not his departure. This pericope could inspire or be inspired by belief in the continuing presence of the Living One to all. On the other hand, Matt 28:16 confines the experience to the eleven, excluding Mary Magdalene and the other women. Pagels discusses the gnostic adaptation of the type of resurrection appearance that Dodd classified as circumstantial (vs. concise). The circumstantial narratives have many of the characteristics found in Matt 28:16–20, except that they are to one person or a few, and there is verbal interchange and recognition, as in John 20:14–18. These lend themselves to being interpreted as visions rather than attestations of a unique historical event which empowers only those witnesses.[388]

In the gnostic/apocryphal Mary materials we have examined, there is mention of an empty tomb only in the Gospel of Peter and the Epistula Apostolorum. As we will see in the next chapter, it is often assumed that the empty tomb tradition associated with her in the Christian Testament would be regarded as irrelevant or crude by those Christians who thought of resurrection as purely spiritual, noncorporeal, as well as by those who believed that the Savior did not really die. In the vision of the crucifixion recounted in Apocalypse of Peter 81:5–30, only the "fleshly part ... the substitution" was put to shame, while the one on the tree "glad and laughing" is "the living Jesus." "Those who did him violence" released his "incorporeal body" (83:7–8). No tomb is mentioned in the vision and revelation (82:4–16) that corresponds to the resurrection of Jesus in the Christian Testament.[389] A body in a tomb and an empty tomb would presumably be of no interest here.

But not all gnostics thought this way. The Letter of Peter to Philip 139:19–20 tries to stress both the reality of Jesus' suffering and the invulnerable glory of his divinity: "He was [crucified] on a tree and he was buried in a tomb. And he rose from the dead. ... My brothers, Jesus is a stranger to this suffering."[390] Here, as in 1 Corinthians 15, though there is burial, there is no mention of discovery of an empty tomb. The description of the risen Christ as a light and voice (134:9–14; 135:3–4; 137:17–19; 138:11–13, 21–22) may represent "a primitive way of depicting the appearances of the risen Lord."[391] That primitive way could indicate an understanding of Jesus as "taken" like Enoch, and Elijah and even like Moses, whose bodies (and graves) are not found. A sophisticated ambiguity should be

---

388. Pagels, "Visions, Appearances, and Apostolic Authority," 418.

389. The vision is of light and a "multitude of ineffable and invisible angels" and the revelation of "the one who gives praise" (*NHL* 377).

390. *NHL* 431–37.

391. Marvin M. Meyer, "The Letter of Peter to Philip," NHL 433.

again recognized. Pagels points out that the author of the Gospel of Philip sees the flesh and spirit as "brothers" (53, 17), and therefore refuses to engage the question of whether resurrection means resurrection "in this flesh" or whether it involves only the spirit or soul. There is "deficiency in both" of these positions (57, 11–12) — "apparently the deficiency inherent in language."[392]

Some critics argue that the empty tomb tradition was a late creation, intended to counter docetic, spiritual understandings of resurrection by emphasis on physicality, or identity: the *same* body that was dead has been raised, is alive again. Others think that the docetic, spiritual understandings oppose an earlier empty tomb tradition, or that these were at some time parallel, non-interactive traditions, whose meanings changed. It is true that the idea that the resurrection had already taken place as a spiritual reality is widespread in gnostic writings (see The Treatise on the Resurrection, The Exegesis on the Soul, The Gospel of Philip and other texts), and true that frequently within gnostic dualistic views the mortal body and matter itself are devalued, as the female is devalued. But it is unhelpful to jump from one document to another, assuming a monolithic system that ridiculed the very idea of bodily resurrection. It is unhelpful to assume we know what bodily resurrection meant, in its wide range of meanings.

In the Gospel of Mary the soul is led inward, set free from the Powers and from the fear of death. This work is about courage in the face of suffering. The Savior's death is real (he was not "spared"), but "there is no promise of, or desire for, a physical resurrection.... In the end, [this work] communicates a vision of a world that is passing away, not toward a new creation or a new world order but toward the dissolution of an illusory chaos of suffering, death, and illegitimate domination,"[393] toward matter dissolving into its own proper "root." "For the nature of matter is dissolved into what belongs to its nature" (2:3–4). It is a vision, one might say, of emptiness, of return to an initial state.[394] But not, perhaps, of annihilation.[395] Peter's question in the Gospel of Mary, "Will matter then be utterly destroyed or not?" can be seen as answered No, if matter is understood as purified, become Light.

It would make sense that Mary, associated with the claim at the empty tomb that Jesus had been raised, however that was understood, and with the claim of a visionary experience of the risen Jesus, would be regarded as a leader in communities that saw resurrection accomplished in this life as a precondition for life after death. In the Treatise on the Resurrection 48:4–5, alluding to the transfiguration

392. Pagels, "The 'Mystery of Marriage' in the Gospel of Philip Revisited," *The Future of Early Christianity* (ed. B. A. Pearson; Minneapolis: Fortress, 1991) 449.
393. King, "Gospel of Mary," 2.610, 628. "The place of rest is beyond the constraints of time and matter and false morality."
394. See Pasquier, *L'Evangile selon Marie*, 49.
395. What "root" means in the Gospel of Mary is not made clear. "Whether that root is matter or nothingness cannot be determined with certainty from the text" (King, "Prophetic Power and Authority," n. 35, p. 37).Compare. Gospel of Philip 53, 14–23; Origin of the World 127, 3–5.

tradition, resurrection is linked with vision: "What, then, is the resurrection? It is always the disclosure of those who have risen." The Gospel of Philip "takes for granted a direct analogy between Christ's experience and that of the initiate"[396] (56, 15–19; 73, 1–7). The theme of Mary as visionary is linked somehow with a tradition of her experience of a resurrection appearance of Jesus, perhaps grounded in mystical practices and ideals of the Jesus movement. Her description in the Gospel of Mary, for example, of a vision perceived through the mind, can be understood as a vision she had during the ministry of the Savior, and/or as an interpretation of a resurrection appearance to her. These should not be insisted on as clear cut alternatives, since belief in resurrection must have sprung from what were experienced as imaginative and spiritual possibilities/realities in the ministry, and belief in the resurrection in turn influenced the memory of the ministry.

Are there Christian Testament connections with other aspects of the gnostic/apocryphal profile — Mary as companion of the Savior, and the disciples' hostility to her? Statements such as "the Savior loved you more than the rest of women" and "he loved her more than us" introduce for some interpreters an erotic element and/or an explicitly sexual element. As we have seen, this is a dominant characteristic in later Magdalene legends and art. There focus is on her overblown and punished sexuality, and on the conflation of her character with that of "the sinner" in Luke 7. I find no evidence that the gnostics drew on Christian Testament traditions about other women — except Mary of Bethany[397] — to fill out the character of Mary Magdalene. They did not use the tropes of weeping, anointing, touching, to link text to text, tradition to tradition.

Unlike the Magdalene of later art and legend, the gnostic/apocryphal Magdalene is not a sinner, not a prostitute. Rather, it is another figure in the gnostic cast, Sophia, who is sometimes associated with a fall through love, and an agony of remorse; she is sometimes linked, as we have seen, with Mary Magdalene. Ward thinks it is possible that the idea of Mary Magdalene as a prostitute was affected by the tradition found, for example, in the Gospel of Philip, in which she is referred to as the intimate companion of Christ.[398] Ruether comments that a primary reason for eliminating the tradition of Jesus' friendship with Mary Magdalene was the late fourth-century depiction of him as a virgin ascetic.[399] With the elimination of mutuality and companionship, her legendary profile develops in a different direction.

---

396. Pagels, "Ritual in the *Gospel of Philip*," 286.

397. For example, in some texts Mary is paired with Martha (Epistula Apostolorum; Manichaean Psalm Book II 192, 21–23; 194, 19–20; Apostolic Church Order 26; Acts of Philip VIII 94; Pistis Sophia I–III; cf. Secret Gospel of Mark which alludes to John 11, the story of the siblings Mary, Martha and Lazarus). The Gospel of Philip 59, 6–8 gives us three Marys.

398. Benedicta Ward, *Harlots of the Desert: a Study of Repentance in Early Monastic Studies* (Kalamazoo, Mich.: Cistercian Publications, 1987) 15.

399. R. R. Ruether, *The New Woman/New Earth* (New York: Seabury, 1975), 49.

I think it likely also that the "fathers'" notion of the gnostic "heretical whore" not-so-subtly came into play, tied with the tradition of Mary's seven demons.[400] Mary could not be condemned completely because of the importance of her role in the works that came to be a part of the Christian Testament. But she was held in esteem by groups considered "heretical," groups which promoted some leadership for women and which were thought to be licentious. "Heretical" women were notorious; Tertullian, for example, charged that Philoumene "became an enormous prostitute," her "erroneous" teachings associated with penetration by evil spirits and therefore sexual pollution.[401] Helena was said to have been a former prostitute from Tyre, rescued by Simon Magus.[402] Epiphanius gives an account of how he barely escaped whorish gnostic women trying to seduce him.[403] (Cf. his interpretation of the Phibionites' stance as involving whoring [*koitais*] and drunkenness.[404]) Mary too came to be thought of as a whore, but a repentant whore, domesticated within "orthodoxy."[405] Her possession by seven devils, mentioned twice in the Christian Testament, has been read as a trace of earlier attempts to dilute her speech, her teaching, and her memory by claiming she had been wild but was tamed. We have the exorcism without the accusation.[406]

For the gnostics, where did the erotic element come from? There is no trace in gnostic/apocryphal literature of the seven demons, or of the intimate recognition and touch in John 20:14–17. Pagels makes the important suggestion that the hint of an erotic relationship between Jesus and Mary Magdalene in the gnostic materials "may indicate claims to mystical communion; throughout history, mystics of many traditions have chosen sexual metaphors to describe their experiences."[407]

400. See above, pp. 77–80. Demon-possession and perhaps a226n implication of wealth are linked in Luke 8:1–3. Jerome, *Ep.* cxxxiii.4 writes of "noble and rich women" seducing communities with money and then polluting them with heresy. Cf. C. Trevett, *Montanism: Gender, Authority and the New Prophecy* (Cambridge: Cambridge University Press, 1996) 153.
401. Tertullian, *de Praescriptione hereticorum* 6 and 30; King, "Prophetic Power," 29–30. Philumena was associated with Apelles, a disciple of Marcion; Hippolytus says Apelles wrote her "revelations" (Hippolytus, *Ref.* 7.38.2). See King n. 61, p. 39 for similar references, to Priscilla and an Asian prophet. The heretical male teacher is depicted as seductive charlatan (see McGuire, "Women, Gender and Gnosis," 263).
402. Justin, *Apology* 1.26.1–3; Irenaeus, *Her.* 1.23.2–24.4; Tertullian, *de Anima* 34; Hippolytus, *Refutatio omnium haeresium*; Epiphanius, *Pan.* 21–22. M. Scopello ("Jewish and Greek Heroines in the Nag Hammadi Library," *Images of the Feminine in Gnosticism,* 90) thinks the role of courtesans probably influenced gnostic writers, surely Simon, in the composition of their myths. Douglas Parrott, responding to Scopello's paper, refers to "the doctrine that ...disclosed the basic attitude about women: the fall of Sophia" (94).
403. Epiphanius, *Pan.* 26.17.4–8. See Williams, "Rethinking 'Gnosticism,'" 179–84. "Perhaps the discovery that these women whom he had thought to be proper Christian virgins were actually getting their inspiration from heretical, demiurgical texts was more than enough" for him to allege they tried to seduce him (182).
404. *Haer.* 26.5.8.
405. See K. J. Torjesen, *When Women Were Priests* (San Francisco: Harper, 1993) 143–49 on women's leadership and the charge of shamelessness in the third-century Didascalia.
406. See Trevett, *Montanism,* 153–58.
407. Pagels, *The Gnostic Gospels,* 18.

Marjanen wonders if the tradition of the Savior's love for Mary as found in the Gospel of Philip and the Gospel of Mary might have a primary source in the "idea of a beloved disciple,"[408] or in "Jesus' love for Mary." Does he mean the historical Jesus' love for the historical Mary? Jesus is not said anywhere in the Christian Testament to have loved Mary Magdalene. Perhaps this motif is borrowed from the statement in John 11:5 about Jesus' love for Mary of Bethany (and for Martha and Lazarus), and a sign of conflation. Love for Mary of Bethany is "projected onto" Mary Magdalene.[409]

One wonders if it is possible — or if it should be possible — to express the idea of the spiritual importance or significance of a woman — in Christian terms, of her intimacy with Jesus — without sexually explicit or implicit overtones. Is romantic love again "the only possible interpreter" of a woman of power,[410] a diminishment, that is, of her power? "And when we are writing the life of a woman, we may, it is agreed, waive our demand for action, and substitute love instead. Love, the poet has said, is woman's whole existence . . . (as long as she thinks of a man, nobody objects to a woman thinking). . . . [L]ove — as the male novelists define it — and who, after all, speak with greater authority? — has nothing whatever to do with kindness, fidelity, generosity, or poetry. Love is slipping off one's petticoat and — But we all know what love is."[411] Levi in the Gospel of Mary says that the Savior's love for Mary is based on his knowledge of her (10:10). It is love that is based on mutual knowledge. The apocryphal/gnostic Mary does not substitute love for action. These depictions do not seem to be about romantic love; but, then, they are ambiguous.

It seems to me that John 20–21 is not the source or inspiration of the widespread tradition of Peter's hostility to Mary. That source is more diffuse, in a certain unspoken rivalry between Peter and Mary Magdalene in — or, better, behind — the Christian Testament. There is no direct confrontation between them in the canonical literature. The hostility of male disciples (especially Peter and Andrew in the Gospel of Mary) toward Mary resonates with the Lukan account of the disbelief that met Mary's attempt to report the empty tomb and the words of the two dazzling men. In Luke 24:10–11 "the apostles" [v. 9 "the eleven and all the rest"] judged her words "an idle tale (*lēros*; cf. "strange teaching" in the Gospel of Mary), and they did not believe them" (v. 24: "some women of our group astounded us"). In the Markan Appendix 16:10–11, Mary Magdalene "went out and told [about the appearance of the risen Jesus to her] those who had been with him, while they were mourning and weeping. But when they heard that he

408. Marjanen, *The Woman*, n. 43, p. 136, referring to H.-M. Schenke's study of the beloved disciple motif ("The Function and Background of the Beloved Disciple in the Gospel of John," *Nag Hammadi, Gnosticism and Early Christianity* [ed. C. W. Hedrick and R. Hodgson, Jr.; Peabody, Mass.: Hendrickson, 1986] 111–25).
409. Marjanen, *The Woman*, n. 43, p. 136.
410. Woolf, *Room*, 87.
411. Woolf, *Orlando*, 268–69.

was alive and had been seen by her, they would not believe it." Cf. Matt 28:17b where "some doubted" the vision of Jesus on the mountain. These accounts, however, do not mention any specific male as hostile to Mary. In fact, in the Western non-interpolation of Luke 24:12 Peter, hearing her words, runs to the tomb, looks in, and verifies that it is empty (cf. the plural in v. 24 where "some of those who were with us" go to the tomb). In the Fourth Gospel, Mary tells Simon Peter and the beloved disciple about the empty tomb, to which they both then run (John 20:2–3).

But in 1 Cor 15:5 and in Luke 24:34, Peter is said to be the first to receive a resurrection appearance In Matt 28:9–10; John 20:14–17; Markan Appendix 16:9, Mary Magdalene is the first. How to explain this discrepancy is one of the great puzzles of Christian Testament scholarship. One possibility is that different groups preserved and developed different traditions, parallel and unknown to each other. Another possibility is that one first-appearance (protophany) tradition may have been created in reaction to the other. Or contemporaneous traditions may have clashed and fought in the early decades. Paul and Luke may have known of the tradition of a first appearance to Mary Magdalene, and omitted it, replacing it with mention (but not a narration) of an appearance to Peter; thus rivalry is reflected in the Pauline and/or Lukan materials. This process can be seen as linked to controversy over women's roles in early communities, as in Corinth in the 50s. Claims to resurrection appearances established the nature and structure of community leadership, which Luke-Acts restricts to the twelve male apostles.

Peter's priority in 1 Corinthians and Luke is commonly explained as "a priority among those who became official witnesses to the resurrection." The "secondary place" given to the tradition about Mary — although that tradition may well be historical — is said by Brown to probably reflect "the fact that women did not serve at first as official preachers of the church — a fact that would make the creation of an appearance to a woman unlikely."[412] But what does the word "official" mean here, when we are speaking of the tradition in 1 Corinthians 15 which may go back to the decade of the 40s or even the 30s? Who in that earliest period could have made a determination about what was "official," and on what basis? This is not about witnessing in court, but about public speaking, preaching, probably at times in synagogues and in homes. We need to enter the exploration of the Christian Testament material in the next chapter without assuming as "fact" that "women did not serve at first as official preachers of the church."

The Mary Magdalene of the Christian Testament is quite unlike the apocryphal Mary. She is important, but not prominent in the Christian Gospels. Like all the characters besides Jesus, she speaks very little; in her case, only to the figures at the empty tomb, to the risen Jesus and then to the disciples about the resurrection, except in Mark where she is said to remain silent out of fear. She has no role

---

412. Brown, *Community*, n. 335, pp. 189–90.

encouraging the disciples, is not said to be a visionary, is never praised, is not a leader. She is not called the companion of Jesus, and in the Gospel of John the "beloved disciple" is a male. Though disbelieved by all the disciples as a whole in Luke, she is never challenged by Peter or any other individual male. She is never defended, nor does she defend herself.

Leaving the world of the apocrypha and entering the world of the Christian Testament is entering a world that is both strange and too familiar, a world loud with women's silence. We know it cannot be a completely different world. In the next chapter I will try to drive from here to that other world, to which at this time there are no well-travelled roads. The Mary(s) of the "heretics" is related in ways that are not yet clear to both the repentant whore of legend and to the demon-possessed, exorcised woman of the Christian Testament. The historian cannot respect the borders of canon, and cannot see the canon as always and everywhere preserving earlier or "better" tradition.[413] The Gospel of Mary and other works may preserve very early tradition that has been filtered out of the canonical materials.

Perhaps it would have been better in this book to make no chapter division between apocrypha and canon, to treat the Christian Testament narratives that mention Mary Magdalene somehow side by side with the texts treated in this chapter. Mary Rose D'Angelo does this in her article on Mary Magdalene when she creates three sets of sources which blend canonical and noncanonical materials: A. narrative and dialogue gospels; B. dialogue and sayings gospels; C. texts with erotic overtones. She abandons the convention of beginning with Mark, and instead begins with the Gospel of Mary because it "casts Mary in a central role, refocusing the more familiar gospel narratives and illuminating the ways in which the concerns of authors and communities affect the narratives."[414] I have begun with Virginia Woolf, with the dirt of Migdal, moving to the legends, and then the apocryphal/gnostic works, also in order to "refocus" by means of a different approach. But I could not see how to transgress canonical boundaries in a formal, structured way in this chapter or the next, although perhaps obvious solutions[415] will occur to my readers. In chapter five, as here, questions about the interplay

---

413. See Good, "Pistis Sophia," 679: "Sound historical research dispenses with the canon entirely." It sees canon as "a fourth-century version of what the first century ought to look like" (678).

414. M. R. D'Angelo, "Reconstructing 'Real' Women from Gospel Literature: the Case of Mary Magdalene," *Women and Christian Origins*, 109. See also the organization of the second volume of *Searching the Scriptures*: Part I: Revelatory Discourses: Manifestations of Sophia; Part II: Epistolary Discourses: Submerged Traditions of Sophia; Part III: Biographical Discourses: Envoys of Sophia. The aim is "both to undo the exclusionary kyriarchal tendencies of the ruling canon and to renew the debate on the limits, functions and extent of the canon" — which does not itself represent the collective experience of early Christian women (E. Schüssler Fiorenza, "Transgressing Canonical Boundaries," *Searching the Scriptures*, 2.5; n. 11, p. 13).

415. Such as: classify texts according to the profile presented in this chapter (Mary is prominent, a visionary, speaks boldly . . .); or according to her presence in the movement; at the crucifixion; empty tomb; her visionary experiences.

between canonical and noncanonical texts are treated. But the chapter separation also recognizes that, for better or worse, canon is a powerful, influential category, to be treated with tremendous suspicion.[416] And research already done on the literary interconnections or lack of connection, the literary and theological characteristics, and the stages of canonical Gospel development mean that the four Gospels of Matthew, Mark, Luke and John present distinctive scholarly tasks and problems, which I want to engage.

This chapter's presentation of gnostic/apocryphal Mary traditions has been extensive, in order to make chunks of the actual texts available to readers, in order to show by contrast the narrowness of and puzzling gaps in the canonical depiction of Mary Magdalene, and in order to give a sense of the struggles that resulted in the distortion, destruction and erasure of women's traditions and in the eventual, multiple exclusions of women from positions of authority. Flawed as she is as a proponent and symbol of egalitarianism, the gnostic/apocryphal Mary destabilizes canon and imperial church. She can teach us to read the canonical texts in new ways, and to work to transform oppressive structures.

The future did depend upon what extent men could be led to stand free speech in women.[417] They could not stand it. The future seems still to depend on it, or on ignoring whether or not they can stand it.

---

416. See King, "Canonization" 29–36. Marginalization was produced in part by canonization. "Canon and 'orthodoxy' were devised in part to exclude women from positions of leadership and authority" (36).

417. V. Woolf, *Women and Writing* (ed. Michele Barrett; New York: Harcourt, Brace, Jovanovich, 1979) 13.

The Christian Testament's Mary Magdalene

Scholarly Versions, Explorations, Erasures

"The history of men's opposition to women's emancipation is more interesting perhaps than the story of that emancipation itself. An amusing book might be made of
it if some young student at Girton or Newnham could collect examples and deduce
a theory — but she would need thick gloves on her hands, and bars to protect her
of solid gold."

V. Woolf, Room, 55

H ISTORICAL, LITERARY, AND SOCIOLOGICAL ISSUES are entangled even more
tightly in scholarly appraisals of the canonical materials concerning Mary
Magdalene, than in appraisals of her treatment in legends and apocrypha. In
spite of this, somehow the "facts" under or within the canonical narratives and
the rhetoric seem closer, more within reach. There is for some the sense that they
must or should be gotten at; and that more is at stake. But these are illusions. We
cannot get at the "facts." History is just as elusive here as in the other materials,
and certainty just as impossible, undesirable, and stifling. Certainty, that is, which
indicates "we have consulted sufficient evidence to come to the conclusion that
no further assessment need be done, and that we can discount the possibility that
further evidence might come to light which would disprove the occurrence."[1]
"Truth is not always historical, and what seems warranted by historical evidence,
does not always turn out to be true."[2] Sometimes, however, truth *is* historical, and
what seems unwarranted by the evidence turns out to be true. The boundaries
of canon do not separate what is valuable from dreck, what is historical from
non-historical, what is true from not true.

In this chapter I am most interested in (1) the ways in which the women
and their contributions disappear from history and early tradition in most major
scholarly treatments, but do not disappear in others, and (2) the ways in which

---

1. P. F. Carnley,"Response," *The Resurrection* (ed. S. T. Davis, D. Kendall, G. O'Collins; New
York: Oxford University Press, 1997) 36.
2. K. Woodward, *Newsweek*, April 1996, quoted by J. Wilkins, "A Summit Observed," *Resurrection*, 1.

the women are diminished in the texts themselves. Woman is "a very queer, composite being.... Imaginatively she is of the highest importance; practically she is completely insignificant. She pervades poetry from cover to cover; she is all but absent from history."[3] Feminist scholars in the field of religion are used to finding only traces of women's lives and contributions, to learning how to read and fill in the gaps when possible. But here, in the Christian Testament texts about the crucifixion and resurrection, is something very strange. Not just traces and gaps. Women, in what seem to be crucial roles, but treated by many scholars as though they were not crucial.

Possible Aims, Motivations, Hopes, Frameworks

An examination of aims is in order as the Christian Testament materials are approached, with the recognition that aims are slippery, never fully conscious. There are several possibilities for the feminist scholar.[4] (1) One aim might be to prove or at least support what is assumed, the historicity of the empty tomb and/or of the first appearance to Mary Magdalene, her role as the first witness to the resurrection, "apostle to the apostles." This would be to begin with what looks like a conclusion (though it might be held lightly as an hypothesis), and arranging the data to lead to it (or seeing if the data would indeed lead to it). This might be a project undertaken to uncover this woman's history, and perhaps to undergird present ecclesiastical reform efforts or efforts to move creatively in new directions. Since 1998, the Roman Catholic organization FutureChurch, in conjunction with Call to Action, promotes services honoring Mary Magdalene on July 22. According to one journalist, "both groups see scholarship and feast-day celebrations as a means rather than end" to the goal of access to the priesthood for all baptized persons who experience a call.[5] Such an aim would be influenced by intuition and faith in women, by suspicion of as well as a good deal of trust in the primary texts. But with such an agenda would one be able to accept or even see alternatives if the case cannot be made, if the data cannot reasonably be so arranged? This aim underestimates the complexities of the Christian Testament materials, and ignores the fact that such historical "proof" is impossible. Further, the goal of access to the priesthood is too limited.

(2) A very different aim might be to demonstrate the possibility or probability that the historical Mary Magdalene is, like the site at Migdal, lost irretrievably. There was something there once, perhaps, but it is overgrown and trampled; there is no money or influence to change this situation, and it is too late. Let

---

3. Woolf, *Room*, 43.

4. The aims of the non-feminist scholar should be articulated by him- or herself.

5. See P. Schaeffer, "Groups promote Mary of Magdala, women's roles," *National Catholic Reporter* (April 7, 2000) 5; cf. H. Schlumpf, "Who Framed Mary Magdalene?" *US Catholic* 65 (April 2000) 12–17.

her memory stand as a warning: there is nothing for women in Christianity and there never was. Let her stand for all the forgotten; and let her be forgotten. The purpose of such work, then, might be to release energies from holding on to what is dead and gone and maybe never was, to redirect energies to other figures. Or it might be to release energies to create a Mary Magdalene of the imagination, like the imaginary park at Migdal. She would be a fantasy based on wishful thinking, desires, and on whatever intuition might remain of something historical, something important. A symbolic Mary Magdalene, a literary character with a past and future. Her mythology ongoing, she too could inspire efforts at reform or breakaway efforts; she could inspire just about anything, or nothing. But this aim, in my opinion, underestimates the historical value of the evidence we do have in the Christian Testament and its importance as a ballast to the imagination, and sidesteps the interesting task of making something of the evidence.

(3) A historical reconstruction of the role of Mary Magdalene would aim to use historical-critical and literary-critical methods in an effort to follow and assess the evidence plausibly but without claiming certainty, keeping the outcome and uses of the reconstruction open to surprises. In the doing there is no sureness about where the analysis will lead or what it will mean to others. There is the effort to deny, suppress, or at least control one's own political interests and not let them dictate either paths followed or results. This aim involves facing the complexity of the evidence, the inadequacy of our methods, and the current situation of male dominance in Christian Testament studies, in which gender analysis and feminist interpretation are not yet the requirements they should be for serious scholarship.

Each of the alternatives described above is not a disinterested project, but an advocacy project. Disinterested examination is impossible, and in fact interest may be most influential when it is ignored or unstated or concealed or unexamined. All work takes place within a framework of assumptions and commitments, about which a scholar may be more or less conscious and forthcoming. (4) My own aim is to produce a feminist reconstruction of the contribution of the historical Mary Magdalene, and an analysis of the uses and suppression of her memory in the Christian Testament. In the next chapter, I will attempt to lay out the framework of my own assumptions. My project runs the risk of expending too much time and energy using the master's tools for my "donkey work."

Five Sets of Problems

Discussion of the Christian Testament Mary Magdalene places us in the midst of great scholarly controversies that cannot be settled or even fully summarized here. I enter this minefield with trepidation, but also with great interest in the way the problems are identified and in the logic of proposed explanations, arguments and counter-arguments. Five major sets of historical problems must be faced. They are often ignored or bypassed in popular treatments which quickly claim Mary Magdalene as "first witness to the resurrection" (happily, not a prostitute), and put that claim at the service of contemporary efforts to reform Christianity. But in some scholarly treatments of the Gospels, these problems and certain solutions to them are, on the other hand, often the apparent reason why Mary Magdalene receives little if any attention, why study of this figure is not at all on the radar screen of most prominent critics. (A hermeneutic of suspicion leads one to ask if this rationale might not sometimes be reversed, with little attention to her leading to certain solutions.) The historical problems arise from serious consideration of the complexities, confusions and puzzling elements in the Christian Testament texts in the following five areas.

1. The Nature of the Jesus Movement, or – Better – the Kingdom of God Movement[6] and Its Gender Makeup, Ideals, Realities

As we have seen, Mary Magdalene and other women are mentioned as having followed Jesus in (Luke 8:1–3) and from (Mark 14:41; Matt 27:55; Luke 23:49, 55) Galilee. There is scholarly disagreement about what if anything[7] can be said historically about the women's involvement. Whether, for example, they should be seen as itinerants travelling with the men or as sympathizers settled in towns; whether they participated as fully as men did or were in only a domestic-like support role or the role of wealthy patrons; whether they were motivated by gratitude for personal healing or by other reasons/emotions; whether or to what extent their needs, insights, questions shaped the movement; whether the women and men worked together, or whether there was gender segregation; whether outsiders, especially the Roman government, could have seen them as full members. A small number of critics, following the lead of Elisabeth Schüssler Fiorenza, claim that the presence of women signals what we would call "a discipleship of equals" and the struggle to live an egalitarian ideal.[8] Others regard this claim as wishful thinking, anachronistic, the product of less-than-rigorous scholarship.[9]

Exploring what may have attracted women to this movement and sustained them in it involves the question of how was it like and/or unlike other Jew-

---

6. D'Angelo prefers the designation "reign-of-God movement," which frees her to think of leadership and creativity being exercised by other members as well as by Jesus ("Reconstructing 'Real' Women," 123).

7. "If today one smiles condescendingly at earlier presentations of Jesus that repeatedly referred to his ethical 'ideals,' one can be assured that future generations will read with comparable amazement today's confident portrayals of him as the leader of a social movement designed to restructure Galilean society" (Keck, *Who Is Jesus?* 9). Keck shows no interest in the women of the movement.

8. See E. Schüssler Fiorenza, "The Biblical Roots for the Discipleship of Equals," *Duke Divinity School Review* 2 (1980) 87; *In Memory of Her* (New York: Crossroad, 1983); *Bread Not Stone* (Boston: Beacon, 1984) 65–92; *But She Said* (Boston: Beacon, 1992) 80–101, and many other publications.

9. See, for example, the widely-used introductory textbook by B. D. Ehrman, *The New Testament* (New York: Oxford, 2000) 364–67.

ish movements, in which what we call politics and religion were embedded in each other, and it inspires the attempt to delineate what Peter Brown calls "the radical Judaism from which Christianity emerged."[10] Was this primarily an apocalyptic movement, or a movement with roots in the wisdom traditions, or was it a movement of wandering Cynic-like philosophers? How one sees the movement influences and may even determine what one thinks is historically possible for its earliest participants to imagine, expect, believe, experience, claim, and express.

Such exploration informs our understanding of how Mary Magdalene might have functioned in the movement, and how she might or might not have been prepared through her participation in its work — its thinking, study, hopes and practices — for any further role at and after the death of Jesus. It also gives us entree into the dynamics of gender and leadership conflicts in earliest Christianities.

2. The Crucifixion and Burial of Jesus

These narratives bristle with historical and literary problems, which overlap and lead scholars to ask whether the role of the women at the cross and burial is historical or not.

A. The narratives are shot through with allusions and quotations from the Hebrew Bible. The catalytic role of biblical texts has long been noted, influencing such motifs as conspiracy by enemies; betrayal by friends; false witnesses; Jesus' silence at the "trial"; mockery by enemies; his innocence, his vindication. The pattern of the "suffering righteous one" is clearly operative in the formulation of the passion narratives.[11] Some have claimed that this is one major indication that the narratives do not represent the memory of eyewitnesses, if there were any, but are, rather, free compositions using passages such as Psalms 2, 22, and 69 to represent what was later thought to have happened. If this is so, the passion narratives are not "history remembered" but "prophecy historicized." "History or propaganda, then, that is the question," and the answer for some is propaganda.[12]

B. There has been intense scholarly disagreement about the extent and very existence of a pre-Markan passion narrative, a narrative, that is, that would predate the war of 66–70, which took place a generation after the death of Jesus. E. Linnemann,[13] for example, argues that there was no pre-Markan narrative.

---

10. P. Brown, "Late Antiquity," in *A History of Private Life*, Vol. I: *From Rome to Byzantium* (Cambridge: Belknap, 1987) 266–67.

11. R. A. Horsley, "The Death of Jesus," *Studying the Historical Jesus* (ed. B. Chilton and C. A. Evans; New York: Brill, 1994) 417. G. W. E. Nickelsburg's hypothesis is that a traditional Jewish "story of the persecution and vindication of the righteous" lies behind the Markan passion narrative, a genre that can accommodate both the pattern of the suffering righteous one and that of the martyr ("The Genre and Function of the Markan Passion Narrative," *HTR* 73 [1980] 153–84).

12. J. D. Crossan, *Who Killed Jesus?* (San Francisco: HarperCollins, 1995) x, xi. He argues that Psalm 2 is especially influential, providing the frame and core of the passion narrative (81–85).

13. E. Linnemann, *Studien zur Passionsgeschichte* (Göttingen: Vandenhoeck & Ruprecht, 1970).

Mark is the creator of the connected form of the story, which may make use of traditional elements. For some scholars the Markan narrative is a fiction based on the pattern of the suffering innocent one or patterns of Jewish and Hellenistic martyrologies.[14] Others, like E. Schweizer,[15] hold that the parallels between Mark and John, which he considers independent, give us access to and delineate a pre-Markan narrative. Crossan argues for a pre-Markan narrative in the source he reconstructs behind the Gospel of Peter; he thinks Mark also used fragments from the Secret Gospel of Mark. M. L. Soards provides an appendix to R. E. Brown's massive *Death of the Messiah*, in which the methods and conclusions of thirty-five scholars are compared.[16] Only thirteen of those surveyed regard as pre-Markan all or part of Mark 15:40, which places at the cross Mary Magdalene, Mary the mother of James the younger and of Joses, and Salome.[17] In addition to the question of pre-Markan source or traditions and Markan creativity concerning the accounts of the crucifixion, burial and empty tomb, are the questions of whether the Mark/Matthew and Lukan accounts are so different that they indicate the existence of independent traditions, and whether John is independent of the Synoptics. Assessment of the sources is essential, traditionally, to assessment of the evidence for the presence of the women.

C. The presence of friends of Jesus at the cross, "standing near" (John 19:25) or even "looking on from afar" (Mark 14:40; Matt 27:55) or "at a distance" (Luke 23:49), has been challenged. Brown regards it as the "most difficult element to verify historically among the activities at the cross."[18] Rome, some think, would not likely allow sympathizers or relatives at the execution. Seutonius reports that "The relatives [of those condemned to death after the fall of Sejanus in 31 C.E.] were forbidden to go into mourning" (*Tiberius*, 61.2; see also Tacitus, *Annals* 6.19), and under various emperors of this period relatives were prohibited from approaching a crucified corpse. The notion that the body of Jesus would have been given a dignified burial, or any burial at all, has also been questioned, since the bodies of the crucified were often left on the cross to be eaten by birds and dogs or wild beasts[19] or thrown into a common grave or lime pit[20] or buried in

---

14. For this position, see B. L. Mack, *A Myth of Innocence: Mark and Christian Origins* (Philadelphia: Fortress, 1988); essays in *The Passion in Mark: Studies in Mark 14–16* (ed. W. Kelber, Philadelphia: Fortress, 1976).

15. E. Schweizer, *The Good News According to Saint Mark* (Richmond: John Knox, 1970).

16. M. L. Soards, "Appendix IX: the Question of a Premarcan Passion Narrative," in R. E. Brown, *The Death of the Messiah* (New York: Doubleday, 1994) 1492–1524.

17. One of these, Nineham, does not make a clear decision about the verse; four of those surveyed do not treat this verse at all.

18. Bown, *Death of the Messiah*, 1028–29.

19. See M. Hengel, *Crucifixion: In the Ancient World and the Folly of the Message of the Cross* (Philadelphia: Fortress, 1977) 9 (Pseudo-Manetho, *Apotelesmatica* 4.198ff), 26 (Tacitus, *Annals* 15.44.4), 54 (Juvenal, *Satires*, 14.77–78), 87.

20. M. Sawicki, *Seeing the Lord* (Minneapolis: Fortress, 1994) 257.

an unknown place.[21] The fact that Mary Magdalene and the other women play no part in the narration of the burial is thought to be further evidence of their absence at the cross. Joseph of Arimathea is often regarded as a fictional character, invented so that an incomplete burial of Jesus by enemies could be changed into a complete entombment by friends.[22]

3. The Empty Tomb

As it stands, the narrative of the empty tomb is the occasion of and vehicle for a primitive form of the Christian confession: "he has been raised" (="God raised Jesus from the dead"[23]). The statement of resurrection, that is, is contained in the story.[24] The relationship between the narratives of the empty tomb and those of appearances is far from clear. As it stands, the finding of the empty tomb precedes narratives of resurrection appearances, and in Matthew and John it can be read to inspire them. In Mark, the women do not tell, and there are no resurrection appearances; in the Markan Appendix and in Luke the women tell and are disbelieved. R. H. Fuller distinguishes between the report of an empty tomb as (a) origin or cause of faith, and (b) vehicle of faith. He argues that historically the basic nucleus of the empty tomb story "was derived from a report given by Mary Magdalene to the disciples," who "received Mary's report not as the origin and cause of their Easter faith, but as a vehicle for the proclamation of the Easter faith which they already held as a result of the appearances."[25]

In Christian Testament scholarship, apart from feminist scholarship, the empty tomb is rarely treated as a pericope of central importance.[26] Historically it is sus-pect. If there was no burial that was witnessed, or no burial at all, or burial in a common pit where bodies were indistinguishable, there could have been no discovery of an empty tomb. The creation of the empty tomb by Mark or before Mark, even the tradition that Jesus was buried at all, has been seen as an "apol-

---

21. H. Grass argues that Jesus had probably been buried with the other two criminals in an unknown place (*Ostergeschehen und Osterberichte* (Göttingen, 1962) 173–86, 233–49.

22. See J. D. Crossan, "Empty Tomb and Absent Lord," *The Passion in Mark* (ed. W. Kelber; Philadelphia: Fortress, 1976) 137.

23. See R. H. Gundry (*Mark* [Grand Rapids: Eerdmans, 1993] 1001, 992) on the question of an underlying early Christian formula, and on contextual support for the passive meaning of *egeirō* in Mark 16:6 ("he has been raised"). See M. Reiser, *Jesus and Judgment* (Minneapolis: Fortress, 1997) 266–73: "Excursus: The So-called *Passivum Divinum* or *Passivum Theologicum* and the Eschatological Passives." "When the events are not, as in Daniel 7, depicted in a visionary manner *as events beheld*, such expressions and descriptions are usually presented in the future tense" (271, emphasis mine). The passive here puts emphasis on resurrection; drawn from apocalyptic, I think it may also signal visionary experience.

24. B. Lindars ("Jesus Risen: Bodily Resurrection but No Empty Tomb," *Theology* 89 [1986] 90) holds that a careful distinction should be made between the statements and the popular stories, including this one, in which they eventually found expression.

25. R. H. Fuller, *The Formation of the Resurrection Narratives* (Philadelphia: Fortress, 1980) 70.

26. See the summary of views by S. T. Davis, "Was the Tomb Empty?" *Hermes and Athena* (ed. E. Stump and H. P. Hint; Notre Dame: University of Notre Dame, 1993) 77–83 and n. 12, pp. 98–99.

ogy" for the failure of Jesus' relatives, disciples and friends to bury him,[27] or as providing a cult aetiology for annual early Christian rites at the tomb of Jesus.[28] It is debated inconclusively whether resurrection language in first-century Judaisms would require or imply the absence of the dead body,[29] and what indeed resurrection in a given time or text would emphasize — whether the new, heavenly or angelic character of a spiritual or symbolic body, or revival or transformation of an earthly body.[30] Nevertheless, the empty tomb is also widely considered a late addition to the story, designed to "prove the reality of the resurrection,"[31] support the resurrection kerygma, or interpret it,[32] or to underline a crassly physical (in contrast to spiritual) notion of resurrection,[33] or a correctly physical understanding (in contrast to spiritual).[34] A. Y. Collins thinks that the author of Mark composed the passage as a whole to narrate and interpret the early Christian proclamation of Jesus' resurrection in "a way that was natural for an author living in the first century."[35]

There is no mention of an empty tomb (as well as no mention of Mary Magdalene in the list of those who saw the risen Jesus) in the early fossil of tradition, perhaps as early as the 30s, embedded in 1 Corinthians 15, written in the 50s. It is debated whether or not the mention of Jesus' burial in 15:4 means that Paul and/or the tradition before him knew of an empty tomb.[36] It is not clear whether or not such a tradition may have been or must have been presupposed by him, or

---

27. Crossan, "Empty Tomb," 137. See Gundry, *Mark*, 980: Mark depicts a dignified burial in order to overcome the shame of the cross.

28. L. Schenke, *Auferstehungsverkündigung und Leeres Grab* (Stuttgart, 1968).

29. Compare these attempts to understand the variety of Jewish beliefs: Lindars, "Jesus Risen," 92; H. C. C. Cavallin, *Life after Death* (Lund, 1974) 139; E. P. Sanders, *Judaism: Practice and Belief 63 BCE–66 CE* (Philadelphia: Fortress, 1992) 298–303; A. Y. Collins, "The Empty Tomb in the Gospel According to Mark," *Hermes and Athena*, 128–30; A. J. M. Wedderburn, *Baptism and Resurrection* (Tübingen: Mohr, 1987) 167–80.

30. A. Y. Collins, "The Empty Tomb in the Gospel according to Mark," 130.

31. R. Bultmann, *History of the Synoptic Tradition* (New York: Harper & Row, 1968) 287.

32. N. Perrin, *Resurrection Narratives according to Matthew, Mark and Luke* (Philadelphia: Fortress, 1977) 82–83.

33. Lindars, "Jesus Risen," 90; M. Goulder, "Did Jesus of Nazareth Rise form the Dead?" *Resurrection* (ed. S. Barton and S. Stanton; London: SPCK, 1994) 58–68.

34. It is seen as a corrective to the tradition of vision-like appearances, which in the beginning could be thought of as purely spiritual appearances from heaven (e.g., Paul's vision or the appearance in Matt 28:16–20). An empty tomb, so this thinking goes, implies the physicality of the resurrection, not spiritual exaltation, not the survival of Jesus' soul or ghost, not necromancy. See Mack, *Myth of Innocence*, 308.

35. *The Beginning of the Gospel* (Minneapolis: Fortress, 1992) 119–48. See M. Borg, "The Irrelevancy of the Empty Tomb," *Will the Real Jesus Please Stand Up?* (ed. P. Copan; Grand Rapids: Baker, 1998) 117–28: it is irrelevant because the resurrection of Jesus has nothing to do with his corpse; it has to do with his ongoing, empowering presence. One can meaningfully affirm the resurrection without an empty tomb, which is only a metaphorical affirmation that he lives.

36. See also Acts 2:24–31; 13:28–37, using Psalm 16:10 to argue that though Jesus died and (in 13: 28–37) was buried, he experienced no corruption. This early preaching may presuppose an empty tomb, but there is no mention of it in Acts, though Luke had narrated the story in his first volume.

whether such a presupposition was unnecessary to his resurrection belief.[37] Lindars thinks the emptiness of the tomb may be assumed in 1 Corinthians 15, "but is not made the grounds for inviting belief in the resurrection. This suggests that the proclamation of the bodily resurrection of Jesus lies behind the empty tomb stories, and not the other way round."[38] Most hold that Paul did not know of the tradition of the women's discovery of the empty tomb, either because it was late or because it had not yet made its way into the male kerygmatic tradition. If, on the other hand, the story of the empty tomb and/or of the appearance to women was known and omitted, the reasons for its suppression are debated.[39] Wire holds that Paul may have suppressed the tradition because of gender controversies in Corinth.[40] Osiek thinks the stories of empty tomb and appearance to Mary Magdalene are passed over by Paul and Acts "precisely *because* they involve the testimony of women," but she argues this may just be the effect of "the assumed androcentric bias of the accounts (which could have operated almost unconsciously and need not presume active misogyny)."[41]

Appearances to men are regarded by most critics as the foundation of the resurrection faith. Lindars, for example, assumes that the series in 1 Corinthians 15 consists of appearances of the exalted Lord which triggered proclamation of the resurrection, the earliest proclamation making no distinction between exaltation and resurrection.[42] For Goulder, the genuine conversion experiences of Peter and Paul and others, experienced as visions, were interpreted according to the widespread belief of the time "that the kingdom of God was coming and that the dead would be raised," as evidence that Jesus had risen from the dead.[43] But visions of other dead persons as far as I can see, even in this period — for example, the visions of Moses and Elijah in the Synoptic transfiguration narratives — did not result in the belief that they *had been resurrected*. Why would these visions?

The empty tomb narratives present a great divergence of detail with regard to the names of the women involved, the number of angels, the message, the

---

37. Contrast Davis, "Was the Tomb Empty?" 90 and A. Y. Collins, "The Empty Tomb in the Gospel according to Mark," 111–12 on the implications of the seed imagery. Against Davis, A. Y. Collins thinks "for Paul and presumably many other early Christians, the resurrection of Jesus did not imply that his tomb was empty" (114).

38. Lindars, "Jesus Risen," 91.

39. On whether or not women could serve as public witnesses, see C. Osiek, "The Women at the Tomb," *Ex Auditu* 9 [1993] 103–4; B. Gerhardsson, "Mark and the Female Witnesses," *DUMU-E2-DUB-BA-A* [ed. H. Behrens et al.; Philadelphia: The University Museum Occasional Publications of the Samuel Noah Kramer Fund II, 1989] 218; J. M. Baumgarten, "On the Testimony of Women in 1QSa," *JBL* 76 (1957) 266–69. Osiek thinks the general reluctance in ancient Mediterranean society to see women as public spokespersons or officeholders explains why there is silence about women's witnesses in the public speeches in Acts; but it does not explain Paul's silence about the women in 1 Corinthians 15 (104).

40. A. Wire, *The Corinthian Women Prophets* (Philadelphia: Fortress, 1990) 159–76.

41. Osiek, "The Women," 105.

42. Lindars, "Jesus Risen," 92.

43. Goulder, "Did Jesus of Nazareth Rise from the Dead?" 65.

women's reaction and response. For Perkins this suggests there was no unified tradition about the empty tomb in early Christianity. "At almost every point the accounts go in separate directions. It is impossible to harmonize them in such a way as to produce a single, simpler tradition that has then been redacted by the narrators."[44] Others disagree because there is a "common thread" to all four canonical accounts: at least one woman companion of Jesus, Mary Magdalene, was the first to come to the tomb after the sabbath, found it empty, and went away. It is also common to the Synoptics that she and at least one other "received a message from someone(s) to interpret the meaning as the resurrection of Jesus."[45]

The age of the empty tomb tradition depends on the literary question regarding its origin.[46] Mark's account has been labeled fiction created entirely or in part by Mark,[47] or composition based on a pre-Markan account that can be reconstructed.[48] In reconstructions, the angelophany is often removed as secondary, reflecting the church's kerygma,[49] so that the original form of the story is said to be that some women arrived first at the tomb, saw the stone rolled back, found the tomb empty, went away confused, and ran to tell the disciples. Without the angelophany ("supernatural intervention") and/or without the appearance of the risen Jesus to the women as in Matthew and John), the explanation of the emptiness "could just as well be that the body was stolen."[50] But both the efforts to

44. P. Perkins, *Resurrection* (New York: Doubleday, 1984) 91, 93, following E. L. Bode, *The First Easter Morning* (Rome: Biblical Institute, 1970) 6–17. I would not expect that the method of "harmonizing" would give us an earlier tradition.

45. C. Osiek, "Women at the Tomb," 97. I will argue below that something similar to this Synoptic "thread" is found also in the Gospel of John.

46. A. Y. Collins, "The Empty Tomb in the Gospel According to Mark," 115.

47. K. Corley, "Women and the Crucifixion and Burial of Jesus," *Forum* 1 (1998) 206: Mark 16:1–8 is "a fictional, anti-translation or deification story." See A. Y. Collins, "The Empty Tomb and Resurrection according to Mark," *The Beginning of the Gospel*, 119–48. She thinks Mark composed 16:1–8, but he did not make up the episode "out of whole cloth." "He regarded the resurrection of Jesus as an event attested by those to whom the risen Jesus had appeared. Since he did not have evidence for the details regarding *how* [emphasis mine] Jesus was raised, he reverently supplied those details in accordance with his sense of what must have happened," probably but not necessarily (if I understand her correctly) in line with his understanding of resurrection as the revival or transformation of an earthly body (as in 2 Maccabees, in contrast to Daniel 12) (126, 129). But Mark does not give a clear impression of *how* Jesus was raised, as the stone being rolled back could be for the purpose of letting the body of Jesus out of the tomb, or of letting the women see inside, as Collins herself says. As I will argue in the next chapter, I do not think the either/or approach to these texts is productive (either translation or revival, either physical resurrection or spiritual resurrection) in discussion of this stage of the tradition.

48. Fuller finds the presence of literary sources in Mark's account (*Formation of the Resurrection Narratives*, 50–70). Crossan thinks material from the Gospel of Peter, which he calls the Cross Gospel, has been redacted by Mark and then by others (*The Birth of Christianity*, San Francisco: Harper, 1998).

49. P. Perkins ('I Have Seen the Lord' (John 20:18)," *Int* 46 [1992] 37) notes that the angelophany is commonly "taken as secondary because the content of the scene reflects the early church's kerygma and the redactional emphases of each Gospel" and even liturgical elements. She thinks, however, that the primitive tradition may have reported an angelophany, that led to the women's departure, in the vicinity of the tomb.

50. Osiek, "The Women," 98,100. She argues that the earlier version referred to a group of women because "mourning and preparation of a body for burial are social activities for women." John has

reconstruct a source and the claim that this passage is a Markan creation face the difficulty that a source can of course be reworded by an author in his or her own way; it can look like creation. Identification of elements of continuity, tension, stylistic variation, legend, and of Semitisms, Markisms in Mark's text does not produce a convincing analysis of what is creation and what, if anything, is tradition or source. Since there is now no consensus on whether or not the Gospel of John is dependent on or independent of Mark or of the Synoptics in general, the method of comparing the empty tomb accounts in Mark and John in order to speak about pre-gospel traditions is rarely used.

Further, it is not clear how the tradition of the empty tomb discovered by women is related to the traditions that precede and follow it. It strikes some critics as secondarily joined to the preceding narrative of crucifixion and burial, because of the naming of the women again in Mark 16:1 after 15:40, 47, because of the variation of the names, and because of the very strangeness of the women's intention stated in Mark (and Luke), to anoint a corpse,[51] even if that anointing is imagined as an honorific sprinkling.[52] Others think the stories of the burial and empty tomb probably circulated together.[53]

Women, not men, are said to be represented at the tomb because this is suggested by the early tradition that Jesus was buried and raised on the third day (1 Corinthians 15), and caring for the dead and visiting tombs is what women did and do. In other words, for some critics they provide verisimilitude.[54] But the narratives are also thought by others to lack verisimilitude in their depictions of the women's purpose: coming to anoint (Mark 16:1; Luke 24:1), to sit (Matt 27:61), to watch or see (Matt 28:1) or simply as coming (John 20:1), rather than to lament. Corley asks, "What keeps the authors from portraying this common custom [women lamenting]?" She answers that a women's lament tradition has been erased because of its necromantic associations. "The association of followers of Jesus (particularly women) going to a tomb on the third day following Jesus' death to commune with the dead through their mournful cries could too closely associate Jesus with everyday 'divine men' or heroes, and his followers

---

reduced this group to Mary Magdalene alone: (1) 20:11–18 was composed as a private encounter, and (2) this focus prefigures her centrality in later apocrypha. The plural in John 20:2 ("we") may be a remnant of the earlier version (101). Without the angelophany, the story is one that enhances the meaning of the resurrection but is not necessary, in that it does not offer any "proof" (105).

51. Bultmann, *History of the Synoptic Tradition*, 285; Osiek, "The Women," 98.

52. See L. Schottroff, "Mary Magdalene and the Women at Jesus' Tomb," *Let the Oppressed Go Free* (Louisville: Westminster/John Knox, 1991) 181, n. 42, p. 200. Osiek ("The Women," 98) remarks that "when this anointing is to be done more than thirty-six hours after burial, it still strains credibility."

53. See Gundry, *Mark*, 996–97.

54. See D'Angelo, "Reconstructing 'Real' Women," 120–21. Against the argument that the stories of the women at the tomb must have been true, since women would not have been invented as witnesses, she argues that their lesser credibility "could be used to enhance the verisimilitude of pious fictions because the supposed unreliability of women witnesses could help explain why the stories became known later.

with magic." The empty tomb story results from the modification of the women's lament tradition by use of the fictional device of an empty tomb, thought to be drawn from Hellenistic translation or deification stories and romances.[55] Doubting that the gravesite of Jesus was ever found, Corley argues further that the Gospels' empty tomb and appearance stories are attempting to obscure the possibility that Christian belief and practice have their origin in dreams, waking dreams and visions (especially women's) following deaths; there is a common link between these and the founding of cults in antiquity. The Gospels obscure this by replacing evidence of this possible origin "with a resurrection theology" and the story of a tomb found empty on the third day. The women should be included in any posited pre-Markan account, but the empty tomb narrative does not contain an oral narrative tradition passed through women's networks;[56] rather, "it may have risen in response to a tradition that implied women's cultic experience."[57]

Mark's final statement in 16:8 that "the women said nothing to anyone because they were afraid" is commonly taken as an answer to the question why the story of the discovery of the empty tomb remained unknown for a long time.[58] The women's fear and silence, with which this Gospel ends, are also often considered their failure, a Markan parallel to the failure of the male disciples who flee in Gethsemane.[59] Contrast the treatments of those critics who think the women told in spite of their fear,[60] or that the ending is carefully crafted to be resolved "outside the story world and in the life of the reader."[61]

If and when it is considered historical in any sense, the story of the finding of the empty tomb is frequently dismissed in various ways: as based on deception, wishful thinking, imagination, hysteria, or as merely ambiguous. In the eighteenth century, for example, Reimarus argued that the disciples of Jesus stole the body

---

55. Corley, "Women and the Crucifixion and Burial," 203–5; cf. A. Y. Collins, "The Empty Tomb in the Gospel according to Mark," 123–28. The women do come to lament in Gospel of Peter 13:55–57, and Mary Magdalene weeps in John 20:11; presumably Corley regards these as remnants of the tradition.

56. Against Osiek ("The Women," 103–4) who thinks the empty tomb stories tell the women's side of an event.

57. Corley, "Women and the Crucifixion and Burial," 207, 209. See also A. Y. Collins, "The Empty Tomb in the Gospel according to Mark," 123–28. See O'Collins (*Resurrection*, 15–17) for criticism of the view that Mark has been so influenced by Greco-Roman literature.

58. Bultmann, *History of the Synoptic Tradition*, 285, following Bousset.

59. The literature on this pericope is enormous. See, for examples, Crossan, *Birth of Christianity*, 557. D. R. Catchpole, "The Fearful Silence of the Women at the Tomb," *Journal of Theology for Southern Africa* 18 (1977) 3–10; E. S. Malbon, "Fallible Followers: Women and Men in the Gospel of Mark," *Semeia* 28 (1983) 229–48; A. T. Lincoln, "The Promise and the Failure: Mark 16:7–8," *JBL* 108 (1989) 293–96; W. Munro, "Women Disciples in Mark?" *CBQ* 44 (1984) 225–41.

60. See M. J. Selvidge, "'And Those Who Followed Feared' (Mark 10:32)," *CBQ* 45 (1983) 396–400; E. S. Malbon, "Disciples/Crowds/Whoever: Markan Characters and Readers," *NovT* 28 (1986) 118; E. Schüssler Fiorenza, *In Memory of Her*, 320–23.

61. P. L. Danove, *The End of Mark's Story* (Leiden: Brill, 1993) 1; T. E. Boomershine, "Mark 16:8 and the Apostolic Commission," *JBL* 100 (1981) 225–39; J. Camery-Hoggatt, *Irony in Mark's Gospel* (Cambridge: Cambridge University Press, 1992) 10–12, 177–78.

and then later proclaimed the lie that he had been resurrected. The eleven did this for economic reasons, ambition, and the desire for power.[62] Others scholars give rationalizing explanations of the empty tomb, arguing that Jesus had been buried alive and returned to consciousness,[63] or that the body was reburied by Joseph of Arimathea in a place unknown to the disciples.[64] E. Renan in *The Life of Jesus* (1863) wrote that "the strong imagination of Mary Magdalene played an important part" in the establishment of the resurrection faith. "Divine power of love! Sacred moments in which the passion of one possessed gave to the world a resuscitated God!"[65] Renan says Mary Magdalene "appears to have been of a very enthusiastic temperament. According to the language of the time, she had been possessed by seven demons. That is, she had been affected with nervous and apparently inexplicable maladies.... [S]he was the principal means by which faith in the resurrection was established."[66] More typical today is the opinion of Gerhardsson, that "the original opinion within early Christianity" was certainly that women first discovered that the tomb was empty; but "it was hard for Early Christianity to make use of their testimony" because of "the traditional attitude" about women, which had a strong hold on the disciples themselves as well as on their audiences. Paul, he thinks, omitted mention of their testimony thinking it of little use. "Not only was the empty tomb a mystery rather than a piece of evidence, in addition, the testimony for it was weak and vulnerable." In this reading, the empty tomb is negative data, carrying no original angelic interpretation or insight; and appearances to the women are late. "The feministic attempts to make the positive data about women [I suppose here he means the interpretation of the empty tomb and the appearances to them] the most original testimonies... are in my opinion the result of considerable wishful thinking, as are the attempt to reconstruct the history of Christian beginnings by believing that in the beginning, in the circle around Jesus and in the very first days of the Church, women were given the same position as men and thus totally lifted up above the restrictions put on the female part of society in Palestine in this time."[67]

Fuller argues that "Whether the women's story was based on fact, or was the result of mistake or illusion, is in the last resort a matter of indifference";[68] what is crucial is not the emptiness of the tomb, but the affirmation that God has raised

---

62. H. S. Reimarus, *Fragments* (ed. C. H. Talbert; Chico, Calif.: Scholars Press, 1970) 243.

63. H. E. G. Paulus, *Kommentar über die drei ersten Evangelien* III (1802) 797, 806, 839–931; *Das Leben Jesu als Grundlage einer Geschichte des Urchristentums* (Heidelberg, 1828) 277–305.

64. Anon., "Versuch über die Auferstehung Jesu," *Bibliothek für Kritik und Exegese des Neuen Testaments und älteste Kirchengeschichte* 2 (1799) 537–51; J. Klausner, *Jesus of Nazareth* (London) 357.

65. E. Renan, *The Life of Jesus* (Buffalo: Prometheus, 1991; translation originally published by Watts & Co., 1935) 215.

66. Renan, *Life of Jesus*, 93.

67. Gerhardsson, "Mark and the Women Witnesses," 224–26. Pagels and Schüssler Fiorenza are cited as examples of scholars who engage in wishful thinking. His short article is fascinating for its gaps in reasoning, its blind spots, and its slippages.

68. Fuller, *Formation of the Resurrection Narratives*, 179.

Jesus. For Craig, the discovery of the empty tomb is the one plausible "historical fact" associated with the resurrection of Jesus. His treatment is unusual in that he not only argues for the historicity of the empty tomb itself, but he also defends the historical veracity of almost all of the details associated with the story in Mark, by harmonizing details found in John's account, and invoking the authority of the Beloved Disciple for divergent Johannine elements.[69]

Controversy about the empty tomb narrative shows a continuing opposition between what Theissen and Merz call "the objective or the chronological priority of the tomb or the appearance tradition,"[70] and a long scholarly history of priority given to the latter.[71] These are commonly regarded as independent traditions,[72] combined at a late stage by the creation of narratives of appearances to women at the empty tomb.[73] When the empty tomb is accepted as prior, it is often seen as only a bare fact, and as reported by the women as a bare fact: it has no internal interpretation. H. von Campenhausen considers it the decisive stimulus to "the course of Easter events," but real insight comes from the male disciples not from the women: the disciples hiding in Jerusalem were told by the women that they discovered the tomb empty "on the third day." Peter immediately believed Jesus had been raised from the dead and led the eleven to Galilee where, first to Peter and then to the Twelve, the appearances took place. Later tradition put the belief in resurrection and sequence of events into the mouth of the angel at the tomb.[74] In this reconstruction, the resurrection faith and the appearances which confirm it belong to the men. The women provide only an enigmatic report of the empty tomb, with no interpretation of that emptiness. Von Campenhausen does not explain why he thinks Peter believed on the basis of the emptiness, but the women did not. He holds that there is "striking support in the tradition" for the

---

69. See W. L. Craig, "The Historicity of the Empty Tomb of Jesus," *NTS* 31 (1985) 39–67. Others who argue for the historicity of the empty tomb include Stauffer, León-Dufour, Stein, Bode. See criticism of Craig by P. Perkins, "The Resurrection of Jesus of Nazareth," *Studying the Historical Jesus* (ed. B. Chilton and C. A. Evans; Leiden: Brill, 1994) n. 57, p. 436. Perkins thinks the pre-Markan tradition did recount the discovery that Jesus' tomb was empty (*Resurrection*, 91–95).

70. G. Theissen and A. Merz, *The Historical Jesus* (Minneapolis: Fortress, 1998) 480. Their survey of interpretations (474–511) is helpful.

71. D. F. Strauss, for example, argued that the visions of disciples in Galilee are the historical origin of the Easter faith, far away from the tomb of Jesus in Jerusalem, which becomes an empty tomb in secondary legend (*The Life of Jesus Critically Examined* [ed. P. C. Hodgson; Philadelphia, 1972] 709–44).

72. Bultmann, if I understand him correctly, thinks that the oldest tradition told of the disciples' flight to Galilee. But Mark 16:7, which commissions the women to tell the disciples to go to Galilee, presupposes that the disciples were still in Jerusalem, and so is secondary. The charge to the women, pointing toward a Galilean appearance conflicts with what he thinks is "the dominant motif of the passage" (to prove the reality of the resurrection by the empty tomb); so the story of the empty tomb and the story of the Galilean appearance had an independent origin (*History of the Synoptic Tradition*, 285–87).

73. Theissen and Merz, *The Historical Jesus*, 484.

74. H. von Campenhausen, "The Events of Easter and the Empty Tomb," *Tradition and Life in the Church* (London: Collins, 1968) 84–85.

notion that Peter may have been "the only one to remain loyal, or, at least, not to have given up everything, perhaps also the first to rekindle hope and to have kept together or regrouped the others"[75] W. Pannenberg also argues that the tradition of the empty tomb is as original as that of the appearances, but the former is dependent on the latter for content: "For only in the light of the appearances does the empty tomb become the witness to the resurrection; without them it remains ambiguous."[76] Theissen and Merz, after a review of arguments for and against the historicity of the empty tomb, conclude that historicity cannot be demonstrated or refuted with historical-critical methods. For them, the balance tilts a little way toward the possibility that the story has a historical nucleus. But the empty tomb (found by women, but about which they kept silent because they did not want to be accused of grave robbery) is enigmatic. It can only be illuminated by the Easter faith (which is based on appearances first in Galilee to the fugitives, secondarily relocated to Jerusalem). "The Easter faith cannot be illuminated by the empty tomb."[77] Again, the women are witnesses to an empty tomb but they do not know what to make of it until Easter appearances to others interpret it; this interpretation is then folded into the story of their discovery by being put on the lips of the Markan young man in white. Perkins finds the nucleus behind the tomb traditions in the discovery of the empty tomb by some women disciples "who then left perplexed." This nucleus did not include an angelophany "since the angel's message reflects the kerygmatic preaching of resurrection and thus requires an understanding of the significance of the empty tomb gained from the appearance traditions. Finding the tomb empty was not the source of early Christian belief that Jesus had been raised."[78] So both the angelophany associated with the empty tomb and the christophany to women in Matthew and John are usually taken as signs of lateness and a well-developed tradition.

In many historical reconstructions of the empty tomb materials, then, Mary Magdalene is either a semi-fictional character (her name comes from ancient tradition, but the story about an empty tomb is theological fiction) or a woman who did not understand the significance of what she found, until men interpreted it for her through their own experience.

4. Resurrection Appearances

These are obviously problematic for the historian, as they involve claims that one who died lived again and acted in time and history, or, rather, acted upon and with those who were in time and history. The appearances are seen as "interventions" into human history, with historical consequences. They are presented as visionary-auditory experiences. But in Luke 24:37–43; John 20:20, 27 the risen

---

75. Von Campenhausen, "The Events," 82.
76. W. Pannenberg, *Systematic Theology*, 2. 343–63.
77. Theissen and Merz, *The Historical Jesus*, 503.
78. Perkins, *Resurrection*, 94.

Jesus is dramatically distinguished from a ghost or a bodiless spirit; his corpore-ality — though transformed — appears to be emphasized. In her groundbreaking 1978 article, Pagels sees these juxtaposed traditions developing by the mid-second century into at least two different lines of tradition: those that "attest the reality of the resurrection," and those that "lend themselves to interpretation as visions." The second type (for example, the appearance to Mary Magdalene in John 20:14–18 and to Paul in Acts 9:3–7) is favored by those condemned as "heretics" by the "orthodox" or "ecclesiastical writers." The two lines "bear different theological interpretations," and "also lead to very different attitudes toward authority — not only in terms of doctrine, but also in terms of the social and political leadership within the communities."[79] We should recognize, however, that the two types of appearances both concern self-manifestations not available to neutral observers, and both deal with a Jesus not immediately recognizable. As Schneiders puts it, "There is nothing naive (however artless they may seem) about the appearances. Those who saw the risen Jesus knew [or, better: those who wrote the appearance narratives described them in a such way] that whatever 'seeing' meant it was not a purely biological, optical event in the natural order, i.e., within the arena of historical cause and effect and governed by the coordinates of space and time."[80]

It is debated how the claims to appearances,[81] if these claims are in any way historical, are to be understood psychologically. Bultmann was not interested in such explanations: "The church had to surmount the scandal of the cross and did it in the Easter faith. How this *act of decision* [emphasis mine] took place in detail, how the Easter faith arose in individual disciples, has been obscured in the tradi-tion by legend and is not of basic importance."[82] But most are not willing to let the rise of the Easter faith remain thus unexplained. Strauss thought the resurrection appearances could be explained by the resolution of conflict between messianic faith and crucifixion: the offense of the cross was overcome by the interpretation of Jesus' death as a necessary and salvific in accordance with scripture, and by visions which Strauss thought could produce pious enthusiasm in situations of oppression.[83] Most recent attempts at explanation focus on Peter and feelings of

79. Pagels, "Visions, Appearances, and Apostolic Authority: Gnostic and Orthodox Traditions," *Gnosis* (ed. U. Bianchi et al.; Göttingen: Vandenhoeck & Ruprecht, 1978) 415–16.

80. S. Schneiders, "The Resurrection of Jesus and Christian Spirituality," *Christian Resources of Hope* (ed. M. Junker-Kenny; Collegeville, Minn.: Liturgical Press, 1995) 90. Schneiders, however, following O'Collins, distinguishes resurrection appearances too sharply from apocalyptic-type visions (91; n. 14, p. 112). For O'Collins, the Easter appearances do not happen at sleep or even at night; do not take place while the recipient is in ecstasy; have no apocalyptic features; are never described as "visions"; and are never silent (G. O'Collins, *The Easter Jesus* [London: Darton, Longman & Todd, 1980] 20–22).

81. That is, the bare claims; obviously apologetic elements have been added to answer questions about the reality of the resurrection: the risen Christ appears through closed doors, eats, and so on.

82. R. Bultmann, *Theology of the New Testament* (New York: Scribners, 1951) 1.45; cf. W. Marxsen, *The Resurrection of Jesus of Nazareth* (Philadelphia: Fortress, 1970) 126–27.

83. Strauss, *Life of Jesus*, 780.

guilt. G. Lüdemann, for example, explains Peter's foundational vision in terms of a mourning process blocked by Jesus' sudden death, a process in which Peter overcomes his guilt feelings toward the Lord whom he has betrayed. Forgiveness of sins is a basic motif of the vision. All the other visions are dependent on the primary visions of Peter and Paul, and can be explained only by mass suggestion.[84] Presumably, feelings of guilt would not be the major psychological trigger or context for the visionary experience of Mary Magdalene, if indeed she is thought to have had such an experience, and if indeed she is thought to have remained loyal to the end. Lüdemann holds that "It seems historically certain that Mary Magdalene was witness to an appearance of the risen Jesus," but the tradition of an appearance to her is late, so he does not discuss her possible feelings.[85]

The Gospel accounts contradict one another and cannot be harmonized temporally or spatially. In Mark, the young man tells the women "to tell his disciples and Peter" that Jesus is going before them into Galilee; "there you will see him as he said to you" (16:7). But this Gospel ends at v. 8 with the women's silence and fear; no seeing of the risen Jesus is narrated. In Matt 28:1–20 an angel and then Jesus himself appears to the women and tells them to inform the disciples (with no mention of Peter) that Jesus is risen. The eleven then go to Galilee, to a mountain which has not been mentioned before, where they are commissioned to make disciples, teach and baptize. This Gospel ends with his promise of presence, but no departure of Jesus. In Luke 24:1–52, the women leave the empty tomb and the two men in dazzling clothes; the women report to the eleven, who disbelieve them. In 24:12, probably an addition to the Lukan text based on John 20:3–10, Peter runs to see the empty tomb; "stooping and looking in, he saw the linen cloths by themselves; then he went home, amazed at what had happened." Appearances to two disciples at Emmaus follow this; on their return to Jerusalem, they learn "the eleven and their companions," are saying "The Lord has risen indeed, and he has appeared to Simon (v. 34)." The whole group then sees the risen Jesus standing among them, are taught by him, and receive the promise of "power." In nearby Bethany he blesses them and is carried up to heaven (Acts 1:1–11 places the ascension of Jesus 40 days later). In John 20–21, Mary Magdalene's discovery of the removed stone is reported to Simon Peter and the beloved disciple, who run to the tomb, and then return home. Jesus appears to Mary Magdalene alone, and she tells the disciples. In the evening of the same day, Jesus appears to the disciples, then again a week later, and afterward in Galilee to Simon Peter and six others. The Markan Appendix places three appearances

---

84. G. Lüdemann, *The Resurrection of Jesus* (Minneapolis: Fortress, 1994) 174–79; *What Really Happened to Jesus?* (Louisville: Westminster/John Knox, 1995) 131–37. Paul the persecutor had an unconscious, repressed fascination with Jesus, which finally breaks through.

85. Lüdemann, *What Really Happened to Jesus*, 66–67. He thinks she was a follower of Jesus, healed of seven spirits, and took part with him and others in the fateful journey to Jerusalem. The identification of her with the sinner of Luke 7 would connect her demon possession with her former life of vice. "Unfortunately [sic] this attractive identification is pure speculation..." (66).

in the Jerusalem area on the first day of the week: the first is said to be to Mary Magdalene who is disbelieved by "those who had been with" Jesus; the second to two walking into the country, who are also disbelieved; and the third to the eleven, who are criticized for not believing, but commissioned and empowered to preach. Jesus is then taken up into heaven, but is said to work with them as they proclaim the good news everywhere.

The claim to have received a resurrection appearance functioned in the early church to authenticate a person's claim to apostleship (Paul asks, "Am I not an apostle? Have I not seen Jesus our Lord?" [1 Cor 9:1]).[86] One wonders, however, if it functioned this way for the "more than five hundred brothers and sisters, most of whom are still alive, though some have died" who are part of Paul's list in 1 Corinthians 15:6 (NRSV). In the Lukan scenario, imposed on traditions that contradict its historicity, legitimate leadership is limited to the circle of "the men who have accompanied us during all the time that the Lord Jesus went in and out among us," that is, to the eleven and Judas' replacement (Acts 1:21). No women are said to receive resurrection appearances or commissions in Luke-Acts, although women do accompany the men in the ministry and do discover the empty tomb. Resurrection appearances are thought of in this framework as different from and superior to visions which might occur outside the forty day framework between Jesus' resurrection and ascension. The commissioning of the male disciples in the canonical Gospels, then, occurs in narratives which emphasize the physicality of the resurrection. The one exception is Matthew 28:16–20, which can be read as a vision from heaven. Apocryphal and gnostic writers develop a visionary understanding of the appearances, which is open to other forms and sources of leadership and continuing revelation.

It is not at all clear how a claim for an appearance to Mary Magdalene relates to the story of the discovery of empty tomb by her and other women. As we have seen, the appearances and empty tomb are usually considered two separate lines of tradition, secondarily joined, and the account of an appearance to her often regarded as late. The appearances are associated with males and the empty tomb with females. In the long scholarly history of priority given to the appearance tradition, Strauss, for example, argued that the visions of disciples in Galilee — none of which, we note, are explicitly to women — are the historical origin of the Easter faith, far away from the tomb of Jesus in Jerusalem, which becomes an empty tomb in secondary legend.[87]

The claim to have received the first appearance (protophany) may have served at some point and in some groups as a manifestation of the primacy of an apostolic witness, and may have been considered the foundation of the church's faith.

86. See W. O. Walker, "Postcrucifixion Appearances and Christian Origins," *JBL* 88 (1969) 157–65.
87. Strauss, *Life of Jesus*, 709–44.

In the Christian Testament, Peter and Mary Magdalene are not explicitly said to be rivals for primacy, but the protophany traditions conflict. The scholarly consensus[88] seems to be that the earlier, stronger, and more important tradition is of the protophany to Peter, because of 1 Corinthians 15:5; Luke 24:34; Mark 16:7 (read as promising it).[89] In John 21, Peter is named with others including the Beloved Disciple as seeing the risen Jesus at the sea of Tiberias; there Peter is given the job of feeding the flock. The Gospel of Peter mentions him with Andrew and Levi as the text breaks off, and this is often taken as retaining a tradition that the first appearance to Peter took place in Galilee. The Synoptic transfiguration narratives, the Lukan scene of the immense catch of fish (5:1–11), and the Matthean story of Peter walking on the water (14:28–33), all often considered transposed resurrection narratives, name Peter as present with other disciples. The scene in which he is called the rock on which the church is to be built (Matt 16:16b–19) likewise may have been postresurrectional in origin, and likewise companions him with other disciples. This text, and Luke 22:31–32, set at the Last Supper and promising Peter will strengthen his brothers "once he has turned back," are regarded as possible fragments of a longer original "lost" narrative of a post-resurrectional appearance to Peter wherein he was rehabilitated after his denials, and given authority in the early Church.[90] Brown sees no reason why an early Christian preacher would have taken a Peter story from the ministry and made it post-resurrectional as in John 21; but Luke's reason for retrojecting can be understood in light of his Gospel's post-resurrectional sequence, in which Jesus ascends on Easter day from the Jerusalem area (not Act's sequence, in which Jesus ascends forty days later).[91] Matthew's scenario of the appearance of the risen Jesus to the eleven in Galilee, which ends that Gospel, may also "leave no room for an earlier appearance to Peter."[92]

Retrojection may make sense in the light of later authority struggles. But still it is strange that there is no narrative of a resurrection appearance, first or otherwise, to Peter alone. There is a "structural oddity" in resurrection testimony, wherein Simon Cephas/Peter is said to be the fountainhead of faith in 1 Corinthians 15, but there is no appearance to him in particular in the Synoptics. "The problem

88. See W. T. Kessler, *Peter as the First Witness of the Risen Lord* (Rome: Gregorian University Press, 1998) 53–62; von Campenhausen, "The Events of Easter," 78–79; Marxsen, *Resurrection*, 58–59, 159; Fuller, *The Formation of the Resurrection Narratives*, 35, 112. Contrast J. Jeremias, *New Testament Theology* (New York: Scribner's, 1971) 306. J. S. Spong popularizes and dramatizes this consensus about "the vision of Christ that started the church," and dramatizes it in "a speculative reconstruction" (*Resurrection: Myth or Reality?* [San Francisco: Harper, 1994]).

89. Alternatively, the reference to him here may be meant simply to include him ("even Peter, who betrayed") rather than to point to a special appearance to him.

90. R. E. Brown, "John 21 and the First Appearance of the Risen Jesus to Peter," *Resurrexit* (ed. E. Dhanis; Vatican City: Libreria Editrice Vaticana, 1974) 251–54.

91. Brown, "John 21," 257.

92. *Peter in the New Testament* (ed. R. E. Brown, K. P. Donfried, J. Reumann; Minneapolis: Augsburg, 1973) 106.

of Simon Peter" is resolved only in John 21, the only appearance that features him.[93] Perhaps silent companions did not preclude the idea that an appearance was primarily to Peter.

Because Mary Magdalene is not mentioned in the list of witnesses in 1 Corinthians 15, many critics argue that the tradition that she did receive one is late, an insertion into the traditions of appearances to males, a kind of bridge between the empty tomb narrative and these accounts. Some argue that the traditions of a protophany to her (John 20:11–18; Matt 28:1, 9–10; Markan Appendix 16:9–11) are late and historically worthless: John 20 is said to be a special tradition from the Johannine community with no historical nucleus; Matthew 28 derives from a concern, late in the history of the tradition, to combine the tomb tradition (in which the women have their fixed place) with the appearance tradition; the Markan Appendix is from the second century. But other critics hold that good arguments can be made for this rival tradition as primary. For Perkins, for example, the women at the tomb are "the primary messengers of the resurrection," and commissioned with the others by the risen Jesus in Luke 24:36–49; Mary Magdalene is acknowledged by John (20:18) as equal with the other disciples as a witness to the resurrection.[94]

There are in the ministry segments of the Gospels no stories of Mary Magdalene's faith or lack of faith, or of her authorization, which might be retrojected fragments of post-resurrection traditions. In fact, she is mentioned otherwise, as we have seen, only in Luke 8:1–3 with other women travelling with Jesus, and in the crucifixion accounts, where she neither speaks nor is spoken to. The conflations studied above in chapter 3, of her with the anointing woman in Mark and John and the anointing "sinner" in Luke, could not function as retrojections. O'Collins and Kendall synthesize the Peter and Magdalene traditions, sidestepping the question of priority. "This synthesis does not deny authority to Peter, nor does it ignore the fact that he was the recipient of a postresurrection appearance. It does, however, show the complementary roles of women, Peter, and the other disciples as witnesses to the risen Christ. Among the female recipients of the appearances, Mary Magdalene is portrayed in Scripture as having the primary role."[95] Peter, says O'Collins, has the primary role as official proclaimer of the resurrection; in that sense Peter's witness is primary, even if it may not be temporally prior.[96] No tension or conflict between primacy traditions is recognized. Contrast the treatment of Schüssler Fiorenza who finds in the canonical texts the root of later debates "on whether women are the legitimate transmitters of apostolic

93. B. Chilton, "Resurrection in the Gospels," *Judaism in Late Antiquity* (ed. A. J. Avery-Peck and J. Neusner; Leiden: Brill, 2000) 4.223.
94. Perkins, *Resurrection*, 129, 167, 177.
95. G. O'Collins and D. Kendall, "Mary Magdalene as Major Witness to Jesus' Resurrection," *TS* 48 (1987) 646.
96. G. O'Collins, *Jesus Risen* (London: Darton, Longman & Todd, 1987) 162.

revelation and tradition."[97] According to Luke 24:34, the appearance to Peter led the other disciples to faith.[98] But the appearance to the women produces nothing: the Gospels record disbelief over their testimony (Luke 24; Markan Appendix) or no response at all to it (Matthew; John). This may be a clear indication of conflict that is all the more powerful for being indirect and subtle.

Lest anyone think acceptance of the tradition of a protophany to Mary Magdalene would undermine the patriarchal structures of Catholicism, we have the 1988 apostolic letter of John Paul II, "Mulieris Dignitatem" (On the Dignity and Vocation of Women). Assuming a harmonized chronology of the Gospels, and meditating on women's "special sensitivity which is characteristic of their femininity," the Pope writes that women being first to meet and proclaim the risen Jesus gives them a mission to the Apostles and a sanctity complementary to the "triple function" of Peter and the apostles, to teach, sanctify and govern. The faith of the first community is built on the primary witness of these "concrete men."[99] Kessler sums up: Peter "has an official, enduring, public leadership, whereas the leadership of Mary Magdalene is more intimate and temporally prior, but not something of which we have any indication of continuity."[100]

J. Lieu "with some relief and with general trends in New Testament study" turns from the historical question to the message of the individual Gospels. But here [too?] she finds "a deliberate minimizing of the testimony of the women. The tradition was too resilient to be effaced, but it could be confined, restrained, and retained so that the women have a voice, but a voice which declares its own limitations. The resurrection witness of the women is a witness to their own confinement." She asks, "Can we then reach behind this to the liberating moment, to the authentic resurrection witness?" but as far as I can see, she seems to answer in the negative.[101] Schüssler Fiorenza, on the other hand, recognizes that "it is difficult to prove which tradition was primary, that of the 'empty tomb' associated with women or that of the 'visionary experience' authorizing men. It is equally difficult to ascertain whether the empty tomb tradition and the narrative account of Jesus' death, burial and resurrection were first articulated and transmitted by women." But, she argues, we can claim our power as readers. "Whatever the case may have been historically, the privileging of the 'women's tradition' can function as a heuristic means to develop and adjudicate our own Christological meaning-making in the face of violence and killing today."[102]

97. Schüssler Fiorenza, *In Memory of Her*, 332, 306.
98. Marxsen, *Resurrection*, 88–90, 95–96.
99. John Paul II, "Mulieris Dignitatem," 67–69; n. 55, p. 133; *Catechism of the Catholic Church*, 641–42, both cited by Kessler, *Peter as the First Witness*, 198–99.
100. Kessler, *Peter as the First Witness*, 200–201.
101. J. Lieu, "The Women's Resurrection Testimony," *Resurrection* (ed. S. Barton and G. Stanton; London: SPCK, 1994) 35.
102. E. Schüssler Fiorenza, *Jesus: Miriam's Child*, 125.

For those interested in the historical and exegetical issues, and in what they may contribute to our understandings of liberation, a key question here is whether the Magdalene appearance traditions are truly independent, offering independent attestation to a protophany to her. If they are independent, is there any sort of literary or traditional relationship between the narrative of the appearance to Mary Magdalene alone in John 20, and the narrative of an appearance to her and two other women in Matthew 28? That is, do the two narratives have enough points in common to sketch a tradition behind them? Obviously there are many other issues tangled here with regard to these strange and complex texts. Questions of literary coherence, of logic and imagination; questions of theological creativity.

5. Differing Depictions of Mary Magdalene

Finally, the different ways Mary Magdalene is depicted, and if/how these different depictions may be related, need explanation. The Magdalene of legend, the Mary of gnostic/apocryphal works, and the Mary Magdalene of the Christian Testament seem at first to be almost totally disconnected. As we have seen, there is great diversity of treatment in the legends and apocrypha. So too in the Christian Testament, where she is not mentioned outside the Gospels: her role in each Gospel is distinctive, in subtle and major ways. She is the speechless witness in Mark, the fearful/joyful messenger in Matthew, the intimate of Jesus in John, the former demoniac in Luke and Markan Appendix, perhaps the wealthy patron in Luke. Analysis is not a matter of determining trajectories, or logical developments or progressions. Different communities are involved, different social, ecclesial, political settings over two thousand years and within specific time frames that make the attempt to find patterns superficial and futile. But there is something tantalizing about the very disconnectedness: it is a dismemberment.

These five problems, whether or not they are mentioned and treated, lie below the surface of anything that is written about the Christian Testament Mary Magdalene. Once you get some idea of where these shoals or imagined shoals are, you can see with what varying degrees of skill scholars navigate the waters. Some plow on through, perhaps oblivious of the problems, running the risk of running aground. Some steer cautiously around them, hesitant — in varying degrees — to make sweeping claims about Mary Magdalene. Some try to avoid these waters altogether. Obviously the historical and literary problems are so complex and extensive that they cannot be treated in detail here. In the next chapter I will risk my own reconstruction. Let us first look at how others have navigated.

Five Scholarly Reconstructions

Following the trajectory of my own book here, I will first examine the efforts of Bovon, Price, Marjanen, King to move from discussion of the apocrypal/gnostic materials into discussion of the Christian Testament materials, to move from one world to another which at first appear to have little in common, and their efforts to make sense of the Christian Testament evidence. To these I will contrast the work of Crossan, who comes from a different direction, that of traditional Christian Testament scholarship, and with different questions.

1. Bovon

François Bovon claims[103] that the historical Mary Magdalene was from Magdala, was exorcised by Jesus and accompanied him from Galilee to Jerusalem. She may have been single and independent, since her name is not linked with that of a husband or father. Without discussion, he appears to accept as historical her presence at the crucifixion, and calls her presence at the tomb on Easter morning a "fact [which] must be archaic indeed." Accounts of the appearance of the risen Jesus to her — alone or in the presence of other women — are of an "official nature" and reflect "an ecclesiastical claim" that seeks to establish her authority as witness — perhaps even, he implies, as the "first leader" of some group. These accounts are not late legendary or popular materials. He thinks there is a tradition which lies behind John 20:1–18 and Matt 28:9–10, which is not easy to reconstruct. "And even if this tradition should be late, it still exists and manifests less the popular imagination than an ecclesiastical if not canonical necessity. . . . In brief, the historic person of Mary of Magdala has always been associated with the Easter event which founded the Church. This recollection was maintained in the form of the empty tomb and kindled in the narration which without a doubt reflected an authentic experience of Easter, the apparition of the resurrected Lord to a woman, according to the exigency of ecclesiastical law and not under any popular pressure."

The woman was "troublesome," however, "in a Jewish environment where only the testimony of men counted; troublesome also to a Church attempting to establish a masculine ministry hostile to prophetism, often incarnated by women" and troublesome to the type of Christianity which depended on Peter and Paul and which ultimately triumphed. Bovon regards her absence from the list of witnesses to the resurrection in 1 Cor 15:5–8 as the first evidence of the exclusion of this troublesome woman. Bovon considers this list as likely "the result of a conciliation between Judeo-Christian group(s) in Jerusalem, still under the direction of Peter and James, and the Pagan-Christian groups of the Hellenists and Paul, to the detriment of the other groups, Johannine in particular." Mary Magdalene's role was minimized and her experience and authority relegated to the background by the primitive community in its process of organization. She "had first to get her revenge- in the fourth Gospel, then in various conventicles and sects." An "old heritage" lies behind the apocryphal/gnostic choice of her as Jesus' partner

---

103. Bovon, "Paschal Privilege," 147–50.

and the ideal believer. "Only recourse to one or several paleo-Christian traditions, discreetly excluded by the orthodox Church, could explain this survival. Cultural, historical, sociological and even mythological influences of the period amplified, modified or even twisted this old heritage, as reading of the later witnesses suffices to show. But it was not they which gave birth to such traditions."[104]

Note Bovon's careful distinguishing between the recollection of "the Easter event," and both the form it took in the story of the empty tomb and the "kindling" provided by the story of an appearance to her. Note the complexity of forces he analyzes as responsible for minimizing the role of Mary Magdalene. It might have been even more complex if we think also of group(s) in the Galilee that may have been source and developer of empty tomb and Magdalene traditions.

One of the problematic aspects of Bovon's work is the contention that only the testimony of men counted in a Jewish environment. Osiek has carefully criticized the "unexamined scholarly commonplace in Christian's exegesis" that women could not be legal witnesses in ancient Judaism, a commonplace which relies heavily on Josephus' remark that Mosaic legislation included a prohibition of women serving as legal witnesses because of their "lightness and presumption" (*Ant.* 4.219). Actually, this prohibition is not found in the Torah and not fully supported by Mishnaic law, which was compiled later. There, women were disqualified from serving as witnesses in a case that entailed bringing an accusation against another; but as Osiek says, this is "an exemption not an exclusion, since those not exempted were required to bear witness when necessary. Women were therefore exempted from being compelled to initiate public testimony of a crime committed," a situation which does not apply to the case of women testifying about the resurrection. However, a woman was allowed to testify in matters of credibility; these would include matters that pertain particularly to women (e.g., female virginity); efforts to free herself or another from a legal obligation; business matters (an oath of deposit and swearing to her own honesty); cases when she was the only one present, and certain cases when men were not present or when their presence was not appropriate. "Women's testimony was valued and drawn upon in the sphere of private affairs, but not in public. . . . That is, in domestic, family and private law (including business contracts) women functioned as legal persons. But the general reluctance in ancient Mediterranean society to see women as public spokespersons and officeholders applies here as well." The women are credibility witnesses in the empty tomb narratives. Their giving witness in a public situation might be discouraged or downplayed, but not their witness in house gatherings.[105]

---

104. Bovon, "Paschal Privilege," 155.
105. Osiek, "The Women at the Tomb," 103–4, citing M. Meiselman, *Jewish Woman in Jewish Law* (New York: KTAV, 1978) 73–80; J. R. Wagner, *Chattel or Person? The Status of Women in the Mishnah* (New York: Oxford, 1988) 120–26, 188–89. See also K. von Kellenbach, *Anti-Judaism in Feminist Writings* (Atlanta: Scholars Press, 1994) 61: the witness of women, children and foreigners

What about in the synagogue? The work of Brooten and others has shown that Jewish women were religious officials and benefactors, honored by inscriptions as leaders or heads of synagogues. The evidence she analyzed is later and from diaspora Judaism (from Crete, Trace, Italy, North Africa),[106] and there is no evidence women functioned in such roles in Palestine at the time of Jesus. But Paul's reference to women in leadership roles, such as Phoebe who functioned as *diakonos* and *prostatis* (Rom 16:1–2) in Rome in the 50s may indicate the Christian community there continued that Jewish tradition of female leadership; the Corinthian correspondence gives information about women prophets. Women's presence was common and segregated seating was not practiced in the ancient synagogue, and it is possible that in Palestine women were called to read from the Torah and participated actively in assemblies.[107] Marginality in the public sector was the norm for women throughout antiquity, but there was a tradition of equality in Judaism[108] that supports us imagining that a woman might speak there.

Note that Bovon apparently regards John and the Synoptics as independent works. Refusing to link simplistically the empty tomb accounts with women and the apparition accounts with men, since the apparition to a woman does not fit such categorization,[109] he can therefore consider the accounts of the appearances to Mary Magdalene as early rather than as secondary accretions, late imitations of male traditions. Bovon sees the gender conflicts such as we studied in chapter four already in process in the early decades of Christianity's existence. The prominence of the Magdalene in John and in the apocryphal materials is "revenge" for a process of her erasure begun early.

---

were allowed to confirm deaths; J. Hauptman, *Rereading the Rabbis* (Boulder, Colo.: Westview, 1998) chapter 9.

106. See, for example, B. Brooten, "*Iael prostatēs* in the Jewish Donative Inscription from Aphrodisias," *The Future of Early Christianity*, 149–62, on a third-century inscription. *Prostatēs* "has three general meanings: (1) leader, chief, president, presiding officer; (2) guardian, champion, patron; (3) one who stands before a deity to entreat him or her, a suppliant" (153). Iael could have been the president or patron of a soup kitchen (or burial institution) or of its governing board; she should be seen as a religious leader engaged in philanthropic activity. Elsewhere also Jewish women held office and made donations to the synagogue. See Brooten, *Women Leaders in the Ancient Synagogue: Inscriptional Evidence and Background Issues* (Chico, Calif.: Scholars Press, 1982); R. S. Kraemer, "A New Inscription from Malta and the Question of Women Elders in the Diaspora Jewish Communities," *HTR* 78 (1985) 431–38.

107. See L. Levine, *The Ancient Synagogue: The First Thousand Years* (New Haven: Yale, 2000). Synagogue officialdom in Jewish Palestine appears to have been different from that of the Diaspora and from that of the hellenized areas of Palestine, but he admits "The study of leadership in the ancient synagogue is fraught with uncertainties" (426, 387). R. A. Horsley (*Galilee* [Valley Forge, Pa.: Trinity Press International, 1995] 237) thinks women's leadership in Galilean village assemblies should not be ruled out, pending possible inscriptional evidence, but it is unlikely in patriarchal village communities.

108. See Levine, *The Ancient Synagogue*, 472, 489, on the apparent equality of women in many ritual ceremonies as set forth in Deuteronomy; but Levine himself thinks women were denied any liturgical function (490). See below, pp. 264–65.

109. Neither does the presence of Peter and John at the empty tomb in John: 20:3–10 (cf. Luke 24:24); but it is more likely that these *are* late additions.

The maintenance of her memory even in the canonical texts is accounted for as "an ecclesial if not canonical necessity," by "the exigency of ecclesiastical law." These are forces which Bovon does not explain. I am puzzled by what he could mean. Bovon mentions but does not explore the "old heritage," "one or several paleo-Christian traditions" he thinks excluded by the orthodox Church. In the next chapter I will propose that one can be found in John 20.

2. Price

In a short article, "Mary Magdalene: Gnostic Apostle?"[110] Robert M. Price sees in the "intriguing scraps" about Mary Magdalene in the Christian Testament enough to give him the impression "that these details are the lingering after-echoes of some great explosion."[111] He tries to show what the "two starkly contrasting bodies of evidence" — the Christian Testament and the gnostic documents — have to do with one another, and with the historical Mary Magdalene. Price's suggestion is that "Both canonical and noncanonical traditions seem to preserve the memory that Mary claimed a privileged disciple relationship with Jesus both before and after the resurrection, that she received unique revelations after the resurrection, and that these revelations included female equality with males based on the transcendence of sexuality in a spiritual union with Christ."[112] For Price, that memory is accurate historically. The historical Mary Magdalene also became an apostle of "an egalitarian, celibate Christianity which preached spiritual marriage with Christ."[113]

Other currents of earliest Christianity "reacted to her radical gospel by minimizing and distorting her role in the ministry of Jesus and the early Christian community." The circles receptive to her, however, "eventually contributed to the great Gnostic movement" which preserved in their circles and texts her apostolic role and her "radical gospel" which entailed equality between women and men. Mary Magdalene in the gnostic/apocryphal works, then, is not a literary creation, not just a mouthpiece for gnostic ideas; she is a woman accurately remembered as having been an apostle, and this memory is a "trajectory" that "evolves" (or really, devolves) through seven basic stages.

Price argues for the "hypothesis that an actual apostolic claim by Mary Magdalene underlies and conditions the various New Testament treatments of her."[114] At issue in all the stories that concern her is how much, if any, apostolic authority is to be granted to her. In his reading, John 20:1, 11–18 is an originally independent pericope in which Mary receives "unique" revelations from the risen Christ.

---

110. *Grail* 6 (1990) 54–76.
111. Price, "Mary Magdalene," 56.
112. Price, "Mary Magdalene," 76. The spiritual union he calls "spiritual marriage."
113. Price, "Mary Magdalene," 57.
114. Price ("Mary Magdalene," 63) speculates that the late medieval Greek life of Mary may have preserved a genuine tradition in its record of a missionary journey of Mary to Marseilles.

In this tradition removed from its context, she alone receives an appearance; the disciples receive only news that he is *going*, a relayed farewell. This, Price suggests, is "an approximation of the original version of the Mary Magdalene Easter tradition and the starting point of the trajectory we traced through the later Gnostic texts."[115]

The six other "stages" are traditions preserved in the following texts:

- the Markan Appendix 16:9–10 (where the appearance to her is given chronological priority in a string of appearances, but all she says to the disciples is that she has seen the risen Lord);

- Matt 28:1–10 (where she is accompanied by other women who also see the risen Jesus who simply reiterates the charge of the angel, that they tell the disciples to meet Jesus in Galilee);

- Luke 24:1–12 (where Mary Magdalene and the other women do not see the risen Jesus, but, without being told to, they do deliver the announcement of the angel to the disciples);

- Mark 16:1–8 (where she and the other women do not see the risen Jesus and disobey the injunction of the angel, saying nothing to anyone because they were afraid);

- John 20:2–10 (where Mary sees neither angel nor the risen Jesus, and receives no revelation; her role is merely to fetch the male disciples);

- 1 Corinthians 15 (where she has been totally omitted because her claim to apostleship has been denied).

Price's thinking about "circles" and groups and "the great Gnostic movement" and "orthodoxy" needs revision, as does his cursory reading of the gnostic texts. He argues, for example, that Mary's "revelations entail equality between women and men, thanks to the enabling grace of the Saviour who has made women as men, i.e., eliminated gender-based subordination by transcending sexuality altogether. This enlightenment is symbolized as sexual union with Christ."[116] An egalitarian message is not one of the elements in my profile of the gnostic/apocryphal Mary, because, as Marjanen and others have shown, the gender situations presupposed and addressed by the different texts are complex and the messages are different. None of them in my opinion, even the Gospel of Mary, amount to a clear statement or platform of gender equality, although some do illustrate gender conflict and explore such notions as male androgyny. I do not find in the gnostic/apocryphal material any clear notion that the symbolism of sexual union with Christ was linked to eliminating sexism by "transcending sexuality altogether." With regard to the Christian Testament and the message of egalitarianism Price thinks the description of the disobedience and failure of the women in Mark 16:8, the ending Mark intended, is a repudiation of a third faction (alongside the Twelve and the relatives of Jesus): the *women* disciples of Jesus

---

115. Price, "Mary Magdalene," 67.
116. Price, "Mary Magdalene," 60.

led by Mary Magdalene. Price reads Luke 8:1–3 to mean that she was the leader of a group of women. He does not say whether he thinks of her later "adherents" as primarily women or as a mixed, egalitarian group.

Price has indeed shown a kind of "logical progression" in the domestication of Mary Magdalene in the Christian Testament texts, and perhaps this logic means something important, something more than an imposition of order on the disorder of real life. He has been careful to insist that he does not mean that the canonical texts discussed were written in the order in which he considers them, but rather that the writers/redactors of the Christian Testament "have severally preserved various stages of a tradition which *evolved* in the order" he reconstructs.[117]

But would that doing history were so simple. It is just as possible that a variety of attitudes toward Mary Magdalene coexisted at the same time and even in the same community, alongside ignorance of her. One wonders if realities such as sexism and racism and hostility really "evolve" in any sense other than grow where permitted. Moreover, if we grant that Price has shown there was some sort of process of erasure, like a spreading stain, possible catalysts and circumstances for the proposed stages must be explored. We need to theorize about why the various positions developed, and why they were incorporated into the texts we have, their redactional meanings and the role of the authors and the authors' communities in their creation. It must be asked why in Price's schema the earliest datable text (1 Corinthians 15) contains the latest stage of evolution, and the latest datable text (John 20) the earliest stage. If, because of her prominence as an associate of Jesus, the Gospel writers and their sources could not omit mention of Mary Magdalene's role in the Easter story but only diminish it, nevertheless something made it possible and desirable for the creators of the tradition embedded in 1 Corinthians 15 and/or Paul to erase her, apparently with impunity. Price contends that "Mary was remembered as a prominent figure by all segments of the Christian movement but in orthodox circles her claims were ignored and the reasons for her obvious prominence were forgotten."[118] Whoever is behind the tradition in 1 Corinthians 15 — and usually this is thought to be the Jerusalem "authorities" Paul consulted at the beginning of his career — may not be part of this "all."

In short, like Bovon, Price points to but does not examine power struggles and issues of authority.[119] He holds that the historical Magdalene and the tradition that remained faithful to her spoke out for the equality of women and men. But he does not explore the traces of what may have been such a stance, in her prominence in the Christian Testament, sayings attributed to Jesus, the sociology of this kingdom of God movement, and in the gender polemics in some

---

117. Price, "Mary Magdalene," 66.
118. Price, "Mary Magdalene," 73.
119. He is especially careless with the term "the Twelve," assuming its presence in texts where it is not present.

gnostic/apocryphal texts. However, he makes the extremely important suggestion, mentioned above,[120] that the claim that Mary had been demon-possessed is a trace of polemics against what was regarded as her heresies, and hence her authority. "[I]t is hard to see how being tagged with the reputation of sevenfold demon-possession would not seriously undermine one's credibility as an apostle." (See John 7:20; 8:48; 10:20 on the charge that Jesus has a demon is leveled against him; and 1 Tim 4:1; 1 John 4:3 against opponents.) This would mean that already in the Christian Testament period, what Mary Magdalene stood for may have been judged as false teaching in comparison to the teachings of some others, but false teaching that had been overcome by the truth. Already she was demonized but exorcised (and silenced, like the slave girl of Philippi in Acts 16:16–19 whose prophesy is silenced by Paul's exorcism). Price suggests also that the later identification of Mary as a prostitute may originate in the epithet "Magdalene" slanderously reinterpreted by her Aramaic-speaking Christian rivals ("early followers of the Twelve") as M'gaddla, the hair curler, a euphemism for prostitute "since elaborate hairstyling was regarded as the mark of a prostitute"; this slur he thinks was then incorporated into rabbinic texts as a slander against Jesus' mother.[121] I think it is as likely that a punning joke about Mary Magdalene's town fed into the identification created by conflation. In any case, the later characterization of her as a reformed prostitute may have been one more way of talking about "heresy" overcome by "orthodoxy."[122] The "heresy" of egalitarianism would have involved not only theory, however the relationship between the sexes was conceived, but also action — women's bold claim of authority in visionary experience and revelation, and the exercise of leadership by them. "When ... one reads of a witch being ducked, of a woman possessed by devils, of a wise woman selling herbs, or even of a very remarkable man who had a mother, then I think we are on the track of a lost novelist, a suppressed poet, of some mute and inglorious Jane Austen, some Emily Bronte who dashed her brains out on the moor or moped and moved about the highways crazed with the torture that her gift had put her to."[123]

Thus with "the paradigm furnished by the noncanonical texts," Price traces his trajectory of increasing polemics forward from the lifetime of the historical Mary Magdalene. Ironically, her absence from 1 Corinthians 15 shows Price that the polemics go back as far as her lifetime. But this reconstruction of the evolution of the tradition is flawed and "contains too many major methodological problems to be plausible," as Marjanen argues. "It is not feasible that the tradition which

---

120. Above, pp. 77–80, 199. See further, below, chaps. 6 and 7.
121. Price, "Mary Magdalene," 73–74.
122. See V. Burrus, "The Heretical Woman as Symbol in Alexander, Athanasius, Epiphanius, and Jerome," *HTR* 84 (1991) 229–48. The figure of the heretical woman is designed to control "unruly" women by threatening them with the labels of heretic and whore, that is, to articulate boundaries between insiders and outsiders.
123. Woolf. *Room*, 49.

must have reached its final stage already before or with the formulation of the list in 1 Cor 15 (if it is a conscious reaction against the Mary Magdalene tradition of John 20:1.11–18, as Price assumes) could have been accessible to the writer of the so-called longer ending of the Gospel of Mark in its second stage, to the author of the Gospel of Mark proper in its fifth stage, and to the Jerusalem Christians formulating the confession in 1 Cor 15 in its final stage." He points out also that Price is making a hypothetical assumption that both Luke and the author(s) of 1 Corinthians 15 were aware of an oral tradition about an appearance of the risen Jesus to Mary Magdalene, and suppressed it. Further, Marjanen thinks there are positive aspects of Luke's and especially Matthew's presentation of the Magdalene which Price has not accounted for. And finally, Price's reconstruction of "the form of Christianity started by the historical Mary Magdalene" is not found in any single Gnostic text but is an arbitrary combination of elements (encratism, her privilege, spiritual marriage) from different texts.[124]

Still, I think Price's treatment has many insights that set an agenda for further work, especially on the Christian Testament Magdalene texts; it is an opportunity to refine methodologies and test hypotheses. Most importantly, it shows that the complexity of gnostic/apocryphal depictions of Mary and of the Christian Testament materials means that no straight "trajectory" can be drawn.

3. Marjanen

Antti Marjanen asks whether the second-century gnostic idea of Mary Magdalene as a prominent disciple reflects "a historical figure who besides having been known to have experienced an appearance of Jesus had a leadership function among early Christians." His answer is: "It may, but there is no real evidence for it."[125] He asks do texts like the Gospel of Mary "reflect a knowledge of the historical role Mary Magdalene had in the early Christian movement which goes beyond what the New Testament traditions tell about her as the obvious leader of Jesus' female followers and as the receiver of the Risen Jesus' appearance? Was she a spiritual authority comparable to some of Jesus' male disciples? Or was Mary Magdalene selected to be the protagonist of the writing because it was written to an audience consisting mainly of women? Or was the author of the book a woman who wanted to give the leading role to a woman? These questions cannot but remain interesting questions. The lack of evidence prevents us from finding answers which could be backed up with sufficient degree of probability."[126]

This attitude seems to me defeatist; the questions are too important to merely remain "interesting"; and we have only begun to look for evidence.

Marjanen accepts that Mary Magdalene was "the obvious leader of Jesus' female followers" because she appears first in all the lists of women in the canonical

124. Marjanen, *The Woman*, 10–12.
125. Marjanen, *The Woman*, 192.
126. Marjanen, *The Woman*, 100.

Gospels, except for John 19:25. But assuming that she led only women may reflect Luke's two lists of male and female leaders, and may be just Luke's assumption or wish. Marjanen also appears to accept (as King does, with caution [see below]) that Mary Magdalene was "the receiver of the Risen Jesus' appearance." He does not explain what he means by the first "the" here, but insists this would *not* mean that controversy between Mary and the male disciples may be projected back to the first century. The male disciples' challenge to her role is regarded by Marjanen as late, due to his staging of the gnostic conflict materials, which I think is flawed. He posits an initial stage based on evidence from Gospel of Thomas 21, the Sophia of Jesus Christ and the Dialogue of the Savior, in which there is no conflict between Mary and male disciples. On the other end of the spectrum, Marjanen argues that nowhere else in early Christian literature is an equally negative view of women found as in Gospel of Thomas 114; this is probably a "mischaracterized" representation of a developing ascetic perspective.[127] I would say rather that the negativity is more overt than, say, the references to the 144,000 "who have not defiled themselves with women" in Revelation 14:4 or the commands/urgings of women to silence in multiple texts. We need taxonomies of gender hostility and its rhetorical strategies for use in different situations, before any such staging is reliable.

Marjanen has not looked at the Christian Testament evidence, even in as sketchy a fashion as Price has. Price sees conflict and suppression there, which needs to be discussed in the light of the gnostic/apocryphal evidence. The tradition of an appearance to her is not simply, as Marjanen would have it, a "story [which] evidently made Mary Magdalene an attractive figure for a Gnostic myth-making process."[128] It — and, I think, the other "intriguing scraps" of the Magdalene tradition — are more in the nature of the "after-effects of some great explosion" that Price posited. In order to see what the gnostic/apocryphal materials and the Christian Testament materials have to do with each other, we need to look more closely at both.

4. King

In a paper for the American Bible Society Multimedia Translation Project on John 20, Karen King argues that "These simple facts are all that can be said of Mary with *a solid probability of historical accuracy:* Mary was Jewish, she came from Magdala, and was an early and notable follower of Jesus, who accompanied him throughout his career and supported him out of her own independent means. She may have been exorcised by Jesus."[129] I am not so certain of two of the elements in this summary. The exorcism, as Price suggested, may rather be evidence of

127. Marjanen, *The Woman*, 192, 45–46.
128. Marjanen, *The Woman*, 192.
129. K. King, "Mary Magdalene in the New Testament and Other Early Christian Literature," working paper, American Bible Society New Media Bible Project (New York, 1998) 1. Emphasis

efforts to tame her and/or tame the memory of her. Luke's claim that she and other women supported Jesus and his followers financially, as patrons, should also not be taken at face value in my opinion.

King assigns a lower level of historical probability to other traditions. "The strength of [the] literary tradition, including its multiple attestation," that mentions her at the crucifixion and empty tomb and claims she was the first to see the risen Jesus, was commissioned to announce the resurrection and was first to do so *"makes it possible to suggest* that historically Mary may have been a prophetic visionary and leader within some sector of the early Christian movement *after the death of Jesus.*"[130] Note King's caution, her use of the criterion of multiple attestation,[131] and her careful indeterminacy ("within some sector"). She does not enter here or elsewhere into a discussion of the historical reliability or dating of the canonical Gospel accounts of Mary's encounter with the risen Jesus, noting only that the story is judged by some to be ancient based primarily on the fact that there are multiple independent witnesses to the tradition. King relies further on the opinions of R. E. Brown: "An argument in favor of antiquity is the primacy all the Gospels give her among the women followers of Jesus whenever they are listed; this may well be because she was the first one to see the risen Jesus." Her absence from the list in 1 Corinthians 15 is not surprising, Brown thinks, because "There is no reason why such a tradition should have included an appearance to a woman who could scarcely be presented as either an official witness to the resurrection or as an apostle."[132] The historical reliability of the resurrection scenes is less important to King "than the fact that, for early Christians, the witness to an appearance of the risen Lord signaled authority for the foundational claim of orthodox Christianity." The "very meagerness of what was known" of Mary Magdalene's life — in contrast to Price's "great explosion" — is for King what fired the imagination of later Christians, "who elaborated her history in story and art according to their spiritual needs and political aims."[133]

Mary "becomes a center around which controversy swirls" in the second and third centuries, as evidenced in gnostic writings, whose controversies "show that the figure of Mary had become a figure to which apostolic appeal could be

---

mine. In her earlier summary in "The Gospel of Mary Magdalene," 2.716, King calls Mary "a woman of color."

130. King, "Mary Magdalene," 2. Emphases mine. In "The Gospel of Mary Magdalene," 2.617, King seems more certain: Mary Magdalene became a leader in the early Christian movement after the death of Jesus.

131. She thinks this criterion does not apply to the tradition that Mary had been a demoniac, since King thinks Mark 16:9 is dependent on Luke 8:2; nevertheless "it seems plausible" (p. 1).

132. R. E. Brown, *The Gospel According to John XIII–XXI* [Garden City: Doubleday, 1970] 1003, 971. King does not discuss Brown's reason for this latter opinion. See above, p. 212, for Osiek's analysis of the issue of women as witnesses.

133. King, "The Gospel of Mary Magdalene," 2. 620, 617.

made."[134] King apparently does not see such controversy in the Christian Testament: "Though her testimony [about the resurrection] is usually questioned or
completely discounted by the male disciples (Mark 16:10–11; Luke 24:10–11), in
the end the Gospels vindicate her and validate the truth and authority of her witness." The response to Mary Magdalene in the Gospel of John "more ambiguous,
but the male disciples clearly do not believe until they see for themselves (John
20:3–10, 19–29)."[135] I will argue in chapter 7, however, that whatever vindication and validation there is is muted, minimized and obscured by shifts of focus
to the males and their mission. Mary Magdalene is incorporated but left behind.
We have seen a similar shift take place at the end of the Gospel of Mary. In the
Christian Testament empty tomb narratives, as Claudia Setzer puts it, there is
already a "soft-pedaling" and "partial erasing" of Mary's Magdalene's role.[136]

These shifts of focus and attention, important aspects of which Price has noticed, are just as much a strategy of dealing with the "dangerous memory"[137] of
Mary Magdalene as other strategies which have been noted. These involve: ignoring her as many early "fathers of the church" did; reinterpreting or revising
her as a former prostitute as the later church did;[138] erasing her by replacing
her with Peter or Mary the mother of Jesus, as some Coptic or Syriac writers or
copyists of apocrypha did.[139] Regarding this last strategy, Brock says such changes
seem to have "a deeper meaning than merely arbitrary substitution" or confusion;
they are purposeful, deliberate and systematic. She relates them to other early
Christian literature which portrays competition between Peter and Mary Magda-

---

134. King, "Mary Magdalene," 6. These "might be instances where we could read inter-Christian
controversy over such issues as the meaning of Jesus' teaching and/or his death and resurrection, the
basis for apostolic authority, or the roles of women."
135. King, "The Gospel of Mary Magdalene," 2.618, 632.
136. Claudia Setzer, "Excellent Women: Female Witness to the Resurrection," *JBL* 116 (1997) 268.
137. See Schüssler Fiorenza, *In Memory of Her*, 31–32. Memory struggles constantly against these
strategies.
138. King, "Gospel of Mary Magdalene," 2.619.
139. See A. G. Brock, "What's in a Name: The Competition for Authority in Early Christian
Texts," *Society of Biblical Literature Seminar Papers* (Atlanta: Scholars Press, 1998) 1.106–24. She
notes an interesting phenomenon in early Christian texts: Mary Magdalene's "position either as an
apostle or as an eyewitness [sic] of the resurrection is often altered, compromised, or eradicated
from the narrative altogether" (123). Substitutions for the figure of Mary Magdalene occur in the
Coptic version of the Acts of Philip (where Peter is substituted for her), the Acta Thaddaei (where
Mary the mother of Jesus "and the other women" receive the first appearance), the Book of the
Resurrection of Jesus Christ by Bartholomew the Apostle (where Mary the mother of Jesus replaces
Mary Magdalene in an elaboration of the garden scene from John 20 and Peter's presence and authority
are highlighted), as well as numerous other Coptic fragments (such as the Revillout Coptic fragment
where Mary the mother replaces Mary Magdalene in an elaboration of the garden scene of John 20,
and is commissioned to tell the disciples of the resurrection); and certain Syriac texts by Ephrem (306–
73; where the same substitution occurs four times in his commentary on the Diatessaron and in his
hymns) and Theodoret (393–466; same substitution in two of the three principal mss of *Quaestiones
et Responsiones ad Orthodoxos*). In the Questions of Bartholomew Mary the Mother, perhaps as a foil
to Mary Magdalene (Parrott, "Gnostic and Orthodox Disciples," 210), is the spokesperson for the
authority of Peter and for male superiority; Mary Magdalene does not appear.

lene.[140] To my mind, these strategies are ways of *avoiding* competition, in contrast to the open competition and confrontation in gnostic/apocryphal texts. Similar avoidance strategies may appear in the Christian Testament: revisioning her role at Easter; relegating or confining her to a role of domestic or financial support during the ministry; and labeling her a former demoniac, a tradition which may carry both ideas of her as a former heretic and (anticipating the label of prostitute) as formerly immoral or sexually licentious, showing that strategies can be intertwined.

King notes that opposition to women's speech draws throughout history on "a rather limited and fixed set of strategies." These include "attacking women's moral character, charging them with sexual license and heresy, and using institutional and legal sanctions. Women's opponents selectively appealed to Scripture, tradition, and patriarchal social norms (often represented as the 'natural' order)." All of this is already seen in 1 Corinthians. Strategies used to support women's public speech were framed in reaction to these attacks and charges. King notes that "The defense of women's character in the face of moral slander was...fraught with ambiguity because judgments about moral character were often based on conformity to patriarchal gender roles."[141] This last remark almost makes me think there might be a certain defense of Mary Magdalene *in* the claim that she was a *repentant* prostitute, or *former* demoniac — patriarchal gender roles much less traditional than the roles of mother or virgin martyr. Other efforts to defend her in Christian Testament times are as lost as the efforts to defend the Corinthian women prophets. The gnostic/apocryphal defenses are framed in such a way as to avoid what we would consider real discussion of gender issues and theology: the Savior will lead her and make her male (Gospel of Thomas); he loved her and who are you to attack her? (Gospel of Mary).

For King, neither the Christian Testament nor the gnostic nor the early patristic materials about Mary Magdalene prepare the way for the later identification of Mary as a prostitute. In light of the strong and consistent tradition portraying her as a prominent disciple and witness to the resurrection, King finds it difficult to understand how this tradition was eclipsed in later centuries by the portrait of Mary as a repentant prostitute. But we can be "fairly certain about the hermeneutical process by which this later portrait was established. The confusion has its base in two difficulties": (1) the large number of women named Mary in the Christian Testament Gospels; and (2) "(muddled) exegetical attempts to reconcile divergences" among the anointing women. King calls this Western Christianity's "mistake" whose motives are difficult to ascertain: "Was it simply a matter of naive and muddled exegetics? Or, as has been suggested, were there polemical motives to undermine a basis for women's claims to apostolic leadership? Or to stamp out

---

140. Brock, "What's in a Name," 111, 113.
141. King, "Prophetic Power and Women's Authority," 336.

views identified with Mary Magdalene's teaching (such as the Gospel of Mary's interpretation of the teachings of the Savior and the resurrection as a spiritual event)?"[142] (How valuable these views might be, if they could be reconstructed: "What genius, what integrity it must have required in face of all that criticism, in the midst of that purely patriarchal society, to hold fast to the thing as they saw it without shrinking."[143])

If, as Price and others argue, the controversy over Mary Magdalene is older than our oldest texts, the claim that she was a repentant prostitute can be seen as one more tactic of suppression, the most successful, prepared for in the Christian Testament's treatment of her as former demoniac, and by Luke's juxtaposition of materials in chapters 7–8. In the Gospel of Mary and elsewhere, Mary's teaching offered interpretation of the teachings of Jesus that implicitly questioned the value of other interpretations. I am interested in what in the Christian Testament texts may prepare the way for interpretations associated with her name and for traditions of her authority. King's sophisticated gender analysis of the gnostic/apocryphal materials has exciting implications for the study of the Christian Testament.

5. Crossan

To Bovon's, Price's, Marjanen's and King's analyses I want to contrast Crossan's, in which the historical Mary Magdalene disappears from the burial and tomb (which themselves also disappear) and in which she is not the recipient of the first or any resurrection appearance (which disappear). She disappears, that is, from his historical reconstruction. Mary and the other women increasingly *appear*, as he reconstructs it, the farther we move away from history. He sees it this way: "The women are not so much being eliminated or reduced as being introduced and emphasized" as one moves from earlier sources (1 Corinthians 15; the Cross Gospel, a source Crossan reconstructs of the Gospel of Peter) to later (Mark 16:9–14; final redaction of Gospel of Peter 11:50–51).[144] With Crossan's work, in which he has treated the passion/resurrection narratives extensively, we move into mainstream, malestream Christian Testament scholarship. "... I found myself walking with extreme rapidity across a grass plot. Instantly a man's figure rose to intercept me. Nor did I at first understand that the gesticulations of a curious-looking object, in a cut-away coat and evening shirt, were aimed at me. His face expressed horror and indignation. Instinct rather than reason came to my help; he was a Beadle; I was a woman. This was the turf; there was the path. Only the Fellows and Scholars are allowed here; the fravel is the place for me. Such thoughts were the work of a moment."[145] I will lay out Crossan's reasoning and

---

142. King, "Mary Magdalene," 7–8.
143. Woolf, *Room*, 74, on Austen and Brontë.
144. Crossan, *Birth of Christianity*, 551. Against Setzer, "Excellent Women," 268.
145. Woolf, *Room*, 6.

assessment of probabilities as carefully as I can here, in preparation for my next chapter.

Crossan proposes that "Jesus' closest followers knew nothing more about the passion than the fact of the crucifixion, that they had fled and later had no available witnesses for its details, and that they were concerned, in any case, with far more serious matters, such as whether that death negated all that Jesus had said and done, all that they had accepted and believed."[146] Of all the followers of Jesus who fled at his arrest, none witnessed what happened to his body, because "In most cases, . . . ordinary families were probably too afraid or too powerless to get close to a crucified body even after death." "Nobody knew what had happened to Jesus' body. . . . [B]y Easter morning, those who cared did not know where it was, and those who knew did not care."[147] Why does Crossan accept as historical the Markan tradition that "all of them deserted him and fled" (14:50)? Not because it is multiply attested (for Crossan it is not), but because there is nowhere a tradition of the burial of Jesus by his companions. "Jesus' companions had fled after his arrest and were not there to see what happened. Their ultimate terror was that he was left unburied. So the process of negating that awful possibility began."[148]

Most probably, he thinks, the corpse of Jesus was left on the cross as carrion, or laid in a shallow grave in a graveyard for executed criminals, and later eaten by wild dogs, or thrown in a lime pit.[149] Josephus' claim that he had three of his own friends removed from crosses after the fall of Jerusalem (*Life* 421) is regarded by Crossan as an exception to Roman practice. The fact that only one skeleton has been found of a crucified person (Yehohanan, in his ossuary at Giv'at ha-Mivtar), out of all the thousands crucified in Jerusalem in the first century, shows that burial was the exception.[150] Mishnah Sanhedrin 6:5–6 mentions that the Sanhedrin "used not" to bury executed criminals in their ancestral tombs but kept two burial places for them; then after a year their bones could be taken and reburied honorably by their families but without public mourning. Crossan says "*If* that was ever operational in real (as distinct from ideal) law, and *if* it was operational in early-Roman Jerusalem, Joseph [of Arimathea] *could* have been

146. J. D. Crossan, *The Historical Jesus* (San Francisco: Harper, 1991) 375.

147. Crossan, *Historical Jesus*, 392, 394. Crossan's focus is not on the companions' concern but on what they knew about the passion events, not on what could have happened but on what did (*Birth of Christianity*, 479).

148. J. D. Crossan, *Who Killed Jesus?* (San Francisco: Harper, 1995) 171.

149. His opinion on the lack of burial and many other points has remained constant, though he has added details and responded to his critics. In 1976 Crossan already held the view that Mark created the empty tomb narrative: "Empty Tomb and Absent Lord," 135–52. See the 1998 extended treatment in Crossan, *Birth of Christianity*, 477–573.

150. Crossan, *Birth of Christianity*, 54. The command that the crucified be removed before sunset (following Deut 21:22–23) found in the Temple Scroll 11Q64:11–13 is regarded by Crossan as a call for reform of what was happening under the Hasmoneans "(and presumably under the Romans as well)" i.e., nonburial of the executed.

the official whose duty it was to bury condemned bodies."[151] But "could" is not good enough. Joseph of Arimathea is a historically unbelievable character, an invention of Mark. "Mark's story presented the tradition with double dilemmas. First, if Joseph was in the council, he was against Jesus; if he was for Jesus, he was not in the council. Second, if Joseph buried Jesus from piety or duty, he would have done the same for the two other crucified criminals; yet if he did that, there could be no empty-tomb sequence.... Unless one imagines three separate tombs, they would all have been buried together in a single tomb or even in a communal tomb for criminals. Were that the case, though, how could you continue into an empty-tomb story? How ghastly to imagine probing among corpses to identify the missing one as that of Jesus."[152]

The idea that there was a tomb at all comes from wishful thinking expressed in the Cross Gospel, material Crossan identifies as the earliest passion narrative, and the source used by the Gospel of Peter.[153] In that source, Roman soldiers and Jewish authorities make the discovery of the empty tomb and receive the vision of the resurrected Jesus. The story of the women discovering the empty tomb but saying nothing about it, Crossan argues, is created by Mark to avoid ending with an apparition of the risen Jesus to the disciples. This would not fit with Mark's severe and relentless criticism of the Peter, the inner three male disciples, and the Twelve.[154] The empty-tomb story "is neither an early historical event nor a late legendary narrative but a deliberate Markan creation."

As for the tradition that Mary Magdalene had an apparition of the risen Jesus, "the so-called protophany of Mary Magdalene has no traditional basis."[155] Matthew created the story of the appearance of the risen Jesus to the women, in order to change Mark's negative ending of the women fleeing in silence to a pos-

---

151. Crossan, *Birth of Christianity*, 554; Sawicki interprets this Mishnah passage to be about confiscation of the corpse by the Sanhedrin and therefore about the loss of the body to the companions of Jesus (*Seeing the Lord*, 257).

152. Crossan, *Birth of Christianity*, 555. Crossan concedes that none of these points is unanswerable, but together they persuade him that Mark created the burial by Joseph of Arimathea.

153. This Cross Gospel, possibly composed at the time of Agrippa I (41–44c.e.) in the Jerusalem community, contained a linked narrative of crucifixion and deposition (1:1–2; 2:5b–6:22), tomb and guards (7:25; 8:28–9:34), resurrection and confession (9:35–10:42; 11:45–49). Mary Magdalene and her friends appear only in the later Gospel of Peter 12:50–13:57. See *Birth of Christianity*, 482–525 for his 1998 analysis; earlier Crossan thought pro-Roman Sepphoris in the fifties was the location for the creation of this narrative (*The Historical Jesus*, 387). See Appendix 7, Strata in the Gospel of Peter (Crossan, *Historical Jesus*, 462–66).

154. Crossan, *Birth of Christianity*, 557. Whether this theme of criticism for the male disciples is interpreted as (a) opposition to the theological viewpoints of other Christian communities, or as (b) consolation for those in Mark's community who have failed Jesus in recent persecutions connected with the war of 66–73/4 and who need to be reassured that "failure, flight and even denial are not hopeless," Crossan believes that Mark could not end with apparitions. This makes more sense to me if (a) is the case, but even so, if Mark can offer the glimmer of hope in 16:7, I fail to see why he could not pen an appearance, especially one that provided theological correction and emphasized forgiveness. If (b) is the case, I fail to see the rigor of this logic.

155. F. Neirynck, *Evangelica II: 1982–1991. Collected Essays by Frans Neirynck* (ed. F. Van Segbroeck; Leuven: Leuven University Press, 1991) 588, cited by Crossan, *Birth of Christianity*, 561.

itive one, and in order to prepare for the apparition to the disciples in Galilee.[156] John then appropriated and changed Matthew's account of the vision to Mary Magdalene. Crossan reasons thus: having already decided that Matt 28:9–10 is a complete Matthean creation, he argues that if any of its "characteristic elements" appear in John 20:14–17, this would make Johannine dependence on Matthew the likeliest explanation. He finds three Matthean elements: the adaptation of tomb dialogue to create vision dialogue, the "holding" of Jesus, and the term "brothers." In both of these narratives, Mary Magdalene and the other women are given "a message-vision (tell the disciples) and not a mandate-vision (change the world)."

There is, therefore, no tradition earlier than Mark, let alone historical information, in any of the three units of burial, tomb and vision to women. Further, Crossan remarks that it is likely that none of the gospel accounts "is describing visions at all. What happened to Paul was certainly a vision, but those gospel accounts are more about establishing an authority than about retrieving an apparition."[157] Crossan does not explore the question of why even the low-level authority of a messenger is given by Mark to Mary Magdalene and the other women.

Where, then, in Crossan's reconstruction, do the women come from, and why? He sees the resurrection appearance narratives taking shape around issues of community and male leadership (Meal and Sea traditions: bread and fish; walking on water; fishing for humans). The tomb story in Mark, with its stone rolling away and young man inside, comes from Secret Mark's story of the young man raised from the dead by Jesus; the boy later comes to Jesus by night robed in white. The Gospel of Peter, as we have seen (and the Cross Gospel behind it) depict no women by the cross, and the Secret Gospel of Mark has no account of Jesus' crucifixion, burial, or resurrection. Crossan argues that Mark's three women at cross and tomb (Mary Magdalene, Mary the mother of James, and Salome) are three women in Jericho ("the sister of the youth whom Jesus loved and his mother and Salome were there, and Jesus did not receive them") from Secret Mark 2r14–16. The triad of an unnamed woman, an unnamed mother, and Salome are part of "the textual debris of a censored incident from *Secret Mark*."[158] The three women in Mark, "inaugurally and therapeutically enveloped among many other women" in Mark 15:40–41, are a "canonical Mark"[159] creation as far as their presence at the tomb goes. They are designed as models of failure, though not of

---

156. See Crossan, *Birth of Christianity,* 560: the worship of the women prepares for the worship of the disciples; the Matthean account presupposes nothing but Mark.

157. Crossan, *Birth of Christianity,* xx.

158. Crossan thinks the account of the raising of the dead man and the mention of his family in Secret Mark are earlier than and incorporated into the first version of the Gospel of Mark composed in the early seventies (*Historical Jesus,* 415, 429–30).

159. Mark originally ended at 15:39 with the centurion's confession, parallel to the anointing woman's action in 14:3–9; 15:40–16:8 comes from "canonical Mark" (Crossan, *Historical Jesus,* 415–16).

hopeless failure. They fail in two ways. First, their failure to anoint the corpse — or, better, their very attempt to anoint, which shows their lack of faith in the resurrection — contrasts with the unnamed woman's success in anointing Jesus in Mark 14:3–9 and her faith.[160] Second, their flight and failure to deliver the message of the young man at the tomb[161] parallels the failure and flight of the male disciples in Gethsemani in 14:32–42.[162] Both the three males in Gethsemani and the three women at the tomb represent for Mark "authority to be criticized" and opposed.[163] Mark's creation of the tomb story is subsequently taken up into the gospels of Matthew, Luke, John, and the final statum of the Gospel of Peter.

"There was a movement. The authorities executed the founder. But the movement continued and spread. Those three points are history. I do not find anything historical in the finding of the empty tomb, which was most likely created by Mark himself — at least I cannot find it anywhere except under his influence. The risen apparitions are not historical events in the sense of trances or ecstasies, except in the case of Paul."[164]

Are Mark's three women "real" in any way? Crossan says they are "as real as are the three men [in Gethsemani], and the very fact that Mark singles out *both* groups for criticism tells me of their importance in those Christian communities to which Mark's gospel offers both correction and hope." They are "real" in that they are not created out of nothing by Mark. "Real" in that they are for Mark "important and authoritative figures."[165] But whence this importance and this authority? Crossan concedes in *The Birth of Christianity*, that the women are "real" also in that they are historical witnesses to "the bare and brutal facts of crucifixion."[166]

---

160. Crossan, *Birth of Christianity*, 558. The Markan women characters are pitted against each other: Crossan finds the anointing by the unnamed woman in Mark 14 "far more startling than to claim that a woman was (or women were) first to *find* an empty tomb or even first to *see* the risen Jesus. Mark says that a woman was first to *believe* in the resurrection. If you are concerned with firsts, that does seem the more significant one" (559; cf. *Historical Jesus*, 416). Here I am startled by Crossan's failure to deal with E. Schüssler Fiorenza's treatment of this woman in *In Memory of Her*, which offers a very different reading of the Markan text and the tradition behind it. He takes this anointing to be something the woman must do now or never, because Jesus will be resurrected.

161. *Birth of Christianity*, 557. Crossan remarks that "While the reaction [in Mark 16:8] could be explained as numinous awe, the text offers a rather negative portrayal of the women." By "the text" he seems to mean his reading of Mark as a whole, and especially the Markan design of failure/success.

162. Crossan, *Who Killed Jesus?* 183; cf. *Birth of Christianity*, 557 where the reference regarding the failure of the males is mistakenly given as Mark 10:32–42. The three named women parallel the three named men sleeping in Gethsemani (Peter, James and John), whose failure is a Markan creation too.

163. The scenes in John 20:3–10 (about Peter), 20:1–2, 11–18 (Mary Magdalene) and 20:19–21 (Thomas) "are John's creations, but they make the same point as do Mark's creations. Criticism and opposition indicate importance and authority," contrasted in the Fourth Gospel with the Beloved Disciple (*Birth of Christianity*, 562).

164. Crossan, *Who Killed Jesus?* 209.

165. Crossan, *Birth of Christianity*, 185–86, 562. For John, Mary Magdalene and Peter and Thomas are "significant leaders in other communities."

166. Crossan, *Birth of Christianity*, 559.

All this sleight-of-hand is tied to Crossan's assessment of the Gospel of Peter and the Secret Gospel of Mark as preserving very early material, and his assessment of the canonical Synoptic and Johannine passion narratives as not independent: "the narrative passion is but a single stream of tradition flowing from the *Cross Gospel*, now embedded within the *Gospel of Peter*, into Mark, thence together into Matthew and Luke, and thence, all together, into John."[167] Crossan adopts as a primary methodological principle that what is allowed as historically authentic should be attested by what he judges to be multiple, independent sources, preferably containing material he has stratified as early. But if there is only one ancient source and one stream, multiple attestation is ruled out from the start, with respect to the passion/resurrection narratives.[168] Crossan knows the risk he is taking: "wrong on sources, wrong on reconstructions."[169] His source analysis has not been accepted by any major scholars. By Crossan's own assessment, the use of proper method should yield some scholarly consensus; the fact that his work has not won wide approval tells against it, though he may argue that convincing others takes time.

What is allowed as historical must coincide with Crossan's assessment of the logic and the psychological aspects of events and claims. For the burial, Crossan does not give any weight to the attestations in 1 Cor 15:33–35; Acts 13:29. Presumably he thinks these also arise — independently? — like the mention of the tomb in the Gospel of Peter 8:30–33 (part of his Cross Gospel)[170] from the male disciples' guilt and wishful thinking, wishing that Jesus had been buried (even by enemies as in the Gospel of Peter) or that they had been there to bury him. The women, then, do not — indeed, cannot — appear either in his reconstruction of the primary stratum of the tomb/resurrection narratives,[171] or in his reconstruction of the history behind the narratives.

167. Crossan, *Historical Jesus*, 376. Matthew, Luke and John are based on both canonical Mark and the Cross Gospel (see the diagram in *The Cross that Spoke*, 18). Contrast H. Koester (*Ancient Christian Gospels* [Philadelphia: Trinity Press International, 1990] 220) who proposes that a single Passion Source was used independently by Mark, John, and the Gospel of Peter. Crossan calls this a major alternative proposal. This source might be not a writing, but an original basic structure that contained accounts of (1) the trial and crucifixion of Jesus; (2) his burial by friends; (3) the women at the empty tomb. It gave rise to three independent oral performances, which gave rise to three independent written versions in Mark, John and the Gospel of Peter ("The Historical Jesus and the Cult of the *Kyrios Christos*," *Harvard Divinity Bulletin* 24 (1995) 13–18. For Crossan, those three extant versions are not mutually independent.
168. Crossan's criticism of Meier's presentation of five criteria of authenticity (John Meier, *A Marginal Jew* [New York: Doubleday, 1991] 1.168–77) voices some important objections, especially to the criterion of discontinuity, and stresses the need for interdisciplinary method. In my opinion, the criteria should be used as checks and counterchecks.
169. Crossan, *Birth of Christianity*, 482.
170. The Cross Gospel has a tomb, but no story of Jesus' burial; Crossan thinks the story which appears Gospel of Peter 6:23–24 is based on the canonical Gospels, and ultimately on Mark, who created it on the basis of Deut 21:22–23; Josh 10:26–27, in order to shift the responsibility for Jesus' burial from his enemies (Gospel of Peter) to his friends.
171. W. L. Craig ("John Dominic Crossan on the Resurrection of Jesus," *The Resurrection* [ed. S. T. Davis, D. Kendall, G. O'Collins; New York: Oxford, 1998] 251): "This ensures agnosticism concerning

The dating and combining of materials this way is not the only reason the women almost completely disappear from history. They disappear also because of a host of unexamined assumptions (what Schüssler Fiorenza calls "cultural gender assumptions"[172]) and so-called "common sense": "...ordinary families were probably too afraid...." "Jesus' closest followers" were concerned with "far more serious matters...," concerned, that is, with themselves. It is "ghastly to imagine" probing among corpses to identify that of Jesus, if he was not buried alone — perhaps too ghastly.[173]

A basic premise goes unchallenged: those males who fled are responsible for the Easter faith. Their fleeing cannot be a loss of faith. "When he was executed, those with him lost their nerve and fled. They did not lose their faith and quit. What they found, even after his execution, was that the empowering Kingdom was still present, was still operative, was still there. Furthermore, and however one expressed it, Jesus' presence was still experienced as empowerment...." For Crossan, there is something "insulting" about the empty tomb and resurrection narratives. Easter faith "did not start on Easter Sunday. It started among those first followers of Jesus in Lower Galilee long before his death.... It is absolutely insulting to those first Christians to imagine either that faith started on Easter Sunday through apparition, or that, having been temporarily lost, it was restored by trance and ecstasy that same Sunday." For Crossan, this faith is "the experience of Jesus' continuing empowering presence...the continued presence of absolutely the same Jesus in an absolutely different mode of existence."[174] I think that Crossan is right to stress continuity. But he does not explore how and why and on what basis faith in this "absolutely different mode of existence" developed after Jesus' death. Aside from guilt and the desire to stay empowered, there is no catalyst. And "insult" to the first Christians seems to carry some sort of contemporary insult, and to be complex, as the anger Woolf dissects: "anger that had gone underground and mixed itself with all kinds of other emotions." "I knew that he was angry by this token. When I read what he wrote about women I thought, not of what he was saying, but of himself."[175]

Who the "real" Mary Magdalene might have been, if there was one, and why her name and those of other women were added, and how and why a tradition developed of an apparition to her — these are apparently issues of no interest to Crossan. He has no discussion of Luke 8:1–3, but he states in that "The only way a woman could have been involved in the earliest Jesus movement as an itinerant prophet, given the cultural situation of the day, was if she travelled with a male

Jesus' burial and resurrection, since, on Crossan's analysis, we lack multiple, independent accounts of the exact sequence of what happened at the end of Jesus' life."

172. Alice Bach, "Elisabeth Schüssler Fiorenza: an Interview," *BiblIcon* 3 (1998) 34.
173. Crossan, *Birth of Christianity*, 555.
174. Crossan, *Who Killed Jesus?* 209–10.
175. Woolf, *Room*, 32, 34.

as his 'wife' (or in some other acceptable female role). As long as she was with a male, nobody would have really cared about the relationship or bothered to ask about it. Such companionship did not threaten patriarchal domination in any way; a woman accompanying a man could be servant or slave, sister, mistress, or wife without male chauvinism caring enough even to ask for definition."[176] That two of the women whose names are remembered in Mark (Mary Magdalene and Salome) are not linked with the names of men, however, remains unexplained. Crossan prefers to speak of Jesus' companions, not disciples because "When a teacher sends out students on their own and tells them to speak exactly, act exactly, and live exactly as their teacher does, they have graduated from students to companions."[177] Is this thought to apply to the women as well as the men? The gender clashes and their relationship to leadership, evident in Gospel of Thomas 114, are noted only with the comment that historically Simon Peter succeeds in denying a leadership role to Mary.[178]

Crossan's work is without sophistication in regard to theories of gender and methodologies of women's history, and shows virtually no acquaintance with feminist scholarship of the last twenty-five years. In this he is not alone among prominent Christian Testament scholars. His discussion of his own background and interests in the epilogue to *Who Killed Jesus?* and in *It's a Long Way from Tipperary*[179] is interesting but strangely thin in this respect. Though he holds that Jesus lived a life of "fundamental egalitarianism, of human contact without discrimination and divine contact without hierarchy," he offers no reflection on gender. He speaks of himself as inside the Roman Catholic or Christian tradition, but keeping his distance from the Roman Catholic hierarchy lest he get trapped in the negativity of pro- or anti-dogmatic agendas.[180]

We choose what elements we investigate and which we allow to disturb our thoughts, our hypotheses, our methods, our active commitments. I am not at all accusing Crossan of conscious sexism or an anti-feminist agenda, though there is still a lot of that in the field. But I am looking for a clearer awareness and presentation of his own gender presuppositions and assumptions. Schüssler Fiorenza, speaking of the new New Quest for the Jesus of history, faults it because "Its refusal to reflect on its own ideological or theological interests and its restoration of historical positivism corresponds to political conservatism. Its emphasis

---

176. Crossan, *Birth of Christianity*, 378–79; he is following Gerd Theissen and others, but speculating that both the women and men were prophets. The mention of "pairs" in Mark 6:7 and Q Gospel 10:1 "means that women could also participate, traveling either in twos or singly with a man; both custom and safety concerns kept women from traveling on their own" (337).
177. Crossan, *Birth of Christianity*, 337.
178. Crossan, *The Historical Jesus*, 411; mentioned with "personage clashes" (e.g., Paul vs. the Jerusalem and Antioch authorities; Thomas vs. Peter and Matthew) and type clashes (e.g., Peter vs. the Beloved Disciple in John 20–21).
179. San Francisco: Harper & Row, 2000.
180. Crossan, *Who Killed Jesus?* 211, 214.

on the *realia* of history serves to promote scientific fundamentalism since it generally does not acknowledge that historians select and interpret archaeological
artifacts and textual evidence as well as incorporate them into a scientific model
and narrative framework of meaning." It also "does not undermine and undo the
literalist desire of christological fundamentalists for a 'accurate' reliable biography of Jesus."[181] O'Collins remarks on "the ongoing habit of some male writers of
minimizing the testimony of the women. By belittling the empty tomb tradition
as a later elaboration, they devalue the witness of women; after all, women, and
not men, were utterly central to the empty tomb tradition." He rightly notes,
however, that Crossan's elimination of the empty tomb tradition is by means of
elimination of the story of Jesus' burial by Joseph of Arimathea. It is, in other
words, a consequence of the elimination of the burial.[182]

There are many aspects of Crossan's analysis that are exciting; many questions
that he raises that must be addressed. His writing is engaging, lucid, confident
and uncluttered; and very popular. But like all biblical and all historical scholarship, his is a house of cards, hypothesis on hypothesis. Some of his hypotheses
simply will not hold the deck. I am one of many scholars not persuaded by his
reconstruction of the passion traditions behind Mark or by his understanding of
the interrelationships of canonical texts, or canonical and noncanonical texts.[183]
His reasoning strikes me often as far less than reasonable. But it is almost always
challenging, and dialogue with it advances work in the field. Most importantly, it
reminds us of the brutal horror of crucifixion, the great complexity of the sources
and the difficulty of historical reconstruction.

There are three major points on which I disagree with Crossan: (1) The older
scholarly consensus that John and the Synoptics are independent gave way in the
1980s to the opposite position, that John knew and used the Synoptics, which is
actually a revival of the traditional view. But now there is no consensus. I am not
convinced that, creative as John is, this author knew and made use of the Synoptics. Rather my working hypothesis is that John is independent, with access to
some pre-Synoptic traditions. Crossan's working hypothesis, that John used the

---

181. Schüssler Fiorenza, in Bach, "Interview," 35–36. See W. E. Arnal's discussion of "epistemic
neutrality" ("Making and Re-Making the Jesus-Sign," *Whose Historical Jesus?* 316–18).

182. G. O'Collins, "The Resurrection: The State of the Question," *The Resurrection,* 14 referring
to Osiek, "The Women at the Tomb."

183. For a critique of Crossan's assumptions, methodology and conclusions regarding the Passion
Narrative, see C. A. Evans, "The Passion of Jesus: History Remembered or Prophecy Historicized?"
Bulletin for Biblical Research 6 (1996) 159–65. The women also disappear from the cross in Evans'
discussion here, however: he finds it probable that Jesus' friends and followers "did find out what
happened, even if only in bits and pieces, and then did their best to show that what happened was
'according to the scriptures'" (161). He holds that the Marcan passion narrative is "in all probability
based on primitive, reliable data" (163). See also H. C. Kee, "A Century of Quests of the Culturally
Compatible Jesus," *Theology Today* 52 (1995) 22, 24; B. Meyer, review of Crossan's *The Historical Jesus,*
CBQ 5 (1993) 576. Craig comments on the fact that the presuppositions from which Crossan works
are at odds with scholarly consensus concerning the development of the Gospels in general ("John
Dominic Crossan on the Resurrection," 250).

Markan passion narrative, depends in great part on seeing the intercalation of Peter's betrayal with Jesus' confession in John 18:13–27 as a Markan fingerprint or DNA (cf. Mark 14:53–72). This is for Crossan a genetic relationship "proved (beyond a reasonable doubt!)" that he argues can be corroborated by redactional confirmation,[184] which, as he presents it in these passages and others, is never convincing to my mind. The argument is skewered by talk of DNA and fingerprints, as though redactional peculiarities or literary devices with theological purposes are irrefutable scientific evidence. Further, as D. Moody Smith points out, since we do not have the tradition that Mark used, we cannot confidently distinguish Markan tradition and redaction, or even say the intercalation is Mark's original idea.[185] Crossan's insistence on dependency at this and other points, whatever its cogency, is certainly not enough to bear the weight of his hypothesis that the whole Johannine Passion Narrative as well as the Johannine story of the empty tomb are dependent on Mark. Nor does his analysis John 20 and Matthew 28 convince me of Johannine dependence on Matthew with regard to the appearance to Mary Magdalene. In the next chapter I will argue that John is independent of Mark and Matthew in these accounts. We have multiple attestation of this tradition, with at least two independent sources.

(2) Even if Crossan's Cross Gospel is an early Passion Narrative — and I am not persuaded that it is[186] — the displacement of the women by soldiers and officials as "discoverers" of the empty tomb and witnesses to the resurrection may be, like 1 Corinthians 15, an early example of suppression or ignorance of the women's testimony, either by the framers of the pre-Pauline tradition or by Paul himself. Crossan does not adequately treat the question of whether "buried . . . was raised" implies an empty tomb; nor does he discuss whether the Pauline use of burial imagery for baptism (Rom 6:4; cf. Col 2:12) implies it. He sees that the basic sequence of death-burial-resurrection-apparition appears with creedal brevity in 1 Corinthians 15:3b–7 and with full narrative detail in Mark 15–16, Matthew 27–28, Luke 23–24 and John 19–21, but holds "there is not the slightest indication that the sequence . . . was a tradition behind any of our present gospel conclusions." I do not know what would count as an "indication" for Crossan. He dismisses the argument that Paul may have known and omitted the traditions of the women's discovery of the tomb and reception of a resurrection appearance. "*Maybe* Paul knew both those items as received tradition but omitted them because of trouble with women prophets at Corinth. (But Paul had far greater trouble with James and Peter-Cephas, according to Galatians 2:11–14, and there

---

184. Crossan, *Birth of Christianity,* 565; see also N. Perrin, *The New Testament* (New York: Harcourt Brace, 1974) 228–29. Crossan holds that John is independent of the Synoptics in its first stage of development; and dependent in a second and third stage (113).

185. See D. M. Smith, *John Among the Gospels* (Minneapolis: Fortress, 1992) 115–16.

186. See above, n. 167 for Koester's proposal. Brown (*Death of the Messiah*) considers the Gospel of Peter a digest from memory of Matthew, Luke and John, along with some popular passion traditions from outside those Gospels.

was even some trouble concerning Peter-Cephas in 1 Corinthians 1:12, yet Paul does not omit either man from officially received tradition.)"[187] However, authority struggles complicated by gender are far from the same thing as male authority struggles; Crossan does not show awareness of this difference and the different dynamics, strategies. Nor does he engage in conversation with two decades of feminist scholarship about early Christian gender "troubles." Even Schüssler Fiorenza's *In Memory of Her* and Antoinette Clark Wire's *The Corinthian Women Prophets* are missing from his immense bibliography.[188]

(3) I have already mentioned unexamined cultural and gender assumptions that flaw Crossan's presentation of what it is "reasonable" to think happened, what is "likely" to have happened. Here is the most important example. Even in Crossan's reconstruction the women do not completely disappear. Their presence at the crucifixion is not Markan creation, but "received tradition." He asks, "But is [it] historical fact? My best answer is yes, because the male disciples had fled; if the women had not been watching, we would not know even the brute fact of crucifixion (as distinct, for example, from Jesus being summarily speared or beheaded in prison)."[189] And if the women were watching, two things seem "reasonable" and "likely" to me and some others, though not to Crossan.

(A) They must have reported more than the "brute fact" of crucifixion (Crossan, actually, does refer once to the "facts "[190]). This "more" surely included aspects which would unsurprisingly evoke or suggest biblical passages: such as stripping the victim, listening for his attempts to speak last words, and cruelty on the part of executioners. This "more" calls into question Crossan's understanding of the development of the passion tradition, by "two equiprimordial processes," "male exegesis" and by "female lament."

One "literate and highly sophisticated stream of tradition," he says, involved an intense search of the Scriptures that could be used to fill in the brute fact of crucifixion. On surface, intermediate and deep narrative levels, Crossan thinks, "biblical models and scriptural precedents have controlled the story to the point that without them nothing is left but the brutal fact of the crucifixion itself."[191] Exegesis was not story or narrative, though story and narrative was created from it,[192] and it continued after there were narratives. "Exegesis was there first. Exegesis became story." What or who turned "prophetic exegesis" into story, who

---

187. Crossan, *Birth of Christianity*, 550.
188. Crossan does mention *In Memory of Her* a couple of times, but in passing.
189. Crossan, *Birth of Christianity*, 559.
190. Crossan, *Birth of Christianity*, 568.
191. Crossan, *Birth of Christianity*, 521. Crossan strips away individual units (lots cast and garments divided as coming from Ps 22:18; darkness at noon from Amos 8:9; gall and vinegar Psalm 69:21), general sequences (the mount of Olives situation from 2 Samuel 15–17; trial collaboration from Psalm 2; abuse description form Leviticus 16) and overall frames (narrative genre of innocence vindicated, etc.).
192. "There is no evidence for a passion-resurrection *story* that does not presume, absorb, embody and integrate *exegesis* as its hidden substratum and basic content" (*Birth of Christianity*, 571).

"created the very idea of the passion-resurrection schema as story...saw over, under, around, and through exegesis to story?" Crossan thinks it likely that *"The group or process that created exegesis is not the same group or process that created story."*[193] Instead, he holds that

> In the absence of a body *and a tomb* [emphasis mine], female ritual lament wove exegetical fragments into a sequential story...turned the male exegetical tradition into a passion-resurrection story once and for all forever. The closest we can get to that story now is the *Cross Gospel*, whose insistence on communal passion and communal resurrection may be strongest index of those origins. The gift of the lament tradition is not just that we know the names of Mary Magdalene and the other women, but that their passion-resurrection story moved into the heart of the Christian tradition forever. And once it was there, within a decade of the death of Jesus, others would compose variations on it, but nobody would ever replace or eliminate it.[194]

It flowed then into a single line of male scribal tradition, from the Cross Gospel to the canonical gospels.

This is Crossan's simultaneous answer to three questions: Why do women appear more frequently but also more negatively in texts at and after the execution of Jesus? Who are those who created biographical story? and Why are there no accounts of female lament or ritual mourning for Jesus in the passion-resurrection tradition? As far as I can see, Crossan does not show clearly how this answers the first and third questions, so we have to try to answer them ourselves. He might mean that the third-stage scribal tradition is backlash and erasure, partially successful. It is something more than "Standard male chauvinism [which] simply ignores women or describes them, when necessary, within the roles, positions, and confined presumed as normal." He might mean that it is backlash against the teaching of women in their laments.[195] Crossan draws on gender stereotypes when he insists that women's laments "operate on a level far more physical and primitive and profound" than male religion, which they bypass; the laments are tears in dialectic with ideas, and "somewhere deep down inside us we wonder if the 'tears' have it right over the 'ideas.'"[196]

---

193. Crossan, *Birth of Christianity*, 571. He does not argue "that the obverse of his conclusion is absolutely impossible, just that it is extremely unlikely."

194. Crossan, *Birth of Christianity*, 571–73.

195. Crossan, *Birth of Christianity*, 571. He implies it is something like the prohibition in 1 Tim 2:12 of women's teaching or controlling men.

196. Crossan, *Birth of Christianity*, 533, drawing on the work of P. L. Fermor, *Mani: Travels in the Southern Peloponnese* (New York: Harper & Row, 1984), G. Holst-Warhaft, *Dangerous Voices: Women's Laments and Greek Literature* (New York: Routledge, 1992), and others. Crossan is mainly using Kathleen Corley's unpublished manuscript (*Lament and Gospel: Women's Voices in the Passion Tradition*, forthcoming, Oxford University Press) in which she suggests that a female lament tradition and liturgical context was a *Sitz im Leben* for an early Passion Narrative. Cf. her article in *Forum*, referred to above, pp. 213, n. 47, 214–15. See also A. Bourke, "More in Anger than in Sorrow: Irish Women's Lament Poetry," *Feminist Messages Coding in Women's Folk Culture* (ed. J. N. Radner; Chicago: Uni-

Let me try to get this straight. As he presents it, there is no connection be-tween the women he holds were historically at the cross, and the women's lament tradition. Women — other women? — mourned in the absence of a body and a tomb, weaving the exegetical fragments (produced by males, not by the witnessing women[197]) into story, which was then developed by male scribal tradition. The passion-resurrection story is not history remembered because, quoting Koester, "the form, structure, and life situation of such a historical passion report and its transmission have never been clarified."[198] But if women witnessed the crucifix-ion, they surely communicated more than the brute fact. It makes more sense to think of a lament tradition, with its biographical material about the death, and its implicit or explicit protest against death and against male injustice, religious and political, as springing from and developing from that witness. Exegesis is not "first," as Crossan would have it. Nor need it be seen as "male." There is no reason why women as well as men could not make use of the Jewish lament tradition, especially the psalms.

(B) If the women were watching, it seems reasonable to me that they, or as Mark says some of them,[199] watched until the end, whether it was burial in a tomb or common grave or pit, or (I think unlikely) until the corpse of Jesus was eaten by birds or dogs. And if they watched until the end, if there was a body or remnants of a body to return to, their return — for whatever purpose — is what I would expect. On what basis do I think that they watched until the end? Not all women are brave, loyal, persistent, capable of caring for corpses. But if these women were present at the crucifixion, these women were brave, overcoming fear of their own arrest and perhaps execution,[200] and overcoming the unforgettable, traumatic horror of watching. They had nothing to lose by seeing it out, finishing it, witnessing what amounted to the final act of Jesus' execution, the deposition from the cross of the corpse and its disposal. If they hoped to be of some help, their hope was thwarted, if the tradition is accurate. This is the world of male privilege and power. If Luke's Joanna was present, even she, the wife of Herod's steward Chuza, may have been without clout with Pilate; perhaps how much more so the other women. Weeping and raw lamenting, standing by, efforts to care afterward for the corpse: these were the jobs assigned to women at executions, the roles

versity of Chicago, 1993) 160–82; N. Loraux, *Mothers in Mourning* (Ithaca: Cornell University Press, 1998).

197. But somehow on the basis of the brute fact(s) of crucifixion reported by the witnessing women?

198. H. Koester, "Apocryphal and Canonical Gospels," *HTR* 73 (1980) 127; quoted by Crossan, *Birth of Christianity*, 521.

199. Mark has three women at the cross but two watch the burial (Mary Magdalene and Mary the mother of Joses); all three return to the tomb. Matthew: three at the cross; two at the burial and two at the return. Luke mentions "the women who had followed him from Galilee" at the cross and at the burial. Three are named as with "the other women" who told the eleven of the empty tomb. John mentions three or four women at the cross; no women are mentioned at the burial; Mary Magdalene (and others; cf. "we" in v. 2) are at the tomb.

200. See below, pp. 276–77.

they were socialized to play, and it is reasonable to think they performed them. The dead one was not loved any less than when he was living. And this does seem to be about love, a certain kind of love, bold and helpless and doing what it can.

The question of how the scribal tradition or traditions relate to the lament tradition and to the possibility of women witnesses, merits, therefore, much more careful attention. Crossan has rightly noted — as Setzer, Price and others have — that there are "negative" elements in the treatment of women in the passion/resurrection narratives. Crossan sees seven of these, but there are more, especially in his reconstructed Cross Gospel[201] and the Gospel of Peter. He lists:

1. the "uncomplimentary" mention of the three women watching the crucifixion "from a distance" in Mark 15:40 (cf. 14:54; Ps 38:11);

2. the naming of Mary Magdalene last in the list of those at the cross in John 19:25;

3. Mark's implicit criticism of the women because of their plan to anoint a corpse, which as Crossan reads it, shows disbelief in the resurrection (15:47–16:8), in contrast to "the Markan ideal" of an anointing woman (14:3–9);

4. the women's failure to deliver the message in Mark 16:8;

5. Mary Magdalene's "immediate and continuing interpretation" in John 20:2, 13, 15 of the empty tomb as due to grave robbery;

6. her mistaking the risen Jesus for the gardener in John 20:15;

7. the fact that even the one positive story in Matt 28:9–10 of the appearance to the women has them receiving "a message-vision rather than a mandate-vision; it is secretarial-level rather than executive-level apparition."

The details of Crossan's exegeses aside, his claim that "All of that, especially in Mark and John, is not a case of ancient tradition being redacted negatively but a case of negative tradition being created before our eyes"[202] is wrong, if the women witnessed and reported more than the bare fact of crucifixion. These accounts need more analysis, and in a different framework.

In 1993 I was invited to the Carleton University Learneds in Ottawa to take part in a Canadian Society of Biblical Studies seminar on the historical Jesus. One of the points I briefly argued in my paper concerned the story of the empty tomb: "Apocalyptic aspects of the New Testament passion/resurrection predictions, the stories of the empty tomb and the witness of women merit, in my judgment, much more careful historical and literary sifting than they have so far received. Instead of being dismissed as legend and later accretion, the empty tomb tradition may

---

201. If the Cross Gospel is the earliest instance of the scribal tradition, later scribal traditions swim strongly against it in giving the women more significant roles (discoverers of the empty tomb; commission; apparition).

202. Crossan, *Birth of Christianity*, 571–72.

prove to be ever more central to a feminist understanding of Christian origins."[203] In the discussion that followed, Crossan turned and said to me, "Jane, if I could give you the empty tomb, I would." Sadly for feminist scholarship, he implied, and maybe sadly for him too, his reconstruction of "what happened" erases the women from the tomb. It would be nice if he could give them to us, but he cannot. There is simply no evidence of their presence. The work of Schüssler Fiorenza, he said he finds "too optimistic." "This was the turf; there was the path."[204] I was stunned into silence by Crossan's wish to "give" me the narrative of the tomb; by the fact that it even occurred to him that he might. I wondered if I had to "take" it. No, I knew I did.

But wait a minute. This giving and not giving, this taking, this grabbing and hoarding, is not what feminist biblical criticism is about. This giving and taking depends, rather, on what Schüssler Fiorenza keeps pointing out is passe because it is positivistic: the insistence — even if one denies it — that only one reading is right, and can bring us to "what really happened" and to "the meaning," irrespective of systemic power differentials and ideological currents in the worlds of historical subjects, writers, historians and readers. She argues that reifying positivism "understands history as depicting 'how it actually was' and as providing evidence for historical facts"; it is a form of determinism. While acknowledging the constructedness of historical knowledge, "[c]ritical historical work must remain central to feminist studies in religion, because it not only allows for change, but also it critically theorizes change" in its attempt to correct the hegemonic notion of history, to tell (his)story differently.[205] Crossan does declare his work a reconstruction "Because there is *only* reconstruction"[206]; but he aims to be as "for-

203. J. Schaberg, "A Feminist Experience of Historical-Jesus Scholarship," *Whose Historical Jesus?* (ed. W. E. Arnal and M. Desjardins; Ottawa: Wilfrid Laurier University Press, 1997) 160. Like Schüssler Fiorenza, today I would use the term "beginnings" rather than "origins," since as King says "appeals to origins are not only ambiguous but potentially dangerous. The logic of appeal to origins depends upon contrasting the purity, power, and goodness of the pristine originary movement with a corrupt, deviant, or wicked foil. Whether such a contrast is explicit or not, it is potentially available for exploitation. And too often it has been used, for example, to praise Jesus' egalitarianism at the expense of denigrating Jewish women, or to uphold pristine Protestant origins in the face of Catholic corruption. Even when anti-Judaism and anti-Catholicism are clearly eschewed as unacceptable appeals in the struggle for justice for women, the contrastive logic of origins remains in place, waiting for a new exploitation." In the case of the egalitarianism of Jesus, a major intended contrast by those a generation ago claiming Jesus as a feminist was between a movement in which men and women participated as equals, and forms of contemporary Christianity, especially Roman Catholicism, in which they do not. "The question," King says, "is less what the basis is for women's authority than what conditions or religious ideas have supported women's taking up public roles" ("Prophetic Power and Women's Authority," 340–41). I do not fully agree with King on this last point, since the issue is also one of *precedent*: the story of a woman from earliest Christianity as precedent for the empowering of women. And also, this figure as precedent for the experience of opposition, backlash. Work on the empty tomb narratives, I think, offers opportunities for exploration of these possibilities.
204. Woolf, *Room*, 6.
205. Schüssler Fiorenza, *Jesus, Miriam's Son*, 82–88; and Bach, "Elisabeth Schüssler Fiorenza," 33–34.
206. Crossan, *Historical Jesus*, 426.

mally objective" as possible.[207] He does not adequately analyze the assumptions behind his reconstruction, or the uses to which his reconstruction is put. If only one reading or reconstruction is right, and it is his, then as Crossan said, the text can't be given away. If only one reading or reconstruction is right, then the text must be wrestled over in an *agōn* along the model of father-son literary struggles. Victory on the literary battleground consists in producing a strong misreading, a revisionary reading, that wrests power from the forefathers. Let the best man win.

But what if I say to Crossan: I don't want your empty tomb. Keep it. Now here is mine — my interpretation, my text, both of which do not belong to me. Maybe then we can talk about this. And let readers decide which is more persuasive, and which parts of which are more convincing. Let readers blow on the houses of cards and bump them gently; let the reader even pound the table with his or her fist. See what falls and see what stands, as "true" and historically sound. More importantly, let the readers see which interpretations spark the readers' own creativity, and move them to liberatory action — which readings are "ethical" in Schüssler Fiorenza's sense.[208]

King argues for this intertwining. "Writing history is engaging in moral discourse; it is a matter of ethics and imagination. How we imagine the past is part of our discourse about the meaning of the present. We are all responsible. The methodological disciplines of historical analysis are basic to this task insofar as they serve the ethics of impartiality and guard against superficiality and arbitrariness. As such, they belong to history as moral discourse."[209] She stresses the importance of ending not with answers, but with an hypothesis, leaving the door open for reflection, for writing the story a different way. Scholarly disagreements can be seen as a sign of the vitality of the field of Christian Testament studies, or as a problem of contentiousness and isolation one from another, or of vague, fundamentally flawed methodologies, or — as I like to see them — all of these. In the next two chapters I will write the interpretation of the empty tomb and appearance to Mary Magdalene in my own way, which I hope will prop the door open a bit. To get that door open wide requires a sensibility that lights on small things and shows "that perhaps they were not small at all." It brings buried to things to light and makes one "wonder why they were buried at all."[210]

---

207. Crossan, "The Historical Jesus: An Interview with John Dominic Crossan," *The Christian Century* 108 (1991) 1200–1204.

208. E. Schüssler Fiorenza, "The Ethics of Biblical Interpretation: Decentering Biblical Scholarship," chapter 1 of *Rhetoric and Ethic* (Minneapolis: Fortress, 1999) 17–30; this is her 1987 SBL presidential address, first published in *JBL* 107 (1988) 3–17.

209. K. King, "Translating History: Reframing Gnosticism in Postmodernity," *Tradition und Translation* (Berlin: de Gruyter, 1994) 275–76; using the work of H. White, "The Value of Narrativity in the Representation of Reality," *The Content of the Form. Narrative Discourse and Historical Representation* (Baltimore: Johns Hopkins, 1987) 27.

210. Woolf, *Room*, 92.

Christian Testament
Converging Possibilities

i

"& as the current answers don't do, one has to grope for a new one; & the process of discarding the old, when one is by no means certain what to put in their place, is a sad one."

V. Woolf, *Diary*, 1.259

"She felt him trying to piece together in a laborious and elementary fashion fragments of belief, unsoldered and separate, lacking the unity of phrases fashioned by the old believers. Together they groped in this difficult region, where the unfinished, the unfulfilled, the unwritten, the unreturned, came together in their ghostly way and wore the semblance of the complete and satisfactory. The future emerged more splendid than ever from this construction of the present. Books were to be written, and since books must be written in rooms, and rooms must have hangings, and outside the windows there must be land, and an horizon to that land, and trees perhaps, and a hill, they sketched a habitation for themselves."

V. Woolf, *Night and Day*[1]

Fantasy and Mysticism

I N THIS CHAPTER I want to enter into the discussion by asking if and how the tradition of an appearance to Mary Magdalene, alone or with other women, may relate to the story of the discovery of the empty tomb. This entails entering a world of social commitment and activism, but also a world of mystical imagination and fantasy. I am reminded often of my experience at the dissertation stage: one of my directors, Raymond Brown, responded to something I had written on Mark 14:62 — a proposal that Merkavah imagery was being used there[2] — by scrawling

---

1. V. Woolf, *Night and Day* (1919; London: Vintage, 1992) 488.
2. See J. Schaberg, "Mark 14:62: Early Christian Merkabah Imagery?" *Apocalyptic and the New Testament* (ed. J. Marcus and M. L. Soards; Sheffield: JSOT, 1989) 69–94; P. S. Alexander ("Comparing Merkabah Mysticism and Gnosticism," *JJS* 35 [1984] 10–11, 17) holds that Merkabah mysticism, though with different emphases than it later has, can be seen as an inner-Jewish development of pre-70 apocalyptic.

"sheer fantasy!" in the margin so hard that the dot on his exclamation point pierced the page. His action was "most rational & impersonal: rather impressive; yet so definite, so emphatic, that I felt convinced: I mean of failure; save for one odd gleam, that he was himself on the wrong tack & persisting for some deep reason. . . . "[3] I kept that page as a reminder that yes, in spite of what Brown thought, the Bible *is* often fantasy literature, and yes, fantasy is a part of life and of history. The fantastic has liberating potential, can be seen as "inverting and subverting the world with hope," in the words of Jack Zipes.[4]

Morton Smith has shown that a knowledge of Jewish mystical traditions can enable a scholar to view as coherent and even sometimes historical what other scholars view as late, complex, and confusing fiction, primarily the product of theological and sociological conflicts.[5] What Smith has shown can be considered apart from the question of whether the scholar believes or disbelieves like Smith in the "reality" which is being claimed or presented as true, as experienced, and also whether or not the scholar has an ear or appreciation for the mytho-poetry of a text. "History," Smith holds, "is a work of the imagination within limits set by the imagination. We must try to imagine what actually happened, that is, what accords both with our image of the preserved evidence and with our image of the real world." He examines two historical problems: "Did Jesus think he had ascended into the heavens? Did he tell his most intimate disciples that he had done so?" Sounding like Khrushchev discussing what the astronauts did not see, Smith presents his presuppositions: "By 'the heavens' I mean a series of regions, one above the other, beginning with the sky, going on up away from the earth, and inhabited by supernatural beings. I don't think there are any such regions or beings, consequently I don't think anybody could have ascended to them, but I do think people could make others and even themselves believe that they had ascended or were actually ascending, and believe so strongly that they experienced by hallucination whatever they expected to experience during an ascent."[6] In the Greco-Roman world of the time of Jesus, it was commonly believed that it was possible for a human being to ascend into the heavens, after death and before it, in dreams, visions, and bodily. Smith holds that the unusual frequency and importance in Palestinian literature of ascent stories, and the insistence in the Qumran Hodayot and Manual of Discipline that the sectarians worshipped with

---

3. Woolf, *Diary*, 5.271, on Leonard Woolf's criticism of her biography of Fry.

4. J. Zipes, *Fairy Tales and the Art of Subversion* (New York: Routledge, 1991).

5. On the praxis of visionary ascent, see M. Smith, "Two Ascended to Heaven — Jesus and the Author of 4Q491," *Jesus and the Dead Sea Scrolls* (ed. J. Charlesworth; New York: Doubleday, 1992) 290–301; "Ascent to Heaven and Deification in 4QMa," *Archaeology and History in the Dead Sea Scrolls* (ed. L Schiffman; Sheffield: JSOT Press, 1990) 181–88. Smith suggests in "Two Ascended" (298–99) that the concept of ascent could clarify the christology of the Fourth Gospel. See also C. A. Evans, "The Recently Published Dead Sea Scrolls and the Historical Jesus," *Studying the Historical Jesus* (ed. B Chilton and C. A. Evans; Leiden: Brill, 1994) 565; J. J. Collins and D. Dimant, "A Thrice-Told Hymn," *JQR* 85 (1994) 151–55.

6. M. Smith, "Ascent to Heavens," *Eranos* 50 (1981) 403.

the angels, indicate that there were practices and techniques that centered on the theme of ascent "and perhaps led the imaginative to believe that they, too, experienced the sort of heavenly ascents they read and wrote of."[7] Jesus, he argues, taught and practiced ascent to the heavens;[8] Christians believed he had ascended after his death and expected to do the same themselves. For Smith the root of this belief is in "some immediate experience."[9] It is an experience I presume Smith does not share, and for which he has a mixture of scorn and deep interest. I do not read all this literally[10] as he does. I think of it as real, in some way, for some people, one out of many ways of describing mystical experience. Which I understand following D. Soelle and others to involve eroticsm, community, suffering, joy, and resistance.[11]

Apocalypticism

Future hope and present experience, contemplation and action are at times in a certain balance that can be found in an apocalyptic outlook, which involves much more than end-of-the-world speculation. John J. Collins has shown in apocalyptic eschatology the intimate connection and mutual interdependence or interpenetration between present depth experience and future hope of transcendence of death. In apocalyptic texts, "while the present experience of righteousness gives rise to the hope of final vindication, it is also true that the hope of final vindication confirms and even makes possible the present experience of righteousness and divine approval."[12] In the logic of eschatology, the present depth experience is one of liberation from the fear of personal loss and death,

---

7. Smith, "Ascent," 411–12. See E. Schuller, "A Hymn from a Cave Four Hodayot Manuscript: 4Q427 7 + ii," *JBL* 112 (1993) 605–28; she thinks it doubtful that deification was the goal or actually believed attainable at Qumran, but the notion of human entry into the heavenly realm and taking a seat among celestial beings deserves careful consideration (she is followed by Evans, "The Recently Published Dead Sea Scrolls").

8. Contrast Smith's view of the transfiguration accounts ("The Origin and History of the Transfiguration Story," *USQR* 36 [1980] 39–44) with Perkins, "Resurrection," 427. Perkins holds that the accounts cannot be read as evidence for a practice of apocalyptic, visionary ascent on the part of Jesus and his disciples because "the episode as it stands does not describe Moses and Elijah as either transfigured or translated to the divine." However, it does present them as alive centuries after their lifetimes; the belief that they had been taken up into God's presence seems to me to be taken for granted. Seeing into (or hearing sounds from, or going into) that presence signal mystical practice.

9. Smith, "Ascent," 416.

10. W. F. Smelik ("On Mystical Transformation of the Righteous into Light in Judaism," *JSJ* 26 [1995] 123) makes a sharp distinction, with which I assume Smith would agree, between metaphor and mysticism (literalism).

11. D. Soelle, *The Silent Cry: Mysticism and Resistance* (Minneapolis: Fortress, 2001); see also G. M. Jantzen, *Power, Gender and Mysticism* (Cambridge: Cambridge University Press, 1995) especially chapters 1, and 339–53 on mysticism and feminism, paying close attention to issues of power. "[T]he idea of mysticism is a social construction, and . . . it has been constructed in different ways at different times" (12).

12. J. J. Collins, "Apocalyptic Eschatology as the Transcendence of Death," *CBQ* 36 (1974) 41.

liberation therefore to pursue a life of righteousness or justice. "It is undoubtedly true that this depth experience can be attained by some without a belief in the heavenly host, immortality of the soul, or resurrection of the body. It is also true that belief in an afterlife does not necessarily involve liberation, or the attainment of a depth-experience. However, if we are to understand the thought pattern of apocalyptic eschatology we must realize that for the apocalypticists, present experience and future hope were intrinsically connected and mutually interdependent."[13]

I want to attempt here to cut through the scholarly tangles discussed in the previous chapter with a general reconstruction of the pre-gospel empty tomb tradition as fragments of an apocalypse, drawing on Daniel 7 and 12 and 2 Kings 2, as these texts may have been used as mystical texts by members, communally and individually, in the *basileia* (Kingdom) movement of Jesus and his companions.[14] By such use of mystical texts I mean use that prompts and inspires the effort to come into direct contact with or to live in and for that "kingdom" believed to be "where" there is victory over injustice and death. Greenspoon finds the origin of the idea of resurrection in belief in Yahweh as the divine warrior who rules over nature, chaos, and death, and in the belief that his followers are incorporated into his kingship of victory over death.[15] The goal of the mystic was coming into presence of God; mystical practices took the form of heavenly ascent to the throne of Glory, or of earthbound visions, and may have involved ascetical preparations. The apocalyptic nature of this *basileia* of Jesus and his companions movement gave such practices an eschatological, ethical and sociopolitical context. Not just transformation of the mystic, but transformation of creation was the desired end.[16]

Some further preliminary remarks. "I am going to develop in your presence as fully and freely as I can the train of thought which led me to think this. Perhaps if I lay bare the ideas, the prejudices, that lie behind this statement you will find that they have some bearing upon women and some upon fiction. At any rate,

---

13. Collins, "Apocalyptic Eschatology," 43.

14. Against the modern view that mysticism is fundamentally individualistic and private, C. Newsom thinks that the purpose of the Shirot, recited at the time of sabbath whole-offering, is to describe "the praxis of something like a communal mysticism" (*Songs of the Sabbath Sacrifice* [Atlanta: Scholars Press, 1985] 19); cf. C. H. T. Fletcher-Louis, "Heavenly Ascent or Incarnational Presence?" *SBL Seminar Papers* (Atlanta: Scholars Press, 1998) 1.398; he argues that in Songs of the Sabbath Sacrifice ritual ascent was a corporate experience, not esoteric but at the heart of the community's liturgical life. On apocalypticism and mysticism, see Segal, *Paul*, 38–39; I. Gruenwald, *Apocalyptic and Merkabah Mysticism* (Leiden: Brill, 1979); *From Apocalypticism to Gnosticism* (Frankfurt am Main: Peter Lang, 1988; C. Rowland, *The Open Heaven* (New York: Crossroad, 1982).

15. L. J. Greenspoon, "The Origin of the Idea of Resurrection," *Traditions in Transformation* (ed. B. Halpern and J. D. Levenson; Winona Lake: Eisenbrauns, 1981) 247–321.

16. See C. Rowland ("In This Place: the Center and Margins of Theology," *Reading from This Place* [ed. Segovia and M. A. Tolbert; Minneapolis: Fortress, 1995] 2.175) on the political dimension of Matthew's perspective — privileging the apparently insignificant and children — given added importance by the mystical tradition. See J. J. Kanagaraj, *'Mysticism' in the Gospel of John* (Sheffield: Sheffield Academic Press, 1998) 157–58 on the correlation of ethics and mysticism in the traditions associated with Yohanan ben Zakkai.

when a subject is highly controversial — and any question about sex is that — one cannot hope to tell the truth. One can only show how one came to hold whatever opinion one does hold. One can only give one's audience the chance of drawing their own conclusions as they observe the limitations, the prejudices, the idiosyncrasies of the speaker."[17]

Four Possibilities in a Feminist Framework

The following are a carefully chosen set of four converging possibilities — about the nature and makeup of this *basileia* movement, the crucifixion and burial of Jesus, the empty tomb, and the appearance to Mary Magdalene and (an)other(s). These possibilities fit together and to my mind reinforce each other. They inter-lock to give us a hypothetical critical basis for historical reconstruction that will (1) account for the evidence in some texts of Mary Magdalene's key participation and agency in the movement; (2) account for the lack of that evidence elsewhere; and (3) be a bridge to portrayals of Mary in gnostic/apocryphal literature and in her legends. My aim is to provide "a set of plausible descriptions within the band of highest probabilities."[18] But it is crucial to ask by whom, and in the context of what possibilities, plausibility and probability are assessed.

My interpretive framework and presuppositions are feminist. In this framework it is possible to place women as agents at the center of historiography,[19] and to understand them as makers as well as bearers of meaning. Feminist histori-cal/critical and literary analysis is grounded in wo/men's[20] experience of oppression and historical agency, that is, in wo/men's participation in and contribution to struggles for justice. This is experience of the agency and intelligence of wo/men, and of the force and strategies of oppression.[21] The assumption that wo/men were there, they suffered, and they prevailed is given methodological priority. I have questioned and rejected reconstructions that deny the possibility of that agency in the early Christian movement. I have accepted probabilities and reconstructions that allow for it. On the basis of what we judge historically possible and probable, we make our educated guesses and speculations. Feminist interpretation reads

---

17. Woolf, *Room*, 4.

18. E. Castelli, "Drawing Large and Startling Figures," *Reimagining Christian Origins* (ed. E. Castelli and H. Taussig; Valley Forge, Pa.: Trinity Press International, 1996) 14.

19. See E. Schüssler Fiorenza, *Jesus and the Politics of Interpretation* (New York: Continuum, 2000) 35, 51–55.

20. Wo/men is Schüssler Fiorenza's term for all women and oppressed and marginalized men (*Miriam's Child*, n. 1, p. 191). See Woolf, *Three Guineas*, 101–2 on destroying the old, vicious, and corrupt word "feminist": "The word 'feminist' is destroyed; the air is cleared; and in that clearer air what do we see? Men and women working together for the same cause."

21. L. Schottroff, "Working for Liberation: A Change of Perspective in New Testament Scholar-ship," *Reading from This Place*, 2.185: she speaks of women reading the Bible as "a document recording the struggles of their female ancestors, and as a document of patriarchal *attempts* to suppress women" (emphasis mine).

against the current of contemporary criticism — as represented by Crossan, Mack, and Brown — in which the women at the tomb disappear from history and/or their role from serious theological consideration. Our educated assumption is that an androcentric telling and stereotypes, and centuries of androcentric interpretation, have garbled and diminished and all but erased the contribution of wo/men.[22] This directs us to read gaps and slippages in the texts, to map out ancient and contemporary strategies of suppression and resistance, to test what Woolf called the "atmosphere"[23] of values. Feminist criticism asks its own questions, and makes its own connections. It does not pretend to be objective in the disinterested sense, but to be fair and to have a say in what is fair. It is work done to empower social change and wo/men's liberation, and work that only wo/men can do.[24]

It is crucial that feminist presuppositions and interests inform historical-critical and literary-critical treatments of the Christian Testament, and that the desire to uncover wo/men's history, making for a fuller human history, enter fully into discussion of these texts. Here come together the massive scholarship on the search for the historical Jesus and Christian origins, over two hundred years old, and scholarship on historical women, only in its second generation. This feminist framework is what makes feminist work done with traditional methodologies seem to some strange and disconcerting, especially to those operating within a framework of unexamined or inadequately examined commitments, priorities, ideologies. "The very assumption that scholarship can stay out of (or above) ideology . . . is ideological itself."[25] I know that the issue is more than competent exegesis; that use of traditional or innovative methods of historical and literary criticism will not convince those who do not or cannot share the basic feminist assumptions behind this work, or who have decided to belittle or ignore feminist scholarship. This, not nostalgia or confusion, is what makes the process a "sad one"[26] for feminist scholars; sad in other ways for other scholars. In the field of Christian Testament studies, men and women cannot yet say "together they groped in this difficult region."[27] The framework determines to a certain extent what is deemed logical, reasonable, possible; what questions are asked; what motivates the writing. A feminist framework requires that the researcher examine and re-examine how and why she is reading, and let her reader know also. In the introduction I have tried to lay out the process of my self-understanding and experiences as they relate to this book. This hermeneutical stance precedes and

22. See T. Ilan, *Integrating Women into Second Temple History* (Tübingen: Mohr Siebeck, 1999) 5.
23. Woolf, *Three Guineas*, 52.
24. W. E. Arnal, "Making and Re-Making the Jesus-Sign: Contemporary Markings on the Body of Christ," *Whose Historical Jesus?* (ed. W. E. Arnal and M. Desjardins; Waterloo: Wilfrid Laurier, 1997) 317: "The ultimate value that undergirds the desire to avoid epistemic bias — hence the most basic and hidden epistemic bias of all — is the desire to conserve the world roughly as it is."
25. M. Bal, "The Politics of Citation," *diacritics* 21 (1991) 26.
26. Woolf, *Diary*, 1.259.
27. Woolf, *Night and Day*, 488.

informs method, so "one can speak not so much of a different method as a differ-ence in which the data gleaned from the application of traditional methods are assessed."[28]

Methodologically, I proceed on the basis of the Synoptic four-source theory and Markan priority, of the hypothesis that John is independent of the Synoptics but shares traditions with them. The three stages of Gospel development (from history to tradition to Gospels) is a general outline within which I work, with an eye con-stantly on apocryphal traditions and writings. Some methods used for "historical Jesus" research are useful in the search for wo/men's history — multiple attesta-tion; knowledge of the socio/cultural/political/economic/religious/gender realities of the time (especially of first-century Judaism[s]); evaluation and comparison of the general tendencies and viewpoints of each Evangelist; reconstruction from Acts and Paul of early phases of church existence. These not just Euro-white men's "ways of knowing," but reasonable approaches to the Gospels, developed by Euro-white men, available to all of us. They can function quite differently for feminists. Take the case of Mary Magdalene's sevenfold demonic-possession. John Meier thinks that the criteria of embarrassment and coherence suggest that historically Jesus performed an exorcism on her.[29] But whose embarrassment? We can suppose the prominence of a flawed female figure was *less* embarrassing to males who opposed her and her memory than an unflawed female, especially when that flaw, even if healed, connotes madness, deviant behavior, and heresy. Fem-inist scholars look at the tradition in a radically different way, as indicating the association of Mary Magdalene with protest against injustice, and with prophetic vision.[30]

1. The Nature of the Basileia (Kingdom) Movement of Jesus and His Companions: Its Gender Makeup, Ideals, Realities

Following Schüssler Fiorenza, I reconstruct the movement[31] as egalitarian, in the sense that women as well as men were full members and active participants

---

28. McGinn, "Acts of Thecla," *Searching the Scriptures*, 2.801.

29. Meier, *Marginal Jew*, 2. 657–59.

30. T. Ilan, "In the Footsteps of Jesus: Jewish Women in a Jewish Movement," *Transformative Encounters*, 134–35. Elisha is called mad in 2 Kings 9:11. See also C. B. Ubieta, "Mary Magdalene and the Seven Demons in Social-Scientific Perspective," *Transformative Encounters*, 203–23; she discusses possession as indirect protest and rebellion strategy of the marginal, as connected with sexual values and gender roles (using the work of I. M. Lewis, C. Kessler, M. Douglas, E. Dio-Bleichmar). Ubieta points out that the number seven points to previous unsuccessful treatment (see Luke 11:24–26, on partial and ultimately unsuccessful healing). She thinks that Mary Magdalene's exorcism by Jesus was historical; by it he reinstated her into her kinship and larger community group, further affirming that she was correct in her protest against society, and introducing her into his group, "where followers lived according to a more kinship-oriented and egalitarian *ethos*" (222). My own tendency is to be more suspicious of Luke, who may present her exorcism as her integration into the patriarchal social order and use it as a means of silencing her memory.

31. On the necessity of a shift of focus away from the historical Jesus to the movement of which he was a part, see Schüssler Fiorenza, *Politics of Interpretation*, 20–25.

(though they are not clearly depicted as such in the canonical Gospels), and that there was an implied, semi-articulated ideal of equality acted upon and struggled toward (which can be detected in the texts). Schüssler Fiorenza speaks of an initial praxis of coequal discipleship and of struggle. She sees the liberatory traces of this utopian moment[32] and ideal leaving traces which remain as a promise for the future. I understand "future" here as the period after the death of Jesus, as well as subsequent centuries. The traces are not remnants of a pristine origin to be contrasted with a corrupt "foil," a move rightly criticized as open to exploitation.[33] The vision or ideal seeks authorization in human need, rather than in sacred scripture or a sacred history. But it draws on the long and broad tradition of prophetic critique, involving internal critique. Jesus did not explicitly attack the power structures that create injustice and oppression, but implicitly subverted them "by envisioning a different future and different human relationships on the grounds that *all* persons in Israel are created and elected by the gracious goodness of Jesus' Sophia-God"[34] Historically this was not a unique, privileged moment of original perfection, not a totally nonkyriarchical community, egalitarian without conflict. Rather, it was egalitarian *in* conflict: men and women in community, struggling. Precisely because it was imperfect, incomplete, unfinished, indeterminate, it is a resource for the future.[35] "[W]e are all in transition to an equality no one has ever known."[36]

This was an emancipatory movement, resisting the domination of Roman and probably Temple establishments, focused on intertwined political, economic, social and theological issues, revolutionary in Segal's sense.[37] It can be reconstructed

---

32. See E. Castelli, "The *Ekklēsia* of Women and/as Utopian Space: Locating the Work of Elisabeth Schüssler Fiorenza in Feminist Utopian Thought," *Wisdom on the Cutting Edge* (ed. J. Schaberg and A. Bach; New York: Continuum, forthcoming). J. J. Collins ("Models of Utopia in the Biblical Tradition," 'A *Wise and Discerning Mind*' [Providence: Brown University Press, 2000] 67) stresses that in the biblical tradition the vision of utopia is concretely embodied in a specific land, is not primarily a no-place. "Even in the new creation [in Revelation], the specificity of place persists" (66).

33. King, "Afterword: Voices of the Spirit," *Women Preachers and Prophets*, 340.

34. Schüssler Fiorenza, *In Memory of Her*, 142. In the introduction to the tenth anniversary edition (1994) she explains further the framework, premise and focus of her feminist critical reconstruction of Christian beginnings (see especially xxiv–xxv, xxx–xxxi). See also the essays in *Discipleship of Equals* (New York: Crossroad, 1998).

35. See J. P. Meier, *A Marginal Jew* (New York: Doubleday, 2001) 3.250–51 and n. 121, pp. 283–84. He can only understand egalitarianism as a lack of order and structure. He sees that the outreach to *all* Israel had "a certain egalitarian thrust to it. But as the inner circle of the Twelve as well as George Orwell reminds us, in an egalitarian society all are equal, but some are more equal than others. The eschatological program of Jesus did not envision the Israel of the future, any more than the Israel of the past, as totally devoid of structure and order." (251). Contrast R. A. Horsley, *Jesus and the Spiral of Violence* (San Francisco: Harper & Row, 1987) 209–84, especially 231–45. Egalitarianism is about working toward and in what Saiving calls "structures that will oppress no one" ("Our Bodies/Our Selves," 117).

36. G. Steinem, "A Great Woman Who Was Everywoman," *New York Times* Op-Ed, Saturday, July 21, 2001, A27.

37. A. Segal, *Rebecca's Children* (Cambridge: Harvard, 1986) 68–95.

as a particular form of the diverse *basileia tou theou* (Kingdom of God) movement in Second Temple Judaism.[38] John the Baptist's movement, the Therapeutae, sporadic Zealot-type groups,[39] apocalyptic conventicles,[40] Pharisaic *havuroth*, and perhaps the Qumran community may be considered other forms. To explore the motives that led Jewish women to join the movement of Jesus and his companions, or any of these movements, we have to look to "the issues that engaged Jews of both genders in the first century (the oppressive presence of the Romans, the corruption of the Herodians, the purity and efficacy of the temple) and to the pressures on women, Jewish and otherwise, to conform to ancient understandings of gender."[41] I think we must also look to the distinctive emphases of Jewish apocalyptic/wisdom texts and traditions. To ignore the theological dimension of a group is as unsound historically as focusing only on it, or as ignoring or focusing only on political and socio-economic issues.

The argument that the movement of Jesus and his companions was egalitarian is not an argument from silence. It is difficult to find more than hints of egalitarianism in the androcentric canonical Gospels, but those hints are present. Women were clearly members of the movement. Table fellowship was inclusive.[42] Some women were with Jesus in Galilee and followed him up to Jerusalem; others seem to have been members who did not travel with him (Martha and Mary [Luke 10]). Some may have travelled at times with him, stayed home at other times. If Horsley is right that this was a social revolution beginning with the renewal of village society,[43] those who remained domiciled agents in villages may have played as primary a role as travelling missionaries.[44] Married women and mothers (Mary the mother of James the younger and of Joses [Mark 15:40], the mother of the sons of Zebedee [Matt 27:56], Joanna the wife of Herod's steward Chusa [Luke 8:3], Mary [the wife?] of Clopas [John 19:25]) and women not identified by such ties — perhaps single or divorced[45] or widowed (Mary Magdalene, Salome [Mark

---

38. Schüssler Fiorenza, *Miriam's Child*, 131.

39. On models for women revolutionaries, T. Ilan points to the women in 1–2–4 Maccabees, and Judith (*Integrating Women*, 77; cf. Schüssler Fiorenza, *In Memory of Her*, 115–18).

40. On Vielhauer's thesis that apocalypses were coventicle literature, some support is possible n. the case of Qumran and the Enoch literature, but this should not be generalized (J. J. Collins, *The Apocalyptic Imagination* [2d ed.; Grand Rapids: Eerdmans, 1998] 38).

41. Kraemer, "Jewish Women and Christian Origins," 46; K. E. Corley, "The Egalitarian Jesus: A Christian Myth of Origins," *Forum* 1 (1998) 291–325. A.-J. Levine stresses that women may have followed Jesus "not because of a problem with the types of Judaism available in Judea and the Galilee, but for one of many other reasons (e.g., his healings, interpretation of Torah, personal welcoming, charisma)" ("Lilies of the Field and Wandering Jews: Biblical Scholarship, Women's Roles, and Social Location," *Transformative Encounters* (ed. I. R. Kitzberger; Leiden: Brill, 2000) 332.

42. K. Corley, *Private Women, Public Meals* (Peabody, Mass.: Hendrickson, 1993) 185.

43. Horsley, *Spiral*, 324.

44. Against A.-J. Levine, "Women in the Q Communit(ies)," *Women and Christian Origins,* 157.

45. Some Jewish women in Roman Palestine divorced their husbands (See J. J. Collins, "Marriage, Divorce and Family in Second Temple Judaism," *Families in Ancient Israel* (ed. L. Perdue et al.; Louisville: Westminster/John Knox, 1997) 119–21.

15:40], Martha and Mary of Bethany [Luke 10; John 11–12]) — were all included in the movement.[46] The Syro-Phoenician woman and the Samaritan woman of John 4 indicate that women were central figures in the early Christian outreach to Gentiles. "It would seem then that the founder of Christianity believed that neither training nor sex was needed for this profession. . . . The prime qualification was some rare gift which in those early days was bestowed capriciously upon carpenters and fishermen, and upon women also."[47]

Both women and men were healed, and the experience and labor of both is used in Jesus' parables and sayings. No sexist or misogynist statement is attributed to him. Some of his sayings can be understood as directly anti-patriarchal: for examples, the prohibition against calling anyone on earth "father" (Matt 23:8) and the call to a different kind of family (Mark 3:35).[48] Other sayings, some from the sayings source Q, criticize patriarchal domination radically, even though from an androcentric perspective.[49] Jesus spoke of the divine "Sophia" as well as "Father."[50] He understood himself and his companions and predecessors as sent by Sophia (Luke 7:35; Luke 11:49; 13:34; Matt 11:28–39).[51]

The Christian Testament provides no evidence Jesus was an outspoken feminist in the contemporary sense, or that he was unique for his time and place in his treatment of women. As Plaskow puts it, "He is never portrayed as arguing for women's prerogatives, demanding changes in particular restrictive laws that affect women, or debating the Pharisees on the subject of gender." Without the bias of anti-Judaism, and without selectively negative and anachronistic use of rabbinic texts to depict first-century C.E. conditions, he can be seen as "simply a Jewish man who treated women like people . . . [who] acted respectfully toward women without ever explicitly defending their cause. . . . [H]is attitudes toward women would represent not a victory *over* early Judaism but a possibility *within* it." Reading the Christian Testament texts as reflecting part of the continuum of first-century Jewish practice with regard to women, "[t]he absence of any overt challenge to Jesus' treatment of or teachings about women suggests that his relation to women and gender norms might not have been so different from

---

46. Against Kraemer, "Jewish Women and Christian Origins," *Women and Christian Origins*, 45: "Missing among the women portrayed as Jesus' close disciples and supporters are married women with husbands and children." The Jewish women in the Jesus movement "are represented as disproportionately unmarried, widowed, childless, possessed, and otherwise physically afflicted."

47. Woolf, *Three Guineas*, 122.

48. See R. A. Horsley, *Sociology and the Jesus Movement* (2d ed.; New York: Continuum, 1994) 123 on the non-literalistic interpretation of these texts.

49. L. Schottroff ("Itinerant Prophetesses: A Feminist Analysis of the Sayings Source Q," *Behind the Gospels: Current Studies on Q* [ed. R. A. Piper; Leiden: Brill, 1995] 354).

50. Schüssler Fiorenza, *In Memory of Her*, 140–54, 132–35.

51. M. Hengel, "Jesus als messianischer Lehrer der Weisheit und die Anfange der Christologie," *Sagesse et Religion* (Paris: Presses universitaires de France, 1979) 147–88; Schüssler Fiorenza, *Miriam's Child*, 139–43.

the relations of his contemporaries."[52] This does not negate but highlights the egalitarianism of the movement, as it contrasts with later understandings of gender relations in patristic Christianity and rabbinic Judaism.

The possibility of egalitarianism *within* Judaism is rooted in the belief, never fully actualized, that the "entire people, and not only a spiritual, intellectual, or clerical elite, are God's children and consecrated" to God. "Hence, biblical religion is for the people as a whole," as Tigay puts it. "The entire citizenry" is to be trained in the nature of justice, and must know its history of freedom from enslavement, and its own rights and duties.[53] Deut 31:9–13 (cf. Josh 8:34–35; Neh 8) commands the public reading of the teaching of Moses every seven years before all the people, "all Israel" — men, women, children, and resident aliens; in talmudic times this was expanded into a year-round system of reading the Torah aloud in the synagogue. Private teaching in the family is urged in Deut 4:9–10; 5:1; 6:6–9, 20–25; 11:18–20 and elsewhere. Oral presentation was the primary method used from the time of Moses down to the invention of printing. Deut 33:4 calls the teaching "a possession for the assembly of Jacob." Because of the androcentrism and patriarchialism of the traditions, and male control of their presentation and interpretation, it might be argued that such education functioned to keep women subordinate;[54] but it must have had leveling power as well, with its focus on "the interior life" and vision of a just community.[55] Whether or not women served as leaders in Galilean village assemblies, they probably participated actively in them and made their own contributions.[56] Accepting this as a possibility *within* Judaism, within the heart of the tradition, does not to my mind make women insiders. Rather, it makes them outsiders in Woolf's sense. It acknowledges their right to trespass. "Let us trespass at once. Literature is no one's private ground.... Let us trespass freely and fearlessly and find our own way

---

52. J. Plaskow, "Anti-Judaism in Feminist Christian Interpretation," *Searching the Scriptures*, 1.119–20, 123–24, 126. She is arguing that Jesus has been seen as a "feminist" only on the basis of a negative view of Judaism.

53. J. F. Tigay, Excursus 28, "The Writing and Reading of the Teaching," *Deuteronomy* (Philadelphia: The Jewish Publication Society, 1996) 498–502. "There are few, if any, counterparts elsewhere in the ancient world to the idea of educating the entire people in religious and civil law.... The idea that the entire people must be instructed in God's law eventually led to the intellectualization of Judaism" and the democratization of leadership. "No other religion is so dependent on all of its adherents being learned" (500–501). Such learning, however, has always been at least partially subject to the control and management of a male elite, whose interests are reflected and promoted in religious and civil law.

54. We have only tantalizing glimpses of women's attendance at synagogues, and women's own religious practices, attitudes and theologies in the first century C.E. (such as Acts 16:16: "On the sabbath day we went outside the gate by the river, where we supposed there was a place of prayer; and we sat down and spoke to the women who had gathered there"). See below, on the Therapeutae (p. 267).

55. King ("Afterword," 341) is clear that "the interior life is not to be confused with a modern individualist ethic."

56. Horsley, *Galilee*, 237.

for ourselves . . . teach ourselves how to read and write, how to preserve and how to create."[57]

Mark and Matthew obscure the women's roles by introducing them late in the story, at the crucifixion. Luke mentions them earlier, but 8:1–3 is puzzling. While the women's "service" may have originally indicated a powerful leadership position, it is most often read as casting them in the roles of financial supporters or servants caring for the physical needs of the men, confining them in private rather than public roles. Schottroff is right, in my opinion, to judge that Luke's "idea that wealthy women were close to Jesus does not originate from otherwise lost traditions of the Jesus movement but from later experiences of the young church in the cities of the Roman Empire outside Palestine, which Luke projects back into Jesus' time (see Acts 16:14–15; 17:4, 12)."[58] The conventional view that Jesus surrounded himself with twelve men,[59] and the restriction of the term "disciple" to men in the Gospels further restricts the readers' view of women.[60] "For one often catches a glimpse of [women] in the lives of the great, whisking away into the background, concealing, I sometimes think, a wink, a laugh, perhaps a tear."[61] "They were certainly . . . ardent listeners to Jesus preaching and teaching" but not disciples, says Gerhardsson.[62] Luke/Acts characteristically depicts women as subordinate, passive, and silent.[63] The Gospel of Matthew opens with the story of an endangered woman, Mary, whose story is told, however, from the perspective of interest in the decision of Joseph. Its focus on Peter and its final commission of the eleven in Galilee leave no room for women at the center.

D'Angelo observes that neither the Gospels of John or Mark — the two Gospels often judged most open to women's traditions — "addresses the issue of gender or foregrounds the participation of women in any coherent or comprehensive way. Neither of the authors or the communities behind them appears to have made the status of women any central focus in their concerns. Nor it is the case that either narrative reflects gender practices that were unheard of or even challenging for their time. . . . Mark and John do seem to accept, indeed to assume,

---

57. V. Woolf, "The Leaning Tower," *A Woman's Essays: Selected Essays* (New York: Penguin, 1992) 1.159–78, lecturing to a working-class audience about how literature will survive the war. See Marder, *The Measure of Life*, 291–92.

58. L. Schottroff, *Let the Oppressed Go Free* (Westminster/John Knox, 1993) 92. Horsley (*Sociology*, 121) notes that people of considerable means would have been the exception even in urban communities. Contrast Meier, *A Marginal Jew*, 3.76.

59. On the twelve as appointed by Jesus during his ministry, and the symbolic meaning of twelve as restoration of the twelve tribes, see Horsley, *Spiral*, 199–208. Horsley interprets their function of judging in Matt 19:29 in terms of liberating and effecting justice. Sir 48:10 lists this restoration as one of the tasks of the returning Elijah.

60. See D'Angelo, "Reconstructing 'Real' Women, 113. She thinks that the verb *diēkonoun* used of Mary Magdalene in Luke 8:1–3 means that they were remembered later as *diakonoi*, like Phoebe.

61. Woolf, *Room*, 44–45.

62. Gerhardsson, "Mark and the Female Witnesses," 219.

63. J. Schaberg, "Commentary on Luke," *Women's Biblical Commentary* (ed. C. Newsom and S. Ringe; Philadelphia: Westminster/John Knox, 1992).

the participation of women in communal life in ways that *would* [emphasis mine] cause dissension, become marginalized, and eventually be eliminated and to offer at least some vivid and dynamic representations of women."[64] My treatment of John 20 will involve an argument that the status of Mary Magdalene was a central focus of some in the community behind that Gospel. The Christian Testament *already* provides ample evidence that the participation of women in the pre-gospel and gospel periods caused dissension, that women were being marginalized and their traditions in process of being eliminated and distorted in the earliest communities; evidence, in other words, of struggle. The Gospels' lack of treatment of gender issues and their depictions of women is part of that struggle. Schüssler Fiorenza's reconceptualizing of biblical studies in rhetorical terms is an insistance that "any historical reconstruction must observe the prescriptive, projective, and perspectival character of its source-texts and artifacts.... Rather than assume that the kyriocentric text is a reflection or record of historical reality, scholars must challenge not only the text's but also their own ideological practices of erasure and marginalization."[65]

In her "reconstruction of 'real' women" behind the "(re)presentations of women" in the Gospels, D'Angelo sees the movement connected with Jesus as one of shared prophecy, based in the shared experiences and shared teaching of co-workers, rather than based only in his teaching.[66] Others besides Jesus may have had powers of exorcism and healing.[67] Nonhierarchical equality in the Spirit would have been expressed in alternating leadership and partnership.[68] The

---

64. D'Angelo, "(Re)presentation of Women," 145.
65. Schüssler Fiorenza, Introduction to tenth anniversary edition of *In Memory of Her*, xxi; cf. Schüssler Fiorenza, *Rhetoric and Ethic* (Minneapolis: Fortress, 1999). I am attempting to work with the sophisticated methodological approach she continues to develop.
66. D'Angelo, "Reconstructing 'Real' Women," *Women and Christian Origins*, 122–25. Though he does not mention her work, Meier would certainly classify it with those who, in spite of the "dearth of data" (he is examining later rabbinic traditions about rabbis teaching women), offer "fanciful hypotheses about the precise way in which women participated in the first generation Christian mission; here we have a primary example of 'historical imagination' which is almost all imagination and no history" (*Marginal Jew*, 3. n. 122, p. 119). In his mind, an excess of imagination mars the work of most women scholars he does mention (Ricci, Munro), and even that of some men (like Horsley, n. 115, p. 117). Meier himself grants that "devoted female followers" of Jesus were viewed and treated by him as disciples; but they were not given the title of disciple because the Evangelists may be "somewhat inhibited" by (1) the fact that there are no call narratives of women (for "whatever reason — androcentric bias or just the chance fluctuations of oral tradition," neither of which he examines); and (2) the philological point that there was no feminine form in Hebrew or Aramaic of the word disciple (73–80). Focused on "a narrow question of historical reconstruction: were the female followers of Jesus thought of or called disciples during the ministry of the historical Jesus, "No attempt is made here to address the larger questions of the historical reality or the theological picture of women in the Gospels or in the NT in general — to say nothing of the still larger project of a feminist hermeneutic of the NT data" (n 113, p. 116). This is a good example of historical reconstruction attempted within an unexamined framework of bias.
67. Horsley, *Sociology*, 140, on Q 10:9. On rabbinic references to women who practiced the art of healing, see Ilan, "In the Footsteps of Jesus," 129. "[I]f Jesus was primarily a healer he could have received some formal education in a professional guild of healers, many of which were women."
68. See Schüssler Fiorenza, *In Memory of Her*, xxxi–xxxii.

members may have thought of themselves as wisdom teachers, prophets of Sophia reaching out to the oppressed and willing to pay the price for that lifework, suffering as her representatives (Luke 11:49).[69] In such a reconstruction, teaching in words and actions centered not on Jesus himself, but on the *basileia* of God, which Schüssler Fiorenza understands as the radically democratic alternative to all systems of domination. This *basileia* was experienced in the context of common meals, healing events, and religious reflection of the community.[70] Jesus himself is reconceived as a man who could learn from and with women. With the death of Jesus and belief in his resurrection, there was a shift in focus, from the *basileia* to Jesus himself.

One result of such a reasonable presumption of egalitarianism is that whatever is argued that the male disciples heard and learned during the ministry, the women may also be thought to have heard and learned.[71] Another result is an openness to the idea of the real participation of members. Jesus and others can be seen as resisting the authoritarian dynamic associated with a charismatic leader whose followers would be dependent and helpless without him.[72] In such a movement a person like Mary Magdalene could be seen as a contributor, partner, and leader, not simply a follower. She may have been Jesus' companion, or his elder, perhaps his teacher or predecessor, in a relationship that may or may not have been sexual.[73] She may also have been seen as his successor.

The community of men and women was not without parallel in other Jewish contexts of the period. The Therapeutae in Egypt seem to have included women and men on an equal or near equal basis, and both may have shared fully in the ecstatic celebrations. Unlike the *basileia* movement around Jesus, however, their scripture study did not, as far as we know, lead them to lives of social involvement.[74] Kraemer remarks that for Philo "the inclusion of women was facilitated by the fact that they were of relative old age (probably menopausal), childless, apparently virgins, and probably never married. That is, while possessing the bodies of women, they were in all significant respects, male."[75] For Philo, perhaps, but his information is not always reliable. As for the communities connected with Qum-

---

69. See my article "Major Midrashic Traditions in Wisdom 1,1–6, 25," *JJS* 13 (1986) 75–101, for the suggestion that in this passage about the fate of the righteous one there is a confluence of traditions from Daniel 2, 7, 12, as well as from 1 Enoch and Isaiah. Hengel ("Jesus als messianischer Lehrer der Weisheit," 175) thinks the Wisdom of Solomon, which uniquely combines Palestinian apocalyptic traditions and sapiential background with Hellenistic vocabulary, is the pre-Christian Jewish key to understanding post-Easter christology.

70. Schüssler Fiorenza, *Miriam's Child*, 90.

71. Contrast Gundry, *Mark*, 998 and others, who think the women at the tomb would not have heard of resurrection predictions.

72. See R. Fenn, *The Death of Herod* (Cambridge: Cambridge University Press, 1992) 145–56.

73. D'Angelo,"Reconstructing 'Real' Women," 123–25.

74. Philo, *On the Contemplative Life*. See R. A. Horsley, "Spiritual Marriage with Sophia," *VC* 33 (1979) 40–41.

75. Kraemer, "Women's Judaism(s)," 70.

ran, Schuller holds that from a feminist perspective women's full membership may be presumed, in the absence of evidence to the contrary,[76] and in the presence of evidence that may support this.[77] At the present time, information about the female skeletons and other archaeological finds from the site is inadequate and confusing. Of the 43 skeletons excavated by DeVaux, it is debated how many are female (arguments range from 1 to 16), how many are of more recent burial, and whether the Northern and Southern cemeteries are to be included; it is debated also whether the graves excavated by Steckoll are to be taken into account. The full physical/anthropological report of Susan Sheridan is not yet published. Further, the items listed by DeVaux have not been adequately studied.[78] Kraemer argues that the extraordinary concern for ritual purity, and the misogynist, gender-specific and sometimes gender-exclusive language makes her wonder how and why adult, premenopausal women would have been a part of such a group.[79] But women have ways of ignoring and moving around what oppresses them in highly androcentric systems. Schuller wisely holds that it may be premature to draw too many conclusions at this stage.[80] As for other groups, Josephus says Simon ben Giora had "a following of women" which included his wife and her female servants (*J.W.* 4.504–6; see 538–44). No rabbinic sources portray women as disciples in earlier, proto-rabbinic circles.[81] But the fact that there is debate in those sources over whether and under what circumstances women should study or be taught Torah shows that women were indeed studying and being taught. *M. Sotah* 3:4 enshrines a debate between Ben Azzai and R. Eliezer about teaching a daughter Torah; cf. *m. Nedarim* 4:3 on teaching scripture to one's sons and daughters. Tal Ilan argues that women were members, not just supporters, of the Pharisaic movement, and that they participated in the activities of the Pharisaic table-fellowships, the *havurot*.[82]

Our gradually increasing knowledge of Jewish women's lives and options indicates the vitality in some circles of the egalitarian impulse within Judaism, based in

76. This is the argument of E. Schuller, *Women in the Dead Sea Scrolls, Methods of Investigation of the Dead Sea Scrolls and the Khirbet Qumran Site* (ed. M. O. Wise; New York: New York Academy of Sciences, 1994) 115–31; See Josephus, *J.W.* 2.160–61; CD 7:6–7; 1QSa 1:4; 1QM 7:4–5;; L. Schiffman, "Women in the Scrolls," *Reclaiming the Dead Sea Scrolls* (Philadelphia: Jewish Publication Society, 1994) 127–43.

77. See J. M. Baumgarten, "4Q502, Marriage or Golden Age Ritual?" *JJS* 34 (1983) 125–35. The fact that there were 8 copies of 4QInstruction at Qumran needs to be addressed; it is almost uniformly positive about women, and fragment 2 addresses a woman.

78. See the papers given by J. Magness, B. G. Wright, M. J. Bernstein, A. Baumgarten at the Qumran Section of the SBL 2000 meeting in Nashville, on the theme Women and Children at Qumran and Related Sites.

79. Kraemer, "Jewish Women and Women's Judaism(s) at the Beginning of Christianity," 69.

80. Response to papers listed in n. 41, SBL 2000. Audio tapes of this session are available from ACTS, Town & Country MO 63017.

81. Kraemer, "Women's Judaism(s)," 71.

82. Tal Ilan, "Paul and Pharisee Women," *Wisdom on the Cutting Edge*, festschrift for E. Schüssler Fiorenza (ed. J. Schaberg and A. Bach; New York: Continuum, forthcoming).

general on the covenantal tradition of Israel. But can more can be said about the source and motivation of the egalitarianism of this *basileia* movement of Jesus and his companions? Some scholars imagine egalitarianism springs from peasant life or from poverty. Crossan speaks of Jesus' "ideal of open or egalitarian commensality," of eating with outcasts and sinners, with "anyone," an "[o]pen commensality [that] profoundly negates distinctions and hierarchies between female and male, poor and rich, Gentile and Jew." This is not, Crossan thinks, a projection of contemporary democratic idealism anachronistically back onto the performance of the historical Jesus. Rather, "such egalitarianism stems not only from peasant Judaism, but, even more deeply, from peasant society as such."[83] However, even such a "romanticized vision of peasant life"[84] as this does not deal with gender inequities.[85] For Schottroff, "The different situation of women and men is not an issue in the Jesus movement of Palestine since experience is determined by the equality that poverty and the common hope of God's kingdom produce."[86] However, although poverty alone may produce an equality of hardship, work and suffering, sometimes a sense of solidarity, it also produces distinct forms of gender oppression. Corley places Jesus' movement with its egalitarian ethic and inclusive meal practice "within some kind of progressive Jewish framework" in Hellenized Palestine.[87]

We can be more precise than this. Egalitarianism is a common and constant characteristic of apocalyptic movements throughout history,[88] and of wisdom communities like the Therapeutae.[89] Apocalypticism characteristically promotes egalitarianism and is motivated by the desire for it: "People who join apocalyptic groups feel deprived of something meaningful or valuable to the society but unavailable to all people equally."[90] Allison reluctantly thinks Jesus' program "may have promoted egalitarianism.... [I]f Jesus may have had a special place for women within his movement (although this is not quite as obvious to me as it seems to be to others), one could relate this to the special attraction of females to many millennial movements" (referring to the works of Cohn, Schwarz, Shepperson, Worsley).[91] Kraemer sees the presence of women

83. Crossan, *Historical Jesus*, 361–63.
84. Corley, "Feminist Myths of Christian Origins," *Reimagining Christian Origins*, 60.
85. See Crossan's citations from the works of James Scott (*Historical Jesus*, 263–64).
86. Schottroff, *Let the Oppressed*, 97.
87. Corley, "Feminist Myths," 60; cf. "Jesus' Table Practice: Dining with 'Tax Collectors and Sinners,' including Women," *SBL Seminar Papers* (Atlanta: Scholars Press, 1993) 445.
88. See the many examples in E. Weber, *Apocalypses: Prophesies, Cults, and Millennial Beliefs through the Ages* (Cambridge: Harvard, 1999); androgynous and gynocentric images and ideals are common also (see pp. 114, 162–63, 173, 199 and elsewhere).
89. Schüssler Fiorenza, *Miriam's Child*, 134–35, following D. Georgi.
90. Segal, *Rebecca's Children*, 71. Besides deprivation of material needs or spiritual status, there are other factors of anxiety, leadership and the propensity to interpret events in a religious framework.
91. D. C. Allison, *Jesus of Nazareth Millenarian Prophet* (Minneapolis: Fortress, 1998) 63; n. 238, p. 64, 86; cf. 108–10. His depiction of the movement, however, is androcentric ("They decided to abandon wives and businesses" [215; contrast 147]).

in the Jesus movement is a consequence of an ascetic lifestyle fostered by an apocalyptic ethic.[92]

I see the movement as one in which Jewish wisdom elements are part of an apocalyptic stance.[93] Its theology is an "Apocalyptic-Wisdom theology."[94] Jewish wisdom and apocalyptic "cannot be cleanly separated from one another" in holistic thinking about the past; they have a "generic compatibility."[95] Apocalypticism and mysticism are also "inextricably bound" in first-century Judaism, "united phenomenologically."[96] Thought and ethical action are intertwined and influence each other. The aim is to transform human community, not simply improve the lives of individuals.

A division between Hellenistic, non-Jewish wisdom and Jewish apocalyptic has become common in contemporary Historical Jesus research, one group of scholars (which includes Crossan, Mack, Funk, Scott) seeing Jesus and the members of the movement as practitioners of radical, pragmatic, subversive wisdom and common sense, and the other (including A. Schweitzer, E. P. Sanders, Allison, Schüssler Fiorenza, Horsley) seeing them as apocalyptic prophets.[97] I find the basic outlook of the second group more persuasive primarily because of its understanding of the Judaism of this movement within a tradition of prophetic critique and apocalyptic vision.[98] D'Angelo rightly notes that if the movement is considered a cyniclike movement of sages, Mary Magdalene's "role in the resurrection narratives must be regarded as later legend or as part of the apocalyptic transformation of the movement."[99] But understanding the movement as apocalyptic more readily ac-

---

92. R. S. Kraemer, *Her Share of the Blessings* (New York: Oxford, 1992) 138–41; cf. "Women's Judaism(s)," 71.

93. See J. J. Collins, *Seers, Sybils and Sages in Hellenistic-Roman Judaism* (New York: Brill, 1997) chapters 19, 23; *The Apocalyptic Imagination*, chapter 9. See above, note 69.

94. Schüssler Fiorenza, *Miriam's Child*, 135. Schottroff ("Itinerant Prophetesses," 347–60) in her critique of Schüssler Fiorenza's work looks only at the Wisdom literature, in which she does not find either criticism of patriarchy or good news for the poor.

95. G. W. E. Nickelsburg, "Wisdom and Apocalypticism in Early Judaism," *SBL Seminar Papers* (Atlanta: Scholars Press, 1994) 717, 729; J. J. Collins, "Wisdom, Apocalypticism, and Generic Compatibility," *In Search of Wisdom* (ed. L. Perdue et al.; Philadelphia: Westminster, 1993). Cf. A. Segal, *Paul the Convert* (New Haven: Yale, 1990) 110, 160; R. A. Horsley, "Wisdom is Justified by All Her Children," *SBL Seminar Papers* (Atlanta: Scholars Press, 1994) 733–51; A. J. Levine, "Women in the Q Communit(ies)," 154. In contrast, some argue that Wisdom material was only combined with the apocalyptic Son of Man tradition in the final redaction of Q (J. S. Kloppenborg, "'Easter Faith' and the Sayings Gospel Q," *Semeia* 49 [1990]; Perkins, "Resurrection," 426).

96. Segal, *Paul*, 158, 165. "Mysticism in first-century Judaism was apocalyptic, revealing not meditative truths of the universe but the disturbing news that God was about to bring judgment" (34).

97. See M. Borg, "Portraits of Jesus in Contemporary North American Scholarship," *HTR* 84 (1991) 1–22 for discussion of the 1980s views of Sanders, Mack, Borg, Schüssler Fiorenza, Horsley.

98. See S. Heschel, *Abraham Geiger and the Jewish Jesus* (Chicago: University of Chicago, 1998) 233–35, on the work of Perrin, Mack, Crossan, Borg and Meier as part of the trend within American scholarship which "continues to de-Judaize Jesus," in contrast to the work of E. P. Sanders. Cf. Arnal, "Markings," 308–16 on the Judaism of Jesus and the issue of apocalypticism.

99. D'Angelo, "Reconstructing 'Real' Women," 123–24; cf. A.-J. Levine, "Women in the Q Communit(ies) and Traditions," 154.

commodates not only a visionary Jesus, but a visionary Mary Magdalene: "It was perhaps her interpretations of the visions [that she had of him], her proclamations of their meaning, that laid the foundation for the new community."[100]

In calling this movement apocalyptic, I do not imply that its members were intellectuals, formally educated scholars, or people of means, or that they dedicated themselves to the study of texts or debate of ideas, or that they were non-activists or suicidal fanatics or escapists or fully egalitarian. But I do think familiarity with the prophetic and apocalyptic traditions, gained in the ordinary course of Jewish life and synagogue attendance, and intelligent, creative application of these traditions energized the mostly-peasant movement. The context of oppression in Roman times united the whole people, peasants and intellectuals, and lived experience of the *basileia* made apocalyptic relevant. In Horsley's terms, their "sense of fulfillment apparently heightened the sense of anticipation of the completion of that fulfillment or renewal."[101] This signals to me the balance between present experience and future vindication that J. J. Collins identified as characteristic of apocalyptic eschatology.[102] Horsley argues that Jesus' social revolution was not a program for elite wandering charismatics, sages or ascetics. Rather, Jesus envisioned a program of concrete socioeconomic cooperation and mutual care on the part of ordinary people in local Galilean villages. The passion, the political analysis, and the courage in face of death that this program demanded are rooted in an apocalyptic orientation and motivation. The apocalyptic imagination is able to remember, to creatively envision, and to demystify.[103]

As in the apocalyptic outlook of the book of Daniel, there was in this movement insistence on taking a sociopolitical, ethical stand in hope of and faith in final justice. Eschatology was not stressed at the expense of ethics, and violence was not an option.[104] Horsley argues that we should assume given movements

---

100. D'Angelo, "Reconstructing 'Real' Women," 124–25. Note that she says nothing of the empty tomb.

101. Horsley, *Sociology*, 126; he sees this in some cases at least. For Horsley, "Such an excitement over or anticipation of fulfillment may be operative also in apocalyptic literature, but it would not necessarily have taken apocalyptic form or adopted apocalyptic perspective and language. . . . [It] could also find adequate expression without an elaborately developed 'Christology' and probably was not what has been conceived of by scholars as 'eschatology.' " (125–26). Doctrine-making and literalistic reading/hearing/speculation about the End are not what I have in mind here either.

102. See above, pp. 256–57.

103. Horsley, *Spiral*, 129–45, 143–44.

104. Human-initiated physical violence is eschewed in Daniel, Revelation, and in the apocalyptic material in the Gospels, though violent imagery is used. On the stance of nonviolent resistance even at the cost of martyrdom in Daniel and T. Moses, and the stance in some Qumran literature which is not one of absolute pacifism but of vengeance exacted on the Day of Revenge, see Collins, *Apocalyptic Imagination*, 114, 131, 170. See T. Pippin and G. Aichele, *Violence, Utopia and the Kingdom of God: Fantasy and Ideology in the Bible* (London: Routledge, 1998) on biblical forms of "verbal violence, language which disfigures, dehumanizes, or erases altogether the human as object and as subject," "mental or spiritual violence caused by hatred or oppression" (7). In his preface to this volume, J. Zipes remarks, "As fantasy, the Bible documents why violence and suffering occur in the name of God, and in this documentation, it proves (thankfully) to be a faulty text" (xi).

were not apocalyptically oriented and motivated "unless there is some compelling evidence to suggest otherwise." For him, it is primarily the sense of struggle between demonic and divine forces that provides such evidence for the Jesus movement. "Precisely because Jewish demonology reflected concrete political-economic conditions, precisely because more generally the apocalyptic perspective was rooted in the concrete historical circumstances, the belief in demons and confidence in God's ultimate deliverance provided an important social condition of and for the emergence and effectiveness of (at least some involved in) the Jesus movement."[105] The compelling evidence for me is the interpretation of the empty tomb in terms of predictions about the Son of Man and resurrection of the dead martyr. Here also — perhaps here above all — we see the apocalyptic perspective rooted in concrete historical circumstances.[106]

I regard the figure of the Son of Man (or better, the Human One)[107] as central to the egalitarian imagination and ideals of this *basileia* movement even before the death of Jesus,[108] and central to earliest understandings of his fate and that of the righteous. I think Jesus anticipated his own *and* a corporate suffering and vindication *as* (an aspect of, a member of) the Human One.[109] A corporate understanding of the figure, rooted in Daniel's link between it and the holy ones/people of the holy ones of the Most High, seems to me to lie behind the strange flexibility of reference that is so confusing, and has led to awkward classifications and historical stagings and layerings of Christian Testament Human One sayings.

Already in Daniel, this link may indicate that an either/or approach to meaning is not the best one. The allusiveness, reticence and deliberate opacity of the visions should be honored.[110] The Danielic figure is not exhausted or closed by identifying it as angelic, as Michael, any more than it is exhausted or closed by seeing it as representative of the maskilim and the righteous.[111] The figure of the human one is inclusive, and the angel Michael is one of its aspects. The holy ones (a single community of angels and human beings) participate in this figure, which is the prototype and *telos* of righteous humanity, in whom Israel sees its own

---

105. Horsley, *Sociology*, 97, 99.

106. In some respects, apocalypticism is not "an utterly alien world-view" for those involved in liberation movements, even if they are academics (cf. Arnal, "Markings," 314).

107. See below, Appendix C.

108. In this I follow A. Y. Collins ("The Origin of the Designation"), though I do not always agree with her analysis of specific texts. See also A. J. B. Higgins, *The Son of Man in the Teaching of Jesus* (Cambridge: Cambridge University Press, 1980); M. E. Boring, *Sayings of the Risen Jesus: Christian Prophecy in the Synoptic Tradition* (Cambridge: Cambridge University Press, 1982) for the argument that Jesus himself was the origin of the Synoptic Son of Man tradition. The fact that these sayings are attributed to Jesus does not mean that their creative insight was his alone.

109. Contrast Perkins ("Resurrection," 430) who thinks pre-Markan tradition behind 14:62 suggests "Jesus anticipated his own *or* a corporate vindication as enthronement *with* [emphasis mine] an angelic figure like the Son of Man in Dan 7:13–14."

110. J. E. Goldingay, *Daniel* (Dallas: Word, 1989) 192, 91.

111. See J. J. Collins, *Apocalyptic Imagination*, 101–7 and *Daniel*, 72–79, 304–9 for surveys of interpretations of the Human One.

transcendence as a being alongside God.[112] Nor, though the figure can function as a symbol, is it merely symbolic, reduceable to a symbol.[113] Daniel 7 describes the persecution of Jews under Antiochus Epiphanes IV, and their vindication in the angelic-like figure of the Human One. The Human One in Daniel can represent, incorporate and be somehow more than the people suffering under Antiochus Epiphanes IV; it can represent, incorporate and be more than the *maskilim* who resist, make others righteous, and who will be vindicated and transformed in resurrection (12:1–3).

In this interpretive tradition, the Human One of the Christian Testament can (at least at a pre-Gospel[114] level) represent, incorporate and be more than Jesus; represent, incorporate and be more than the suffering righteous, those Matt 25:40 calls "the least of these who are members of my family" (NRSV). He is are not "identified with" the figure, because "identity" or selfhood is not conceived as individualistic. It is also not conceived as human in total and permanent distinction from the angelic, since the earthly and heavenly dimensions are to some extent permeable. The notion of the corporate Human One is not an anthropological one from "primitive" tribal cultures,[115] but to my mind a political, poetic one. To think of it as simply the close linking of "an extraordinary human being with a heavenly figure,"[116] is to omit the communal dimension of the figure which is a strong element in its tradition-history.[117] The term "corporate" is preferable to

112. A. Lacocque, *The Book of Daniel* (Atlanta: John Knox, 1979) 242, 131–13, 127–28.

113. Against Kanagaraj, 'Mysticism,' 172–77.

114. H. Odeberg, *The Fourth Gospel* (Uppsala: Almqvist & Wiksell, 1929; repr. Chicago: Argonaut, 1968) argued that in John the believers were included in the Son of Man. But R. Schnackenburg, *The Gospel according to St. John* (New York: Crossroad, 1968) 1.321 holds that such inclusive mysticism contradicts the Johannine soteriology which calls for faith in Jesus and attachment to him. Kanagaraj agrees: Odeberg's idea of "inclusiveness" in the Son of Man "does not complement John's emphasis on 'believing' and the subsequent ethical responsibility of Jesus' followers" ('Mysticism,' 190). In my opinion, the earlier understanding has been obscured and distorted by the Gospels' focus on Jesus.

115. The idea of "corporate personality" as used by H. W. Robinson and others is applied to an aspect of "ancient Hebrew thought" said to involve the ideas of corporate responsibility and representation and of "psychic community" or "psychical unity" (H. W. Robinson, *Corporate Personality in Ancient Israel* [Philadelphia: Fortress, 1964]). See the criticisms of J. W. Rogerson, "The Hebrew Conception of Corporate Personality: a Reexamination," *JTS* 21 (1970) 1–16. J. J. Collins ("Heavenly Representative," 113–14) notes that the idea of corporate personality has been rightly criticized by Rogerson and Mowinckel (*He That Cometh* [Nashville: Abingdon, 1955] 381) in so far as it implies this 'psychical unity' and rests on outdated and widely discredited anthropological theories; but he accepts Mowinckel's understanding of "representative unity." C. F. D. Moule, wrestling with what "the understanding and experience of Christ as corporate" might mean in the intellectual context of the twentieth century, speaks of Christ as an inclusive person, more than individual, more than representative; in short, like the omnipresent God (*The Origin of Christology* [Cambridge: Cambridge University Press, 1977] 47–96); cf. T. W. Manson, *The Teaching of Jesus* (Cambridge: Cambridge University Press, 1963; reprint of 1935 edition) 35, 227–28, 232–35.

116. A. Y. Collins, "Origin of the Designation," 155, on Moses (in Ezekiel the Tragedian and Philo's *On the Birth of Abel* 9–10), Melchizedek (in 11 QMelchizedek), and Enoch (in 1 Enoch 70–71).

117. See J. J. Collins, "The Heavenly Representative: the 'Son of Man' in the Similitudes of Enoch," *Ideal Figures in Ancient Judaism* (ed. G. W. E. Nickelsburg and J. J. Collins; Chico, Calif.: Scholars Press, 1980) 111–33. The Similitudes projects an ideal of righteousness onto a heavenly and mythological figure.

"representative" because "corporate" evokes "embodiment" and thus points toward the resurrection faith with which the figure is already linked in Daniel. C. H.
Dodd and C. F. D. Moule rightly think that the Christian Testament concept of
the Human One "challenges the mind to discover a doctrine of personality, which
will make conceivable this combination of the universal and the particular in a
single person."[118] Woolf challenges the mind in a similar way: "I wished to add
some remarks to this, on the mystical side of this solitude; how it is not oneself
but something in the universe that one's left with."[119] "I dig out beautiful caves
behind my characters; I think that gives exactly what I want; humanity, humor,
depth. The idea is that the caves shall connect & each comes to the daylight at
the present moment."[120]

The use of the figure of the Danielic Human One in the Christian Testament traditions is an exercise of what Fishbane calls "the exegetical imagination"
in which there is an interrelationship between exegesis and religious ideas or
values, and the process is connected with the renewal of the world. The ideal
is "an authentic doublevoicedness: to speak about the text with an intimacy
and understanding achieved through philological persistence, but in a voice
that is also shaped by the conceptions and concerns of one's own time and
place.... [T]heological attitudes or thoughts become practical theological actions
through forms of meditation or right attitude" and are also "embedded in public
practices."[121] "The exegetical imagination," then, has Scripture and current experience as its two points of departure, and in a reciprocal process that takes different
forms.[122] "Theological persistence" might be a better phrase for the movement
studied here than "philological persistence." This was not limited to a scribal class
or even to the literate (if any) of the companions of Jesus, and not limited to men.
Jesus and the other members of the movement understood the Book of Daniel to
refer to their own time and to the near future, and referred to the Human One
known on the basis of that text; they need not have been scribes or professional
interpreters of scripture to have known the major characters and basic contents
of the text.[123]

---

118. C. H. Dodd, *Interpretation of the Fourth Gospel*, 249; cited by Moule, *Origin*, 1.

119. Woolf, *Diary* 3.93. See *Mrs. Dalloway*, 11; Zwerdling, *Virginia Woolf and the Real World*, 281
comments on Clarissa's vision of the possibility of human unity and her own survival in it: "People
melt into each other, into the buildings, into the trees, into the air itself, and yet we do not lose the
feeling of Clarissa Dalloway thinking." He discusses the vision of community as an inalienable part of
Woolf's identity, and the emotional basis of her pacifism.

120. Woolf, *Diary*, 2.263.

121. M. Fishbane, *The Exegetical Imagination* (Cambridge: Harvard, 1998) ix, 2, 5, 7. See below,
p. 340.

122. G. Vermes (*Jesus the Jew* [Philadelphia: Fortress, 1973]) tries to categorize the Human One
sayings with regard to their relationship to Dan 7:13: those that cite it; allude to it indirectly; have
no link. A. Y. Collins argues that this is not satisfactory since none of the sayings is "exegetical in
form. They do not take Scripture as their point of departure" ("Origin of the Designation," 145).

123. Compare A. Y. Collins, "Origin of the Designation," 154.

My hypothesis is that the movement's integration of study and work and mystical experience[124] was preparation for the earliest attempts to make sense of the death of Jesus. In particular, very general predictions of the suffering and resurrection of the Human One could have been produced before the death of Jesus, given knowledge of the fate of John the Baptist, popular expectation of the martyrdom of prophets, and the experience of mounting establishment hostility. These would be simple statements of impending doom and vindication, evoked by and evoking Dan 7:13, 25; 12:2: the Human One would be delivered into the hands of enemies, and be raised "after three days," which I see as an interpretation of Daniel's measurement of the final suffering, "a time, two times and half a time."[125] One positive reason for attributing such Human One sayings to this period is the subsequent resurrection faith as articulated in empty tomb traditions.[126] The innovation of these general predictions would be in their stress on the idea of a suffering Human One not understood as other than the community of righteous. If the Similitudes of Enoch are contemporaneous or earlier,[127] the innovation moves beyond the ideal figure of the Human One found there, whose "withdrawal" parallels the suffering of the righteous ones, but who is not said to suffer or die. J. J. Collins holds that "The fact that [the Human One of the Similitudes] is preserved from their sufferings makes him a figure of pure power and glory and an ideal embodiment of the hopes of the persecuted righteous. The efficaciousness of the 'son of man' figure requires that he be conceived as other than the community, since he must possess the power and exaltation which they lack."[128] But if the Human One was understood in Jesus' *basileia* movement as more "corporate" than that — as really "corporate" — then a rethinking of power is involved, and a denial of such "otherness."

Such innovation would not rule out what Segal calls "the utter unexpectedness of Jesus' death and resurrection"[129] but it would help to explain how his death was

---

124. See Kanagaraj, '*Mysticism*,' 179–80 for a list of fourteen elements of the mystical experience, later called "Merkabah mysticism," as he claims was practiced in the late first century. I see no reason to think it was "probably instigated" by the war of 70, though of course the war had a tremendous impact.

125. See J. Schaberg, "Daniel 7, 12 and the New Testament Passion-Resurrection Predictions," *NTS* 31 (1985) 208–22, on the Synoptic and Johannine passion/resurrection predictions. Cf. Brown, *Death*, 2.1468–91, Appendix VIII: Jesus' Predictions of His Passion and Death.

126. P. Vielhauer ("Gottesreich und Menschensohn in der Verkundigung Jesu," *Aufsatze zum Neuen Testament* [Munich: Kaiser, 1965]) holds that the identification of Jesus with the heavenly Son of Man was the result of an attempt by his followers to make sense of his death, and their conviction that God had vindicated him. Cf. A. Y. Collins, "The Origin of the Designation," 155.

127. Greenfield, Suter, J. J. Collins, A. Y. Collins and others regard the Similitudes (1 Enoch 37–71), which were not found at Qumran, as a Jewish work written sometime between the reign of Herod the Great and the fall of Jerusalem in 70 C.E.

128. See J. J. Collins, "The Heavenly Representative," 115–16.

129. Segal, *Paul*, 111.

understood and his resurrection believed in.[130] The bond between Jesus, others and the Human One (who was and was more than the suffering people of the Most High) would be the base of the conviction that God had vindicated him, as that was articulated in traditions associated with the empty tomb. Smith suggested that the disciples experienced ascent as part of an initiation in which they were "magically and psychologically identified with" Jesus.[131] My suggestion is that the mystical experiences and practices of this group focused on an incorporation into the Human One that expanded "identity" beyond the individual, and that involved struggle against injustice and a belief in vindication.[132]

2. The Crucifixion and Burial of Jesus

"I saw all the violence & unreason crossing in the air: ourselves small; a tumult outside: something terrifying: unreason."[133]

"I said to L.: I dont want to die yet. . . . I've got it fairly vivid — the sensation: but cant see anything but suffocating nonentity following after. I shall think — oh I wanted another 10 years — not this — & shant, for once, be able to describe it. It — I mean death; no, the scrunching & scrambling, the crushing of my bone shade in on my very active eye & brain: the process of putting out the light, — painful? Yes. Terrifying. I suppose so — then a swoon; a drum; two or three gulps attempting consciousness — & then, dot dot dot."[134]

I regard it historically likely that in spite of the danger to themselves some women — most prominently Mary Magdalene — were present at the crucifixion. Tacitus (*Ann.* 6.19) and Seutonius (*Tiberias* 61) tell us that when rebels were punished, Rome thought it wise to keep an eye on their sympathizers, friends and relatives, even women and children. Josephus (*J.W.* 2.253, 305–8)[135] and Philo (*In Flaccum* 72) report Roman and Jewish arrests of women and even their crucifixions. Pliny the younger, in his correspondence with Trajan, writes of women and men accused and attacked for being Christians in Bithynia, mentioning his torture of two female slaves "who are called deacons" (*Letters* 10.96–97). If we think of this *basileia* movement as "totally dependent on one single charismatic man, one single sovereign leader," as Gerhardsson and others do, we might regard the women at the cross to have exposed themselves to no great risk, or

---

130. Contrast A. Y Collins ("Origin of the Designation," 154): she holds that it is credible "that Jesus spoke of a heavenly Son of Man and that, after his death and *presuming his exaltation* [emphasis mine], some of his followers identified him in his exalted state with that being."
131. M. Smith, "Ascent to the Heavens" 420.
132. Cf. T. W. Manson, *The Teaching of Jesus* (Cambridge: Cambridge University Press, 1963; reprint of 1935 edition) 35, 227–28, 232–35.
133. Woolf, *Diary*, 4.103.
134. Woolf, *Diary*, 5.326–27.
135. Josephus (*Ant.* 12.256) says Jewish women persecuted under Antiochus Epiphanes IV (see 1 Macc 1:60–61) were crucified.

less risk than the male disciples.[136] But if the movement was egalitarian, the risk was shared, whether or not Rome perceived it. Although "Jesus has never been presented [in Mark] as a leader of a revolutionary movement and no attempt by either Jewish police or Roman soldiers to arrest any of his followers has been reported,"[137] still the male disciples fled in real or imagined fear of death or arrest, a flight likely historical.[138] In John 19:25, a male, the Beloved Disciple, is present at the cross, probably some sort of corporate or symbolic figure.[139] Luke 23:49 claims "all those known to Jesus" stood at a distance, and the women from Galilee, "watching these things." The feminine participle, *horosai*, signals Luke's insertion;[140] no acquaintances are mentioned at the burial. The women's anxiety about rolling away the stone from the door of the tomb (Mark 16:3) highlights their aloneness. The fact that the women are not said in any account to be mourning or lamenting reflects Rome's prohibition of this act for the crucified (Tacitus, *Ann.* 6:19–10; Suetonius, *Tiberias* 61; *Digestae* 3.2.11.3; Philo, *In Flaccum* 72).

Mark 14:50, pars Matt 27:55; Luke 23:49 reports that the women watched "from a distance,"[141] a phrase that is often taken as an allusion to Ps 38:11 ("My friends and companions stand aloof from my affliction, and my neighbors stand far off"); cf. Ps 88:8 ("You have caused my companions to shun me; you have made me a thing of horror to them"); for some that allusion tells against the notion that Mark holds the women up as examples of bravery.[142] But clearly the women are not "aloof," nor are they "shunning" Jesus, as the psalm parallelisms would indicate. The distance is most likely a realistic feature of a political execution, and not so great as to mitigate the effect this form of terrorism was intended to have on spectators, especially on the companions of the crucified. Brown sarcastically rejects Markan — and one supposes any historical[143] — comparison between

---

136. Gerhardsson, "Mark and Women Witnesses," 220–21. On the execution of women., cf. Schottroff, *Let the Oppressed,* 171–72; Corley, "Women and the Crucifixion," n. 66, p. 189; J. Efron, "The Deed of Simeon ben Shatah in Ascalon," Appendix to A. Kasher, *Jews and Hellenistic Cities in Eretz-Israel* (Tübingen: Mohr Siebeck, 1990) 318–41; J. M. Ford, "The Crucifixion of Women in Antiquity," *Journal of Higher Criticism* 9 (1997) 291–309.

137. Brown, *Death,* 2.1157. He argues that this means the women were not in danger.

138. So Brown, *Death,* 1.9, 14; 2.1194 n. 136 on the Twelve. Schottroff (*Let the Oppressed,* 171) thinks the women were included in the "all" who fled in Mark; I think it more likely the "all" may be androcentric blindness and/or hyperbole (cf. 14:55, 64; 15:1).

139. See below, pp. 344–45.

140. Brown (*Death,* 2.1169, n. 73) says this participle "is feminine by attraction" but surely meant to apply as well to the acquaintances.

141. John 19:25 places followers of Jesus near the cross, but it is unlikely Rome would permit this.

142. Brown, *Death,* 2.1157: "Observing 'from a distance' is scarcely an opening description designed to make readers think of bravery" or "of noble behavior"; cf. Mark 14:54 on Peter, who did not want to be recognized as a disciple, following at a distance.

143. The purpose of Brown's commentary is "*to explain in detail what the evangelists intended and conveyed to their audiences by their narratives of the passion and death of Jesus*" (*Death,* 1.3). He has no analysis of his own position as a reader. He regards the Gospels as rooted in history and discusses in detail the historicity of many aspects of the Passion Narratives, but has no extended treatment of the historicity of the women's role.

"[c]owardly males [who] fled; [and] noble women [who] remained." "[W]hat evidence is there that Mark's narrative would encourage readers to contrast male disciples whose fleeing was mentioned some sixty [66] verses before with these women who are not said to have *remained* (precisely because we have been told nothing of their previous presence)?" The contrast he sees in Mark is between the women at a distance who are silent and give no evaluation of Jesus, and the centurion who has been standing at the cross opposite Jesus and who confesses him as God's son after he dies (15:39, one verse before the women are mentioned). His thesis, that "Mark has not portrayed the role of these women observers so positively as many have assumed," is tested and confirmed for him by examination of the women's lack of "any helping intervention by word or deed" in Jesus' burial (15:42–47), their failure to anoint the corpse (16:1), and their fear and silence as they flee the tomb ("[T]hey do not have the courage to obey.... The three women are not moved to proclaim Jesus even when they are directed to do so by heavenly intervention!")[144] There's that exclamation point again. Brown's treatment here is also curious, in view of the fact that he has just understood the distance at which the women stood by comparison with the distance with which Peter followed, some sixty-three verses earlier.[145]

Sarcasm and Markan redaction aside, Mark and John bear independent witness to a pre-Gospel tradition of Galilean women, Mary Magdalene among them, present at the crucifixion. John's list and ordering of names (Jesus' mother's sister, Mary of Clopas, and Mary Magdalene) is not borrowed from Mark's (Mary Magdalene, Mary the mother of James the younger and of Joses, and Salome). Constant in the canonical accounts is the name of Mary Magdalene and another Mary; a third name varies (Salome in Mark, the mother of the sons of Zebedee in Matthew, Joanna in Luke, and Jesus' mother's sister in John). These women witnessed Jesus' death by crucifixion.[146]

But was their historical witness to the brute fact alone, or also to some details? I think it reasonable to assume it was to some details. In Mark and Matthew the dying Jesus utters a cry in Aramaic or a strange combination of Hebrew and Aramaic: *"Eloi, Eloi, lama sabachthani"* (Mark 15:34); *"Eli, Eli, lema sabachthani?"* (Matt 27:46),[147] a quotation — though neither Evangelists notes this — of Ps

---

144. Brown, *Death*, 2.1158.

145. See also D. Senior, "The Death of Jesus and the Meaning of Discipleship," *The Death of Jesus in Early Christianity* (ed. R. E. Van Voorst, J. Marcus, D. Senior; Peabody, Mass.: Hendrickson, 1995) n. 29, p. 249.

146. On staying with the dying as "the hardest thing there is," see A. Lingis, *The Community of Those Who Have Nothing* (Bloomington: Indiana University Press, 1994) ix, 155–79. Saiving sees this staying-with as a power which can enable affirmation of finite life in its totality ("Our Bodies/Our Selves," 124–25).

147. On the combinations of Hebrew and Aramaic in these two versions, the Hebrew original and the Greek translations, and the parallel in Gospel of Peter 5:19, see Brown, *Death*, 2.1051–56. Mark's transliteration may represent Aramaic or an Aramaic dialect; Matthew may have changed *Eloi* to *Eli* to conform to prayer usage, and to clarify the misunderstanding (1052–53).

22:1, "My God, my God, why have you forsaken me?" The cry is misunderstood by some of the bystanders as a cry to Elijah. In Mark, someone runs, fills a sponge with *oxos* (vinegary wine), puts it on a reed and gives it to Jesus to drink, saying "Wait, let us see whether Elijah will come to take him down" (15:36). The act is strange, perhaps an act of mercy to postpone death; but *oxos* is bitter, cheap rotgut and mockery might be indicated, as in Ps 69:21 ("They gave me poison for food, and for my thirst they gave me vinegar to drink"), to which many see an allusion. The confusion between *Eloi/Eli* and Elijah (*Elijah* in Hebrew) may be understandable given that this is a death scene: the garbled speech of one suffocating is heard in terms of a popular expectation that Elijah will help the oppressed,[148] and will returns before "the day of the Lord ... the great and terrible day" (Mal 3:23; 4:5). More specifically, a tradition seems to be drawn on here that Elijah comes to the dying righteous one: Sirach 48:1 can be read "Blessed is he who shall have seen you before he dies."[149]

But it is not clear why a perceived mention of Elijah would prompt the offering of *oxos*, or how that would effect the timing of Elijah's coming.[150] Two early traditions, *Eloi/Eli*/Elijah and the *oxos*, have been awkwardly combined by Mark.[151] The first has been omitted by Luke, and does not appear in John, whereas the second appears in both. John 16:32 may be evidence that Evangelist knew of the tradition of the cry of forsakenness, and rejected it. The Gospel of Peter has another form of the first tradition: a citation of Ps 22:1, which understood *eli* not as "my God" but as "my strength" (*dynamis*); and instead of the misunderstanding about Elijah, the statement that when Jesus said this, "he was taken up." The verb *anelēphthē* may be a euphemism for death, or may refer to an ascension into heaven, that is, a rescue/exaltation. Or both, as in John. Crossan points out that

---

148. J. T. Walsh, "Elijah," *ABD* 2.465; see L. Ginzberg, *The Legends of the Jews* (Philadelphia: Jewish Publication Society of America, 1954) 4.202–11.

149. Translation by P. Skehan, *The Wisdom of Ben Sira* (introduction and commentary by A. DiLella; AB 39; New York: Doubleday, 1987) 530. See A. E. Crowley and A. Neubauer, *The Original Hebrew of a Portion of Ecclesiasticus (XXX.15 to XLIX.11)* (Oxford: Clarendon, 1897); 36. The second colon of this verse is missing in the Hebrew ms B; it should have contained a reasons of sorts for the paradoxical statement of 11a. GI (Greek translation of the grandson) has "for we too shall certainly live." The corresponding Sryriac reads "(Blessed is he who shall have seen you and died;) but he shall not die, but shall certainly live." (Hebrew reconstruction by Segal: *ki 'ap hu' hayoh tihyeh*; by Smend: *we'asreka ki hayoh tihyeh*.) Smend understands Elijah to be the person spoken of in 11b; Segal thinks it is the individual who sees Elijah before dying. Skehan comments, "In view of the strong evidence that Ben Sira did not believe in the resurrection of the dead, Segal is hard put to conjure up the possibility of a few meritorious individuals (he does not say, like Elijah himself) for whom the author might have allowed an exception." Skehan suggests the original of 11b may have read "for we too shall certainly come to rest (*ki 'ap 'anahnu noah nanuah*)" (cf. Sir 30:17b), possibly ameliorized by the grandson's day as "we will surely live (*hayoh nihyeh*)." See further, below p. 309, n. 54.

150. Matthew redacts the scene so that one of the bystanders performs the act, more clearly hostile, but others say,"Wait, let us see whether Elijah will come to save him" (27:49; cf. 27:40, 42).

151. Contrast Brown (*Death*, 2. 1084) who thinks two separate traditions were (a) the last cry of Jesus combined with the offering of *oxos*, and (b) the mocking about Elijah. But the Elijah motif is naturally connected with the cry, and awkwardly connected to the *oxos*.

all the canonical authors also avoid the term "died."[152] This achieves a connection with Elijah in a very different way (cf. 2 Kings 2:9, 11 on the taking up of Elijah). My suggestion is that the women's witness to the crucifixion may have included the tradition that Jesus cried out the words of Ps 22:1 or similar words,[153] and that they were misunderstood as a cry to Elijah. Two developments later occurred: (1) Psalm 22 was explored for connections with this crucifixion, giving a theological depth and meaning to normal execution aspects like mockery, stripping the crucified and distributing garments, thirst.[154] If there developed a women's lament tradition, as Corley has suggested, Psalm 22 may have provided a likely beginning not available only to "scribes." The raw grief and trauma and, even more so, the ritualized grief of Jewish women would make use of traditional words, though not confine itself to them.[155] Sharp protest, despair, fear, anger are part of this tradition, which women may have helped to create. Psalm 22, like many others, is of mixed form (lament and thanksgiving-eschatological hymn of praise[156]); the transition is abrupt at v. 22 with the statement that God has responded to the cry of abandonment: "You have answered me" (MT, missing in LXX and Tg).[157] A lament in the Jewish tradition would be open to this turn-around structure of reversal. Ps 22:22 ("I will tell of your name to my brothers") may be evoked in the reference to Jesus' "brothers" in the commission to the women (Matt 28:10) or to Mary Magdalene alone (John 20:17). (2) Elijah traditions, as we will see, very early provided a way to believe in and understand the vindication of Jesus.

In my reconstruction, women also witnessed the burial performed as a religious duty by Joseph of Arimathea, a prominent member of the Sanhedrin, not a follower of Jesus. The common Roman practice was to deprive executed criminals of a decent burial and to leave their corpses exposed on the cross for many days to be eaten by birds (see Suetonius, *Augustus* 13.1–2; Tacitus, *Ann.* 6.29; Petronius, *Satyricon* 111–12; Horace, *Epistle*, 1.16.48). It is unlikely that Pilate would have turned over the body of Jesus to his followers, friends or family. But Deut 21:22–23 regulated that a person who had been executed and hanged should not be left hanging after sunset; he (or she) should be buried on the same day.

---

152. Crossan, *The Cross That Spoke*, 223.

153. Words such as *Eli atta* or just *Eli*, which subsequently were linked with Ps 22:1 (see H. Sahlin, "Zum Verstandnis von drei Stellen des Markus-Evangeliums," *Biblica* 33 (1952) 62–66; X. Léon-Dufour, "Le dernier cri de Jesus," *Etudes* 348 (1978) 666–82; cf. G. Rossé, *The Cry of Jesus on the Cross* (New York: Paulist, 1987) 42–44.

154. See Brown, *Death*, 2.1455–65 for discussion of twelve proposed parallels.

155. Contrast Crossan, *Birth of Christianity*, 541: "female laments totally ignore and bypass institutional religion." He is basing his opinion on studies of modern Greek women who are ignoring official, orthodox Christian belief and dogma.

156. On the illustration in vv. 30–32 of belief in divine justice with regard to human life and death, see J. Schaper, *Eschatology in the Greek Psalter* (Tübingen: Mohr (Siebeck), 1995) 50–52.

157. See A. Lacocque, "My God, My God, Why Have You Forsaken Me?" and P. Ricoeur, "Lamentation as Prayer," in A. Lacocque and P. Ricoeur, *Thinking Biblically: Exegetical and Hermeneutical Studies* (Chicago: University of Chicago, 1998) 187–88, 217–21.

Josephus insists three times on Jewish concern for proper burial: of those crucified by Rome, suicides, enemies, and those put to death under Jewish law (*J.W.* 4.5.2, #317; 3.8.5, #377; *Ant.* 4.8.24, ##264–65; 4.8.6 #202).[158] In later rabbinic literature, leaving a corpse unburied is a case of *niwwul*, disgrace.[159] Observing the law, Joseph of Arimathea gave Jesus the quick, minimal burial of a criminal in a nearby tomb. In other words, the Sanhedrin took custody of Jesus' corpse through its delegate, and laid it in a tomb. Presumably the same was done for the other two crucified with Jesus; but the Evangelists are not interested in this. Such a burial bore the marks of shame: no public mourning rites were observed and the burial was not in a family tomb.[160] The Sanhedrin is later said to have maintained burial places (not a common pit) for the bodies of those executed to undergo decomposition; a year later the bones would be released to the family for burial in an ossuary (*m. Sanh.* 6:5–6; cf. *t. Sanh.* 9.8).[161] This may have been what happened to the crucified Yehohanan, whose bones were found in a ossuary at the first-century burial place Giv'at ha-Mivtar.[162] After the Sabbath the women returned to the tomb of Jesus at the Sanhedrin burial ground for criminals.

It is reasonable — to me — to suppose that women who had been present throughout the execution would stay to witness the burial even if they did not, because they were not allowed to, participate in it. And reasonable that they would note the burial site, and reasonable that they would return to it.[163] This would mean that the tradition of crucifixion, burial, and tomb could be a pre-Markan, complex unit, linked by the witness of women. But this is not to claim there is a recoverable pre-Markan narrative.[164]

---

158. See Brown, *Death*, 2.1209.

159. D. Daube, *The New Testament and Rabbinic Judaism* (London: Ahlone, 1956) 302. He makes the interesting point that between 100 B.C.E. and 100 C.E., the Pharisees carried through radical reform of traditional modes of execution, a kind of "humanization" which damaged the body less; this should be seen against the background of belief in bodily resurrection. For most rabbis, God's power to raise the dead did not depend on the integrity of the skeleton, but the reform may have been undertaken "in order to strengthen the belief in physical resurrection among the masses: the masses would accept the dogma more readily if the religious leaders did everything to emphasize the importance of the body, everything to save the most durable parts, the bones, from destruction" (307)

160. B. R. McCane, "'Where No One Had Yet Been Laid': The Shame of Jesus' Burial," *SBL Seminar Papers* (Atlanta: Scholars Press, 1993) 482.

161. Brown, *Death*, 2.1209; Sawicki, *Seeing the Lord*, 257.

162. See above, p. 239. His bones would not have been identified as those of a crucified person, if not for the fact that a large iron nail piercing his heel bone had been embedded in a knot of wood (J. Zias and E. Sekeles, "The Crucified Man from Giv'at ha-Mivtar: A Reappraisal," *IEJ* 35 [1985] 28).

163. Against Crossan, see above, pp. 248–51.

164. See Brown, *Death*, 2.1236, n. 74 on whether a pre-Markan narrative contained an empty tomb segment, or whether the burial and the empty tomb were originally separate. He is not certain there was a pre-Gospel narrative of the latter. His commentary on the Passion Narratives is "from Gethsemane to the grave" (burial) because of "practicality" (to extend it to the empty tomb scene would involve discussion of resurrection) and "perceived utility" (those who reflect, study or preach about the passion do not think of the resurrection as part of the subject matter). But he cautions

Brown thinks that there were two older traditions: (1) of three women at the crucifixion (Mary Magdalene, another Mary, and a third woman who was not identified in the pre-Gospel tradition, since every Gospel names her differently[165]) and (2) Mary Magdalene (and vaguely other women; cf. "we" in John 20:2) at the empty tomb. Mark lists three women at the crucifixion, but only two of them at the burial (Mary Magdalene and Mary of Joses), and the three again at the empty tomb. Matthew has three at the crucifixion, and only the two (Mary Magdalene and "the other Mary") at the burial and empty tomb, as though he is correcting Mark in the third scene. The women are not said to observe the burial in John, and clearly for Mark they are mentioned in order to stress the continuity of their witness. But I do not think their presence in the burial tradition is a logical "back-formation" from their presence in the empty-tomb tradition.[166] It seems logical that at least Mary Magdalene witnessed the burial, since she is never depicted as ignorant or confused about the location of the tomb she visits on the third day. The action of returning to the tomb involved great risk, just as other activities did that revealed an affiliation with someone crucified, since Rome feared the graves of executed political enemies could become "a gathering spot of conspiring elements."[167]

3. The Empty Tomb

"Such confusion everywhere!" exclaimed Better Flanders, bursting open the bedroom door.
Bonamy turned away from the window.
"What am I to do with these, Mr. Bonamy?"
She held out a pair of Jacob's old shoes."[168]

Rather as if [Julian] were jerked abruptly out of sight, without rhyme or reason; so violent & absurd that one cant fit his death into any scheme."[169]

Can the empty tomb tradition be considered historical? As we have seen, Paul mentioned neither the women at the tomb nor an appearance to them. But if he knew of these, he may have omitted them possibly because of reported conflicts regarding women in the Corinthian assembly and in marriages, disputes over status and authority.[170] He did not stand by these women in support of their prophetic speech. It is possible, given what we know of later gender debates among

readers that the evangelists may have had a different understanding of what constituted Jesus' passion (1.37).
165. Or, alternatively, who was named differently in pre-Gospel traditions.
166. Against Brown, *Death*, 2.1241, n. 86; 2.1275–77.
167. Schottroff, *Let the Oppressed*, 172, quoting J. Blinzler, *Der Prozess Jesu* (4th ed; Regensburg, 1969) 386, n 14.
168. V. Woolf, *Jacob's Room* (New York: Harcourt Brace & Company, 1922) 176.
169. Woolf, *Diary*, 5.122.
170. M. Hengel, "Maria Magdalene und die Frauen als Zeugen," *Abraham unser Vater* (ed. O. Betz et al.; Leiden: Brill, 1963) 251; H. E. Heron, "Eyewitness Communities: A Proposal Concerning Mary Magdalene and 1 Corinthians 15," unpublished paper, Pacific Region SBL 1994, revised 1996.

the "gnostics" which pit Peter against Mary (Magdalene), that the women of Corinth were basing their authority and citing as their precedents the experience of women in this Galilean and Judean *basileia* movement, in particular the women at the tomb. The inclusion of Peter and James in Paul's list in 1 Corinthians 15 of epiphany recipients may be the result of the particular traditions that had prominence in Jerusalem, where Peter and James were honored as "pillars," and where Paul received his initial but brief training in Christianity from these very two men (Gal 1:18–19).[171] Mary Magdalene's omission from the list may indicate Paul was not told about the tradition of her epiphany, which suggests her exclusion from this in-group, and/or her absence from Jerusalem. 1 Corinthians 15 is one of six texts in which either Peter or Mary Magdalene receives an individual resurrection appearance. The Gospel of Luke, the Gospel of Peter and 1 Corinthians 15 are Petrine texts; Matthew, John and the Markan Appendix are Magdalene texts. This indicates to Brock — and I agree — that the tension between these two figures portrayed in the apocryphal literature may exist already early in first century conflicting traditions. "[W]ith respect to apostolic authority, it appears that the greater the prominence of Peter in a text, the more diminished is the role of Mary Magdalene and most other female leadership."[172] The reverse is not true, that the greater prominence Mary Magdalene has, the more diminished the role of Peter and other males.

Paul's tradition, however, that Jesus "was raised on the third day" implies some discovery or revelation or insight that was dated. It does not clearly appear to be drawn from any "scripture" like Hos 6:2, nor from sayings of Jesus himself like John 2:22. I have suggested that the third day motif draws on Daniel 12's expression for the length of the time of oppression, "a time, two times, and half a time," meaning "soon." Under pressure of history, the motif is modified from *after* three days in the earliest passion/resurrection prediction (meaning "soon") to *on* the third day (meaning on the third day after the crucifixion).[173] Rowland calls *egeirō* in 1 Cor 15:4 a "technical term" the use of which would not be justified by mere visions of Jesus. He finds it likely that Paul did presuppose the tradition of an empty tomb or something like it that had to do with the transformation of Jesus' body. That tradition, then, would be part of the oldest stratum[174] Marked also by the verb *egerthē* in Mark 16:6 and parallels, a radical reinterpretation and surpassing of apocalyptic expectation has begun in the belief that the end is already inaugurated.

Overlapping ideas of resurrection and translation, resurrection and angelic exaltation, physical body and spiritual body, appear in contemporaneous passages

---

171. See A. G. Brock, "Peter, Paul and Mary: Canonical vs. Non-Canonical Portrayals of Apostolic Witnesses," *SBL Seminar Papers* (Atlanta: SBL, 1999) 199.
172. Brock, "Peter, Paul and Mary," 196.
173. Schaberg, "Daniel 7, 12," 210–11. See above, pp. 275.
174. C. Rowland, *Christian Origins* (London: SPCK, 1985) 188–92.

and often even in the same passages.[175] It is difficult, even impossible, to say what a first-century Palestinian Jew must have held with regard to the fate of the body of the vindicated Jesus. For some, the absence of the body might be required in order for one to speak of resurrection; for others, not. What seems logically distinct to us (or some of us) may not have seemed so to them; or, more to the point, they may not have been thinking and imagining logically. We cannot say with total certainty, for example, that belief in the resurrection must have implied belief that the tomb was empty, or that it must have been compatible with a rotting corpse. Vindication, even vindication by resurrection, was expressed in a variety of ways by different writers and even sometimes by the same writer. Josephus' statement about the belief of the Pharisees: "the soul of the good …passes into another body" (*J.W.* 2.8.14#163) could be understood in terms of transmigration, or as a "rather thinly veiled reference to the Jewish idea of resurrection of the body." It might be a reference to what Paul calls a spiritual body.[176]

I propose we turn the riddle around and ask, rather than what implies emptiness of a tomb, what emptiness might imply to someone who was trained in this *basileia* movement, and who had witnessed a brutal execution. I align myself with those who think the emptiness of the tomb is historical.[177] But I do not think this commits me to the belief that the resurrection must be thought of as the resuscitation of a corpse; rather, it is compatible with a lost or stolen corpse, and compatible with exaltation/ascent, and compatible with the mystery of the unknown fate of the corpse, and compatible with the destruction of a corpse. Noting the absence of dead bodies on the screen in Claude Lanzmann's "Shoah," Shoshana Felman asks what would it mean "to bear witness from inside the witness's *empty* grave," empty "because the witness who did die was, consequent to his mass burial, dug up from his grave and burned to ashes — because the dead witness did not even leave behind a corpse or dead body?"[178] The fact that the

---

175. Dan 12:1–3; Jub 23:30–31; 4 Ezra 7:32–34; 4:34–35; 1 Enoch 22, etc. Mark 12:18–27, in the context of a discussion about resurrection, speaks of the dead as like angels in heaven.

176. J. D. Tabor, " 'Returning to the Divinity': Josephus's Portrayal of the Disappearances of Enoch, Elijah, and Moses," *JBL* 108 (1989) 232. He thinks that Josephus "meant to obscure, or even reinterpret, a traditional Jewish way of expression which would clearly refer to resurrection in a literal fashion" (n 15, p. 232). Cf. "a renewed existence" (*Ag. Ap.* 2.30#218).

177. Archaeological evidence is compatible with this stance (see O. Nicholson, "Holy Sepulchre, Church of," *ABD* 3.258–59).

178. S. Felman, "The Return of the Voice: Claude Lanzmann's *Shoah*," *Testimony* (ed. S. Felman and D. Laub; New York: Routledge, 1992) 225. In one of the film's most powerful scenes, survivor Richard Glazar remembers the night they began to burn the bodies in Treblinka, November 1942: "Suddenly, from the part of the camp called the death camp, flames shot up. Very high. In a flash, the whole countryside, the whole camp, seemed ablaze. It was already dark. We went into our barracks and ate. And from the window, we kept on watching the fantastic backdrop of flames of every imaginable color: red, yellow, green, purple. And suddenly one of us stood up. We knew…he'd been an opera singer in Warsaw. His name was Salve, and facing that curtain of fire, he began chanting a song [in Yiddish]I didn't know: "My God, my God, why has Thou forsaken us? We have been thrust into the

death of Jesus was a brutal execution must always be kept in mind, and our minds must be responsible to their own times. Texts like 2 Maccabees insist that the bodies of martyrs which were destroyed must be restored. Faith in resurrection functions differently in different texts: in Daniel and 2 Maccabees God raises the righteous dead because they suffer for God's sake; in 1 Enoch simply because they suffer unjustly. Resurrection also speaks to the problem of suffering and oppression even when it has not resulted in death. In Test Benj 10:5–11, all are resurrected, not only the persecuted righteous. In 4 Maccabees, immortality and eternal life begin at death; in the Wisdom of Solomon, God makes the righteous immortal already in their earthly life (1:12–16). In some texts like 2 Baruch and 4 Ezra, the purpose of resurrection may not be participation in the messianic kingdom but individual judgment, reward and punishment.[179] It is most important that we not be distracted from the insight of A. Geiger, that resurrection had political connotations that shifted over time,[180] and continue to shift. This is true even — especially — when the belief seems apolitical.

To summarize how I am building my house of cards: the *basileia* movement of Jesus and his companions was apocalyptic, with a stress on wisdom. It was egalitarian in some sense, and its combined study, prayer and actions of resistance were the intellectual/spiritual preparation for the resurrection faith of women who found the tomb empty. No standard, clear expectation of resurrection or vindication was available to them in which to process this emptiness, but rather belief in the suffering and resurrection/exaltation of the Human One, understood as corporate.

Must historians and theologians must leave it at this: that the presence of the women at crucifixion, burial and empty tomb can be credibly reconstructed as historical? Must we leave it open whether or not the ambiguous emptiness remained ambiguous to the women until it was clarified by the mysterious and unexplained "decision" Bultmann spoke of, that is, until it was clarified by the claims of male disciples to have received appearances of the risen Jesus? Schüssler Fiorenza argues no. She holds that "it is difficult to prove which tradition was primary, that of the 'empty tomb' associated with women or that of the 'visionary experience' authorizing men. It is equally difficult to ascertain whether the empty tomb tradition and the narrative account of Jesus' death, burial and resurrection were first articulated and transmitted by women." But we can claim our power as readers. "Whatever the case may have been historically, the privileging of the 'women's tradition' can function as a heuristic means to develop and

---

fire before, but we have never denied Thy Holy Law" (C. Lanzmann, *Shoah: An Oral History of the Holocaust; the complete text of the film* (New York: Pantheon, 1985) 14.

179. See G. W. E. Nickelsburg, *Resurrection, Immortality and Eternal Life in Intertestamental Judaism* (Cambridge: Harvard University Press, 1972) 19, 124; W. S. Vorster, "The religio-historical context of the resurrection of Jesus and resurrection faith in the New Testament," *Neotestamentica* 23 (1989) 166, 169.

180. See Heschel, *Abraham Geiger*, 90.

adjudicate our own Christological meaning-making in the face of violence and killing today."[181] She reads that women's tradition, *with the essence or insight of its angelophany,* the proclamation that Jesus is going before them to Galilee, as a base of the conviction that the executed Jesus was the vindicated or resurrected one.[182] Read this way, it is a statement of presence ahead, not of absence. This is not a tradition that glorifies, justifies and glamorizes suffering and injustice, or that "proves" the resurrection. Rather it is a statement of faith in the context of a terrible ambiguity, which remains. It is a call to act in spite of that ambiguity.[183] A "sublime courage and optimism" breaks through "the ultimate horror."[184] "Against you I fling myself, unvanquished and unyielding, O Death! *The waves broke on the shore.*"[185]

It is possible to say more.

The angelophany is integral to this tradition when Mark 16:1–8 is read as a little apocalypse or a fragment of an apocalypse.[186] It can be outlined in this way:

A. As in Daniel 7, 4 Ezra 13, and elsewhere the situation is one of grief[187] because of perceived oppression.

B. Something strange is seen: a stone rolled back, a "young man" in white inside the tomb in place of the expected corpse.

C. The sight causes amazement.[188]

---

181. Schüssler Fiorenza, *Miriam's Child,* 125. But because of the tradition of an appearance to women or to a woman at the tomb, and the tradition of men at the tomb, we cannot neatly connect women with the tomb and men with appearances (R. Atwood, *Mary Magdalene in the New Testament Gospels and Early Tradition* (Bern: Peter Lang, 1993).

182. Schüssler Fiorenza, *Miriam's Child,* 90.

183. Cf. R. J. Miller, "What Do Stories about Resurrection(s) Prove?" *Will the Real Jesus Please Stand Up?* (ed. P. Copan; Grand Rapids: Baker, 1998) 98: "Empty tombs don't prove anything, except to insiders. Nor do reports of appearances of risen leaders."

184. C. W. Bynum, *The Resurrection of the Body in Western Christianity, 200–1336* (New York: Columbia University Press, 1995) 343.

185. Woolf, *The Waves,* 297.

186. Schottroff (*Let the Oppressed,* 183–84) calls Mark 16:1–8 an epiphany story, from a form-historical viewpoint. The story is about the women and how they are changed (cf. Acts 9:1–9 about Paul). However, she understands the resurrection here "in the religio-historical aspect primarily from the context of apocalyptic hopes."

187. D. Merkur ("The Visionary Practices of Jewish Apocalyptists," *The Psychoanalytic Study of Society* 14 [1989] 119–48) discusses the seer's use of exaggerated mourning and lamentation to induce ecstasy (1 En 14:7; Dan 9:3–4, 20–22; 10:2–5; 4 Ezra 5:13, 20; 6:30–31, 35; 2 Bar 5:6–6:4a; 9:2–10:1; 81:2–4; 3 Bar 1:1–3 Gk) in terms of the unconscious bipolar mechanism: ecstasy manifested in defense against depression. Mark 16:1–8, of course, is not a scene about ritualized mourning or deliberate use of visionary techniques. The "real" grief implied here is that of witnesses who were loyally present at a bloody execution but helpless, not the grief of those who betrayed or were absent out of fear.

188. In the Christian Testament, only Mark uses the verb *ekthambeomai,* to express some kind of awe (the crowd sees Jesus after the transfiguration, 9:15) or agitated distress (Jesus in Gethsemane, 14:33).

D. An explanation (Jesus has been raised) is given by the young man, an angelic interpreter.[189]

E. The women are commissioned to tell the disciples of Jesus about a future reunion.

F. The women respond with fear[190] and silence.

In comparison, Daniel 7 can be outlined in a somewhat similar way:

A. The context is one of grief, the oppression of Israel by Antiochus Epiphanes IV.

B1. Strange things are seen: visions of four beasts, of the Ancient of Days sitting in judgment, of destruction of the fourth beast, of the Human One receiving authority (vv. 2–14).

C. Daniel reacts: his spirit was troubled, visions terrified him, and he asked an attendant about the truth of all this (vv. 15–16a).

D. An angelic interpretation is given (vv. 16b–18);[191]

B2. Second request and second vision: of fourth beast warring with the holy ones, Ancient of Days judging for them, their reception of the kingdom (vv. 19–22).

D2. Second angelic interpretation is given (vv. 23–27). The second vision and interpretation are like a close-up of the first; or do they correspond to a commission?

F. Daniel's response is terror, silence (v. 28: "As for me, Daniel, my thought greatly terrified me, and my face turned pale; but I kept the matter in my mind"); cf. Dan 12:9, where Daniel is told by "the man clothed in linen" to go his way, "for the words[192] are to remain secret and sealed until the time of the end."

Mark 16:1–8 meets the proposed definition of an apocalypse as "a genre of revelatory literature with a narrative framework, in which a revelation is mediated by an otherworldly being to a human recipient, disclosing a transcendent reality which is both temporal, insofar as it envisages eschatological salvation, and spatial insofar as it involves another, supernatural world.[193] It provides an excellent example of what J. J. Collins called "apocalyptic eschatology as the transcendence of death."

---

189. The *neaniskos* is not presented as a human being, in spite of the parallel some have seen to the young man who flees naked in Gethsemane (14:51–52). Angels are called "men" in Daniel (8:15–16; 9:21; 10:5); *neanias* (also translated "young man") is used of angels in 2 Macc 3:26; Josephus, *Ant.* 5.277. Cf. Herm. Vis 3.1.6.8; 3.2.5; 3.4.1; Gospel of Peter 13:55. White clothing signals otherworldly existence or access (Dan 7:9; 2 Macc 11:8–10; Acts 1:10; Mark 9:3 pars).

190. If this is apocalyptic fear, it is fear of the numinous, that is, appropriate fear. But what does Mark mean? Fear of the demand placed on them, which leads to their failure? Fear of the disciples' response (justified if Mark knows of the tradition found in Luke 24:11; Mark 16:11). There is a lot of interesting irony here: who is really afraid of whom? The history of tradition indicates the disciples were afraid of the women and their testimony; fear is projected onto the women.

191. In Daniel, an angelic interpreter sometimes interprets a vision and sometimes explains a situation. Luke uses the device to comment on the significance of the ascension (A. Y. Collins, "The Empty Tomb in the Gospel According to Mark," n. 54, p. 136).

192. These words are about the length of time of the persecution; Daniel hears but cannot understand (12:6–13).

193. J. J. Collins, *Apocalyptic Imagination*, 5.

The women's silence in Mark may be taken as a kind of apocalyptic signature: those who saw now (in the Gospel) break their silence.[194] But there are major differences with regard to the motif of silence in Mark and Daniel. Daniel's silence in 7:28 signifies that he is overwhelmed and must ponder.[195] The women in Mark are told to tell, but do not tell anyone anything (the Greek double negative is emphatic). Daniel has no such immediate commission; rather in 12:4, 9 (cf. 8:26–27) he is told not to tell. The revelation to him involves an implicit, eschatological commission. But as in Mark, the book itself breaks the silence.

Resurrection language drawn from Daniel 12 ("he has been raised") explicates the absence of the corpse of the executed Jesus. The prediction in Mark 16:7, that Jesus is going before the disciples to Galilee, where they will see him, is a reminder of Jesus' prediction in 14:28 ("After I am raised up I will go before you to Galilee"), which Luke 24:6, removing reference to an appearance in Galilee, explicitly links to a prediction of the passion/resurrection of the Human One ("Remember how he told you, while he was still in Galilee, that the Human One must be delivered into the hands of sinful men, and be crucified, and on the third day rise"). In contrast, Matthew moves forward from the story of the empty tomb to the appearance of the risen one on the mountain in Galilee, which I have argued elsewhere is based on a midrashic treatment of Daniel 7.[196] The insight presented as angelic revelation, then, can be seen as formulated under pressure from passion/resurrection predictions which use Daniel 7, 12.

Other imagery and language was also available to explicate belief in the vindication of Jesus, that drawn from the tradition of Elijah's translation (he was "taken" 2 Kings 2; cf. Gen 5:24). Luke 24:3 may allude to this with the phrase "they did not find the body" (cf. 2 Kings 2:17).[197] Here comes one of my major cards. Not finding the body is the catalyst for a radical modification of the Danielic tradition, with resurrection understood as translation, and vice versa.[198] In John

194. E. S. Malbon thinks the narrator is leading the audience to assume that the story has been told to him or his intermediaries by those who heard the women tell it (see *NovT* 28 [1986] n. 27, 118). Gundry (*Mark*, 1013) counters that here the author may be thought of as omniscient.

195. See also Asc Isaiah 11:39–40; 4 Ezra 14:44–48, where the works can be read in the last generation. M. G. Reddish, *Apocalyptic Literature* (Peabody, Mass.: Hendrickson, 1995) 290.

196. J. Schaberg, *The Father, the Son and the Holy Spirit* (Chico, Calif.: Scholars Press, 1982); cf. W. D. Davies and D. C. Allison, "Matt 28:16–20: Texts Behind the Text," *RHPR* 72 (1992) 89–98; *The Gospel According to St. Matthew* (Edinburgh: T. & T. Clark, 1997) 676–89.

197. E. Bickermann ("Das leere Grab," *ZNT* 23 [1924] 281–92) argued Mark used a "translation story" or "removal story." Bultmann found insufficient evidence of this (*History of the Synoptic Tradition,* 290, n. 3). A. Y. Collins ("The Empty Tomb in the Gospel According to Mark," n. 42, p. 136) thinks that the literary form "translation story" does not define Mark 16:1–8 or its alleged source, but this does not mean that such stories or the notions they express had no influence on the passage. Her focus, however, is on the translation accounts of Greco-Roman heroes as a literary influence.

198. Daniel 7, 12 and 2 Kings 2 have powerful thematic affinities (the throne/chariot, fire, human or human-like figure, and ascent [see Schaberg, "Mark 14:62," 79–84; *The Father, the Son,* 169, 179–80]). A. Y. Collins ("The Empty Tomb in the Gospel According to Mark," 131) remarks that "The interpretation of the resurrection of Jesus as a type of translation has an effect on one's reading of the apocalyptic discourse of chapter 13. That discourse has its climax in the prediction of the coming of

20:7–8, 17 resurrection and ascent (translation) language appear together. I see the emptiness of the tomb rather than the resurrection appearances as the trigger of the resurrection faith.[199] The emptiness is not the expression (necessary or un-necessary) of that faith.[200] In other words, the emptiness is not demanded by or created by resurrection faith, nor is it a response to resurrection faith. The empti-ness is, rather, an inspiration of that faith. Here I am reversing the usual terms of the discussion (whether or not resurrection implied for some or for all empty tomb) and arguing that although emptiness (a missing body) did not necessarily imply resurrection, it may have been the (or an) occasion for insight, a "revela-tion" of resurrection. I am in agreement here with Rowland. "[T]he finding of the tomb empty on the first Easter morning may have been one of those 'signals of transcendence,' as Peter Berger has called them. We cannot know what effect such a discovery would have had on the disciples [sic]. It is not impossible that it may have led to the conviction that Jesus had been raised and provoked visions of him. As Rowan Williams has suggested: 'Something must have provided a first stimulus, and, more importantly, a structure of presuppositions within which sub-sequent experiences could be organized. The empty tomb tradition proposes just such a stimulus and structure....' "[201] This does not reduce the resurrection to the women's spiritual experience (which is to be distinguished from theological insight, intuition, and certainly from deduction[202]). Rather, their experience leads them to believe that something happened to Jesus. Intersubjectivity and trusting self-transcendence (were and) are involved in accepting their Easter testimony as veracious.[203]

The past tense, aorist passive, of the verb in Mark 16:6 — he has been raised — jolts. One might have expected the future tense as in Daniel 12:2–3 ("your people shall be delivered...many of those who sleep in a land of dust shall awake...those who are wise shall shine...") or in John 11:24 (Martha knows that her brother Lazarus "will rise again in the resurrection on the last day"). But the traumatic grief of the women, embedded in a belief in injus-tice done to Jesus[204] and in ultimate, eschatological justice for the Human

---

the Son of Man with the clouds with great power and glory" and his gathering of the faithful. The empty tomb narrative activates other Son of Man sayings as well, such as 14:62 (p. 123).

199. Contrast Lindars, "Jesus Risen," 92.

200. The Hellenistic and Jewish motif of translation emphasizes *dis* appearance; the empty tomb story features resurrection as well as absence (See Gundry, *Mark*, 994–95).

201. Rowland, *Christian Origins*, 193, quoting R. D. Williams, *Resurrection*, 106–7. Contrast Spong, *Resurrection*, 228–29: "the women's visit had nothing to do with the first Easter...Easter occurred first in Galilee. It focused primarily on the experience of Peter."

202. Cf. Segal, *Paul*, 143.

203. Francis Schüssler Fiorenza, "The Resurrection of Jesus and Roman Catholic Fundamental Theology," *Resurrection* (ed. Davis et al.; New York: Oxford, 1998) 213–48.

204. Perkins ("Resurrection," 424) sees the primitive form of the confession that God raised Jesus from the dead as also a statement about the goodness and innocence of Jesus' life.

One,[205] produces this theological leap, the claim that "resurrection" had taken place.[206]

What could this have meant? (1) Contemporary Jewish apocalyptic thought did not consistently or clearly make either/or distinctions between spiritual survival, immortality, ascent, and bodily resurrection. We note again that variations of these ideas can appear in the same texts, side by side or in some blend. Dan 12:1–3, for example, stresses resurrection and the ascent and astral transformation of the *maskilim*. In Daniel and I Enoch a resurrection of the spirit or spiritual body is envisioned, "and its relation to the physical body that died is not clarified." Later writings adapt this tradition in different ways (2 Baruch, for example, insisting those who rise are recognizable but are subsequently transformed).[207] Speculations about the nature of the resurrected body and the mechanics of resurrection miss the point, as Paul insists in 1 Cor 15:35–49. What kind of body? who knows? who cares?[208] The point of resurrection language, in the context of Jewish apocalypticism, is that the whole, recognizable person will live in some manner by the power of God, the whole person will be vindicated, the suffering and oppression he or she experienced — from civil and religious authorities — as a result of his or her dedication to justice and as a result of God's dedication, will be overturned. In this case, though it is not the way we commonly use the term,[209] " 'body' names the reality of the human being, soul and all."[210]

205. The non-availability of the bodies of Enoch, Moses, Elijah did not arise from nor give rise to notions of corporeal resurrection or corporeal transcendence, in that, as far as I know, there was no real speculation about the *bodies* of these characters in heaven. On Elijah as a Moses redivivus in 2 Kings 17–19; 2 Kings 2, see J. T. Walsh, "Elijah," *ABD*, 2.464–65.

206. Cf. Sawicki, *Seeing the Lord*, 257: Grief *over the loss of the body* [emphasis mine; in a limed pit, or confiscated in a common tomb] was the starting point of the reflection that culminates in the 'finding' of the empty tomb and a 'seeing' of Jesus as already risen from the dead."

207. J. J. Collins, "The Afterlife in Apocalyptic Literature," *Judaism in Late Antiquity: Part 4: Death, Life-After-Death, Resurrection and the World-to-Come in the Judaisms of Antiquity* (ed. A. J. Avery-Peck and J. Neusner; Leiden: Brill, 2000) 137.

208. Segal ("Some Observations about Jewish Mysticism," 397) thinks Paul's talk about spiritual bodies may be "a way of mediating between Greek notions of soul or spirit and the Jewish apocalyptic notion that the body of the martyr is to be resurrected. In any event, it is Paul's own insight that is clearest here." And in 2 Cor 12:1–4, probably speaking of his own ascent — "whether in the body or out of the body, I do not know; God knows" — "Paul is frankly stumped by the mechanism. He will not risk a guess." Cf. M. Wyschogrod, "Resurrection," *Pro Ecclesia* 1 (1992) 107: "The enemy here is system." Talk about being "like the angels" is another way of dealing with resurrection (Mark 12:25 and pars.; cf. 2 Enoch 22; Apocalypse of Paul 7 on "the angel of each man and woman" ("the familiar angel" 16). See C. R. A. Morray-Jones, "Transformational Mysticism in the Apocalyptic-Merkabah Tradition," *JJS* 43 (1992) 1–31; D. Daube, "On Acts 23: Sadducees and Angels," *JBL* 109 (1990) 493–97; and the forthcoming Oxford dissertation by K. Sullivan.

209. S. Schneiders ("The Resurrection of Jesus and Christian Spirituality," *Christian Resources of Hope* [ed. M. Junker-Kenny; Collegeville, Minn.: Liturgical, 1995] 97–98) inquires into the nature of the body "as symbol of the self." This signifies at least four things: 1. "body grounds and manifests *identity through change* "; is "the principle of *personal consistence*"; "provides the condition of possibility and ground of *interaction with others* "; and "allows the individual to constitute the node of a *network of relations among others.*"

210. Sawicki, *Seeing the Lord*, n. 1, p. 187. See D. Boyarin, "Behold Israel According to the Flesh: On Anthropology and Sexuality in Late Antique Judaisms," *Yale Journal of Criticism* 1 [1992] 30) on

(2) The claim that Jesus had been resurrected is about more than — but not less than — one person's passage through death. As the resurrection of the Human One, it is in some sense a corporate resurrection. A. Y. Collins notes that the Son of Man is "a powerful political symbol ... of a specific way of being, living, and hoping *embodied by* [emphasis mine] Jesus and his followers. The Son of Man is an alternative to other symbols of authority, such as the Roman emperor and his agents, the heirs of Herod the Great, and the messianic pretenders who attempted to overthrow Roman rule by force." It is a symbol used consistently by the author of Daniel, the Qumran community, the author of Revelation and other writers, teachers and prophets as well as Jesus, none of whom advocated violence, and none of whom was content with accommodation to the status quo. "All called for resistance to the current unjust order by creating an alternative symbolic universe which sustained an alternative way of life."[211] The empty tomb traditions, as I read them, draw on such symbolism — which is believed to be not just symbolism — to express this political faith in the resurrection and vindication of the executed Jesus and of all others who live this alternative way of life. It expresses also the belief that the risen Jesus breaks through the limitations of time, space, gender, ethnicity.[212]

4. A Resurrection Appearance to Mary Magdalene

" ... Julian who stalks beside me, in many different shapes."[213]

"Yes, but my happiness isn't blind. That is the achievement, I was thinking between 3 & 4 this morning, of my 55 years. I lay awake so calm, so content, as if I'd stepped off the whirling world into a deep blue quiet space, & there open eyed existed, beyond harm; armed against all that can happen. I have never had this feeling before in all my life; but I have had it several times since last summer: when I reached it, in my worst depression, as if I stepped out, throwing aside a cloak, lying in bed, looking at the stars, those nights at Monks House."[214]

There is no appearance to Mary Magdalene, or to anyone at all, in Mark's enigmatic final pericope, 16:1–8. Scholars debate whether or not it was Mark's

Paul's consideration that some kind of body, positively valued, is necessary but transformed and not of "flesh"; Boyarin contrasts this with rabbinic Judaism's definition of the human being as a animated body and not as a soul trapped or housed in a body, the body and soul forming a whole rather than a polarity. Boyarin argues that Christianity developed out of a Hellenistic Jewish cultural koine rather than out of Palestinian Jewish apocalyptics (n 5, p. 52). I am interested here in the (or an) original insight, not its development, and I do not make a sharp distinction between Palestinian and Hellenistic.

211. A. Y. Collins, "Origin of the Designation," 158. The judgment that belief in and hope for the future activity of this heavenly being is "a failure to work with the realities of politics and history, or as the wishful thinking of the powerless" Collins regards as hasty and based on modern preferences, ignoring the political dimension of the symbol (157).
212. See Schneiders, "The Resurrection of Jesus and Christian Spirituality," 108. "His bodiliness is not physical."
213. Woolf, *Diary*, 5.107.
214. Woolf, *Diary*, 5.78.

intended ending. If it was, its meaning and integrity are not agreed upon. If it was not, can an intended ending be reconstructed? Many explanations have been suggested for the women's silence in Mark 16:8 based on the assumption that this is Mark's intended ending:

- Mark has an anti-Jerusalem bias, and is saying the disciples and Peter never received the message and did not believe in the resurrection;

- or Mark is describing all the disciples (men and women) as failures, in his attack on a divine man christology;

- or Mark or his source is signaling that Christian belief is not dependent on the testimony of women;

- or Mark is downplaying resurrection in favor of belief in the believers' vindication at the (perhaps immediate) parousia;

- or the silence is a literary device which throws the commission to the reader;

- or the silence emphasizes the secret character of the revelation;

- or the silence is not meant to be taken literally, but is "a conventional expression of the human reaction to the numinous" and is only temporary.[215]

Some have argued that silence makes sense if 16:7 is removed. The promise in v. 7, that the disciples will see the risen Jesus, is therefore seen as secondary, Mark's insertion into his source of a link with the prediction about Galilee in 14:28. Mark achieves here a bridge to traditions — but not narratives — of appearances in Galilee.[216] The tension between the command to tell in v. 7 and the women's silence in v. 8 is considered by many the best argument for the presence of a source.[217] A "latent incoherence" makes the theory of a lost ending difficult. Verse 8 "has effectively dismissed the women from further immediate participation in events, while v. 7 urgently demands their intervention." If v. 8 was the original ending; Mark inserted v. 7 into a traditional unit without noticing the problem, that the silence would make it impossible for the narrative to continue; but then Mark may have had no intention of continuing it.[218]

---

215. Gundry, *Mark*, 1013–20 gives a helpful survey of interpretations. On this last point, see 1008–9 (Gundry believes, however, that this is not the original Markan ending).

216. Bultmann, *History of the Synoptic Tradition*, 185, 187; also J. Delorme cited by Perkins, *Resurrection*, 121, 143 n. 41. Fuller cited by Fuller and Pesch, cited in Perkins 143 n. 41. Fuller, Kremer, Delorme, Lindemann and Perkins agree that this verse was added to a source (Perkins, *Resurrection*, 116, 120–21 and 140 nn 16,17).

217. Bousset, cited by Bultmann, *History of the Synoptic Tradition*, 285; Perkins, *Resurrection*, 120–21. Contrast A. Y. Collins, "The Empty Tomb in the Gospel according to Mark," 120: she holds that "the hypothesis of a source is unnecessary to explain or resolve the tensions in the passage," apparently accepting Perkins' explanation that we have here a "paradoxical affirmation" that the women will be Jesus' witnesses in spite of their incomprehension and fear; this is also an implicit warning to the audience not to repeat the failure of the male and female disciples (Perkins, *Resurrection*, 121–23).

218. J. M. Creed, "The Conclusion of the Gospel according to Saint Mark," *JTS* 31 (1930).

In the Markan text as it stands, then, the women's fear suits the angelophany, but "their silence does not suit the angelic commission and therefore needs reversal by an assuring appearance of Jesus to them. . . . The women's silence goes against a command and thereby raises an expectation of further material that will keep the silence from frustrating a fulfilment of Jesus' prediction."[219] But even without the command to tell in v. 7, the reader/hearer acquainted with or even unacquainted with apocalyptic literature knows there is an implicit commission, as in Daniel; the story must move beyond the silence. With or without 16:7, the narrative moves beyond v. 8.[220] It may have been continued in the source, or in a Markan original, with the silence broken.

Those who think Mark did not originally end at v. 8 argue that the author died before the Gospel was finished; or the text was deliberately mutilated; or mutilated by accident. Conjectures are made about what the intended ending might have contained, and how it would be possible to move beyond the women's silence.[221] I agree tentatively with the suggestion is that there may have been deliberate suppression of an ending. Whether Mark suppressed a tradition, or Mark's own ending was suppressed, cannot be explored in any detail here.

Some of the arguments that support the idea that Mark omitted appearances (and so ended at v. 8) can just as well supply motivation for another person or persons censoring an ending Mark wrote: for example, to curtail an over-realized eschatology (Achtemeier) or a theology of glory (Lindemann) or "gnostic connotations" (Kelber) or visionary claims of Christian prophets (Boring).[222] This last seems to me the most likely, especially if the visionaries in question were women, or a woman. With the ending at v. 8, those claims would be suppressed, and the silence would also sever any link between the empty tomb traditions and appearances to the disciples, which then owe nothing to the testimony of women. Whoever suppressed the ending may have doubled the negative in v. 8 to intensify it: literally "they said to *no one (oudeni) nothing (ouden)*."

I think it may be possible to reconstruct, from Matthew, John and perhaps the Markan Appendix and other Markan endings, fragments of an original ending to Mark which involved a christophany. In contrast, Gundry sees traces of Mark's original ending in Matthew and Luke, especially in Matthew's narratives of appearances to the women as they flee and to the disciples in Galilee. "To reconstruct the lost ending of Mark, we should use Matt 28:9–10, 16–20 (but not 28:11–15, for it complements Matthew's redactional insertion in 27:62–66);

---

219. Gundry, *Mark*, 1014.
220. With 16:7, which promises an appearance in Galilee, an appearance to the women in Jerusalem is in some tension (see Lindars, "Jesus Risen," 94).
221. See J. Fenton, "The Ending of Mark's Gospel," *Resurrection* (ed. S. Barton and G. Stanton; London: SPCK, 1992) 1–7.
222. See summaries, Gundry, *Mark*, 1017. What would be curtailed especially in the first three suggestions is an ending that reverses the expectations set up in the Gospel itself.

Luke 24:9b–12 (but not 24:13–54, for it breathes the atmosphere of Jerusalem, wheres Mark 16:7 points to Galilee). . . . Presumably the lost ending of Mark contained a version of the Great Commission, but one devoid of characteristically Matthean diction and references. It would probably be foolhardy to speculate any further. . . . "[223] I see two problems here: (1) Gundry does not make any use of John in developing his theory; (2) it is difficult to imagine Matthew and Luke both having access to a full, original Mark (where? when?) before the loss of the ending, which Gundry seem to think was accidental. My proposed reconstruction is based on extant narratives of an appearance to Mary Magdalene. A full analysis of this reconstruction, its provenance and the reason(s) and timing of its suppression or loss, are obviously beyond the scope of this study. But an examination of these narratives is a preliminary step in that direction.

Such an examination suggests to me that a tradition of an appearance to her may form an intricate fit with the empty tomb tradition. The appearance to her, in that case, is not a late creation designed to be a bridge to the appearances to the disciples, as many have suggested.[224] The angelic announcement at the tomb in the Synoptics is enough of a bridge to appearances. It is more probable that an original tradition of a protophany to Mary Magdalene has been suppressed, than that it came into being later. I agree with those scholars who see Matthew and John as independent witnesses to an early tradition of an appearance to her,[225] locating it at or near the tomb. The third mention of a protophany to her, the Markan Appendix, is generally regarded as resulting from a late recombination of canonical material, though this is far from certain.[226]

In the early decades of the Christian movement there were competing claims and counterclaims based on visionary experiences, and an effort to cap off the list of authorized ones and present them as different from "ordinary" visions. The appearance to Mary Magdalene is involved in this competition. Independent

---

223. Gundry, *Mark*, 1021, 1020.

224. Neirynck, for example, holds that Matthew created this bridge to prepare for the appearance to the eleven in Galilee, and John took over Matthew's appearance to the women and redacted it for his own purposes. He argues that in more than one aspect, the reconstructions of the Johannine source come close to the text of the Synoptics (F. Neirynck, "John and the Synoptics: the Empty Tomb Stories," *Evangelica II* [ed. F. van Segbroeck; Leuven: Leuven University Press, 1991] 571–78); Not so in my analysis. Neirynck's theory that John knew and used Matthew here is followed by Crossan, as we have seen. J. E. Alsup (*The Post-Resurrection Appearance Stories of the Gospel Tradition* [London: SPCK, 1975] 114) thinks Matthew created his bridge based on the angelophany.

225. See C. H. Dodd, "The Appearances of the Risen Christ," *More New Testament Studies* (Manchester: Manchester University Press, 1968) 18–19, 32–33; Fuller, *Formation of the Resurrection Narratives*, 156–77; R. E. Brown, *The Gospel according to John* (Garden City: Doubleday, 1970) 2.967.

226. P. A. Mirecki argues that 16:9–15, 20a contains an underlying core narrative made up of a cycle of three post-resurrection appearance scenes. This text is carefully written, and not a set of borrowed phrases from other gospels. It was not the original ending of Mark but might have been an early gospel ending, perhaps even one that Mark intentionally displaced (*Mark 16:9–20: Composition, Tradition and Redaction*, Harvard University dissertation 1986).

witnesses are reminiscences of different communities to a protophany to Mary Magdalene[227] which authorized her in an extraordinary way. John may preserve fragments of the earliest or a very early version, and give us some indication of its explosive nature.

In the simple procedure of comparing the three canonical accounts, and distilling the common elements, we find the following. The Markan Appendix v. 9 agrees with Matthew and John on four, perhaps five, points: (1) the risen Jesus appears; (2) the first appearance is to Mary Magdalene;[228] and (3) that appearance is timed "when he rose early on the first day of the week" (Matt 28:1: "toward the dawn on the first day of the week"; John 20:1: "on the first day of the week...early"); (4) she is said to have gone and told "those who had been with him" (v. 10; they are described, as in the Gospel of Mary, as mourning and weeping). (5) The location as at the tomb, though not mentioned, is perhaps taken for granted by the author of the Appendix, as the women have just fled from the tomb in Mark 16:8.

Matt 28:9–10 and John 20:1, 11–18 have eighteen points of contact:

1. The risen Jesus appears

2. to Mary Magdalene (with the other Mary in Matthew, following Mark 15:47 instead of 16:1; alone in John, but see the plural "we" in 20:2)[229]

3. early on the first day of the week.

4. The encounter takes place in the vicinity of the tomb (or as Neirynck has it, "the christophany is connected with the visit to the tomb").[230]

5. In contrast to Simon Peter and the beloved disciple, and in contrast to the women in Mark and Luke, Mary Magdalene does not enter the tomb, but looks into it (the women are invited to look into it in Matthew).

6. It is the first appearance narrated.

---

227. The first appearance is to three women also in the Epistula Apostolorum 10, which has no angelophany.

228. The Markan Appendix identifies her, as neither of the other two do, as she from whom Jesus had cast seven demons (cf. Luke 8:2). The demons are not said in Luke to have been exorcised by Jesus.

229. G. W. Trompf ("The First Resurrection Appearance and the Ending of Mark's Gospel," *NTS* 18 [1972] 309) sees a process of "individualization," from a group of women (in original, lost Mark, followed by Matt 28:9–10) to the isolated figure of Mary Magdalene. He thinks this process served as an antidote to the tradition which prioritized Jesus' mother as one of those women (cf. Mark 6:3 with 15:40, two mentions of a Mary with sons named James and Joses), and hence her family, especially James, thus challenging the leadership of Peter (313). The tradition of a protophany to Mary Magdalene, in this reading, serves to promote the authority of Peter by diluting the authority of Jesus' family. Luke is "more destructive" and pro-Petrine than Matthew or John, in that the appearance to the women simply disappears (325). If the other Mary at the cross, burial and tomb is not the mother of Jesus, however, as almost all other scholars think, it is not a case of one woman neutralizing another, and the authority struggles must be seen differently.

230. Neirynck, "The Empty Tomb Stories," 581.

7. The emptiness of the tomb is explained as due to theft or removal of the corpse (in Matthew a false report that disciples have taken it; in John Mary Magdalene's first, mistaken impression that enemies have removed it).

8. Jesus utters a greeting (*chairete* [Rejoice!] in Matthew; "Mary"[231] in John).

9. He repeats words of the angel(s), thereby showing some duplication with the angelophany.

10. He is recognized (immediately in Matthew, slowly in John[232]).

11. 11. Touching or holding him is mentioned (the women grasp [*ekratēsan*] his feet in Matt v. 9; Mary is told "Do not hold me" [*mē mou haptou*] in John 20:17), with two verbs which may be synonyms.[233]

12. Mary Magdalene is given a commission to speak Jesus' own words to the disciples, that is, to be the voice of the risen Jesus.[234] Of the canonical Gospels, only John gives a direct quotation as part of her report. The second part of the verse in indirect discourse fits awkwardly with the first. The verse reads literally: "Mary Magdalene went and announced to the disciples, 'I have seen the Lord,'" and he said these things to her." The source verse was probably "Mary Magdalene went and announced to the disciples that he had said these things to her." The Evangelist may have opened up the sentence and inserted the creedal formula,[235] or may have shortened a saying such as "I have seen the Lord ascending" or "I have seen the Lord and he said 'I am ascending.'"

13. The disciples in this commission are referred to as "my brothers," perhaps an allusion to Ps 22:23 [22]).[236] In neither Gospel does this term refer to the Twelve or the Eleven.[237]

14. The commission is fulfilled (implied in Matthew, since the disciples go where they are sent;[238] explicitly in John v. 19 as she gives her report).

15. There is no verbal response to the women/woman's message on the part of the disciples. But the response of believing acceptance is implied in that in John 20:20

231. See Brown, *John*, 2.990 on the fluctuations of textual witnesses in the five times she is named in this Gospel.
232. Her wrong identification of him as the gardener gives the occasion for recognition that follows Jesus speaking her name (cf. 10:3).
233. Compare Mark 1:31 with Matthew 8:15. Neirynck calls them "interchangeable" ("Empty Tomb Stories," 583).
234. D'Angelo ("Reconstructing 'Real' Women," 111) considers this message a prophetic oracle.
235. S. Schneiders, "John 20:1–18: The Encounter of the Easter Jesus with Mary Magdalene — A Transformative Feminist Reading," in *What Is John?* (ed. F. Segovia; Atlanta: Scholars Press, 1996) 167. Contrast Fortna, *The Fourth Gospel*, 193.
236. S. Schneiders ("John 20:1–18," 161) argues that *adelphoi* in v. 17 should be translated "brothers and sisters." I think this may well be a correct interpretative translation of the source behind these two accounts.
237. On Matthew, see N. B. Stonehouse, *The Witness of Matthew and Mark to Christ* (Grand Rapids: Eerdmans, 1944) 175–76. On John, Trompf comments that the term "brothers" is unusual "for an evangelist without a theology of 'brotherhood'" ("First Resurrection Appearance," 322).
238. The mountain, however, is not mentioned in the commission to the women.

the disciples "were fully prepared to recognize and accept Jesus' appearance in their midst that evening," and in Matt 28:16 the eleven show up for the Galilean 'appearance.[239]

16. The Holy Spirit is mentioned in the following scene (in the triadic formula in Matt 28:19; breathed on the disciples in John).

17. The role of Mary Magdalene is subordinated or obscured. In Matthew this is by the subsequent appearance to and the world-wide commissioning of the eleven; in John by insertion of vv. 2–10 concerning Simon Peter and the beloved disciple[240] — the latter said to be the first to believe (v. 8) and widely seen as "an exemplar of the faith that needs no appearances of the Lord to recognize that Jesus has entered his glory (v. 9),"[241] and by the appearance to her not being mentioned when the appearances are counted. John 21:14 says that the appearance on the shore of the Sea of Tiberias was "the third time that Jesus had appeared to the disciples after he had risen from the dead." Either Mary Magdalene is not considered a disciple, or her vision is discounted. The verse may have come from a source that enumerated only appearances it recounted, and did not include hers (cf. the numbering of signs in 2:11 and elsewhere), or it may be counting only appearances to groups. But wherever the explanation, 21:14 now discounts 20:11–18. V 14 "may reflect less participation in leadership among women in the community in its later years, or the desire to restrict women's participation on the part of the appendix or its audience"[242]

18. Neither account is followed by a narrative of ascension. Ascension narratives are found only in Luke/Acts (cf. Markan Appendix v. 19). Paul's mention of himself as "last of all" to receive an appearance in 1 Cor 15:8 implies an ending of official appearances.

It seems to me that these eighteen points — plus differences between the narratives and inconsistencies within them — indicate a common pre-Matthean, pre-Johannine tradition.[243] I do not think that they indicate that John is re-

---

239. Schneiders, "John 20:11–18," 161; Schneiders ("Women in the Fourth Gospel and the Role of Women in the Contemporary Church," *BTB* 12 [1982] 44) contrasts the disciples in John "who give no indication of not accepting Mary's testimony," with those in Matt 28:17 ("some doubted"); Mark 16:11; Luke 24:10–11.

240. Brown (*John*, 2.998) finds traces of three narratives behind vv. 1–18 (two visits to the empty tomb [an early form in vv. 1–2 and a later truncated form in vv. 11–13], and the narrative of an appearance to Mary Magdalene); he is unable to say if these were combined by the Evangelist or before. His reason for holding the two Magdalene scenes were independent is the "we" in v. 2 (999): a link would not have been created which contradicts v. 1. But v. 2 is part of the Peter/beloved disciple material; it may use the plural "we" drawn from Synoptic sources or memories. The tradition of the empty tomb involving her and another women may have been the original context of an appearance to her.

241. Perkins, " 'I Have Seen the Lord,' " 39. The Thomas episode (20:24–29) "is connected to the Magdalene story by the demand to touch Jesus' wounds. The reader knows that such a request is illegitimate, as is the demand for a sign (cf. John 4:48, cp. 20:25). Thomas apparently comes to belief without actually taking up the challenge to touch Jesus" (citing Brown, *John*, 1044–46).

242. D'Angelo, "(Re)presentations of Women," 137.

243. H. E. Hearon, *Witness and Counter-Witness: the Function of the Mary Magdalene Tradition in Early Christian Communities*, Graduate Theological Union dissertation, 1998. She argues, I think correctly, that an account behind these Gospels derives from oral tradition.

fashioning Matthew. As will be clear from my treatment of John 20 in the next chapter, John may be using a source which he does not fully use, or does not see or draw the implications of. The distinctive characteristics of that source are not evident in Matthew, who may have inherited an already diluted version. How the Markan Appendix and a hypothetical lost ending of Mark might fit into this process of dilution cannot be explored here. But note that in the Markan Appendix Mary Magdalene, without a commission, tells "those who had been with" Jesus, and they would not believe "that he was alive and had been seen by her" — two elements that may bear some relationship to numbers 14 and 17 above. Davies and Allison hold that the Matthean passage is a shortened form of "a story" which has been expanded in John.[244]

Schneiders has pointed out that "Until quite recently, post-patristic commentators have, virtually to a man (and I use the word designedly), treated the appearance to Mary Magdalene as a minor, private, personal, or unofficial encounter between Jesus and his (hysterical?) female follower, in which he kindly consoles her before making his official and public Easter appearances to male witnesses and commissioning them to carry on his mission in the world. More recently, commentators, under the influence of feminist scholarship, have tended to recognize the raw sexism of this traditional interpretation, which ignores the plain content and intent of the Johannine text, because patriarchal bias and the ecclesiastical power agenda blinded the interpreters to the apostolic identity of a woman witness and its potential repercussions on contemporary Church order."[245] But too few scholars are under the influence of feminist scholarship; and the repercussions of feminist scholarship are much, much wider. In the following, final chapter I will indicate that "the plain content and intent" of this text turn out to be not so plain.

The above reconstruction and the treatment of John 20 that follows accept as possible that women were the — or a — primary source of the resurrection faith. It accepts as possible that the pagan authors who were convinced, as MacDonald puts it, "that female initiative was central to Christianity's development"[246] were reflecting not just second-century controversy and ongoing

244. Davies and Allison, *Gospel According to St. Matthew*, 668. L. M. Wills (*The Quest of the Historical Gospel* [London: Routledge, 1997] 156) argues that by using John and Mark as lenses though which we can perceive the refracted image of an earlier gospel tradition, we can hypothetically reconstruct its outline.

245. Schneiders, "John 20:1–18," 159. Her examples of the blinded scholars are R. E. Brown, *The Virginal Conception and Bodily Resurrection of Jesus* (London: Chapman, 1973) n. 170, p. 101; X. Léon Dufour, *Resurrection de Jésus* (Paris: Seuil, 1971) 272; A. George, "Les récits d'apparitions aux onze à partir de Luc 24, 26–53," *La Resurrection du Christ et l'exégèse moderne* (Paris: Cerf, 1969), 76. More recent examples could be found as well. She refers to the article of G. O'Collins and D. Kendall ("Mary Magdalene as Major Witness to Jesus' Resurrection, *TS* 48 [1987] 631–46) as "an excellent marshalling of the data for reinterpretation."

246. MacDonald, *Early Christian Women*, 2.

ambivalence about women's roles, but indirectly acknowledging women's active and creative witness from the beginning. The charge of naivete and lack of sophistication can be leveled against any treatment that so reconstructs women's history.[247] More often the charge is "too much optimism" or "imagination." We have to be willing to risk these charges in order to enter a history shaped by apocalyptic mysticism.

---

247. Cf. T. Ilan's (far too) brief reconstruction, which leads her to conclude that "women were extremely instrumental at the most critical moment of Christian history.... [T]he initial momentum seems to have begun with the people who interpreted the events following Jesus' death as a resurrection. The Gospels unanimously agree that these people were women. Thus, the basic creed of Christianity, namely that Jesus after his death had come back to life, is in fact a woman's idea." She thinks her suggestion "promotes a rather positivist approach to the words of the Gospels, taking them more as historical descriptions than is usually merited today. In fact, this approach could be viewed as naive and unsophisticated" unless incorporated into "a wider historical perspective" — which she attempts to provide with "the application of some source criticism and some onomastic methodology" ("In the Footsteps," 116, 123). I am in sympathy with some of her insights, but not her approach, which does not move beyond positivism. See D. LaCapra, *Writing History, Writing Trauma* (Baltimore: Johns Hopkins, 2001) 1–42, on two approaches to historiography: a documentary or self-sufficient research model, of which positivism is the extreme form, and radical constructivism. His own view falls between the two. His notion of "empathetic unsettlement" (41–42), which involves affectivity and provides a barrier against closure, has important connections with feminism.

SEVEN

Mary Magdalene as Successor to Jesus

"A scene always comes to the top; arranged; representative. It will not stand argument — that we are sealed vessels afloat upon what is convenient to call reality; at some moments, without a reason, without an effort, the sealing matter cracks; in floods reality."

V. Woolf, "A Sketch of the Past"[1]

"I am not concerned with the single life, but with lives together. I have — am trying to find, in the folds of the past, such fragments as time having broken the perfect vessel, still keeps safe. The perfect vessel? But it was not by any means made of durable stuff. For it was only when the thing had happened and the violence of the shock was over that one could understand, or really live; only when one had left the room and was walking home at the dead of night. Then in that darkness, which had no limit, very dark, whose shores were invisible, whatever had happened, expanded, and something dropped away. Then without a companion one loved; spoke with no one to hear; and carried on an intercourse with people who were not there more completely than [when] chair was drawn close to theirs."

V. Woolf, Draft of The Waves[2]

$\mathbf{S}$ ARAH COAKLEY ASKS, "What was it about Mary Magdalene's testimony that was both formative and yet in need of being downplayed?" She wants us to answer her question in ways that do not shore up gender stereotypes — as, for example, Thomas Aquinas shores them up when he argues that women's greater capacity for love and fidelity was seen in their presence at the cross and tomb, and will earn them a quicker share than men in the beatific vision (ST 3a, 55, 1 ad 3). She is interested in the epistemic significance of the probability "that women first witnessed the resurrection, first 'saw' the risen Christ," and in "questioning the resistance, in philosophical circles, to probing *beneath* the level of epistemic functioning taken as normative for the 'generic male' — that

---

1. V. Woolf, "A Sketch of the Past" *Moments of Being*, 142.
2. V. Woolf, Draft I of *The Waves*, 9 (Berg Collection, New York Public Library; see Moore, *Short Season*, 140 and n. 14, p. 144 for pagination).

is, the vision of selfhood supposedly abstracting from gender differentiation, but actually showing a marked predilection for characteristics honoured culturally as 'male.' That seems to me quite important for understanding the appropriate mode for recognizing the risen Christ. What levels of the self — what affective or intuitive interpersonal mysteries of human response, what dimensions of bodily existence (themes normally downplayed in 'masculinist' philosophical discussion [and biblical studies]) — are unavoidable in their epistemic implications if the true *richesse* of encounter with the risen Christ charted in the New Testament is to be grasped? How are 'normal' understandings of perception and rationality to be *revised* in the light of the resurrection narratives, and to what extent is that necessary revision entangled with questions of gender? In this, as in other areas of current analytic philosophy of religion, my suspicion is that no spiritually profound advances can be made here unless some of the lessons of feminist critique (both theological and philosophical) are assimilated."[3]

Her questions sharpen a sense of discovery. I argued in the previous chapter that the mysticism expressed in the empty tomb tradition assumes a non-individualistic understanding of selfhood that is grounded in corporateness and full humanity, and that is stronger than death. This is to use the concept "humanity" in a way that radically displaces the Western kyriarchal frame of reference which understands gender as a biological given and masculinity as the paradigm for being human.[4] Coakley urges an understanding of "the ontological *seriousness* of metaphorical speech."[5] The resurrection faith is communal and personal, a matter of the vindication of the Human One, that is, of Jesus and of all who suffer and stand up against injustice. Traces of a communal idea of death[6] and resurrection are found in Matt 27:52–53 and the preaching to the dead in Gospel of Peter 10:41–42, as well as in talk such as Paul's of Jesus as the "first fruits of those who have died" (1 Cor 15:20–23, 51–55). Two elements are constant in the Jewish literature of the time: that resurrection is a collective event and that it is an event of the future that involves the renewal of all creation.[7]

What became the source of conflicting interpretations, as for example at Corinth, was the past tense ("has been raised") in its potential in the present for energizing and en-couraging individuals to understand themselves as able now to face down death, to act (as the women are said to have at the crucifixion and tomb) in spite of the fear of death, and to act together. 2 Tim 2:17–27 expresses

3. S. Coakley, "Response" to W. P. Alston, "Biblical Criticism and the Resurrection," *The Resurrection* (ed. S. T. Davis, D. Kendall, G. O'Collins; Oxford: Oxford University Press, 1998) 189–90.
4. Schüssler Fiorenza, *Miriam's Son*, 47.
5. Coakley, "Response," 188.
6. Contrast Mr. Ramsey's view in Woolf's *To the Lighthouse* (165): "We perish, each alone."
7. A. Y. Collins, "The Empty Tomb in the Gospel According to Mark," 128. She speaks of the claim that God raised "a single individual, Jesus" as one of the innovations of the Christian movement. I would argue that the resurrection in the empty tomb tradition is not originally seen only as the raising of a single "individual," because of its connection with the tradition of the Human One.

a "hostility to those who preach a realized eschatology," which may refer to a conviction shared by some in Corinth that they were already enjoying the fruits of the resurrection (cf. 1 Cor 15:12–20), claiming that they were already risen and a new creation in Christ (cf. Gal 3:27–28).[8] The Corinthian community is confident that Christ has "activated" resurrection for them in their present existence. This gives them the strength and courage to live differently and transgress the barriers that separate them.[9] The past and present tense of the claim and its corporateness were formative for some early Christians.

But it was threatening to others.[10] The testimony of the women can be seen as democratic and challenging to structures of domination. As Schüssler Fiorenza reads the account of the empty tomb, the testimony of the women contains a demand: that one who hears it go on to Galilee to continue the work of economic and social justice, for the poor, ill, oppressed, women, slaves. The work of the liberation of the exploited is to be continued in the vision of a world free of hunger, poverty, death and in the action taken to implement that vision. It is work done not in a privatized, depoliticized, spiritualized way, but in the way of this *basileia* movement. The root of the resurrection faith is an apocalyptic vision of the present reality and future hope of a renewed world free of suffering and death. "Resurrection does not simply spell the survival of the soul but requires the transformation of the world as we know it."[11] The claim of vindication derives its authority from and is validated in continuing struggles against injustice and against the many forms of death.[12] Arguments and speculation focused on Jesus' vindication alone, or on what happened to his body, or on whose appearance story is best or earliest, or who is boss now, distract from this apocalyptic meaning.

The testimony is threatening also because it springs from the interpreted experience[13] and insight of historical Jewish women. Their belief may have been in the "taking" of Jesus' body, something we would call miraculous, hard for the historian to accept.[14] But the historian must deal with the possibility of their belief, as well as with the possibility that their belief was mistaken. That interpreted experience and insight comes to us distorted and framed by androcentric interests and

8. L. Maloney, "The Pastoral Epistles," *Searching the Scriptures,* 2.372, 376.

9. S. Matthews, "2 Corinthians," *Searching the Scriptures,* 2.206, 210.

10. L. Ross-Bryant ("Imagination and the Re-Valorization of the Feminine," *The Archaeology of the Imagination* [ed. C. E. Winquist; JAAR Studies vol. 48/2 (1981)] 109) explores three new centers of imagining: "deepened historicity, renewed participation, and concrete embodiment."

11. Schüssler Fiorenza, *Miriam's Son,* 121. The empty tomb tradition signifies that "Jesus is going ahead — not going away" (126).

12. Schüssler Fiorenza, *Miriam's Child,* 128: the authorization of theological discourse about Jesus "must be articulated and proven 'right' again and again within the continuing struggles for survival, justice and well-being."

13. J. Scott ("The Evidence of Experience," *Critical Inquiry* 17 [1991] 777) argues that "experience" should be redefined as "at once always already an interpretation and something to be interpreted."

14. Lindars, "Jesus Risen," 90–91.

emphases,[15] passing through the process of conceptualization, tellings, retellings, writings, redactions, readings, interpretations. I wonder in particular how much scholarly emphasis on the empty tomb traditions as crassly physical is attributable to male notions of female piety, and sexist identification of women with the flesh and death (womb/tomb), the uncanny. In spite of the process of reformulating the tradition, the four canonical gospels still present women as the primary witnesses to Jesus' execution and the first proclaimers of the resurrection, Mary Magdalene the most prominent among them. I have argued here that we must posit a mind and spirit with what Woolf called "the shock-receiving capacity":[16] a mind and spirit prepared by work and study and mystical experience, prepared by struggle against oppression, to produce and receive the "jolt" of revelation or apocalypse. That jolt's communal and personal dimension is stressed.

The traditions of the empty tomb and appearance to the women can be reasonably assessed as ancient and primary. It is not at all clear how this tradition related to the traditions of appearances to male disciples, and to "more than five hundred." We may be tempted to think almost of parallel universes inhabited by men and women, of separate origins, different dynamics (psychological, exegetical, sociological). Or we may think of the women's testimony winning enough initial acceptance — mingled perhaps with rivalry — to become an inspiration for appearances to others. Which was possibly more original, an appearance to several women or to one woman, Mary Magdalene? This cannot be answered by appeal to some supposed rule (that names tend to be added, or that they tend to disappear), especially as the context here is competing authorizations. We may think beyond this either/or. Matthew 28:1 and John 20:2 preserve a tradition of women companions of Mary Magdalene, which may be original. But that she alone is named as receiving the protophany in John 20 and the Markan Appendix may indicate she is the source of the empty tomb tradition complete with its insight/revelation, that is, its interpretation. The threatening thought appears: that Mary Magdalene can be considered a — or the — founder of Christianity, if one wants to use such a term; that she was "a creator of the Christian belief in the resurrection,"[17] and has a better claim than Paul to the title "the first great interpreter of Jesus."[18] This, of course, runs counter still to "the enormous body of masculine opinion to the effect that nothing could be expected of women intellectually. . . . Yet genius of a sort must have existed among women as it must have existed among the working classes."[19]

---

15. On this problem in later material, see E. Castelli, "Visions and Voyeurism: Holy Women and the Politics of Sight in Early Christianity," Protocol of the Colloquy of the Center for Hermeneutical Studies (Berkeley: GTU and University of California at Berkeley, 1992) 20.

16. Woolf, "A Sketch of the Past," 72. She supposed that this capacity is what made her a writer.

17. Macdonald, *Early Christian Women*, 124, 250, on Celsus' accusation.

18. B. Chilton, "Resurrection in the Gospels," *Judaism in Late Antiquity* (ed. A. J. Avery-Peck and J. Neusner; Leiden: Brill, 2000) 4.217.

19. Woolf, *Room*, 54, 48.

John 20 and 2 Kings 2

In this chapter I want to explore a larger threat, "formative [for some] and yet [for others] in need of being downplayed." In John 20 I see fragments of the claim that Mary Magdalene was a successor of Jesus. This, I think, was the explosion Price was looking for, that explains the subsequent fragmentations and distortions and strength of her memory.[20] Speaking of rabbinic texts, Boyarin insists "We must very carefully tease out ... the different strands of discourse and counter-discourse which they preserve and suppress, and sometimes preserve *by* suppressing — complicating our reading of ancient ideology and not simplifying it."[21] Identifying the techniques of suppression and preservation is basic to a study of the figure of Mary Magdalene.

In the framework of feminist thought, my suggestion is that the tradition behind Matthew 28 and John 20 (and perhaps also the Markan Appendix) of an appearance to Mary Magdalene at or near the tomb, whether alone or with others,[22] is intimately connected to the empty tomb and explicated it. Traces of an early telling found in John show an imaginative reuse of 2 Kings 2:1–18, Elisha's witnessing of Elijah's ascent. What leads me to turn to this text as subtext is the risen Jesus' statement that he has not yet ascended (that is, he is in the process of ascending [*anabaino*][23]) and that Mary Magdalene is to tell his "brothers" that she saw him and he said to her, "I am ascending." This is the "marker"[24] that activates the allusion for me.[25]

The claim to have witnessed an ascent is powerful stuff biblically and is particularly powerful in the mystical tradition represented, for example, by the Testament of Job. The witnessing of Elijah's ascent is the condition upon which, or assurance, or sign that what Elisha has asked his "master" — to inherit a double share of his spirit, the oldest son's share[26] — will be granted him by God. "Elijah said to Elisha, 'Tell me what I may do for you before I am taken (*laqah*) from you.' Elisha said, 'Please let me inherit a double share of your spirit.' He responded, 'You have asked a hard thing; yet, if you see me as I am being taken from you, it

---

20. See above, p. 229.

21. D. Boyarin, "Reading Androcentrism against the Grain: Women, Sex and Torah-Study," *Poetics Today* 12 (1991) 51.

22. Cf. accounts in Acts of Paul's Damascus experience.

23. The present tense used here is translated by G. R. Beasley-Murray (*John*, [Dallas: Word, 1987] 377) as "I am on my way." Jesus is "already in the process of ascending, but has not yet reached his destination" (Brown, *John*, 2.994). See R. Schnackenburg, *The Gospel according to St. John* (New York: Crossroad, 1982) 3.319.

24. Z. Ben-Porat, "The Poetics of Literary Allusion," *PTL: A Journal for Descriptive Poetics and Theory of Literature* 1 (1976) 108–9.

25. Jonathan Draper, in a paper for the 1999 SBL which he kindly shared with me, sees different details of the scene, such as the two angels, one at the head and one at the feet (John 20:12), indicating that Isaiah 6, read in a Targumic fashion, is evoked here to present Jesus at the tomb "on the *merkabah* with the angels poised to fly up to the father to be enthroned in the heavenly temple."

26. J. Walsh, "Elijah," *ABD*, 2.465. Deut 21:17.

will be granted you; if not, it will not.' As they continued walking and talking, a chariot of fire (*rekeb-esh*) and horses of fire separated the two of them, and Elijah ascended ('*lh*) in a whirlwind (*basearah*) into heaven.[27] Elisha kept watching and crying out, 'My father, my father! The chariot[28] of Israel and its horsemen!' But when he could no longer see him, he grasped his own clothes and tore them in two pieces. He picked up the mantle of Elijah[29] that had fallen from him, and went back and stood on the bank of the Jordan. He took the mantle of Elijah that had fallen from him, and struck the water, saying, 'Where is the Lord, the God of Elijah?' When he had struck the water, the water was parted to the one side and to the other,[30] and Elisha went over.[31] When the company of the prophets who were at Jericho saw him at a distance, they declared, 'The spirit of Elijah rests on Elisha.' They came to meet him and bowed to the ground before him."

With the reuse of this text, Mary Magdalene's *claim to have seen the risen Jesus ascending carries with it the implicit claim to have inherited a double portion of the spirit that was in him.* The scene in 2 Kings 2 evokes Joshua's succession of Moses. "Joshua the son of Nun was full of the spirit of wisdom, because Moses had laid his hands on him, and the Israelites obeyed him, doing as the Lord had commanded Moses" (Deut 34:9; cf. 1:37–38; 3:28; 31:7–8, 14–15, 23; Num 27:16–23).

I am not aware of anyone else suggesting this textual and imaginative connection, but I will be surprised if no one else has, if indeed allusions " 'program' texts in such a way that the anticipated reader inevitably connects them."[32] But allu-

---

27. Targum Pseudo-Jonathan: "he ascended as if to the sky" (see A. Wiener, *The Prophet Elijah in the Development of Judaism* [London: Routledge & Kegan Paul, 1978] n. 50, p. 205. Re'uyot Yezezqe'el describes God descending to judge in "the chariots of fire and storm (*merkebot esh u-searah*) (ed. I. Gruenwald in *Temerin* 1 [1972] 137–39; cited by Gruenwald, "Jewish Merkavah Mysticism and Gnosticism," *Studies in Jewish Mysticism* (ed. J. Dan and F. Talmage; Cambridge: Association for Jewish Studies, 1982] 47). On the chariot of God as an expression of natural phenomena, see M. Lieb, *The Visionary Mode* (Ithaca: Cornell University Press, 1991) 28. Some critics distinguish the whirlwind, emblematic of the presence of God, from the chariot and horses, symbolic of the prophetic task (e.g., T. E. Fretheim, *First and Second Kings* [Louisville: Westminster/John Knox, 1999] 138), but this is too prosaic. 3 Enoch 6:1 describes Enoch's translation to heaven "in great glory on a fiery chariot, with fiery horses and glorious attendants," the image borrowed from 2 Kings 2 (P. Alexander, "3 (Hebrew Apocalypse of) Enoch," *OTP* 1.246, 261, n. c). See also A. Kuyt, *The 'Descent' to the Chariot* (Tübingen: Mohr, 1995) 235, 355, 357.

28. *Rekeb* is sometimes used as a plural, chariotry (*BDB* 939); it is often translated this way in 2 Kings 2:12; 13:14.

29. A mantle of animal skins was often worn by prophets (1 Kings 19:13; 2 Kings 1:8 [belt]; Zech 13:4; Mark 1:6 [belt also]).

30. As it had for Elijah in v. 8.

31. 4Q481A, one of three tiny fragments which reproduces 2 Kings 2:14–16 with paraphrastic supplements, reads "Elisha went up" (G. Vermes, *The Complete Dead Sea Scrolls in English* [4th ed.; New York: Penguin, 1997] 554).

32. A. R. Winsor, *A King Is Bound in the Tresses: Allusions to the Song of Songs in the Fourth Gospel* (New York: Peter Lang, 1999) 1. Holding that an oral version has been incorporated into the Johannine text without problem, she thinks "the process of literary allusion virtually requires the reader to make the textual connections programmed into the narrative" (3), though she acknowledges that allusions can be overlooked or disregarded (11). I see the process as more subtle than this, and the process I am suggesting here is full of conflict.

sions do not always function in this way; they can be further obscured, and their connections lost or partially broken. Others have argued that a source borrowed by the author of the *Grundschrift* behind John 20 alludes to the assumption of Moses in a Jewish-Christian view of Jesus as the prophet like Moses,[33] and also that the command that Mary not touch Jesus (John 20:17) has a parallel in Adam's instruction to Eve (Apocalypse of Moses 31:3–4) that she not touch his body after his death, but permit the angel of the Lord to dispose of it; angels then bring it to the earthly paradise for burial (37–41).[34]

Objections

1. Did Elijah Die?

It might be immediately objected that the taking of Elijah, unlike the story of the empty tomb and appearance, is not about death or resurrection, but about escaping death. N. T. Wright warns: "Remember, resurrection does not mean being 'raised up to heaven' or 'taken up in glory.' Neither Elijah nor Enoch had been resurrected in the sense that Daniel, 2 Maccabees and the rabbis meant it; nor, for that matter, had anyone else. Resurrection will happen only to people who are already dead. To speak of the destruction of the body and the continuing existence, however blessed, of something else (call it a 'soul' for the sake of argument) is not to speak of resurrection, but simply of death itself. 'Resurrection' is not simply death from another viewpoint; it is the reversal of death, its cancellation, the destruction of its power," a belief justified "by reference to the creator God and this God's passion for eventual justice." Although the doctrine remained "quite imprecise and unfocused" and the idea of resurrection could be used metaphorically by early Christians, resurrection was "the overcoming of death by the justice-bringing power of the creator God . . . [it] was seen to consist of passing *through* death and out the other side into a new sort of bodily life." The resurrection hope "turned those who believed it into a counter-empire, an alternative society"[35]

Yet even in the Hebrew Bible and LXX, Elijah's translation may be understood as a death. In 2 Kings 19 the verb *lqh* is used three times. Because his enemies are seeking his life "to take it away" (vv. 10, 14), Elijah asks "that he might die: 'It is enough; now, O Yhwh, take away my life" (v. 4). After Elijah ascends in 2:11,

---

33. G. Richter, "Der Vater und Gott Jesu und seiner Bruder in Joh 20,17," *Münchener Theologische Zeitschrift* 24 (1974); reprinted in *Studien zum Johannesevangelium* (Regensburg, 1977) 266–80; cited by Neirynck, "Empty Tomb Stories," 585–86.

34. M. R. D'Angelo, "A Critical Note: John 20:17 and Apocalypse of Moses 31," *JTS* 41 (1990) 529–36. She thinks v. 17 emphasizes that "the state of Jesus is different when he encounters Mary from when he meets the disciples and Thomas and invites Thomas' touch"; it is possible that this uniqueness may confer on her a unique privilege (535). This needs further exploration.

35. See N. T. Wright, "The Resurrection of Resurrection," *BR* 16 (2000) 10, 63.

Elisha tears his clothing into two pieces, a sign of mourning.[36] The persecuted prophet is now removed beyond his enemies' reach (cf. Wisd 4:10, 16, often · read as referring to Enoch,[37] in which "taken up" is clearly synonymous with "died"). His translation provides him with a new kind of bodily life, beyond time and decay, available for return, recognizable. Gruenwald points out that this is not an ascent during lifetime as we find in apocalyptic literature, but "As far as we know, his ascension marked his death... the termination of his lifespan on earth."[38] The cry "My father, my father! The chariot of Israel and its horsemen!" is repeated by the weeping King Joash before the dying Elisha (2 Kings 13:14).[39] It is repeated also by R. Akiba in his funeral address for R. Eliezer (*b. Sanh.* 68a; *Avot of Rabbi Nathan* [A] 25; *Semahot* 9:2)[40] and by Joshua ben Hananiah for R. Eliezer ("my Rabbi," *p. Shab.* 5b).[41] Elijah's disappearance did not preclude his death for Josephus, who remarks that "Elijah disappeared from among men and no one knows until today anything of his death" (*Ant.* 9.2.2).[42] Buber relates the taking of Enoch and Elijah to the death "turned into a mystery" in Ps 73:24; 49:15.[43] R. Abahu (*Ber. R.* 25, 1) relates the "taking" of Enoch and Elijah to the God "taking" away from Ezekiel the desire of his eyes, that is, to the death of his wife (Ezek 24:16).[44]

Pseudo-Philo's Liber Antiquitatum Biblicarum 48:1 refers to the death of Elijah (identified as Phinehas), Enoch, and perhaps others, after their eschatological return, but it is not a reference to their martyrdom.[45] In 1 Enoch 89:51–53, the sheep (Elijah) survived a murder attempt on the part of the other sheep, and fled away "and they wanted to kill him, but the Lord of the sheep rescued him from

36. Gen 37:34; 2 Sam 1:11; 13:3; Job 1:20. See D. Daube, *The New Testament and Rabbinic Judaism* (London: Athlone, 1956) 24–25 on rabbinic traditions about rending garments in two pieces on the occasions such as the death of a parent, a teacher of Torah. See *Mo'ed Qatan* 26a: "Resh Lakish asked R. Yohana: 'Isn't Elijah still alive? Why did Elisha mourn for him?' R. Yohanan answered, 'Since Elisha could not see him any more, he considered him good as dead.'" (S. M. Segal, *Elijah: A Study in Jewish Folklore* [New York: Behrman's Jewish Book House, 1935] 56.

37. M. Black, "The 'Two Witnesses' of Rev 11:3f," *Donum Gentilicium* (ed. E. Bammel, C. K. Barrett, W. D. Davies; Oxford: Clarendon, 1978) 233–34.

38. Gruenwald, *From Apocalyptic to Gnosticism*, 19, 127. The idea of a heavenly ascent of the soul is sometimes wrongly traced back to the Hebrew Bible (70; see n. 20 on Gen 5:24 in Onqelos and elsewhere). See R. E. Friedman and S. D. Overton, "Death and Afterlife: The Biblical Silence," *Judaism in Late Antiquity*, 4.52: the story of Elijah's ascent "may be precisely the account of his death."

39. In 6:17 an army of horses and chariots (*rekeb*) of fire is seen around Elisha.

40. C. R. A. Morray-Jones, *Merkabah Mysticism and Talmudic Tradition* (dissertation Cambridge University 1988) 298–301. My thanks to him for providing this reference.

41. Daube, *The New Testament and Rabbinic Judaism*, 26.

42. Contrast Philo, *Questions and Answers on Genesis* 1:86.

43. M. Buber, *The Prophetic Faith* (New York: Harper & Row, 1960) 201–2.

44. R. T. Herford, *Christianity in Talmud and Midrash* (Clifton, N.J.: Reference Book Publishers, 1966) 271.

45. R. Bauckham, *The Climax of Prophecy* (Edinburgh: T. & T. Clark, 1993) n. 60, p. 276. On Phinehas as a pattern for martyrs, however, see 4 Macc 18:12 (H. A. Fischel, "Martyr and Prophet," *JQR* 37 [1947] 273, 373).

the sheep and caused him to ascend and settle down."[46] Chariot imagery is used to speak of death in Apocalypse of Moses 33:34 (Eve sees Adams soul taken "in a chariot of light" borne by four bright eagles, with angels going before it). The death chariot appears also in the Testament of Abraham 14, again with the soul separated from the body: "And chariots of the Lord God came and took his soul into the heavens.... And Isaac buried his father Abraham near his mother...."[47] Cf. 2 Baruch 46:4: speaking of his coming death, Baruch says "The throne of the Mighty One I cannot resist." Enoch's final translation is described in 1 Enoch 70:2: "he was raised aloft on the chariots of the spirit and his name vanished among them."[48] Many centuries later, the Negro Spiritual "Swing Low, Sweet Chariot" understood 2 Kings 2 in terms of death and/or a code of resistance and liberation. A song "of freedom and of faith in the inevitability of freedom,"[49] sometimes involving a return to Africa,[50] it was beloved by Harriet Tubman, and sung by her friends the evening she died, March 10, 1913.[51]

The association of Elijah with resurrection (probably made because of the revival of the widow's son in 1 Kings 17:22[52]) is found in *Pirke de R. Eliezer*, chap. 33 (Warsaw 1912); *Pesahim* 68a; *Tanhuma Emor.*, sec. 13 (ed. Buber); *Midrash Canticles Zuta*, chap. 7, pp. 38–39 (ed. Buber).[53] His association with an eschatological

---

46. Translation by E. Isaac, *OTP* 1.67.

47. *OTP* 1.902, E. P. Sanders translation (MSS E, C).

48. See also Odes of Solomon 38:1–4: "I went up into the light of Truth as into a chariot, and the Truth... set me on the place of immortal life."

49. S. A. Floyd, Jr., *The Power of Black Music* (New York: Oxford, 1995) 41. The chariot trope was repeated and revised many times. Floyd found eleven spirituals with the word "chariot" in their titles (e.g., "Good News, de Chariot's Coming," "Going the [sic] Ride Up in the Chariot, "Going Home in the Chariot." 279) and twenty-three others whose texts include it, some of these using Ezekiel 1. Eventually the new chariot of the train appeared (213–25). For discussion of the delicate balance between focus on transcendent life in the present and focus on the reality of death and reunion with the beloved dead, see A. C. Jones, *Wade in the Water: The Wisdom of the Spirituals* (Maryknoll, N.Y.: Orbis, 1993) 86–88. On the River Jordan as death, see A. J. Raboteau, *Slave Religion* (New York: Oxford, 1978) 262. Thanks to my colleague Prof. Stephanie Mitchem for these references.

50. M. M. Fisher, *Negro Slave Songs in the United States* (New York: Russell & Russell, 1953) 145, citing E. A. Pollard, *Black Diamonds Gathered in the Darkey Homes of the South* (New York, 1859) 115.

51. C. L. Blockson, *The Underground Railroad* (New York: Hippocrene, 1994) 337–38. J. W. Work (*Folk Song of the American Negro* [New York: Negro Universities, 1969; first published 1915] 59) classifies "Swing Low" as one of the "sorrow songs with note of joy," and mentions the tradition that it was composed by Mrs. Hannah Shepard of Tennessee (79–80).

52. Sir 48:5 interprets the reviving of the son as "raising a corpse from death and from Hades." Epiphanius claimed (*Adv. Haer.* 42) that the quotation in Eph 5:14 ("Awake, O Sleeper, and arise from the dead, and Christ shall give you light") is a passage found "in Elijah," perhaps a reference to an unknown book or a comment on the raising of the son.

53. Segal, *Elijah*, 30–31, 168. See *Sukkah* 5a: "R. Josse said that God's divine presence never came down on earth and that Moses and Elijah never went up to heaven; for this he offers the testimony of the verse, 'The heavens are the heavens of the Lord, but the earth hath He given to the children of man (Deut 19:15).' But how do we reconcile the verse concerning Elijah, 'And Elijah went up by a whirlwind to heaven'? The answer is, he ascended to the heavens but retained ten hand-breadths beneath the throne of God" (Segal, *Elijah*, 57). For parallels between Moses and Elijah, see *Pesikta Rabbati*, sec. 4, p. 13a–b (ed. Friedmann); *Sifre Deuteronomy*, sec. 342, p. 142a (ed. Friedmann); Segal, *Elijah*, 60–61. For traditions of Elijah as psychopomp, and as one who defeats the angel of death,

resurrection may be found earlier, in Ben Sira 48:11: "Blessed is he who sees you before he dies, f[or] you give l[if]e and he will live." This is Puech's restoration of the Hebrew text from the Cairo Genizah; he interprets it as meaning that the righteous who die after the return of Elijah will be resurrected.[54] See also 4Q521, which speaks of an anointed one probably through whose hand God will "give life to the dead" this may be an eschatological prophet, either Elijah or a prophet like Elijah.[55] Mark 9:11 gives us another early witness to this association between Elijah and resurrection: "Why do the scribes say that Elijah must come first?" — before, that is, the Human One's "rising from the dead" (v. 10).[56]

This Markan passage and its Matthean parallel sound what Robinson calls "a further theme, the deep mystery that a *suffering* Elijah was of a piece with a suffering Son of man."[57] Mark 9:13 ("... Elijah has come, and they did to him whatever they pleased, as it is written about him") seems to be a reference to a written tradition of the martyrdom of Elijah,[58] understood in the light of the murder of John the Baptist. This tradition is assimilated to — or an instance of — "how [it is] written of the Human One, that he should suffer many things and be treated with contempt" (v. 12). Matthew, however, while retaining the link between Elijah and the Human One, removes the references to writings in Mark 9:12 and 13. If Elijah is thought of as one of the two witnesses in Revelation 11, there he is said to be murdered. His body lies unburied for three and a half days, after which he is resurrected and ascends on a cloud (cf. the Coptic Apocalypse of Elijah 4:7–19: Elijah and Enoch return to earth, fight the shameless one, are killed, rise up, "lay down the flesh for the spirit," and "will shout up to heaven as they shine" [cf. Dan 12:3]).[59] Their enemies witness their ascent in Rev 11:12; "all

---

see Ginzberg, *Legends of the Jews*, 200–202, 227–29; on Elijah as teacher of the Kabbalah, pp. 229–33; Elijah as performing the miracle of resurrection, to confirm his identification of the Messiah, p. 234–35; see also Wiener, *The Prophet Elijah*, chapters 3, 4.

54. E. Puech, "Ben Sira 48:11 et la Resurrection," *Of Scribes and Scrolls* (ed. H. Attridge, J. J. Collins and T. H. Tobin; Lanham, Md.: University Press of America, 1990) 81–90. Cf. Sir 48:5 NRSV ("You raised a corpse from death and from Hades, by the word of the Most High"). For other readings of 48:11, see above p. 279, n. 149.

55. J. J. Collins, *The Scepter and the Star* (New York: Doubleday, 1995) 116–23. J. E. Taylor (*The Immerser: John the Baptist within Second Temple Judaism* [Grand Rapids: Eerdmans, 1997] 286) reads this with 4Q541 where it is said that the atoning figure will suffer at the hands of those who spread lies about him; "his fire will spring forth to all the ends of the earth."

56. J. A. T. Robinson, "Elijah, John and Jesus," *NTS* 4 (1958) 268.

57. Robinson, "Elijah," 276.

58. Black ("'Two Witnesses,'" 237) the allusion is probably to "some apocalyptic scripture, late echoes of which have reached us in the Pseudo-Philo and the Coptic Elijah apocalypse," rather than to 1 Kings 19:2, 10. See also Taylor, *The Immerser*, 285–88.

59. The Sahidic text says "lay down the flesh of the body"; cf. 5:32 "They will lay down the flesh of the world and they will receive their spiritual flesh." The narrator, an unnamed prophet, is addressed as "son of man" in the Akhmimic of 1:1; cf. Ezekiel 2:1. Translation by O. S. Wintermute, *OTP* 2.748, 752. Both the Coptic and the Hebrew Apocalypse of Elijah show evidence of a complex reediting of earlier material that may go back to the first or second century C.E.; the Coptic was reworked in a Christian community, the Hebrew in a Jewish community. Resurrection is a theme in both. (O. S. Wintermute, "Elijah, Apocalypse of," *ABD* 2.487). Wintermute thinks that the two times Elijah and

the people and all the world see them" in Apocalypse of Elijah 4:19.[60] Whether the tradition of Elijah's death is pre-Christian or not, John the Baptist's fate made an impact on that tradition, for those who saw him as Elijah, as well as for those who saw Jesus as Elijah.[61]

2. A Woman as Visionary, as Successor?

Another initial and major objection to my claim that 2 Kings 2 is evoked in John 20 might be that the very idea of a woman visionary, or a woman inheriting the "mantle"[62] of spiritual authority was unthinkable in the Judaism or Jewish Christianity of the period. There are no examples of female characters ascending to the heavens in the extant literature of this period; mysticism seems to be a male thing. The possible cultic background for accounts of mystical ascent, such as in 1 Enoch 14, may be regarded as a reminder that access to holy places was limited to men, and there is explicit reference to impurity caused by menstrual blood in *Hekaloth Rabbati* 18 (cf. Lev 21–22).[63] However, ritual impurity did not disqualify a woman from *ever* entering the Temple.[64] Though women may not have functioned as priests in the Jerusalem Temple,[65] they were allowed in every area of the Temple precincts in which men were allowed, passing through the

---

Enoch are mentioned may be Christian interpolations, influenced by Rev 11:1–12, into an earlier Jewish work ("Apocalypse of Elijah," *OTP* 1.721). He discusses the "apparent discrepancy" between chapter 1 (where the righteous who die are led to a heavenly city by angels) and elsewhere (where those who flee the lawless one will lie down as one who sleeps; their spirit and soul return to the Lord but their body is turned to stone until the day of the judgment when they will be resurrected) (731). This may not have appeared as a discrepancy to the writer.

60. R. Bauckham ("The Martyrdom of Enoch and Elijah: Jewish or Christian?" *JBL* 95 [1976] 447–58) argues that if there were a pre-Christian tradition, it must have included martyrdom and resurrection or have included neither; he concludes it included neither. Contrast Black, "The 'Two Witnesses,'" 236: because of the motif of three and a half days, language borrowed from Ezekiel 37, and the repetition of the ascension, he argues for an independent source for the legend of the death, resurrection, and ascension of the witnesses, possibly a pre-Christian one. "The story, as told in Revelation, need not be modelled on the story of Christ's death, resurrection, and ascension."

61. Meier (*Marginal Jew* 3.623–24; cf. 2.509–1038) summarizes his position that the historical Jesus consciously took upon himself the role of Elijah. Cf. Taylor, *The Immerser*, 281–94.

62. I am not aware of other examples of the motif of passing along a garment to anyone as a way of depicting prophetic succession.

63. C. Rowland, "Apocalypticism, Mysticism and the New Testament," *Geschichte — Tradition — Reflexion* (ed. P. Schafer; Tübingen: Mohr-Siebeck, 1996) 1.417. The Hekaloth texts explicitly allow only men to take part in the ascents and adjurations (*Synopse zur Hekhalot-Literatur* [ed. P. Schafer; Tübingen: Mohr-Siebeck, 1981] 623, 684).

64. S. J. D. Cohen, "Menstruants and the Sacred in Judaism and Christianity," *Women's History and Ancient History* (ed. S. B. Pomeroy; Chapel Hill: University of North Carolina, 1991) 271–99; A.-J. Levine, "Discharging Responsibility: Matthean Jesus, Biblical Law and Hemorrhaging Women," *Treasures New and Old: Recent Contributions in Matthean Studies* (ed. D. R. Bauer and M. A. Powell; Atlanta: Scholars Press, 1996) 379–97.

65. See, however, B. Brooten, *Women Leaders in the Ancient Synagogue* (Chico, Calif.: Scholars Press, 1982) 73–99. On the basis of an inscription mentioning "Marin, priestess (*hierissa*) she suggests that the Jews of Leontopolis may have accepted the cultic participation of Jewish women who claimed descent from Aaron (88). Cf. Luke 1:5 where Elisabeth is called "one of the daughters of Aaron."

Israelites' Court to offer sacrifices at the altar in the Priests' Court. In the Court of the Women, men mixed freely with them except during the Water Drawing Ceremony held on the Feast of Tabernacles.[66] Luke 2:36–37 depicts the widowed, ancient prophet Anna living in the Temple. As Joan Taylor points out, in the Therapeutae's sacred ceremony, involving music and eating the holy food of the shewbread, this group of women and men saw themselves conceptually as spiritual priests within the Temple Sanctuary.[67]

In any case, exclusion need not stunt the imagination or the spirit. Women were certainly as capable as non-priestly men of knowing themselves not excluded from the holy, and of imagining themselves entering the Holy of Holies. Paul's transfer of cultic imagery to communities of men and women shows "that ritual impurity does not seem to have been a disqualification from access to the nascent Christian communities."[68] That openness was Jewish also. An agenda of power and struggle for authority are inherent in the discussion of mysticism, since "a person who was acknowledged to have direct access to God would be in a position to challenge any form of authority,"[69] doctrinal, political, familial, religious.

The Testament of Job is a Jewish work that presents contact with heaven as a possibility for women, and values women's prophetic, ecstatic activity and leadership. Chapters 45–53 show not only chariot imagery used in or before the Christian Testament period to portray a death, but also shows women, Job's three daughters, witnessing an ascent — that is, engaging in mystical practice, capable of connection with the divine realm *and* of inheriting spiritual power. If one strand of thought in early Judaism regarded only men as capable of communication with heaven, another strand, represented by the Testament of Job, regarded both women and men capable. Exploration of this work and others[70] helps "to break down the monolithic picture of a patriarchal Judaism that results from reading androcentric texts such as the Mishna with an uncritical eye."[71]

Job's three daughters ask why they did not receive part of his estate, as their seven brothers did. He tells them, "Do not be troubled, my daughters: I have not

---

66. Josephus, *J.W.* 5; *m Middot* 2.5; E. P. Sanders, *Judaism: Practice and Belief 63 BCE–66 CE* (London: SCM, 1992) 61; D. F. Sawyer, *Women and Religion in the First Christian Centuries* (London: Routledge, 1996) 73–75, 77–78; S. Safrai, "The Role of Women in the Temple," *Jerusalem Perspective* (July/August 1989) 5–6; "The Place of Women in First Century Synagogues," *Jerusalem Perspective* (Sept/Oct 1993) 5–6, 14.

67. J. Taylor, "The Women 'Priests' of Philo's *De Vita Contemplativa*: Reconstructing the Therapeutae," *Wisdom on the Cutting Edge*, forthcoming.

68. Rowland, "Apocalypticism, Mysticism and the New Testament," 417.

69. Jantzen, *Power, Gender, and Christian Mysticism*, 1–2, 157. She points out that "A feminist analysis of the social construction of mysticism has hardly begun" (18).

70. See R. D. Chestnutt, "Revelatory Experiences Attributed to Biblical Women in Early Jewish Literature," *'Women Like This,'* 107–25 on Rebekah in Jubilees, Aseneth in Joseph and Aseneth, and the daughters in the Testament of Job. See above, on Eve's vision in Apocalypse of Moses 33:34.

71. R. Lesses, "The Daughters of Job," *Searching the Scriptures*, 2.140–43, 147.

forgotten you. I have already designated for you an inheritance better than that of your seven brothers" (46:4). The whole of T. Job can be seen as a midrashic development of Job 42:15b ("And their father gave them inheritance rights like their brothers"), although some see no particular use made of the notion of inheritance.[72] I think the inheritance here is spiritual, symbolized by cords. The daughters each receive a shimmering, heavenly, multicolored cord from the sash or belt God gave Job with which to "gird up his loins" and by which he was cured (T. Job 47:2–9; cf. Job 38:3; 40:7; 42:4). These cords, Job says, "will lead you into the better world, to live in the heavens" (46:3). Job himself has a throne in this better world ("my kingdom is forever and ever, and its splendor and majesty are in the chariots of the Father" [33:2–9; cf. 36:3]). The daughters too will now share in his kingdom, receiving "another heart,"[73] ecstatically singing hymns in the language of angels (48:3; 49:2; 50:2).

The cords or charismatic sashes are "wearable 'charms' with therapeutic, economic, evil-averting, glossolalic and apocalyptic-visionary powers."[74] They enable the daughters "to see those who are coming for [their father's] soul" (47:11). After three days, Job and his daughters "saw the gleaming chariots which had come for his soul.... After these things the one who sat in the great chariot got off and greeted Job as the three daughters and their father himself looked on, though certain others did not see.[75] And taking the soul he flew up, embracing it, and mounted the chariot and set off for the east. But his body, prepared for burial, was borne to the tomb as his three daughters went ahead girded about and singing hymns to God" (52:8–12).[76]

This female visionary tradition is linked with the town of Migdal or Magdala, where, in rabbinic tradition, the daughters of Job are said to have died (Migdal Seb'iya; see *Pesiqa de Rab Kahanah* [*Pisqa* 7]; *Wayyikrah Rabbah* 17:4; *Ruth Rabbah* 1:5]). The Testament of Job, "a primitive form of Merkabah mysticism,"[77]

---

72. R. P. Splitter, "Testament of Job," *OTP* 1.864, n. c.

73. Job himself "forgot the pains in his heart" when he was cured (47:8); for Spittler the changed heart in 48:2; 49:1; 50:2 refers not to conversion, but rather describes the onset of the ecstatic state, 'the descent of the Merkabah'" ("Testament of Job," n. d, p. 865). Cf. 1 Sam 10:9 where Saul becomes ecstatic.

74. Spittler comments ("Testament of Job," n. i, p. 865) this is "a case of restrained Jewish magic." The cords "are not traditional phylacteries such as those found at Qumran, but it is striking that the daughters wore them at all, since slaves, mourners, and women were exempted from the use of phylacteries in talmudic tradition (*Kid* 34a; *MK* 15a; *Tefillin* 3)."

75. "It was a property of the charismatic sash (47:11) that gave the daughters access to the vision. Restrictions of the vision of the assumption also appears in an earlier, Gk. form of the AsMos (in Clement of Alexandria, *Strom* 6.15), where only Joshua and Caleb witness the sight. In the finally edited form, Moses' assumption is not mentioned and he dies in the presence of all the people, As Mos 1.15" (Spittler, "Testament of Job," n. j, p. 868).

76. Translation by R. P. Spittler, "Testament of Job," *OTP* 1.864–68. The hymns are said to have been preserved by Job's brother, Nereus (chapter 51).

77. See also H. C. Kee, "Satan, Magic, and Salvation in the Testament of Job," *SBL Seminar Papers* (Missoula, Mont.: SBL, 1974) 1.53–76, on the origin of the Testament in a circle of Judaeo-Greek merkabah mystics. Contrast P. Nicholls, *The Structure and Purpose of the Testament of Job*, unpublished

is dated by Spittler to the first century B.C.E. or C.E.. He thinks it was written in Greek, possibly among the Therapeutae, and may have been reworked in the second century by Montanists, who created chapters 46–53 and possibly inserted chapter 33, to give precedence to ecstatic female prophecy.[78] But P. W. van der Horst counters that chapters 46–53 are dependant on a source from an otherwise unknown Jewish ecstatic-mystical group "in which women played a leading role by their greater ecstatic gifts and their superior spiritual insight into heavenly reality." This haggadah may have been created to legitimate their leading role when it was assailed.[79] Whatever its provenance, I agree with Lesses that the Testament of Job 46–53 is a "discarded source" for Jewish history, part of the heritage of Greek-speaking Judaism, largely lost with the ascendency of the rabbinic tradition.[80] "Rejected by the rabbis and the Church, the Testament of Job not surprisingly has been virtually unnoticed till modern times and has had little detectable effect on the development of Western culture."[81]

The inheritance of the daughters of Job can be compared to Joshua's reception of Moses' "garments of wisdom" and "belt of knowledge" as God appoints him the prophetic successor of Moses after the latter's death, in Pseudo-Philo's account (*L.A.B.* 20:2–3). "And when he clothed himself with it [the belt of understanding], his mind was afire and his spirit was moved, and he said to the people...." This may be a case of a "non-interdependent" use of the motif of "the reception of a girdle from or of a person who had been endowed with God's Spirit and the ensuing inner change."[82] Perhaps by the first century C.E. it had become a standard way of depicting prophetic succession.

---

dissertation, Jerusalem 1982, cited with approval by P. W. van der Horst, "Images of Women in the Testament of Job," *Studies on the Testament of Job* (ed. M. A. Knibb and P. W. van der Horst; Cambridge: Cambridge University Press, 1989) n. 57, p. 112, arguing that the element of the throne-vision is not prominent in this work. "There are no points of contact between it [T. Job] and the wide range of texts which deal with speculation about the merkabah. What evidence there is would suggest that the circle in which Test. Job arose had little interest in this form of mysticism" (Nicholls, 258).

78. Spittler, "Testament of Job," 836, 833–34, with regard to the Therapeutae, following K. Kohler and M. Philonenko. I see nothing to indicate the daughters are like Philo's notion of the Therapeutae, "aged virgins" who reached spiritual heights by abandoning the traits of their womanhood (*On the Contemplative Life* 68).

79. Van der Horst, "Images," 107–9, 113, 114. In spite of its negative and positive depictions of women and other tensions, the Testament has also been regarded as a unity. J. J. Collins argues for this ("Structure and Meaning in the Testament of Job," *SBL Seminar Papers* [Missoula, Mont.: Scholars Press, 1974] 44), as does S. R. Garrett ("The 'Weaker Sex' in the Testament of Job," *JBL* 112 [1993] 55–70) who both think "a fundamentally negative view of females as preoccupied with that which is earthly and corruptible underlies the document form beginning to end" (57). This is an overstatement. It is true that the daughters receive the cords from Job and not from God; but their changed hearts are like his own; moreover they replace him in the leading role in chaps. 46–53 (van der Horst, "Images," 106).

80. R. Lesses, "The Daughters of Job," 139.

81. Spittler, "Testament of Job," 836.

82. Van der Horst, "Images," 113.

Enlightening Allusions

John 20 can be read as part of this strand of Jewish tradition. C. H. Dodd seemed fascinated by this narrative of the appearance of the risen Jesus to Mary Magdalene. He reasoned that

> This story never came out of any common stock of tradition; it has an arresting individuality. We seem to be shut up to two alternatives. Either we have a free, imaginative composition based upon the bare tradition of an appearance to Mary Magdalene, akin to that represented by Matt. xxviii.9–10, or else the story came through some highly individualized channel, directly from the source, and the narrator stood near enough to catch the *nuances* of the individual experience. It would be hazardous to dogmatize. The power to render psychological straits imaginatively with convincing insight cannot be denied to a writer to whom we owe the masterly character-parts of Pontius Pilate and the Woman of Samaria. Yet I cannot for long rid myself of the feeling (it can be no more than a feeling) that this *pericope* has something indefinably first-hand about it. It stands in any case alone. There is nothing quite like it in the gospels. Is there anything quite like it in all ancient literature?[83]

Yes, there is, I submit, in the Elijah-Elisha story. Both 2 Kings 2 and John 20 are about an intense and erotic — though perhaps not romantic or sexual — bond. They are about grief and loss and about empowering, the transformation and sending of the visionary. It is necessary to explore more than Dodd's two alternatives to discuss the possible provenance and development of the tradition, but Dodd's haunting "feeling (it can be no more than a feeling)" — is the expression of something rare and valuable in this field, important to pay attention to, and to follow up.

If 2 Kings 2 is behind or beneath John 20, several elements of the latter text, other than Mary Magdalene witnessing the ascent of Jesus, begin to coalesce:

1. the strangely "low" christology of Mary Magdalene's address to Jesus: *"Rabbouni"* (v. 16, cf. *Kyrios* in v. 18; in 2 Kings 2 the company of prophets warn Elisha twice, "Do you know that today the Lord will take your master [*adoneika*] away from you?'). The terms *rabbouni* and *adoneika* seem roughly equivalent here. In the Targum Elisha's cry "my father" is changed into "my rabbi."[84] Elisha is a pupil, fellow-prophet, companion

---

83. C. H. Dodd, *More New Testament Studies* (Manchester: Manchester University Press, 1968) 115; *Historical Tradition in the Fourth Gospel* (Cambridge: Cambridge University Press, 1965) 148. In particular he was impressed by the dialogue between Jesus and Mary, which "has no analogue, and it shows a psychological subtlety which is quite exceptional in these stories. We can only say that if a traditional unit underlies this *pericope* [vv. 11–17], it has been fairly completely remoulded." The story of Mary Magdalene "represents a good tradition, unknown to Luke, better preserved here than in Matt xxviii (though the evangelist has written it up in his own manner)" (*Tradition*, 146, 149).

84. Daube, *The New Testament and Rabbinic Judaism,* 25; he does not cite the text, but refers to Strack-Billerbeck, 1.919.

and follower of Elijah; Mary Magdalene is a pupil,[85] fellow-prophet, companion[86] and follower of Jesus;

2. the statement that she should not "hold" or "cling to" him (v. 17; in 2 Kings 2 Elisha refuses to leave his master, as they travel from Gilgal to the Jordan, where Elijah will be taken. Three times Elijah says "Elisha, stay here [*sheb-na poh*], for the Lord has sent me . . . ;[87] three times Elisha responds, "As the Lord lives, and as you yourself live, I will not forsake you [*e'ezbeka*]."[88] They cross the Jordan together);

3. the motif of seeking (v. 15 Jesus asks her "whom do you seek?" She has continued a search which is successful;[89] fifty men seek for Elijah for three days but do not find him, a seeking Elisha knows is useless [2 Kings 2:16–18]);[90]

4. only one witness, in the presence of others who do not see (other women in the empty tomb scene; fifty sons of the prophets[91] in 2 Kings 2 who stand at a distance);

5. Mary Magdalene's being sent to the disciples as Jesus' agent and voice (vv. 17–18; Elisha replaces Elijah);

6. Jesus speaking of "my father and your father" and designating the disciples his "brothers" (v. 17; Elisha cries out "my father, my father" [*abi, abi*]) to Elijah, and the band is called "sons of the prophets," family language used also in a spiritual sense). These are expressions of equal privilege in the family of God, and are part of the Merkabah tradition's notion of the transformed mystic and angels in a "celestial family" (3 Enoch 12:5), echoing the "communal mysticism" of Qumran. In the Gospel of John, mystical union is with the "angelomorphic Son of Man by means of Jesus' ascent, not in the sense of absorption in him [or deification] but in the sense of sharing the same relationship with God."[92] John 20:17 does not award the

---

85. M. Scott (*Sophia and the Johannine Jesus* [Sheffield: Sheffield Academic Press, 1992] 233) holds that Mary Magdalene's seeking, her use of the title *rabbouni*, and the stress in this scene on intimacy show that it is as a teacher that she recognizes Jesus Sophia. He thinks, however, that her faith and recognition move beyond that to the confession of him as *kyrios* in v. 18.

86. The term *havera* (or perhaps *r'yytw* [see 4Q502 i 7] might lie behind the Coptic *koinōnos* applied to Mary Magdalene (see above, pp. 152–53). See Ilan, "Paul and Pharisee Women," 8, 16 on *t. Demai* 2, which describes the initiation process of a sect or fellowship, possibly Pharisees, which placed special emphasis on purity and food regulations, and which Ilan thinks included women. She suggests that *havura* was the name the Pharisees chose for themselves. Perhaps it was general enough to be applied to other groups as well.

87. The impression is given that Elijah is trying to get rid of Elisha (see R. D. Nelson, *First and Second Kings* [Louisville: John Knox, 1987] 158).

88. As three times Mary Magdalene inquires about the whereabouts of Jesus. Also twice the sons of prophets engage Elisha prior to Elijah's ascent, and twice Mary Magdalene engages or is engaged by others (disciples, angels) about her search for Jesus. H. Hearon suggested to me these might indicate a more formal connection between the two narratives.

89. Mark 16:6: "you seek Jesus of Nazareth . . . "; par Matt 28:5; Luke 24:5 "Why do you seek the living among the dead?"

90. Luke 24:12, 24 places the seeking by other disciples after the report of the women about the empty tomb *and resurrection*; John 20:3–10 places the seeking by Peter and the beloved disciple after Mary Magdalene's report only of an empty tomb.

91. Nine of the ten uses of this phrase in the Hebrew Bible occur in connection with Elisha and probably refer to a particular prophetic organization opposing the Omride dynasty (J. R. Porter, "Notes and Studies," *NTS* 32 [1981] 423, 429).

92. Kanagaraj, 'Mysticism,' 211, 213.

disciples a new status but rather reminds them of the destination they share with Jesus.[93]

Further objections to this intertextual connection could be made. Though the thematic and visual similarities are strong, the verbal connections are slight and tenuous.[94] This is no quotation, but allusion, which is oblique, subtly signaled, sometimes concealed. Signals "may consist of isolated terms, patterns and motifs taken from the independent text alluded to."[95] Although difficult to recognize, allusions are as relevant for the understanding of a given text as explicit quotations; the identification of allusions is absolutely necessary. They differ from mere reminiscences in that allusions show "some degree of strangeness or peculiarity in their context," and their identification sheds light on a given text, making obscure details meaningful. The reader's role in recognition and activation is crucial.[96]

The association between the texts here is somewhat in the nature of what Daniel Stern calls a "twice told tale."[97] In 2 Kings 2:1–18, Elisha becomes the legitimate inheritor of the spirit of Elijah and the one in whom Elijah's own three-part commission in 1 Kings 19:15–16 will be accomplished.[98] We have no account of Jesus being told to anoint Mary Magdalene, or of Jesus calling her by throwing his mantle over her as Elijah does to Elisha in 19:19–21.[99] In the canonical

---

93. M. R. D'Angelo, "Imitating Deity in the Gospel of John: Theological Language and 'Father' in 'Prayers of Jesus,'" *Semeia* 85 (1999) 68.

94. Still, it does not seem to me to be a case of "Parallelomania," see S. Sandmel, *JBL* 81 (1962) 1–13.

95. D. Dimant, "Mikra in the Apocrypha and Pseudepigrapha," *Mikra: Text, Translation, Reading, and Interpretation of the Hebrew Bible in Ancient Judaism and Early Christianity* (ed. M. J. Mulder and H. Sysling; Philadelphia: Fortress, 1988) 410.

96. L. Painchaud, "The Use of Scripture in Gnostic Literature," *JECS* 4 (1996) 131–32, 135–36. On the reader's role, see below, pp. 351–52. See *Reading Between Texts: Intertextuality and the Hebrew Bible* (ed. D. N. Fewell; Louisville: Westminster/John Knox, 1992) for the glossary by T. Beal for definitions of Inner-biblical Exegesis, Intertextuality, Intertext, Intratextuality, Poetic Influence, and Trace (22–24); and D. Penchansky, "Staying the Night: Intertextuality in Genesis and Judges," for definitions of intertextuality as (1) the literary text; (2) the social text, (3) the interpretive text (77–88). G. A. Phillips, "Sign/Text/Differance: the Contribution of Intertextual Theory to Biblical Criticism," *Intertextuality* (ed. H. F. Plett; New York: Walter de Gruyter, 1991) 78–97 For canonical criticism, see J. A. Sanders, *Torah and Canon* (Philadelphia: Fortress, 1972); idem, *From Sacred Story to Sacred Text* (Philadelphia: Fortress, 1987); idem, "Extravagant Love," *New Blackfriars* 68 (1987) 278–84.

97. D. Stern, *One Day's Perfect Weather* (Dallas: SMU, 1999) xi. See Dimant, "Mikra," 406 for the use of implicit quotations in "free narrative" such as Tobit and Judith; and 417–19 for models and motifs such as Job as model in Tobit. "In implicit compositional uses biblical elements are part of the materials forming the texture of the composition. Authors employing biblical elements in this way aim at re-creating the biblical models and atmosphere, and identify themselves with the biblical authors" (419).

98. Elijah is told to anoint Hazael to be king over Syria (see 2 Kings 8:7–15 where this is accomplished by Elisha), and to anoint Jehu to be king over Israel (see 2 Kings 9 where Elisha does this), as well as to anoint Elisha prophet in Elijah's place (2 Kings 2).

99. Elisha is plowing a field with 12 pair of oxen when he is called (cf. the 12 stones Elijah uses to build an altar in 18:31); the 12s place both of them in relation to the history and theology of Israel (J. A. Todd, "The Pre-Deuteronomistic Elijah Cycle," *Elijah and Elisha in Socioliterary Perspective* [Atlanta: Scholars Press, 1992] 16).

Gospels she is not said to replace Jesus or fulfill his mission. (Her following him to his death may in some way be seen as equivalent to crossing the Jordan with him. But there is no evidence that crossing the Jordan was at that time a metaphor for death.) Mary Magdalene receives no mantle of the ascending Jesus; she performs no feat like the parting the waters of the Jordan to demonstrate her empowerment. Elisha's empowering is explicit and acknowledged; Mary Magdalene's is not. In fact, there is no response at all to her report,[100] and the spirit of Jesus is said in the subsequent scene to have been breathed by him not on her, but on the disciples (John 20:22–23).

Only Shards

Read the way I am suggesting, John 20 contains only remnants, large shards of a prophetic succession tradition. The expressions characteristic of ancient references to succession, the semantic field discussed by Talbert and Stepp, is not found with reference to Mary Magdalene in John 20, which does not have the conventional form of a succession story ([1] the naming of what is to be passed on; [2] the symbolic acts which accompany succession; and [3] confirmation that the succession has taken place). The notion of succession is usually associated with "the desire to show continuity in a given area, to guarantee preservation of something, to legitimate or authenticate." The LXX stories of succession function to show the true line of leadership in salvation history, often not the expected line but the one willed by God. A role or office is passed on, a tradition or lifestyle, and sometimes a combination of these. "The centrality of the concept of succession to a document may be determined by whether or not it seriously affects the form of a document."[101]

In Luke/Acts that centrality is evident, where Talbert and Stepp find echoes of the Elijah-Elisha transfer unmistakeable.[102] The succession from Jesus to the Twelve is central to the Lukan plot, which stresses the correspondences between the career of Jesus and that of the apostles in Acts, and which creates a schema of death — resurrection — ascension.[103] As we have seen, this Gospel particularly diminishes Mary Magdalene.[104] There the three requisite components are present in multiple ways, and a number of linguistic signs of the semantic field. Luke is aware of an Elijah christology (9:4; 4:25–26; 7:11–16), and of female prophecy

---

100. Lee ("Partnership," 39) notes that there no narrative impact is made by the beloved disciple's response in v. 8. But he and Peter appear again in chapter 21 in key roles.

101. C. H. Talbert and P. L. Stepp, "Succession in Mediterranean Antiquity, Part I: the Lukan Milieu and Part II: Luke-Acts," *SBL Seminar Papers* (Atlanta: Scholars Press, 1998) 167–68, 171, 175.

102. Allusions to Elijah's commissioning of Elisha appear in 9:57–62 (Q).

103. This is not the schema of the Synoptics (as S. Schneiders says [*Written That You May Believe* [New York: Crossroad, 1999] 57) or John; it only appears in Luke/Acts and in the Markan Appendix.

104. Brock ("Peter, Paul and Mary," 173) shows that Luke has more in common with the Gospel of Peter than with its three canonical Gospel counterparts.

(Anna in 2:36; Acts 2:17 "your sons and daughters shall prophesy"; the daughters of Philip in 21:9; cf. the slave girl in 16:16), but he makes no link between the two which would empower women. In their treatment of Elijah and Elisha, Talbert and Stepp do not mention 2 Kings 2:10, the necessity of witnessing the ascent. But Luke has made sure this element is included — twice: the witnesses are "the eleven and their companions" (24:51) and "the apostles" (Acts 1:9–11). John 20:1, 11–18 has obvious affinities with the ascension scenes in Luke/Acts. Is the Magdalene tradition in John a pale and weak imitation of this notion, or has Lukan appropriation overwhelmed and blotted out a rival? I think the latter.[105] According to Perkins, "[T]he living presence of the risen Jesus made it unnecessary for the early community to resolve the problem of succession by discovering a disciple to whom its leader's charisma had passed. The source of life is not found in ancestral and social ties."[106] This may be the ideal, but I see no period in which it was taken seriously.

Connection with 2 Kings 2 is virtually erased in the appearance to the women in Matthew 28 and to Mary Magdalene in the Markan Appendix. Dodd thinks there is some connection between the accounts in John and Matthew, but not the slightest ground for supposing that this contact was literary. He judges — as I do — the Johannine appearance to Mary Magdalene better preserved than the shorter Matthean appearance to the women.[107] Access to the prophetic tradition as I am reconstructing it may have been very limited, perhaps denied to Matthew and the author of the Markan Appendix (and rejected by Luke). Or, on the other hand, someone associated with the Johannine community in an early stage may have turned a simple visionary report into a succession narrative. On the basis of the eighteen similarities between Matthew 28 and John 20, the non-Matthean elements in Matthew 28 and the non-Johannine elements in John 20, I think the former possibility is more likely. As we have seen, the two and maybe three independent witnesses testify to the earliness and strength of the tradition of an appearance to Mary Magdalene[108] that elucidated the empty tomb and her role.

105. Luke, I think, is particularly good at "deal[ing] with the threat of female power by incorporating it" (the process analyzed by T. Modleski, *Feminism Without Women* [New York: Routledge, 1991] 7–9).

106. Perkins, "Resurrection," 441.

107. Dodd, *Tradition*, 147–49. So also P. Benoit, who thinks the christophany to Mary Magdalene is primitive tradition, "plus archaïque en somme que l'angélophanie de Mc 16:1–8 par., et mieux conservée qu'en Mt 28:9–10" ("Marie-Madeleine et les disciples au tombeau selon Jean 20, 1–18," *Judentum, Urchristentum, Kirche* [ed. W. Eltester; Berlin: Topelmann, 1964] 152). Schnackenburg (*John* 3.321) thinks there is a common tradition used by Matthew and John, but it "cannot be pronounced ancient and reliable" because Luke does not know of an appearance to the women.

108. Benoit ("Marie Madeleine," 141–52) holds that the version in John of Mary Magdalene's report of the empty tomb derives from the most primitive layer of tradition. R. Fortna (*The Fourth Gospel and its Predecessor* [Philadelphia: Fortress, 1988] 187–90) thinks the source already had its own well-developed tendencies. Perkins sees vv. 11–18 is founded on an earlier tradition difficult to reconstruct, perhaps one that repeated only in concise form the tradition of an appearance to her, like other references to individuals, Peter, Paul and James (" 'I Have Seen the Lord,' " 40).

The remnants of a prophetic succession tradition survive in John incorporated, like other aspects of an identification of Jesus with Elijah,[109] into a christology of the descending/ascending Human One. They bear witness to a community that valued the participation and leadership of women. But because they are only remnants, what is lost is recognition of a tradition of the empowering of Mary Magdalene as successor of Jesus. Note that the commission of Mary Magdalene here does not contain a promise that the disciples will see the risen Jesus. In fact, she is just to inform them that he is going. If the text is read on it own, apart from the subsequent Johannine scenes, it is clear they will not see him, "but are only relayed Jesus' farewell."[110] Her role then, is not a preliminary or transitional one. In any work that may have ended with this scene, Mary Magdalene would be the only guarantor of the vindication of Jesus, and this the final message. That message implicitly says who she is, as well as who they are as "brothers"; it does not empower them for a worldwide mission. A. Reinhartz imagines the narrative continuing with a series of events consolidating Mary's authority (the rejoicing of the disciples, the conferring of the holy spirit on Mary). But the narrative does not continue in this way. Instead, the Gospel is completely silent about the disciples' reception of her proclamation. This silence dismantles her authority and makes her report "superfluous and abortive."[111]

Survivals of the Tradition

1. The Gospel of Mary

The empowering of Mary Magdalene was a tradition that apparently did not stand a chance of surviving fully and openly in the circles in which the canonical materials were produced.[112] What remains are traces, erasure marks, which "lead readers to stray into the margins and off the page."[113] But the tradition survived

---

109. See J. L. Martyn, "We Have Found Elijah," *The Gospel of John in Christian History* (New York: Paulist, 1979) 9–54.

110. Price, "Mary Magdalene: Gnostic Apostle?" 67. He refers here to the disciples as "the Twelve," but this is not a common Johannine designation for the disciples (it is used only in John 6:70; 20:24, identifying Judas and Thomas). Contrast A. Jasper, "Interpretative Approaches to John 20:1–18, *ST* 47 (1993) 113: she holds that in the full Gospel of John Mary is no more than a messenger, the vehicle for a message addressed to Jesus' brothers, not to her. F. Segovia calls 21:1–23 the Gospel's "final farewell" ("The Final Farewell of Jesus," *Semeia* 53 [1991] 167–91).

111. A. Reinhartz, "To Love the Lord: An Intertextual Reading of John 20," *The Labour of Reading* (ed. F. C. Black, R. Boer, E. Runions; Atlanta: SBL, 1999) 59–60.

112. Brown, *John*, 2.971 argues for the historicity of an appearance to her; there is no reason why the tradition from the mid-thirties mentioned in 1 Corinthians 15 should mention her, since a woman "could scarcely be presented as either an official witness to the resurrection or an apostle." On "official witnesses," see above pp. 212, 216, 227–28; Junia is listed as an apostle in Romans 16:7. But Brown's reasons may have been held by some first-century Christians.

113. T. K. Beal, "Glossary," *Reading Between Texts*, 24.

embattled in the circle in which the Gospel of Mary was produced. That gnostic work opens in the time between Jesus' death/resurrection and his departure.[114] After the departure, Mary claims to have had a vision of Jesus, and to have spoken with him of ascent. There is recognition and rejection of the implication of that claim, which in this case shows the Savior's preference for her, and defense of it by Levi.[115]

2. Elijah and Lilith

Another gnostic tradition may be confusedly reacting to John 20 or the source behind it or a development of it, with great hostility toward Mary Magdalene and all she represents (and perhaps also with hostility to an Elijah christology?). Epiphanius tells of a lost gnostic story about Elijah and Lilith (*Adv. Haeres.* 26.13.228): "And thus runs their frivolous and fanciful stories, how they even make bold to blaspheme about the holy Elijah, and to claim that a story tells how, when he had been taken up (*anelēphthē*), he was cast back (*kateblēthē*) into the world. For, it says, a female demon (*mia daimon*) came and laid hold (*ekratese*) upon him, and said to him, 'Where are you going? For I have children (*tekna*) from you, and you can't go up into heaven and leave your children here.' And he said — so the story goes — 'How do you have children from me? For I was always chaste.' The demon says (according to this book), 'But I do! When you were dreaming dreams (*enupviois enupniazomenos*), you often were voided by an emission from the body; and I was the one who took up the seeds from you, and begot you children.' Vast is the stupidity of those who say this sort of thing."[116] There is no Elijah Apocalypse or tradition otherwise known that fits the description of this exchange, but it clicks into place as a possible response to the Magdalene tradition I have reconstructed. In this response she is not prophetic successor, but sexy, thieving Lilith. She not only *had* demons, she *is* the frightening female demon, in a weird, one-sided sexual "relationship" with Elijah/Jesus. Not his companion, as in the Gospel of Philip, not the one he loved more than others, as in the Gospel of Mary, but the one who stole his seed.[117]

Kaja Silverman holds that a text operates as a verbal mirror, in which a reader perceives his or her subjectivity and a structure of identity, formed and promoted

---

114. Similarly, in the Sophia of Jesus Christ, Mary Magdalene is one of seven women and twelve men gathered to hear the Savior between the resurrection and the ascension.

115. See further, my article in the E. Schüssler Fiorenza festschrift, *Wisdom on the Cutting Edge.*

116. Translation by M. Stone and J. Strugnell, *The Books of Elijah,* Parts 1 and 2 (Missoula, Mont.: Scholars Press, 1979) 88–89. They comment that it is not certain whether the tale was found in the same work as preceding fragments they present; "it might have derived from independent Gnostic tradition, or even a distinct Gnostic Apocalypse/Ascension/of Elijah."

117. Cf. the stories of the children or child of Mary Magdalene and Jesus in the Merovingian legends (M. Baigent, R. Leigh, H. Lincoln, *Holy Blood, Holy Grail* [New York: Delacorte, 1982]) and fantastic interpretations of Qumran texts by B. Thiering. Above, pp. 100–101.

by a specific social ideology through learned conventions and expectations and responses.[118] A woman seeing herself and/or being seen by others, women and men, as an Elisha, would be reading herself into 2 Kings 2 in accordance with some ideology and against another. She might be identifying with a male figure in the text, repressing her femaleness ("becoming a 'man' "); or identifying with and claiming the authority of the figure, discounting its maleness. A woman seen as an evil Lilith is another matter, as unlikely a woman's creation as the legendary Magdalene.

Resisting Distortion and Dismemberment

A great deal of effort is required to resist distortion of the nearly-lost tradition of an appearance to Mary Magdalene. I see this appearance or vision tradition as following on and explicating the revelation/insight about resurrection, itself triggered by the emptiness of the tomb, and interpreted or understood in the memory of passion/resurrection predictions about the Human One. This resurrection involves ascent. The two notions, resurrection and ascent, are logically and imaginatively distinct, since the former but not the latter necessarily involves death. They can represent different theological beliefs, and were not ever before, as far as I know, represented by the same kinds of narratives. We have seen that it is usually argued that the empty tomb was part of a widely held legendary motif in the ancient world, the rapture or disappearance into heaven of a revered figure, *rather than* his resurrection from the dead and reappearance on earth. In the reconstruction of many critics, the empty tomb is totally separate in origin and intention from the resurrection, and also appears earlier (or later) in the Christian tradition.[119] But the combination resurrection/ascent may be original to the early Christian tradition of the empty tomb.[120] Perhaps it is not unprecedented in connection with Elijah. In Elijah traditions examined above, ascent and reappearance, death and resurrection combine and coalesce, though not in any known narrative unity. We must reckon with the loss or suppression of Elijah traditions in

118. See K. Silverman, *The Subject of Semiotics* (New York: Oxford, 1983); *The Acoustic Mirror: The Female Voice in Psychoanalysis and Cinema* (Bloomington: Indiana University Press, 1988), cited by J. Tarlin, "Toward a 'Female' Reading of the Elijah Cycle: Ideology and Gender in the Interpretation of 1 Kings 17–19, 21 and 2 Kings 1–2.18," *A Feminist Companion to Samuel and Kings* (ed. A. Brenner; Sheffield: Sheffield Academic Press, 1994) 208–9. Tarlin, a "male" scholar produces a "female" reading by focusing on "female" aspects of the Elijah texts — "fragmentation, contradiction, ambiguity, lack of closure" (212).
119. E. Bickermann, "Das leere Grab," *ZNW* 23 (1924) 281–92, followed in part by A. Y. Collins.
120. See C. Rowland, "Interpreting the Resurrection," *The Resurrection of Jesus Christ* (London: Darton, Longman & Todd, 1993) 76–79 on the themes of resurrection and exaltation as intimately interwoven themes in the Christian Testament.

Judaism due to Christian use, and in Christianity due to Jewish Christian use.[121] We must reckon as well with Christian innovation.

In the rich context of early Jewish mysticism, catalyst, insight, and vision can be read as part of one process. The empty tomb tradition and the visionary tradition, then, are not two separate sources of belief. The latter, however, may have been appropriated quite early on as a predominantly male tradition, in the interest of claims to authority. The appearance to Mary Magdalene is not originally foreign to the empty tomb tradition.[122] The empty tomb by itself, of course, does not convey the idea of resurrection, but I think it may never have existed without some sort of angelophany-revelation, and never without the appearance which clarifies and strengthens the revelation. The commission to tell is implicit in the very notion of revelation.

The threads of this imaginative unit I am proposing would be (1) not finding the body (as Elijah's body was not found) as the context for (2) the insight about resurrection *having occurred,* as the context or provocation[123] for (3) a vision of the resurrected one ascending (as Elijah ascended).[124] Contrast the schema proposed by some: (1) finding an ambiguous empty tomb; (2) appearances of risen Jesus as foundation of belief in his resurrection; (3) reading that faith back into the tomb accounts by creation of an angelophany.[125] In the Fourth Gospel the link I propose is tighter in the presentation of death/resurrection *as* ascent. The "lifting up" of the Human One (3:14–5) is the lifting up of Jesus on the cross and his exaltation or return to heaven. As Brown remarks, it might have been more logical if John had had Jesus go directly to the Father from the cross, "for the resurrection does not fit easily into John's theology of the crucifixion.... If John reinterprets the crucifixion so that it becomes part of Jesus' glorification, he dramatizes the resurrection so that it is obviously part of the ascension." He sees the story of the appearance to Mary Magdalene as used by John as the

121. I owe this insight to C. Morray-Jones. It is odd that Elijah is hardly ever mentioned in the pseudepigrapha, or in the Merkabah mysticism materials (see *j Berakot* 5:1; Wiener, *The Prophet Elijah,* 82 and chap. 4). K. H. Lindbeck ("Non-Rabbinic Sources for Elijah Legends in Rabbinic Literature," *SBL Seminar Papers* [Atlanta: Scholars Press, 1994] 753) speaks of "the whole body of Elijah traditions which circulated in oral and written forms now lost." The phrase "descender to the Chariot" (*yored merkabah*) however, may derive from Elijah's posture, putting his head between his knees, as a preparation for mystical experience (1 Kings 18:42; see M. Idel, *Kabbalah: New Perspectives* [New Haven: Yale, 1988] 90). See P. Schafer, *The Hidden and Manifest God* (Albany: SUNY, 1992) 42–43 on the allusions to the messenger of Mal 3:1–5 in the description of the *yored merkabah* in *Hekaloth Rabbati* 86. The "sound of sheer silence" Elijah hears at Horeb (1 Kings 19:12) is like the whisper that implies esoteric tradition (*Gen R* 3.4).

122. Against L. M. Wills, *The Quest of the Historical Gospel* (New York: Routledge, 1997) 155.

123. Rowland, *Christian Origins,* 193.

124. For further study: the exploration of possible relevance of patterns in prophetic literature, such as the progression in Amos from seeing an ordinary sight ("a basket of summer fruit [*qayits*]") via wordplay to insight/revelation ("The end [*qets*] has come upon my people Israel") to vision ("I saw the Lord standing on the altar..."), or in apocalyptic literature, such as the pattern of double vision in Daniel 7, with explanation, further clarification.

125. For example, Schneiders, *Written That You May Believe,* 181.

vehicle for his reinterpretative dramatization of the resurrection.[126] But obviously it is a reinterpretation that causes much confusion. For Meeks, "since the fourth evangelist's dramatic compression of exaltation and crucifixion motifs into one has left the traditional Easter appearances in a kind of limbo," the strange statement in 20:17 "imparts to that limbo a sacred liminality. Jesus is no longer in the world, but has not yet ascended; he belongs to the intermediate zone that violates these categories and renders him untouchable."[127] I see the resurrection/ascension complex as pre-Johannine. In Luke/Acts, it is split apart, and ascent is used both to end the chain of authorizing appearances, and to underline the authorization of (mainly) the Eleven apostles.

The traditional unit must extend backward to also include burial and crucifixion.[128] The women's witness of the burial is necessary to explain their presence at the tomb; their witness at the burial presupposes their presence at the crucifixion scene. There they witness the cry of Jesus from the cross, *"Eloi, Eloi, lama sabachthani"* (Mark 15:34), interpreted by some of the bystanders as a cry for or a crying to Elijah. We have seen that this misunderstanding of the cry may reflect the tradition of Elijah as helper of the oppressed or more specifically that Elijah comes to the dying righteous one.[129] Elijah traditions, then, connect or undergird crucifixion, tomb, and appearance.[130]

The sequence I am suggesting as early is not present in John. There is no cry of desolation from the cross. Angels do not interpret the empty tomb, do not reveal he is resurrected; "they simply interrogate."[131] Mary Magdalene is weeping (vv. 11a, 11b, 13, 15) when she sees the risen Jesus, before she recognizes him. Perkins, like Brown, thinks there were two early forms of women as resurrection witness: (a) an angelophany, symbolizing divine revelation, to a group of women, and (b) an appearance to Mary Magdalene. Their report of the first has a crucial role in the process of "community founding," "and may have been the impetus for the group's return to Galilee, as Matthew's account suggests, and the

---

126. Brown, *John*, 2.1013–14. Schnackenburg sees the tension here between the theology of John and what he calls "the traditional view of the primitive Church" (*John*, 3.319).
127. W. A. Meeks, "The Man from Heaven in Johannine Sectarianism," *JBL* 91 (1972) 66.
128. R. Pesch (*Das Markusevangelium* [Freiburg: Herder, 1977] 2.519–20) proposes that the passion narrative concluded with the finding of the empty tomb as evidence that Jesus had been vindicated. G. W. E. Nickelsburg ("The Genre and Function of the Markan Passion Narrative," *HTR* 73 [1980] 153–84) holds that the story could have ended at the crucifixion, with vindication expressed by the statement of the centurion that Jesus was the Son of God. I agree; the genre did not dictate such a dramatic ending as the empty tomb. But the righteous ones in Isaiah 52–53 and Wisdom 2–6 are known to be vindicated when they are seen by their enemies.
129. See above, p. 279.
130. Daube, *The New Testament and Rabbinic Judaism*, 24–25 also connects the tearing of the temple veil to Elisha's tearing of his garment, and the centurion's confession to Elisha's cry. The narrative of the crucifixion is "a much more closely knit pericope than has hitherto been realized."
131. A. Jasper, "Interpretative Approaches," 111. These angels are "semiotically speaking, much weaker than their synoptic counterparts at the tomb."

recollection of what Jesus taught there, as Luke's version has it."[132] In contrast, I see the angelophany (which interprets the empty tomb as meaning resurrection) and the appearance to Mary Magdalene as originally joined expressions of a Danielic-Elijah mysticism that John or someone before him has inherited and changed. Fortna does reconstruct a pre-Johannine source with angelophany and christophany. His reconstruction retains the prohibition about clinging, but not the reference to Jesus ascending,[133] and so the thought-field I am suggesting is broken up.

Other scholarly analyses of the tradition, as we have seen, separate these segments, and then attempt to show a development from more to less primitive notions of resurrection, or to show the opposite, from less to more primitive. The fragmentation of this material in contemporary scholarship is of special interest to feminist scholars. We are accustomed to having to argue that women were present where they are not mentioned or are only briefly mentioned (at Sinai, in prophetic movements, in early Christian communities, in leadership roles). But here in the crucifixion, burial and empty tomb narratives, where women are actually said to be present and central to the story, many scholars remove them from history and minimize or overlook whatever contribution is associated with their presence in the narrative.

It should not be surprising, perhaps, that the argument for women's inclusion and agency is most difficult when the role is crucial. Male guilt and shame about abandonment are involved here, as well as the courage to remember and transmit the stories of betrayal. These traditions are built on traumatic memories and their aftermaths. In the canonical texts, the women's role can be seen as deformed by the attempt to hide (Luke, maybe John[134]) or redistribute (Mark[135]) guilt, and even more by the attempt to overcome it by the emphasis on forgiveness (Luke, John) and empowerment (Matthew, Luke, John, Markan Appendix) of the male disciples.

---

132. Perkins, "'I Have Seen the Lord,'" 41. Mary Magdalene's witness (b), Perkins says, should have placed her alongside other witnesses in creedal formulas; it did not because of "first-century prejudice against women as public witnesses." Perkins does mention that feminists readings such as Wire's suggest other reasons why Mary Magdalene does not appear in 1 Corinthians 15 (n 53, p. 41).

133. See Fortna, *Predecessor*, 187–88: 20:1 Early on Sunday (while it was still dark) Mary Magdalene [and...] came to the tomb and saw the stone taken from the tomb. 2 And she [or they] ran and came to Simon Peter and told [him], "They have taken the Master from the tomb, and we don't know where they have laid him." 3 So Peter went out, and they came to the tomb. 6b And he went into the tomb and he saw the burying cloths lying. [And he wondered.] 9 For as yet they did not know the scripture that he must rise from the dead. 10 So [he] went home again. 11 Mary was standing outside the tomb, weeping. As she wept she stooped to look into the tomb, 12 and she saw two angels in white sitting (one at the head and one at the feet) where Jesus' body had laid. 13a And they said to her, "Woman, why are you weeping?" 14a She turned away, and saw Jesus standing! 15a Jesus said to her, 'Whom are you looking for, 16 Mary?" She said to him in 'Hebrew,' "Rabbouni!" 17 Jesus said to her, "Do not cling to me, but go to my brothers and tell them [. . .]. 18 Mary Magdalene went and announced to the disciples, "I have seen the Master." [*The disciples disbelieve.*]

134. By the appearance of male acquaintances or a male disciple of Jesus at the crucifixion. But see below, pp. 344–45, Schneiders' understanding of the Beloved Disciple at the cross.

135. By emphasizing that the women did not deliver the message.

John's Use of the Tradition

The appearance to Mary Magdalene was short-circuited in circles that became dominant. John has incorporated and (he or someone before him) diluted the Magdalene tradition. The appearance to her seems prepared for earlier in the Gospel. In John 6:62 Jesus asks those complaining about the difficulty of the teaching regarding eating the flesh and drinking the blood of the Human One: "Does this offend you? Then what if you were to see the Human One ascending to where he was before?" "Though hypothetical, [the saying] alludes to 'some occurrence by which a revelation of high importance' will be given by virtue of the ascension of the Son of Man.... The point in 6.62 is that if Jesus' 'disciples' do not believe (6.64) but take offense at the life-giving effect of his incarnation and death, they can scarcely believe his ascension, which will exhibit even greater glory — the glory that he had in heaven with God (17.5) — and hence that they will stumble even more (cf. 3.12)."[136] Mary Magdalene in the Gospel of John is represented as the believer who sees the ascending. But the insertion[137] of Peter and the Beloved Disciple into the narrative interrupts the sequence of the source. She is upstaged by the Beloved Disciple who is the first to come to belief by virtue of the sight of the grave cloths (20:9). His faith "is to be understood as all the more exemplary since it was not prepared for even by scriptural prophecy."[138] The Beloved Disciple's faith is also not dependent on angels, "the voice of an intermediary."[139] Mary Magdalene is the first person to see the risen Jesus, but "someone else already believes."[140] The Beloved Disciple is superior to her in faith, and also in authority (21:25). She is upstaged also by the disciples who receive the Spirit from Jesus (20:22),[141] who may then seem to have been glorified only *after* the appearance to her (cf. 7:39).

This staging of the giving of the Spirit (conditional upon his glorification in 7:39; or "going away" in 16:7) has led some to ask if the appearance to her took place before the ascension, and those to the disciples after it. This would

---

136. Kanagaraj, 'Mysticism,' 207, quoting W. H. Cadman, *The Open Heaven* (New York: Herder and Herder, 1969) 90. Brown (*John*, 2.1015) points out that with the continuation of the saying in v. 63 ("It is the Spirit that gives life") John makes "an intimate connection between the ascension of the Son of Man and the giving of the Spirit." However, the spirit/flesh contrast here ("the flesh is useless" [NRSV]) does not carry the full reference to Jesus' Spirit.

137. Contrast Neirynck, "John and the Synoptics," 595.

138. Fortna, *Predecessor,* 191.

139. J. Ashton, *Understanding the Fourth Gospel* (Oxford: Clarendon, 1991) 506; G. O'Day, "John," *Women's Bible Commentary*, 841. See, however, C. M. Conway, *Men and Women in the Fourth Gospel: Gender and Johannine Characterization* (SBLDS 167; Atlanta: Scholars Press, 1999) 190–92 on belief here meaning belief that the tomb is empty (cf. Luke 24:12).

140. J. Rena, "Women in the Gospel of John," *EgT* 17 (1986) 143.

141. It is true that the Spirit and Paraclete is given to the whole group of disciples, not to a specific figure, and "[t]his would tend to suggest a collective and not a hierarchical understanding of leadership in the Johannine community" (J. Draper, "The Sociological Function of the Spirit/Paraclete in the Farewell Discourses in the Fourth Gospel," *Neot* 26 [1992] 22). But until recently commentators have not seen women as part of this leadership.

mean it was not the glorified Jesus who appeared to her, "and thus she was granted only an inferior-grade appearance.... [T]he Jesus of the Magdalene is earthbound... [Jesus] still has his dead body."[142] Against this, Brown argues that John's emphasis "is on the identification of the resurrection and the ascension, not on the accidental time lag." "I am ascending" is a theological statement "contrasting the passing nature of Jesus' presence in his post-resurrectional appearances and the permanent nature of his presence in the Spirit." It draws attention "to what his glorification will mean to men, namely, the giving of the Spirit that makes them God's children.... Jesus' ascension will make possible the giving of the Spirit who will beget the believing disciples as God's children," so that they are referred to in anticipation as "my brothers." Mary Magdalene's authorization is not part of this narrative.[143]

Her proclamation, "I have seen the Lord," in v. 18 is appropriated by the disciples in v. 25. This short form of the resurrection kerygma (cf. 1 Cor 9:1) which does not repeat anything from v. 17 may replace a more original report, a remnant of which may be found in the second half of v. 18. This verse is an awkward blend of direct discourse (focusing on her vision) and indirect (focusing on what the risen Jesus said to her).[144] As Tovey puts it, "In the story's 'double ending,' the implied author brings together two challenges: the challenge to believe (represented in Jesus' encounter with Thomas) and the challenge to follow (Jesus and Peter).... The disciples receive the Holy Spirit and are sent by Jesus to continue his ministry; the beloved disciple and his book take over the testimony of John."[145] The gift and democratization of the Spirit/Paraklete, available to all members of the community owes nothing to her.[146] At the end, Mary Magdalene fades from view, even more completely than she does in the Gospel of Mary.

Many commentators move on from this scene, as does the Gospel, to focus on the implications of the ascent of Jesus for the disciples[147] and on their empowering. The scenes in 20:19–31 may have been added "precisely to undercut the impression that the definitive interpretation of Jesus' departure was delivered only through a woman," and the Appendix supplied later to define the relative

---

142. Brown, *John*, 2.1014 mentions Schwank and Kraft as holding these views, with which he disagrees.

143. Brown, *John*, 2.1014–15. He does not discuss why the contrast is not a factor in the other resurrection appearances in John. He cites with approval Dodd's thought that the resurrection is emphasized as the renewal of personal relations with the disciples.

144. Contrast Perkins, "'I Have Seen the Lord,'" 39: she thinks "I have seen the Lord" may have been taken from the source used here, or from the angelophany tradition.

145. D. Tovey, *Narrative Art and Act in the Fourth Gospel* (Sheffield: Sheffield Academic Press, 1997) 261.

146. I do not understand what Brown means when he says that Mary Magdalene "could serve as an example to Christians of the Johannine community at the end of the 1st century whose contact with the risen Jesus is through the Paraclete who declares to them what he has received from Jesus (xvi 14)" (*John*, 2.1009–10).

147. Brown, *John*, 2.1004, 1011–17.

roles of Peter and the Beloved Disciple.[148] It is possible, however, that Johannine redaction and hearers'/readers' androcentrism and prejudices did not conceal from every hearer or reader the tradition of Mary Magdalene's contribution and empowerment. It is widely held that her importance in gnostic literature and circles stems somehow from John 20. Brown thinks the story of an appearance to Mary Magdalene is ancient, "a story that came down from early times but was not part of the official teaching."[149] But whose "official teaching"? More correctly, it was not part of the teaching presented as official in the canonical materials such as 1 Corinthians 15. Other circles can be imagined which treasured, taught, developed and acted in response to this story in its ancient or Johannine forms, in different, more inclusive ways.[150]

Demeaning Interpretations

As told in its Johannine form, the story is enigmatic, puzzling, and most often read to demean rather than authorize Mary Magdalene. She is understood in the garden scene as the woman who misunderstands, whose knowledge is inadequate.[151] Several aspects of the account are said to illustrate this. (1) Her concern for the body of Jesus and her fear that it is stolen are taken to indicate her ignorance about the resurrection.[152] (2) In contrast to her recognition of the risen Jesus in Matthew 28, in John 20 she fails to recognize him, thinking he is the gardener. This may be an example, though not typical, of the Johannine motif of misunderstanding.[153] Or, by basing her recognition of Jesus on hearing rather than seeing, it may serve to bring her tradition in line with the Gospel emphasis (20:29). Her

148. D'Angelo, "Reconstructing 'Real' Women," 112. Conway (*Men and Women*, 199) thinks the role of Peter and the beloved disciple is to corroborate Mary's discovery, and they are intentionally placed in a secondary position to her. She sees all the female characters in this Gospel presented in a positive light, clearly superior to the male characters; the women stand outside recognized structures of authority, to which they represent a challenge (205). This literary reading is interesting but it strikes me as not suspicious enough of the surface of the text and the strategies of oppression.

149. Brown, *John*, 2.1014. Alsup (*The Post-Resurrection Appearance Stories*, 206–11) posits a traditional christophany on the basis of vv. 14b–16, omitting the difficult v. 17.

150. Perkins ("'I Have Seen the Lord,'" 40) thinks the prominence Mary enjoyed "among the female followers of Jesus reflects the special place she held as one of the first to see the Lord." But perhaps she was prominent at one time among both women and men.

151. See Bultmann, *John*, 686: she is foolish; P. S. Minear, "'We Don't Know Where...'" John 20.2," *Int* 30 (1976) 129: her grief is obsessive and she is befuddled over graves; B. Witherington, *Women in the Earliest Churches* (Cambridge: Cambridge University Press, 1988) 179: she blunders. Contrast D. A Lee, "Partnership in Easter Faith: the Role of Mary Magdalene and Thomas in John 20," *JSNT* 58 (1995) 38: she sees misunderstanding in the Johannine narratives "as an authentic marker on the journey of faith."

152. Conway, *Men and Women*, 194.

153. Fortna (*Predecessor*, 198) sees it as non-typical, but probably Johannine. See S. Van Tilborg, *Imaginative Love in John* (Leiden: Brill, 1993) 202: "searching for a dead body Mary can not recognise Jesus in this living person.... She can not recognise Jesus because she can not imagine him as 'living.' One could call that a defect."

mistake may function positively to defend the community against the charge of credulity (cf. Luke 24:11),[154] but it serves to diminish her role.

(3) She calls the risen Jesus *"Rabbouni."* The form is that of early Palestinian Aramaic, as shown by its appearance in the Targum fragments from the Cairo Genizah.[155] The expression has been described as a caritative, that is, a diminutive form of endearment: "my dear rabbi," or "my little rabbi." (The diminutive is particularly interesting: "my little master" undercuts the idea of mastery.) In 1:38 Jesus asks the disciples of John the Baptist, "What are you looking for?" and they address him as "Rabbi."[156] Mary Magdalene's use of title *Rabbouni* is often thought of as another sign of her ignorance.[157] It is a "modest" title, says Brown, "characteristic of the beginning of faith rather than of its culmination," certainly falling far short of Thomas' 'My Lord and my God' in v. 28.[158] He is tempted to theorize that by using this "old" title the Johannine Magdalene is showing her misunderstanding of the resurrection: she thinks she can now follow Jesus in the same way she did during the ministry. Such thinking may indicate she has an inferior faith, and does not possess the Spirit: "[O]ne may wonder if her use of an inadequate title does not imply that only when the Spirit is given (vs. 22) is full faith in the risen Jesus possible." Her use of the title "Lord" in v. 18 makes this reasoning less plausible,[159] but it is nevertheless common, in spite of her use of "Lord" in v. 2 also.

(4) Most important is the risen Jesus' command (v. 17), "Do not touch me" or "Do not go on touching me." The present imperative implies that she is already touching him, or is trying to.[160] The verb *haptō* may have the notion of grasping or clinging.[161] F. Perles thinks that the original meaning, which is mistranslated in

---

154. D'Angelo, "Reconstructing 'Real' Women," 111.

155. M. Black, *An Aramaic Approach to the Gospels and Acts* (Oxford: Clarendon, 1946) 21. Jesus' use of the Semitic form of her name *Mariam* in v. 16 and possibly v. 18 (instead of *Maria* which is used for her in 19:25; 20:1, 11) may correspond to *Rabbouni*, and be indicative of a source. See J. D. M. Derrett, "Miriam and the Resurrection (John 20, 16)," *Downside Review* 111 (1993) 174–86. It is the only time in John that Jesus refers to a female character with her proper name (Conway, *Men and Women*, 194).

156. See further, below, pp. 341–43.

157. R. Bultmann, *The Gospel of John* (Philadelphia: Westminster, 1971) 687: she thinks he has "simply 'come back' from the dead, and that he is again the man she knew as 'Teacher.' "

158. J. H. Charlesworth (*The Beloved Disciple* [Valley Forge, Pa.: Trinity Press International, 1995] 300) sees Thomas resisting "easy belief, whether before an empty tomb (20:1–10), from claims that angels had been seen in the tomb (20:12), from the testimony of a woman (20:17–18), or the ecstatic enthusiasm of other disciples (20:24–25). The narrator thus allows Thomas to stand for reliable belief."

159. Brown, *John*, 2.992, 1010.

160. Perkins reads the touching with Matt 28:10 as originally an attempt to worship Jesus, prohibited because he has not yet returned to the Father (*Resurrection*, 175–76).

161. Dodd (*Interpretation*, 443, 2) on the aorist. See B. Violet, "Ein Versuch zu Joh 20 17," *ZNW* 24 (1925) 78–80 for references to LXX *haptesthai* translating *dabaq (dabeq)*, "to cling to, cleave to" and *ahaz*, "to seize," *qarab (qareb)*, "to come near, approach."

John, was "Don't follow me,"[162] which would bring us even closer to the storyline in 2 Kings 2, where Elisha is following Elijah. The command of the risen Jesus in John 20:17, however, is most often taken to signal of Mary Magdalene's spiritual and intellectual inadequacy, her earthiness. Minear's interpretation is one of the most extreme: her touch is an attempt to restrict and entomb Jesus.[163] The point of 20:17 is for some that mere resuscitation of a corpse is not what resurrection means.[164] Or, by telling her not to cling to him, the Johannine Jesus indicates that his permanent presence is not by way of appearance as she mistakenly thinks but by way of the gift of the Spirit that can come only after he has ascended.[165] Brown cites Bultmann's "penetrating observation that the 'not yet' of Jesus' 'I have not yet ascended' is really applicable to Magdalene's desire — she cannot yet have Jesus' enduring presence. Instead of trying to hold on to Jesus (not that she could actually have prevented his ascension), she is commanded to go and prepare his disciples for that coming of Jesus when the Spirit will be given."[166] De Conick's treatment is unusual: she argues that "Mary, by recognizing Jesus, acknowledges his victory over death." Touching him enables her to identify him as *"Rabbouni"* (v. 16; cf. v. 18: "the Lord").[167] But this does not explain the prohibition against touching.

(5) Mary's double "turning" in vv. 14, 16 is sometimes read as a turning backward toward Judaism, then turning in a spiritual conversion from it. Schneiders' view[168] is that Mary's "turning" in 20:14 is a turning toward "the dispensation which came to a close with the glorification of Jesus on the cross. In the historical context of the Johannine community, it is probably also to turn back toward the synagogue, toward religious experience governed by the coordinates of Judaism, toward Moses as teacher of the way." Rema holds that Mary Magdalene could be a representative of Brown's "Jewish Christians of inadequate faith" or an "apostolic Christian group." "She serves as a positive example for people whose faith

---

162. F. Perles, *ZNW* 25 (1926) 287; against Brown, *John*, 2.992. See also Violet, "Ein Versuch," 79–80.

163. P. S. Minear, "'We don't know where...' John 20.2," *Int* 30 (1076) 130.

164. King, "Mary Magdalene," 4.

165. Brown, *John*, 2.1010.

166. Brown, *John*, 2.1012; cf. Bultmann, *History of the Synoptic Tradition*, 533; cf. Bultmann, *John*, 687–89. Bultmann thinks of Jesus as already ascended rather than ascending: Do not touch me yet because I have ascended. But see R. G. Maccini, *Her Testimony is True* (Sheffield: Sheffield Academic Press, 1996) 213: we would expect *gar* to follow rather than precede *anabebeka*.

167. A. D. De Conick, "'Blessed Are Those Who Have Not Seen' (JN 20:29): Johannine Dramatization of an Early Christian Discourse," *The Nag Hammadi Library After Fifty Years*, 392–93, using scenes from classical Greek and Latin literature where the hero is identified through exposure of his wounds and the touching of his body. The scenes in John 20 are not demonstrations of Jesus' corporeality, unlike Luke 24:37–42 (395; against G. J. Riley (*Resurrection Reconsidered* [Minneapolis: Fortress, 1995] 107–26).

168. Schneiders, "John 20:11–18," 163; see also W. Howard-Brook, *Becoming Children of God: John's Gospel and Radical Discipleship* (Maryknoll, N.Y.: Orbis, 1994) 451; he finds it a possible reading that Mary's clinging to Jesus be seen in terms of Song of Songs 3:4 and the desire to bring him back to the mother's house, the synagogue. Countered by Reinhartz, "To Love the Lord," 62.

is curtailed by traditional or reasonable expectations. Although she asks for no sign, she thinks only about things that can be seen. The futility of living by sight alone is emphasized by the fact that her blindness persists even in the presence of the living Lord."[169]

Neyrey points to the instances in which Mary is painfully "not in the know": 20:2 ("we do not know where they have laid him"); 20:13 ("I do not know where they have laid him"); 20:14 (She did not know that it was Jesus); 20:15 ("Supposing him to be the gardener.... Tell me where you have laid him"). He sees her transformed, however, into "a disciple supremely 'in the know'" by her recognition of Jesus when he speaks her name; she then "serves as a conduit of esoteric christological information" to the disciples. Neyrey holds that her knowledge of secrets about Jesus (such as "where he is going") indicates that she enjoys very high status within the Johannine group.[170] I think this may have been true for some members of the group, even after her insight was muted by being incorporated into a narrative which (1) does not respond to it and (2) appropriates and overwhelms it by focus on the male disciples. This incorporation results in a distorted stress on her ignorance, not her knowledge.

The Erotic

The patristic and modern history of the interpretation of John 20:1–2, 11–18 is a fascinating record full of distraction, obsession, romance and misogyny — as well as more interesting insights and debate over the nature of the resurrected Jesus' body and over leadership. The narrative is wide open to being read as centered on Jesus' rebuff of the touch of Mary Magdalene, correcting her and illustrating her stupidity, obsession, physicality, unseemliness, inferiority, and lust. We have seen that the admonition not to touch him was interpreted as an absolute injunction against all women teaching or administering the sacraments.[171] The erotic element is often narrowed to her sexuality, with implications for his. The theory of Kastner, for example, is that the risen Jesus was naked, so Mary had turned away from him; his nakedness is also seen as the reason why her touch was inappropriate.[172] This theory may be "[n]otable as a curiosity,"[173] but it is a

169. Rema, "Women," 144–45; see R. E. Brown, *Community of the Beloved Disciple* (New York: Paulist, 1979) 71–88.

170. J. Neyrey, "The Sociology of Secrecy and the Fourth Gospel," *What Is John?* (ed. F. Segovia; Atlanta: Scholars Press, 1998) 2.104–5. Conway (*Men and Women*, 199) sees Peter's dominant character trait in 20–21 as his inability to understand Jesus.

171. Above, pp. 86–87, 96.

172. K. Kastner, "Noli me tangere," *BZ* 13 (1915) 344–53.

173. See Brown, *John*, 2.990–93, for a variety of readings. Some treatments show no awareness of Johannine irony or dramatic misunderstandings; others are more sophisticated. For attempts to repunctuate v. 17 see M. McGehee, "A Less Theological Reading of John 20:17," *JBL* 105 (1986) 299–302 ("Do not cling to me. Since I have not yet ascended to the Father, go to my brothers and tell them"). Riley (*Resurrection Reconsidered*, n. 86, p. 98) suggests the sentences mean "Let go of me now,

subliminal message in many interpretations, and many artistic representations of the scene, especially those in which a kneeling and/or groveling Mary reaches toward the groin of Jesus, and he recoils.[174]

D'Angelo remarks that although Jesus' "rebuke" functions primarily to draw attention to his liminal state, "it cannot be excluded that the danger of a touch between Mary and Jesus involves the sexual connotations of the word 'touch': they are well attested in the period." Although Mary of Bethany is the only character in this Gospel who touches Jesus,[175] other interactions between Jesus and both male and female characters of John also display a "dialectic of erotic and ascetic overtones" and "anxieties about physicality, particularly the physicality of Jesus, that frequently accompany prophecy."[176] This dialectic needs to be further explored, especially in relation to the "masculinity" or lack of "masculinity" of Jesus, understandings of the risen body, and the gender power-struggles over prophetic authority. D'Angelo thinks that in its earlier stages the community of John contained their anxieties about the flesh by relegating eros to the spiritual realm, where ascetic practice enabled its fuller exploitation and a relatively wide realm of participation for women. But "the identification of women with flesh and sexuality remained, and ascetic ambitions helped to lay the groundwork for future tensions about women's roles. . . . In so far as ascetic and spiritualist tendencies liberated women from these categories, they do so [sic] only by limiting them as actors in the world."[177] It is important to ask whose anxieties we are discussing, whose identifications, whose power to relegate, and to insist that men and women experienced these quite differently. In an androcentric mystical tradition with rigid purity conventions (cf. *Hekaloth Rabbati* 15), a *woman's* touch might be thought of as the touch of someone ritually impure, unable to enter the

---

for I need to go to my Father, and you need to go to the other disciples." Schnackenburg thinks an act of worship such as that in Matt 28:10 is prohibited because Jesus has not yet returned to the Father (*John*, 3.317). Schneiders (in "John 20:11–18," 164) takes v. 17 as a rhetorical question expecting a negative answer ("Am I not yet ascended?"); in *Written That You May Believe*, 112, she translates "I ascend to my Father and [who is now] your Father, to my God and [who is now] your God," but believes it would be clearer to translate it paraphrastically as "my ascension is to my Father who is now your Father. . . . " The emphasis, she thinks, "is not on the ascension but on the disciples' sharing in Jesus' relation to God, which is effected by this ascending" (n 42). She thinks the pronoun "me" should be emphasized: "Not me (emphatic) continue to touch" — that is, not Jesus the individual; rather she should encounter him in the community (197–98).

174. See, for example, Titian's *Noli me tangere*, 1550 (London's National Gallery) and its 1989 spinoff by Wayne Forte, *Really Waana Touch You* (private collection), both reproduced in M. W. Holmes, "To Be Continued . . . The Many Endings of the Gospel of Mark," *BR* 17 (August 2001) 16.

175. A. Reinhartz, *Befriending the Beloved Disciple: A Jewish Reading of the Gospel of John* (New York: Continuum, 2001) 119.

176. D'Angelo, "Reconstructing 'Real' Women," 120, 136. Other examples include the anointing scene in John 12, which casts Mary of Bethany in the role of the woman lover from the Song of Songs; Martha and Lazarus said to have been loved by Jesus (11:5); the unnamed one called the Beloved Disciple.

177. D'Angelo, "(Re)presentations of Women," 137, citing H. Koester, *Ancient Christian Gospels* (Philadelphia: Trinity Press International, 1990) 274–76.

realm of the sacred. The heavenly body of Jesus, that is, would be threatened by uncleanness.[178] But in an egalitarian mystical tradition, I suggest, concerns about touching or holding would be quite different, and a woman's mystical seeing could be accepted.[179]

Both scenes in 2 Kings 2 and John 20 are erotic.[180] In 2 Kings 2 the bond is between two men, in a father-son, teacher-student relationship; in John 20 the bond is between a man and a woman, not a relationship of father-daughter. (It may or may not be a relationship of lovers. Many commentators have seen allusions to the Song of Songs: in the garden setting, the woman seeking the absent man, holding him and not being willing to let him go, the question addressed to the watchmen; in the motifs of peering, turning, night, spices, arise, touch,[181] and voice).[182] Along these lines, Mary Magdalene is thought by some readers to display "the blind folly, tough-minded devotion, desperate despair, and rapturous joy of the ardent lover."[183] She is considered by others to display a stereotypical subordinate and supportive role in relation to the hero-bridegroom.[184] According to Reinhartz, a reading that focuses on the tropes of physicality and sensuality, whether or not intended by the author(s), casts Mary and Jesus in the role of lovers, even though the Gospel says nothing about their prior physical relationship. In the context of love, John 20:17 can be and has been read as the prohibition against her touching him; it is either a rejection of intimacy or a mild chastisement. In either case, this verse aborts "the Canticles paradigm," since the woman and man are never together again and never achieve the consummation of their relationship.[185]

---

178. C. Rowland, personal communication, December 2000.

179. C. Afzal ("'Early Jewish and Christian Mysticism'" A Collage of Working Definitions,"ed. A. DeConick; *SBL Seminar Papers* [Atlanta: Scholars Press, 2001] 281): "Mysticism is erotic theology...Mystical texts are texts reflecting a desire for God."

180. Fishbane (*Exegetical Imagination*, 19) speaks of the "spiritual eros that animates midrashic exegesis."

181. "I held him and would not let him go..." (Song of Songs 3:4).

182. M. Cambre, "L'Influence du Cantique des Cantique sur le Nouveau Testament," *RThom* 62 (1962) 5–26; A. Feuillet, "La recherche du Christ dans la Nouvelle Alliance d'apres la Christophanie de Jo 20, 11–18," *L'Homme devant Dieu* (Paris: Aubier, 1963) 1.93–112; Schneiders, "John 20:11–18," 161; Winsor, *A King Is Bound*. See Nicolas Wyatt, "'Supposing Him to Be the Gardener,'" *ZNW* 81 (1990) 21–38 for the paradise motif. Reinhartz (*Befriending*, 106–7) argues that Mary is not the new Eve, although she is called "woman" (cf. Gen 2:23), called by name (cf. Gen 3:20) and clings to Jesus (cf. Gen 2:24). The Genesis echo, however, "suggests a contrast between the sexual relationship that developed between the first man and woman and the relationship of devotion between Jesus and Mary. In doing so, it also draws attention to the sexual potential of an encounter between this man and woman in a garden" (108).

183. Schneiders, *Written That You May Believe*, 99. Spong (*Resurrection*, 92) thinks Mary's laying claim to the body, an action appropriate only for the nearest of kin, might be John's hint of a romantic relationship, his portrayal of her as Jesus' wife and now his widow. "It makes for a fascinating and, I believe, life-affirming speculation powerfully and innocently lifting women into the account of the resurrection." Her subsequent status derives from her relation to this male (243).

184. A. Fehribach, *The Women in the Life of the Bridegroom* (Collegeville, Minn.: Liturgical, 1995).

185. Reinhartz, *Befriending*, 110.

Inspired by the work of Mieke Bal, Alison Jasper gives a fascinating reading of John 20 which brutally aborts the paradigm. She maintains a primary focus on the figure of Mary Magdalene. From the viewpoint of Mary Magdalene, this is "a chapter of horrors." She is failed by Peter and the beloved disciple (who do not share what they see with her or make any gesture toward her), by angels (who do not deliver a message of hope or comfort or resurrection), by Jesus (who harshly spurns her at the moment of reunion) and perhaps also by the narrator (who implants signs of her failures, for example, to recognize Jesus). An increasing sense of isolation, confusion, violation, and rejection pervades the narrative. Her concern that the corpse has been desecrated, and the physical expression of her love are seen as inappropriate and wrong. It is hard to avoid the conclusion that Jesus does violence to her in v. 17–18, which like Genesis 2–3 is "a story about a brutal expulsion from innocent intimacy subsequent upon the demonstration of inappropriate knowledge." The message she is commissioned to deliver is for others, not for her; she is bypassed. Her final remark, "I have seen the Lord," might bear more or less than the sense of good news: it indicates her "measured perception of what the risen Christ has to offer," but her witness is not said to convince the disciples. "Perhaps because it has not convinced her."[186]

Turning to Rembrandt's painting of this scene,[187] Jasper notes the configuration of Mary Magdalene's confusion in her unconnectedness to others, her unprotectedness and surprise, the lack of tenderness toward her, her hands raised as if fearing attack, the disordered clothing (the grave cloth is in her hand). This last detail, not from the text, may have special significance: "In her hand, could disordered clothing become the sign of Mary's disordered clothing, the suspected violation of Jesus' body become at that moment another sort of experienced violation?" Mary's experience of great pain and loss in these verses is a direct consequence of her love for Jesus. She is one who suffers, and who has reason for her anguish and pain: what she loved had been violently and without pity taken from her.

Unlike other readings, this one does not silence the nature of her longing for the physical presence of Jesus by making it "an example or lesson of how not to behave or think in the community of the Risen Christ." Jasper thus considers her reading a "counter-reading which runs against the prevailing theological configurations." Her reading runs also counter to the efforts of some contemporary interpretations which attempt to heighten Mary Magdalene's importance in the text as it stands in this Gospel as a whole, and to integrate her into the implied authority structure. Many of these efforts, as well as the long history of interpretation and of artistic depictions of this scene, minimize or dismiss her ignorance

---

186. Jasper, "Interpretative Approaches," 112–13.
187. Panel; 61. 5x50cm. Signed and dated: Rembrandt f. 1638. London, Buckingham Palace (Royal Collection). Reproduced in H. Hoekstra, *Rembrandt and the Bible* (Utrecht: Magna Books, 1990) 418, and B. Bernard, *The Bible and Its Painters* (London and Sydney: Macdonald & Co., 1988) 241.

and anguish, theologically desensitizing them, thus continuing the violation Jasper sees in the text. She thinks that the text read in her way is capable of registering what feminist critics know "about the damaging polarities of a gendered discourse we cannot easily escape, and at the same time revealing the memorial of a protest and a refusal to be silenced."[188] The protest represented by Mary Magdalene, as I understand it, is against death, against the loss of the body, against separation. It urges: "telling the truth about my own experiences as a body, I do not think I solved, I doubt that any woman has solved it yet."[189]

Reinhartz offers a very different reading which is instead a confirmation of the Canticles paradigm in a new definition of consummation. Now consummation is in terms of speech and vision rather than touch, in terms of Mary's testimony to the disciples rather than an embrace. In this line of interpretation, 20:17 does not abort the paradigm. "Although the beloved is not accessible in the flesh, she has his image in her mind's eye and his words upon her lips." Intimacy, through the experience of Mary Magdalene, is accessible to the reader who acknowledges the subtext; the reader, that is, can see, hear and almost touch the risen Lord through "the signs that are written in this book" (20:30–31). The subtext creates "an authority structure that is at odds with that which plays on the text's surface. Whereas on the surface the Beloved Disciple[190] apparently upholds the authority of the disciples as an exclusive group within the community of Jesus' followers, his allusions to the Song of Songs implicitly define Mary as the one who exemplifies the intimacy and love between the believer and the risen Lord."[191]

Both of these readings, in my opinion, help bring the whole issue of body and touch into the context of death in a different way. They are not focused on the nature or corporeality of the risen Jesus. Mary Magdalene's desire is not an example of "inappropriate knowledge" or lack of knowledge, or of "how not to behave and think." Rather, her desire is for the relationship that does not break off, for connection with the whole, non-dichotomous person, whatever the cost in terms of anguish.[192] "Such she often felt herself—struggling against terrific odds to maintain her courage; to say: 'But this is what I see; this is what I see', and so to clasp some miserable remnant of her vision to her breast, which a thousand forces did their best to pluck from her."[193] I am reminded of the opposite of this

---

188. Jasper, "Interpretative Approaches, 115–16. Recent interpretations of the Song of Songs, as soft pornography, sado-masochistic eroticism, or a continual play of absence and presence, seeking and finding, bring new dimensions to the interpretation of John 20. See abstracts by C. Exum and S. Moore (*AAR/SBL Abstracts*, Denver 2001) 3–4.

189. V. Woolf, "Professions for Women," *The Death of the Moth*, 241.

190. For Reinhartz, the implied author.

191. Reinhartz, *Befriending*, 111.

192. See Ruddick, "Private Brother," 192–93 on the affirmation of Woolf's novel, *Jacob's Room*: we are right to care, to embrace the shadows; occasionally, we will be rewarded with connection.

193. Lily Briscoe in Woolf, *To the Lighthouse*, 46.

desire, expressed in the assessment by Corliss Lamont that no one he had ever known, including himself, was worth survival after death.[194]

In the context of the apocalyptic/mystical thought world we have explored, Mary Magdalene's search is successful. It illustrates the belief that "love is strong as death,/passion fierce as the grave" (NRSV Cant 8:6). But Reinhartz recognizes that although the allusions to the Song of Songs powerfully portray the mutual love of Mary and Jesus, "the text falls short of describing her as an important leader among the disciples, and therefore we cannot say that she represents a leader within the Johannine community."[195] In fact, the association of the Song of Songs with Mary Magdalene can be so nonthreatening that 3:1–4 is a reading used for her feastday Mass in Roman Catholicism.[196] When love is "the only possible interpreter" of a woman, both love and the woman are diminished.

We need not make an either/or choice here: to see John 20 drawing either on the Song of Songs or on 2 Kings 2. The Song of Song allusions may overlap in John 20 with allusions to merkabah mysticism traditions. Four men, Ben Azzai, Ben Zoma, Elisha Ben Abuyah and R. Aquiba enter a garden (*pardes;* cf. Song of Songs 4:13 [*pardes rimmonim*]) in the Tosefta and both Talmuds. These texts are read by Scholem and others in terms of visionary ascent in this tradition.[197] *Pardes* is variously interpreted as the garden of Eden, or the heavenly or earthly temple, or heaven (cf. 1 Enoch 60:8, the garden where the elect and righteous dwell). Well before the third century C.E. "a complex web associating Ezekiel 1 and the Song of Songs with the Sinai revelation" was developing in which *pardes* was used as a technical term for the Holy of Holies in the highest heaven, where God appears in his glory upon the merkabah. The original author of the tradition about the four men evidently expected readers to understand this usage, "which was deeply rooted in the prerabbinic and pre-Christian tradition of the visionary ascent."[198] It is possible that the author of the tradition used in John had the same expectation. With the imagery of the temple and the Holy of Holies at the heart of the ascent-to-paradise tradition,[199] we should not miss the significance of a woman's presence there in the garden. The Gospel of John proposes friendship as the bond of the community, and perhaps something like that was communicated by the use of Song of Songs allusions ("This is my beloved, and this is my friend, O daughters of Jerusalem" 5:16).

194. C. Lamont, *Atheism;* this book, from the 1950s, has not been available to me.
195. Reinhartz, *Befriending,* 122.
196. An alternate reading is 2 Cor 5:14–17.
197. *T. Hag* 2:l; *y. Hag* 77b; *b. Hag* 14b–15b; *Cant. R.* 1:28. But see J. Dan, *Three Types of Jewish Mysticism* (Cincinnati: University of Cincinnati, 1984) 10–11 for the attribution to R Akiba himself of a new mystical attitude and interpretation of the Song of Songs, later fused with the ancient Merkabah tradition.
198. C. R. A. Morray-Jones, "Paradise Revisited (2 Cor 12:1–12): The Jewish Mystical Background of Paul's Apostolate, Part 1" *HTR* 86 (1993) 193, 183, 208.
199. As Morray-Jones holds (2 Cor 12:1–12): The Jewish Mystical Background of Paul's Apostolate, Part 2: Paul's Heavenly Ascent and its Significance," HTR 3 [1993] 285–86).

Johannine Disputes about Mysticism

Can we fit the ideas I am proposing about this source (or fragment of a source), and its use by the Johannine author, into the position that the author was in dispute with mystical pre-mortem ascent theology and its sometimes concomitant belief in the divinization or immortalization of the visionary?[200] John 1:18; 3:3; 3:13; 5:37; 6:46 are the major texts read in terms of such a polemic. To these De Conick adds the series of verses where Jesus proclaims that he will not be able to be followed into heaven (at least not before the Eschaton). Four times (7:33–34; 8:21; 13:33; 13:36), Jesus tells different audiences that "you will seek me . . . (but) where I am going, you cannot come." If we add John 20:17 ("Do not cling to me") to this list, and read it in the context of seeking to follow (rather than to hold back a departure), this verse too may be thought to oppose the notion of ecstatic pre-eschatological ascent and visionary experience. That might be a meaning intended by the Johannine author, of a tradition that originally and in earlier readings validated more fully the mystical experience of Mary Magdalene as another Elisha. Elisha, after all, saw the chariot, "crossed the Jordan" with Elijah, then crossed back, with Elijah's mantle and the double portion of his spirit. In this sense 2 Kings 2 is an at least partially successful attempt to follow, more than an attempt to hold Elijah back. Mary Magdalene's seeing in John 20 may fulfill in some way the promise to Nathanael in 1:51,[201] and the promises at the supper in 14:19, 21; 16:16, 21.

The readings of John's text, then, which suggest an ignorant attempt to hold Jesus back miss even John's point. For John, Mary Magdalene is not stupid. But the tradition of her as visionary must be contained and disguised, diverted. It may have been as powerful or even more powerful than the tradition of Thomas ("the hero of Syrian Christianity"), if he is presented in 20:24–29 as "the Fool who does not have the correct understanding of the way to heaven or of the manner of encountering God since he insists on visions," a fool "who misunderstands salvation as ascent and vision mysticism." Was Thomasine Christianity less acceptable for the Johannine community than Magdalene Christianity? De Conick argues that fragments of the discourse between the Thomasine and Johannine communities "tell us that the Thomasine tradition expected theophany experiences whereas the Johannine Christians did not."[202] Belief in the

---

200. See De Conick, "'Blessed Are Those," 381–83 for a brief summary of the varieties within this position. For Odeberg (*The Fourth Gospel*, 89) the saying of R. Yose ben Halafta (ca. 150 C.E.) is relevant here, in which the descent of the Shekinah and the ascensions of Elijah and Moses are denied; for Moses "there was a distance of ten fingers' breadth"; for Elijah, three (*Sukkah* 5a; see above n. 53).
201. The second "you will see" is plural.
202. De Conick, "'Blessed Are Those," 390, 382–83, 390.

incorporation of the believer into the Human One, however, would qualify that statement.[203]

It is not clear what fragments associated with the Magdalene tell us. Certainly the insertion of the episode with Peter and the Beloved Disciple at the tomb, and stress on the latter's faith downgrade the importance of her visionary experience, and the Thomas episode's stress on faith without seeing downgrades it further. It seems possible that a Magdalene Christianity stressed pre-mortem visionary ascents, some sort of proleptic, "spiritual" resurrection, and prophetic empowerment, and these were regarded as incompatible, or only partly compatible, with the developed Johannine stress on faith. In the Gospel of the Savior 107.1–108.64, DeConick finds a visionary mystical tradition that appears to hold that vision is a necessary basis for faith and salvation. The risen Jesus' insistence that Mary Magdalene not hold or touch him (John 20:17) is echoed, and the reason given: because his glorified body is identified with fire, an image commonly connected to the *kabod*, the manifestation of God.[204] I can only raise here these issues and questions about mysticism in John. Exploration of similarities and distinctions between the Gospel of John and the Gospel of Mary, and their communities, and their connections with Merkabah mysticism will surely prove fruitful for furthering this discussion.[205]

Mary Magdalene in the Gospel of John

Positive (or semi-positive) readings can be given of the Johannine depiction of Mary Magdalene. In this Gospel, the tradition about Mary Magdalene serves as "the capstone" to a series that begins with the mother of Jesus at Cana and includes a missionary, the Samaritan woman, and Martha, who confesses him as Messiah, the Son of God, and "the coming one" (*ho erchomenos*).[206] Mary Magdalene joins the other women in this narrative who come to faith through their

---

203. Kanagaraj, 'Mysticism,' 211, 213. In the Gospel of John, mystical union is with the "angelomorphic Son of Man by means of Jesus' ascent, not in the sense of absorption in him [or their deification] but in the sense of sharing the same relationship with God."

204. A. DeConick, *Voices of the Mystics: Early Christian Discourse in the Gospels of John and Thomas and Other ancient Christian Literature* (Sheffield: Sheffield Academic Press, 2001) 148–49.

205. See Gruenwald, *From Apocalypticism to Gnosticism*, chaps 7 and 8. He argues that in the case of at least texts from Nag Hammadi (The Hypostasis of the Archons and On the Origin of the World) we have to assume some kind of knowledge of Merkabah material. He holds that in both apocalypticism and gnosticism the ascent to heaven is in order to learn, to acquire gnosis in the wide sense of the term; the ascent is not a flight from the world ("Merkavah Mysticism and Gnosticism," 52). See also M. Himmelfarb, "Heavenly Ascent and the Relationship of the Apocalypses and the *Hekhalot* Literature," *HUCA* 59 (1988) 73–100; P. Alexander, "Comparing Merkavah Mysticism and Gnosticism: An Essay in Method," *JJS* 35 (1984) 1–18; A. Y. Collins, "The Seven Heavens in Jewish and Christian Apocalypses," *Death, Ecstasy and Other Worldly Journeys* (ed. J. J. Collins and M. Fishbane; Albany: SUNY, 1995) 59–91.

206. In context, she is assenting also to Jesus' description of himself as "the resurrection and the life" (11:25).

own experience.[207] The Johannine community appears to have been independent from other early Christian groups, and to have had a less authoritarian structure. The powerful depictions of women in this Gospel apparently were "enabled by the communal prophetic experience that made every believer a source of spirit and life. What little leadership and structure there was seems to have been charismatic and dynamic in character. This did not exclude conflict over communal roles."[208]

Mary Magdalene can be seen to stand with Peter and the Beloved Disciple in a kind of triadic leadership. She does not appear, however, after 20:18. The appendix, John 21, authorizes Peter to feed the lambs and sheep, representing Jesus the good shepherd. Mary Magdalene becomes then only "the indispensable link to apostolic Christians under Peter's leadership."[209] It is possible that her prominence signals the presence of women leaders in the Johannine community at some stage(s), and her absence from the final scenes signals conflicts over such leadership, and signals who has won. T. K. Seim finds in the Johannine story of the empty tomb "a strange and rather entertaining apportionment among the persons involved. It makes sure that none of them becomes 'the winner' of the search. Each of them is given some priority, and only when their various pieces of evidence are gathered together does the witness become complete." This apportionment among Mary Magdalene, Peter, and the beloved disciple, she thinks, could imply an egalitarian interest in the leadership of the Johannine community, in which men and women would share the responsibilities of authority, witness, and proclamation. For Seim, "the tension and contrast that exists in the synoptic tradition of the empty tomb between the group of women disciples and the men is not [to] be found in John."[210] Perhaps she is right that in the treatment of the empty tomb, this Gospel provides more evidence of egalitarianism than the Synoptics. And perhaps such egalitarianism, such balance, is a point of Johannine redaction. But "the story's double ending"[211] nevertheless overpowers the Magdalene traditions. It is too much to say that "the Johannine version represents a merger and an equalization of one tradition focusing on Peter and another focusing on the women [Mary Magdalene]"[212] If that were the case, she would reappear, as Peter does, in the scenes where the spirit and commissions are given. Grassi sees all this in dualistic terms: the beloved disciple and Mary Magdalene are "inner successors" to Jesus. Their special relationships to him give them the mission of bringing a deep inner understanding of him. They are counterparts to

207. Perkins, "'I Have Seen the Lord,'" 41; cf. R. Kysar, *John the Maverick Gospel* (Louisville: Westminster/John Knox, 1995) 148–54
208. D'Angelo, "(Re)presentations of Women in the Gospels," 137
209. J. A. Grassi, *The Secret Identity of the Beloved Disciple* (New York: Paulist, 1992) 85.
210. T. K. Seim,"Roles of Women in the Gospel of John," *Aspects of Johannine Literature* (ed. L. Hartman and B. Olson; Uppsala: Almqvist & Wiksell, 1987) 67.
211. See above, p. 326.
212. Seim, "Roles of Women," n. 23, p. 67.

Peter and the twelve "who were outer successors in regard to authority and the apostolate."[213]

Mary Magdalene behind the Gospel of John: Jewish Christian Source(s)?

A positive reading of the appearance to Mary Magdalene in John is nice, but I think it is not enough. Not enough to be true to the reconstructed tradition of her empowerment, not enough for the feminist historian and reader aware of the gaps and distortions and their implications. I have boldly speculated that a traditional source used in John 20:1, 11–18[214] emphasized Elijah-Elisha traditions. Allusions to Elijah and Elisha in 1 and 2 Kings are numerous throughout the Gospel of John: the changing of water into wine; healing of the nobleman's son; feeding of the multitude; healing of the man born blind; and perhaps Jesus' prayer at the raising of Lazarus; the expectation of the "coming one."[215] These allusions occur within the signs source postulated by many scholars.[216] Martyn holds that Jesus was the eschatological Elijah in a Jewish Christian source used by the author of the Fourth Gospel. In John 1:21 John the Baptist denies he is Elijah, opening the way for an identification of Jesus with Elijah, but this identification never happens in the finished Gospel.[217] The hypothetical source that I have suggested is incorporated into chapter 20 may have been a part of a larger work, which ended with Mary Magdalene's report of her encounter with the risen Jesus,[218] or with conflict and (partial) resolution, like the Gospel of Mary.

That there is no anti-Jewish polemic in all the passages in which women play a prominent role "strongly suggests that the community did not experience the role of women within it as a source of tension with the Jewish communities it knew."[219] But these passage may have functioned in a different way in various stages of

213. Grassi, *Secret Identity*, 116.
214. I think likely these were joined and not two separate traditions.
215. Martyn, "We Have Found Elijah," 20–28.
216. See G. Reim, *Studien zum alttestamentlichen Hintergrund des Johannesevangeliums* (Cambridge: Cambridge University Press, 1974) 207.
217. Martyn, "We Have Found Elijah," 9–54.
218. See D'Angelo, "(Re)presentations of Women," 191: "It is possible to postulate an early version of John ending with the figure of Mary Magdalene, charged with the message of Jesus' ascension, in which the voices of the Samaritan woman, of Martha and Mary, and of the mother of Jesus were even more prominent. To imagine a woman author of these works does not change the gendered arrangements they reflect. But it does cast the stories about women as signatures, as ways in which the writer declares herself within the narrative, placing a particular emphasis upon women of the final scenes. And this is a speculation that points the twentieth-century reader to what these gospels certainly had: women readers and women hearers for whom the gender of Mary Magdalene could be good news." She thinks a first edition of John was contemporary with and independent of Mark ("Reconstructing 'Real' Women," 131).
219. D'Angelo, "Reconstructing 'Real' Women," 135.

composition and in the Gospel as a completed whole.[220] They certainly do so now for some critics, for example, those who interpret Mary Magdalene's "turning" in 20:14 as a turning backward to Judaism, the synagogue, an inadequate Mosaic faith, a blindness.[221] If such interpretations represent the viewpoint of the finished Gospel (and I am not convinced they do), they are not the views represented in the earlier Mary Magdalene tradition. Brown comments that "giving to a woman a role traditionally associated with Peter [being the first to see the risen Lord] may well be a deliberate emphasis on John's part," since Martha's confession of Jesus' messiahship substitutes for the Synoptic Peter's.[222] Historically, perhaps this substitution should be reversed.

My hypothetical source is produced by what Fishbane calls "the inner texture of Jewish thinking as an ongoing exegetical process": a new text is created that interprets an old text, as existence is textualized "by having the ideals of (interpreted) Scripture embodied in everyday life."[223] The hearers/interpreters are meant to read and hear the connections, to retrieve the past acts of exegetical imagination.[224] Fishbane holds "that Jewish thought and theology arise in the thickness of exegesis and are carried by its forms. The theologians thought with these elements."[225] The possible source used in John 20:1, 11–18 presented the startling claim that Mary Magdalene was a successor of Jesus. If this claim — and the allusion that carried it[226] — was then obscured by the Evangelist or someone

220. R. Kysar, "John, Gospel of," *ABD* 3.918–22 discusses dating and stages of development.
221. See above, pp. 329–30, the views of Schneiders and Rema.
222. R. E. Brown, "Roles of Women in the Fourth Gospel," *TS* 36 (1975) 693.
223. Fishbane, *Exegetical Imagination*, ix, 4.
224. This is so even if for a feminist interpreter like myself the texts are not "Scripture" in the rabbinic or Christian ecclesiastical sense. Fishbane holds that "The task for the interpreter is therefore to examine carefully the exegetical reasoning manifest in the text at hand — in the thickness of its citations and expression — and to re-imagine the earlier exegete's habit of mind. Only thus will a truly historical theology be retrieved" (4). Cf. T. R. Hatina, "Intertextuality and Historical Criticism in New Testament Studies: Is There a Relationship?" *BibInt* 7 (1999) 28–43. Fishbane's inner-biblical exegesis, which starts with received Scripture and moves forward to interpretations, is to be distinguished from tradition-historical criticism which is interested in the oral source(s) behind the text.
225. Fishbane, *Exegetical Imagination*, 8.
226. M. Fishbane (*Biblical Interpretation in Ancient Israel* [New York: Oxford, 1985] 10) argues that the Gospels, Pauline writings, and writings from Qumran are "an innovative *traditio* [subsequent interpretation of Scripture], continuous with the Hebrew Bible but decidedly something new; something not 'biblical,'" not quite like inner-biblical exegesis. They are not properly studied in an intertextual relationship with the Hebrew Bible, because "the dominant thrust of these documents is that they have fulfilled or superseded the ancient Israelite *traditum* [Scripture]." However, G. O'Day ("Jeremiah 9:22–23 and 1 Corinthians 1:26–31," *JBL* 109 [1990] n. 35, p. 267) counters that Paul's use of the Israelite tradition "seems to proceed from the same textual-exegetical imagination as that of his scribal and prophetic forebears." I understand what Fishbane is saying. The Christian Testament is not biblical in his sense of the term, and especially where the Christian imagination "supersedes" the Hebrew Bible, the relationship is in a sense broken. But I am primarily interested here in pre-Gospel stage(s), before there was a Christian scripture, as well as in John's reuse of earlier material. Reinhartz discusses the impact of the scriptures on the author of John, and "the profound and playful role of biblical allusion in John 20:1–18" (*Befriending*, 106–7). She understands intertextuality as "the reading of one text against the background of another, at the discretion and choice of the reader" ("To Love the Lord," 53).

before him, it can be argued that women did not gain in importance as stories were retold in the Johannine community.[227]

What sort of leadership might have been envisioned for Mary Magdalene is unknown. Was her "double portion" of the spirit understood to elevate her hierarchically? Or was the spirit understood as available to all in some way through her message? The second option is more probable, since the risen Jesus is *Rabbouni*, not judge or ruler; his God and father is the God and father of all the "brothers and sisters." Mary Magdalene, then, would not be not *the only* successor to Jesus either in this source or in this basically or quasi-democratic Gospel, in which all receive the Paraklete[228] and all will do great works (14:12). John 20:19–31; 21:1–25 could be appreciated for recognizing and emphasizing this, if not for the fact that Mary Magdalene is written out.

But it may be possible to write her back into other sections behind the Gospel. An Elijah component in the christology of John's source may have served as a kind of rudimentary Gospel in John's community. In this source (as in material behind the Gospel of Mark), Jesus as eschatological prophet Elijah healed and helped the needy, suffered and died.[229] In John 1:35–51, two disciples of John Baptist are presented as the first followers of Jesus; one is Andrew and the other is not named. Andrew then brings his brother Simon Peter to Jesus; the next day Philip is called, and Philip brings Nathanael to Jesus. There is a pattern to the first and third calls:

A. One disciple identifies Jesus to the new recruit: "We have found the Messiah" (v. 41); "We have found him about whom Moses and the prophets wrote" (v. 45);

B. The disciple brings the recruit to Jesus;

C. Jesus identifies the new disciple: "You are Simon son of John. You are to be called Cephas" (v. 42); "Here is an Israelite in whom there is no deceit" (Nathanael, v. 47).

This pattern is broken in the second call: Jesus himself finds Philip and says to him, "Follow me" (v. 43).

Further, John 1:35–51 bears some relation to 1:20–28, where John the Baptist denies he is the Messiah, Elijah, or the (Mosaic) prophet. The first and third of these expectations are applied to Jesus in 1:41, 45, but the second is not. These broken patterns and parallels signal the use of a source which has been edited. Who is the unnamed disciple of John the Baptist? Why is the pattern broken in the second call and what might have stood there originally? And why does an identification of Jesus with Elijah never happen in the finished Gospel?[230]

---

227. Contrast R. T. Fortna, *The Gospel of Signs* (Cambridge: Cambridge University Press, 1970) 236–45.

228. My thanks to Robert G. Hall for raising this point (SBL meeting, 2000).

229. J. L. Martyn, *The Gospel of John in Christian History*, 42, following Haenchen and R. Fortna. Also, in a pre-Marcan catenae of miracle stories, the underlying paradigm for healings and exorcisms appears to be the Elijah-Elisha narratives. See Mack, *Myth of Innocence*, 91–93, 217–18, 222–24.

230. Martyn, "We Have Found Elijah," 9–54.

By reconstructing a source, the patterns and parallels can be hypothetically restored. There is a chain of disciples recruiting disciples, and John the Baptist's three denials are matched by three affirmations about Jesus. On the basis of "a remarkable degree of structural similarity" evidenced in John 1:20–21 and 1:41–47, and 1:41–42 and 45–57,[231] the identification of Jesus with Elijah would originally be made in 1:43. Martyn reconstructs it this way: "He (Andrew — making a second recruit)[232] found Philip and said to him, 'We have found Elijah who comes to restore all things.' He led Philip to Jesus. And, looking at him, Jesus said, 'Follow me!'" and/or something identifying an essential characteristic of Philip (cf. 1:42, 47). The affirmation of Jesus as Elijah in this reconstruction is the counterpart of the denial by John the Baptist in v. 21 that he is Elijah.

Let me suggest another possibility: that in the source, the second unnamed disciple of John the Baptist took the initiative to find Philip, and that disciple was originally a woman (Mary Magdalene).[233] In this case, the news would pass from Andrew to Simon Peter, from Mary to Philip, from Philip to Nathanael.[234] This would be a link early in the story between her and Jesus-as-Elijah, and make her a companion of both John the Baptist and Jesus. It would represent Mary Magdalene as active and called (1:35–39), and indicate the type of Judaism from which some women members of the movement came.[235] (Matt 21:31–32 is the only mention of women among the disciples of John the Baptist; they are called prostitutes — a term that could be applied to a woman for a number of reasons besides accepting money for sex.[236]) Mention of Mary Magdalene in a source behind John 1 would, if used by the Evangelist, have introduced her — as the mother of Jesus and the Beloved Disciple are — before the crucifixion. But if Mary Magdalene appeared in this or any earlier scene, she has been erased, replaced by an unnamed person, an "empty set."[237]

---

231. Martyn, "We Have Found Elijah, 38–42.

232. This would be Andrew's second outreach, the first being to his brother Simon Peter (so also Bultmann and Fortna). Martyn thinks Peter is also possible here, in which case there would be a simple chain: from Andrew to Simon Peter, from Simon Peter to Philip, from Philip to Nathanael.

233. O'Day, "John," 301: she sees that the question Jesus asks her in 20:15 ("Whom are you seeking?") evokes the call of the first disciples in 1:38 ("What do you seek?").

234. Against M.-E. Boismard, "Les traditions johanniques concernant le Baptiste," *RB* 70 (1963) 40: he identifies the unnamed disciple of John the Baptist as Philip, so that both of the Baptist's disciples become apostles: to the Jewish world (to Simon, v. 41; to Nathanael, v. 45) and to the Gentile world (12:20–22). V 43 is excised as the work of the redactor. A footnote in the NRSV suggests the beloved disciple may have been the unnamed disciple of the Baptist.

235. Morray-Jones suggests that the transformational aspect of heavenly ascent was at an early period transferred to the rite of baptism ("Paradise Revisited, Part 2," n. 27, p. 273; cf. his "Transformational Mysticism in the Apocalyptic-Merkabah Tradition," *JJS* 43 [1992] 1–31. G. Scholem noted that "at important turning points in the history of Jewish mysticism — precisely at those times when something new appeared — constant reference was made to revelations of the prophet Elijah" (*Origins of the Kabbalah* [ed. R. J. Werblowsky; Philadelphia: Jewish Publication Society, 1987] 36).

236. Taylor, *The Immerser*, 119–23.

237. Schneiders (*Written That You May Believe*, 217–32): the "other disciple" here and elsewhere is "the evangelist's creation of an 'empty set' into which the reader, who is called to become a beloved

So too has the Elijah christology been deliberately suppressed. John 3:13 is regarded as polemic not only against the identification of Jesus with Elijah but also against the belief that Elijah was translated. Only Jesus is the ascended one, as the Human One.[238] "The evangelist could leave Elijah-like traits strewn among the miracle stories, very probably not merely out of reverence for his source. But he could scarcely allow the explicit identification and at the same time maintain the integrity of his own massive christology; for, in the frame of *his* christology, to do so would have implied that the logos experienced successive incarnations. We can be very nearly certain that this latter idea never seriously presented itself to John as a usable scheme, not because it was *religionsgeschichtlich* inconceivable (note the successive incarnations of the 'true prophet' in the Kerygmata Petrou) but because it would have diluted what for him could not be diluted: Jesus Christ the eternal Son as the sole mediator of God's revelation. In short, the Elijah christology of the source had to give way to the christology of eternal preexistence, expressed initially in the figure of the logos, and then dominantly in the figure of the descending and ascending Son of Man."[239]

But there may have been other reasons as well why the Elijah christology was suppressed: perhaps its association with the leadership of Mary Magdalene and other women; and/or with a corporate understanding of the Human One. Martyn asks if one could identify this pre-existent figure, "the sole locus of communication between heaven and earth (1:51)," with Elijah. "To ask the question is to answer it" (in the negative. though Elijah christology may have led to the notion of preexistence).[240] However, the Similitudes seem to identify the preexistent Human One with Enoch (1 Enoch 71); why not some identifying that figure with Elijah? The Human One may have been inclusive of Elijah at some stage in the Johannine community.[241] The political dimension of the Elijah-Elisha tradition has been seen as important to the *basileia* movement of Jesus and his companions "perhaps even as a historical prototype for their own mission of restoring or revitalizing the people of Israel."[242]

Martyn's work pushes us to think more about reasons for the suppression of an Elijah christology, and to try to reconstruct a fuller text of the source's account of Mary Magdalene's encounter with the risen Jesus. What might have appeared in the source as Jesus' identification of her essential characteristic? As we have

---

disciple, is intended to insert him- or herself"; it is a "cipher for the implied reader." This is not *the* Beloved Disciple, whom she sees as an historical but also a representative figure, not necessarily exclusively male. See below, pp. 344–45.

238. Martyn, "We Have Found Elijah," 20–21.
239. Martyn, "We Have Found Elijah," 52–53.
240. Martyn, "We Have Found Elijah," 52–53.
241. Mark 9:9–13 seems to identify Elijah (John the Baptist) with the Human One. Martyn thinks the Fourth Gospel's Jesus can be identified with the prophet *like* Moses because this affirms only "a typological relationship between two distinct figures" ("We Have Found Elijah," n. 88, p. 53).
242. Horsley, *Sociology and the Jesus Movement*, 143.

seen, gnostic/apocryphal materials identify her as the woman who understood everything, the net-caster, the loved one. This early scene of a call of Mary can be imagined to be related to the tradition of the resurrection appearance to her. A positive response to her report to the disciples is expected there, but missing: their recognition that "the spirit of Jesus rests on Mary." Perhaps it was articulated in some segment of the Johannine community, for some time.

All this is guesswork. Neither the literary evidence used for the study of Jewish Christianity by Daniélou, Schoeps, Klijn, nor the archaeological data collected by Bagatti and Testa have shown the identification of Jesus with Elijah was a Jewish Christian motif. But while this silence does not help a hypothesis like Martyn's, neither does it damage it "if one bears in mind that our attempts to reconstruct the history and thought of Jewish Christianity are being made, thus far, on the basis of data which put us in touch with a *very* small fraction of the original picture(s) — shall we say one-tenth or one-onehundredth?"[243] And even that small fraction, I would add, may yield surprises when viewed by different eyes, with different questions.

The Beloved Disciple

Schneiders has suggested that Mary Magdalene be identified with the Beloved Disciple, who is not the Evangelist of the Fourth Gospel. The crucifixion scene is most crucial for identification of the Beloved Disciple. As Schneiders reads it, there are three women witnesses, not three women and one man; a Beloved Disciple does not stand beside the women, but includes or represents two or one of them. This figure may be Mary of Clopas and Mary Magdalene as a community, or Mary Magdalene herself. The Beloved Disciple is both a literary device and "a pluralistic historical reality (a plurality of actual disciples presented as unique and diverse incarnations of this paradigm)." This figure guarantees the truth of this Gospel: "If there is an eyewitness source behind the Fourth Gospel, the most clearly designated embodiment of that role in the text itself is Mary Magdalene."[244]

The deliberate obscuring of Beloved Disciple's identity by the Evangelist and then by the ecclesiastical redactor can be explained in part by such an iden-

243. Martyn, "We Have Found Elijah," n. 76, p. 45.
244. Schneiders, *Written That You May Believe*, 221. She calls the Beloved Disciple "neither a pure literary symbol nor a single historical individual," but "a kind of textual paradigm who concretely embodies in the text the corporate authority of the Johannine school" (225). Mary Magdalene and other real disciples share this role of ideal disciple, and realize it in diverse ways. Grassi (*Secret Identity*, 85–90) calls Mary Magdalene a "counterpart" of the beloved disciple. Cf. my Appendix on the corporate understanding of the Human One. To Schneiders' view, contrast Reinhartz, *Befriending*, 23, 32. A. Culpepper (*John, the Son of Zebedee* [Columbia: University of South Carolina, 1994] 59) holds that the unnamed disciple of 1:40 cannot be John or the beloved disciple.

tification. Mary Magdalene is "the problematic woman protagonist in [gnostic] literature regarded as heretical at precisely the time that this Gospel was beginning to circulate at the beginning of the second century" when the "orthodox" were attempting to silence women. Schneiders finds it difficult not to recognize the features of the Johannine Beloved Disciple in the Mary of gnostic/apocryphal literature.[245] This recognition is made even easier when we see the scene at the cross as some sort of a succession scene before the death of Jesus,[246] and when we see the figure of Mary Magdalene downplayed and implicitly in conflict with Peter in this Gospel, as it contrasts with the hypothetical source I have posited.[247] Such a source may have been composed from early testimony to support the leadership of the Beloved Disciple, perhaps in memory of her, perhaps to justify and legitimate the leadership of later women. "Beloved" can indicate not only righteous and dear to God (*Ant.* 14.22–24 on Honi the Circle-Drawer) but also one who understands or acquires wisdom (Prov 4:3) and "comprehends the vision" (Dan 9:23; cf. 10:11–12, 19), a prophet especially chosen, treasured by God.[248]

There is, however, a major problem with understanding Mary Magdalene as an aspect of the Beloved Disciple: she would be split into two in the empty tomb scene, at least in 20:2b and 10 (the plural). Without elements of those two verses, the narrative can be read as Mary Magdalene (the Beloved Disciple) telling Peter about the tomb, beating him in a race, and believing first though not with full understanding.[249] (Cf. Luke 24:12, a "western non-interpolation," possibly dependent on a common source: in response to the report of the women, Peter alone[250] runs to check out the tomb and sees the cloths.) But if Mary Magdalene and the Beloved Disciples are two figures in the Gospel of John, the latter is preferred.[251] All this complicates an attempt to understand the motivation and intent of the Evangelist and redactor, but raises new questions.

---

245. Schneiders, *Written That You May Believe*, 223–24, 228. Contrast K. Quast, *Peter and the Beloved Disciple* (Sheffield: Sheffield Academic Press, 1989).

246. Quast, *Peter and the Beloved Disciple*, 95–97 on the theories of Titus, Dauer, Snyder, Goguel.

247. Contrast Schneiders, who sees in the Gospel as it stands the conflict between the Beloved Disciple and Peter but not between Mary Magdalene and Peter, and the obscuring of the Beloved Disciple but not of Mary Magdalene. See *Written That You May Believe*, n. 15, p. 99 on her brief response to the view of Fehribach, who finds the women in the Fourth Gospel presented in stereotypical feminine roles in relation to the bridegroom.

248. See Taylor, *The Immerser*, 269–72.

249. Schneiders sees the belief of the Beloved Disciple as belief in the glorification of Jesus (he has returned to the Father) but not in his resurrection (his return to his disciples). She sees the material about the empty tomb and the material about the appearances as intrinsically and necessarily interrelated ("The Resurrection of Jesus and Christian Spirituality," 94, 87), but does not explain how. Cf. my proposal, above pp. 294, 322.

250. But see the plural in Luke 24:24.

251. Van Tilborg, *Imaginative Love*, 207. "At decisive moments Jesus retreats from [his] relation with women: he finds refuge in his relation with the male disciples...retires into himself...goes back to his relation with the beloved disciple" (208).

Matthew's Use of the Tradition
of an Appearance to Women

Let us briefly ask what Matthew may have done with whatever aspects of the tradition he inherited. The appearance near the tomb to two women, Mary Magdalene and the other Mary, conforms to the pattern of Dodd's "concise narrative." The pericope is strangely anticlimactic, and lacks information about the mountain of meeting, information which is assumed in 28:16. If there was an appearance in a lost ending of Mark that had the essential function of overcoming the women's fear and silence (Mark 16:8), in Matthew the appearance has no such function, and in fact seems to have no function at all. The women run from the tomb "with fear and great joy," supposedly needing no reassurance. The appearance to them interrupts the movement to Galilee, and the words of Jesus almost exactly[252] repeat the angel's words. The women have been given a commission to tell the disciples they will see the risen Jesus in Galilee, and in Galilee "the eleven" (v. 16) are subsequently commissioned to "make disciples of all nations," baptizing and teaching them (v. 19). That commission to tell the disciples, which many hold was absent from a pre-Markan account of the empty tomb,[253] makes the women's role there as in Matthew and Luke preliminary, "secretarial," and of temporary importance. They are apostles (only) to the apostles, and fade out in contrast to the role of the empowered "eleven."

Some critics have seen a marked difference also between the approachable, recognized, risen Jesus whose feet the worshipping women seize, and the exalted Jesus, worshipped and doubted, who appears on the mountain and who is always with the eleven, never said to depart. That mountain — the seventh in this Gospel — may be a symbol for God's kingdom or God's throne, and may indicate knowledge and use of Enochic imagery and traditions (cf. 1 Enoch 18:6–8; 24:3; 25:3).[254] The risen Jesus in Matt 28:16–20 is apparently thought of as having been given "all power in heaven and on earth" at his ascent/assumption/resurrection from the grave. There is no evidence to support an argument that Matthew is reworking a tradition of the witnessing of Jesus' ascent and the empowering of the witness. Matthew perhaps did not know of or chose to ignore the ascent theme and the prominence of Mary Magdalene. But the possibility is tantalizing that further analysis might suggest a connection between the pre-Johannine Magdalene tradition and the Matthean or pre-Matthean mountain scene. And that this connection might illustrate an interpretation of Jesus' Elijah-like ascent,[255] not as his disappearance but as his permanent presence. Further, in spite of Matthew's emphasis on the authority of Peter (16:18–19) and the commission of the

---

252. The disciples are called Jesus' "brothers" by the risen Jesus but not by the angel.
253. E.g., Brown, *John*, 2.978.
254. See Schaberg, *The Father, the Son and the Holy Spirit*, 228–29, 237–38, 321–22.
255. Cf. Markan Appendix 16:9, 19b.

eleven (28:16–20), critics have noticed a certain non-hierarchical structure as characteristic of the Matthean community,[256] similar in some ways to that of the Johannine community.

It is interesting to speculate where a Galilean Magdalene tradition might have come from, and been cherished. As Lindars remarks, the beginnings of the church in Galilee were suppressed in Acts. Jerusalem became the headquarters of the church before Paul, with James in charge.[257] Nickelsburg has pointed out the long history of the area around Dan and Hermon as sacred territory associated with visionary activity ("it served as a locus that was catalytic of revelation"). The transfiguration narratives, the commission of Peter at Caesarea Phillipi, and the final appearance of the risen Jesus in Matthew indicate some early Christian fascination with this general area. But it is associated with male figures, especially Peter. Citing Marxsen, Fuller and Brown, Nickelsburg says "That Peter was a primary (or the first) witness to the resurrection of Jesus is widely conceded." A Galilean location of a christophany to him is suggested by several Christian Testament passages (especially Matt 28:16–20), and it might be placed in the environs of Mount Hermon. Nickelsburg further suggests "a historical connection between some members of the primitive Christian community and those apocalyptic Jewish circles in which the Enoch-Levi materials circulated . . . a continuing association between the Petrine and Enochic traditions."[258] Hopefully, future scholarship will tell us something about the early church in Galilee, and the leadership of Mary Magdalene and other women will be seen as part of it. Study of the ascent section of the Gospel of Mary may eventually be elucidating in this regard, challenging the primacy of Peter.

Magdalene Christianity

If we can brave our ways through the charge of "sheer fantasy!," and the anger of professors jabbing pens on paper,[259] we may come to know more about the role of women in apocalyptic and mystical groups. Even if we may not be able to

---

256. See B. T. Viviano, "Social World and Community Leadership: the Case of Matthew 23:1–12, 34," *JSNT* 39 (1990) 14–15; E. Schweizer, "Matthew's Church," *Interpretation of Matthew* (ed. G. Stanton; Philadelphia: Fortress, 1983) 140; E. Wainwright, *Towards a Feminist Critical Reading of the Gospel according to Matthew* (New York: Walter de Gruyter, 1991) 341–42; H. Hearon, "Eyewitness Communities: A Proposal Concerning Mary Magdalene and 1 Corinthians 15," Pacific Region SBL Presentation 1994, revised 1996; D. Duling ("Matthew and Marginality," *SBL Seminar Papers* [Atlanta: Scholars Press, 1993] 661) thinks Matthew's church is moving toward hierarchical structure.

257. B. Lindars, "Risen Jesus," 93.

258. G. W. E. Nickelsburg, "Enoch, Levi and Peter: Recipients of Revelation in Upper Galilee," *JBL* 100 (1981) 586, 599–600.

259. Woolf, *Room*, 31. See J. Marcus, "Art and Anger: Elizabeth Robins and Virginia Woolf," *Art & Anger* (Columbus: Ohio State University Press, 1988) 132–35 for an analysis of Professor von X's anger ("the attendant sprite of power") and of Woolf's own angry response and its deflection, demonstrating the scapegoating process.

locate its center(s), we will be able to imagine more clearly a Magdalene group or groups continuing to exist and create, on the basis of wo/men's insight, revelation, and leadership. Examination of the rivalry posed by Petrine (and perhaps James) traditions will give a fuller picture of the struggle of and for early Christian egalitarianism. This struggle must be situated in several contexts: (1) within individual ancient Christian communities, and in their different stages, (2) among them in their efforts to define orthodox and heretical, inside and outside, and (3) with outsiders like Celsus who ridiculed the resurrection faith as based on the witness of "a hysterical female, as you say, and perhaps some other one of those who were deluded by the same sorcery" (Origen, *Contra Celsum* 2.55). (4) The struggle is also situated within our own time, and has many dimensions. Maccini's comment (though he does not intend it this way) is about the success that was and is really a failure, in early Christianity and later: "In no case does John present a woman as a witness in a way that so tramples the religious, social and legal boundaries that readers would feel compelled to reject her. Quite the contrary, all the women witnesses, regardless of whether their testimonies are limited, corroborated or surpassed, are true and acceptable within the conventions of their culture."[260] In the case of Mary Magdalene, in order to accomplish this, John has had to trample her — her and her Judaism — within an illusion of Jewish boundaries and conventions. And in the tradition of Luke 8:3 and the Markan Appendix 16:9 she is acceptable as exorcised of the seven demons.

Whatever else Magdalene Christianity may have stood for, at the beginning and in subsequent centuries, it is possible that the struggle for egalitarianism was central. Community structures and tensions presupposed by the Gospels of Matthew and John and Mary bear witness to this. Its resurrection insight was not prompted by guilt or forgiveness, but by standing with the oppressed. Its focus was not on sacrifice or what Woolf called "the emotional excitement of death, glory, etc."[261] A vision of the Human One was central, and imaginations wide and generous and healthy enough to view this figure as inclusive. Gal 3:26–28, commonly regarded as an early baptismal formula, may have been in use. As a rhetorical strategy, the claim to prophetic succession would have functioned

---

260. Maccini, *Her Testimony*, 249. Reinhartz notes that women characters in this Gospel are "disciples" in the general sense of this term, followers of Jesus; but they are never called disciples, and hence may not have been leaders in the Johannine community historically. She sees Mary Magdalene excluded from the group of disciples, and senses "considerable tension between her and that group," as well as great ambiguity in the Gospel's portrayal of women (*Befriending*, 120–24; cf. the view of Meier, above, p. 261, n. 35, p. 266, n. 66). My own view is that reconstruction of sources is important because it indicates there were different stages of increasing tension and struggle.

261. V. Woolf, "Reminiscences of Julian," Monk's House Papers A 8:9, University of Sussex Library, quoted by Zwerdling, *Virginia Woolf and the Real World*, 273. See N. Jay, "Sacrifice as Remedy for Having Been Born of Woman," *Immaculate and Powerful: The Female in Sacred Image and Social Reality* (ed. C. W. Atkinson, C. H. Buchanan, M. R. Miles; Boston: Beacon, 1985) 283–309, on the links between priesthood, blood sacrifice, and apostolic succession.

quite differently than the claim to apostolic succession,[262] in that it would have privileged surprise over order. I see Magdalene Christianity as disconcerting, demanding, and horribly vulnerable. It attempted the impossible. It represented wo/men's empowering speech, and sanity.[263]

Summary

To summarize, as I read the narratives of the empty tomb and the appearance to the women, then, Daniel 7, 12 and 2 Kings 2 are the primary texts that inform the "exegetical imagination" that produced the Easter faith and eventually produced Christian texts that flow from and channel in new ways the streams of mystical tradition. In this reconstruction, resurrection and translation, side by side or overlapping, are expression of belief in the vindication of Jesus and of all those incorporated into the Human One. That the insight or revelation about the resurrection of Jesus is exegetical is recognized in John 20:9 ("for they as yet did not know the scripture that he must rise from the dead") as well as in 1 Cor 15:3–4 ("according to the scriptures"). This intellectual and spiritual component is every bit as important as the psychological and sociological aspects of the beginnings of the Easter faith. In the case of the empty tomb and the appearance to Mary Magdalene, we do not have "a rational explication" of the scripture, of course, but an innovation decided by "a specific revelation"; the texts, contemplated beforehand, were "re-experienced" in waking visions, possibly preceded by a "night vision of lamentation," to use Segal's expressions.[264] This I think, not a gradual, rational realization, produced the "jolt" of Easter. The textual presentations are multilayered, but at bottom there is "no reason to believe that people did not have these experiences" — mystical experiences which "made the transformation of thought and consciousness possible," to quote Segal again.[265]

Further, in John 20 fragments of the claim that Mary Magdalene was successor of Jesus is a burst of energy that occasioned other bursts. An assumption articulated by Boyarin is relevant here: the amount of energy which a culture expends in order to suppress or marginalize a voice "forms a reliable index to the effectiveness of that voice as posing a threat to the hegemonic practices of that culture."[266] Previous chapters have shown the tremendous amount of energy ex-

---

262. On genealogical reasoning, see Buell, above, pp. 35–36.

263. See M. Caminero-Santangelo, *The Madwoman Can't Speak: Or Why Insanity Is Not Subversive* (Ithaca: Cornell University Press, 1998).

264. Segal, "Some Observations about Mysticism," 389. He sees the enormous changes in interpretation between Ezekiel 37 and Isaiah 24–27 as needing "to be justified not merely by exegesis but by *revelation*" (390).

265. Segal, "Some Observations about Mysticism," 390, 399. See J. J. Collins and M. Fishbane, "Introduction," *Death, Ecstasy and Other Worldly Journeys*, xii: "Visionaries see what is believed in their culture to be possible."

266. D. Boyarin, "Reading Androcentrism against the Grain: Women, Sex and Torah-Study," *Poetics Today* 12 (1991) 31. He calls it "an ideological voice."

pended through a succession of cultures and a variety of art forms and scholarship with regard to the "voice" of Mary Magdalene. The memory of claims made for and perhaps by her was not only downplayed; it was murdered. The number of critical articles and books on Mary Magdalene has rapidly increased in the past fifteen years, dealing with her legends, her images in art history and film, her appearances in gnostic/apocryphal materials, and the Christian Testament texts. Her representation or icon, like that of Virginia Woolf, continues to change as it meets different needs, comes under different control, is enacted and marketed and appropriated in different ways. Many recent works make a positive contribution to the resurrection of the dangerous memory explored here. To let the Magdalene of history live again, however, they often slay the Whore in the House and Street, the Whore in the church, who "died hard.... She was always creeping back when I thought I had dispatched her."[267] Though she is a killer herself, she is ourselves,[268] this Outsider. I have argued that her creeping back has something to say. Let her, let us, stay.[269]

My reconstruction privileges the tradition of the women at the tomb and of the appearance to Mary Magdalene. It warns our imagination not to confine Mary Magdalene to a romantic relation to Jesus, to a personal, private, emotional relationship, whether sexual or spiritual or both; not in fact to confine her to *any* type of relationship with Jesus but to try to see her in her own right. She is not to be restricted to the stereotypical feminine tasks of domestic service, mourning, caring for the dead, or playing a subordinate, "non-official" role to the male apostles who alone have a world-changing mission. Her apocalypse or revelation of the resurrection and vindication of Jesus is embedded in the reality of struggles against domination. Without the struggle, no meaningful belief in resurrection.

I have tried to mount convincing, coherent arguments that this is possibly bedrock tradition: that women were at the crucifixion, burial and tomb. That they found it empty, and that they — or Mary Magdalene alone — claimed to receive a revelation interpreting that emptiness as resurrection. That Mary Magdalene claimed — or it was claimed by others — that she had a visionary experience of Jesus which empowered her with God's spirit. In some ways it does not matter if this tradition is historical or not, or if it can be persuasively shown to be historical or not. If Mary Magdalene was a fictional, literary character, and these claims for her legendary, she could still empower and be a resource for contemporary wo/men. We can read the Gospels any way we want and need to, as every previous generation has done; we can seek to grasp what the texts once meant and mean, and to participate in their seemingly inexhaustible capacity to bear many

---

267. Woolf, "Professions for Women," 238, on the Angel in the house.
268. See Modleski, *Feminism Without Women*, 16, in conversation with D. Riley ("Am I That Name?" — woman, or [as in *Othello*] whore).
269. Above, pp. 103–7.

meanings. Our history is not determined by powerful precedents nor by bleakness. Both history and literature can inspire work for social transformation.

But I am not willing to stop trying to do history, to let go of possible evidence of both historical power and the lack or weakening of power. In my judgment, historians have not made a reasonable case for the absence of the women at the cross and burial and tomb, or for the lateness of the claim that Mary Magdalene received a resurrection appearance. So I have taken my turn with the texts, situating my imaginative, historical reconstruction in the context of early Jewish mysticism and social/political struggle, following the insight of Gruenwald that "Not all mysticism comes from 'a failure of nerve.' In Fact [sic], the early manifestations of mysticism in Jewish Apocalypticism can be shown to come from a struggling, not a resigning, spirit."[270] That struggle at the origins of Christianity is part of its debt to Judaism, and evidence — not that we need more — that the hierarchical structures of the church distort its origins[271] and its promise.

Continuity with the prophetic and mystical tradition of Israel is claimed by my analysis here. 2 Kings 2 reused as I have suggested gives that text a powerful and unsuspected dimension, but such reuse does not supersede or displace or replace or undo or overcome this text, though it may aim to alter an exclusivist interpretation.[272] The reuse signals conflict, but among Johannine contemporaries, not with the precursor. This is the world of "texts claiming authority, granting authority, supporting authority, and wrenching authority away. Texts form the backbone of the status quo . . . ; texts are also the weapon of those . . . who seek change."[273] The reuse of 2 Kings 2 signals to me the existence and efforts of those seeking or continuing change, claiming the prophetic tradition for wo/men. I understand this claim as a characteristic of the *basileia* movement of Jesus and his companions

The role of the reader is of central importance, since the presence of 2 Kings 2 in John 20 is meaningless unless recognized. Identification of biblical elements in later compositions "depends on the ability of the reader to recognize the scriptural elements and to see their meaning in the new context."[274] As a rhetorical device, implicit quotations or allusions "are intended to create complicity between the author and the reader"; an "open space for the sagacity of the reader. . . . The more concealed an allusion is, the closer this complicity between the author (or the text) and the intended reader will be."[275] Those who catch the allusion and agree with its implications, are complicit down through the centuries. The implied reader who catches the allusion in the twenty-first century is complicit with the implied

270. Gruenwald, *From Apocalypticism to Gnosticism*, 1.
271. See Ruotolo, *The Interrupted Moment*, 211.
272. Cf. P. D. Miscall, "Isaiah: New Heavens, New Earth, New Book," *Reading Between Texts*, 44–45.
273. Fewell, "Introduction," *Reading Between Texts*, 12.
274. Dimant, "Mikra," 400.
275. Painchaud, "Use of Scripture," 135.

readers of the source I have posited, and of the Gospel of John who recognize its incorporation. They share a certain sense of human possibilities and tasks, and an alienation from "non-knowing readers"[276] with whom a struggle is enjoined.

I am well aware my treatment will not be convincing to everyone. A scholar I respect thanked me for sending him part of this work in progress, and commented only: "It puzzles me, but you know of my abiding respect for you personally. With cordial greetings. . . ." After I read this, I went into the kitchen and gashed my leg open by tripping on a kitty litter pail; then I reflected. Puzzlement can be good; perhaps I should have used this note as a blurb on the jacket. When I delivered an earlier draft of these arguments at the Society of Biblical Literature meeting in 2000, one of the respondents helpfully said he was *able* to imagine such a reading of John 20 with 2 Kings 2, but found no reason why he *should*.[277] Perhaps that is enough, since I do not aim to push my reading as the only possible one, nor can I restrict the reader's freedom. Sometimes it is possible to think of something, "though without the encouragement of contemporary experience no one would have been likely to do so."[278] The contemporary experience that encouraged this work is the women's movement and feminist scholarship. If I have failed to present a convincing, comprehensive reconstruction or reading, I hope I have failed well enough to destabilize existing "authoritative" readings and the oppressiveness of the whole Magdalene tradition, to suggest at least to some readers new lines of research, and encourage the desire to continue undermining and trespassing. The deepest knowledge results from dialogue that involves the largest number of differing vantage points, all partial, rather than from a singular perception regarded or regarding itself as authoritative.[279] That dialogue has only begun in religious studies, and in the life of religious communities, which impact all of us.

Mary Magdalene traditions focus the issue of changing attitudes toward the vulnerable, ambiguous human body: how these influence women's opportunities for public leadership; how they influence systems of transcendence and social arrangements; how they influence us to live in the face of death; how they influence understandings and expressions of sexuality. Obsession with Mary Magdalene's sexuality had and has many functions: it turns Jesus into a real guy, it signals her illicit knowledge, allows a certain kind of female sexuality expression in the realm of the "sacred." In this book, I let lie the issue of the sexuality of Mary Magdalene, in that I let it remain ambiguous whether or not she and Jesus were lovers. But does tolerating ambiguity erase this figure's sexuality? That is not my intent. And it is not what I want John 20 to mean.[280] To resist the reduction and

---

276. Painchaud, "Use of Scripture," 146.

277. The feminist methodology of reading of gaps seemed to him strange, bifocal.

278. J. Barton, *Oracles of God* (New York: Oxford University Press, 1986) 262.

279. Floyd, *The Power of Black Music*, 176, 277. The destabilized "authoritative" voice is part of the dialogue.

280. See Winsor, *A King Is Bound*, n. 6, p. 29.

fragmentation of Mary Magdalene is to resist seeing her only as protagonist in a love or porno story, as madwoman, or victim, or lone hero, and also only as religious intellectual and leader. Attempting such resistance is resisting our own fragmentation. Powerful forces of fragmentation within and outside us aim to destroy "that curious sexual quality which comes only when sex is unconscious of itself."[281] This phrase of Woolf's may be, I think, about sexuality that has eluded and forgotten gender constraints: unhindered sexuality, creative wholeness. Let us insist on this, for Mary Magdalene as for ourselves. "[W]e long sometimes to escape from the incessant, the remorseless analysis of falling into love and falling out of love.... We long for some more impersonal relationship. We long for ideas, for dreams, for imaginations, for poetry."[282]

Some may find the historical Mary Magdalene or the Mary Magdalene of biblical criticism boring, compared to the flamboyant character of legends and art. That assessment differs from my own. I would like to have "found" a Mary Magdalene as bold and courageous as Woolf, or as Woolf's Ethel Smyth: "She is of the race of pioneers, of pathmakers. She has gone before and felled trees and blasted rocks and built bridges and thus made a way for those who come after her."[283] But history can most often merely tantalize with such possibilities. I am drawn to what it does provide: only shadows and traces, and the impossibility of knowing with certainty.[284] The Christian Testament's narratives of the empty tomb and of an appearance to Mary Magdalene are in many ways like the site at Migdal. They too are our necessary ruin, one of many. They have been looted, dug at, abandoned, endangered. Many luxury hotels have been built on them. They are a site from which many have been excluded. But we can climb the fences, walk on it, dig and sift and treat it with respect, even foolishly imagine buying it and owning it. Underneath it lies part of our history. In boxes too: Stanislao Loffreda has finally answered me via email that yes, there are more artifacts and notes from the digs he did there with Corbo. It is stored in boxes in his office in Jerusalem. The material "has been packed and nobody knows when I will be able to publish it." No excavations at Migdal are foreseen.[285] No response to my request to know more.

---

281. Woolf, *Room*, 93. She is discussing the author she invented, Mary Carmichael, "writing as a woman," with "a sensibility that was very wide, eager and free."
282. V. Woolf, "The Narrow Bridge of Art," 55.
283. V. Woolf, 1931 speech reprinted in *The Pargiters: The Novel-Essay Portion of The Years* (ed. M. Leaska; London: Hogarth, 1977) xxvii.
284. D'Angelo "Reconstructing 'Real' Women," 125: there are only snippets of memories and expectations "embedded in the distant conversations of long-dead authors with long-dispersed communities...."
285. Now see H. Shanks, "Is It or Isn't It — A Synagogue? Archaeologists Disagree Over Buildings at Jericho and Migdal," *BAR* 27 (2001) 51–57; summarizing the article by E. Netzer, "Did the Water Installation in Magdala Serve as Synagogue?" *Synagogues in Antiquity* (ed. A. Kasher et al.; Jerusalem: Yad Izhak Ben Zvi, 1987) in Hebrew, with undated photos.

Like Judith Shakespeare, Mary Magdalene who died for the sins of patriarchy is buried at a crossroads: "Behind us lies the patriarchal system; the private house, with its nullity, its immorality, its hypocrisy, its servility. Before us lies the public world, the professional system, with its possessiveness, its jealousy, its pugnacity, its greed."[286] Retreat is possible, or going forward, or going forward on a road that transforms these alternatives,[287] or standing still. Actually, in the area near the South London crossroads Woolf had in mind, women who worked in the "stewhouses" or brothels — Magdalenes — were buried in the fifteenth century and earlier. The memory of nineteenth-century prophet Joanna Southcott also haunts the area.[288] "Now my belief is that this poet who never wrote a word and was buried at the crossroads still lives. She lives in you and in me, and in many other women who are not here tonight, for they are washing up the dishes and putting the children to bed. But she lives; for great poets do not die; they are continuing presences; they need only the opportunity to walk among us in the flesh. This opportunity, as I think, it is now coming within your power to give her." With economic security, solitude, "the habit of freedom and the courage to write exactly what we think," with seeing in relation to reality, looking past Milton's bogey ("for no human being should shut out the view") "the opportunity will come and the dead poet who was Shakespeare's sister will put on the body which she has so often laid down. As for her coming without that preparation, without that effort on our part, without that determination that when she is born again she shall find it possible to live and write her poetry, that we cannot expect, for that would be impossible. But I maintain that she would come if we worked for her, and that so to work, even in poverty and obscurity, is worthwhile."[289]

As she imagined the future, Virginia Woolf described the work of Outsiders as that of critics and artists, making their own contributions, preserving and creating. One thing they are preserving and creating is an "emergent religion."[290] They make marginal notes and insertions into her description: "The novel [religion] of a classless and towerless world should be a better novel [religion] than the old novel [religion]. The novelist [theologian] will have more interesting people to describe — people who have had a chance to develop their humor, their gifts, their tastes; real people, not people cramped and squashed into featureless masses by hedges."[291] And a more interesting God. In that democratic space, the democratic voice of Anon reborn can be heard in 2001 as in 1941, the creator who speaks for

---

286. Woolf, *Three Guineas*, 86.
287. See A. Snaith, *Virginia Woolf: Public and Private Negotiations* (New York: St. Martin's, 2000) 12–13, 161–63.
288. K. Koenigsgberger, "Excavating the Elephant and Castle," *Virginia Woolf and Her Influences, Selected Papers from the Seventh Annual Conference on Virginia Woolf, 1997* (ed. L. David and J. McVicker; New York: Pace University Press, 1998) 98–103.
289. Woolf, *Room*, 113–14.
290. Hussey, *The Singing of the Real World*, xx.
291. Woolf, "The Leaning Tower," 2.179, 181.

and is part of the community.[292] "Anon is sometimes man; sometimes woman. He is the common voice singing out of doors, He has no house."[293] In this space, even the space of the empty tomb, the nameless spirit, "haunter and joiner," creator of "what is not mind or body, nor surface or depths, but a common element in which the perishable is preserved, and the separate become one," is absent presence.[294]

As a student of Woolf, I can — and must — comfortably resist the desire to clarify, unify, and end with "one profound, all-encompassing statement." The unintentionally final words of her last, unfinished essay, "The Reader," are, fortunately: "We are in a world where nothing is concluded."[295]

•

I meet Harvey Klein, to end this book as it began. The restaurant on the upper west side is long gone, so we have drinks in TriBeCa. The air still stinks of dust and rot, and the work of recovering the bodies goes on. He has read the whole manuscript, and is mellow.

"A nice piece of work; makes me wish I were back in biblical studies — the feminist kind. Almost wish. I made a killing, you know, in auto parts."

"Get off the auto parts. What else?"

"The part about falling over the kitty litter pail. I thought you were finished punishing yourself like that."

"I thought so too. What else?"

"No, really now. The voice doesn't quite work, the voices. I see what you're trying to do, with the creative and the analytic. But it's ok that it doesn't quite work — maybe it can't right now. You're right Woolf would get a hoot out of this; that's the way to go, voices from outside so-called "re-li-gi-on." But what? you think the people in the leaning tower will start for the stairwells? (He glances downtown.) This Hannah Cullwick Magdalene, she sticks in my mind. The hypothetical, maybe, possible, reconstructed stuff — wish you could get it as strong as her. Wish she'd get off her knees; and get that dogchain off her neck. And Migdal, do you realize how much it's like the abandoned Detroit you showed me? Hey, let's go to Jerusalem, knock on Loffred's door, grab the boxes."

---

292. Moore, *The Short Season*, 32.

293. V. Woolf, Anon. Typescript fragment, with the author's ms. corrections, unsigned and undated, pp. 1–2, Berg Collection, New York Public Library. B. A. Silver, " 'Anon' and 'The Reader': Virginia Woolf's Last Essays," *Twentieth Century Literature* (Fall/Winter 1979).

294. "[T]his spirit, this haunter and joiner, who makes one where there are two, three, six or seven, and preserves what without it would perish, is nameless. Nameless it is yet partakes of all things named; it is rhyme and rhythm; is dressing and eating and drinking; is procreation and sensation; is love and hate and passion and adventure; partakes of the dog and the cat; of the bee and the flower and of bodies in coats and skirts." *Between the Acts* typescript with author's corrections, unsigned, 2 April '38–July 30 '39 (earliest dated draft) Berg Collection, in M. A. Leaska, *Pointz Hall* (New York: University Publications, 1983) 61–62. See Hussey, *Singing of the Real World*, 153.

295. Snaith (*Public and Private Negotiations*, 156) gives this reference as A, 429.

"Loffreda. Harvey, more on my hypothetical, maybe, possible, reconstructed stuff."

"I can see that I *could* read John 20 like that, but I just don't see that I *should*. Great line, it really happened?

"Yeah."

"Actually, I do think I *should*. All this — all this — war — this waste — this.... Well, Magdalene Christianity: we — you — have to invent it. Maybe it wouldn't have to be called Christianity; something new, outside. I might even...."

"Yeah, I might even too."

Works That Mention Mary Magdalene, Not Found at Nag Hammadi

- The Pistis Sophia[1] (Faith Wisdom, standing for the Redeemed Redeemer[2]), a third-century or earlier Egyptian text in Coptic, was contained in a parchment manuscript, the Codex Askewianus, bought by a Dr. Askew in a London book shop in 1773 and passed on to the British Museum. It was published around eighty years later.

- A small parchment codex containing part of the Gospel of Peter in Greek was found in 1886 by a French archaeological team in a Christian monk's grave at Akhmim in Upper Egypt, about 60 miles north of Nag Hammadi. Two small papyrus fragments (P Ox 2949) published in 1972 were identified in 1981 as fragments of this gospel. Whether the work is gnostic at all is debated, as is its date and relationship to the canonical gospels.[3]

- The Gospel of Mary was (with the Sophia of Jesus Christ[4]) part of the 1896 find, Papyrus Berolinensis 8502, not published until 1955.[5] This gospel is often considered with the Nag Hammadi texts because the Apocryphon of John and the Sophia of Jesus Christ, found there were also included in the Berlin codex.

- In 1930 the Psalms of Heracleides were discovered in Egypt in the Manichaean Psalm Book II; Manichaeans are usually considered gnostic or a gnostic offspring.

---

1. Pistis Sophia I–III and Pistis Sophia IV are two independent works. See Puech, NTA 1.362, revised by Blatz; Marjanen, *The Woman*, 148.
2. D. Good, "Pistis Sophia," *Searching the Scriptures*, 2. n. 2, p. 704. Good does not treat I–III and IV as separate works.
3. On whether and to what extent it is gnostic, compare Mauer in NTA 1. 180–83 (1963 edition) with W. Schneemelcher in NTA 1.220 (revised edition 1991). The latter is more cautious, arguing that this is not a gnostic or even a docetic work if one uses a very exact definition of docetism based on its original usage, according to which the historical and bodily and human form of Jesus was pure semblance without any reality. Because they do not seem to be gnostic or related to gnostic sources (building on them or reacting against them), Marjanen does not treat the Gospel of Peter, the Secret Gospel of Mark, and the Epistula Apostolorum (*The Woman*, 20–24). Bovon treats all three.
4. The codex contained also the Apocryphon of John, the Sophia of Jesus Christ, and the Acts of Peter.
5. As well as the Coptic version, two Greek fragments survive of this work (P. Ryl. 463 and P. Oxy. 3525), which show that there were at least two different Greek versions in circulation.

Three of these Coptic psalms, from the second half of the fourth century refer to Mary Magdalene.[6]

• Coptic fragments of the Epistula Apostolorum were found in 1895, and later the entire Ethiopic translation of the lost Greek original. Dated to the mid-second century, it opposes some gnostic ideas and the leaders Simon and Cerinthus,[7] but at the same time adapts some of their thought forms and motifs.[8]

• The fourth-century Apostolic Church Order 1.26, 1–2 mentions a laughing Mary. This work — or fragments of it — appear in Greek, Ethiopic, Arabic, Bohairic, Sahidic, Syriac and Latin, in libraries all around the world.[9]

• The Acts of Philip is a fourth-century Greek work in two parts which are probably independent (I–VII a collection of legends concerning Philip the evangelist, and VIII dealing with Philip the apostle[10]). There is a critical edition dating from 1903, but manuscripts in Athens and Athos, recently edited by Bovon, Bouvier and Amsler, are crucial to understanding it.[11] This work shows the survival, re-use and reinterpretation of gnostic motifs associated with Mary Magdalene,[12] who appears in the second part as the sister of Philip.

• At the other end of the time spectrum, in 1958 Morton Smith found in the Greek Orthodox monastery of Mar Saba, south-east of Jerusalem, a handwritten text at the back of a 1646 edition of the works of Ignatius of Antioch. The text contains an extract of a letter said to be from Clement of Alexandria, warning against a "more spiritual" gospel of Mark produced by the gnostic Carpocratians, and quoting from it twice.[13] Some have considered an unnamed woman who appears in the quotations to be Mary Magdalene. Scholars are divided about the authenticity of the letter, and almost universally have rejected Smith's contention that the quotes go back to the Aramaic original version of Mark, a source used by the authors of canonical Mark and canonical John.[14] This Secret Gospel of Mark, as Smith called it, may be evidence only of the existence of an expanded version of canonical Mark in Alexandria around 170 C.E.; but in that it is important for our study of the conflation of the Magdalene figure in the late second century.

---

6. The Coptic translates a work in Syriac or Greek from the end of the third or middle of the fourth century.

7. See *The Earliest Christian Heretics* (ed. A. J. Hultgren and S. A. Haggmark; Minneapolis: Fortress, 1996) 15, 34.

8. C. Detlef G. Mueller NTA 1.251: it is not free of gnostic motifs, but has a bluntly anti-docetic tendency.

9. See T. Schermann, *Die allegemeine Kirchenordnung, fruhchristliche Liturgien und kirchliche Überlieferung. Erster Teil: Die allegemeine Kirchenordnung des zweiten Jahrhunderts* (Paderborn: Druck und Verlag von F. Schoningh, 1914); A. J. Maclean, *Ancient Church Orders* (Cambridge: Cambridge University Press, 1910) 26–29; G. Horner, *The Statutes of the Apostles or Canones Ecclesiastici* (London: Oxford University Press, 1915); J. P. Arendzen, "An Entire Syriac Text," *JTS* 3 (1902) 59–80; W. H. Frere, "Early Ordination Services," *JTS* 16 (1915) 323–71.

10. VIII is called Acts of Philip the Martyr.

11. *Acta Philippi* (ed. F. Bovon, B. Bouvier, F. Amsler; Turnhout: Brepols, 1999); see Bovon, "Paschal Privilege," 156; Marjanen, *The Woman*, 41.

12. See Aurilio de Santos Otero, "Later Acts of Apostles," NTA 2.468–73.

13. M. Smith, *Clement of Alexandria and a Secret Gospel of Mark* (Cambridge: Harvard University Press, 1973); *The Secret Gospel* (New York: Harper & Row, 1973).

14. See H. Merkel, NTA1.106–9.

- In addition, one fourth-century patristic testimony gives us access to another Magdalene tradition, from the second or third century. Epiphanius refers to her in connection with an "abominable" gnostic work known to him, the Great Questions of Mary (*Pan.* 26. 8, 1–3).[15] Here she is the recipient of a vision of Jesus as Adam, who produces Eve and then has sex with her. (As we have seen, Origen's Celsus mentioned groups that regarded themselves as disciples of Mary Magdalene or Salome or Martha [*C. Celsum* 5.62], and Hippolytus said the Naassenes traced their secret traditions through her to James [*Ref.* 5.7.1; 10.7,9].)[16]

---

15. The Great Questions are to be distinguished from the lesser questions which some have identified with the Pistis Sophia; so Bovon, "Paschal Privilege," 154.

16. Jansen ("Maria," n. 111, p. 95) argues against E. Moltmann-Wendel (*The Women Around Jesus* [New York: Crossroad, 1986] 80–81) that there is no evidence to support the theory that the Cathar women were proponents of the cult of the Magdalene, particularly the apostolic Magdalene. Indeed, one of their alleged blasphemous beliefs was that she was Christ's concubine." But "concubine" may be an interpretation of "companion" (on which, see above, pp. 152–53).

1 Enoch 70–71

1 Enoch 70–71 narrates what is probably the final translation of Enoch's spirit (his "name" 70:1) and his exaltation. The narration careens dizzily between third person and first person. In the passage 71:14–17 "which has caused untold anguish to the commentators,"[1] Enoch is told by an angel, " 'You are the Son of Man who was born to righteousness, and righteousness remains over you, and the righteousness of the Head of Days will not leave you' ... 'And all ... will walk according to your way, inasmuch as righteousness will never leave you; with you will be their dwelling, and with you their lot, and they will not be separated from you, for ever and for ever and ever. And so there will be length of days with that Son of Man, and the righteous will have peace, and the righteous will have an upright way in the name of the Lord of Spirits for ever and ever.' "[2] Some of the unsuccessful attempts to emend and rearrange this passage arise from judgments such as that of R. H. Charles, that it is incomprehensible that the translated Enoch should be identified with the preexistent Son of Man of the Similitudes.[3] I

1. F. Borsch, *The Son of Man in Myth and History* (Philadelphia: Westminster, 1967) 151.
2. Translation by M. A. Knibb in consultation with E. Ullendorf, *The Ethiopic Book of Enoch* (Oxford: Clarendon, 1978) 2.166–67. Contrast E. Isaac, "1 (Ethiopic Apocalypse of) Enoch," *OTP* 1.50. He translates the first line this way: "You, son of man, who are born in righteousness ..." in order to distinguish "son of man" from the "Son of Man," because the Ethiopic distinguishes by using different terms for "man" (*be'esi,* "a masculine person") and Man (*sab'e,* "people," or *'eg^uula-'emma heyyāw,* "son of the mother of the living," i.e., "human being" [n. s, p. 50]). Isaac does not comment on the connection between the two. He thinks that 1 Enoch already contained the Similitudes (37–71) by the end of the first century C.E. (p. 7).
3. R. H. Charles, "Book of Enoch," *APOT* 2.237. J. J. Collins ("the Son of Man in First Century Judaism," *NTS* 38 [1992] 448–66, 451–59) argues that in 1 Enoch 71:14 Enoch is not at all identified with the Son of Man, who is a preexistent, individual messiah not a collective symbol in this vision. Contrast my treatment in *The Father, the Son and the Holy Spirit,* 224–28; C. Rowland, *The Open Heaven* (London: SPCK, 1982) 106–7; and see A. Y. Collins, "Origin of the Designation," 155–56: The patterns behind the identification of Enoch and the Son of Man could be as follows: "There was a preexistent. heavenly being, known from Daniel 7, who was to have an eschatological role. Enoch began as an ordinary human being. Instead of dying like other humans, he was exalted to heaven and identified with (merged with or replaced) that heavenly being. Enoch then would exercise the predetermined eschatological role. Alternatively, the logic may be that Enoch himself was the

do not find it incomprehensible, but rather part of a development of a corporate understanding of the heavenly figure, Daniel 7's "one like a son of man" (or, as DiLella translates, "one in human likeness").[4] The dead, transformed righteous (Dan 12:1–3) are, in some sense, the heavenly figure of Dan 7:14.[5] The identification of Enoch with the enthroned Son of Man in 1 Enoch 70–71 may be a version of the transfiguration of the visionary, and an influence on Paul's understanding of his mystical experience.[6] Traces of this corporate tradition can be seen also in Christian Testament interpretations of the Human One[7] (or Son of Man), which are central to the resurrection faith.

Inclusive translation may be appropriate in 1 Enoch 71, as in Daniel 7, but it is not demanded by the explicit content of either of these works. The Gospel of Philip 57–58 employs androcentric language in a similar, related vein: "Jesus took them all by stealth, for he did not appear as he was, but in the manner in which [they would] be able to see him... some indeed saw him, thinking that they were seeing themselves.... The heavenly man has many more sons than the earthly man. If the sons of Adam are many, although they die, how much more the sons of he perfect man, they who do not die but are always begotten." In contrast, the greater centrality and importance of Mary in the Gospel of Mary and the gender dynamics of the story means that inclusive translation is necessary there. "The heavenly human being... the perfect human being" I see as a development of the corporate Danielic figure. This is one of the great metaphors with the potential to shape the understanding of what humanity is, to widen the boundaries of who counts as humanity.[8] Within the context of resurrection faith, from Daniel onward, the figure is in some sense(s) corporeal, however that is understood.

The "identification mysticism" of the Gospel of Philip centers on the identification between the initiate and Christ. Pagels notes that this is "evinced in Philip's characterization of Christ as *ptelios ᵉrrome* (55.14), and of the initiate, conversely, as having the potential to become, through sacramental transformation, a Christ

---

heavenly, preexistent being, who became human, or took human form for a time, and then returned to heaven. The identity of the heavenly Son of Man as Enoch has been revealed only to the elect." She does not explore the corporate dimensions of the Son of Man of the Similitudes.

4. See A. DiLella, "The One in Human Likeness and the Holy Ones of the Most High in Daniel 7," *CBQ* 39 (1977) 1–19.

5. Cf. 2 Enoch 22:9–10: In the seventh heaven, Enoch is transformed: "And I gazed at all of myself [how? as in a mirror?] and I had become like one of the glorious ones, and there was no observable difference."

6. A. Segal, "Angelic Mediator Figures," 304–8. See also Segal, *Paul the Convert* (New Haven: Yale University Press, 1990) 45–46: "Exemplary men [sic] can... ascend to divinity by identification with or transformation into the enthroned figure." Cf. 11 Q Melchizedek, where Melchizedek is the counterpart of a heavenly being, spirit or angel called Belial.

7. My preferred translation of *ho huios tou anthropou*. See below Appendix C.

8. See G. M. Jantzen, *Power, Gender and Christian Mysticism* (Cambridge: Cambridge University Press, 1995) 349–50. She stresses that the metaphors and the ideas and practices that literalize them must be always deconstructed to expose their power to oppress.

(*ou* ᵉ*khrs*, 67.27)."[9] The ancient tradition of transformation of the righteous by vision, and/or by ascent in life or in death underlies the sacramental element, and breaks gender boundaries.[10] This tradition, in my opinion, undercuts our notions of individuality, self, soul, and identity, and blurs the "orthodox" line between the human and divine, the self and the Christ.[11]

"'I' rejected; 'We' substituted: to whom at the end there shall be an invocation?"[12]

---

9. Pagels, "Ritual in the *Gospel of Philip*," 287. She distinguishes between an identification between the initiate and Christ, and an identification between the soul and "some sort of 'given' essentially divine self."

10. See McGuire, "Women, Gender and Gnosis," 281, on the Gospel of Thomas reflecting the notion of ritual initiation or visionary ascent effecting a restoration of the primordial, pre-mortal Adam (understood in two different ways in logia 22 and 114).

11. See Williams, *Rethinking*, 271, on "the idea of the divine consubstantiality of the spark [in human beings, "the divine counterpart of the self"] that is in need of being awakened and reintegrated." To my mind, neither the self nor the Christ are a "given." Merkur quotes Buber's reflection on the experience of a state in which the bonds of the personal nature of life seem to have fallen away, and one experiences an undivided unity. For Buber and for Merkur, to imagine this is union with the primal being or godhead is "an exaggeration no longer permitted to the responsible understanding." It can be called the attainment of "an original prebiographical unity" of a creature, not of the soul of the All (Merkur, *Gnosis*, 20, citing M. Buber, *Between Man and Man* [New York: Macmillan, 1965] 24). Woolf goes further, exploring the sense of "souls" joined.

12. Woolf, *Diary*, 5.135.

The Human One

"[A]nother picture has imposed itself upon the foreground. It is the figure of a man; some say, others deny, that he is Man himself, the quintessence of virility, the perfect type of which all the others are imperfect adumbrations. He is a man certainly. His eyes are glazed; his eyes glare. His body, which is braced in an unnatural position, is tightly cased in a uniform. Upon the breast of that uniform are sewn several medals and other mystic symbols. His hand is upon a sword. He is called in German and Italian Fuhrer or Duce; in our own language Tyrant or Dictator. And behind him lie ruined houses and dead bodies — men, women and children. . . . [T]he human figure . . . suggests that we cannot dissociate ourselves from that figure but are our-selves that figure. It suggests that we are not passive spectators doomed to unresisting obedience but by our thoughts and actions can ourselves change that figure. A com-mon interest unites us; it is one world, one life. How essential it is that we should realize that unity the dead bodies, the ruined houses prove."

Woolf, Three Guineas[1]

"Let us try to drag up into consciousness the subconscious Hitlerism that holds us down. It is the desire for aggression; the desire to dominate and enslave."

Woolf, "Thoughts on Peace in an Air Raid"[2]

For *kebar enash* in Dan 7:13 Di Lella prefers the translation "one in human like-ness" or "one like a human being" or "what looked like a human being" because these "allow the possibility of women being included in the symbol." Hartman comments that the Aramaic phrase means a member of the human race, not a male human being.[3] On the translation problem in Daniel 7, and in related texts in the Similitudes of Enoch, and the Christian Testament, A. Y. Collins argues

---

1. Woolf, *Three Guineas*, 142.
2. V. Woolf, "Thoughts on Peace in an Air Raid," August 1940, *Death of a Moth*, 245. See S. Oldfield, *Women Against the Iron Fist: Alternatives to Militarism 1900–1989* (London: Blackwell, 1989) 96–130 on Woolf.
3. A. DiLella and L. F. Hartman, *The Book of Daniel* (AB 23; Garden City: Doubleday, 1978) 87, 218.

that translation should depend on the aim of the translator: if the aim is historical accuracy, then gender-exclusive language should be used; if the aim is "to serve the process by which an ancient text becomes living Word for the worshipping community and to foster equity," then gender-inclusive language is appropriate and is "in line with the primary intention of the tradition in which these texts stand, to overcome the division between the human and the divine, the material and the spiritual."[4] Her aim is historical accuracy in her essay, "The Influence of Daniel on the New Testament"; there she uses "Son of Man" "in part because masculine terms were probably significant in the historical contexts in which the relevant phrases were used and in part because of scholarly tradition."[5]

She is right that a translation should not prejudge or ignore historical and interpretive issues. But I see these texts, beginning with Daniel, as having a horizontal "intention" as well: to overcome certain divisions among humans. Later traditions about the Maccabean war, during which Daniel 7, 12 was written, pay some attention to the courage and suffering of women as well as men. 1 Macc 1:60–61 mentions women put to death who circumcised their sons; and corpses of infants hung from their mothers' necks. In 2 Maccabees 7, seven brothers are arrested with their mother, who urges them to accept death (vv. 20–29), and then herself is martyred (v. 41) cf. 4 Maccabees 14–17 for praise of this mother.[6] Although the author of Daniel does not mention this dimension of the resistance, it is possible he was aware of it, and that early and later audiences were also. In light of this, an inclusive translation has even historical justification. The figure of *kebar enash* is a promise of vindication for true Israel, a call to unity, authenticity and courage. The only known examples of re-use of the figure of the Human One depict it as male (cf. 1 Enoch 71; 4 Ezra 13), but it stands for more than an individual.

I think that in the Christian Testament, and in the Gospel of Mary and else-where in "gnostic" materials,[7] Son of Man traditions strain to become expressions of full humanity, inclusive of men and women. But the fact remains that the word used is "son," not "child" because only a male figure "could function rhetorically as a general or universal type."[8] Modern inclusive translations from Daniel and 1 Enoch on into the Christian and "gnostic" texts challenge this rhetorical custom in the name of alerting us to a possible ideal.

---

4. A. Y. Collins, "The Origin of the Designation of Jesus as 'Son of Man,'" *HTR* 80 (1987) 391–406.

5. A. Y. Collins, "The Influence of Daniel on the New Testament," in J. J. Collins, *Daniel* (Minneapolis: Fortress, 1993) n. 1, p. 90.

6. See R. D. Young, "The 'Woman with the Soul of Abraham,'" *'Women Like This'* (ed. A-J. Levine; Atlanta: Scholars Press, 1991) 67–81; G. S. Oegema, "Portrayals of Women in 1 and 2 Maccabees," *Transformative Encounters*, 245–64.

7. See above, pp. 170–71, especially the translations of K. King.

8. See E. Castelli, "Romans," *Searching the Scriptures*, 2. 287; she is discussing whether Eve rather than Adam could have been a type of Christ, of the one to come.

In a sense the Human One has no face. This figure, I think, can and should be understood by a woman to refer to herself. Surely it was — and is — more difficult for a man to understand it to refer to a woman. And most difficult for all to understand it as wo/man. As both Tyrant and the Human One are "us," both can be changed.

Index

NEW TESTAMENT APOCRYPHA AND PSEUDEPIGRAPHA

DEAD SEA SCROLLS

Also by Jane Schaberg
from Sheffield Academic Press
an Imprint of Continuum

THE ILLEGITIMACY OF JESUS
A Feminist Theological Interpretation
of the New Testament Infancy Narratives

In *The Illegitimacy of Jesus,* Schaberg explores the questions some other scholars hesitate to raise. In this bold and controversial counter-reading of the Christmas story, both Matthew and Luke hand down and rework a tradition, likely to be historical, in which Jesus was conceived during the period of Mary and Joseph's betrothal, and in which his biological father was unnamed. Allusions to Deuteronomy 22:23–27 nudge the reader toward suspicions of rape. God stands by the endangered woman and child.

"Foundational for feminist theology . . . a stimulus for further creative expansion, for a feminist reimagining."
— Louise Schottroff in *Lydia's Impatient Sisters*

"Demonstrates how the familiar dimensions of careful textual exegesis can be placed in the service of a nuanced, feminist reading . . . meticulously documented and forthrightly argued . . . a persuasive reading. Schaberg's exegesis retrieves a repressed story, breaking 'the silence of the "silent night"'; it provides the outline for the theological transformation of the figure of Mary . . . transforms the theological resonances traditionally associated with Mary."
— Elisabeth Castelli in the *Journal of Feminist Studies of Religion*

CONTINUUM INTERNATIONAL
370 Lexington Avenue
New York, NY 10017

1-800-561-7704
www.continuumbooks.com